LEGAL PRACTICE TECHNOLOGY AND LAW

Cases and Materials

FIRST EDITION

Willy E. Rice

cognella® | ACADEMIC PUBLISHING

Bassim Hamadeh, CEO and Publisher
Kassie Graves, Director of Acquisitions
Jamie Giganti, Senior Managing Editor
Jess Estrella, Senior Graphic Designer
Bob Farrell, Senior Field Acquisitions Editor
Gem Rabanera, Project Editor
Elizabeth Rowe, Licensing Coordinator
Chelsey Schmid, Associate Editor

Printed in the United States of America

ISBN: 978-1-5165-0824-2 (pbk) / 978-1-5165-0825-9 (hc)

cognella® | ACADEMIC PUBLISHING

www.cognella.com 800-200-3908

TABLE OF CONTENTS

INTRODUCTION

Immediately after the Stock Market Crash of 2008, many large corporations, financial institutions, businesses, and auxiliary occupations suffered. Millions of employees and professionals were fired. However, the financial collapse did not immediately affect large law firms and lawyers. Then, the lag effects of the 2008 Crash arrived with a vengeance—crippling, destroying, dismantling, and decimating national and international law firms.[a] Thousands of senior partners as well as newly minted associate attorneys were given pink slips. The latter were thrown into long unemployment lines—looking for work in the legal profession.[b]

To illustrate the extent of the post-2008 devastation among traditionally and extremely profitable mega law firms, consider excerpts from a widely read article that appeared in the *New York Times* on June 24, 2013:

> Layoffs are a brutal reality of corporate America. During fallow periods, publicly traded companies, including the big banks, routinely cull their ranks. The country's largest law firms, by contrast, have historically taken a kinder, gentler approach, rarely firing employees en masse. The news on Monday that *Weil, Gotshal & Manges*—among the nation's most prestigious and profitable law firms—was laying off a large number of lawyers and support staff while also reducing the pay of some of its partners, sent shock waves through the industry and underscored the financial difficulties facing the legal profession. Sixty junior lawyers, known at firms as associates, lost their jobs. That amounts to roughly 7 percent of *Weil's* associates. Annual compensation will be reduced for roughly 30 of the firm's 300 partners, in many cases by hundreds of thousands of dollars. And 110 non-lawyers—

---

[a] See Peter Lattman, *Mass Layoffs at a Top-Flight Law Firm*, New York Times, June 24, 2013
http://mobile.nytimes.com/blogs/dealbook/2013/06/24/big-law-firm-to-cut-lawyers-and-some-partner-pay/

[b] *Id.*

> roughly half of them secretaries—were let go. ... The "new normal," in the view of *Weil*'s management and echoed by legal industry experts, is that the market for high-end legal services is continuing to shrink. Dan DiPietro, chairman of the law firm group at Citi Private Bank, said he believed that the profession could experience a wave of job cuts. He said that there were too many lawyers at the country's largest firms, estimating the excess capacity at as much as 10 percent of the lawyer population. ... [C]urrent market dynamics ... have shifted starkly from the boom years leading up to the financial crisis. Pre-2008, profitability exploded and the number of lawyers grew at the country's top firms as demand increased about 4 percent a year. But demand has been flat to down for the last five years, according to several industry reports, and shows little sign of picking up.[c]

Consequently, in light of the post-2008 "new normal" within the legal profession, the number of solo and small-firm practitioners increased substantially—nearly doubling a year after the 2008 Crash. In 2012, Hanover Research published a report—*Law School Solo Practice Incubators and Legal Residency Programs*. The findings revealed:

> Many new law school graduates are foregoing the law firm or corporate attorney route upon graduation, instead deciding to "go solo" and open their own law firms. Indeed, the number of law graduates following this path into solo practice is on the rise. ... [T]he number of recent law graduates going solo increased from 3.5 percent in 2008 to 5.5 percent in 2009— the biggest one-year jump since 1982 [according to] the National Association for Law Placement. ... That percentage increased to 5.7 percent of all private practice jobs for the class of 2010, the highest it's been since 1997.
>
> "Going solo" or working in small law firms is a reality for many lawyers, both new graduates and accomplished professionals. Indeed, in a January 2012 news release, the American Bar Association

---

[c] *Id.*

> notes that about 70 percent of American lawyers in private practice work in solo offices or in small law firms with 20 or fewer members. As the ABA explains, "it is estimated that the United States has about 435,000 solo law practitioners—comprising about 48 percent of private-practice lawyers—and about 200,000 lawyers in firms of between two and 20 lawyers, about 22 percent of lawyers in private practice." [d]

Also, given the "new reality," the ABA created an online Solo and Small Firm Resource Center.[e]

"The ... Center provides online articles, CLE programming, a discussion list for solo and small firm lawyers and other information from groups throughout the ABA—including the ABA General Practice, Solo and Small Firm Division and Law Practice Management Section. The website offers practice management advice, business development strategies, career guidance, advice for handling problem cases and clients, *technology reviews*, networking events and more."[f]

More impressive, increasingly large numbers of law schools are offering courses and programs, which are designed to help law students to become competent and ethical solo and small-firm practitioners. Examples of such efforts are too numerous to outline and discuss here. The reader, however, is strongly encouraged to visit numerous law schools and professional websites—which discuss extraordinary solo and small-firm curricula and programs.[g]

---

[d] Hanover Research: *Law School Solo Practice Incubators and Legal Residency Programs* (July 2012) http://www.americanbar.org/content/dam/aba/administrative/legal_aid_indigent_defendants/ls_sclaid_hanover_report.authcheckdam.pdf

[e] http://www.americanbar.org/portals/solo_home/solo_home.html

[f] http://www.examiner.com/article/aba-serves-solo-and-small-firm-lawyers-with-new-online-resource-center (emphasis added)

[g]
http://www.americanbar.org/content/dam/aba/administrative/legal_aid_indigent_defendants/ls_sclaid_hanover_report.authcheckdam.pdf
http://www.americanbar.org/groups/delivery_legal_services/initiatives_awards/program_main/program_profiles.html
http://www.sddt.com/news/article.cfm?SourceCode=20150305cze&_t=Law+school+deans+praise+legal+incubators#.VeySPVVViko
http://www.americanbar.org/groups/delivery_legal_services/initiatives_awards/program_main/program_news.html
http://www.udmercy.edu/news_events/news/by-year/2015/articles/08-03-law-center-solo-small-firm-practice-program_print.htm
http://www.charlestonlaw.edu/Career-Services/For-Students-and-Alumni/Solo-and-Small-Firm-Practice-Program.aspx

But even more relevant major development occurred in the legal profession four years after the Crash of 2008. Rule 1.1 of the ABA Model Rules of Professional Conduct reads: "A lawyer shall provide competent representation to a client. Competent representation requires the legal knowledge, skill, thoroughness, and preparation reasonably necessary for the representation." In 2012, the ABA amended Model Rule 1.1 and added Comment [8]: "A lawyer should keep abreast of changes in the law and its practice, *including the benefits and risks associated with relevant technology.*"

Many states have adopted the amendment. Other states are presently weighing whether to adopt the amendment or to form a substantially equivalent or modified version of the amendment. And the message is clear: Law firms, in general, as well as solo and small-firm practitioners, in particular, must employ increasingly sophisticated *law-practice technologies and learn how to use such technologies more efficiently and ethically.* In light of Comment [8], law schools are being forced increasingly to add "legal practice technology and law" courses to their general as well as their solo and small-firm practice curricula.[h]

Without a doubt, law schools offer "technology and law" courses. In fact, before the ABA fashioned and adopted Comment [8], many law schools offered "technology and the law" courses.[i] And the explanation is simple: During the "dot-com" boom, law schools introduced new courses which were "devoted to rapidly emerging

---

https://www.law.csuohio.edu/careerplanning/solopracticeincubator
https://www.kentlaw.iit.edu/alumni/solo-and-small-practice-incubator
http://www.thefacultylounge.org/2015/02/maimonides-had-it-right-law-schools-must-teach-students-to-fish.html

[h] *See generally,* Johnathan Jenkins, *What Can Information Technology Do For Law,* 21 Harvard Journal of Law & Technology 589 (2008) (presenting theoretical and legal discussions of the legal risks and economic benefits of law-practice technology); Richard S. Granat and Stephanie Kimbro, *The Teaching of Law Practice Management and Technology In Law Schools: A New Paradigm,* 88 Chi.-Kent L. Rev. 757 (2013) (law and theoretical aspects); Brittany Stringfellow Otey, *Millennials, Technology, and Professional Responsibility: Training A New Generation In Technological Professionalism,* 37 J. Legal Prof. 199 (2013) ("theoretical"); Ash Mayfield, *Decrypting the Code of Ethics: The Relationship Between An Attorney's Ethical Duties And Network Security,* 60 Okla. L. Rev. 547 (2007) ("theoretical"); James C. Melamed, *Computer Uses In Legal Practice—Yesterday, Today, And Tomorrow,* 93 Or. L. Rev. 913 (2015) (practical aspects of employing legal-practice technologies); and, Catherine Palo, *Computer Technology in Civil Litigation,* 71 American Jurisprudence Trials 1 ("theoretical" and "practical").

[i] *See* Thomas M. Steele, *The MacCrate Report: Its Impact On Education in Law Firm Management,* 23 Pace L. Rev. 613, 628 (2003) ("The National Network of Law School Officers' ... e-mail survey polled that American law schools offer fifty-two law and technology classes, which is more than two times the number of law practice management courses.") *Id.* at 636.

technology and intellectual property law issues."[j] Put simply, "technology and the law" courses cover legal disputes involving patents, copyrights, computer technology, intellectual property, trademarks, and trade secrets.[k]

On the other hand, "legal practice technology and law" courses cover legal disputes surrounding solo and small-firm practitioners' *purchasing, using, designing, sharing, invading, misappropriating,* and/or *abusing* legal-practice or law-office technologies: desktop, laptop, and network computers; smartphones; short messaging services (sms); multimedia messaging service (mms); electronic tablets; office and cloud-based computing and printing services; the Internet; website design and maintenance services; social-media services; office production software; billing, invoicing, and accounting programs; document automation and assembly programs; document management systems; document sharing systems; and portable document format (PDF) software and files.

Therefore, in light of the ABA's decision to amend Model Rule 1.1 and add Comment [8], this casebook discusses common-law and statutory rules which state and federal courts employ to resolve law-office-technology disputes. In particular, PART I of the casebook outlines the types of legal and/or ethical actions that solo and small-firm attorneys commence against four groups of defendants: (1) clients; (2) allegedly third-party victims; (3) state disciplinary boards; and (4) the designers, manufacturers, suppliers, and providers of technological goods and services. PART I also discusses common-law and statutory affirmative defenses as well as general and specific denials that defendants employ in courts of law and equity. Conversely, PART II covers the types of technology-generated legal and equitable actions that clients and other parties commence against solo and small-firm attorneys. Finally, the

---

[j] *See* Curtis E. A. Karnow, *Rhetoric of Academe,* 41 U. S. F. Law Rev. 135, 143 (2006).

[k] https://www.law.berkeley.edu/academics/courses/law-technology/. *See also,* Richard Granat & Marc Lauritsen, *Teaching the Technology of Practice: The 10 Top Schools,* 40 Law Practice Magazine (2014) ("Academic attention to the 'law of technology'"—including intellectual property, defamation, product liability, software transactions, computer crime, Internet policy, and related topics—has been widespread for decades. Most law schools have courses ... that address the rich fabric of legal, ethical and policy issues presented by the use of technology in business, government and society. Harvard has the Berkman Center for Internet & Society. Stanford has the CodeX Center for Legal Informatics. Both schools have cyberlaw clinics. Brooklyn Law School has an Incubator & Policy Clinic. Northern Kentucky University Chase College of Law ... received a $1 million grant to establish ... the W. Bruce Lunsford Academy for Law, Business+Technology. ... Many schools have a ... law and technology [law review].") http://www.americanbar.org/publications/law_practice_magazine/2014/july-august/teaching-the-technology-of-practice-the-10-top-schools.html

chapters in PART III discuss a fairly unique class of affirmative defenses that solo and small-firm attorneys are likely to encounter and use—when litigating law practice technology disputes.

Of course, this introduction would be incomplete if it failed to address three frequently raised questions: 1) whether virtual and technologically rich legal practices are likely to replace traditional brick-and-mortar law practices; 2) the benefits and risks of solo practitioners' accelerating use and reliance on law practice technology; and 3) whether existing common-law, statutory, and ethical rules—those governing brick-and-mortar law practices—may be applied to resolve virtual-practice or law-office technology disputes. Some plausible answers appear in the following sections:

SECTION ONE: THE RISE OF VIRTUAL LAW PRACTICE AND THE SLOW DEMISE OF TRADITIONAL BRICK-AND-MORTAR LAW PRACTICE

Who's Afraid of the Virtual Lawyers? The Role of Legal Ethics in the Growth and Regulation of Virtual Law Offices

25 Geo. J. Legal Ethics 575 (2012)

Jordana Hausman

Technology often outpaces the law Virtual legal practice is a growing and inevitable segment of the profession in many states. In a 2010 survey, 14 percent of lawyers practiced virtually, reporting that rather than working from a traditional brick-and-mortar law office, they worked with clients via the Internet and only rarely met clients in person. ...

While some worry about the ethical and practical implications of virtual legal practice, it is likely that the growth of virtual practice within the legal community will bring more good than harm to the legal profession over the long term by providing an additional method of delivering legal services that can be more responsive to twenty-first century conditions. Virtual practices have the ability to offer greater flexibility and efficiency for both attorneys and clients: benefitting practitioners by allowing them to set up a practice with a low outlay for overhead costs and more control over their location and hours, and benefitting clients looking for more economical or unbundled legal services and on-the-go accessibility to their attorney's work product.

The traditional brick-and-mortar law office is in some sense not so traditional after all—in the nineteenth century, many lawyers (including a young Abraham Lincoln) made their living by "riding the circuit." The modern brick-and-mortar legal office can be seen as a byproduct of the Industrial Revolution—a manifestation of the idea that an aggregated workforce increases production. While such justifications may still be true, to some extent, in large firm settings, changing technological capabilities have altered many of the traditional moorings of the brick-and-mortar legal practice. A Virtual Legal Office (VLO) is a creature of the twenty-first century. It is a law office existing purely online without a physical location where attorneys use secure online portals to communicate with clients, share and access documents, and conduct business transactions. ...

What Is a Virtual Law Office?

Many law firms ... maintain an Internet presence. This presence includes firm websites, email communications with clients, online advertising through websites or virtual worlds, blogs, and the use of social networking sites. Some traditional firms also offer legal services over the Internet in addition to their other services. These activities comprise the broad and growing area of eLawyering, of which virtual practice is a subset.

VLOs are distinct from traditional firms that maintain an online presence. ...VLOs lack a brick-and-mortar counterpart although both confront many of the same concerns. Some virtual practitioners may appear like traditional practitioners, for example, by using shared meeting spaces or receptionist services to interact with clients or even having a physical address. However, these aspects are ancillary to the central embodiment of the VLO, which is the secure client portal. A physical address is usually given only where required by the state for service of process purposes. In fact, marketing materials will usually reference a URL or sometimes a P.O. Box rather than a traditional address.

VLOs deliver legal services via the Internet through the use of a secure online portal. This delivery is ideally through software-as-a-service (SaaS), a form of cloud computing by which secure software applications are hosted on third-party servers and accessed via the Internet. SaaS allows for high quality data encryption and backup, regular software updating, and secure access from any Internet-accessible location at a relatively low cost. By effectively outsourcing the services of an information technology professional to the SaaS provider for rates ranging from $50 to $300 per month, this model allows VLOs to be a viable option for solo practitioners and small firms.

VLOs maintain security through the use of unique client user names and passwords to access the virtual office. The website uses end-to-end encryption to protect the security of client documents, and client communications are accessible through the portal. In setting up a virtual office, attorneys must make sure that (1) the website is secure; (2) the website features a disclaimer stating practice limitations; ((3) the public area of the site has a terms and conditions statement explaining services and when a lawyer-client relationship is established; (4) the client accepts a clear retainer agreement; (5) online payment of legal fees complies with applicable state rules; and (6) client confidences are protected. This multitude of concerns faced by new virtual practitioners is further complicated by the differing ways some states deal with VLOs when determining compliance with the state's ethical rules.

VLOs offer a number of practical benefits to both attorneys and clients. Attorneys can gain flexibility—the significant difference in overhead costs increases the ease with which a lawyer can "hang her own shingle." The attorney can also work from the location and during the hours that are best for her. Such benefits play a large role in the growing use of VLOs. Virtual practice is, however, a better supplement than a substitute for more traditional practice structures. Even the loudest supporters of VLOs acknowledge that in some areas, for example criminal defense, where private in-person consultations with clients are needed, and elder law, where clients may have trouble accessing or using a VLO, brick-and-mortar offices are still preferable to their virtual counterparts.

SECTION TWO: THE EVOLUTION AND ATTORNEYS' ACCELERATING USE OF LAW PRACTICE TECHNOLOGIES

1. EVOLVING LAW TECHNOLOGIES' RADICAL TRANSFORMATION OF SEVERAL TRADITIONAL AND ESSENTIAL LEGAL TASKS AND SERVICES

The Great Disruption: How Machine Intelligence Will Transform the Role of Lawyers in the Delivery of Legal Services

82 Fordham L. Rev. 3041

John O. McGinnis and Russell G. Pearce

Law is an information technology. ...Information technology is growing exponentially in power, not only in hardware, but also in the software capacity of the programs that run on computers. As a result, the legal profession faces a great disruption. Information technology has already had a huge impact on traditional journalism, causing revenues to fall by about a third and employment to decrease by about 17,000 people in the last eight years. ... Because law consists of more specialized and personalized information, the disruption is beginning in law after journalism. But, its effects will be as wide ranging. Indeed they may ultimately be greater, because legal information is generally of higher value.

The disruption has already begun. In *discovery*, for instance, computationally based services are already replacing the task of document review that lawyers have performed in the past. But computational services are on the cusp of substituting for other legal tasks—from the *generation of legal documents* to predicting outcomes in litigation. And when machine intelligence becomes as good as lawyers in developing some service or some factor of production that contributes to a service, it does not stop improving. Intelligent machines will become better and better, both in terms of performance and cost. ... These developments have enormous implications for every aspect of law—*legal practice, jurisprudence,* and *legal education.* Lawyers who can change their practice or organization to take advantage of lower cost inputs made available by machines will be able to serve an expanding market of legal services for middle-class individuals and small businesses, meeting previously unfulfilled legal needs.

Five Areas of Law on the Cusp of Machine Intelligence Invasion

1. Discovery

Machine intelligence is most advanced in discovery—probably because legal discovery represents the application of general methods of machine search to the review of legal documents. In its simpler form, electronic discovery or e-discovery is the process by which computers search a database for keywords that lawyers agree are marks of relevance. But keyword search is a relatively blunt instrument. Such searches may be both over- and under-inclusive. ... Predictive coding has fundamentally transformed the prospects for e-discovery. In predictive coding, lawyers look at a sample of the larger set of documents. Computer technicians help construct algorithms that predict whether a document is relevant. ... Some courts have approved predictive coding as a tool of discovery that essentially will make the final decisions of relevance. ... E-discovery is already changing the discovery practices of large commercial litigation—which consumed much time of junior litigation associates years ago.

2. Legal Search

Searching for the law—by combing through precedents—has been an important part of legal work for centuries. Computerized legal research began in the mid-1960s. That system became the foundation for the LEXIS legal search system, which was introduced to the public in 1974. WESTLAW was offered soon after; but its utility was limited, because it did not allow researchers to search the full text of legal opinions. These problems have largely been corrected, and both WESTLAW and LEXIS are now staples of legal research. Previously, computerized legal search depended on search for the right keywords. That limitation disappeared with the rise of semantic search—allowing lawyers to use natural language queries. Machine intelligence will not only uncover precedent but will also guide lawyers' judgments about the use of precedent. Most lawyers can neither comprehensively evaluate the strength of precedent nor recall all possible precedents to mind.

3. Documents as Forms

Legal forms are hardly new. Since the middle ages when lawyers used forms of action, templates helped reduce the cost of law. But machine intelligence will revolutionize the use of legal forms. Most obviously, machine intelligence will help tailor these forms to meet individual situations. For instance, a client of LegalZoom can already submit information about his assets and his intentions for disposal of his estate to generate a draft of a will. Trust and estate planning is already ripe for this kind of mechanization because this area of law has relatively few kinds of forms and unique factual situations that arise for the large majority of people. ... In the future, documents will also improve. With the growing interconnectedness of data, machines can relate specific contracts to all court decisions about them—creating a dynamic of practical critique for continual improvement of legal forms. And, machine processing will be able to automate a form, tailor it according to the specific facts and legal arguments, and track its effect in future litigation.

4. Documents as Briefs and Memos

Legal forms are easier to automate than *legal memos or briefs*—because the latter often depend on more formulaic inputs. Nevertheless, computer-generated drafts can still be valuable. They are comparable to the efforts of associates—even research assistants without law degrees—who generate drafts. Thus, an experienced associate can then shape into a far more polished product. ... Analogous programs already encroach on traditional journalism. ... Ultimately, these kinds of programs will be able to provide drafts of briefs and memos and connect to legal research programs—which will provide data for the writing program. As with legal search, we expect substantial progress in programs over the next fifteen years until they deliver very useful drafts.

5. Legal Analytics

Predictive analytics is a new discipline that combines data with analysis to make predictions. Computational power allows substantial data to be collected and organized. Patterns can then be found among the data. Machine learning can help analyze regularities within the patterns. With the help of these models, known data can be used to predict what will happen in situations that have not yet occurred. The missing data may be unknown and indeed unknowable if the data consists of future events, like the outcome of a legal case. Predictive analytics is all the rage across the corporate world. ...

Predictive analytics is now coming to law. Indeed, law—with its massive amounts of data from case law, briefs, and other documents—is conducive to *machine data mining*. ... Legal analytics is not a distant prospect. Academics and companies are putting it into action. To be sure, legal analytics will still leave a role for lawyers. A lawyer's judgment may still add some value to the predictions derived from machine intelligence—even if the machine's prediction alone is better than the lawyer's prediction alone. Over time, however, legal analytics will reduce the value of a lawyer's assessment in some cases. The rise of legal analytics will also have an effect on the number of cases that go to trial and the amount of discovery. Whenever parties agree on the amount a case is worth, the case is likely to settle. ... As legal analytics provide better estimates of a case's value, parties will converge more rapidly toward an agreement that falls within the settlement window created by legal fees and risk aversion.

2. Lawyers' Embracing "New" Mobile and Online Technologies

Millennials, Technology, and Professional Responsibility: Training a New Generation in Technological Professionalism

37 J. Legal Profession 199 (2013)

Brittany Stringfellow Otey

In recent years, attorneys have begun adopting new technologies at a staggering rate. These numbers are only expected to rise as the technologically inclined Millennial generation continues to join the practice. As technology advances quickly, so does the need for attorneys to keep pace. In large part, they are doing so. The American Bar Association's (ABA) annual technology survey produced eye-opening statistics on the uptake of new technology by law firms.

"According to the ABA's 2011 survey, 23.2 percent of lawyers use online platforms to create and share documents, 22.8 percent use online services for messaging and communication, 17.2 percent for invoicing and bill payment, and 15.3 percent for scheduling and calendaring," says ... [the] attorney and author of the ABA's *Cloud*

Computing for Lawyers. Attorneys are involving their clients in the use of technology, as well: 23 percent of survey respondents allow their clients to access their case files online, through a secure portal. Mobile technologies are also on the rise, with a significant increase in smart phone and tablet usage among attorneys. The ABA survey indicates that 88 percent of responding attorneys are using smart phones, a 9 percent increase over the previous year. Fifteen percent of respondents are using tablets for their work while outside of the office; in firms of over 500 attorneys, the number jumps to 25 percent. Eleven out of the seventeen books published by the ABA in fiscal year 2012 were technology related.

Online practice management services are seeing growth as well, as an increasing number of firms are establishing a presence in the "cloud." Larry Port, CEO of Rocket Matter, one such cloud-based service, reports that "growth in [their] user base has approximately doubled every year since 2008, with growth expected to be in the 'high double digits' if it does not 'double again.'" Practice management site Total Attorneys has seen a 9,000 percent growth over the last eight years. In a survey by research company CompTIA, one in five law firms reported that they were already using a "software-as-a-service" ("SaaS") solution. Fourteen percent of firms planned to invest in a cloud or software-as-a-service solution in the next year. Nearly half of respondents to a survey by *The American Lawyer* who are already using cloud services have increased such use since the year before.

It appears, then, that adoption of some kind of cloud technology by law firms is inevitable. Cloud computing, or SaaS, is a relatively new software model that is very different from the traditional software model in a few important ways. Traditionally, a user would purchase a license to use a software program and install that program on the user's computer. With SaaS, the software is accessed over the Internet through a web browser, instead of locally on the user's machine. All of the data is stored on an off-site server, rather than with the user. Often, these services charge a subscription fee, rather than the large upfront cost of the traditional software model. Whether it is to access documents remotely, to interact with clients outside of the workplace, or to move a firm's Information Technology (IT) department from an internal department to an external service-based department, these new technologies are being adopted at a fast pace.

There are numerous benefits to adopting cloud-based or "virtual law office" technologies to a firm. Lower overhead, less office waste [and] the ability for clients to log into a site to view their case ... are just a few positive aspects. ... Cloud systems also allow increased scalability; as a law practice grows, having a cloud service means that there is no need to increase either local storage space or IT staff. Client and firm information is encrypted and backed up off-site, providing security and peace of mind were anything to happen to the office or equipment. While these potential benefits are inviting, there are also potential risks associated with these new technologies. ... [V]arious ethical obligations, particularly with respect to confidentiality and competence [can occur]. There are trade-offs to relinquishing the ultimate control of data, mostly in security and privacy. Additionally, no cloud service will guarantee 100% access to one's data. ...

Other technologies and practices [also] ... provide benefits and potential risks. The increased usage of individuals' personal devices ("Bring Your Own Device") for work-related activities is becoming the norm rather than the exception. This allows employees to work more/flexible hours, and do their work from anywhere. Tablets and smartphones are becoming more powerful and able to handle important office tasks on the go. Though, with mobility comes increased risk of loss and theft. Issues also arise with the use of applications used on devices, the wireless networks that connect the devices to the Internet, and the security of the devices themselves. This new freedom leads to increased employee productivity and morale. ... User error creates difficulties as well. It is not unusual for a user to use a new technology as a shortcut without fully investigating the possible shortcomings and security holes. This is especially true for Millennials who have grown up in a digital era and "trust" technology easily. As technology is constantly changing and evolving, the onus is on the user to keep up with new issues associated with that technology. Such vigilance is not always practiced.

Section Three: The Applicability and Sufficiency of Existing Common Law Rules to Resolve Law-Office Technology Disputes

Ouellette v. Viacom

2011 WL 1882780
(D. Mont. 2011)

Jeremiah C. Lynch, United States Magistrate Judge. Plaintiff Todd Ouellette is proceeding *pro se* in this action.

Plaintiff's Allegations

Count I—"Interference"

The allegations ... in Ouellette's Amended Complaint stem from his use of various Internet websites—such as YouTube.com and Myspace.com—for the purpose of uploading and publishing (or posting) videos that he has produced. In general, Ouellette contends Defendants have *interfered* with his ability, and his asserted legal right, to post his videos on the Internet.

Defendants' alleged *interference,* however, stems from accusations made against Ouellette asserting that his videos infringe upon various copyrights owned by other parties, including some of the Defendants named in this action. Nonetheless, Ouellette alleges Defendants have wrongfully accused him of infringing upon copyrights they own, have improperly removed his videos from the internet, and have refused to replace his videos on the internet as required by federal law. Ouellette's specific additional claims set forth in his Amended Complaint are summarized as follows:

Count II—"Misrepresentations"

Ouellette alleges Defendants Google, YouTube, BayTSP, Audible Magic and Myspace improperly used "scanning software"—which located videos he posted on YouTube and Myspace—and misidentified those videos as infringing upon existing copyrights. As a result, Ouellette's videos were removed from the internet, and "strikes" were imposed against Ouellette's YouTube and Myspace accounts.

Ouellette alleges these Defendants are liable because they "operated outside of" the provisions of the Digital Millennium

Copyright Act of 1998 (DMCA), and they failed to comply with those provisions. He also asserts Defendants are liable because they made *misrepresentations* as to copyright violations committed by Ouellette, and violated Ouellette's "fair use rights." Ouellette further contends Defendants "maliciously refused to restore [Ouellette's] Fair Use videos" to the internet.

Counts III and IV—"Violation of Fair Use Rights"

After Ouellette's videos were removed from the internet as described in Count II, Ouellette states he submitted "substantially complete" counter notices to Defendants Google and YouTube in accordance with the DMCA. But those entities refused to process Ouellette's counter notices due to minor errors in the notices. Ouellette asserts he advised the Defendants that he suffers from a reading disability that led to the minor errors. Ouellette claims the Defendants' actions deprived him of his "right to fair access to [Defendants'] public accommodation— i.e., the "on-line theater," in violation of the Americans with Disabilities Act (ADA). In Count IV, Ouellette further contends that Defendants Google and YouTube's failure to process his DMCA counter notices violated his asserted right to make *fair use* of others' copyright materials.

Count V—"Fraudulent Assertion"

Ouellette states that after YouTube refused to process his counter notices as described in Count III, he sent counter notices to Defendant Viacom under the DMCA. According to Ouellette, Viacom refused to process those counter notices, and refused to comply with Ouellette's request that it retract its *fraudulent assertion* that Ouellette had violated its copyrights.

Count VI—"Harassment and False Accusations"

Ouellette alleges that various provisions of the Terms of Service (TOS) agreement that Defendants Google and YouTube require subscribers to sign are unfair or illegal. First, Ouellette contends the Defendants violated his rights under the ADA because the block lettering used in the TOS is impossible for him to read. And the Defendants do not provide an audio version of the TOS as an alternative. According to Ouellette, these Defendants have thus deprived him of his right to access their "place of public accommodation" as protected under the ADA.

Second, Ouellette alleges the TOS unlawfully requires a subscriber to consent to an improper jurisdiction and venue for a lawsuit initiated by a copyright owner against a YouTube subscriber. Third,

Ouellette alleges the TOS bars him from exercising his "fair use" right to download news videos for the purpose of critiquing those videos. Fourth, the TOS permits Google and YouTube to violate the "safe harbor" provisions of the DMCA. Finally, Ouellette contends the TOS gives third parties the right to *harass him with false accusations* of copyright infringement.

Count VII

Ouellette advances similar claims under the ADA against Defendant Myspace stemming from provisions of its Terms of Use (TOU) agreement that Ouellette signed. Again he claims the TOU agreement contains block lettering which is impossible for Ouellette to read, and Myspace does not provide an audio version of the TOU. Consequently, Myspace's TOU agreement violates Ouellette's rights under the ADA.

Ouellette also alleges Defendants Audible Magic and Myspace engaged in conduct in violation of provisions of the DMCA. Those Defendants employ "filter blocks" to remove copyright-infringing videos from websites on the internet, and that procedure fails to comply with the "takedown" procedures established in the DMCA. Additionally, Myspace has refused to replace two of Ouellette's videos in response to Ouellette's counter notices. Thus, Defendants' conduct violates Ouellette's right to make fair use of others' copyright materials.

Count VIII

Ouellette's allegations in Count VIII appear to duplicate his allegations in Count VII. Ouellette again refers to two videos he posted on the internet through his Myspace account. Defendants Viacom and NBC Universal—through their agent, Audible Magic—asserted that Ouellette's videos infringed upon their copyrights. Consequently, Viacom and NBC Universal caused Ouellette's videos to be removed from the Myspace website, and Ouellette's right to post videos was suspended. Ouellette contends the removal of his videos was not in compliance with the "safe harbor" provisions of the DMCA.

Ouellette attempted to have the two referenced videos replaced on his Myspace account. He alleges that because Viacom and NBC Universal's claims of copyright infringement were false and improper, he submitted counter notices to Myspace requesting that the videos be replaced on his account. Myspace refused to process the counter notices, and refused to re-post Ouellette's videos. Ouellette alleges Defendants' conduct violated his fair use rights.

Discussion

B. Fair Use Doctrine

Ouellette's various claims allege Defendants have violated his right to make fair use of others' copyrighted materials. Ouellette's theory of liability, however, is not recognized under the law. The common law doctrine of fair use — now codified at 17 U.S.C. § 107 — is only an affirmative defense to a claim of copyright infringement. [It is] not an affirmative right on which a cause of action may be premised. *Eldred v. Ashcroft,* 537 U.S. 186, 219–220 (2003) (discussing the doctrine as a defense); *Perfect 10, Inc. v. Amazon.com, Inc.,* 508 F.3d 1146, 1163 (9th Cir.2007) (same).

A defendant's fair use of copyrighted material is merely an exception to the copyright owner's exclusive rights to that material. *Hustler Magazine, Inc. v. Moral Majority, Inc.,* 796 F.2d 1148, 1151 (9th Cir.1986). Such fair use does not constitute an infringement of a copyright. 17 U.S.C. § 107. Because the fair use doctrine is only an affirmative defense, it does not afford a person an enforceable, guaranteed, or constitutionally protected right to engage in any particular use of another's copyrighted material. *See 321 Studios v. Metro Goldwyn Mayer Studios, Inc.,* 307 F.Supp.2d 1085, 1101 (N.D.Cal.2004) and *Suntrust Bank v. Houghton Mifflin Co.,* 268 F.3d 1257, 1260 n. 3 (11th Cir.2001) (recognizing that the fair use doctrine is not an affirmative right).

Ouellette's allegations that Defendants' conduct violated his alleged "fair use rights" are frivolous, and fail to state a claim on which relief may be granted. Those claims should be dismissed.

C. Americans with Disabilities Act

Ouellette alleges Defendants Google, YouTube, and Myspace have violated his rights under the ADA. In substance, he alleges those Defendants discriminated against him based on his reading disability, and deprived him of access to their internet services and their "online theater"—a "place of public accommodation" governed by the ADA. The Court disagrees.

Title III of the ADA prohibits an owner of a place of public accommodation from engaging in discrimination, and the relevant provision of the ADA states as follows: No individual shall be discriminated against on the basis of disability in the full and equal enjoyment of the goods, services, facilities, privileges, advantages, or accommodations of any place of public accommodation by any person who owns, leases (or leases to), or operates a place of public accommodation. 42 U.S.C. § 12182(a).

To state a claim for relief under the ADA an individual must allege and establish that: (1) [he] is disabled within the meaning of the ADA; (2) the defendant is a private entity that owns, leases, or operates a *place of public accommodation;* and (3) the plaintiff was denied public accommodations by the defendant because of [his] disability. *Molski v. M.J. Cable,* 481 F.3d 724, 730 (9th Cir.2007).

The Ninth Circuit Court of Appeals has held that a "place of public accommodation"—under Title III of the ADA—must be an "actual, physical place where goods or services are open to the public, ... or a place where the public gets those goods or services." *Weyer v. Twentieth Century Fox Film Corp,* 198 F.3d 1104, 1114 (9th Cir.2000). Under the ADA, "some connection between the good or service complained of and an actual physical place is required." ...

Generally, an internet website, by itself, is not an actual place, or a physical, concrete structure that would qualify as a place of public accommodation under the ADA. *Access Now, Inc. v. Southwest Airlines, Co.,* 385 F.3d 1324, 1329 (11th Cir.2004). Absent allegations that a website impedes the plaintiff's "access to a specific, physical, concrete space[,]" and absent allegations establishing a nexus between a website and a physical place of public accommodation, a plaintiff's allegations fail to state a claim upon which relief could be granted. Services ... on an internet website that have no connection to a physical place of accommodation do not fall within the ADA's "place of public accommodation" requirement. *Peoples v. Discover Financial Services, Inc.,* 2009 WL 3030217, *2 (E.D.Pa.2009).

Ouellette's allegations ... do not state a claim on which relief could be granted. His allegations fail to identify any actual, physical place where Defendants' services are made available. [Additionally, there is no evidence of] any connection between the internet websites he sought to access, and any actual, physical structure or facility through which Defendants' services could be accessed or provided. To the contrary, Ouellette alleges only that Defendants' conduct has impeded his access to certain internet websites—the "online theater." Without more, a website does not constitute a physical "place of public accommodation" as required for a cognizable ADA claim. Accordingly, Ouellette's allegations under the ADA should be dismissed.

D. Digital Millennium Copyright Act of 1998

Ouellette claims the Defendants engaged in conduct that violated certain procedures mandated by the DMCA. The procedures established by the DMCA ... , however, do not create liability exposure for internet service providers, or other entities, in the circumstances alleged by Ouellette. The procedures do not create liability that does not already exist independent of the DMCA.

Congress enacted the DMCA to address the application of copyright law and liability for infringement in the context of "the online world." *Ellison v. Robertson,* 357 F.3d 1072, 1076 (9th Cir.2004). Title II of the DMCA, enacted as the Online Copyright Infringement Liability Limitation Act (OCILLA), set forth in 17 U.S.C. § 512, seeks to "facilitate cooperation among Internet service providers and copyright owners 'to detect and deal with copyright infringements that take place in the digital networked environment.' S. Rep. 105–190 at 20 (1998) and H.R. Rep. 105–551, pt. 2 at 49 (1998).

The procedural mechanisms established under the DMCA and OCILLA are designed to facilitate the identification and removal of material placed on the internet that infringes upon a copyright. If a copyright owner identifies an infringement committed by an individual who subscribes to an internet service, the owner may serve a notice of the claimed infringement on the service provider, commonly referred to as a "takedown notice." 17 U.S.C. § 512(c)(1)(C) and (c)(3). In response, the service provider must remove the infringing material from the provider's website. 17 U.S.C. § 512(c)(1)(C).

After a takedown notice is issued and the material is removed from the website, the service subscriber may then challenge those actions through a counter notice. 17 U.S.C. § 512(g)(2)(C) and (g)(3). The subscriber may issue a counter notice which informs the service provider that the material was improperly removed from the website "as a result of a mistake or misidentification." 17 U.S .C. § 512(g)(3)(C). Upon receipt of the counter notice the service provider must replace the subscriber's material on the website. 17 U.S.C. § 512(g)(2)(C).

The intent of the DMCA, OCILLA, § 512, and the foregoing procedures is to limit the liability of internet service providers, not to create liability that could not otherwise be imposed under existing law independent of the DMCA. The statutory intent is "to provide greater certainty to service providers concerning their legal exposure for infringements that may occur in the course of their activities." S. Rep. 105–190 at 20 (1998) and H.R. Rep. 105–551, pt. 2 at 49 (1998).

In establishing that certainty, however, Congress chose not to rewrite or modify *the existing doctrines* that impose liability for copyright infringement as those doctrines apply to the online world. Instead, Congress elected to create various "safe harbors" in five specific circumstances, or categories of activity, which limit internet service providers' liability for copyright infringement—liability that could be founded upon the existing doctrines of copyright infringement law. *Ellison,* 357 F.3d at 1076–1077; *See* 17 U.S.C. § 512(a), (b), (c), (d), and (g) (identifying the safe harbors).

Thus, rather than establish new grounds for claims of copyright infringement against online service providers, Congress chose to create "limitations of liability [which] apply if the provider is found to be liable under *existing principles of law.*" *Ellison,* 357 F.3d at 1077 (quoting from, and adding emphasis to S. Rep. 105–190 at 19). The "safe harbors" established under the DMCA "do not affect the question of ultimate liability under the various doctrines of direct, vicarious, and contributory liability that could otherwise be imposed under copyright law. *Perfect 10, Inc. v. CCBill, LLC,* 488 F.3d 1102, 1109 (9th Cir.2007). The safe harbor provisions of 17 U.S.C. § 512 do not serve to imply that a service provider either is, or is not liable, either for conduct that qualifies for a safe harbor limitation, or for conduct that fails to qualify for the limitation. *Viacom International, Inc. v. YouTube, Inc.,* 718 F.Supp.2d 514, 520 (S.D.N.Y.2010).

The procedural mechanisms of the DMCA on which Ouellette relies for the imposition of liability against Defendants are procedures that exist within two of the DMCA safe harbor provisions. The takedown notice procedures protect a service provider against liability to a copyright owner as long as the provider removes the infringing material in response to the copyright owner's takedown notice. 17 U.S.C. § 512(c)(1). … Ouellette's reliance on the takedown and counter notice safe-harbor procedures in the DMCA is misplaced. The Defendants' alleged compliance, or non-compliance with the procedures does not provide a basis for liability. Defendants' liability to Ouellette, if any, could only be imposed under existing principles of law independent of the DMCA's procedural requirements. Ouellette's allegations, however, do not invoke any independent theory of liability. Therefore, his claims founded upon the DMCA should be dismissed.

E. Misrepresentation Under the DMCA

In Count II, Ouellette alleges Defendants Google, YouTube, BayTSP, Audible Magic, and Myspace made misrepresentations asserting that Ouellette infringed upon certain copyrights. ... Misrepresentations made in takedown notices—issued in accordance with the DMCA—could give rise to liability against a defendant who issued the takedown notice. 17 U.S.C. § 512(f).

Ouellette's allegations, however, fail to state a claim of misrepresentation under 17 U.S.C. § 512(f). Ouellette does not allege in Count II that any Defendant made a misrepresentation in a takedown notice issued pursuant to the DMCA. To the contrary, Ouellette alleges Defendants engaged in conduct "outside of the DMCA rules." Therefore, Ouellette's claims of misrepresentation should be dismissed.

F. Terms of Service/Terms of Use Agreements

Ouellette's allegations in Counts VI and VII challenge provisions of Google and YouTube's TOS agreement, and provisions of Myspace's TOU agreement. To the extent Ouellette alleges those agreements violate his rights under the ADA, Ouellette has similarly failed to allege that Defendants' conduct impeded his access to any actual, physical place of public accommodation. Ouellette's allegations do not establish any connection between the agreements and Ouellette's impaired access to any physical facility. Therefore, Ouellette's ADA claims are subject to dismissal.

Ouellette also challenges the provisions of Google and YouTube's TOS which require him to consent to an improper jurisdiction and venue for any lawsuit that might be filed by a copyright owner. Ouellette, however, fails to suggest that the referenced provision is presently being enforced against him. Therefore, Ouellette's challenge to the provision fails to state a claim upon which relief could be granted.

Finally, Ouellette alleges Google and YouTube's TOS improperly grants third parties a right to harass him with false accusations of copyright infringement. Under the facts alleged by Ouellette, however, Google and YouTube cannot be liable for the conduct of any third party. Therefore, this claim in Count VI should be dismissed.

Conclusion

For the reasons stated, it is hereby recommended that Ouellette's claims advanced in Counts II through VIII of his Amended

Complaint should be dismissed as frivolous and for failure to state a claim on which relief could be granted. 28 U.S.C. § 1915(e)(2)(B)(i) and (ii).

NOTES & QUESTIONS

1) Common Law Principles Are Sufficient to Resolve Legal-Practice Technology Claims. Consider dissenting Judge Mosk's opinion in *Intel Corp. v. Hamidi*, 30 Cal. 4th 1342, 1391-92 (2003):

> [O]wners of computer systems—like owners of other private property—have a right to prevent others from using their property against their interests. That principle applies equally in this case. By his repeated intermeddling, Hamidi converted Intel's private employee e-mail system into a tool for harming productivity and disrupting Intel's workplace. Intel attempted to put a stop to Hamidi's intrusions by increasing its electronic screening measures and by requesting that he desist. ... I believe that existing legal principles are adequate to support Intel's request for injunctive relief. But even if the injunction in this case amounts to an extension of the traditional tort of trespass to chattels, this is one of those cases in which ... [t]he creative element in the judicial process finds its opportunity and power in the development of the law.
>
> The law has evolved to meet economic, social, and scientific changes in society. The industrial revolution, mass production, and new transportation and communication systems all required the adaptation and evolution of legal doctrines. ... The court must now grapple with proprietary interests, privacy, and expression arising out of computer-related disputes. ... That the Legislature has dealt with some aspects of commercial unsolicited bulk e-mail should not inhibit the application of common law tort principles to deal with e-mail transgressions not covered by the legislation. ... Before the computer, a person could

> not easily cause significant disruption to another's business or personal affairs through methods of communication without significant cost. With the computer, ... one person can at no cost disrupt, damage, and interfere with another's property, business, and personal interests. Here, the law should allow Intel to protect its computer-related property from the unauthorized, harmful, free use by intruders.

2) **Conflicting Rules Governing Attorney's Advertising and Soliciting on the Internet.** *See* Amy Haywood and Melissa Jones, *Navigating A Sea of Uncertainty: How Existing Ethical Guidelines Pertain to The Marketing of Legal Services Over the Internet,* 14 Geo. J. Legal Ethics 1099, 1111-1114 (2001)

> Not only do states' rules relating to advertising and solicitation vary from state to state, each state has formed its own opinions on how existing rules and case law should extend to the new medium of the Internet. For example, at least eight states currently require advertisements to include disclaimers with exact language. ...
>
> At least fourteen states place a prohibition—a general restriction or a disclosure requirement on testimonials— and sixteen states impose some restrictions on direct mail solicitations. ... [A]few states single out electronic media and restrict advertising through that media. At least two states, Texas and Florida, have gone as far as to incorporate specific language relating to Internet solicitation into their rules of conduct. Massachusetts has incorporated language relating to "computer-accessed" communications into the comment of its Rule 7.2 relating to advertising, suggesting that the rules should be applied to "computer-based" communication by "analogizing the communication to its hard copy form."
>
> Many state bar association committees have issued advisory opinions to interpret these rules, and because there have been relatively few opinions indicating that the rules are inapplicable, it can be assumed that Internet use in the context of legal marketing will generally invoke all ethics rules

> relating to advertising and solicitation. ... States have also taken different stances in their interpretation of interactive electronic devices such as e-mail and chat rooms. ... A new Florida rule considers all e-mail messages to be direct mail communications. An e-mail to a prospective client is considered to be a targeted mailing whether it [is] sent as a general e-mail or to a specific individual. Finally, states have varied in determining whether a chat room—where computer users can type in "real time" with others in that particular cyberspace location—is the same form of communication as an in-person conversation. ...
>
> A law firm's seeking to utilize the Internet in its practice must be careful to note when communications may be construed as advertisements or as solicitations. Because of the possibility of subjecting themselves to new jurisdictions, lawyers and firms must look not only at the rules which a state has adopted, but also at how the state is currently interpreting those rules relating to Internet communications. As the above examples illustrate, wide variation exists among jurisdictions in analyzing how the Internet fits into current governing law. This lack of uniformity coupled with a still evolving technology leads to the need for extreme caution in following state rules.

PART I.
Solo and Small-Firm Practitioners' Technology-Based Claims and Actions

CHAPTER ONE: Solo and Small-Firm Attorney's Contract-Based and Breach of Warranty Actions

In recent years, about seven percent of small-firm and solo practitioners "opened" a virtual law office on the world-wide web. Virtual offices are computer-simulated environments—which allow attorneys, clients, third-party vendors, and legal assistants to engage in business activities over the Internet. For example, reasonably secure "client portals" and passwords allow clients to visit virtual offices at will to deliver and/or retrieve legal documents. Additionally, lawyers may interact "face-to-face" with clients using Skype—a video chat protocol—or another voice-over-Internet-protocol service (VOIP). And, solo practitioners may access fee-for-service electronic databases —WESTLAW, LEXIS-NEXIS or libraries—to research legal issues.

Even larger numbers of attorneys have structured a quasi-virtual practice. These latter practitioners employ various types of modern technologies—including the Internet—to serve clients, interact with opposing attorneys, produce legal documents, store documents on cloud-based platforms, advertise services, and manage their law practices. And, those same attorneys also employ traditional brick-and-mortar, law-practice technologies—stand-alone fax machines, desktop telephones, paper folders and metal file cabinets. Essentially, quasi-virtual practitioners integrate both online and traditional office technologies to communicate with clients, create legal documents, print and share documents, review documents, plan tasks, monitor deadlines, prepare for trial, fashion financial statements, and send bills.

Still, like purely traditional brick-and-mortar attorneys, virtual and quasi-virtual lawyers are exposed to risks. However, the latter are likely to confront a slightly different set of technological risks: (1) Internet service providers breaching "high speed internet" contracts by throttling attorneys' abilities to upload or download data at a bargained-for-exchange speed; (2) Internet operators breaching attorneys' cloud-based storage contracts—by destroying privileged information or causing clients' electronic files to disappear; (3) website designers breaching express or implied warranties—which undermine attorneys' abilities to advertise effectively over the Internet; (4) domain-name owners and operators breaching implied warranties—which expose virtual and quasi-virtual attorneys to third-party lawsuits; and (5) sellers delivering defective of technological goods—office-management software and hardware—which impair virtual attorneys' abilities to access the Internet quickly, securely, and legally.

In this chapter, the cases illustrate the types of legal actions that quasi-virtual and virtual attorneys have commenced against Internet service providers, Internet operators, website designers, domain-name owners, and sellers of technological goods and services. Consider carefully the courts' breach-of-contract and breach-of-warranties analyses and rulings. Those should help solo and small-practice attorneys to assess technology-based risks and implement effective strategies and tools to reduce such risks.

A. Attorneys' Breach of Contract Actions

1. Minimum-Contact Issues Involving Internet Marketing Entities

Kelly Law Firm, P.C. v. An Attorney for You

679 F.Supp.2d 755
(S.D. Tex. 2009)

Sim Lake, District Judge. Plaintiffs—The Kelly Law Firm, P.C. ("Kelly"), A. Daniel Woska & Associates, P.C. ("Woska"), and The Law Offices of Robert H. Weiss, PLLC ("Weiss")—filed this action alleging breach of contract and unjust enrichment—against defendants: An Attorney for You, Calliope Media, L.P., and Calliope Media, Inc. (collectively, "Calliope").

The claim concerns defendants' [allegedly unsatisfactory] Internet marketing services that the defendants provided to the plaintiffs. Pending before the court is Defendants' Motion to Dismiss, or, in the Alternative, to Transfer to the Southern District of California. Defendants argue that this action should be dismissed for lack of personal jurisdiction pursuant to Federal Rule of Civil Procedure 12(b)(2) or, alternatively, for failure to state a claim under Rule 12(b)(6).

I. Factual and Procedural Background

This action concerns a dispute over Internet marketing services that the defendants provided to the plaintiffs—a group of plaintiff's law firms that contracted with the defendants to provide leads on clients for mesothelioma and birth injury lawsuits. Plaintiff Kelly is a Texas Professional Corporation with its principal place of business in Houston, Texas. Plaintiff Woska is an Oklahoma Professional Corporation with its principal place of business in Oklahoma City, Oklahoma. Plaintiff Weiss is a District of Columbia law firm incorporated pursuant to the laws of the District of Columbia—with branch offices in Jericho, New York, and Atlanta, Georgia.

Defendant—An Attorney for You—is not a legal entity. It is a name used by Calliope Media, Inc., a California Corporation doing business in La Jolla, California. Defendant Calliope Media, L.P., is an inactive California limited partnership that merged into Calliope Media, Inc., prior to the filing of this action. Since Calliope Media, Inc. is the only active legal entity that is a defendant in this action, the court will refer to the three named defendants as "Calliope."

The parties disagree about several aspects of the factual background to this action. What is not in dispute is that in mid-2007 and early 2008, Kelly and Calliope entered into two agreements— "the personal injury agreements" under which Kelly paid Calliope for referrals of potential personal injury plaintiffs from its website, *anattorneyforyou.com*. Kelly and Calliope entered into two additional agreements— "the mesothelioma and birth injury agreements"—in July of 2008 under which Calliope agreed to refer potential mesothelioma and birth injury plaintiffs from its websites to Kelly, Weiss, and Woska in exchange for payment. It is not disputed that the contracts were negotiated and executed between Calliope and Kelly. At some point, Kelly brought in the Woska and Weiss firms to share in the costs and the administrative requirements of the marketing campaigns. The parties dispute precisely when Woska and Weiss became involved in the transaction and what roles they played in it. The parties also disagree as to who initiated the contract negotiations, where the work under the contract was performed, and whether the leads provided by Calliope fulfilled Calliope's contractual obligations. ...

Procedural Background

A dispute arose between the parties soon after the mesothelioma and birth injury campaigns began because, according to plaintiffs, the leads provided by Calliope did not meet plaintiffs' expectations. Plaintiffs allege that "none of the leads that were forwarded by Defendants have resulted in an actionable case." Plaintiffs filed their original petition against defendants in Harris County District Court on September 9, 2009—alleging fraud, breach of contract, unjust enrichment, and violation of the TDTPA. On October 9, 2009, defendants removed the action to this court on the basis of diversity jurisdiction. On October 29, 2009, defendants filed the pending motion to dismiss or transfer the action.

II. Motion to Dismiss for Lack of Personal Jurisdiction

Calliope argues that this action should be dismissed for lack of personal jurisdiction pursuant to Federal Rule of Civil Procedure 12(b)(2). Plaintiffs respond that the defendants' contacts with Texas were sufficient to support the court's assertion of personal jurisdiction over them. …

Applicable Law

Exercise of personal jurisdiction over a nonresident defendant comports with federal due process guarantees when the nonresident defendant has established minimum contacts with the forum state, and the exercise of jurisdiction "does not offend 'traditional notions of fair play and substantial justice.'" *International Shoe Co. v. State of Washington, Office of Unemployment Compensation and Placement*, 326 U.S. 310 (1945).

1. Texas Long-Arm Statute

Texas courts may assert personal jurisdiction "over a nonresident if (1) the Texas long-arm statute authorizes the exercise of jurisdiction, and (2) the exercise of jurisdiction is consistent with federal and state constitutional due process guarantees." *See Moki Mac River Expeditions v. Drugg*, 221 S.W.3d 569, 574 (Tex. 2007).The Texas long-arm statute authorizes service of process on nonresidents "[i]n an action arising from the nonresident's business in this state." Tex. Civ. Prac. & Rem. Code § 17.043. The statute provides, in part: In addition to other acts that may constitute doing business, a nonresident does business in this state if the nonresident (1) contracts by mail or otherwise with a Texas resident and either party is to perform the contract in whole or in part in this state; (2) commits a tort in whole or in part in this state. *Id.* at § 17.042.

The Texas Supreme Court has stated that the long-arm statute's "broad doing-business language allows the statute to "reach as far as the federal constitutional requirements of due process will allow." *Guardian Royal Exchange Assurance, Ltd. v. English China Clays, P.L.C.*, 815 S.W.2d 223, 226 (Tex.1991).

2. Minimum Contacts Analysis

"There are two types of 'minimum contacts': those that give rise to specific personal jurisdiction and those that give rise to general personal jurisdiction." *Lewis v. Fresne,* 252 F.3d 352, 358 (5th Cir. 2001). A court may exercise specific jurisdiction over a nonresident defendant if the lawsuit arises from or relates to the defendant's contact with the forum state. *ICEE Distributors, Inc. v. J & J Snack Foods Corp.*, 325 F.3d 586, 591 (5th Cir.2003). Specific jurisdiction exists where a defendant "purposefully avails itself of the privilege of conducting activities within the forum state, thus invoking the benefits and protections of its laws." *Burger King,* 105 S.Ct. at 2185.

The Texas Supreme Court has recently explained that there are three parts to a purposeful availment inquiry. First, only the defendant's contacts with the forum are relevant, not the unilateral activity of another party or a third person. Second, the contacts relied upon must be purposeful rather than random, fortuitous, or attenuated. Finally, the defendant must seek some benefit, advantage, or profit by availing itself of the jurisdiction. In contrast, a defendant may purposefully avoid a particular forum by structuring its transactions in such a way as to neither profit from the forum's laws nor subject itself to jurisdiction there. *Moki Mac,* 221 S.W.3d at 575 (citing Burger King, 105 S.Ct. at 2182). ...

General jurisdiction exists when a non-resident defendant's contacts with the forum state are substantial, continuous, and systematic. *Helicopteros Nacionales de Colombia, S.A. v. Hall,* 104 S.Ct. 1868, 1872-74 (1984)). "The continuous and systematic contacts test is a difficult one to meet—requiring extensive contacts between a defendant and a forum." *Id.* "General jurisdiction can be assessed by evaluating contacts of the defendant with the forum over a reasonable number of years, up to the date the suit was filed." *Access Telecom, Inc. v. MCI Telecommunications Corp.*, 197 F.3d 694, 717 (5th Cir.1999). The court views all the defendant's contacts in toto. *Id.* "[V]ague and overgeneralized assertions that give no indication as to the extent, duration, or frequency of contacts are insufficient to support general jurisdiction." *Gardemal v. Westin Hotel Co.*, 186 F.3d 588, 596 (5th Cir.1999).

3. Minimum Contacts and Internet Services

Internet-based businesses can present challenges to the traditional minimum-contacts analysis because such businesses can conduct business in a state without ever having a physical presence there. In *Mink v. AAAA Dev. LLC,* the Fifth Circuit established a "sliding scale" to evaluate whether a nonresident defendant's Internet contacts are sufficient to subject it to the jurisdiction of the forum state. *Mink,* 190 F.3d at 336 (citing Zippo Mfg. Co. v. Zippo Dot Com, Inc., 952 F.Supp. 1119, 1124 (W.D.Pa.1997). *See also Revell v. Lidov,* 317 F.3d 467, 470 (5th Cir.2002) (applying the *Mink* standard to a website selling journal subscriptions and advertising).

At one end of the scale is "a passive website that does nothing more than advertise on the Internet"—which does not support a finding of minimum contacts. *Mink,* 190 F.3d at 336. At the other end of the scale are websites through which "a defendant clearly does business over the Internet by entering into contracts with residents of other states which 'involve the knowing and repeated transmission of computer files over the Internet.'" *Zippo,* 952 F.Supp. at 1124. Defendants that own or maintain such websites will be subject to the forum state's jurisdiction. *Id.* In the middle of the spectrum are instances where a defendant has allowed users "to exchange information with a host computer." *Id.* at 336. Whether the contacts generated by sites in this middle ground are sufficient to support a finding of minimum contacts "is determined by the level of interactivity and commercial nature of the exchange of information that occurs on the Website." *Zippo,* 952 F.Supp. at 1124.

III. Analysis

Calliope has moved for dismissal pursuant to Federal Rule of Civil Procedure 12(b)(2), arguing that this court lacks personal jurisdiction over Calliope because it has no physical presence in Texas and because its performance under the mesothelioma and birth injury campaigns was directed primarily at New York. Plaintiffs argue that Calliope is subject to both general and specific personal jurisdictions in Texas because it has actively and continuously sought out business in Texas and because this action arises from Calliope's business activities in Texas. ...

Did Calliope contract to perform in Texas? The record establishes that Calliope contracted with Kelly—a Texas party—in the personal injury agreements as well as the mesothelioma and birth injury agreements. Calliope does not dispute that it contracted with a Texas party; what it disputes is that the contracts were to be performed in whole or in part in this state. The court concludes that they were.

Plaintiffs have provided a screen shot of the website *anattorneyforyou.com* that targets potential legal clients for "attorneys in the state of Texas," and states that the attorneys in the "An Attorney For You Legal Network" serve all 254 counties in the state of Texas. Kelly's declaration states that Calliope sought to recruit Texas lawyers to subscribe to its listing service. The personal injury agreement reflects that Calliope contracted with Kelly to provide e-mails from potential personal injury plaintiffs in exchange for a fee. Since Calliope's duties under this contract required it to collect information from potential plaintiffs in Texas and to send that information to an attorney in Texas, performance under the contract took place, at least in part, in Texas. … The court concludes that Calliope contracted with a Texas resident and that it performed the contract, at least in part, in Texas. Therefore, the Texas long-arm statute is met under Tex. Civ. Prac. & Rem. Code § 17.042(1). …

V. Motion to Dismiss for Failure to State a Claim

Calliope … moves to dismiss plaintiffs' breach of contract claims under Rule 12(b)(6). Calliope argues that it is entitled to dismissal of plaintiffs' breach of contract claims regarding the birth injury agreement because plaintiffs breached that agreement by failing to complete their payments due under it. Calliope further argues that plaintiffs' breach of contract claims regarding the mesothelioma agreement should also be dismissed because Calliope actually fulfilled its obligations under that contract. These arguments, however, are breach of contract defenses and are not relevant to a Rule 12(b)(6) motion, which deals solely with whether or not the plaintiffs have stated a claim upon which relief can be granted. Plaintiffs have stated adequate breach of contract claims. Therefore, Calliope's Rule 12(b)(6) motion to dismiss the breach of contract claims will be denied.

For the reasons stated above, Defendants' motion to dismiss, or, in the alternative, to transfer to the Southern District of California is denied.

2. Breach of Contract Actions Against Internet Advertising and Marketing Services

Ogletree, Abbott, Clay & Reed Law Firm, L.L.P. v. FindLaw

2014 WL 2611862
(D. Minn. 2014)

Richard H. Kyle, District Judge. Plaintiff Ogletree, Abbott, Clay & Reed Law Firm, L.L.P. (Ogletree) hired Defendants FindLaw, Westlaw Publishing Corporation, and Thomson Reuters Holdings, Inc. (FindLaw) —to develop three of Ogletree's websites to increase traffic from search engines. Rather than enhance the quality of the websites, Ogletree alleges Findlaw diminished it and injured Ogletree's business as a result. After the parties failed to resolve their dispute amicably, Ogletree filed the instant action against FindLaw. ... FindLaw now moves to dismiss.

Background

FindLaw provides online advertising services to attorneys. One of its services is website development—aimed at helping attorneys increase their exposure to potential clients online. Ogletree is a law firm specializing in personal-injury matters. In 2012, it hired FindLaw to help develop three of its websites: *www.ogletreeabbott.com*, *www.1800jonesact.com*, and *www.complawyers.net* ("Ogletree Websites").

Between November 2012 and June 2013, FindLaw and Ogletree entered into a series of contracts to redesign and improve the "search engine optimization" (SEO) of the Ogletree Websites. Ogletree paid FindLaw $61,965.69 for its services. FindLaw launched the revised Ogletree Websites in late April and early May 2013. Ogletree was not satisfied with the revised websites and alleges that their quality and SEO deteriorated rather than improved.

Ogletree alleges FindLaw did not utilize and migrate all of the existing indexed content and webpages from the original Ogletree Websites to the revised sites. For example, the number of indexed webpages was reduced from 612 pages to 184 pages on *www.ogletreeabbott.com*, from 598 to 81 on *www.1800jonesact.com*, and from 1,358 to 157 on *www.complawyers.net*. The more indexed pages with quality content on a website, the more opportunities there are for the website to be relevant to a user's search terms, potentially increasing the website's page ranking in Google and thus its visibility in the search results.

When redesigning the Ogletree Websites, Ogletree alleges that FindLaw ignored its webpage-naming conventions—creating error messages when users followed inbound links set to the prior page names. For example, it alleges *www.complawyers.net* contained 234 "page not found" errors. If the information at the old webpage address was useful to users, FindLaw's changes and resulting errors would "cause the Ogletree website to lose the beneficial page rank that ... inbound links [to those pages] would have otherwise provided."

FindLaw also added software code to the Ogletree Websites that required users to download a large amount of data in order to view certain pages. Whereas the previous websites required users to download only .5 MB of data to view them, the revised websites required users to download more than 1.5 MB of data in some instances. The revised websites also required users to load twice as many files as the previous websites. This affected the websites' load time—which is a factor for Google's ranking. In addition to adversely impacting Google rankings, these changes resulted in users' abandoning the Ogletree Websites before they had loaded and causing Ogletree to lose out on potential clients.

Ogletree alleges it told FindLaw not to place outbound links on its websites. But in October 2013, it discovered that FindLaw had "secretly inserted at least one outbound link on every page of the Ogletree websites which were directed to FindLaw's website." As outbound links are generally beneficial to the site that receives them and may decrease the value of the website that posts it, these links diminished the value of Ogletree's Websites and improved the SEO of FindLaw's. When Ogletree demanded FindLaw remove the outbound links, it did so. But FindLaw offered no acknowledgement of or explanation for its conduct.

FindLaw "represented that it would build inbound links to the Ogletree Websites that would meet and conform to Google's SEO Guidelines." But Ogletree alleges FindLaw obtained paid links to the Ogletree Websites—which violate Google policy. As a result, it alleges Google has "significantly penalized the Ogletree websites."

Finally, Ogletree used Google Analytics to track its website performance, such as how many visitors used the websites, where the users had navigated from, and what they were doing on the websites. Ogletree used this information to improve its websites and attract more users (potential clients). When FindLaw launched the revised Ogletree Websites, the sites did not have Google Analytics code installed for the first 27 to 45 days (depending on which site).

Ogletree alleges that FindLaw represented its "goods or services had characteristics or benefits" that they did not and that their "agreement conferred or involved rights, remedies, or obligations" that it did not. It alleges Findlaw "failed to disclose information concerning goods or services which was known at the time of the transaction thereby intending to induce Ogletree into entering into the referenced agreement—knowing that it would not have entered" but for these alleged misrepresentations. It also alleges that FindLaw promised to improve the Ogletree Websites so it could get "more clients and more money" and "better results and more business." However Ogletree has fewer clients and less money. Finally, Ogletree alleges FindLaw "misrepresented that it "produces results" with "custom content" developed by "expert copy writers" and a "dedicated team of attorney SEO experts." But FindLaw outsources to Bangalore, India, and FindLaw cut its staff in January 2013 by 25%."

Dissatisfied with FindLaw's revisions to the Ogletree Websites, Ogletree stopped payment in September 2013. During a span of three weeks in November 2013, Ogletree removed the sites from FindLaw's servers and launched them on its own servers. Then, in an attempt to resolve the matter, it relaunched the sites from FindLaw servers. And when the parties did not reach resolution, it again removed them from FindLaw's servers and launched them on its own. In February 2014, Ogletree filed the instant action—asserting claims for fraud, misrepresentation, deceptive trade practices, negligence, breach of warranties, and breach of contract. FindLaw now moves to dismiss all but the breach-of-contract claim. ...

Analysis

"Breach of Contract" versus "Negligent Breach of Contract"

Ogletree alleges FindLaw "was negligent in the promotion and sale of its website redesign, SEO marketing services, and Internet attorney marketing services." FindLaw challenges whether it owed Ogletree any "duty" that could provide the basis for this claim. Whether a defendant owed a duty to a plaintiff is a question of law. *Woehrle v. City of Mankato*, 647 N.W.2d 549, 551 (Minn.Ct.App. 2002).

Ogletree alleges FindLaw breached its "duty of reasonable care by its words and actions against [Ogletree]." Ogletree provides no further elaboration of or authority for this alleged duty. Under Minnesota law, a negligence claim cannot be based on a breach of duty that is indistinguishable from the breach of contract. *Lesmeister v. Dilly*, 330 N.W.2d 95, 102 (Minn.1983) (stressing that Minnesota does not recognize negligent breach of contract). A plaintiff may only maintain a negligence claim in the context of a contract action if "a relationship would exist— which would give rise to the legal duty—without enforcement of the contract promise itself." *Hanks v. Hubbard Broad., Inc.*, 493 N.W.2d 302, 308 (Minn.Ct.App.1992).

As Ogletree has not alleged such a relationship, it appears that any duty FindLaw owed it was "only as a result of the parties' contractual relationship." Thus Ogletree's allegations are "properly analyzed as part of [its] breach-of-contract claim, not as a negligence claim." *Nat'l Broom Co. of Ca. v. Target Corp.*, 2012 WL 4856295, at *4 (D. Minn. Oct. 12, 2012).

NOTES AND QUESTIONS

1) Negligently Designing and Maintaining Attorneys' Websites: Consider the issue and court's analysis in *Ferris & Salter, P.C. v. Thomson Reuters Corporation,* 889 F.Supp.2d 1149 (D. Minn. 2012). West Publishing Corporation does business as Findlaw. Ferris & Salter law firm filed an action against Findlaw—alleging that Findlaw breached a contract and negligently designed and managed the law firm's website. Under Minnesota law, a professional negligence action does not lie against computer engineers and technicians. Therefore, Findlaw moved to dismiss the professional negligence claim under Rule 12(b)(6). The court granted the motion.

2) Computer Consultants' Protection from Professional Malpractice Suits: Other courts also bar professional malpractice actions against computer consultants. *See e.g. Columbus McKinnon Corp. v. China Semiconductor Co., Ltd.*, 867 F.Supp. 1173, 1182 (W.D.N.Y.1994) ("There is no basis in law for extending the doctrine of professional malpractice to cover independent computer consultants."); *Hosp. Computer Sys., Inc. v. Staten Island Hosp.*, 788 F.Supp. 1351, 1361 (D.N.J.1992) (rejecting the argument that

New York law supports a claim of professional malpractice against computer consultants); *Racine Cnty. v. Oracular Milwaukee, Inc.*, 767 N.W.2d 280, 286, 289 (Wis. 2009) ("There is no evidence in the record that lets us decide if the occupation of computer consultants is a 'profession.' From our own experience, we know that many computer skills are learned 'hands on' and not during long and intensive training. We also know that the state of Wisconsin does not license computer consultants. We are not aware of any enforceable code of ethics governing computer consultants."); and *Heidtman Steel Prods., Inc. v. Compuware Corp.*, 2000 WL 621144, at *14 (N.D. Ohio Feb. 15, 2000) ("There is no precedent in Michigan to recognize computer consultants as professionals.").

3. Breach-of-Express-Contract Actions Against Internet Service Providers for Throttling Bargained-for-Exchange "High Internet Speed"

Lyons v. Coxcom, Inc.

718 F.Supp.2d 1232
(S.D. Cal. 2009)

Marilyn L. Huff, District Judge. On November 4, 2008, Plaintiff Lynn Lyons ("Lyons") filed a class action complaint against Defendant Coxcom, Inc.— doing business as Cox Communications, Inc. ("Cox"). On February 6, the Court granted Defendant Cox's motion to dismiss and granted Plaintiff leave to amend.

Background

Plaintiff instituted this class action against Cox, an internet service provider in California, 21 other states, and the District of Columbia. Plaintiff, after seeing and reading Cox's advertisements regarding faster internet speeds, upgraded her internet service to Cox's High Speed Internet Premier with PowerBoost Package in order to obtain faster uploads and downloads to and from the internet. Plaintiff alleges that Cox advertises "blazing fast" internet with PowerBoost speeds up to 20 Mbps for Premier Tier and 12 Mbps for Preferred Tier customers.

She alleges Cox also advertises that with PowerBoost "you can now enjoy doubled upload speeds and up to 33% faster downloads," and that Cox provides "Racing Speeds: 2.3 X Faster than 3 Mbps DLS."

Plaintiff alleges that Cox's terms of service promise to provide specific speed tiers that vary in price based on the speed tier purchased. Plaintiff alleges that Cox breaches its promise to provide high speed internet access and specific speeds by selectively targeting and severely impeding the use of certain peer-to-peer ("P2P") file sharing internet applications ("Blocked Applications") by transmitting unauthorized hidden messages known as reset packets to customers' computers who use such applications, which slows such applications to a mere crawl or stops them altogether.

Plaintiff alleges that she uses the Blocked Applications to download and upload large files such as music and video files and that she has experienced severe limitations on the speed of service when she uses such applications. Plaintiff alleges that Cox impairs use of Blocked Applications irrespective of bandwidth consumption or network congestion. Plaintiff alleges that she has performed her obligations under the terms of the agreements by paying her monthly charges and by not engaging in activities prohibited under the agreements. As a result of this alleged conduct by Cox, Plaintiff alleges causes of action for: (1) breach of contract; and (2) breach of the implied covenant of good faith and fair dealing ...

Defendant Cox moves the Court to strike Plaintiff's class allegations and to dismiss the FAC based on lack of subject matter jurisdiction — as the Court's basis for subject matter jurisdiction rests on the Class Action Fairness Act of 2005. Defendant also moves to dismiss the FAC for failure to state a claim for relief and for failing to plead fraud with specificity. In support of its motions, Cox relies on the terms and conditions of the subscriber agreement referenced by Plaintiff in the FAC. In order for a subscriber to purchase Cox's service, the subscriber is required to check two "Customer Authorization" boxes confirming that he or she has read and accepted the Cox Terms and Conditions of Service, Subscriber Agreement ("SA"), and Acceptable Use Policy ("AUP").

Cox contends that it is permitted to manage the network under the terms of the subscriber agreement and never promised in its advertising unlimited uploading and downloading ability at the maximum speeds offered. The SA sets forth the terms and conditions of the internet service and as part of the contract the subscriber agrees that Cox provides "Network Management" for the "greatest benefit of the greatest number of subscribers including, specifically, traffic prioritization, and protocol filtering." Cox asserts that the contractual provisions directly contradict Plaintiff's allegations, and therefore Plaintiff's claims for breach of contract and inadequate disclosure should be dismissed.

Discussion

A. Breach of Contract

Plaintiff's first cause of action alleges Cox breached a written or implied contract.) In a breach of contract claim under California law, a plaintiff must allege (1) a contract, (2) plaintiff's performance, (3) defendant's breach, and (4) damages. *McDonald v. John P. Scripps Newspaper,* 257 Cal.Rptr. 473, 475 (Cal.Ct.App.1989). Under the terms of the SA, however, the agreement "shall be exclusively governed by, and construed in accordance with, the laws of the State of Georgia." Under Georgia law, "[t]he elements of a right to recover for a breach of contract are the breach and the resultant damages to the party who has the right to complain about the contract being broken." *Budget Rent-a-Car of Atlanta, Inc. v. Webb,* 220 Ga.App. 278, 280 (1996). A contract of adhesion is strictly construed against the drafter and as reasonably understood by the consumer. *See Hosp. Auth. of Houston County v. Bohannon,* 272 Ga.App. 96, 98-99 (2005) and *Graham v. Scissor-Tail, Inc.,* 28 Cal.3d 807, 820 (1981).

Plaintiff alleges that she entered into a written or implied contract with Defendants to pay monthly fees in order to obtain the service, which Defendant promises will provide high speed access to the internet for uploads and downloads at specified speeds, that she performed her obligations under the contract by paying monthly fees and by not engaging in any activities prohibited by the Agreement, that Defendant breached the contract by restricting Plaintiff's access to, and use of, the service at speeds promised in the Agreement, and that she was damaged by the breach because she did not receive the service at the speeds for which she paid.

Plaintiff further alleges that the Terms and Conditions, SA, and AUP are required to be accepted by a subscriber in order to purchase the service, the terms of the service explicitly promise specific internet access speeds, and Defendant charges more for faster speeds. Plaintiff alleges that the "Limitations of Service" state that the Preferred with PowerBoost Package has a maximum downstream speed of 5 to 9 megabits per second and maximum upstream speed of 512 kilobits to 2 megabits per second and that the Premier with PowerBoost Package has a maximum downstream speed of 10 to 20 megabits per second and maximum upstream speed of 1 to 2 megabits per second. Plaintiff alleges that she reasonably believed—based upon the fact that each progressive tier of the service costs more—that each tier of the service will attain a minimum speed that is at least as fast as the maximum speed promised for the tier below.

The SA also contains a provision that Cox has "the right to manage its network for the greatest benefit of the greatest number of subscribers including, without limitation, the following: rate limiting, rejection or removal of 'spam' or otherwise unsolicited bulk email, anti-virus mechanisms, traffic prioritization, and protocol filtering." Plaintiff alleges that none of the posted policies or terms of service or use state that Defendant can or will impede, limit, discontinue, block or otherwise impair or treat differently the Blocked Applications, and that Defendant impairs and blocks the Blocked Applications in an arbitrary and discriminatory manner and irrespective of the bandwidth consumed by a user of the Blocked Applications.

Plaintiff also alleges that by specifically enumerating the circumstances in which Defendant reserves the right to manage the network, Defendant implicitly promises Plaintiff that they will have otherwise unlimited use of the service at the promised speeds, including with respect to the Blocked Applications.

The court concludes that Plaintiff fails to sufficiently plead a breach of contract —as she points to no term of the contract that was breached by Cox. Plaintiff alleges that Cox promised specific speeds of internet access. But as Plaintiff alleges in her complaint and as the Limitations of Service state, the speeds are maximum speeds attainable by each tier of service, not a promise that at all times a customer's service will deliver those maximums. The Limitations of Service also states: "[T]he limitations set forth herein are approximate and may vary from time to time."

Contrary to Plaintiff's assertions, Cox never promised a minimum speed for each tier of service and such an implied term cannot be read into a fully-integrated contract. *See Collins v. Abel Holding Co.*, 89 Ga.App. 337, 341–426 (1953) ("This Agreement constitutes the entire agreement and understanding between the parties with respect to its subject matter and supersedes and replaces any and all prior written or oral agreements."). Furthermore, Plaintiff does not allege that she never obtained the specified maximums, only that occasionally Defendant sent reset packets that disrupted certain P2P applications while Plaintiff was downloading or uploading large files.

The contract specifically states that a user "must ensure that your activities do not improperly restrict, inhibit, or degrade any other user's use of the Service, nor represent (in Cox's sole judgment) an unusually great burden on the network itself," and Cox specifically reserves the right to manage its network. Cox also does not warrant "the service will be uninterrupted or error free … or any files sent by or to you will be transmitted in uncorrupted form or within a reasonable period of time." Plaintiff subscribed to a service and even construing the contract through the lense of the reasonable consumer as Plaintiff urges, subscribers plainly agreed to use limitations and Cox's discretion to manage its network, including traffic prioritization and decisions concerning overburdening of the network. The agreement makes no promises regarding minimum speeds and never promises that all applications will function at certain speeds at all times.

Accordingly, the court dismisses with leave to amend Plaintiff's breach of contract claim, as she fails to plead a breach of any contract term under Georgia or California law.

B. Implied Covenant of Good Faith and Fair Dealing

Plaintiff's second cause of action is for a breach of the covenant of good faith and fair dealing. California recognizes that every contract contains an implied covenant of good faith and fair dealing, "[imposing] upon each contracting party the duty to refrain from doing anything which would render performance of the contract impossible by any act of his own, but also the duty to do everything that the contract presupposes that he will do to accomplish its purpose." 1 Witkin, Summary of California Law, Contracts § 798 (10th ed.2005). In order to state a claim for relief on an implied covenant theory, there must first be a contractual relationship between the parties. § 800. "The essence of the good faith covenant is objectively reasonable conduct." *Id.* § 801. A breach of the implied covenant of good faith and fair dealing requires something more than a breach of the contractual duty itself. *Careau & Co. v. Security Pacific Business Credit, Inc.,* 222 Cal.App.3d 1371, 1394 387 (1990). This "implies unfair dealing rather than mistaken judgment." *Id.*

According to the Georgia Supreme Court, "[e]very contract imposes upon each party a duty of good faith and fair dealing in its performance and enforcement." *Brack v. Brownlee,* 246 Ga. 818, 820 (1980). Under Georgia law, where a party cannot maintain a cause of action for breach of contract, that party cannot maintain an independent cause of action for a breach of good faith, because the implied covenant of good faith and fair dealing "is not an independent contract term." *Stuart Enter. Intern., Inc. v. Peykan, Inc.,* 252 Ga.App. 231, 234 (2001).

The court concludes that Plaintiff fails to plead a cause of action for a breach of the implied covenant of good faith and fair dealing. Plaintiff's claim for breach of contract fails, and thus under either California or Georgia law her claim for breach of the implied covenant must also fail. Accordingly, the Court dismisses with leave to amend Plaintiff's claim for breach of contract.

It is so ordered.

NOTES AND QUESTIONS

1) Implied Covenant of Good Faith and Fair Dealing. The majority of state supreme courts have embraced the rule that appears in *Coxcom. See e.g., Wood v. N.J. Mfrs. Ins. Co.*, 206 N.J. 562, 577 (2011) ("[E]very contract in New Jersey contains an implied covenant of good faith and fair dealing that is, neither party shall do anything which will have the effect of destroying or injuring the right of the other party to receive the fruits of the contract[.]"), *Cantwell v. City of Boise*, 191 P.3d 205, 213 (Idaho 2008) ("Idaho law recognizes a cause of action for breach of an implied covenant of good faith and fair dealing); and, *In re Hennepin Cnty. 1986 Recycling Bond Litig.*, 540 N.W.2d 494, 502 (Minn.1995) ("Under Minnesota law, every contract includes an implied covenant of good faith and fair dealing. ...").

2) Texas Common Law Duty of Good Faith and Fair Dealing. In *Natividad v. Alexsis, Inc.*, 875 S.W.2d 695, 697-699 (Tex. 1994), Justice Gonzalez wrote: "[T]his court has declined to *impose* an implied covenant of good faith and fair dealing in every contract. ... [But] we have recognized that a duty of good faith and fair dealing may arise as a result of a *special relationship* between the parties governed or created by a contract."

3) Proving a Cause of Action Based on a Breach of a Covenant of Good Faith and Fair Dealing. *See New Breed Logistics, Inc. v. CT INDY, NH TT, LLC,* 2011 WL 4909116 (Conn. Super.) ("An action for breach of the covenant of good faith and fair dealing requires proof of three essential elements: (1) that the plaintiff and the defendant were parties to a contract under which the plaintiff reasonably expected to receive certain benefits; (2) that the defendant engaged in conduct that injured the plaintiff's right to receive benefits it reasonably expected to receive under the contract; and (3) that when committing the acts by which it injured the plaintiff's right to receive under the contract, the defendant was acting in bad faith.")

4) Contracting Parties' Reasonable Expectations, Good Faith, and Fair Dealing. In *Magnan v. Anaconda Industries, Inc.*, 193 Conn. 558, 567 (1984), the Supreme Court of Connecticut addressed the essential purpose of the implied covenant of good faith and fair dealing: "[It is] a rule of construction designed to fulfill the reasonable expectations of the contracting parties as they presumably intended. The principle, therefore, cannot be applied to achieve a result contrary to the clearly expressed terms of a contract, unless, possibly, those terms are contrary to public policy."

4. Breach-of-Implied-Contract Actions Against Internet Service Providers for Throttling Bargained-for-Exchange "High Internet Speed"

Fink v. Time Warner Cable

810 F.Supp.2d 633
(S.D.N.Y. Oct. 28, 2011)

Laura Taylor Swain, District Judge. Plaintiffs Jessica Fink ("Fink") and Brett Noia ("Noia") (collectively, "Plaintiffs") bring this putative nationwide class action pursuant to 18 U.S.C. § 1030. Plaintiffs allege principally that Defendant wrongfully limits Plaintiffs' use of certain peer-to-peer applications without authorization and thereby causes damage to Plaintiffs' computers. Plaintiffs also assert various state law claims ... concerning the nature and quality of its internet service. This Court has jurisdiction of this action pursuant to 28 U.S.C. §§ 1331, 1332 and 1367.1

Defendant moves to dismiss certain of Plaintiffs' claims pursuant to Rule 12(c) of the Federal Rules of Civil Procedure and for summary judgment as to certain of Plaintiffs' claims pursuant to Federal Rule of Civil Procedure 56(a).2 Plaintiffs move—pursuant to Rule 12(f) of the Federal Rules of Civil Procedure—to strike portions of certain documents submitted by Defendant in support of its motion for summary judgment. The Court has considered carefully all of the parties' submissions.

Background

In their Complaint, Plaintiffs assert claims for … breach of contract (Count V) and breach of implied-in-fact contract (Count VI). … Plaintiffs sue on their own behalf and on behalf of a nationwide class of persons, which includes all people who subscribed to Defendant's Road Runner internet service from November 7, 2003, to the date of class certification, pursuant to Rules 23(a), (b)(2), and (b)(3) of the Federal Rules of Civil Procedure. Fink also sues on behalf of a subclass of New York residents. Noia sues on behalf of a subclass of California residents.

The Complaint

The following allegations are drawn from the Complaint and are assumed to be true for the purposes of adjudicating Defendant's Rule 12(c) motion. Defendant—headquartered in New York—is one of the world's largest media and entertainment conglomerates. And it serves as an internet service provider (ISP) to subscribers of its Road Runner High Speed Online internet service (Road Runner). Defendant provides Road Runner service to millions of subscribers in most states across the United States—including New York, Texas, Maine, Ohio, and California.

Plaintiff Jessica Fink is a citizen of New York and resides in New York County, New York. Plaintiff Brett Noia is a citizen of California and resides in Los Angeles County, California. During the Class Period, both Plaintiffs Fink and Noia subscribed to Defendant's Road Runner service.

Defendant used advertisements in order to sell its Road Runner service. Defendant's Road Runner service is named after a cartoon character best known for its lightening speed. Defendant purported to provide internet service with "blazing speed" and an "always on connection" that was the "fastest, easiest way to get online." Defendant advertised that "Road Runner Honors Your Need for Speed; You'll Never Get Road Rage with Road Runner." Further, Defendant advertised in its online promotional materials that it would provide premium service as compared to its competitors—stating that its service is "up to 3 times the speed of most standard DSL packages and up to 100x faster than dial-up so your family can spend their time on the computer learning, experiencing, and playing instead of waiting."

These representations allowed Defendant to charge consumers a premium of up to more than 100% of the fees charged by its competitors. Both Plaintiffs Fink and Noia relied on Defendant's advertisements in deciding to purchase Defendant's service and pay a premium for it. Defendant did not disclose that it would interfere with or limit their internet connections or their attempts to engage in peer-to-peer communication. Had Defendant disclosed that its Road Runner service did not live up to the advertised descriptions, or that it would intentionally interfere with their internet access, Plaintiffs would not have paid a premium for the service.

Defendant engaged in a network management practice that Plaintiffs refer to as "throttling" to interfere with and limit subscribers' internet communications. This practice of throttling was not authorized by Plaintiffs. Throttling interferes with subscribers' ability to share content through peer-to-peer (P2P) transmissions. Computers exchange information on the internet by using Transmission Control Protocol (TCP)—which delivers a stream of bytes from one program on one computer to another. TCP is often used in P2P transmissions, which tap into multiple other participating computers and exchange the data, allowing its users to share content files and real-time data with each other over the internet. When a computer finds that a P2P transmission is being blocked, it communicates TCP messages called reset packets that cause inbound internet connections to close down and abort the transmission of P2P content. One method of throttling is accomplished by sending forged reset packets to computers, which cause the computers engaged in P2P file sharing to abort file transfers and stop the relevant communication. The forged reset packets are disguised as communications from the computers themselves.

Defendant uses the practice of throttling to frustrate its subscribers' efforts to share online content via P2P networks. In particular, Defendant's practices affect BitTorrent peer-to-peer file sharing communications, Gnutella, Skype, and other protocols or applications that communicate audio, video, voice, and other data content online. The types of information whose availability is affected include information about other computers around the world participating in a P2P network; information about query terms and results of searches across P2P networks; data contents of files; and data encapsulating the content of text and voice communications.

Defendant's conduct was motivated by a desire to maximize its profit. Defendant misrepresented the qualities of its service in order to lure subscribers into paying a premium price, steer consumers to its added-price content by throttling access to similar content available for free elsewhere on the Internet, and avoid the costs of infrastructure upgrades by throttling transmissions while recruiting additional customers.

Plaintiffs have sustained the following damages and losses as a result of Defendant's conduct. First, Plaintiff Noia relied on the Road Runner service to upload large image and vector files for his work as a freelance designer; to download files; and to watch licensed media. However, he consistently found that uploads from his internet connection would drop to extremely low speeds: he should have been able to upload at up to 300 kB/s, but instead he could not usually upload faster than 10kB/s and never faster than 30 kB/s. For this reason, he regularly rented a computer at Kinko's using his own money.

Noia lost work opportunities because he was unable to respond to client requests and meet professional deadlines, due to having to drive to Kinko's. He also lost the value of this time. Plaintiff Noia estimates these losses for one year to be between $5,500 and $7,000. Second, Noia tried subscribing to Verizon's cellular data service as an alternative means of transmitting his large files, at $59.99 per month. Verizon's service was, however, by its nature slower than Defendant's.

Third, both named Plaintiffs used Skype—which allows users to make free voice calls over the internet through a P2P protocol. Fink and Noia were unable to make and receive Skype calls allegedly due to Defendant's throttling, which allegedly compromised the integrity of their computer systems. It also impaired the availability of data because their computers were unable to send or receive information from other Skype users. Fourth, both named Plaintiffs wasted time and effort in determining what was causing the slow connection. They rebooted their computers or made repeated attempts to reconnect to various people on Skype. They also incurred costs for using land lines and cell phones to call these people.

Evidentiary Proffers

The following facts are undisputed except as otherwise indicated. Plaintiff Fink has been a subscriber to Time Warner Cable's internet service since on or around December 4, 2007. Plaintiff Noia was a subscriber to Time Warner Cable's internet service from on or around March 31, 2008, through on or around January 5, 2009. He is not currently a subscriber to Time Warner Cable's internet service.

Defendant contends that detailed service terms and agreements that included express provisions permitting the network management practices at issue here were delivered to Plaintiffs in connection with installations and at other times. Plaintiffs dispute certain allegations concerning the content and delivery of these documents. In light of Defendant's withdrawal of the aspects of its motions that were premised on the content of these documents, the disputes are not material.

Discussion

Motion for Judgment on the Pleadings

Defendant moves for judgment on the pleadings pursuant to Federal Rule of Civil Procedure 12(c) on ... Plaintiff's claims for breach of contract and breach of implied-in-fact contract. The standard governing a Rule 12(c) motion is equivalent to that governing motions under Rule 12(b)(6) of the Federal Rules of Civil Procedure. In deciding a motion to dismiss a complaint for failure to state a claim pursuant to Rule 12(b)(6) of the Federal Rules of Civil Procedure, the Court must "accept as true all factual statements alleged in the complaint and draw reasonable inferences in favor of the non-moving party." *McCarthy v. Dun & Bradstreet Corp.*, 482 F.3d 184, 191 (2d Cir. 2007) "To survive a motion to dismiss, a complaint must contain sufficient factual matter, accepted as true, to state a claim to relief that is plausible on its face." *Ashcroft v. Iqbal*, 129 S.Ct. 1937, 1949 (2009). "Where a complaint pleads facts that are merely consistent with a defendant's liability, it stops short of the line between possibility and plausibility of entitlement to relief."...

Count V—Breach of Contract Claim

Plaintiffs claim: (1) they entered into a contract with Defendant to pay monthly fees in exchange for its high-speed internet service, (2) they performed their obligations under the contract by paying their monthly fees, and (3) Defendant breached the contract by intentionally interfering with their access to and use of the high-speed internet service. Defendants argue that the breach of contract claim must be dismissed because Plaintiffs have neither attached what they consider to be the contract to the Complaint nor referred to or cited the specific contract terms at issue.

To properly plead a breach of contract claim under New York law, a party must identify (1) the existence of a contract; (2) performance by one party; (3) breach of the contract by the other party; and (4) resulting damages. *Rexnord Holdings, Inc. v. Bidermann*, 21 F.3d

522, 525 (2d Cir.1994). The plaintiff does not need to attach a copy of the alleged contract to his complaint or quote directly from the contract alleged to have been breached. *See Griffin Bros., Inc. v. Yatto*, 415 N.Y.S.2d 114 (3rd Dept.1979). However, a breach of contract claim will be dismissed where a plaintiff fails to allege "the essential terms of the parties' purported contract, including the specific provisions of the contract upon which liability is predicated." *Martinez v. Vakko Holding A.S.*, 2008 WL 2876529, at *2 (S.D.N.Y. 2008). The plaintiff must allege the essential terms in nonconclusory language. *Sirohi v. Trustees of Columbia University*, 162 F.3d 1148 (2d Cir.1998).

Here, Plaintiffs have not set forth with specificity the essential terms of the contract that they allege Defendant has breached with requisite specificity. Plaintiffs claim that they entered into a contract with Defendant to pay monthly fees in exchange for "high-speed" internet service. This simple characterization of the nature of the promise, and the equally simplistic allegations that Defendant failed to perform, are insufficient to make the requisite plausible factual demonstration of the basis of Plaintiffs' claim. Defendant's motion for judgment on the pleadings as to Count V is therefore granted.

Count VI—Breach of Implied-in-Fact Contract Claim

In its reply papers, Defendant seeks judgment on the pleadings as to Plaintiffs' breach of an implied-in-fact contract and breach of the implied covenant of good faith and fair dealing causes of action (Count VI). Under New York law, an implied-in-fact contract requires "consideration, mutual assent, legal capacity and legal subject matter" to be established. *Maas v. Cornell University*, 94 N.Y.2d 87, 94 (1999). There is no dispute as to the parties' legal capacity to enter into such a contract or that the alleged contract was regarding a legal subject matter. The Plaintiffs allege that they paid for and received cable services on a monthly basis from Defendant. This is sufficient to meet both the "mutual assent" and "consideration" aspects of the alleged contract. *See Berlinger v. Lisi*, 731 N.Y.S.2d 916 (3rd Dep't 2001) ("As a general rule, the performance and acceptance of services can give rise to the inference of an implied contract to pay for the reasonable value of such services.").

However, Plaintiffs' claim relies on advertisements to supply the terms of the alleged implied-in-fact contract. Plaintiffs assert that the implied-in-fact contract was breached because the "Defendant's practice of offering 'low-speed' internet service" was in conflict with

"Defendant's promises regarding the quality of its high-speed internet service," which they alleged were the basis of the implied-in-fact contract. Because the advertisements referred to by Plaintiffs do not contain sufficient specific, concrete, factual representations such that they could be interpreted to supply the terms of an implied contract, Plaintiffs have failed to state a cause of action in this regard. Defendant's motion for judgment on the pleadings as to Count VI is therefore granted. …

Conclusion

For the foregoing reasons, Defendant's motion for judgment on the pleadings is … granted as to Counts V and VI. … Plaintiffs' request for leave to replead Counts V and VI is granted. Any second amended complaint must be filed by September 30, 2011. Failure to timely file a further amended complaint by this date will result in dismissal of Counts V and VI with prejudice.

So ordered.

B. Attorneys' Breach of Warranty Actions

Once more, consider the relevant facts in *Ogletree, Abbott, Clay & Reed Law Firm, L.L.P. v. FindLaw*, 2014 WL 2611862, *4 (D. Minn. 2014). Ogletree Law Firm hired FindLaw—a subsidiary of West Publishing Corporation and Thomson Reuters Holdings, Inc.—to develop Ogletree's websites. Ogletree alleged that FindLaw decreased the traffic on the websites and injured Ogletree's business. More specifically, Ogletree alleged that FindLaw ignored Ogletree's webpage-naming conventions—which created error messages when users followed inbound links set to the prior page names.

Also FindLaw added software code to Ogletree's websites that required potential clients "to download a large amount of data in order to view certain pages. … [T]he previous websites required users to download only .5 MB of data to view them. The revised websites, however, required users to download more than 1.5 MB of data in some instances." The revised websites also required users to load twice as many files as the previous websites. The revisions affected the websites' load time—a factor which determines one's Google's ranking. "In addition to adversely impacting Google rankings, these changes resulted in users abandoning the Ogletree Websites before they had loaded, causing Ogletree to lose out on potential clients."

Ogletree filed a breach-of-warranties action against FindLaw. Now, consider the federal district judge's cursory analysis and conclusion after citing *Master Blaster, Inc. v. Dammann,* 781 N.W.2d 19, 35 (Minn.Ct.App. 2010) and *Cargill, Inc. v. Ron Burge Trucking, Inc.,* 2013 WL 608520, at *3 (D.Minn. Feb. 19, 2013):

> Ogletree asserts that FindLaw breached its warranties by selling services that were not "of *merchantable* quality" and not fit for their intended use. Although the claim is styled as "breach of *expressed and implied warranty,*" Ogletree has not identified any *express warranty* pleaded in the Complaint. It pleaded only *implied warranties.* But its claim fails on this front too, because *implied warranties* arise in contracts for the *sale of goods, not services.* Ogletree's contracts with FindLaw were for services. *Ogletree,* 2014 WL 2611862, *4.

To be sure, in *Ogletree,* West Publishing Corporation, Thomson Reuters Holdings and FindLaw provided allegedly defective technological services rather than technological goods. But, an important question arises: When sellers deliver inferior technological services or goods, are solo practitioners or small-firm attorneys generally precluded from commencing breach-of-express-warranty and breach-of-implied-warranty actions under the common law and the Uniform Commercial Code? Did the district judge in *Ogletree* reached the wrong conclusion? Or did the *Ogletree* court embrace an exception to a general rule? For answers, consider the following cases and materials.

NOTES AND QUESTIONS

1) "Common Law Warranty"—A Contractual Term. "A warranty is a contractual term concerning some aspect of the sale—such as title to the goods, or their quality or quantity." *Windham at*

Carmel Mountain Ranch Assn. v. Superior Court, 109 Cal.App.4th 1162, 1168 (2003). "[A warranty is] an assurance by one party to a contract of the existence of a fact upon which the other party may rely. ... [I]t amounts to a promise to indemnify the promisee for any loss if the fact warranted proves untrue. ... [A] warranty is not a promise of performance, but a statement of present fact." *First Bank of the Americas v. Motor Car Funding, Inc.*, 690 N.Y.S.2d 17, 21 (A.D. [1st Dept.] 1999);

2) "Common Law Warranty"—A Promise or an Affirmation. "A warranty is defined as an affirmation of fact or promise by the seller of items possessing certain characteristics." *Alpine Climate Control, Inc. v. DJ's, Inc.*, 78 P.3d 685, 690 (Wyo. 2003); and (4) "A warranty is an agreement—collateral to the sale of goods or service—by which the seller undertakes to vouch for the condition or quality of the goods sold or service provided. Even though a warranty is a part of a sales contract, it is an independent subsidiary promise, collateral to the main object of the contract, the breach of which gives rise to a cause of action for damages." *Glockzin v. Rhea*, 760 S.W.2d 665, 669 (Tex. App.–Hous. [1st Dist.] 1988)

3) "Express Warranties" Under the Uniform Commercial Code. Under the UCC § 2–313, each of the following acts creates an express warranty: (1) an affirmation of fact or promise made by the seller to the buyer relating to the goods that becomes the basis of the bargain, (2) a description of the goods that becomes part of the basis of the bargain, and (3) a sample or model made part of the basis of the bargain.

---

1. Vendors' Defective Office Equipment and Attorneys' Breach of Express Warranty Actions

In re HP Inkjet Printer Litigation

2006 WL 563048
(N.D. Cal. 2006)

Jeremy Fogel, Judge. Hewlett-Packard Co. (HP) manufactures printing supplies and inkjet printers. Nicklos Ciolino (Ciolino) and Daniel Feder (Feder) (collectively, Plaintiffs) both own HP printers purchased from CompUSA and Best Buy that use "smart chip" technology. "Smart chip" technology is designed to inform the consumer of the remaining ink level in an HP ink cartridge and when to reorder ink for an HP printer. For instance, once the "smart chip" reads that the cartridge's ink level is low, the "smart chip" sends a warning message to the consumer's printer that the ink level is low and new ink needs to be ordered.

Plaintiffs allege that HP engaged in unfair and deceptive conduct in connection with the "smart chip" technology in its ink cartridges. Plaintiffs contend that the "smart chips" are "programmed to prematurely register ink replacement long before depletion of the ink supply. Frequently, these cartridges can register as empty when they in fact have substantial ink remaining." Plaintiffs also contend that HP's "smart chip"—without regard to the actual supply of remaining ink—"is capable of rendering a cartridge unusable through the use of a built-in expiration date that is concealed from consumers. An external date stamp instead only discloses the end of warranty date, but not the date in which the cartridge is rendered unusable."

In addition, HP allegedly "fails to explain the expiration feature at the point of purchase and omits such information in their marketing materials." Specifically, HP's "SureSupply" campaign and website omit such information. First, HP's "SureSupply" campaign promotes the "smart chip" technology as "a free user-friendly tool enabled through Smart printing technology that provides ... an easy way to manage and purchase HP genuine printing supplies."

Second, HP's website claims that "SureSupply automatically tracks and manages customers' toner or ink level usage, and provides alerts via email or cell phone when toner or ink is low. With a couple of clicks of a button, customers can access cartridge information, pricing and purchasing options that best meet their needs from the reseller of their choice." Plaintiffs contend that HP's "SureSupply" campaign is false because the actual design of the "smart chip" limits consumers' use of ink cartridges and makes consumers believe that their cartridges are empty or expired and must be replaced. In sum, Plaintiffs assert that "HP has deliberately withheld from its consumers information about the true functioning of the smart chip."

On October 31, 2005, Plaintiffs filed an amended class action complaint against HP. Plaintiffs asserted a claim for breach of express warranty. On January 6, 2006, HP filed a motion to dismiss and in the alternative a motion to strike. HP claims that Plaintiffs have not alleged an actual injury. HP also contends that the *breach of express warranty* claim fails for lack of notice and insufficient facts. On February 3, 2006, Plaintiffs filed opposition and HP filed a reply on February 10, 2006. Having considered the briefs, relevant evidence, and the oral arguments at the hearing on February 24, 2006, the Court will grant in part and deny in part the motion to dismiss and deny the motion to strike. ...

Breach of Express Warranty

HP contends that Plaintiffs' breach of express warranty claim should be dismissed because there are not sufficient facts to justify such a claim. "In order to plead a cause of action for breach of express warranty, one must allege the exact terms of the warranty, plaintiff's reasonable reliance thereon, and a breach of that warranty which proximately causes plaintiff injury." *Williams v. Beechnut Nutrition Corp.*, 185 Cal.App.3d 135, 142 (1986). The court agrees that Plaintiffs' amended complaint does not comply with the requirements of *Williams*. While Plaintiffs state that HP breached warranty obligations with the use of an expiration date as to the "smart chip" cartridges, it is unclear what precise terms of the warranty were supposedly breached. Nor do Plaintiffs identify any specific warranty provision upon which they allegedly relied. For example, paragraph 26 of the amended complaint provides: "According to the Limited Warranty for HP Inkjet Print Cartridge Printerheads and Ink Supplies, HP will void the warranty on any printer or cartridge if a cartridge was refilled using a third party device."

HP further contends that Plaintiffs cannot recover for breach of express warranty because timely notice of such breach was not given. The California Commercial Code § 2607(3)(A) provides that a "buyer must—within a reasonable time after he discovers or should have discovered any breach—notify the seller of breach or be barred from any remedy." Cal. Com.Code § 2607(3)(A). "The requirement of notice of breach is ... designed to allow the defendant opportunity for repairing the defective item, reducing damages, avoiding defective products in the future, and negotiating settlements." *Pollard v. Saxe & Yolles Dev. Co.*, 12 Cal.3d 374, 380 (1974).

However, timely notice of a breach under California law is no longer required where the action is against a manufacturer on a warranty that arises independently of a contract of sale—such as a manufacturer's express warranty. *Greenman v. Yuba Power Prods.*, 59 Cal.2d 57, 61 (1963). The *Greenman* court explained: "The notice requirement ... is not an appropriate one for the court to adopt in actions by injured consumers against manufacturers with whom they have not dealt." According to *Greenman*, the notice requirement "becomes a booby-trap for the unwary. The injured consumer is seldom steeped in the business practice which justifies the rule, and at least until he has had legal advice it will not occur to him to give notice to one whom he has had no dealings."

In the instant case, Plaintiffs bought their HP printers from retail sellers. HP's express warranties were not contained in the contract of sale between the Plaintiffs and the retail sellers, but instead were created independently in HP's brochure. Thus, even if Plaintiffs did not give timely notice of breach of express warranty to HP, the claim is not barred. *Corp. of Presiding Bishop of Church of Jesus Christ of Latter-Day Saints v. Cavanaugh*, 217 Cal.App.2d 492, 514-15 (1963) (finding that "even if the plaintiff did not give timely notice of breach of warranty to the manufacturer, the cause of action should not be held to have been barred").

Regardless, "notice otherwise given within a reasonable period of time can under California law follow commencement of suit—provided it is subsequently and properly pleaded." *Hampton v. Gebhardt's Chili Powder Co.*, 294 F.2d 172, 174 (9th Cir.1961). On November 7, 2005, Plaintiffs subsequently provided notice to HP contained in a letter from Plaintiffs' counsel, Bruce L. Simon. The letter provided that Plaintiffs "hereby demand that within 30 days ... HP cease to engage in and rectify the wrongful business practices detailed above." In addition, plaintiffs demand that HP refund, replace, and correct the defective inkjet printers and printer cartridges sold to plaintiffs. ..." The letter, therefore, provided HP with notice and an opportunity to cure its breaches, which HP allegedly has failed to do. Accordingly, Plaintiffs will be given leave to amend their claim for breach of express warranty to remedy the deficiencies described above.

Unjust Enrichment

Here, Plaintiffs assert that, "the express warranty at issue is not a binding agreement between the parties. There has been no bargain-for-exchange between plaintiffs and HP. Rather, the bargain for exchange occurred between the retail seller and the plaintiffs." Further, "Plaintiffs received the written warranties subsequent to their purchases of HP's products. Thus, the warranty itself was not specifically contracted for and cannot, by any means, limit plaintiffs' right to recover for unjust enrichment." Moreover, although the terms of HP's written warranty agreements may govern the relationship between HP and Plaintiffs, Plaintiffs may plead an unjust enrichment claim in the alternative. Accordingly, HP's motion to dismiss Plaintiffs' unjust enrichment claim will be denied.

Order

Good cause therefore appearing, it is hereby ordered HP's motion to dismiss is granted in part and denied in part and HP's motion to strike is denied. Plaintiffs may file an amended complaint on or before March 31, 2006, that addresses the deficiencies identified herein.

It is so ordered.

NOTES AND QUESTIONS

1) **Breach-of-an-Express-Warranty Action—Establishing a Prima Case Using Different Elements.** In Texas, a plaintiff must prove five elements to establish a breach-of-an-express-warranty action: (1) the defendant sold services to the plaintiff; (2) the defendant made a representation to the plaintiff about the characteristics of the services by affirmation of fact, by promise, or by description; (3) the representation became part of the basis of the bargain; (4) the defendant breached the warranty; (5) the plaintiff notified the defendant of the breach; and (6) the plaintiff suffered injury. *See Paragon General Contractors, Inc. v. Larco Const., Inc.,*227 S.W.3d 876, 886 (Tex. App. Ct. – Dallas 2007), citing *Sw. Bell Tel. Co. v. FDP Corp.*, 811 S.W.2d 572, 576–77 & n. 3 (Tex.1991) (embracing some of the U.C.C.'s elements). However, under New Jersey law, a breach of express warranty action has four elements: (1) proof a contract between the parties; (2) proof of a breach of contract; (3) proof of damages flowing from the breach; and (4) proof the complainant performed its contractual obligations. *Hemy v. Perdue Farms, Inc.*, 2011 WL 6002463, *23 (D.N.J.). On the other hand, in Minnesota, an action for breach of express warranty requires a complainant to establish three elements: (1) a warranty's existence; (2) a breach of the warranty; and (3) a causal link between the breach and the harm. *Peterson v. Bendix Home Sys., Inc.*, 318 N.W.2d 50, 52–53 (Minn. 1982).

2) **A Breach-of-Warranty Action Sounds Only in Tort.** *See Iacono v. Anderson Concrete Corp.*, 326 N.E.2d 267, 270 n.1 (Ohio 1975) ("This court has recognized that, historically, an action

grounded on breach of warranty sounded in tort rather than contract. It is a mistaken notion that use of the term 'warranty' always carried the implication of a contractual relationship."); and, *Humber v. Morton,* 426 S.W.2d 554, 556 (Tex.1968) (under Texas law, breach of implied warranties of merchantability and fitness for a particular purpose sound in tort and not in contract).

3) **A Breach-of-Warranty Action Sounds Only in Contract.** *See Fried v. Freeman*, 176 S.E.2d 458, 460 (Ga. App. 1970) ("An action for mere breach of warranty unmixed with fraud sounds in contract, not tort"); and, *Rucker v. Hagar et al.,* 230 P. 70, 71 (Kan. 1924) ("Warranty sounds in contract ... and liability predicated on breach of warranty is contract and not tort liability.").

4) **A Breach-of-Warranty Action Sounds in Both Contract and Tort.** *See Reid v. Eckerds Drugs, Inc.,* 253 S.E.2d 344, 347 (N.C.1979) ("It is now generally acknowledged that the action for breach of warranty is an offspring of mixed parentage, aspects of it sounding in both tort and contract, but following strictly the rules and precedents of neither."); and, *Mitchell v. Pearson Enterprises*, 697 P.2d 240, 247 (Utah 1985) ("An action for breach of warranty may sound in either contract or tort.").

5) **Whether a Breach-of-Warranty Action Sounds in Contract or Tort Depends.** *See Evans Laboratories, Inc. v. Roberts*, 423 S.W.2d 271, 272 (Ark. 1968) ("Whether a suit for breach of warranty sounds in contract or in tort depends upon the nature of the suit, the nature and extent of the warranty, and the effect or results of the breach."); and, *Gazija v. Nicholas Jerns Co.,* 543 P.2d 338, 340 (Wash. 1975) ("Whether an action sounds in contract or tort is determined from the pleadings and complaint as a whole and the evidence relied upon, not by particular words and allegations, the form adopted by the pleader, what the pleader calls it, or the understanding of counsel or the trial court.").

2. Vendors' Inferior Technological Goods and Actions for Breach of an Implied Warranty of Merchantability Under the UCC

Damashek, P.C. v. Wang Laboratories, Inc.

150 A.D.2d 151
(N.Y. Sup. App. Ct. 1989)

Walter M. Schackman, Judge. Plaintiff—Philip M. Damashek, P.C.—purchased a computer system from defendant—Wang Laboratories, Inc. The system was installed in April 1981. During the ensuing months, the system became inoperative on numerous occasions. Although defendant serviced the system and replaced many components, problems persisted. Plaintiff contends that the disk drive was defective. Defendant maintains that the electrical supply was "dirty" and caused the system to fail, a situation for which defendant could not be held accountable.

In November 1981, the system was still not functioning properly. Therefore, plaintiff commenced the present action, seeking damages for breach of implied warranty of merchantability, and for breach of an alleged oral servicing agreement. On December 17, 1981, after service of the complaint, defendant delivered a new disk drive. This disk drive was never installed [and] removed together—along with the other equipment—to storage.

After trial, the jury—in answering special interrogatories—found that the original disk drive was unfit for its ordinary purpose. However, this breach of warranty was not the proximate cause of any damages. The jury responded in the negative to the compound question whether a service contract existed, and whether the contract had been breached. At the foot of the verdict sheet, the jury, not responding to any interrogatory, wrote that it believed that plaintiff should be permitted to retain the computer equipment—including the replacement disk drive—without any further payment to defendant.

We do not find the jury's verdict inconsistent. The jury might have found that any defect in the disk drive was promptly repaired by defendant, and that the continuing breakdowns were caused by "dirty" electricity. The jury might also have found that the delivery of the replacement disk drive was a "cure" within the meaning of UCC § 2–508. Nor should damages be automatically recovered upon proof of a breach of warranty. There must also be proof of damages which are proximately caused by the breach. *See* Comment 13 to UCC § 2–314, UCC § 2–715(2)(b); *Wullschleger & Co. v. Jenny Fashions, Inc.,* 618 F.Supp. 373, 376 (S.D. N.Y. 1985).

We cannot hold—as urged on appeal—that the jury found, contrary to the weight of the evidence: No service contract existed. The compound question answered by the jury can be interpreted as meaning: A service contract did in fact exist, but that the contract was not breached by defendant.

Nevertheless, we reverse, because we are persuaded: The supplemental charge to the jury—that the delivery of the replacement disk drive "would affect the issue of damages in this case"—failed to adequately advise the jury of the law applicable to this case. We assume—for the purposes of this appeal and absent an argument to the contrary: [The] delivery of goods which breach an implied warranty of merchantability constitutes the delivery of non-conforming goods for which the seller could effect a cure. Viewing the case in this manner, the jury should have been charged: Any attempt to cure had to comply with the requirements of UCC § 2–508, including the requirement that the cure be made within a reasonable time. Since the delivery of the replacement disk drive may have formed the basis for the jury's refusal to award damages, we cannot find that this error did not prejudice plaintiff.

We are also in agreement that the jury may have been confused by the court's refusal to advise the jury: The counterclaim for conversion had been dismissed. The notation made by the jury on the verdict sheet may reflect: The jury's belief that they were in some fashion awarding damages by permitting the plaintiff to keep the replacement disk drive—a matter which was no longer in the case. We concur with the trial court's dismissal of the counterclaim, since, among other reasons, we discern no basis in the evidence to permit a finding that plaintiff converted merchandise which was delivered either as an attempted cure, or in compliance with a servicing agreement to repair and replace defective parts.

The question—whether the original contract was modified, so that a limited warranty contained therein to repair or replace defective parts applies to the facts of this case, or whether a new contract was made, so that an implied warranty of merchantability applies—raises questions of fact which should be determined upon a re-trial. We note, however, in the latter instance, that even such a limited remedy, if it should apply in this case, may be avoided when the warrantor fails to correct a defect within a reasonable time. *Chatlos*

Systems Inc. v. Nat. Cash Reg. Corp., 635 F.2d 1081, 1084 (3rd Cir. 1980).

3. Vendors' Inferior Technological Goods and Common Law Action for Breach of Implied Warranties of Fitness and Merchantability

In re HP Inkjet Printer Litigation

2006 WL 563048
(N.D. Cal. 2006)

Jeremy Fogel, Judge. Hewlett-Packard Co. (HP) manufactures printing supplies and inkjet printers. Nicklos Ciolino (Ciolino) and Daniel Feder (Feder) (collectively, Plaintiffs) both own HP printers purchased from CompUSA and Best Buy that use "smart chip" technology. "Smart chip" technology is designed to inform the consumer of the remaining ink level in an HP ink cartridge and when to reorder ink for an HP printer. For instance, once the "smart chip" reads that the cartridge's ink level is low, the "smart chip" sends a warning message to the consumer's printer that the ink level is low and new ink needs to be ordered.

Plaintiffs allege that HP engaged in unfair and deceptive conduct in connection with the "smart chip" technology in its ink cartridges. Plaintiffs contend that the "smart chips" are "programmed to prematurely register ink replacement long before depletion of the ink supply. Frequently, these cartridges can register as empty when they in fact have substantial ink remaining." Plaintiffs also contend that HP's "smart chip"—without regard to the actual supply of remaining ink—"is capable of rendering a cartridge unusable through the use of a built-in expiration date that is concealed from consumers. An external date stamp instead only discloses the end of warranty date, but not the date in which the cartridge is rendered unusable."

In addition, HP allegedly "fails to explain the expiration feature at the point of purchase and omits such information in their marketing materials." Specifically, HP's "SureSupply" campaign and website omit such information. First, HP's "SureSupply" campaign promotes the "smart chip" technology as "a free user-friendly tool enabled through Smart printing technology that provides ... an easy way to manage and purchase HP genuine printing supplies."

Second, HP's website claims that "SureSupply automatically tracks and manages customers' toner or ink level usage, and provides alerts via email or cell phone when toner or ink is low. With a couple of clicks of a button, customers can access cartridge information, pricing and purchasing options that best meet their needs from the reseller of their choice." Plaintiffs contend that HP's "SureSupply" campaign is false because the actual design of the "smart chip" limits consumers' use of ink cartridges and makes consumers believe that their cartridges are empty or expired and must be replaced. In sum, Plaintiffs assert that "HP has deliberately withheld from its consumers information about the true functioning of the smart chip."

On October 31, 2005, Plaintiffs filed an amended class action complaint against HP. Plaintiffs asserted a claim for breach of implied warranty. ... On January 6, 2006, HP filed a motion to dismiss and in the alternative a motion to strike. HP claims that Plaintiffs have not alleged an actual injury. HP also contends that the breach of implied warranty claim fails because Plaintiffs were not in privity with HP. Having considered the briefs, relevant evidence, and the oral arguments, the Court will grant in part and deny in part the motion to dismiss and deny the motion to strike. ...

Breach of Implied Warranty

HP argues that Plaintiffs' breach-of-implied-warranty claim should be dismissed—both for lack of notice and for lack of privity. As to the second part, HP is correct: "Vertical privity is a prerequisite in California for recovery on a theory of breach of implied warranties of fitness and merchantability." *U.S. Roofing, Inc. v. Credit Alliance Corp.*, 228 Cal.App.3d 1431, 1441 (1991). "The term vertical privity refers to links in the chain of distribution of goods. If the buyer and seller occupy adjoining links in the chain, they are in vertical privity with each other." *Osborne v. Subaru of America, Inc.*, 198 Cal.App.3d 646, 656 n.6 (1988). For example, in *Anunziato v. eMachines, Inc.*, 402 F.Supp.2d 1133, 1141 (C.D. Cal. 2005), the court found: Under California law, a laptop-computer buyer—who purchased a computer from a retailer— lacked vertical privity with the computer manufacturer, requirement to state a claim for breach of implied warranty of merchantability.

In line with *Anunziato,* the Plaintiffs in the instant case purchased HP products from CompUSA and Best Buy. Thus, Plaintiffs lacked vertical privity with the manufacturer, HP. However, "privity is not required where plaintiff relied on defendant's promotional materials." The court concludes that Plaintiffs' breach of implied warranty claim is inadequate as presently pled: Plaintiffs have not alleged that they relied on HP's advertisements or promotional materials in purchasing their HP products. It is also unclear to the court whether Plaintiffs directly bought ink cartridges from HP's website using the "SureSupply." Plaintiffs, therefore, are given leave to amend to remedy the deficiencies outlined above. ...

Order

Good cause therefore appearing, it is hereby ordered HP's motion to dismiss is granted in part and denied in part and HP's motion to strike is denied. Plaintiffs may file an amended complaint on or before March 31, 2006, that addresses the deficiencies identified herein.

It is so ordered.

NOTES AND QUESTIONS

1) **Various Types of Implied Warranties.** Depending on the jurisdiction and contracting parties' undertaking, one or a combination of implied warranties may attach to a contract. There are several types: (a) an "implied warranty of merchantability," (b) an "implied warranty of fitness for a particular purpose," (c) an "implied warranty of workmanship," (d) an "implied warranty of good and workmanlike service," (e) an "implied warranty of workmanlike performance," (f) an "implied warranty of the plans and specifications," (g) an "implied warranty of the adequacy of specifications," (h) an "implied warranty of design," (i) an "implied warranty of eviction," (j) a "statutory implied warranty of title," (k) an "implied warranty of suitability," and (l) an "implied warranty of habitability."

2) **Implied Warranty of Particular Quality or Fineness.** In *Gardiner v. Gray,* 171 Eng. Rep. 46, 47 (1815), the defendant sold twelve bags of allegedly "waste silk" at 10s. 6d. per pound. When it arrived, the buyer discovered that the quality of the silk could not be sold under the "waste silk" label. Writing for the court, Lord Ellenborough concluded:

> [T]he plaintiff cannot recover on the count alleging that the silk should correspond with the sample. The

> written contract containing no such stipulation, I cannot allow it to be superadded by parol testimony. This was not a sale by sample. The sample was not produced as a warranty that the bulk corresponded with it, but to enable the purchaser to form a reasonable judgment of the commodity. I am of opinion, however, that under such circumstances, the purchaser has a right to expect a saleable article answering the description in the contract. Without any particular warranty, this is an implied term in every such contract. Where there is no opportunity to inspect the commodity, the maxim of *caveat emptor* does not apply. He cannot without a warranty insist that it shall be of any particular quality or fineness; but the intention of both parties must be taken to be, that it shall be saleable in the market under the denomination mentioned in the contract between them. The purchaser cannot be supposed to buy goods to lay them on a dunghill.

3) **An Action for Breach of an Implied Warranty of Merchantability.** In *Para-Chem Southern, Inc. v. Sandstone Products, Inc.,*2009 WL 276507, *14 (Tex. App.-Hous. [1st Dist.], the Texas Appellate Court in Houston stated that a plaintiff who files a breach of implied warranty of merchantability action must prove that (1) a product was defective for its purpose; (2) the alleged defect existed when the product left the defendant's possession; and (3) the alleged defect proximately caused the injuries and damages.

4) **An Action for Breach of an Implied Warranty of Good Workmanship.** *See Cocke v. White*, 697 S.W.2d 739, 743 (Tex. App.-Corpus Christi 1985, writ ref'd n.r.e.) ("The elements that a plaintiff must prove [in a breach of implied warranty claim] are (1) the implied warranty of good workmanship, (2) the breach thereof, and (3) that such breach was the proximate cause of the plaintiff's damages.").

5) **Breach-of-an-Implied-Warranty Action in Tort.** *See Smith v. E. R. Squibb & Sons, Inc.*, 273 N.W.2d 476, 479-80 (Mich. 1979) ("A manufacturer of a prescription drug has a legal duty to warn the medical profession, not the patient, of any risks inherent in the use of the drug which the manufacturer knows or should know to exist. ... Breach of implied warranty, on the other hand, is established when plaintiff proves that a product defect attributable to the manufacturer has a causal relationship to plaintiff's injuries. ... The distinction between the elements of negligence and breach

of implied warranty is that in the former plaintiff must prove that the defect was caused by the manufacturer's negligence, whereas under the warranty theory, plaintiff need only establish that the defect was attributable to the manufacturer, regardless of the amount of care utilized by the manufacturer.")

4. Vendors' Defective Computers and Common Law Action for Breach of Implied Warranties of Fitness for Intended Use

Lovely v. Burroughs Corporation

527 P.2d 557
(Mont. 1974)

Haswell, Justice. In 1953, Plaintiff Orvis Lovely commenced an accounting practice in Livingston, Montana. In 1964, he formed a partnership with the other plaintiff—Donald Laubach. In 1966, the partnership purchased an additional practice in nearby Big Timber, Montana, and maintained an office there. The addition of this practice increased the workload of the partnership to the point where additional help had to be hired or the work had to be automated.

Plaintiffs were approached by David Larsen—a sales representative for the defendant—concerning the use of Burroughs equipment in their expanded practice. A series of meetings, correspondence and demonstrations of available equipment ensued—resulting in a purchase order for a small Burroughs computer. That order was superseded in February 1967 by a similar order for a larger, more expensive computer. The second order bore a handwritten notation that it was to be converted into a lease prior to delivery.

Although the computer was delivered and installed in June 1967, no formal lease was ever executed. In November of 1967, Plaintiffs submitted an application and a check—through Larsen—for consideration by a third-party leasing firm. Plaintiffs forwarded a second check in December for the same amount to Burroughs before learning that the application had been denied. Defendant then offered to lease directly to plaintiffs at a higher monthly rental. Plaintiffs' rejection of this offer prompted the removal of the computer in February of 1968.

The district court found that defendant—at the time of the order—knew the particular purposes for which the equipment was required and that plaintiffs were relying on defendant's judgment in furnishing suitable goods. It further found that the equipment delivered was not fit for the purposes intended, and that plaintiffs were damaged.

These findings of fact are amply supported by the record. During the course of Plaintiffs' negotiations with Larsen, the latter became thoroughly familiar with the operations of their accounting practice. Plaintiffs testified that they relied heavily on Larsen's assessment of the computer's suitability for their particular needs. That reliance prompted Plaintiffs to solicit additional business from their customers which was to be provided by the expanded capabilities of the new machine.

Following installation and debugging of the machine, a number of customer accounts were transferred to the automated process. Within a short time, problems arose in the operation of the computer—requiring numerous visits by Burroughs' repairmen. These difficulties occurred daily and often necessitated shutting down the computer until repairs could be made. The problems experienced adversely affected Plaintiffs' ability to promptly and accurately service their customers' accounts. The damage to the reputation of the firm was one of the factors which led to the sale of the practice.

Given this evidence, the district court concluded that defendant had breached both express and implied warranties of fitness for intended use. It further concluded that this breach was the proximate cause of the damages which we shall deal with later.

Defendant argues: (1) there was no transactional basis for any warranty; (2) the breach of warranty, if such warranty existed was not established by the record; and (3) if there was a breach of warranty, the plaintiffs waived their claim for relief. Defendant maintains that the transaction here amounted to nothing more than a gratuitous bailment—giving rise to no express or implied warranty of fitness for intended use. We disagree.

At the very least, a bailment for mutual benefit arose as both parties received the benefits of the transaction. *Global Tank Trailer Sales v. Textilana-Nease, Inc.*, 496 P.2d 1292, 1294-95 (Kan. 1972); and, *Miller v. Hand Ford Sales, Inc.*, 340 P.2d 181, 183-185 (Or. 1959). Plaintiffs had the use of the computer, while the defendant had the expectation of profit from a lease directly with the Plaintiffs or from a sale to the third-party leasing company. Defendant further benefitted by receiving two checks as well as by selling forms for the computer. To argue that defendant gratuitously placed a $38,000 computer at the disposal of the Plaintiffs—without an expectation of profit—does not square with the facts.

Bailments for mutual benefit fall within the scope of the Montana Rev. Civ. Code § 42-101(1947), which provides: "Hiring is a contract by which one gives to another the temporary possession and use of property, other than money, for reward, and the latter agrees to return the same to the former at a future time." The Legislature—by the use of the word "reward"—obviously contemplated benefits other than money as being included in a hiring. We find no sound reason for excluding anticipated rewards from the scope of the statute.

Montana Rev. Civ. Code § 42-211 provides: "One who lets personal property must deliver it to the hirer, secure his quiet enjoyment thereof against all lawful claimants, put it into a condition fit for the purpose for which he lets it, and repair all deteriorations thereof not occasioned by the fault of the hirer and not the natural result of its use." This statute expresses the common law of bailments—requiring fitness for use in bailments for mutual benefit. *Atlantic Tug & Equip. Co. v. S. & L. Paving Corp.*, 334 N.Y.S.2d 532, 533 (App.Div. 1972). When a bailor has reason to know the use for which the property is required, there arises an implied warranty of fitness for that use. This rule applies particularly when the bailee relies upon the bailor's expertise as to the suitability of that property for that use.

Accordingly, Defendant's delivery of the computer created a bailment for mutual benefit, and that relationship gave rise to an implied warranty of fitness for use in Plaintiffs' practice. The district court found, and the evidence clearly shows: That warranty was breached. From the time of installation to the time of removal, the computer suffered malfunctions—which made it incapable of providing timely and accurate information. Defendant's protestations—that a complex piece of equipment such as this is expected to have such problems—are not persuasive. While the problems might be normal for this machine, and we are not convinced of that, Defendant should have known: The computer would never be suitable for Plaintiffs' needs. His representations to the contrary would then be fraudulent.

Defendant further suggests: Plaintiffs waived their claim of breach of warranty by failing to reject the computer during the approximately eight months after delivery. We cannot agree. Even if the defense of waiver had been timely raised, the evidence does not conform to the theory. While the Plaintiffs did retain possession for almost eight months, the evidence clearly shows: They did not accept the computer in its defective condition. The record is replete with repeated complaints made by the Plaintiffs, resulting in numerous service calls directed at remedying the many problems. Plaintiffs' actions amount to a good faith attempt to permit defendant to remedy the defects, not an acceptance of them. We therefore find no waiver of the protection of warranties of fitness for intended use.

The district court awarded damages in the following amounts:

1) $4,000 for time spent attempting to make the computer work and time spent correcting the mistakes made by the computer—time which otherwise could have been billed to clients;

2) $1,302.37 for hiring additional help required by the computer problem;

3) $3,000 in wages for hiring another accountant to conduct the Big Timber practice since the computer demanded Plaintiffs' time in Livingston;

4) $139.40 for costs of preparing a room for installation of the computer;

5) $1,596 which was the amount of the two checks which Plaintiffs sent to Defendant during lease negotiations;

6) $64.05 for telephone charges expended in informing defendant's repairmen that the computer was malfunctioning;

7) $3,391 for loss sustained on the sale of the Big Timber business.

8) $3,268 for loss sustained on the sale of the Livingston business.

* * *

It follows that the judgment of the district court must be affirmed in part and reversed in part. The judgment is sound except for damages dealing with the Livingston practice loss, and the assessment of costs.

We must remand for a redetermination of the amount of damages arising from the loss on the sale of the Livingston business. Judgment should be then entered reflecting that amount, and costs should be awarded in an amount consistent with this opinion.

CHAPTER TWO: Attorneys' Tort-Based Actions Against Competitors and Sellers of Technological Goods and Services

IEthics: How Cloud Computing Has Impacted the Rules of Professional Conduct

88 N.D. L. Rev. 453 (2012)

Andrew L. Askew

Years ago, attorneys were most commonly found in traditional brick-and-mortar law offices, which were crowded with dozens of shelves filled with legal reporters and digests and countless file cabinets containing droves of confidential information. During these times, attorneys were confined within the walls of their law offices and routinely interacted with clients, colleagues, and the judiciary in person, by phone, or by letter. Today, [using] devices like the iPhone and Blackberry, web-based e-mail such as Gmail and Yahoo! Mail, and products such as SharePoint, Google Docs, or Dropbox, attorneys have been able to step outside the walls of the traditional brick-and-mortar law offices and revolutionize ... the way clients are able to access legal services [and] ... how those services are performed and delivered.

Each year, attorneys continue to move away from traditional legal offices and transition to virtual law practices—which can be based from any location where an Internet connection is available. From these virtual law practices, various forms of cloud computing are used to communicate with clients and colleagues, draft work-product, electronically file court documents, and manage legal information. As a result of the increased use of cloud computing technology, attorneys have been able to reduce costs and legal fees, increase efficiency, deliver various unbundled legal services, and, perhaps most importantly, allow for increased access to justice. Despite the many benefits derived from virtual law practice and ...

cloud computing technology, [there are] … many unique ethical and security risks associated with this technology. …

Rule 1.1 of the ABA's *Model Rules of Professional Responsibility* [reads]: "A lawyer shall provide competent representation to a client." "Competent representation requires the legal knowledge, skill, thoroughness and preparation reasonably necessary for the representation." In order to comply with Rule 1.1, the commentary of the rule suggests "a lawyer should keep abreast of changes in the law and its practice, including the benefits and risks associated with relevant technology, engage in continuing study and education and comply with all continuing legal education requirements. …"

As a result, an attorney who chooses to integrate various forms of cloud-computing technology into his or her virtual law practice or traditional brick-and-mortar practice is responsible for obtaining the requisite level of expertise with the respective technology. If the attorney is unable to do so, that attorney is required to seek out qualified individuals who can ensure competency. Although this requirement seems fairly easy to satisfy, many of the latest cloud-computing technologies, such as cloud-based data storage, can be highly complex and may be beyond some attorneys' comprehension. Therefore, before an attorney chooses to use a form of cloud-computing technology, that attorney must take various precautions to ensure the service is adequate and conducive to practicing law.

To repeat, opening a virtual law practice, generally, or employing cloud-computing technology, in particular, exposes a solo practitioner to various professional risks, harms, property damage, and even personal injuries. For example, a trespasser may invade the practitioner's cloud-based storage files and steal privileged information. A third party might intercept attorney-client private email communications and use sensitive information to defame the attorney and/or the attorney's client. Or third parties might violate attorneys' reasonable expectation of privacy by using Google Hangout, Skype, or another virtual-chat service to intrude virtually into attorneys and clients' private conversations.

In this chapter, selected cases illustrate the types of intentional torts that solo and small-practitioners may commence against various parties—those who use law-practice technologies to defame and injury attorneys' persons or to invade and misappropriate attorneys' tangible and intangible properties.

A. Conversion of Electronic Property and Private Right of Action

1. The Evolving Common-Law Tort of Conversion and Protection for Attorneys' Data on Various Types of Computers

Thyroff v. Nationwide Mutual Insurance Company

864 N.E.2d 1272
(N.Y. 2007)

Raffeo, J. The United States Court of Appeals for the Second Circuit has certified a question to us that asks whether the common-law cause of action of conversion applies to certain electronic computer records and data.

I

Plaintiff Louis Thyroff was an insurance agent for defendant Nationwide Mutual Insurance Company. In 1988, the parties entered into an Agent's Agreement that specified the terms of their business relationship. As part of the arrangement, Nationwide agreed to lease Thyroff computer hardware and software—referred to as the agency office-automation (AOA) system—to facilitate the collection and transfer of customer information to Nationwide. In addition to the entry of business data, Thyroff also used the AOA system for personal e-mails, correspondence and other data storage that pertained to his customers. On a daily basis, Nationwide would automatically upload all of the information from Thyroff's AOA system—including Thryoff's personal data—to its centralized computers.

The Agent's Agreement was terminable at will. In September 2000, Thyroff received a letter from Nationwide informing him that his contract as an exclusive agent had been cancelled. The next day, Nationwide repossessed its AOA system and denied Thyroff further access to the computers and all electronic records and data. Consequently, Thyroff was unable to retrieve his customer information and other personal information that was stored on the computers.

Thyroff initiated an action against Nationwide in the United States District Court for the Western District of New York, asserting several causes of action—including a claim for the conversion of his business and personal information stored on the computer hard drives. In response to Nationwide's motion to dismiss, District Court held that the complaint failed to state a cause of action for conversion because Thyroff did not allege that Nationwide exercised dominion over the electronic data to his exclusion and it was undisputed that Nationwide owned the AOA system.

In his appeal to the United States Court of Appeals for the Second Circuit, Thyroff sought reinstatement of his conversion cause of action, along with other relief. Nationwide countered that a conversion claim cannot be based on the misappropriation of electronic records and data because New York does not recognize a cause of action for the conversion of intangible property. The Second Circuit determined that the issue was unresolved in New York and therefore certified the following question of law to this Court: is a claim for the conversion of electronic data cognizable under New York law? ...

III

As history reveals, the common law has evolved to broaden the remedies available for the misappropriation of personal property. As the concept of summary execution and wager of battle became incompatible with emerging societal values, the law changed. Similarly, the courts became willing to consider new species of personal property eligible for conversion actions. Conversion and its common-law antecedents were directed against interferences with or misappropriation of "goods" that were tangible, personal property. This was consistent with the original notions associated with the appeals of robbery and larceny, trespass and trover because tangible property could be lost or stolen. By contrast, real property and all manner of intangible rights could not be "lost or found" in the eyes of the law and were not therefore subject to an action for trover or conversion

Under this traditional construct, conversion was viewed as "the unauthorized assumption and exercise of the right of ownership over goods belonging to another to the exclusion of the owner's rights." Thus, the general rule was that "an action for conversion will not normally lie, when it involves intangible property" because there is no physical item that can be misappropriated. *Sporn v. MCA Records,* 58 N.Y.2d 482, 489 (1983).

Despite this long-standing reluctance to expand conversion beyond the realm of tangible property, some courts determined that there was "no good reason for keeping up a distinction that arose wholly from that original peculiarity of the action" of trover (that an item had to be capable of being lost and found) and substituted a theory of conversion that covered "things represented by valuable papers, such as certificates of stock, promissory notes, and other papers of value." *Ayres v. French,* 41 Conn. 142, 150, 151 (1874). This, in turn, led to the recognition that an intangible property right can be united with a tangible object for conversion purposes. *Agar v. Orda,* 264 N.Y. 248, 251 (1934) *Iglesias v. United States,* 848 F.2d 362, 364 [2d Cir.1988]).

In *Agar,* which involved the conversion of intangible shares of stock, this Court applied the so-called "merger" doctrine because: "for practical purposes [the shares] are merged in stock certificates which are instrumentalities of trade and commerce. ... Such certificates are treated by business men as property for all practical purposes. ... Indeed, this court has held that the shares of stock are so completely merged in the certificate that conversion of the certificate may be treated as a conversion of the shares of stock represented by the certificate." 264 N.Y. at 251. More recently, we concluded that a plaintiff could maintain a cause of action for conversion where the defendant infringed on the plaintiff's intangible property right to a musical performance by misappropriating a master recording—a tangible item of property capable of being physically taken. *Sporn v. MCA Records,* 58 N.Y.2d at 489.

IV

We have not previously had occasion to consider whether the common law should permit conversion for intangible property interests that do not strictly satisfy the merger test. [Some] some courts have adhered to the traditional rules of conversion. *Allied Inv. Corp. v. Jasen,* 354 Md. 547, 562 (1999) [interests in partnership and corporation]; *Northeast Coating Tech., Inc. v. Vacuum Metallurgical Co., Ltd.,* 684 A.2d 1322, 1324 (Me.1996); *Montecalvo v. Mandarelli,* 682 A.2d 918, 929 (R.I.1996). Others have taken a more flexible view of conversion and held that the cause of action can embrace intangible property. *Kremen v. Cohen,* 337 F.3d 1024, 1033–1034 (9th Cir.2003) (Internet domain name; applying California law); *Shmueli v. Corcoran Group,* 9 Misc.3d

589, 594 (Sup.Ct., N.Y. County 2005) (computerized client/investor list].

A variety of arguments have been made in support of expanding the scope of conversion. Some courts have decided that a theft of intangible property is a violation of the criminal law and should be civilly remediable. *National Sur. Corp. v. Applied Sys., Inc.*, 418 So.2d at 850; that virtual documents can be made tangible "by the mere expedient of a printing key function." *Shmueli v. Corcoran Group,* 9 Misc.3d at 592); that a writing is a document whether it is read on the computer or printed on paper. *Kremen v. Cohen,* 325 F.3d 1035, 1048 ([9th Cir.2003) (Kozinski, J., dissenting from certification); and that the expense of creating intangible, computerized information should be counterbalanced by the protection of an effective civil action. *National Sur. Corp. v. Applied Sys., Inc.,* 418 So.2d at 850.

On the other hand, the primary argument for retaining the traditional boundaries of the tort is that it "seems preferable to fashion other remedies, such as unfair competition, to protect people from having intangible values used and appropriated in unfair ways." Nonetheless, advocates of this view readily concede that "[t]here is perhaps no very valid and essential reason why there might not be conversion of" intangible property and that there is "very little practical importance whether the tort is called conversion, or a similar tort with another name" because "[i]n either case the recovery is for the full value of the intangible right so appropriated." Restatement [Second] of Torts § 242, Comment *e*). The lack of a compelling reason to prohibit conversion for redress of a misappropriation of intangible property underscores the need for reevaluating the appropriate application of conversion.

V

"[I]t is the strength of the common law to respond, albeit cautiously and intelligently, to the demands of commonsense justice in an evolving society." *Madden v. Creative Servs.,* 84 N.Y.2d 738, 744 (1995); *Hymowitz v. Eli Lilly & Co.,* 73 N.Y.2d 487, 507 (1989). That time has arrived. The reasons for creating the merger doctrine and departing from the strict common-law limitation of conversion inform our analysis. The expansion of conversion to encompass a different class of property—such as shares of stock—was motivated by "society's growing dependence on intangibles."

It cannot be seriously disputed that society's reliance on computers and electronic data is substantial, if not essential. Computers and digital information are ubiquitous and pervade all aspects of business, financial and personal communication activities. Indeed, this opinion was drafted in electronic form, stored in a computer's memory and disseminated to the Judges of this Court via e-mail. We cannot conceive of any reason in law or logic why this process of virtual creation should be treated any differently from production by pen on paper or quill on parchment. A document stored on a computer hard drive has the same value as a paper document kept in a file cabinet.

The merger rule reflected the concept that intangible property interests could be converted only by exercising dominion over the paper document that represented that interest. Now, however, it is customary that stock ownership exclusively exists in electronic format. Because shares of stock can be transferred by mere computer entries, a thief can use a computer to access a person's financial accounts and transfer the shares to an account controlled by the thief. Similarly, electronic documents and records stored on a computer can also be converted by simply pressing the delete button. "It would be a curious jurisprudence that turned on the existence of a paper document rather than an electronic one. Torching a company's file room would then be conversion while hacking into its mainframe and deleting its data would not."

Furthermore, it generally is not the physical nature of a document that determines its worth, it is the information memorialized in the document that has intrinsic value. A manuscript of a novel has the same value whether it is saved in a computer's memory or printed on paper. So too, the information that Thyroff allegedly stored on his leased computers in the form of electronic records of customer contacts and related data has value to him regardless of whether the format in which the information was stored was tangible or intangible. In the absence of a significant difference in the value of the information, the protections of the law should apply equally to both forms—physical and virtual.

In light of these considerations, we believe that the tort of conversion must keep pace with the contemporary realities of widespread computer use. We therefore answer the certified question in the affirmative and hold that the type of data that Nationwide allegedly took possession of—electronic records that were stored on a computer and were indistinguishable from printed documents—is subject to a claim of conversion in New York. Because this is the only type of intangible property at issue in this case, we do not consider whether any °of the myriad other forms of virtual information should be protected by the tort.

Accordingly, the certified question should be answered in the affirmative.

NOTES AND QUESTIONS

1) **Proving a Common-law Tort of Conversion.** To prove conversion, a claimant must establish: "(1) it owned or had legal possession of the property or entitlement to possession, (2) the defendant unlawfully and without authorization assumed and exercised dominion and control over the property to the exclusion of, or inconsistent with, the claimant's rights, (3) the claimant demanded return of the property, and (4) the defendant refused to return the property." *Hunt v. Baldwin,* 68 S.W.3d 117, 131 (Tex.App.-Houston [14th Dist.] 2001). Originally, the tort of conversion applied only to tangible property. Gradually, the doctrine expanded from its common-law roots—allowing actionable claims for various forms of converted property. On the other hand, a claim for the conversion of intangible property is limited. *See Famoloqy.com Inc. v. Perot Sys. Corp.*, 158 F.Supp.2d 589, 591 (E.D.Pa. 2001) and *Northcraft v. Michener,* 466 A.2d 620, 625 (Pa. Super.1983).

2) **Common Law Tort of Conversion, Intangible Rights and the Application of the Merger Doctrine.** The RESTATEMENT (SECOND) OF TORTS § 242 outlines the "merger" theory. It reads:

> (1) Where there is conversion of a document in which intangible rights are merged, the damages include the value of such rights.
>
> (2) One who effectively prevents the exercise of intangible rights of the kind customarily merged in a document is subject to a liability similar to that for conversion, even though the document is not itself converted.

Some courts have approved an action for conversion by applying the merger doctrine. *See e.g., Astroworks, Inc. v. Astroexhibit, Inc.,* 257 F.Supp.2d 609, 618 (S.D.N.Y.2003) (conversion of an idea that appeared on an Internet website). Courts have also approved conversion actions without considering the historical barriers. *See Cole v. Control Data Corp.*, 947 F.2d 313, 318 (8th Cir.1991) (alleged conversion of computer software program); *National Sur. Corp. v. Applied Sys., Inc.*, 418 So.2d 847, 850 (Ala.1982) (conversion of computer program); and *Mundy v. Decker*, 1999 WL 14479, *4 (Ct.App.1999) (conversion of WordPerfect documents).

2. Statutory Tort of Conversion and Attorneys' Right to Commence a Private Action Under States' Computer Crimes Statutes

Perk v. Vector Resources Group, Ltd.

485 S.E.2d 140
(Va. 1997)

Stephenson, Justice.

The principal issue in this appeal is whether the trial court erred in sustaining the defendants' demurrer to the plaintiff's motion for judgment.

On June 21, 1990, Leo J. Perk—a practicing attorney at law—filed a multi-count motion for judgment against Vector Resources Group, Ltd. (Vector), Charles Michael Monahan—a Vector employee—and the law firm known as Sheffield & Bricken, P.C. (the Firm) (collectively, the Defendants). The Defendants filed demurrers to the motion for judgment which the trial court sustained, ruling that none of the counts in the motion for judgment stated a cause of action against the Defendants. ... We awarded Perk an appeal.

Perk entered into an at-will contract with Tidewater Memorial Hospital, Inc. (Tidewater) to undertake the collection of Tidewater's more than 3,000 delinquent accounts receivable. Sometime thereafter, Tidewater was acquired by what is now Riverside Tappahannock Hospital, Inc. (Riverside). The collection contract continued with Riverside for a period of time without change. On November 10, 1989, Riverside terminated the contract and instructed Perk to forward all payments thereafter received by him directly to Riverside without any fee deduction. Riverside also instructed Perk to deliver all the delinquent accounts to either it or Monahan. ...

Count IV of the motion for judgment alleges that Perk had "invested substantial amounts of his personal time and money in creating, designing, and developing his own customized computer programs, computer databases, and computer software" and that Monahan and the Firm "knowingly, willfully, deliberately, and without justification stole and converted Perk's computer programs, computer databases, computer software, and computer data."

Count IV further alleges that—"as a direct and proximate result of the ... theft and conversion"—Perk was damaged "to the extent of the value of his efforts in creating the computer programs, computer databases, computer software, and computer data, of the fair market value of the computer programs, computer databases, computer software, and computer data, and of the loss of his profits that [Perk] would have enjoyed had [Monahan and the Firm] not stolen his ... property." ...

We ... consider Count IV of the motion for judgment. In this count, Perk alleges the theft or conversion by Monahan and the Firm of his computer programs, data, and software. Perk also alleges that he has lost the value of his efforts in creating the converted items, the fair market value of the items, and future profits.

Pursuant to Code § 18.2-152.8 of the Virginia Computer Crimes Act, Code § 18.2-152.1 *et seq.*, "computer data, computer programs, [and] computer software" are "personal property subject to embezzlement" for the purposes of Code § 18.2-111. Clearly, Count IV alleges that Monahan and the Firm stole or converted such personal property belonging to Perk.

Monahan and the Firm assert ... that the items allegedly converted are "nothing more than lists" of Riverside's debtors, which belong solely to Riverside; that Perk consented to the taking of the items; and that the lists were of no value to Perk once the contract had been terminated. The character of the items allegedly converted and the question whether these items had value to Perk aside from his contractual obligations and professional services to Riverside are, however, matters of proof which cannot be decided by demurrer.

We conclude, therefore, that Count IV states a cause of action. Consequently, we hold that the trial court erred in sustaining the demurrer as to Count IV. ... Accordingly, the trial court's judgment will be affirmed in part, reversed in part, and the case remanded for further proceedings consistent with this opinion.

NOTES AND QUESTIONS

1) **Statutory Tort of Conversion.** There is a common-law tort of conversion and a statutory tort of conversion. Consider the Michigan court's brief analysis *Lawsuit Fin, LLC v. Curry,* 261 Mich.App 579, 591–593(2004): In the present case, plaintiff failed to state a claim for common-law conversion because it failed to allege that defendant's initial exercise of domain over the property was in fact wrongful. "The defendant must have obtained the money without the owner's consent to the creation of a debtor and creditor relationship." ... A mere statement of a pleader's conclusions—unsupported by allegations of fact—will not suffice to state a cause of action. *Churella v. Pioneer State Mut. Ins. Co.*, 258 Mich.App. 260, 272 (2003). ... We also believe that plaintiff failed to state a claim of statutory conversion. Statutory conversion consists of knowingly buying, receiving, or aiding in the concealment of any stolen, embezzled, or converted property. M.C.L. § 600.2919a. This court has ruled that simply retaining money does not amount to "buying, receiving or aiding in the concealment of stolen, embezzled or converted property." *Hovanesian v. Nam,* 213 Mich.App. 231, 237 (1995).

2) **Stolen or Converted Domain Names and Conflicting Right-of-Action Rulings Under the Common Law.** Courts are divided over whether a party or an attorney may commence an action against the conversion of a domain name under the common law. *Compare Carson v. Dynegy, Inc.*, 344 F.3d 446, 456 (5th Cir.2003) (precluding an action under Texas and stressing that a conversion must involve "physical property")—citing *Waisath v. Lack's Stores,* 474 S.W.2d 444, 447 (Tex.1971); and *Emke v. Compana, L.L.C.*, 2007 WL 2781661, *3 (N.D. Tex. 2007) (stressing that "Texas does not recognize a claim for intangible property such as a domain name") *with Kremen v. Cohen,* 337 F.3d 1024, 1033-34 (9th Cir. 2003) (applying California law and holding that domain names—intangible property—may be the basis for a conversion claim); and *Emke v. Compana, L.L.C.*, 2007 WL 2781661,*3 (N.D. Tex. 2007) (applying California and concluding that the plaintiff may commence an action for the conversion of a domain name).

B. Electronic Thieves' and Intruders' Liability for Misappropriating Attorneys' Tangible and Intangible Commercial Property

Unfair competition is an unlawful business injury which consists essentially of one's expressly or impliedly *passing off* or attempting to *pass off* to the public another person's goods or business reputation in order to sell his own goods or services. Generally, the doctrine of unfair competition is designed to ensure business integrity and honest practices among industrial, professional and commercial actors. *American Heritage Life Ins. Co. v. Heritage Life Ins. Co.*, 494 F.2d 3, 14 (5th Cir. 1974). "[N]o one has a right to avail himself of another's favorable reputation in order to sell [one's] goods. Or stated slightly differently, "[a] competitor may not use a name—whether fictitious or real—or a description—whether or not true—which is intended or calculated to represent to the world that his business is that of another, and by such fraudulent misstatements deprive the latter of business which would otherwise come to him." *Oliver Gintel, Inc. v. Koslow's, Inc.*, 355 F. Supp. 236, 239 (N.D. Tex. 1973).

Unfair competition laws have three objectives: (1) to protect the honest trader in business which fairly belongs to him; (2) to punish the dishonest trader who is taking his competitor's business away by unfair means; and (3) to protect the public from deception. 87 C.J.S. Trade-Marks, Trade-Names, and Unfair Competition, §§ 13-14, 89. The doctrine of unfair competition is governed by laws of each state. *General Adjustment Bureau v. Fuess*, 192 F.Supp. 542, 547 (S.D.Tex.1961). And an injured party does not have to prove intentional wrongdoing to prevail. *McCarley v. Welch*, 170 S.W.2d 330, 332 (Tex.Civ.App.-Dallas 1943).

Furthermore, an unfair competition claim is a tort-based claim. In fact, several unfair competition laws have evolved under the common law: tort of misappropriation, common-law tort of palming off, and common law tort of trade-secret misappropriation. Additionally, many states and Congress have enacted statutes which forbid unfair competition. *State ex rel. North Carolina Milk Commission v. National Food Stores, Inc. Supreme Court of North Carolina,* 154 S.E.2d 548, 556-557 (N.C. 1967).

But consider the definition of an "electronic storage location"—which includes "computer hard drives, external hard drives, portable hard drives, thumb drives, flash drives, zip drives, CDs, DVDs, memory sticks, e-mail servers, e-mail accounts, network file servers, network shares, scanners, printers, internet-based storage, web-based storage, cloud-based storage, and all other devices, media or locations that retain electronic documents or data." *Aequitas Solutions, Inc. v. Anderson*, 2012 WL 5304155, *2 n.6 (Del. Ct. Chan. 2012). Therefore, given the rise of the virtual law office, important questions have emerged: Do unfair competition laws protect solo and small-firm practitioners' intangible commercial property—names, likeness, images, words, marks, phrases and designs—which appear on all "electronic storage locations"? Do unfair competition laws prohibit thieves from exercising control or ownership over attorneys' commercial hardware or tangible "electronic storage" property? The cases in this section address these and related questions?

1. Videotaping and Common-Law Misappropriation of Attorney's Name and Likeness

Geragos v. Borer

2010 WL 60639
(Cal. Ct. App. [2nd Dist.] 2010)

Kitching, J.

Defendant and appellant—Jeffrey Borer—surreptitiously and illegally videotaped the noted entertainer Michael Jackson and his two criminal defense lawyers, plaintiffs and respondents Mark Geragos and E. Pat Harris (plaintiffs). [The videotaping occurred when] Jackson and Mark Geragos were flying in a chartered airplane. Borer planned to sell the videotape to a media company for a large sum of money. Before he could do so, however, plaintiffs filed a suit against Borer and obtained an injunction prohibiting the sale of the videotape. Plaintiffs asserted causes of action [were] invasion of privacy and use of name and likeness in violation of Civil Code section 3344. After a bench trial, plaintiffs obtained a judgment against Borer for compensatory damages in the cumulative sum of $2.25 million and for punitive damages in the cumulative sum of $9 million. Borer contends that there was insufficient evidence to support the amount of damages ...

Background

1. The Videotape

In November 2003, Geragos and Harris of the law firm of Geragos & Geragos represented Michael Jackson with respect to criminal charges brought by the Santa Barbara District Attorney. The Jackson case was a matter of intense international media coverage. In light of safety concerns, the Santa Barbara Sheriff's Department and Geragos negotiated a date, time, and place for Jackson's arrest. Geragos and Jackson's assistant arranged to charter an airplane from defendant XtraJet, Inc. (XtraJet) to fly Jackson, Geragos, Harris and Jackson's assistant from Las Vegas, Nevada, to Santa Barbara County so that Jackson could be arrested. Geragos decided to charter a private airplane because he wanted a confidential setting in which he could communicate with Jackson.

On or about November 19, 2003, Borer—the owner of XtraJet—instructed Arvel Jett Reeves to install audio-video recording equipment on the airplane chartered by Jackson. Shortly afterwards, Reeves purchased two mini-camcorders, extension microphones, and remote lenses for the camcorders. Borer and Reeves intended to create audio and video recordings of Jackson and his attorneys, and then sell these recordings to the media for a large sum of money.

Reeves and another unidentified individual worked into the early morning hours of November 20, 2003—installing the camcorders on the airplane. Reeves was unable to install remote microphones because he failed to purchase the proper connections. On November 21, 2003, Jackson, Geragos, Harris, and Jackson's assistant flew on an XtraJet airplane from Las Vegas to Santa Barbara County as planned. During that flight the passengers were secretly videotaped.

2. Defendants Were Enjoined From Selling the Videotape

The videotape first came to the attention of Geragos and Harris when Geragos received a call from Greta Van Susteren of Fox News regarding the matter. Geragos then called Lloyd Kirschbaum—Borer's and XtraJet's lawyer—and demanded that Kirschbaum turn over the videotape. Kirschbaum, however, denied that request. Instead, he advised Geragos something to the effect that his clients were going to "hit the lottery" or that it was their "pay day." Kirshbaum further stated that the videotape was worth "more than a million" or "millions" of dollars. Kirshbaum also told Geragos that he could place a "bid" on the videotape. The existence of the videotape and speculation about its contents became a matter of public discussion on cable news programs and elsewhere. Geragos received approximately 50–100 calls from reporters regarding the videotape.

On November 25, 2003, Geragos and Harris commenced this action and sought a temporary restraining order (TRO) to enjoin the dissemination of the videotape. The court granted the TRO. At the TRO hearing, Kirshbaum argued on behalf of Borer that the plaintiffs should be required to post an undertaking. Kirshbaum claimed that assuming the videotape could be sold, "it may have an extremely high value." He further advised the court that media companies were willing to pay between $10,000 and $15,000 merely to take pictures of the empty airplane where the videotape was recorded, and upwards of $20,000 to $30,000 for an interview regarding the videotape. The court required plaintiffs to post a $20,000 bond.

3. Plaintiffs' First Amended Complaint

Plaintiffs' operative pleading is the first amended complaint. The named plaintiffs are Jackson, Geragos, Harris, and Geragos & Geragos, APC. The named defendants are Borer, XtraJet, Pavair, Inc.—a company affiliated with Borer—Cynthia Montgomery, a travel agent allegedly involved in the scheme to videotape Jackson and his lawyers, and Travel 21, Inc., a company affiliated with Montgomery. The first amended complaint [outlines several] causes of action: for (1) common law misappropriation of name and likeness, and (2) use of name and likeness in violation of Civil Code section 3344....

4. Borer's Conviction of a Federal Crime

Borer's participation in the plan to videotape Jackson and his lawyers resulted in criminal charges against him in federal court. On March 6, 2006, in the United States District Court for the Central District of California, Borer pleaded guilty to one count of conspiracy to intercept an oral communication in violation of 18 U.S.C. § 2511(1)(b)(iv) and 18 U.S.C. § 371. Judge A. Howard Matz accepted Borer's plea and found Borer guilty of the charge.

5. The Trial, Judgment and Motion for New Trial

The superior court conducted a bench trial. Geragos and Harris were the only percipient witnesses called by plaintiffs. Professor Stanley Goldman also testified as an expert witness regarding media issues. In addition, plaintiffs played the videotaped deposition of Reeves and submitted the plea agreements of Borer and Reeves. Borer did not call any witnesses or present any evidence. An important issue at trial was the value of the videotape. Geragos testified about his conversation with Kirshbaum, and Kirshbaum's statement that the videotape was worth "more than a million or millions." He also testified that he received a call from reporter Greta Van Susteren "telling [Geragos] that somebody at Fox [News] had relayed to her that somebody was shopping [the videotape] around for $1 million or $2 million." Borer objected to this testimony as hearsay but the trial court overruled the objection. …

There was also no evidence regarding the content of the videotape. The trial court admonished the parties and the witnesses against discussing the content of the videotape in open court in order to protect Michael Jackson's attorney-client privilege. For the same reason, the trial court declined to accept Borer's request to review the videotape in camera.

The trial court entered judgment in favor of plaintiffs on [the]causes of action. Defendants XtraJet, Borer and Montgomery were ordered to destroy the original and all copies of the videotape, and were permanently enjoined from the sale or further dissemination of the videotape. The trial court awarded Geragos $2 million in compensatory damages against XtraJet, Borer and Montgomery, $8 million in punitive damages against Borer, and $8 million in punitive damages against XtraJet. The court awarded Harris $250,000 in compensatory damages against XtraJet, Borer, and Montgomery, $1 million in punitive damages against Borer, and $1 million in punitive damages against XtraJet. … After the judgment was entered Borer moved for a new trial, which the trial court denied. This appeal followed.

Contentions

Borer's principal argument is that there was insufficient evidence to support the trial court's awards of compensatory and punitive damages. He contends that plaintiffs were only entitled to nominal compensatory damages and no punitive damages. He also contends that the award of punitive damages violates his due process rights under the Fourteenth Amendment to the United States Constitution. Borer further contends that … the trial court erred by refusing to view the videotape in camera, by admitting hearsay statements about the value of the videotape, by finding that there was an audio component to the videotape, and by failing to differentiate between the high commercial value of Jackson's image and the limited commercial value of Geragos's and Harris's images.

In addition, Borer argues that there was no substantial evidence supporting the trial court's ruling on liability with respect to plaintiffs' third cause of action for common law misappropriation of name and likeness and fourth cause of action for use of name and likeness in violation of Civil Code section 3344. Finally, Borer argues that the trial court's denial of his motion for a new trial was error because the compensatory and punitive damages awarded were not supported by substantial evidence.

Discussion

Common Law Action for Misappropriation of Name or Likeness

"In California the right of publicity is both a common law right and a statutory right. The common law right of publicity has been recognized in this state since 1931. In 1971, the Legislature enacted [Civil Code] section 3344, which authorized recovery of damages by any living person whose name, photograph, or likeness was used for commercial purposes without his or her consent." *Gionfriddo v. Major League Baseball*, 94 Cal.App.4th 400, 408 (2001). Plaintiffs have asserted both rights here.

Plaintiffs'... cause of action is for misappropriation of name and likeness. The elements of this tort, at common law, are: (1) the defendant's use of the plaintiff's identity; (2) the appropriation of plaintiff's name or likeness to defendant's advantage, commercially or otherwise; (3) lack of consent; and (4) resulting injury." *Eastwood v. Superior Court*, 149 Cal.App.3d 409, 417 (1983).

Statutory Action for Misappropriation Under Civil Code Section 3344

Plaintiff's next cause of action is for use of name and likeness in violation of Civil Code section 3344. Civil Code section 3344, subdivision (a) provides, in part: "Any person who knowingly uses another's name, voice, signature, photograph, or likeness, in any manner, on or in products, merchandise, or goods, or for purposes of advertising or selling, or soliciting purchases of, products, merchandise, goods or services, without such person's prior consent, or, in the case of a minor, the prior consent of his parent or legal guardian, shall be liable for any damages sustained by the person or persons injured as a result thereof."

Relying mainly on *Eastwood* and *Solano v. Playgirl, Inc.*, 292 F.3d 1078 (9th Cir.2002), plaintiffs argue that defendants tortuously "used" their names and likeness. In *Eastwood*, the defendant publisher made a "telecast advertisement" in which it featured the plaintiff's name and photograph and mentioned prominently an article regarding the plaintiff in the defendant's newspaper. 149 Cal.App.3d at p. 415. The defendant ... clearly used the plaintiff's name and photograph to sell newspapers. Similarly, in *Solano*, the defendant published a photograph of the plaintiff and the plaintiff's name on the cover of its magazine without the plaintiff's consent. There was evidence that the defendant used the plaintiff's name and likeness in a knowingly false manner in order to promote the magazine's sales. 292 F.3d at 1086, 1089.

The present case is distinguishable from *Eastwood* and *Solano*. Plaintiffs base their common law and statutory causes of action on defendants' alleged use of their likeness as depicted in the videotape. There was no evidence, however, that Borer used the videotape or plaintiffs' likeness for commercial purposes—i.e., on or in products, merchandise, or goods, or for purposes of advertising or selling, or soliciting purchases of, products, merchandise, goods or services. Defendants did not sell the videotape or make profits from the videotape or use it to their advantage in any manner. Accordingly, there was insufficient evidence supporting plaintiffs' ... causes of action, and the trial court's ruling in plaintiffs' favor on those causes of action was error.

Plaintiffs' Compensatory Damages Were Excessive as a Matter of Law

Our determination that the trial court erred with respect to plaintiffs'... causes of action is not, by itself, reason to reverse the judgment. An appellant has the burden to show not only that the trial court erred but also that the error is prejudicial. *Pool v. City of Oakland*, 42 Cal.3d 1051, 1069 (1986).) An error is not prejudicial if independent grounds unaffected by the error support the judgment. *D'Amico v. Board of Medical Examiners*, 11 Cal.3d 1, 19 (1974). ... Except as expressly provided by the Civil Code, the measure of tort damages "is the amount which will compensate for all the detriment proximately caused [by the tortious conduct], whether it could have been anticipated or not." Civ. Code, § 3333. ... Borer argues that plaintiffs only submitted evidence of nominal damages. We reject that argument. Geragos presented his own testimony to prove his damages. He testified as follows. The incident was "embarrassing," "extremely upsetting" and "enormously offensive" to Geragos. Geragos did not, however, receive any treatment or counseling for his injuries.

The incident also affected Geragos's law practice. Part of Geragos's practice involved representing high profile people. Indeed, after November 2003, Geragos always had at least one client who was subject to media attention. Accordingly, in response to Borer's misconduct, Geragos went to "almost paranoid lengths" to safeguard his communications with his clients. He met clients in hotel rooms, hotel conference rooms, under freeways and under bridges. He hired a private investigator to work full-time for his firm. One of the reasons he relocated his office was so that he could maintain better security.

Harris too testified regarding plaintiffs' damages. He testified as follows. The incident was "very embarrassing" and made Harris and Geragos "look less than professional." Harris "felt like it [the videotape] damaged [plaintiffs'] reputation a great deal." Further, the incident created an "air of paranoia" within plaintiffs' law firm. Harris often conducted face-to-face meetings with clients because he was afraid of being taped. On one occasion, Harris flew to "Moldavia" to meet an attorney in order to engage in a secure conversation. Finally, Harris was upset about the incident because it offended his sense of ethics.

This testimony constitutes substantial evidence that both Geragos and Harris sustained damages beyond a nominal amount. Plaintiffs had good reason to be very upset about Borer's outrageous and illegal conduct. However, ... the amount of compensatory damages awarded went far beyond any reasonable amount in light of the evidence presented. The amount awarded to the plaintiffs was so great that it shocks the conscience. The most serious gap in plaintiffs' evidence is that there was virtually no evidence that anyone actually viewed the videotape. Plaintiffs' expert, Stanley Goldman, testified that he saw a "small excerpt" of the videotape as part of his work at Fox News. There was also evidence that Borer solicited bids for the videotape from the media. Thus, if the evidence is viewed in a light most favorable to plaintiffs, plaintiffs proved at most that a handful of people within the media viewed the videotape but the videotape was never seen by the public at large.

Further, because the videotape did not contain an audio component and because there was no evidence about the content of the videotape, there was no evidence that any third party ascertained any statements made by Geragos, Harris and Jackson to each other during their flight from Las Vegas to Santa Barbara. In addition,

Harris's conclusionary statement that he "felt" the videotape damaged plaintiffs' reputation was not supported by any other evidence. Plaintiffs did not present any evidence that they lost a single client as a result of the videotape or that any clients or potential clients expressed concern about plaintiffs' professionalism. There was also no evidence anyone perceived that plaintiffs acted in a less than competent and professional manner in connection with the recording of the videotape. Indeed, it is difficult to find fault with plaintiffs' conduct because plaintiffs were the victims of a crime and had no reason to believe that they could not speak in confidence with their client in a privately chartered airplane. Accordingly, there was no objective reason to conclude that plaintiffs' reputation was greatly harmed by the unlawful recording of a silent videotape that almost no one saw. …

We conclude that plaintiffs' compensatory damages were excessive as a matter of law. Having reached that conclusion, this court may "(1) remand for a new trial on all issues or on the issue of damages alone [citation], or (2) issue a remittitur conditioning affirmance of the judgment on plaintiff's agreement to remit part of the award." *Cunningham v. Simpson*, 1 Cal.3d 301, 310 (1969). We shall give plaintiffs Geragos and Harris a choice of whether to pursue a new trial on damages or whether to accept reduced compensatory damages in the amount of $100,000 for Geragos and $50,000 for Harris. …

In this case, Borer's misconduct was sufficiently reprehensible to warrant punitive damages. There was abundant evidence that Borer acted with malice, that is, he engaged in despicable conduct with a willful and conscious disregard of the rights of others. Civ. Code, § 3294, subd. (c)(1). The right violated here was the right of plaintiffs to engage in confidential communications without a third party unlawfully recording such communications. See Pen. Code, § 630. What makes matters worse is that Borer tried to record the confidential communications between criminal defense lawyers and their client. "While it is perhaps somewhat of a hyperbole to refer to the attorney-client privilege as "sacred," it is clearly one which our judicial system has carefully safeguarded with only a few specific exceptions." *Solin v. O'Melveny & Myers*, 89 Cal.App.4th 451, 457 (2001).

Borer not only sought to violate the attorney-client privilege, he did so in order to make a profit. … Most of the reprehensibility factors, however, weigh against a high punitive damages award. Borer's conduct did not endanger the health or safety of others and did not cause any physical harm, though plaintiffs were embarrassed and upset. The target of Borer's conduct—Michael Jackson and his lawyers—were not financially vulnerable. Rather, Jackson was sufficiently wealthy to charter a private airplane and his lawyers were sophisticated and presumably well-compensated professionals. Further, there was no evidence of repeated misconduct by Borer; this appears to be an isolated incident. Under the totality of the circumstances, the reprehensibility of Borer's conduct was not particularly egregious compared to other conduct that justifies punitive damages.

In present case, as we have explained, the evidence adduced at trial cannot support compensatory damages greater than $100,000 for Geragos and $50,000 for Harris. In light of the reprehensibility of Borer's conduct, punitive damages greater than a four-to-one ratio cannot be justified. Because the punitive damages awarded Geragos and Harris exceed that ratio, Borer's due process rights were violated. ...

NOTES AND QUESTIONS

1) **Misappropriation Under Federal Common Law.** In *International News Service v. Associated Press,* 248 U.S. 215 (1918), the Court established a theory of recovery for federal common law misappropriation. *International News Service,* however, "is no longer good law." *Barclays Capital Inc. v. Theflyonthewall.com, Inc.,* 650 F.3d 876, 894 (2d Cir.2011). "Purporting to establish a principle of federal common law, the doctrine law was abolished in *Erie R.R. Co. v. Tompkins,* 304 U.S. 64 (1938)." Thus, the ruling in *International News Service* survives only "as a description of a tort theory, not as precedential establishment of a tort cause of action." *Id.*

2) **Establishing a Prima Facie Case of Trade-Secret Misappropriation.** "One who discloses or uses another's trade secrets, without a privilege to do so, is liable to the other if (a) he discovers the secret by improper means, or (b) his disclosure or use constitutes a breach of confidence reposed in him by the other in disclosing the secret to him." *Hyde Corp. v. Huffines,* 314 S.W.2d 763, 769 (Tex.1958), citing 4 Restatement of Tort § 757. In Texas, the elements of trade-secret misappropriation are: "(1) the existence of a trade secret, (2) the breach of a confidential relationship or the improper discovery of a trade secret, (3) the use

of the trade secret, and (4) the award of appropriate damages." *Hurst v. Hughes Tool Co.*, 634 F.2d 895, 896 (5th Cir. 1981). "[A] trade secret may consist of any formula, pattern, device or compilation of information which is used in one's business, and which gives him an opportunity to obtain an advantage over competitors who do not know or use it. It may be a formula for a chemical compound, a process of manufacturing, treating or preserving materials, a pattern for a machine or other device, or a list of customers." *Kewanee Oil Co. v. Bicron Corp.*, 416 U.S. 470, 474-475 (1974), citing Restatement of Torts § 757 cmt. b (1939). "The subject of a trade secret must be secret, and must not be of public knowledge or of a general knowledge in the trade or business. *National Tube Co. v. Eastern Tube Co.*, 3 Ohio Cir. Ct. R., N.S., 459, 462 (1902). However, if the holder of the trade secret reveals the trade secret to another in confidence, and under an implied obligation not to use or disclose it, this element of secrecy is not defeated. *Cincinnati Bell Foundry Co. v. Dodds*, 10 Ohio Dec. Reprint 154, 156, 19 Weekly Law Bull. 84 (Super.Ct.1887).

2. Common Law Action Against Misappropriating Attorneys' Internet Domain Names and Their "Trade Value"

DeGidio v. West Group Corporation

191 F.Supp.2d 904
(N.D. Ohio 2002)

Katz, District Judge. Pending before this Court are cross-motions for summary judgment filed by Defendants—West Group Corporation, The Thompson Corporation, and West Licensing Corporation (Defendants or West)—and Plaintiff Anthony DeGidio), who is proceeding *pro se.*

I. Background

Plaintiff is the registrant of the domain name "lawoffices.net" and alleged founder and owner of the corresponding website—which provides an attorney directory, legal information relating to cyberlaw issues, a vanity email service, listings of domain names for sale, and a hosting service for legal related websites. In the instant action, Plaintiff asserts trademark protection for the designation LawOffices.net—which is the moniker attached to the website lawoffices.net. However, Plaintiff does not own either a federal or state registration for the LawOffices.net designation. The essential features of Plaintiff's putative trademark are: (1) a capitalization of the letters "l" and "o;" (2) pluralization of "lawoffice;" and (3) placement of the term "LawOffices.net" in black font in a horizontal rectangular box that is shaded in marbled white and light gray:

Defendants utilize the designation *Law* office.com and the domain name "lawoffice.com" to market the West Legal Directory—described by Defendants as "a one-stop online resource for useful information pertaining to law and lawyers for businesses, professionals and consumers." Defendants' website offers information on over four hundred legal topics, a directory of attorneys and other legal professionals, an online searchable legal dictionary, and a frequently asked questions section. In addition to the aforementioned services, West also offers fee-based services—including email, website creation and hosting, and sponsorship packages.

However, these fee-based services are not advertised at the *Law* office.com website. The essential features of the designation *Law* office.com are: (1) capitalization of the letter "l"; (2) singular—as opposed to plural— "lawoffice"; (3) italicization of "law"; (4) placement of *Law* office.com in white font in a dark blue rectangular box; (5) a multicolored open door emblem situated over the "dot"; and (6) the text "from West Legal Directory" placed in smaller white font beneath *Law* office:

Plaintiff asserts that Defendants' use of the designation *Law* office.com—in conjunction with the website lawoffice.com—infringes upon his alleged rights in the designation LawOffices.net and the affiliated lawoffices.net website. Specifically, Plaintiff pleads [several] causes of action, alleging: (1) common law unfair competition; (2) common law dilution; and (3) common law misappropriation.

Defendants moved for summary judgment, asserting *inter alia* that the "designation LawOffices.net is descriptive, devoid of secondary meaning, and therefore not entitled to trademark protection." Defendants also argue that even if this Court determines that there is a genuine factual dispute as to the trademark status of the designation of LawOffices.net, Plaintiff still cannot prevail on his dilution claims because he cannot establish that his mark is famous. Defendants further assert that Plaintiff cannot maintain his Ohio state law claims because he does not own an Ohio registration for the LawOffices.net designation. Plaintiff not only opposes Defendants' motion. …

II. Discussion

A. Summary Judgment Standard

"Summary judgment is just as appropriate in a trademark infringement case as in other litigation and is granted or denied on the same principles." *Freed v. Farag,* 994 F.Supp. 887, 889 (N.D. Ohio 1997) (citing *WSM, Inc. v. Tenn. Sales Co.,* 709 F.2d 1084, 1086 (6th Cir.1983); Summary judgment must be entered "against a party who fails to make a showing sufficient to establish the existence of an element essential to that party's case, and on which that party will bear the burden of proof at trial." *Celotex Corp. v. Catrett,* 477 U.S. 317, 322 (1986). Of course, the moving party always bears the initial responsibility of informing the district court of the basis for its motion, and identifying those portions of "the pleadings, depositions, answers to interrogatories, and admissions on file, together with the affidavits, if any," which it believes demonstrate the absence of a genuine issue of material fact. The burden then shifts to the nonmoving party who "must set forth specific facts showing that there is a genuine issue for trial." *Anderson v. Liberty Lobby, Inc.,* 477 U.S. 242, 250 (1986), *quoting* Fed. R. Civ. P. 56(e).

Once the burden of production has so shifted, the party opposing summary judgment cannot rest on its pleadings or merely reassert its previous allegations. It is not sufficient "simply [to] show that there is some metaphysical doubt as to the material facts." *Matsushita Elec. Indus. Co. v. Zenith Radio Corp.,* 475 U.S. 574, 586 (1986). Rather, Rule 56(e) "requires the nonmoving party to go beyond the unverified pleadings" and present some type of evidentiary material in support of its position. *Celotex,* 477 U.S. at 324. Summary judgment shall be rendered if "the pleadings, depositions, answers to interrogatories, and admissions on file, together with the affidavits, if any, show there is no genuine issue as to any material fact and that the moving party is entitled to judgment as a matter of law." Fed. R. Civ. P. 56(c).

"In considering a motion for summary judgment, the Court must view the facts and draw all reasonable inferences therefrom in a light most favorable to the nonmoving party." The Court is not required or permitted, however, to judge the evidence or make findings of fact. The purpose of summary judgment is not to resolve factual issues, but to determine if there are genuine issues of fact to be tried. Ultimately, this Court must determine "whether the evidence presents a sufficient disagreement to require submission to a jury or whether it is so one-sided that one party must prevail as a matter of law." *Anderson,* 477 U.S. at 251–52. …

Common Law Misappropriation

[Regarding] common law misappropriation, Defendants argue that the Court should analyze this claim as an unfair competition claim. However, Plaintiff does not premise this claim upon the alleged infringement of his putative common law trademark. Instead, Plaintiff asserts a claim for misappropriation of the "trade value" of the lawoffices.net designation and website. Therefore, the Court disagrees with Defendants' assertion that this claim is subject to the trademark analysis applicable to Plaintiff's other claims. …

Plaintiff alleges that "Defendants have appropriated the trade value of the lawoffices.net mark in a manner that constitutes reaping where he has not sown, and seeks to take a free ride from the Plaintiff's promotion of the lawoffices.net mark and website." Defendants assert that [misappropriation] is a claim for unfair competition and accordingly should be disposed of pursuant to federal trademark principles as applied to analogous state claims. Plaintiff asserts that facts pertaining to this claim are disputed and thus summary judgment is not appropriate. …

As support for their position that Plaintiff's misappropriation claim should be analyzed as an unfair competition claim, Defendants cite to *George P. Ballas Buick–GMC, Inc. v. Taylor Buick, Inc.,* 5 Ohio Misc.2d 16 (1981) in which Defendants assert that the court "labeled plaintiff's claim under § 4165.02 as a "misappropriation claim." Defendants' reliance upon *Taylor Buick* is misplaced. First, in *Taylor Buick,* the court did not hold that misappropriation claims are to be treated as [Ohio Deceptive Trade Practices Act] claims. Second, the ODTPA itself provides that "[t]his section does not affect unfair trade practices that are otherwise actionable at common law or under other sections of the Revised Code." Ohio Rev.Code § 4165.02(C).

Third, the cases are distinguishable on their respective facts. In

Taylor Buick, the plaintiff alleged that "the defendants misappropriated its research, design and advertising by copying and duplicating its advertising design on ... [a] billboard thereby appropriating plaintiff's property rights in this advertising design." *Taylor Buick,* 449 N.E.2d at 807. Plaintiff also alleged infringement upon his common law service mark. In the instant action, Plaintiff alleges appropriation of a much more amorphous concept— *i.e.,* "the 'trade value' of the lawoffices.net mark," a term which this Court construes as encompassing Plaintiff's good will, reputation, labor, business methods, and other intangibles that are not otherwise protectable by trademark law.

In the instant action, the Court admittedly finds no Ohio case discussing the misappropriation of "trade value." However, Ohio courts have recognized a separate tort of misappropriation in other contexts—such as misappropriation of trade secrets and misappropriation of another's name or likeness. ... Relying upon Supreme Court precedent and the common law of misappropriation as developed in numerous states, this Circuit has concluded that "there has been, and perhaps continues to be, a body of law which gives meaning to the term 'misappropriation of advertising ideas or style of doing business.'" *Advance Watch Co. v. Kemper Nat. Insurance Co.,* 99 F.3d 795, 802 (6th Cir.1996).

The court in *Advance Watch* further clarified that "[m]isappropriation of advertising ideas or style of doing business" does not necessarily refer only to the common-law tort of misappropriation recognized by the Supreme Court in *International News Service v. Associated Press,* ... but we conclude, it does refer to the unauthorized taking or use of interests other than those which are eligible for protection under statutory or common-law trademark." *See also Circle Communications, Inc. v. Hinton,* 1975 Ohio Misc. LEXIS 43, at *9, *17 (June 2, 1945) (recognizing that the Supreme Court has distinguished misappropriation as a separate cause of action, which "adopts protectable quasi-property values to such things as ideas, information, formulas, designs, and artistic creations").

While the Court makes no determination as to whether Plaintiff has successfully pled a cause of action for this tort, the Court notes that Defendants offer no grounds for summary judgment on this count, other than their claims as to the status of Plaintiff's trademark. *See Advance Watch,* 99 F.3d at 805 (distinguishing between trademark infringement on the one hand, and "misappropriation of advertising ideas or style of doing business" on the other, and noting that "it is common practice, but not legally precise, to refer to misappropriation of a trademark").

As the Court has no reason to determine that the Ohio Supreme Court would not recognize this cause of action, the Court will deny Defendants' motion for summary judgment. It is so ordered.

NOTES AND QUESTIONS

1) The Conversion of Stored Computer Records and Conflicting Right-of-Action Decisions Under the Common Law. Some courts allow aggrieved parties to commence a common-law cause of action against violators who convert or steal electronic records. *See In re Yazoo Pipeline Co., L.P.*, 459 B.R. 636, 653 (Bankr. S.D. Tex. 2011) (finding that the company's proprietary and converted seismic data had physical manifestation, humans could access the electronic data like accessing traditional tangible property, and concluding that the company stated a claim for conversion under Texas law); and, *Terarecon, Inc. v. Fovia, Inc.*, 2006 WL 1867734, *10 (N.D. Cal. 2006) (holding that a claim for conversion of a company's computer code and other intangible intellectual property was actionable because California law recognizes such claims). Other federal and state courts, however, have reached a contrary conclusion. *See Apparel Business Systems, LLC v. Tom James Co.*, 2008 WL 858754, *18 (E.D. Pa. 2008) (finding that the conversion of software data claim was essentially a copyright violation claim and declaring that copyrights and software claims were precluded under Pennsylvania law of conversion); and, *In re TJX Companies Retail Sec. Breach Litigation*, 527 F. Supp.2d 209, 213 (D. Mass. 2007) (declaring that Massachusetts law does not recognize an action for conversion if the claim is on the theft of intangible computerized credit card and account data).

2) Unauthorized Use of Commercial Trademarks and the Common Law Doctrine of Palming Off. An unfair competition claim may also commence under the doctrine of palming off. In *Bristol–Myers Squibb Co. v. McNeil–P.P.C.*, 786 F.Supp. 182, 216 (E.D.N.Y. 1992), the court explains: "The gravamen of an unfair competition claim for 'palming off' is that the labors and expenditures of the plaintiff have been misappropriated by the defendant, and are likely to cause confusion among the purchasing public as to the origin of the product." In *Attorney's*

Process and Research Service Inc. v. American Process and Research Corp., 177 Misc.2d 292, 294-295 (Sup. Ct. N.Y. 1998), the plaintiff used the mark "APRS" or "A.P.R.S." to advertise services for attorneys. Eight years after plaintiff's mark appeared, the defendant acted willfully and deliberately to prevent plaintiff from using the mark—by registering the same acronym for defendant's business and by trying to prevent plaintiff from using the mark in a publication. The plaintiff filed a tort action—asserting that defendant's action was "palming off" and unfair competition. The court agreed.

3) **Establishing a Prima Facie Case Under the Doctrine of Palming Off.** To prevail on a claim for palming off, a plaintiff must establish two elements: (1) the plaintiff's trade name has acquired a secondary meaning through usage; and (2) the similarity of the name used by the defendant would be likely to confuse the public. *Hudgens v. Goen,* 673 S.W.2d 420, 423 (Tex. App.-Fort Worth 1984). Courts are more likely to apply the "likelihood of confusion" test rather than a "fraudulent" standard to establish passing off. *Sicilia Di R. Biebow & Co. v. Cox,* 732 F.2d 417, 431 n.10 (5th Cir. 1984). Therefore, under the doctrine of palming off, an allegedly injured party does not have to prove that defendant's trademark infringement or palming off was intentional. *Line Enters., Inc. v. Hooks & Matteson Enter., Inc.,* 659 S.W.2d 113, 117 (Tex. App.-Amarillo 1983).

4) **Distinguishing Common-Law Palming-Off Claims and Statutory Trademark-Infringement Claims.** The common law of trademarks is a part of the broader law of unfair competition. *S. C. Johnson & Son v. Johnson,* 175 F.2d 176, 178 (2d Cir.1949). "It is a changing and expanding area of the law, but its fundamental purpose is to prevent a person from passing off his goods as the goods of another. The critical question is whether customers are, or may be, misled. Is the defendant taking advantage of the goodwill and business reputation established by the plaintiff? ... There is, however, a fundamental distinction to be drawn between trademark infringement and unfair competition. ... The essential element of a trademark is the exclusive right of its owner to use a word or device to distinguish his product. On the other hand, a claim of unfair competition considers the total physical image given by the product and its name together. Thus unfair competition exists if the total impression of package, size, shape, color, design and name upon the consumer will lead him to confuse the origin of the product." *Jean Patou, Inc. v. Jacqueline Cochran, Inc.*, 201 F. Supp. 861, 863 (S.D.N.Y. 1962).

3. Social Media, Social Websites and the Statutory Misappropriation of Attorneys' and Others' Names and Likeness

Fraley v. Facebook, Inc.

830 F.Supp.2d 785
(N.D. Cal. 2011)

Lucy H. Koh, District Judge. Facebook, Inc. (Facebook) owns and operates Facebook.com, a social networking site with over 600 million members worldwide and over 153 million members in the United States. While members join Facebook.com for free, Facebook generates its revenue through the sale of advertising targeted at its users. ... In this putative class action, Plaintiffs—Angel Fraley [and] Paul Wang (collectively "Plaintiffs") on behalf of themselves and all others similarly situated—allege that Facebook's Sponsored Stories violate California's Right of Publicity Statute, Civil Code § 3344 [and] that Facebook unlawfully misappropriated Plaintiffs' names, photographs, likenesses, and identities for use in paid advertisements without obtaining Plaintiffs' consent. Defendant filed a motion to dismiss pursuant to Federal Rules of Civil Procedure 12(b)(1) and 12(b)(6) arguing lack of Article III standing ... and failure to state a claim upon which relief can be granted ...

I. Background

Facebook allows members to share information with their Friends in a variety of ways: members may "Post" by adding text, images, videos, and hyperlinks to their own profile page; "Check-in" by announcing their geographical location within the feature "Places"; and "Like" content by clicking on a thumbs-up button that appears next to certain items on the Internet, both within Facebook.com and on external sites. Whenever members take one of these actions, Facebook generates a "Story," which then appears on their Friends' "News Feed."

Facebook earns revenue primarily through the sale of targeted advertising that appears on members' Facebook pages. Plaintiffs challenge one of Facebook's advertising services in particular—known as "Sponsored Stories," which Facebook ... was enabled for all members by default. A Sponsored Story is a form of paid advertisement that appears on a member's Facebook page and that generally consists of another Friend's name, profile picture, and an assertion that the person "likes" the advertiser. A Sponsored Story may be generated whenever a member utilizes the Post, Like, or Check-in features, or uses an application or plays a game that integrates with the Facebook website, and the content relates to an advertiser in some way determined by Facebook.

For example, Plaintiff Angel Fraley—who registered as a member with the name Angel Frolicker—alleges that she visited Rosetta Stone's Facebook profile page and clicked the "Like" button in order to access a free software demonstration. Subsequently, her Facebook user name and profile picture—which bears her likeness—appeared on her Friends' Facebook pages in a "Sponsored Story" advertisement consisting of the Rosetta Stone logo and the sentence, "Angel Frolicker likes Rosetta Stone." Plaintiffs Susan Mainzer [and] Paul Wang were similarly featured in "Sponsored Story" advertisements after clicking on a "Like" button on a company's website. ...

Unlike ordinary "Stories" that appear in a member's News Feed, Sponsored Stories are offset along with other advertisements paid by Facebook advertisers. The Second Amended Complaint (SAC) quotes Facebook CEO Mark Zuckerberg explaining that "[n]othing influences people more than a recommendation from a trusted friend" and that "[a] trusted referral is the Holy Grail of advertising." On average, actions taken by Facebook members are shared with 130 people—the average number of friends [for each] member. ... Plaintiffs assert that Sponsored Stories constitute "a new form of advertising which drafted millions of [Facebook members] as unpaid and unknowing spokespersons for various products," for which they are entitled to compensation under California law. ...

Plaintiffs allege that Facebook's practice of misappropriating their names and likenesses for commercial endorsements without their consent violated their statutory right of publicity under California Civil Code § 3344. ... Plaintiffs bring this putative class action on behalf of all persons in the United States who were registered members of Facebook.com as of January 24, 2011, and whose names, photographs, likenesses, or identities associated with their account were used by Facebook in a "Sponsored Story" advertisement. ...

IV. Discussion

Defendant moves to dismiss on grounds that (1) Plaintiffs fail to allege a cognizable injury and therefore lack Article III standing necessary to maintain an action in federal court; and (2) Plaintiffs fail to state a claim for misappropriation under California Civil Code § 3344 because they have not alleged any actionable injury, they consented to the use of their names and likenesses, and the republished content is newsworthy under § 3344(d). …

A. Article III Standing

To establish Article III standing, Plaintiffs must demonstrate that they satisfy three irreducible requirements: (1) they have suffered an "injury in fact"—i.e., "an invasion of a legally protected interest which is (a) concrete and particularized, and (b) actual or imminent, not conjectural or hypothetical"; (2) the injury is "fairly traceable to the challenged action of the defendant"; and (3) it is "likely, as opposed to merely speculative, that the injury will be redressed by a favorable decision." *Lujan v. Defenders of Wildlife*, 504 U.S. 555, 560–61 (1992). … Here, there is no dispute that Plaintiffs satisfy the second and third requirements of constitutional standing. … Furthermore, Plaintiffs' alleged injury is both "concrete and particularized," as well as "actual or imminent, not conjectural or hypothetical." *Lujan*, 504 U.S. at 560–61. … Defendant's motion to dismiss for lack of constitutional standing is accordingly denied. …

C. Misappropriation Action Under California Civil Code § 3344

California has long recognized a right to protect one's name and likeness against appropriation by others for their advantage. *Downing v. Abercrombie & Fitch*, 265 F.3d 994, 1001 (9th Cir. 2001). California law provides two vehicles for asserting such a right: a common law cause of action for commercial misappropriation, and a statutory remedy for commercial misappropriation under California Civil Code § 3344. To state a common law cause of action for misappropriation, a plaintiff must plead sufficient facts to establish "(1) the defendant's use of the plaintiff's identity; (2) the appropriation of plaintiff's name or likeness to defendant's advantage, commercially or otherwise; (3) lack of consent; and (4) resulting injury." To state a statutory cause of action under § 3344, a plaintiff must plead all the elements of the common law action and must also prove (5) "a knowing use by the defendant," and (6) "a direct connection between the alleged use and the commercial purpose."

The SAC alleges that Facebook's nonconsensual use of Plaintiffs' names, photographs, and likenesses in Sponsored Stories violates § 3344, which provides, in relevant part:

> Any person who knowingly uses another's name, voice, signature, photograph, or likeness, in any manner, on or in products, merchandise, or goods, or for purposes of advertising or selling, or soliciting purchases of, products, merchandise, goods or services, without such person's prior consent, or, in the case of a minor, the prior consent of his parent or legal guardian, shall be liable for any damages sustained by the person or persons injured as a result thereof. Cal. Civ. Code § 3344(a).

The statute further provides that a party in violation of § 3344 "shall be liable to the injured party or parties in an amount equal to the greater of [$750] or the actual damages suffered by him or her as a result of the unauthorized use," and shall disgorge "any profits from the unauthorized use that are attributable to the use and are not taken into account in computing the actual damages." *Id.*

Defendant moves to dismiss on grounds that (1) Facebook's actions fall within § 3344(d)'s "newsworthy" exception for which consent is not required; (2) in any event, Plaintiffs consented to the use of their names, photographs, and likenesses; and (3) Plaintiffs fail to allege sufficient injury under § 3344(a). Notably, Defendant does not at this juncture dispute that it knowingly used Plaintiffs' identity, or that the use of Plaintiffs' names or likenesses was to Defendant's advantage.

a. Newsworthiness

Defendant argues that Plaintiffs' § 3344 claim must be dismissed for failure to state a claim because the Sponsored Stories fall within the newsworthy exception under § 3344(d) for which consent is not required. Section 3344(d) provides that the "use of a name, voice, signature, photograph, or likeness in connection with any news, public affairs, or sports broadcast or account, or any political campaign, shall not constitute a use for which consent is required under [§ 3344(a)]." Cal. Civ. Code § 3344(d). Under California law, the "newsworthiness" exception under § 3344(d) tracks the constitutional right to freedom of speech under the First Amendment. *See Shulman v. Group W. Prods., Inc.*, 18 Cal.4th 200, 214–16 (1998).

A statutory cause of action for commercial appropriation therefore will not lie for "the publication of matters in the public interest, which rests on the right of the public to know and the freedom of the press to tell it." *Montana v. San Jose Mercury News, Inc.*, 34 Cal.App.4th 790, 793(1995). ... Because Facebook's publication of Plaintiffs' "Likes" is alleged to be for commercial advertising purposes and not part of "any news, public affairs, or sports broadcast or account, or any political campaign," the Court does not find it appropriate to dismiss the claim under the newsworthiness exception provided in § 3344(d).

b. Consent

Defendant next argues that even if consent was required, Plaintiffs gave the necessary consent by registering for and using the Facebook website under its Terms of Use—which informs members: "You can use your privacy settings to limit how your name and profile picture may be associated with commercial, sponsored, or related content (such as a brand you like) served or enhanced by us. You give us permission to use your name and [Facebook] profile picture in connection with that content, subject to the limits you place." According to Facebook, "Sponsored Stories are only delivered to your confirmed friends and respect the privacy settings you configure for News Feed." ... Facebook's Statement of Rights and Responsibilities, Privacy Policy, or Help Center ... remains a disputed question of fact and is not proper grounds for dismissal at this time.

c. Injury

The right to prevent others from appropriating elements of one's identity for commercial gain has evolved from the common law right of privacy, which is often described as comprising four separate and distinct torts: "(1) intrusion upon the plaintiff's seclusion or solitude; (2) public disclosure of private facts; (3) placing the plaintiff in a false light in the public eye; and (4) appropriation, for defendant's advantage, of plaintiff's name or likeness." *Motschenbacher v. R.J. Reynolds Tobacco Co.*, 498 F.2d 821, 824 (9th Cir. 1974) and *KNB Enterprises v. Matthews*, 78 Cal.App.4th 362, 366 (2000).

While violation of one's right to privacy may result in "injury to the feelings" that is wholly mental or subjective, California law has long recognized that "where the identity appropriated has a commercial value, the injury may be largely, or even wholly, of an economic or material nature." *Motschenbacher,* 498 F.2d at 824. The right of publicity has therefore "become a tool to control the commercial use and, thus, protect the economic value of one's name, voice, signature, photograph, or likeness." *KNB Enterprises v. Matthews,* 78 Cal.App.4th at 366.

Here, Plaintiffs allege ... that they suffered economic injury because they were not compensated for Facebook's commercial use of their names and likenesses in targeted advertisements to their Facebook Friends. Defendant does not deny that Plaintiffs may assert economic injury, but insists: [B]ecause they are not celebrities, they must demonstrate some preexisting commercial value to their names and likenesses—such as allegations that they "previously received remuneration for the use of their name or likeness, or that they have ever sought to obtain such remuneration."

First, the Court finds nothing in the text of the statute or in case law that supports Defendant's interpretation of § 3344 as requiring a plaintiff pleading economic injury to provide proof of preexisting commercial value and efforts to capitalize on such value in order to survive a motion to dismiss. The plain text of § 3344 provides simply that "[a]ny person who knowingly uses another's name, voice, signature, photograph, or likeness, in any manner ... for purposes of advertising or selling ... without such person's consent ... shall be liable for any damages sustained by the person or persons injured as a result thereof." Cal. Civ. Code § 3344.

The statutory text makes no mention of preexisting value, and in fact can be read to presume: [A] person whose name, photograph, or likeness is used by another for commercial purposes without his consent is "injured as a result thereof." Consistent with this reading, at least one court has suggested: "[C]ourts generally presume that the fourth element of the applicable test has been established if there is sufficient evidence to prove the first three elements." *Del Amo v. Baccash,* 2008 WL 4414514, *6 (C.D. Cal. 2008). ... Nor does the Court find any reason to impose a higher pleading standard on non-celebrities than on celebrities. California courts have clearly held that "the statutory right of publicity exists for celebrity and non-celebrity plaintiffs alike." *KNB Enterprises,* 78 Cal.App.4th at 373 n. 12. ... Moreover, even if non-celebrities are subject to a heightened pleading standard under § 3344, the Court finds that Plaintiffs' allegations satisfy the requirements for pleading a claim of economic injury under § 3344. ...

Thus, Plaintiffs have alleged that, in the same way that celebrities enjoy commercially exploitable opportunities among consumers at large, they enjoy commercially exploitable opportunities to advertise among their immediate friends and associates because "[i]n essence, Plaintiffs are celebrities—to their friends." ... At this stage, the Court finds their allegations of provable commercial value sufficient to survive a motion to dismiss and accordingly denies Defendant's 12(b)(6) motion with respect to the § 3344 claim. ...

V. Conclusion

For the reasons discussed herein, Defendant's motion to dismiss the Complaint based on lack of Article III standing [and] failure to state a claim under California Civil Code § 3344 ... is denied.

C. Solo and Small-Firm Attorneys' Defamation Actions Against Competitors and Others

Defamation is an intentional tort. And attorneys and others have a fairly long history of suing newspapers and magazines for defamation. For example, in *Cochran v. NYP Holdings, Inc.,* 58 F.Supp.2d 1113, 1116 (C.D. Cal. 1998), Johnnie L. Cochran, Jr.—a well-known trial attorney who successfully defended former football player O.J. Simpson—sued the *New York Post* for defamation. Andrea Peyser—a columnist for the *Post*—wrote: "[H]istory reveals that [Cochran] will say or do just about anything to win, typically at the expense of the truth." At that time, Cochran had not disclosed that he would join the legal team for and file a lawsuit on behalf of Abner Louima—a Haitian immigrant. Allegedly, Brooklyn police officers tortured Louima. Peyser stated: "Louima—a sympathetic plaintiff—would weaken his otherwise strong case by allowing Cochran—a 'legal scoundrel'—to join his team." *Id.*

Cochran's complaint alleged: When read in the context of the entire column, the statement implied that Cochran has a record of lying and unethical conduct. The district court dismissed the action—holding that Andrea Peyser was not liable for defaming attorney Johnnie Cochran. The Court of Appeals for the Ninth Circuit affirmed. *Cochran v. NYP Holdings, Inc.*, 210 F.3d 1036, 1038 (9th Cir. 2000). The Ninth Circuit adopted district court's conclusion: Peyser's statements were opinions or commentary or about Cochran's trial strategy. Thus, the First Amendment prevented

Peyser's "loose, figurative and hyperbolic" statements from serving as the foundation for a defamation claim. 58 F.Supp.2d, at 1114-1117.

Just eight years after the *Cochran* decision, Richard Pérez-Peña penned an article entitled, "Newspaper Circulation Continues to Decline Rapidly." *N.Y. Times*, Oct. 28, 2008 at B4. The article disclosed: Newspaper circulation has fallen annually for years and continues to accelerate. Weekday circulation for the largest metropolitan dailies fell from 1.9 to 13.6 percent. And the circulation at the nation's biggest newspapers "fell 10 percent or more." And "[t]he "Internet—where newspapers are generally free—has siphoned off circulation and advertising even as it made papers more widely read than ever before."

Perhaps, courts will and should apply established legal principles to resolve Internet-defamation claims—those which arise against large publishing houses, newspapers and "traditional" mass media. But, consider the numerous and various Internet, media-sharing and social-media websites—live online forums, blog-comment forums, social networks, bookmarking sites, social-news sites and microblogging websites. Put simply, on these electronic websites and forums, everyone is a publisher when s/he posts allegedly defaming information about attorneys or other persons. Thus, two questions have arisen: (1) Should solo and small-firm attorneys have a private right of action to file defamation lawsuits against competitors or others who post "derogatory" statements about attorneys on social networks or on social-news sites?; and (2) if the answer is yes or a qualified yes, should courts apply current common-law rules or novel legal principles to address attorneys' Internet-defamation claims? Consider the defamation claims, analyses and rulings in the following cases.

1. Attorneys' Defamation Actions Against Anonymous Social-Media Posters, Website Owners, and Internet Service Providers

Thomson v. Doe

356 P.3d 727
(Wash. Ct. App. 2015)

Appelwick, J. What showing must be made by a defamation plaintiff seeking disclosure of an anonymous speaker's identity? This is an open question in Washington. Thomson brought a defamation suit against Doe—an anonymous poster who wrote a negative review of Thomson on Avvo.com. Thomson then subpoenaed Avvo seeking Doe's identity. When Avvo refused to provide the information, Thomson moved to compel Avvo's compliance with the subpoena. The trial court denied Thomson's motion, finding that Thomson had not made a *prima facie* claim of defamation. Thomson appealed.

Facts

Deborah Thomson is a Florida attorney. Avvo Inc. operates an online lawyer review and rating system. On May 21, 2014, Thomson filed a *pro se* lawsuit in Florida against Jane Doe—an anonymous individual who posted a review on Thomson's Avvo profile. The review, posted by "Divorce client," stated:

> I am still in court five years after Ms. Thomson represented me during my divorce proceedings. Her lack of basic business skills and detachment from her fiduciary responsibilities has cost me everything. She failed to show up for a nine-hour mediation because she had vacation days. She failed to subpoena documents that are critical to the division of assets in any divorce proceeding. In fact, she did not subpoena any documents at all. My interests were simply not protected in any meaningful way.

Thomson's complaint alleged that Doe was not a client and that the post was designed to impugn Thomson's personal and professional reputation. Thomson alleged four causes of action: defamation, defamation *per se*, defamation by implication, and intentional infliction of emotional distress (IIED).

On June 25, 2014, Thomson filed a subpoena in King County Superior Court requesting from Avvo the anonymous poster's identification. On July 3, Thomson received an e-mail from Joshua King—Avvo's vice president of business development and general counsel. King told Thomson: "I've received your subpoena seeking records on an anonymous review. Our policy on handling such subpoenas is to let the reviewer know, so that they can move to quash if they want. They may also provide me with more information about the representation, in which case we may ask you to withdraw the subpoena." Thomson replied: "Thank you for letting me know. … I am pretty certain I am aware who wrote it, so I am eager to obtain the records."

On July 8, King e-mailed Thomson: "I have received a response. While I can't give you the specifics, it included information sufficient for me to believe the reviewer was a client of yours. Given this information, I ask that you withdraw the subpoena." Thomson responded, "Please be advised that I will not be withdrawing my subpoena. Please provide the documents requested therein."

On July 16, Thomson moved to compel Avvo to comply with the subpoena. She asserted that Doe's speech was libel and defamation. Specifically, she alleged that each of the sentences in the Doe post was either a false statement of fact or a combination of fact and opinion that was provably false. She did not submit a declaration, affidavit, or any other evidence in support of her motion. Avvo opposed the motion, arguing that Thomson failed to show that the post was defamatory and failed to provide evidence of damages. On July 28, the trial court denied Thomson's motion to compel. It stated that Thomson "failed to make a *prima facie* showing regarding her defamation claim." Thomson appeals. Avvo and Doe each filed a response.

Discussion

The First Amendment protects the right to speak anonymously. *McIntyre v. Ohio Elections Comm'n,* 514 U.S. 334, 342 (1995). This right applies equally to online speech. *In re Anonymous Online Speakers*, 661 F.3d 1168, 1173 (9th Cir.2011). However, defamatory speech does not enjoy the protections of the First Amendment. *Chaplinsky v. New Hampshire,* 315 U.S. 568, 571–72 (1942). Accordingly, when faced with a defamation claim, courts aim to strike a balance between the right to protect one's reputation and the constitutional right to free speech. *See Dun & Bradstreet, Inc. v. Greenmoss Builders, Inc.*, 472 U.S. 749, 759–60 (1985); *Gertz v. Robert Welch, Inc.*, 418 U.S. 323, 346–48 (1974); *New York Times Co. v. Sullivan*, 376 U.S. 254, 279–80 (1964).

To that end, the United States Supreme Court has considered the type of speech at issue when determining the appropriate standards to apply in defamation cases. For example, when a defamed plaintiff is a public figure, the standard of fault is more stringent; such a claim requires a showing of actual malice. *See New York Times*, 376 U.S at 279–80; *Curtis Publ'g Co. v. Butts*, 388 U.S. 130, 155, 162–63 (1967). This heightened standard reflects the constitutionally protected "interchange of ideas for the bringing about of political and social changes desired by the people." *New York Times*, 376 U.S. at 269. By contrast, when the challenged speech involves a purely private concern, "[t]here is no threat to the free and robust debate of public issues" and thus the First Amendment provides less stringent protection. *Dun & Bradstreet*, 472 U.S. at 759–60.

Here, we are asked to determine whether the trial court struck the proper balance in reviewing Thomson's motion to disclose Doe's identity. To answer this question, we must address two issues: first, whether the trial court applied the correct standard in reviewing a motion to reveal an anonymous speaker's identity, and second, whether Thomson met that standard.

Whether the trial court applied the correct legal standard is a question of law that we review *de novo*. *Hundtofte v. Encarnación*, 181 Wash.2d 1, 13 (2014). If the correct legal standard was applied, we generally review a trial court's denial of a motion to compel for an abuse of discretion. *Lake Chelan Shores Homeowners Ass'n v. St. Paul Fire & Marine Ins. Co.*, 176 Wash.App. 168, 183 (2013). This is because the trial court is "better positioned than another" to decide discovery issues. However, when the trial court's ruling involves libelous speech, the United States Supreme Court has indicated that independent appellate review is proper. *Bose Corp. v. Consumers Union of U.S., Inc.*, 466 U.S. 485, 499 (1984). This is because the constitutional values at issue warrant review by judges—including appellate judges—rather than the trier of fact. … Accordingly, we hold that *de novo* review is the proper standard of review when considering the trial court's decision on a motion to reveal an anonymous speaker's identity.

We now turn to the requisite showing a defamation plaintiff must make on a motion to unmask an anonymous defendant. This is an open question in Washington. However, many other courts—both federal and state—have considered this issue. The two leading cases are *Dendrite Int'l, Inc. v. Doe No. 3*, 342 N.J.Super. 134, 140 (2001) and *Doe No. 1 v. Cahill*, 884 A.2d 451, 456 (Del. 2005). In *Dendrite*, an anonymous speaker posted messages on an online bulletin board criticizing Dendrite's stock performance. Dendrite sued the anonymous speaker and sought disclosure of the speaker's identity. The New Jersey intermediate appellate court set out a four-step process for determining whether to compel disclosure of the speaker's identity:

> [First,] the trial court should … require the plaintiff to undertake efforts to notify the anonymous posters that they are the subject of a subpoena or application for an order of disclosure, and withhold action to afford the fictitiously-named defendants a

> reasonable opportunity to file and serve opposition to the application. These notification efforts should include posting a message of notification of the identity discovery request to the anonymous user on the ISP's pertinent message board.
>
> [Second,] the court shall ... require the plaintiff to identify and set forth the exact statements purportedly made by each anonymous poster that plaintiff alleges constitutes actionable speech.
>
> [Third,] the complaint and all information provided to the court should be carefully reviewed to determine whether plaintiff has set forth a *prima facie* cause of action against the fictitiously-named anonymous defendants. In addition to establishing that its action can withstand a motion to dismiss for failure to state a claim upon which relief can be granted ..., the plaintiff must produce sufficient evidence supporting each element of its cause of action, on a prima facie basis, prior to a court ordering the disclosure of the identity of the unnamed defendant.
>
> Finally, assuming the court concludes that the plaintiff has presented a prima facie cause of action, the court must balance the defendant's First Amendment right of anonymous free speech against the strength of the *prima facie* case presented and the necessity for the disclosure of the anonymous defendant's identity to allow the plaintiff to properly proceed. *Id.* at 141–42.

The *Dendrite* court stated that the test "must be undertaken and analyzed on a case-by-case basis. The guiding principle is a result based on a meaningful analysis and a proper balancing of the equities and rights at issue." *Id.* at 142, 775 A.2d 756.

In *Cahill*, the Delaware Supreme Court considered the proper standard to apply when faced with a public-figure plaintiff's request to unmask an anonymous defendant. The *Cahill* court adopted a "modified *Dendrite* standard consisting only of *Dendrite* requirements one and three: the plaintiff must make reasonable efforts to notify the defendant and must satisfy the summary judgment standard." In concluding that summary judgment was the appropriate evidentiary standard, the *Cahill* court expressed concern "that setting the standard too low will chill potential posters from exercising their First Amendment right to speak anonymously." *Id.* at 457. The court recognized that there was an "entire spectrum" of evidentiary standards that could be applied, with varying levels of severity. It rejected the least stringent standard, the good faith test:

> Plaintiffs can often initially plead sufficient facts to meet the good faith test applied by the Superior Court, even if the defamation claim is not very strong, or worse, if they do not intend to pursue the defamation action to a final decision. After obtaining the identity of an anonymous critic through the compulsory discovery process, a defamation plaintiff who either loses on the merits or fails to pursue a lawsuit is still free to engage in extra-judicial self-help remedies; more bluntly, the plaintiff can simply seek revenge or retribution. *Id.*

It also rejected the next level of evidentiary showing, the motion to dismiss standard:

> [E]ven silly or trivial libel claims can easily survive a motion to dismiss where the plaintiff pleads facts that put the defendant on notice of his claim, however vague or lacking in detail these allegations may be. Clearly then, if the stricter motion to dismiss standard is incapable of screening silly or trivial defamation suits, then the even less stringent good faith standard is less capable of doing so. *Id.* at 459.

By contrast, the court noted: The summary judgment standard would "more appropriately protect against the chilling effect on anonymous First Amendment internet speech that can arise when plaintiffs bring trivial defamation lawsuits primarily to harass or to unmask their critics." *Id.*

As a threshold matter, we agree with *Dendrite* and *Cahill* that notice is a crucial element of the standard. In the interest of due process—or, at the very least, in the interests of fairness and judicial economy—a plaintiff should attempt to notify a Doe defendant that his or her identity might be unmasked. Here, although Thomson did not attempt to provide notice to Doe, Doe acknowledges that Avvo cured this problem by notifying her. The choice of whether to apply the standard of either *Dendrite* or *Cahill* is less clear. Most federal and state courts [considering] this question have adopted some form of the *Dendrite* and *Cahill* tests. In addition, two state courts have determined that adopting *Dendrite* or *Cahill* would be unnecessary because their state procedural rules provided equivalent protection.

Only one court has significantly strayed from *Dendrite* and *Cahill*. The Virginia Court of Appeals declined to adopt either test, instead applying a state statute that required a lower standard of proof. *Yelp, Inc. v. Hadeed Carpet Cleaning, Inc.*, 62 Va. App. 678, 695–97 (2014). Under the Virginia statute, a defamation plaintiff's seeking an anonymous speaker's identity must establish a good faith basis to contend that the speaker committed defamation. In rejecting *Dendrite* and *Cahill*, the *Hadeed* court stated that the legislature had "considered persuasive authority from other states and made the policy decision to include or exclude factors that other states use in their unmasking standards." *Id.* at 703.

Thomson argues that we should follow Virginia's lead and apply the good faith test, while Doe and Avvo advocate the heightened standard under *Dendrite* and *Cahill*. In this way, the parties frame the issue before us as an either/or decision. But, in doing so, the parties bypass an important threshold question: what is the nature of the speech at issue?

The Ninth Circuit has suggested that this question is crucial when reviewing a motion to disclose an anonymous speaker's identity. In *Anonymous*, the plaintiff sought to unmask anonymous online posters who disparaged the plaintiff and its business practices. Applying *Cahill*, the district court granted the plaintiffs motion. The posters filed a *writ of mandamus* challenging the decision. The Ninth Circuit denied the writ, finding that the posters had not demonstrated a need for the extraordinary remedy of mandamus. In doing so, the *Anonymous* court also discussed the link between the type of speech at issue and the appropriate evidentiary standard:

> Because *Cahill* involved political speech, that court's imposition of a heightened standard is understandable. ... [We] suggest that the nature of the speech should be a driving force in choosing a standard by which to balance the rights of anonymous speakers in discovery disputes. For example, in discovery disputes involving the identity of anonymous speakers, the notion that commercial speech should be afforded less protection than

> political, religious, or literary speech is hardly a novel principle. The specific circumstances surrounding the speech serve to give context to the balancing exercise. *Id.* at 1176–77

We agree with *Anonymous*: the evidentiary standard should match the First Amendment interest at play. This aligns with the United States Supreme Court's treatment of the standard of fault in defamation cases. *See, New York Times,* 376 U.S at 279–80 (requiring plaintiffs to meet a higher bar in cases of protected speech); *Dun & Bradstreet,* 472 U.S. at 758–60 (recognizing that commercial speech warrants lesser protection). We therefore hold: When addressing a defamation motion to unmask an anonymous defendant, the court must consider the nature of the speech at issue when determining the evidentiary standard to apply.

Here, the parties treat the type of speech as a peripheral question, only cursorily disputing whether Doe's statements constituted commercial speech. If Doe's speech was commercial, it would warrant a lower evidentiary bar. *See Cent. Hudson Gas & Elec. Corp. v. Pub. Serv. Comm'n of New York,* 447 U.S. 557, 562–63 (1980) ("The Constitution therefore accords lesser protection to commercial speech than other constitutionally guaranteed expression.").

Commercial speech is "expression related solely to the economic interests of the speaker and its audience" or "speech proposing a commercial transaction." *Id.* at 561–62. Doe's speech does not meet this standard: Although her economic interests might have been affected by the behavior her review describes, her act of speech impacts more than her economic interests. While Doe's speech is not commercial, warranting the lowest protection, it is also not political, warranting the highest. Thus, Doe's speech is entitled to an intermediate level of protection.

As such, we reject Thomson's assertion that a good faith showing—the least stringent standard—would be appropriate here. We likewise reject the next level of evidentiary showing—the motion to dismiss standard. As *Dendrite* and *Cahill* persuasively argue, this standard would be inadequate to protect this level of speech. … This leaves the two remaining standards considered by other courts: *prima facie* and summary judgment.

The *Cahill* court's treatment of its summary judgment standard as equivalent to *Dendrite*'s *prima facie* standard has caused some confusion in subsequent cases in other jurisdictions. … Despite this confusion, the "important feature of *Dendrite* and *Cahill* is to emphasize that the plaintiff must do more than simply plead his case." Considering the speech at issue here, we agree that supporting evidence should be required before the speaker is unmasked. …

The final issue we address is Avvo's attempt to serve as the arbiter of Doe's identifying information. Obtaining information from the anonymous poster allowed Avvo to make an informed response to Thomson. Once in that position, Avvo should have afforded the trial court the opportunity for in camera review, so that it too could ground its decision in fact rather than speculation.

The trial court applied the proper standard in reviewing Thomson's motion. Under that standard, Thomson's motion must fail. As Thomson freely admits, she presented no evidence to support her motion. Therefore, the trial court properly denied Thomson's motion for failure to make a *prima facie* showing of defamation. We affirm.

NOTES AND QUESTIONS

1) Internet-Defamation and Attorneys' Action for Injunctive Relief. In *Romero v. Erik G. Abrahamson, P.A.*, 113 So.3d 870, 871 (Fla. 2012), the client sued to collect money he claimed that the law firm owed him. In turn, the law firm filed a defamation action against Romero. According to the firm, Romero posted "derogatory comments about the law firm and the pending case online." Twice, the law firm sought a temporary injunction to prevent Romero from dispersing defamatory information about the firm. Originally, the trial court denied both motions. But the second motion was denied in conjunction with a case management hearing, which allegedly prevented "Romero from speaking about the case in the future to anyone other than court personnel." On review and citing the doctrine of prior restraint, the appellate court "reversed the trial court's order that prevents Romero from engaging in future case-related speech."

2) Anonymous Internet Postings, Defamation Claims, and Duty to Notify Anonymous Posters—Conflicting Decisions. Under both *Dendrite* and *Cahill* and before filing an Internet-defamation suit, a plaintiff should attempt to notify an anonymous Internet poster and disclose that the poster's identity might be unmasked. Due-process requirements, fairness and judicial economy require such notice. However, whether courts should apply the four-pronged *Dendrite* or the competing *Cahill* standard is less clear. *See SaleHoo Grp., Ltd. v. ABC Co.*, 722 F.Supp.2d 1210, 1215 (W.D.Wash.2010) (adopting a *Dendrite*-style test); *Doe I v. Individuals*, 561 F.Supp.2d 249, 255–56 (D.Conn.2008) (adopting the *Dendrite prima facie* showing, because *Cahill*'s test is "potentially confusing and also difficult for a plaintiff to satisfy"); *Highfields Capital Mgmt., LP v. Doe*, 385 F.Supp.2d 969, 974 n. 6, 975 (N.D.Cal.2005) (relying on *Dendrite* and *Cahill* in holding that it "is not enough for a plaintiff simply to plead and pray"); *Mobilisa, Inc. v. Doe*, 217 Ariz. 103, 111 (2007) (adopting *Cahill*'s summary judgment standard and *Dendrite*'s balancing test); *Krinsky v. Doe 6*, 159 Cal.App.4th 1154, 1172 (2008) (compelling plaintiff to make a *prima facie* showing of the elements of libel"); *Solers, Inc. v. Doe*, 977 A.2d 941, 954 (D.C. 2009) (adopting a test that "closely resembles the 'summary judgment' standard articulated in *Cahill*"); *In re Indiana Newspapers*, 963 N.E.2d 534, 552 (Ind.Ct.App.2012) (finding that "the test that draws the most appropriate balance between protecting anonymous speech and preventing defamatory speech is the *Dendrite* test"); *Doe No. 1 v. Coleman*, 436 S.W.3d 207, 211 (Ky.Ct.App.2014) (adopting the *Dendrite test* "as modified by" *Cahill*); *Indep. Newspapers, Inc. v. Brodie*, 407 Md. 415, 454–55 (2009) (adopting the *Dendrite* test); *Mortg. Specialists, Inc. v. Implode–Explode Heavy Indus., Inc.*, 160 N.H. 227, 239 (2010) (endorsing the *Dendrite* test); *Pilchesky v. Gatelli*, 12 A.3d 430, 442–46 (Pa. Super. 2011) (adopting a "modified version of the *Dendrite/Cahill* test"); and *In re Does 1–10*, 242 S.W.3d 805, 821 (Tex.Ct.App.2007) (finding itself "in alignment with the formulations set out in Cahill").

---

2. Attorneys' Internet-Defamation Actions Against Clients' Third-Party Adversaries and Consumers

Feuerstein v. Simpson

582 Fed. Appx. 93
(10th Cir. 2014)

Rendell, Circuit Judge. Appellant George Simpson—acting *pro se*—appeals a jury verdict against him for defamation of character.

I. Background

Simpson was the owner of a condominium unit in the Sapphire Bay Condominiums West in St. Thomas (SBCW). Simpson and SBCW have been involved in multiple lawsuits against one another for over a decade. SBCW was represented in some of these lawsuits by Appellee Alan Feuerstein. In 2003, Simpson instituted a lawsuit against another SBCW condominium owner— Myrna Golden— regarding her ownership of cats. Mrs. Golden was represented by Feuerstein in that litigation.

In September 2004, Simpson sent a letter to Mrs. Golden's husband in which he, among other things, accused Feuerstein of being dishonest in connection with his representation of Mrs. Golden. Feuerstein demanded that Simpson retract the statement, but Simpson refused. Accordingly, on October 14, 2004, Feuerstein filed the instant lawsuit against Simpson in the District Court for the Virgin Islands for ... defamation of character.

Feuerstein alleges that, shortly after he filed his lawsuit against Simpson, Simpson published several websites geared toward defaming and harming Feuerstein's professional reputation. Simpson linked these websites to other websites, also allegedly published by Simpson and containing defamatory material regarding SBCW and certain members of the SBCW Board of Directors. Feuerstein contends that Simpson also published a defamatory website targeting the SBCW's previous attorney—Andrew Capdeville—and that Mr. Capdeville was forced to withdraw as SBCW's counsel to litigate against Simpson with respect to the defamatory website.

Simpson raises four issues on appeal. The most compelling ... is his claim that because no formal amendment of the complaint to include the websites occurred prior to trial, the verdict, based as it was on the websites, cannot stand.

II. Discussion

A. Amendment of the Pleadings

On September 20, 2010, Feuerstein served responses and objections to Simpson's interrogatories and document requests. In response to an interrogatory stating, "[s]et forth each and every utterance, which you claim is defamatory by Defendant against Plaintiffs. State specific sentence(s) which you claim are defamatory and why," Feuerstein identified the websites and the specific defamatory statements on the websites.

Simpson was questioned extensively at his deposition ... regarding the defamatory websites. Feuerstein designated that deposition testimony in his deposition designations for trial. ... In addition, Feuerstein filed a motion in limine ... in which he stated: "This case ... claims damages from defamatory websites erected and maintained by the Defendant George R. Simpson and his nominees. Simpson opposed the motion in limine and filed one of his own ... On the first day of trial, after the jury was empaneled but before it began hearing evidence, the District Judge denied Simpson's motion in limine regarding the websites and stated that he believed that the existing complaint alleged a pattern of harassment sufficient to encompass the websites.

Despite this, he stated that he would permit the complaint to be amended to include allegations regarding the websites. He noted that amendments to complaints are to be liberally granted, and stated, "I think everybody is aware of the issue [of the websites]." At no time did Feuerstein actually make a formal motion to amend his complaint; however, he filed an amended complaint that included allegations regarding the websites that same day. Simpson mounted a defense at trial regarding the websites—namely, that though he agreed with them and supplied some of their content, he was not the one who actually published them. Simpson did not object to questioning regarding the websites at trial, and, indeed, questioned Feuerstein extensively about them. ...

After three days of trial, the jury returned a verdict in favor of Feuerstein—finding by special interrogatory that Simpson published the defamatory websites and was their owner, and awarded Feuerstein $6,600,000 in damages. Feuerstein consented to a reduction of the award to $1,175,000. Simpson appealed.

We review the Court's ruling to permit the amendment for abuse of discretion. *Douglas v. Owens*, 50 F.3d 1226, 1235 (3d Cir.1995). ... Feuerstein argued—and the District Court agreed—that the complaint as originally pled was broad enough in alleging an ongoing pattern of libel and defamation to include the websites. ... Accordingly, in absence of any evidence of unexplained delay, bad faith or undue prejudice, we cannot say that the District Court abused its discretion in permitting Feuerstein to amend his complaint to include the websites. ...

Throughout the proceedings in the District Court and here, Simpson has claimed that he cannot be held liable for the allegedly defamatory statements contained on the websites because he did not publish the websites. Rather, he claims, the websites were owned and published by a company called North American Alliance for Honest Corporate Management, and/or by a man named Randolph Lindsey. Simpson claims that Feuerstein's failure to join Lindsey and North American Alliance for Honest Corporate Management in this lawsuit was in violation of Fed.R.Civ.P. 19, which provides in relevant part: "A person who is subject to service of process and whose joinder will not deprive the court of subject-matter jurisdiction must be joined as a party if: (A) in that person's absence, the court cannot accord complete relief among existing parties." Fed.R.Civ.P. 19(a)(1).

Feuerstein claims that Randolph Lindsey is actually George Simpson's alter ego and does not exist as a separate person, and at the very least, Lindsey and the North American Alliance for Honest Corporate Management are agents of Simpson. He notes that the jury found by special interrogatory that Simpson was responsible for the content of the websites. The burden of showing that joinder is necessary is on the party advocating for joinder. *See Hood ex rel Mississippi v. City of Memphis*, 570 F.3d 625, 628 (5th Cir.2009). And Simpson does not point to any evidence—other than his own testimony—that Randolph Lindsey and/or the North American Alliance for Honest Corporate Management are the true owners of the websites at issue, or that these entities even exist.

In any case, the fact that Simpson may not have been the actual owner of the websites is of no moment. To prevail on a defamation claim under Virgin Islands law, a plaintiff must show that the defendant published the alleged defamatory statement to a third party. *VECC, Inc. v. Bank of N.S.*, 296 F.Supp.2d 617, 622 (D.VI.2003). In a legal sense, to "publish" a defamatory statement merely means to communicate that statement to a person other than the person who is defamed. *See* BLACK'S LAW DICTIONARY 1428, (10th Ed.2014) (defining publish as "to communicate [defamatory words] to someone other than the person defamed.").

Simpson admits that he supplied content for publication on the websites; and there was sufficient evidence for the jury to find that he "published" the allegedly defamatory statements contained therein. Simpson offers no support for his argument: The joinder of Randolph Lindsey, the North American Alliance for Honest Corporate Management, or any other party was necessary for the complete adjudication of Feuerstein's claim that Simpson "published" the defamatory statements. Accordingly, Simpson has failed to sustain his burden with respect to joinder.

Inflammatory Statements in the Presence of the Jury

Finally, Simpson claimed that Feuerstein's statements—labeling Simpson a "hallucinating lunatic," "bizarre," "sociopathic," and "schizophrenic," and referencing Simpson's involvement with the extraterrestrial community—biased the jury against him. The record is clear, however, that it was Simpson, and not Feuerstein or his counsel, who put these labels before the jury by repeatedly quoting from Feuerstein's deposition testimony. By affirmatively raising this inflammatory deposition testimony before the jury, Simpson—not Feuerstein—caused the purported bias of which he now complains. In other words, Simpson cannot complain on appeal of an error that he himself invited.

Accordingly, for the reasons set forth above, we will affirm the judgment of the District Court.

---

3. Attorneys' Internet-Defamation Actions Against Other Law Firms and Solo Practitioners

Salyer v. Southern Poverty Law Center, Inc.

701 F.Supp.2d 912
(W.D. Ky. (2009)

John G. Heyburn, II, District Judge.

Robert E. Salyer brought this action in Jefferson County Kentucky Circuit Court alleging that Defendant—The Southern Poverty Law Center, Inc.—published defamatory statements about him in its 2006 "Intelligence Report." The statements were published in a print magazine and online. ...Defendant removed the case to this court on diversity grounds. The pending motions raise novel and interesting issues concerning allegedly defamatory statements on the internet and what might constitute republication of them. Specifically, the parties dispute the narrow issue of whether the one-year statute of limitations applicable to defamation actions in Kentucky bars Plaintiff's claim. Because the article was originally published more than one year before commencement of this action, the critical question is whether the article was "republished" within that one-year window. ...

I.

Plaintiff is an attorney practicing primarily in Kentucky. On July 7, 2006, Defendant posted its "Intelligence Report"—a comprehensive examination of extremist groups in the military—on its website. The report contained an article entitled "A Few Bad Men." It alleged that Plaintiff was a member of an extremist group, dishonorably discharged from the military, and disbarred from practicing before military courts. The report, including the article, was then published in a print version on August 14, 2006, and mailed to various subscribers. Plaintiff alleges that the statements in the article relating to him were defamatory.

[T]he article remained accessible on Defendant's website indefinitely. [However], it was not altered until July 21, 2008, when Plaintiff asked Defendant [to remove] all mention of Plaintiff's name. Several articles—which were published on Defendant's website between the original publication of "A Few Bad Men" and the removal of Plaintiff's name—referenced the article and included hyperlinks to its original version. Those referencing articles were published on July 21, 2006, July 25, 2006, September 1, 2006, November 23, 2006, and July 18, 2008. Additionally, Defendant's Winter 2008 quarterly print edition contained an article that referred to "A Few Bad Men." Finally, at some time in 2008, Defendant mailed an unedited copy of the August 14, 2006, print publication to a researcher. Plaintiff alleges that these actions constituted republication of the article for purposes of the statute of limitations.

II.

In an April 23, 2009, this court found that all actions for defamation in Kentucky must be brought within one year of the defamatory material's publication date. *See* KRS § 413.140(1)(d); *Caslin v. Gen. Elec. Co.*, 608 S.W.2d 69, 70 (Ky.App.1980). The court further predicted that Kentucky would follow the "single publication rule" for all mass publications of allegedly defamatory materials, including those materials published on the internet. That rule provides: "[A]ny form of mass communication or aggregate publication … is a single communication and can give rise to only one action for libel." On its face, the single publication rule bars this action. The lawsuit was filed on December 18, 2008, and the allegedly defamatory statements were originally published on July 7, 2006, on the internet and August 14, 2006, in print.

However, a narrow exception to the single publication rule called "republication," could provide a way for Plaintiff to avoid dismissal.

As the court previously noted: Republishing material in a new edition—editing and republishing it, or placing it in a new form—resets the statute of limitations. This exception protects Plaintiff by providing a remedy where the defendant edits and retransmits the defamatory material, or distributes the defamatory material for a second time with the goal of reaching a new audience. Therefore, if Defendant republished the article within one year of commencement of Plaintiff's action, the claim is not time barred.

Plaintiff argues that two of Defendant's actions each constitute republication: (1) the posting of articles referencing and hyperlinking to "A Few Bad Men," and (2) the mailing of an additional copy of the "Intelligence Report" to a researcher in 2008. With discovery on the issue now complete and all parties having sufficiently briefed the issue, the Court can now fully address the issues.

III.

The difficulty here is applying the traditional republication exception in the context of material published on the internet—a form of communication certainly not envisioned when the republication and single publication rules were created. Very little case law, either from Kentucky or other jurisdictions, directly addresses these issues. Thus, the court found its analysis on two important principles: (1) conforming to the basic purpose of the single publication rule, and (2) applying analogous examples of traditional republication law.

As the court held in its April 23, 2009, Memorandum Opinion, "[u]nder the single publication rule, the statement is considered published and the statute of limitations runs as soon as the communication enters the stream of commerce." The single publication rule satisfies numerous purposes: to avoid multiplicity of actions; to protect the defendant from excessive liability based on a single publication run; to allow the plaintiff to recover all of his damages at once; and to reduce the chilling effect that the common-law rule might have on the mass communication of ideas. Moreover, the single publication rule is designed to prevent "endless retriggering of the statute of limitations." *Firth v. State of New York*, 775 N.E.2d 463, 466 (N.Y. 2002). As the New York Court of Appeals held: In the absence of the single publication rule, "the statute of limitations would never expire so long as a copy of such book remained in stock and is made [available to] the public. Such a rule would thwart the purpose of the Legislature to bar [actions filed after the limitations period had run]."

IV.

Plaintiff first argues that posting new articles—referencing and hyperlinking to "A Few Bad Men"—republished the article for purposes of the statute of limitations. The referencing articles were published July 21, 2006, July 25, 2006, September 1, 2006, November 23, 2006, and July 18, 2008. The first four of these articles are irrelevant to the pending motion as each was published more than one year before Plaintiff commenced this action. Even if those 2006 articles with hyperlinks republished "A Few Bad Men," this lawsuit would still be time barred. Therefore, only the July 18, 2008, article need be discussed.

Plaintiff does not contend that the new articles—including the references to "A Few Bad Men" themselves—were defamatory. The new articles made no specific mention of Plaintiff. Rather, Plaintiff contends: By referencing and hyperlinking to "A Few Bad Men," the new articles republished the defamatory statements contained therein. Plaintiff cites no case law finding that referencing or hyperlinking to a previous statement republishes that statement. However, that fact alone does not foreclose Plaintiff's argument. The court's research has found a significant dearth of case law on republication generally—as the term is used in this context—and specifically with regard to republication by reference or hyperlink. In analyzing the issue, the court will examine both the reference and the hyperlink.

A.

The reference itself is not a republication of the original article. This court has been unable to find any Kentucky or Sixth Circuit law directly on point. In 1946, the New York Court of Appeals addressed the question directly in *Klein v. Biben*, 69 N.E.2d 682 (N.Y. 1946). There, the defendant published an article in its May 12, 1944, publication and referenced that article in a subsequent article published on June 23, 1944. Asking the certified question—"Does the publication of June 23, 1944, republish the libel published on May 12, 1944, by specific reference thereto," the court simply stated that "question certified [is] answered in the negative." *Id.* at 682.

This court agrees with New York Court of Appeals. Republication, at its core, includes actions such as "publishing a second edition [of] a book or periodical, editing and republishing defamatory material, or placing it in a new form." *Davis v. Mitan*, 347 B.R. 607, 611 (W.D.Ky.2006), citing RESTATEMENT (SECOND) OF TORTS § 577A. The republication "exception provides the plaintiff with a remedy where the defendant edits and retransmits the defamatory material, or distributes the defamatory material for a second time with the goal of reaching a new audience." *Firth*, 775 N.E.2d at 466–67. It appears that the common thread of traditional republication is that it presents the material—in its entirety—before a new audience. A mere reference to a previously published article does not do that. While it may call the existence of the article to the attention of a new audience, it does not present the defamatory contents of the article to that audience. Therefore, a reference, without more, is not properly a republication.

B.

Plaintiff's stronger argument is that the hyperlink republished the original article. According to Plaintiff, a hyperlink is nothing more than an attempt by the original publisher of an online statement to present that statement to a new audience. If the goal was not to present the prior statement to a new audience, according to Plaintiff, there would be no purpose in the hyperlink. After all, the original audience has, in theory, already read the article.

Plaintiff's argument has some logical appeal, especially in light of the facts of this case. Defendant published the July 18, 2008, article in a new section of its website entitled the "Hate Blog." This blog was created well after the 2006 Intelligence Report and appeals to a different type of audience. The purpose of the hyperlink was certainly to entice new readers—who had not previously read "A Few Bad Men"—to click on the link and [direct them] to the article. The RESTATEMENT (SECOND) OF TORTS § 577A specifically states the justification for the republication exception to the single publication rule: "[T]he second publication is intended to and does reach a new group." *Id.* at cmt. d.

The intent element of republication certainly appears when a publisher creates a hyperlink like the one involved here. However, the critical feature of republication is clear: [T]he original text of the article was changed or the contents of the article presented directly to a new audience. That did not occur here. Rather, the hyperlink is simply a new means for accessing the referenced article. Making access to the referenced article easier does not appear to warrant a different conclusion from the analysis of a basic reference. The Western District of Kentucky has considered republication on the internet. In *Davis v. Mitan*, 347 B.R. 607 (W.D.Ky.2006) (*Davis II*), Judge Coffman stated:

> The mere act of editing a website to add unrelated content does not constitute republication of

> unrelated defamatory material that is posted on the same website. Similarly, mere technical changes to a website, such as changing the way an item of information is accessed, is not republication. These rules are consistent with a public policy that encourages the free transmission of information and ideas. In contrast, where substantive material is added to a website, and that material is related to defamatory material that is already posted, a republication has occurred. *Id.* at 611–612. …

[I]t is undisputed that the actual webpage containing the "A Few Bad Men" article was never modified in any manner until Plaintiff's name was removed. While other portions of Defendant's website may have changed, those portions were unrelated to the defamatory statements found in "A Few Bad Men." Thus, the substantive changes that triggered republication in *Davis II* do not indicate republication in this case. In fact, the lack of substantive changes strongly suggests an absence of republication.

The court has found only two cases directly discussing hyperlinks to former articles on the internet in the context of republication. In the first, *Sundance Image Technology, Inc. v. Cone Editions Press, Ltd.*, 2007 WL 935703, *7 (S.D. Cal. 2007), the court dismissed the republication by hyperlink argument without extensive discussion. The court stated: "Plaintiffs appear to argue that the statements were republished when IJM's website provided links to the statements in March 2005. … Plaintiff cites no authority holding that providing links to statements already published on the Web, without more, republishes those statements. Rather, the court finds that such linking is more reasonably akin to the publication of additional copies of the same edition of a book, which is a situation that does not trigger the republication rule."

The issue was also discussed in *Churchill v. State of New Jersey*, 378 N.J.Super. 471, 477 (2005). There, a press release posted on the defendant's website—within the one-year limitations period—directly referenced a defamatory report posted over one year before the action was initiated and "invited visitors to the site to view the report." The plaintiff argued that this press release republished the initial report—thus retriggering the statute of limitations period. Again, the court disagreed in a summary fashion—finding that changes to the website and the press release merely "altered the means by which website visitors could access the report, [rather than altering] the substance or form of the report." *Id.* at 483. Because the substance or form of the report was not altered, the court determined that merely linking to the report did not constitute republication.

Although these cases are certainly not binding on Kentucky courts, this court predicts that Kentucky would follow their rationale. Traditional republication occurs when the substance of previously published defamatory statements is altered or defamatory statements are put in a new form. Neither of those methods of republication occurred in this case. The hyperlinks—while adding a new method of access to "A Few Bad Men"—did not restate the allegedly defamatory statements and did not alter the substance of that article in any manner.

Finally, the court believes that finding republication by hyperlink would undermine the purposes of applying the single publication rule to the internet: The single publication rule is designed to prevent stale claims and to ensure the legislature's intent in passing statutes of limitations is met. By enacting a statute of limitations, the legislature clearly [wanted] lawsuits [to commence] within a specified time of initial publication. Websites are frequently … updated. Methods of access to portions of the website can change on a regular basis and links to previous posts on a website are constantly added and taken away from sites. Therefore, to find that a new link to an unchanged article posted long ago on a website republishes that article would result in a continual retriggering of the limitations period. … The court will issue an order consistent with this Memorandum Opinion.

NOTES AND QUESTIONS

1) Establishing a *Prima Facie* Case of Internet Defamation. To prove a common law defamation action, a private individual must establish: (1) defamatory statements, (2) a nonprivileged communication to a third party, (3) falsity, (4) reference to the complainant, (5) at least the publisher's negligence, and (6) resulting injury. Syl. pt. 6, Miller v. City Hosp., Inc., 475 S.E.2d 495, 503 (W.Va.1996)

2) Judges' Liability for Defaming Solo and Small-Firm Attorneys on the Internet. In *Yoder v. Workman*, 224 F. Supp. 2d 1077, 1078-1081 (S.D. W. Va. 2002), the following statement appeared in a press release and Judge Margaret Workman posted it on the court's Internet website:

> *Mr. Chafin and his stable of lawyers* have engaged in a vitriolic campaign of judge-shopping. This campaign of spurious and unethical legal actions and false allegations against me has been designed to stalk, harass and defame me as a member of the Judiciary because the legal rulings in which I participated with the other Justices of the Supreme Court did not suit them.

Attorney John Yoder alleged that statements were defamatory and targeted him. The court agreed: "[T]he allegedly defamatory statements are neither rhetorical hyperbole nor constitutionally-protected 'opinion.'… [A] reasonable factfinder [could conclude] that Yoder performed spurious and unethical legal actions, made false allegations, and stalked, harassed and defamed the [Judge]."

3) Third-Party Litigant's Liability for Defaming Solo and Small-Firm Attorneys on Electronic Social Media and Forums. In *Versaci v. Richie*, 30 A.D.3d 648, 649 (2006), Attorney Romolo Versaci's client and Diane Richie were opposing litigants in an underlying lawsuit. Later, Richie posted an allegedly defamatory message on *www.SchenectadyNY.info*—a public forum website. She referred to Versaci as a "so called attorney." Citing that phrase, the attorney filed an action for defamation. The supreme court ruled that Richie's published comment was a "nonactionable personal opinion and rhetorical hyperbole." The court dismissed the complaint. Why? The court stated:

> The particular [Richie's posted message] was a rambling commentary about litigation relating to home improvements performed by [Versaci's] client in which [Richie] used the word "real" to refer to a secretary, an attorney, a judge and a court. In reference to [Versaci] and an apparent incident with a pipe, [Richie] stated, "[s]omeone tell Scoobie's so called attorney there is a smoking law in New York State." Clearly, no reasonable reader of [Richie's] statement would construe this phrase to be a false assertion that [Versaci] was not, in fact, an attorney.

D. Intruders' Liability for Tortiously Interfering with Attorneys' Prospective Business Advantages and Contractual Relations

One's intentional interference with a person's contractual relations is a tort. *Korea Supply Co. v. Lockheed Martin Corp.*, 31 Cal. Rptr. 2d 29, 63 P.3d 937 (2003). Also, one commits a very different tort if she intentional interferes with an individual prospective business advantage. *Maloney v. Home and Investment Center, Inc.*, 994 P.2d 1124 (Mont. 2000). Generally, courts characterize one's interference with another's contractual relations as a subset of the broader tort—the interference with a person's prospective business advantage. *TMK Associates v. Landmark Development Group*, 2003 WL 22133151, *9 (Conn. Super. Ct. 2003).

Significantly, evidence of an express or implied contract is not required to prove that an intruder interfered with a party's prospective business venture. *Harry Finman & Son v. Conn. Truck & Trailer Ser.*, 169 Conn. 407, 414-15 (1975). Consider Connecticut Supreme Court's declaration in *Skene v. Carayanis*, 103 Conn. 708, 714 (1926): "The law ... protect[s] rights resting upon completed contracts. ... [And] it also forbids unjustifiable interference with any [person's] right to pursue his lawful business or occupation and to secure ... the earnings of his industry. ... No [person] can justify an interference with another's business through fraud or misrepresentation, nor by intimidation obstruction or molestation."

Examine the nearly-century-old *Carayanis* rule carefully. May a solo attorney collect tortious-interference damages if the attorney cites *Carayanis* and establishes that an Internet service provider (ISP) blocked the attorney's access to a "lucrative international pro-terrorists" website? Would the ISP be liable under *Korea Supply* or *Carayanis* if the ISP prevented an allegedly "unethical" attorney from creating a virtual-law office and offering to represent allegedly "international terrorists"? Or would an ISP be liable for preventing two financially strapped law graduates from soliciting start-up funds on several global crowdfunding websites—www.chipin.com, www.gofundme.com, www.clickandpledge.com? In this section, the select cases illustrate how courts are applying hundred-year-old principles to address attorneys' claim: Clients, competitors as well as sellers of goods and services intentionally use the Internet and other modern technologies to interfere with attorneys' prospective business advantages and ongoing contractual relationships.

1. Tortious Interference with Prospective Business and Attorneys' Actions against Legal-Marketing-Website Operators and Online-Marketing-Services Providers

Allen v. IM Solutions, LLC

94 F.Supp.3d 1216
(E.D. Okla. 2015)

James H. Payne, District Judge. Before the court is Defendant Reed Elsevier Inc.'s motion to dismiss several counts in the Class Action Complaint under Federal Rules of Civil Procedure 12(b)(6).

I. Background

This lawsuit arises out of pop-up advertisements for legal services that appear on Plaintiffs' websites. Plaintiffs Allen & Wiser, LLC and Blount Law Firm PLLC are law firms located in Oklahoma and Tennessee, respectively. Plaintiffs Anthony Allen and James Blount are lawyers and members of those respective law firms (collectively Plaintiffs). According to the Complaint, Defendants IM Solutions (IMS) and LeadingResponse, LLC (RME) are limited liability corporations—engaged in the business of using the Internet to generate leads for law firms to obtain potential clients. Further, according to the Complaint, Defendant Reed Elsevier Inc. (Reed) is the owner and operator of LexisNexis Martindale Hubbell, Lawyers.com, Attorneys.com, and LawyerLocator. Defendant Internet Brands, Inc. (Internet Brands) owned and operated Nolo Legal divisions and over 150 web properties providing marketing services for lawyers and consumer-facing legal information. The Complaint also alleges that Reed and Internet Brands created a joint venture combining its above-described business with Internet Brands's online marketing services.

Plaintiffs filed their Class Action Complaint against Defendants on June 3, 2014. In the Complaint, Plaintiffs claimed that Reed tortiously interfered with prospective advantage under Oklahoma and Tennessee law. For purposes of ruling on a motion to dismiss, the court considers the allegations of the Complaint to be true.

The Complaint alleges that IMS generates its client leads by utilizing a "hidden browser plug-in," placed on consumers' computers by unnamed "affiliates" through advertising, referred to as "adware" or "malware" plug-ins. The plug-ins cause a pop-up window to appear in a separate window when one of these consumers visits the websites of Plaintiffs. If a consumer clicks on the first pop-up window that appears, a second pop-up window appears setting forth a questionnaire about the legal services the consumer seeks. Upon completing the questionnaire and clicking "Speak to lawyers," the results are routed to Reed, and Reed places a telephone call to the consumer. Following the phone call, Reed sends an email to the consumer referring them to IMS who matches the consumer with a law firm. Plaintiffs allege that this lead generating process improperly diverts potential customers away from Plaintiffs' websites, allowing Defendants to capture the business. …

II. Discussion

Tortious Interference

Reed argues that Count III of the Class Action Complaint should be dismissed with prejudice because Plaintiffs have no prospective business relationship with consumers who visit Plaintiffs' websites, holding them akin to window shoppers on a busy commercial street. Additionally, Reed contends that even if such window-shopping gave rise to a prospective relationship, the Complaint is void of any facts which would amount to Reed using improper means to interfere with these prospective customers. Specifically, Reed asserts that without any allegations that Reed was involved with the creation or generation of the pop-up advertisement, Plaintiffs cannot allege that Reed utilized improper measures of interference. In opposition, Plaintiffs argue the mere fact that consumers sought out their websites is sufficient to establish a prospective relationship. Plaintiffs also contend that Reed's alleged participation in the conspiracy alone is sufficient to establish improper means to interfere for purposes of a tortious interference claim.

Oklahoma and Tennessee laws impose substantially similar requirements to state a claim for tortious interference with a prospective business relationship: (1) an existing business relationship or prospective relationship with an identifiable class of third persons; (2) defendant's knowledge of that relationship; (3) the intent by defendant to cause a termination of the relationship; (4) the use of improper means; and (5) damages. *See Trau–Med of Am., Inc. v. Allstate Ins. Co.*, 71 S.W.3d 691, 701 (Tenn. 2002) and *RSF Partners, LLC v. Silvermine Opportunity Funding, LLC*, 2014 WL 360009, *4 (N.D. Okla. Feb. 3, 2014). This court finds that

Plaintiffs have failed to satisfy the pleading requirements for elements one and four.

Plaintiffs' assertion that consumers' visits to their websites create a sufficient expectancy in a business relationship is without merit. Consumers' visits to their websites create nothing more than a mere hope that the consumers will ultimately contract with Plaintiffs for legal services. The law is clear that such a hope or wish is not sufficient to allege a prospective business relationship. *Klein v. Grynberg*, 44 F.3d 1497, 1506 (10th Cir.1995) (finding that plaintiff had no ongoing relationship with any of the investors, therefore, prospective business advantage was a "mere hope" and too speculative to support a tort claim). A plaintiff must show a likelihood or probability that a contract would have resulted. Plaintiffs have not alleged facts which would allow the court to make the inference that a contract with the visiting consumers is likely or probable.

Moreover, Plaintiffs fail to allege sufficient, non-conclusory facts, to establish that Reed used improper means to interfere. Plaintiffs do not allege that Reed participated in the creation or generation of the pop-up—which is allegedly the improper act that diverted customers away from its websites. Rather, Plaintiffs admit throughout the Complaint that IMS was solely responsible for the pop-up—i.e., the alleged interference. Contrary to Plaintiffs' contention, both Oklahoma and Tennessee require that the alleged interferer have an intent to injure the plaintiff. *See Trau–Med of Am., Inc.*, 71 S.W.3d at 701 (tortious interference claims are only actionable if an action is "hurtful to another, intentional and without legal justification, it is malicious in the true legal sense") and *RSF Partners, LLC*, 2014 WL 360009, at *4 (finding that the complaint "fails to plausibly state that Silvermine's actions were malicious, intentional, illegal or otherwise improper"). Plaintiffs presented no such allegations of intent against Reed. ...

III. Conclusion

Accordingly, Plaintiffs' Complaint fails to state claims for violation for tortious interference against Defendant Reed Elsevier Inc., and Defendant's Motion to Dismiss is granted in its entirety.

NOTES AND QUESTIONS

1) Proving a *Prima Facie* Case–The Intentional Interference with One's Prospective Business or Economic Advantage. An intruder is liable for intentionally interfering with a party's prospective business advantage if the plaintiff proves: (1) a prospective contractual relation between a third party and the plaintiff, (2) the intruder's intent to harm plaintiff by preventing the relationship from occurring, (3) the absence of privilege or justification on behalf of the actor, and (4) actual harm or damage as a result of the intruder's conduct. See *Buckaloo v. Johnson,* 14 Cal.3d 815, 827 (1975).

2) Proving a *Prima Facie* Case–The Intentional Interference with One's Contractual or Business Relations. To establish a *prima facie* case of interference with one's contractual or business relations, the complainant must prove that the action (1) was intentional and willful, (2) was calculated to cause damage to the plaintiff in his or her business, (3) was done with the unlawful purpose of causing damage or loss, without right or justifiable cause on the part of the actor, and (4) caused actual damages and loss resulted. *Bermil Corp. v. Sawyer,* 353 So.2d 579, 585 (Fla. App. 3rd Cir. 1977).

2. Tortious Interference with Prospective Business and Attorneys' Actions Against Legal-Marketing-Website Operators and Online-Marketing-Services Providers

Huon v. Breaking Media, LLC

75 F.Supp.3d 747
(N.D. Ill. 2014)

John J. Tharp, Jr., United States District Judge. The plaintiff—Meanith Huon—brings state law ... torts against two groups of defendants: (1) the Above the Law (ATL) defendants—Breaking

Media, LLC a/k/a Breaking Media; Breaking Media, Inc. a/k/a Breaking Media; David Lat; Elie Mystal; John Lerner; and David Minkin; and (2) and the Gawker defendants—Gawker Media, LLC a/k/a Gawker Media; Blogwire Hungary Szellemi Alkotast Hasznosito KFT; Gawker Media Group, Inc. a/k/a Gawker Media; Gawker Entertainment; Gawker Technology; Gawker Sales, LLC; Nick Denton; Irin Carmon; and Gaby Darbyshire. ...

The Fourth Amended Complaint (the Complaint) seeks relief against all defendants for ... the tortious interference with prospective economic advantage (Count VIII). ... The ATL defendants have moved to dismiss the claim under Federal Rule of Civil Procedure 12(b)(6). Several of the Gawker defendants have likewise moved to dismiss the claim against them.

Background

Meanith Huon is an attorney licensed to practice law in Illinois. On July 2, 2008, Huon was charged with two counts of criminal sexual assault, two counts of criminal sexual abuse, and one count of unlawful restraint. The charges arose out of his alleged interactions with "Jane Doe" on June 29, 2008, in Madison County, Illinois. Approximately one year later, on July 17, 2009, Huon was charged with cyberstalking and witness harassment based on allegations involving the same Jane Doe. Huon was tried on the 2008 sexual assault charges in May 2010 in Madison County. The trial began on May 4 and ended on May 6 with his acquittal on both charges. The 2009 cyberstalking and witness harassment charges were ultimately dismissed in December 2011.

The charges against Huon and his criminal trial received publicity in local media and legal news sources; several of the resultant articles are relevant to the instigation of this case. On July 2, 2008, the day the sexual assault and related charges were filed, an article about those charges appeared in the *Madison County Record* (the "Madison County Article"). The following day, July 3, 2008, the legal blog AboveTheLaw.com published a post by defendant Lat (the "2008 ATL Post") that included the one-line statement "Lawyer of the Day: Meanith Huon"—along with a link to the Madison County Article. Next, on August 24, 2009, a post discussing both the 2008 and 2009 charges appeared on the blog LawyerGossip.com (the "Lawyer Gossip Post"). Finally, on May 6, 2010, AboveTheLaw.com published an article by defendant Mystal titled "Rape Potpourri" (the "ATL Article").

The ATL Article provided information and commentary on two "rape stories": (1) the arrest of former New York Giants linebacker Lawrence Taylor based on a rape allegation, and (2) the allegations at issue in Huon's criminal trial and the opening statement made by Huon's defense lawyer at trial. The section of the ATL Article on Huon purported to link to and quote, *inter alia,* the Lawyer Gossip Post, the Madison County Article—which was also linked to in the 2008 ATL Post, and an article in the *Belleville News Democrat* titled "Testimony: Woman Says She Was Raped by Attorney Posing as Scout for Models" (the "BND Article"). At some point following the ATL Article's initial publication, an update was added toward the end of the piece indicating that Huon had been acquitted of the charges discussed. AboveTheLaw.com allows readers to post comments on its articles—subject to certain terms of use—and the ATL Article eventually generated over 107 comments or replies from users.

On May 6, 2011, one year after publication of the ATL Article, Huon sued the ATL defendants and the John Does who posted comments on the ATL Article for defamation, intentional infliction of emotional distress, and false light invasion of privacy. The filing of this suit—like the criminal charges against Huon—generated its share of publicity. On May 11, 2011, an article by defendant Carmon entitled "Acquitted Rapist Sues Blogger for Calling Him Serial Rapist" appeared on the women's interest blog Jezebel.com (the "Jezebel Article"). The Jezebel Article discussed Huon's criminal trial for sexual assault, his lawsuit against local law enforcement authorities for prosecutorial misconduct, and his initial complaint against the ATL defendants in the instant suit.

The Jezebel Article mentioned the title of the ATL Article and included links to the ATL Article and other relevant sources. The Jezebel Article also included an image containing Huon's arrest photograph superimposed over a screenshot of the start of the ATL Article. Users—who are invited by Gawker Media editors or by previously invited users—may post comments on Jezebel.com articles subject to certain terms of use. The Jezebel Article eventually generated over 80 comments or replies from such users. According to Huon, some of the user comments were written by employees of the Gawker defendants, posting under aliases. ... On November 15, 2012, Huon filed the current [amended] Complaint. The ATL defendants and certain of the Gawker defendants filed respective motions to dismiss, which are now under consideration.

Discussion

Tortious Interference with Prospective Economic Advantage

Huon alleges that the defendants tortiously interfered with his business interests by publishing the ATL Article and the Jezebel Article. To state a claim for tortious interference with prospective economic advantage under Illinois law, a plaintiff must allege: "(1) a reasonable expectancy of entering into a valid business relationship, (2) the defendant's knowledge of the expectancy, (3) an intentional and unjustified interference by the defendant that induced or caused a breach or termination of the expectancy, and (4) damage to the plaintiff resulting from the defendant's interference." *Voyles v. Sandia Mortgage Corp.,* 751 N.E.2d 1126, 1133–34 (Ill. 2001). A reasonable expectancy "requires more than the hope or opportunity of a future business relationship." *Bus. Sys. Eng'g, Inc. v. Int'l Bus. Machines Corp.,* 520 F.Supp.2d 1012, 1022 (N.D.Ill.2007) and *Fredrick v. Simmons Airlines, Inc.,* 144 F.3d 500, 503 (7th Cir.1998).

The Complaint states that Huon "held a reasonable expectation of entering into valid business relationships both in his legal practice and in business," and that he had an "expectancy of entering into valid business relationships with members of the public including, but not limited to, his retention as an attorney." The Complaint also alleges that Huon has suffered "a decline in prospective business" and "remains concerned that individuals and organizations including prospective legal clients will choose not to utilize his services." These conclusory statements, which are unsupported by any facts other than the assertion that Huon is a licensed attorney, are insufficient to allege that Huon had a reasonable business expectancy. *See Del Monte Fresh Produce, N.A., Inc. v. Kinnavy,* 2010 WL 1172565, at *6 (N.D. Ill. 2010) ("*Twombly* does require that Kinnavy set forth facts that make it plausible that she had a reasonable expectancy. …").

At best, the statements establish—when read in the light most favorable to the plaintiff—that Huon *hoped* to obtain legal clients or enter into other business relationships. As Huon has thus failed to adequately allege a reasonable business expectancy, it is unnecessary to consider whether he has satisfied any of the other elements of a tortious interference claim. *See Fredrick,* 144 F.3d at 503 (affirming dismissal of a tortious interference claim where the plaintiff "failed to allege any reasonable expectation of a business relationship" and instead alleged "merely that he wished to continue working as a commercial pilot"); *Pulliam v. Am. Express Travel Related Servs. Co.*, 2009 WL 1586012, at *6 (N.D. Ill. 2009) (dismissing a tortious interference claim where the plaintiff failed to allege facts sufficient to support a reasonable business expectancy); *Emery v. Ne. Ill. Reg'l Commuter R.R. Corp.*, 2003 WL 22176077, at *10 (N.D. Ill. 2003) (dismissing a tortious interference claim where the plaintiff alleged "no more than the mere hope [of obtaining] concrete opportunities").

Accordingly, this count is dismissed with prejudice as to all defendants.

NOTES AND QUESTIONS

1) **Ad-Blocking Software and Third-Party Tortious Interference with Advertising Contracts.** Assume that programmers' and vendors' ad-blocking software interfere with solo and small-firm attorneys' existing contractual relationships. More specifically, assume that a vendor's ad-blocking program prevents clients from accessing attorneys' virtual-office website. Would the attorneys prevail in a court of law—assuming that they commenced a tortious interference action against the ad-blocking vendors? Consider *Penthouse International, Ltd. v. Koch*, 599 F. Supp. 1338, 1341 (D.C.N.Y. 1984). The New York City transit authority prevented *Penthouse* Magazine from posting advertisements on trains and buses. *Penthouse* filed an interference action, alleging that the transit authority interfered with *Penthouse* and a third-party advertising contract. The transit authority prevailed, because (1) *Penthouse* could not prove a breach of contract, and (2) *Penthouse's* contract contained a governmental-action exclusion clause. *See also Daisy Outdoor Advertising Co., Inc. v. Abbott*, 473 S.E.2d 47,48-52 (S.C. 1996) (finding that an advertiser intentionally interference with contract rights when the advertiser displayed unregulated "for sale" signs on two parcels of land to block two other advertisers' billboards).

2) **Computer and Internet-Services Interruptions and Third-Party Tortious Interference with Authorized Users' Business Relations.** Assume that a "hacker" intentionally sends a set of instructions to an attorney's business computer and the codes modify, record, or transmit information without the attorney's permission. In the process, the hacker instructions

unintentionally contaminate the computer—transmitting an electronic virus or worm that self-replicates and contaminates the attorney's synchronized smartphone and tablet. Would the attorney prevail in a court of law—assuming that the practitioner commences a tortious interference action against the hacker for interrupting contractual agreements? *Cf. United States v. Morris*, 928 F.2d 504, 506-509 (2nd Cir. 1991). Robert Tappan Morris—a 23-year-old, first-year graduate student in Cornell University's computer science Ph.D. Program—used University's computer and developed the Internet "worm" or "virus." Morris *intended to release* the "harmless" worm to demonstrate the inadequacies of security measures on governmental and other computer networks. However, Morris *did not intend* to "crash" thousands educational and military computers or to prevent the latter from functioning. Still, Morris was criminally liable under the Computer Fraud and Abuse Act § 1030(a)(5)(A)—which prohibits one's "intentional unauthorized access" to federal computers. He was fined $10,050 and placed on probation for three years.

CHAPTER THREE: Solo and Small-Firm Attorneys' Deceptive Trade Practices Actions

Cyberjacking, Mousetrapping, and the FTC Act: Are Federal Consumer Protection Laws Helping or Hurting Online Consumers?

3 Vand. J. Ent. L. & Prac. 221
Kenneth Sanney

Law & Practice; Kenneth Sanney

Your law firm just launched a website to increase its exposure in the local community and beyond. The team who designed the site invested endless hours, effort, and resources conducting market research, perfecting program design, and performing technical upgrades of the support systems. The finished product reflects their hard work; the site is sleek and sophisticated, yet user-friendly and reliable. And best of all or at least from one perspective, you have a profile page on the site. One evening while working on your monthly bills, it dawns on you that you haven't shown your family the new site. Eager to show off a bit, you minimize the program you are working on and open your web browser. You call to your wife, your twelve-year-old daughter and your seven-year-old son.

When [they] arrive, you click the search icon on your browser—to show [your family] how prospective clients can find your firm's website. ... Using the search engine, you type a few words that best describe your firm's area of practice, your city, and the word "law." The results do not disappoint. ... You double-click on [the link for your firm's website] and the site downloads—leaving you, your wife, and your two children looking at three naked women. The address of the site you are on is not your firm's website, but "*www.taboo.com.*" You stab at your browser's back button, but another porn site pops up. This time, it is "*TabooSisters.com.*" More explicit images fill your screen.

Surprise now gives way to anger as you thrash with the mouse—trying to click the close button of your browser. The second you succeed, "*Daily Sexgames.com*" appears—complete with banner ads for companion sites offering pictures of unnatural sexual acts with animals. You ask aloud: "What's going on?"—as your wife hurries your children from the room [with anger]. You click on the browser's back button again, and another porn site pops up. Each attempt to leave these sites or to close your browser causes another porn site to open. You then attempt to restore the minimized program in order to save your work. But the deluge of porn sites has caused your computer to freeze up. You contemplate shutting down your computer, but you know doing so will cause you to lose all of the unsaved work. Additionally, you know that shutting down your computer with programs open can damage its operation, not to mention your hard drive. But then again, you see no other option at this point. So, frustrated and dejected, you slowly press the power button and watch as the monitor goes dark.

To make matters worse, your wife returns looking for an explanation. She thinks that you were visiting these pornography sites before she and the kids came into the room. You declare your innocence, but you have no explanation of how these sites appeared. ... Unbeknownst to you, a company specializing in cyberscams engineered your entire World Wide Web ordeal by catching you in a "web" of its own. First, they hijacked or "cyberjacked" your firm's website by reposting a version that redirects unsuspecting visitors to the never-ending series of pornographic sites. ... Having captured you inside that ring, the pornography company used a technique called "mousetrapping" to frustrate all efforts to leave—keeping you firmly held in its grip. In short, you've just fallen victim to the latest rage in Internet fraud—a scam as effective as it is invisible, as simple to execute as it is hard to regulate.

Currently, only the Federal Trade Commission (FTC) can bring a federal cause of action against a company whose business practices or actions deceive consumers. However, the FTC's power is limited; it can intervene on behalf of consumers only when there is a pattern of misconduct ... that threatens the public interest. But ... patterns may be virtually impossible to establish. Moreover, even successful FTC actions may yield little ... preventative or compensatory benefit for the individual user. ... [Therefore] the Federal Trade Commission Act should be amended to give private citizens a cause of action against deceptive trade practices and fraud on the Internet. ... [S]uch an amendment should offer enhanced damages and attorneys' fees in order to encourage [private attorneys general to file a federal] action.

Section 5 of the Federal Trade Commission Act, 15 U.S.C. § 45(a) was fashioned to protect consumers from "unfair or deceptive acts or practices in commerce." And, under the FTC, the Commission has authority to enforce § 5. On the other hand, aggrieved consumers may not file private actions. To be sure, the Federal Trade Commission has sued on behalf of consumers—including solo and small-firm attorneys—to reduce deceptive trade and unfair practices on the Internet. For example, in *FTC v. Toysmart.com,* 2000 WL 34016434, *1 (D. Mass. July 21, 2000), the Commission sued Toysmart for allegedly violating section 5. The Commission asserted: The toy *e*-retailer engaged in deceptive acts or practices by "disclosing, selling or offering to sale customers' personal information" to third parties.

Additionally, in *FTC v. D Squared Solutions, L.L.C.*, 2003 WL 22881377, *3 (D. Md. 2003), the FTC sued to prevent pop-up ads or spam—which exploited a Windows-software defect on consumers' computers. And, in *FTC v. Zuccarini*, 2002 WL 1378421, *1 (E.D. Pa. 2001), the Commission sued to prevent "mouse trapping." This latter deceptive practice displays an advertisement in a browser on, say, an attorney's laptop computer. And when the attorney tries to close the original window, additional windows open and present even more advertisements. Quite simply, the attorney will waste a considerable amount of precious time because "mouse trapping" makes it very difficult to escape from ad-ridden websites.

Still, among consumers generally and attorneys in particular, a common view persists: "The FTC has been ineffective ... as a consumer protection agency. ... The sole enforcement weapon available [for] the FTC to police most consumer frauds is the cease-and-desist order, which has proved inadequate." *Carlson v. Coca-Cola Co.,* 483 F.2d 279, 281-282 (9th. Cir. 1973). *See also Johnson v. Tele-Cash, Inc.,* 982 F.Supp.2d 264, 266 (D. Del. 1999) (citing evidence of the FTC's historically inadequate enforcement resources).

However, it is important to stress: Over the past fifty years, an impressive development has occurred. Every state has adopted a Consumer-Protection or a Deceptive Trade Practices Act (DTPA). *See United HealthCare Ins. Co. v. AdvancePCS,* 2002 WL 432068, *18 (D. Minn.) (Every jurisdiction has "legislation that prohibits the use of deceptive tactics in business and/or prohibits the deception of consumers."). Generally, most states have modeled their DTPAs after the Federal Trade Commission Act, the Uniform Consumer

Sales Practice Act, or the Uniform Deceptive Trade Practices Act (UDTPA). And twelve states have adopted the 1964 or 1966 version of the UDTPA. In a nutshell, DTPA statutes "make it unlawful [for any person] to use or otherwise engage in unfair or deceptive acts or practices in the conduct of trade or commerce." *Cf.* Carolyn L. Carter, CONSUMER PROTECTION IN THE STATES—A 50-STATE REPORT ON UNFAIR AND DECEPTIVE ACTS AND PRACTICES STATUTES, National Consumer Law Center, Inc. (*http://perma.cc/3ezp-bweu).*

Consequently, on behalf of themselves and their firms, attorneys and other professionals have filed all types of technology-based claims under DTPAs. *See* e.g., *Dash v. Seagate Technology (US) Holdings, Inc.,* 2015 WL 4257329, *1 (E.D.N.Y. 2015) (plaintiff's alleging that defendant violated New York's DTPA by using deceptive speedometer icons to market and sell external computer hard drives); *QVC Inc. v. Your Vitamins Inc.,* 439 Fed. Appx. 165, 167-168 (3d Cir. 2011) (plaintiff-merchant's alleging that defendant-merchant violated Delaware's Uniform Deceptive Trade Practices Act, by "trolling" or by posting wilfully inflammatory, off-topic and stupid remarks about plaintiff's business and profession on a *Yahoo*-website message board); *Vulcan Golf, LLC v. Google* Inc., 552 F.Supp.2d 752, 774 (N.D. Ill. 2008) (finding that an Internet-search-engine operator, domain-name registrants, and companies violated Illinois Uniform Deceptive Trade Practices Act by aggregating consumers' domain names, allowing an advertising service to license and monetize the domain names, and directing Internet users to a deceptive domain); *KEG Technologies, Inc. v. Laimer*, 436 F.Supp.2d 1364, 1380 (N.D. Ga. 2006) (awarding injunctive relief under Georgia DTPA, after finding that defendants accessed KEG's computer without authorization and copied files—those "containing KEG's customer lists, financial information, design drawings, product orders, profit margins and pricing information"); and, *Sotelo v. DirectRevenue, LLC,* 384 F.Supp.2d 1219, 1233-34 (N.D. Ill. 2005) (holding that defendants violated Illinois DTPA, by downloading "phishing" spyware onto plaintiff's personal computer without plaintiff's consent).

This chapter outlines the types of DTPA actions that brick-and-mortar, quasi-virtual, and virtual attorneys have commenced and may commence against sellers of technological goods and services, Internet service providers, Internet operators, website designers, domain-name owners, and others. Necessarily, the cases and materials in this chapter highlight an array of procedural and substantive questions which have generated less-than-clear answers and analyses. To repeat, our goal is clear: to help solo and small-practice attorneys to avoid technology-based risks—which often include legal disputes and the costs of commencing lawsuits. Therefore, when reading the materials in this chapter, consider carefully the standards of proof that attorneys must satisfy to prevail in a technology-based DTPA lawsuit.

NOTES AND QUESTIONS

1) **States' Adopting the Uniform Deceptive Trade Practices Act**. Twelve states have adopted the 1964 or 1966 version of the UDTPA: Colo. Rev. Stat. Ann. § 6-1-105 (West 2000); Del. Code Ann. tit. 6, §§ 2532-2536 (West 2000); Ga. Code Ann. §§ 10-1-370 -375 (West 2000); Haw. Rev. Stat. §§ 481a-1-5 (West 2000); 815 Ill. Comp. Stat. Ann. §§ 510 / 1-7 (West 2001); Me. Rev. Stat. tit. 10, §§ 1211-1216 (2000); Minn. Stat. Ann. §§ 325d.43-48 (West 2000); Neb. Rev. Stat. Ann. §§ 87-301-303.06 (West 2001); Nev. Rev. Stat. Ann. §§ 598.0905-0915 (West 2001); Ohio Rev. Code Ann. §§ 4165.01-04 (West 2000); Okla. Stat. Ann. tit. 78, §§ 51-55 (West 1999); and Or. Rev. Stat. § 646.608 (West 1999). *(http://perma.cc/l2u9-y5xv).*

2) **States' Modeling Their DTPA After the Uniform Deceptive Trade Practices Act.** The remaining states have enacted DTPA statutes which are "substantially equivalent" or "fairly similar" to the UDTPA: Ala. Code § 8-19-5 (2014); Alaska Stat. Ann. § 45.50.471 (West 2014); Ariz. Rev. Stat. Ann. § 44-1211 (2014); Ark. Code Ann. § 4-88-107 (West 2014); Id. § 4-101-201 (governing the sale of fracture-filled and clarity-enhanced diamonds); Cal. Bus. & Prof. Code § 17200 (West 2014); Conn. Gen. Stat. Ann. § 42-110b (West 2014); D.C. Code § 28-3904 (2014); Fla. Stat. Ann. § 501.204 (West 2014); Idaho Code Ann. § 48-603 (West 2014); Ind. Code Ann. § 24-5-0.5 (West 2014); Iowa Code Ann. § 714.16 (West 2014); Kan. Stat. Ann. § 21-4403 (West) (repealed 2010); Ky. Rev. Stat. Ann. § 367.170 (West 2014); La. Rev. Stat. Ann. § 51:1405 (2014); Md. Code Ann., Com. Law § 13-301 (2014); Mass. Gen. Laws Ann. ch. 93A, § 2 (West 2014); Mich. Comp. Laws Ann. § 445.903 (West 2014); Miss. Code Ann. § 75-24-5 (West 2014); Mo. Ann. Stat. § 407.020 (West 2012); Mont. Code Ann. § 30-14-103 (West 2013); Nev. Rev. Stat. Ann. § 598.0915 (West 2014); N.H. Rev. Stat. Ann. § 358-A:2 (2014); N.J. Stat. Ann. § 56:8-2 (West 2014); N.Y. Gen. Bus. Law §§ 349, 350 (McKinney 2014); N.C. Gen. Stat. Ann. § 66-74 (West 2014); N.D. Cent. Code Ann. § 51-15-02 (West 2013); 73 Pa. Cons. Stat. Ann. § 201-3 (West 2014); R.I. Gen. Laws

Ann. § 6-13.1-2 (West 2014); S.C. Code Ann. § 39-5-20 (2013); S.D. Codified Laws § 37-24-6 (2014); Tenn. Code Ann. § 47-18-104 (West 2014); Tex. Bus. & Com. Code Ann. § 17.46 (West 2013); Utah Code Ann. § 13-11-4 (West 2014); Vt. Stat. Ann. tit. 9, § 2453 (West 2014); Va. Code Ann. § 59.1-200 (West 2014); Wash. Rev. Code Ann. § 19.86.020 (West 2014); W. Va. Code Ann. § 46A-6-104 (West 2014); Wis. Stat. Ann. § 100.20 (West 2013); Wyo. Stat. Ann. § 40-12-105 (West 2014).

Baldwin's Ohio Revised Code

Title XLI. Labor and Industry
Chapter 4165. Deceptive Trade Practices

§ 4165.03 Injunction; Damages

(A) (1) A person who is likely to be damaged by a person who commits a deceptive trade practice that is listed in division (A) of section 4165.02 of the Revised Code may commence a civil action for injunctive relief against the other person, and the court of common pleas involved in that action may grant injunctive relief based on the principles of equity and on the terms that the court considers reasonable. Proof of monetary damage or loss of profits is not required in a civil action commenced under division (A)(1) of this section.

(2) A person who is injured by a person who commits a deceptive trade practice that is listed in division (A) of section 4165.02 of the Revised Code may commence a civil action to recover actual damages from the person who commits the deceptive trade practice.

(B) The court may award in accordance with this division reasonable attorney's fees to the prevailing party in either type of civil action authorized by division (A) of this section. An award of attorney's fees may be assessed against a plaintiff if the court finds that the plaintiff knew the action to be groundless. An award of attorney's fees may be assessed against a defendant if the court finds that the defendant has willfully engaged in a trade practice listed in division (A) of section 4165.02 of the Revised Code knowing it to be deceptive.

(C) The civil relief provided in this section is in addition to civil or criminal remedies otherwise available against the same conduct under the common law or other sections of the Revised Code.

Vernon's Texas Statutes and Codes

Business and Commerce Code
Chapter 17. Deceptive Trade Practices

Subchapter E. Deceptive Trade Practices and Consumer Protection

§ 17.50—Relief for Consumers

(a) A consumer may maintain an action where any of the following constitute a producing cause of economic damages or damages for mental anguish:

(1) the use or employment by any person of a false, misleading, or deceptive act or practice that is:

(A) specifically enumerated in a subdivision of Subsection (b) of Section 17.46 of this subchapter; and

(B) relied on by a consumer to the consumer's detriment;

(2) breach of an express or implied warranty;

(3) any unconscionable action or course of action by any person; or

(4) the use or employment by any person of an act or practice in violation of Chapter 541, Insurance Code.

(b) In a suit filed under this section, each consumer who prevails may obtain:

(1) the amount of economic damages found by the trier of fact. If the trier of fact finds that the conduct of the defendant was committed knowingly, the consumer may also recover damages for mental anguish, as found by the trier of fact, and the trier of

fact may award not more than three times the amount of economic damages; or if the trier of fact finds the conduct was committed intentionally, the consumer may recover damages for mental anguish, as found by the trier of fact, and the trier of fact may award not more than three times the amount of damages for mental anguish and economic damages;

(2) an order enjoining such acts or failure to act;

(3) orders necessary to restore to any party to the suit any money or property, real or personal, which may have been acquired in violation of this subchapter; and

(4) any other relief which the court deems proper, including the appointment of a receiver or the revocation of a license or certificate authorizing a person to engage in business in this state if the judgment has not been satisfied within three months of the date of the final judgment. The court may not revoke or suspend a license to do business in this state or appoint a receiver to take over the affairs of a person who has failed to satisfy a judgment if the person is a licensee of or regulated by a state agency which has statutory authority to revoke or suspend a license or to appoint a receiver or trustee. Costs and fees of such receivership or other relief shall be assessed against the defendant.

(c) On a finding by the court that an action under this section was groundless in fact or law or brought in bad faith, or brought for the purpose of harassment, the court shall award to the defendant reasonable and necessary attorneys' fees and court costs.

(d) Each consumer who prevails shall be awarded court costs and reasonable and necessary attorneys' fees.

(e) In computing additional damages under Subsection (b), attorneys' fees, costs, and prejudgment interest may not be considered.

(f) A court may not award prejudgment interest applicable to:

(1) damages for future loss under this subchapter; or

(2) additional damages under Subsection (b).

(g) Chapter 41, Civil Practice and Remedies Code, does not apply to a cause of action brought under this subchapter.

(h) Notwithstanding any other provision of this subchapter, if a claimant is granted the right to bring a cause of action under this subchapter by another law, the claimant is not limited to recovery of economic damages only, but may recover any actual damages incurred by the claimant, without regard to whether the conduct of the defendant was committed intentionally. For the purpose of the recovery of damages for a cause of action described by this subsection only, a reference in this subchapter to economic damages means actual damages. In applying Subsection (b)(1) to an award of damages under this subsection, the trier of fact is authorized to award a total of not more than three times actual damages, in accordance with that subsection.

A. Technology-Based Disputes and Attorneys' "Pure" DTPA Actions

1. Proving One's Standing to Sue as a Consumer Under the DTPA

Hugh Symons Group, PLC v. Motorola, Inc.

292 F.3d 466
(5th Cir. 2002)

Robert M. Parker, Circuit Judge. Appellant Hugh Symons Group, PLC appeals the district court's grant of summary judgment to appellee Motorola, Inc. In 1995, representatives of Concept Technologies, Ltd. and Motorola met at an electronics trade show in Las Vegas, Nevada. Concept was a wholly-owned subsidiary of Hugh Symons—both based in the United Kingdom. Concept was seeking electronic components for development of its conceptual handheld computer—the "Pic Pocket." Motorola described its MPC-821 microprocessor as a possible component.

Motorola provided a circuit card and a few MPC-821 chips for Concept's suitability determination. Concept found that the MPC-821 was too slow; but Motorola asserted that the next version would be substantially faster. By 1997, Concept also found that the chip produced screen flicker and had cache/memory problems—making it unsuitable for the Pic Pocket. Motorola continued to indicate that future versions would be improved. In June 1998, however, Motorola announced that it would not produce any new versions of the MPC-821, because Motorola's other users were digital camera manufacturers who did not rely on the features that Concept wanted to improve.

Motorola suggested another microprocessor, the MPC-823. Concept found that it was slower and required a complete hardware re-design. Motorola replied that version "823e" would fix the problems. In early 1999, however, Motorola announced a six-month delay of the MPC 823e. Concept missed its marketing window for the Pic Pocket and abandoned the concept.

In April 2000, Concept sued Motorola under federal diversity jurisdiction in the Western District of Texas for violating Texas's Deceptive Trade Practices Act (DTPA). On December 29, 2000, Hugh Symons was substituted by motion as plaintiff of record. The parties consented to trial by a magistrate judge. In April 2001, Motorola filed a motion for summary judgment.

On August 2, 2001, the magistrate judge issued a Memorandum Opinion and Order with a Final Judgment granting summary judgment to Motorola. He found that Hugh Symons was not a "consumer" under the DTPA, because it had over $25 million in gross assets. ... Hugh Symons appealed.

Standard of Review

We conduct a *de novo* review of a grant of summary judgment, ensuring that no genuine issue of material fact exists and that judgment in favor of the appellee was warranted as a matter of law. *See St. Paul Guardian Ins. Co. v. Centrum GS Ltd.,* 283 F.3d 709, 712-13 (5th Cir.2002); *Haynes v. Pennzoil Co.,* 207 F.3d 296, 299 (5th Cir.2000). Under Fed. R. Civ. P. 56(c), summary judgment is appropriate when the evidence—viewed in the light most favorable to the non-movant—reflects no genuine issues of material fact. *See Celotex Corp. v. Catrett,* 477 U.S. 317, 322-23, (1986); *Hall v. Gillman, Inc.,* 81 F.3d 35, 36-37 (5th Cir.1996).

Unsubstantiated assertions are not competent summary judgment evidence. *Celotex,* 477 U.S. at 324; *Forsyth v. Barr,* 19 F.3d 1527,

1533 (5th Cir.) (Unsubstantiated assertions, improbable inferences, and unsupported speculation are not competent summary judgment evidence). Mere conclusory allegations are not competent summary judgment evidence and are insufficient to overcome a summary judgment motion. *Eason v. Thaler,* 73 F.3d 1322, 1325 (5th Cir.1996).

DTPA Claim

The DTPA, Tex. Bus. & Com. Code § 17.44(a) reads:

> This subchapter shall be liberally construed and applied to promote its underlying purposes, which are to protect consumers against false, misleading, and deceptive business practices, unconscionable actions, and breaches of warranty and to provide efficient and economical procedures to secure such protection.

Hugh Symon claims that Motorola violated §17.44—by "misrepresenting the quality, grade and characteristics of its MPC-821 micro processing chip." The elements of a valid DTPA complaint are: (1) the plaintiff is a consumer; (2) the defendant engaged in false, misleading, or deceptive acts; and (3) these acts constituted a producing cause of the consumer's damages. *Chamrad v. Volvo Cars of North America,* 145 F.3d 671, 672 n. 3 (5th Cir.1998), citing *Doe v. Boys Clubs of Greater Dallas, Inc.,* 907 S.W.2d 472 (Tex.1995).

Under DTPA § 17.45(4), a consumer is defined as:

> [A]n individual, partnership, corporation, this state, or a subdivision or agency of this state who seeks or acquires by purchase or lease, any goods or services, except that the term does not include a business consumer that has assets of $25 million or more, or that is owned or controlled by a corporation or entity with assets of $25 million or more.

Therefore, a complaining plaintiff must be a consumer, meeting the definition of § 17.45(4). *Flenniken v. Longview Bank & Trust Co.,* 661 S.W.2d 705, 707 (Tex.1983).

"Assets" for the purposes of § 17.45(4) means "gross assets." *See Eckman v. Centennial Savings Bank,* 784 S.W.2d 672, 673 n. 3, 674 (Tex.1990). Hugh Symons's total gross assets exceed $25 million, disqualifying it as a "consumer" capable of bringing a claim under the DTPA. It contends, however, that Concept Technologies was the interested party bringing the DTPA suit and that Concept had less than $25 million in assets. Further, Hugh Symons asserts that it transferred its shares in Concept to Elata, PLC, on October 17, 2000. Symons then substituted as the plaintiff on December 29, 2000. Later, Concept assigned its interest in the DTPA suit to Symons on March 5, 2001.

Where a DTPA plaintiff is asserting a claim acquired by assignment, the assignor's consumer status controls. *PPG Indus., Inc. v. JMB/Houston Ctr. Partners Ltd. Partnership,* 41 S.W.3d 270, 279 (Tex.App.—Houston [14th Dist.] 2001, no pet.). Therefore, Hugh Symons contends: Since Concept held less than $25 million in assets, it was a consumer under the DTPA. And Hugh Symons—its assignee—may pursue the suit. We disagree. At all pertinent times—at the time of the alleged violation of the DTPA and when the lawsuit was brought—Concept was a wholly-owned subsidiary of Symons. Despite the later transfer of shares within the Hugh Symons family of businesses, § 17.45(4) bars an entity—controlled by another with assets of greater than $25 million—from bringing a DTPA suit ... Hugh Symons and Concept were not consumers under the DTPA.

For the reasons stated herein, we affirm the trial court's grant of summary judgment on each issue.

NOTES AND QUESTIONS

1) Private Actions Under Texas DTPA and Proof of "Consumer" Status. Consider the Texas Supreme Court's analysis in *Flenniken v. Longview Bank & Trust Co.,* 661 S.W.2d 705, 706 (Tex.1983): It is clear that only a "consumer" has standing to maintain a private cause of action for treble damages and attorney's fees under section 17.50(a) of the DTPA. *Knight v. International Harvester Credit Corp.,* 627 S.W.2d 382, 388 (Tex.1982); *Cameron v. Terrell & Garrett, Inc.,* 618 S.W.2d 535, 538 (Tex.1981); *Riverside National Bank v. Lewis,* 603 S.W.2d 169, 173 (Tex.1980). Section 17.45(4) defines a consumer as "an individual ... who seeks or acquires by purchase or lease, any goods or services." Under the DTPA, goods include "real property purchased ... for use," Tex. Bus. & Com. Code § 17.45(1). And services include "services furnished in connection with the sale ... of goods." *Id.* §

17.45(2). Section 17.45(4), however, only describes the class of persons entitled to bring suit under section 17.50. It does not define the class of persons subject to liability under the DTPA. The range of possible defendants is limited only by the exemptions provided in § 17.49. Section 17.50(a)(3), for example, allows a consumer to "maintain an action if he has been adversely affected by ... any unconscionable action or course of action by any person."

2) Competing Standards for Establishing One's Standing as a DTPA. In *Melody Home Manufacturing Company v. Barnes*, 741 S.W.2d 349, 351 (Tex. 1987), the Texas Supreme Court reaffirmed: DTPA plaintiffs must qualify as consumers—as that term is defined in Tex. Bus. & Com.Code Ann. § 17.45(4)— to maintain a private cause of action under section 17.50 of the Act. We have recognized at least two requirements to establish DTPA consumer status. First, the plaintiffs must have sought or acquired goods or services by purchase or lease. *Cameron v. Terrell & Garrett, Inc.*, 618 S.W.2d 535, 539 (Tex.1981). Second, the goods or services purchased or leased must form the *basis of the complaint.* It is uncontroverted that the Barneses purchased goods and thus were "consumers" when they originally bought the home. Melody Home's attempts to repair the defects in the home were, by definition, "services" under the DTPA. Section 17.45(2) defines "services" as "work, labor or service purchased ... for use including services furnished *in connection with* the sale or repair of goods." Melody Home argues that the Barneses were not "consumers" with regard to the repair services because they did not purchase them with cash. The absence of a cash transfer is not determinative because DTPA plaintiffs establish their standing as consumers in terms of their *relationship to a transaction*, not by their *contractual relationship* with the defendant."

2. The Particularity Doctrine and Attorneys' DTPA "Laundry List" Actions against Website Developers and Internet Marketing Firms

Ogletree, Abbott, Clay & Reed Law Firm, L.L.P. v. FindLaw

2014 WL 2611862
(D. Minn. 2014)

Richard H. Kyle, District Judge. Plaintiff Ogletree, Abbott, Clay & Reed Law Firm, L.L.P. (Ogletree) hired Defendants Findlaw–West Publishing Corporation, and Thomson Reuters Holdings, Inc. (FindLaw)—to develop three of Ogletree's websites to increase traffic from search engines. Rather than enhance the quality of the websites, Ogletree alleges FindLaw diminished it and injured Ogletree's business as a result. After the parties failed to resolve their dispute amicably, Ogletree filed the instant action against FindLaw. ... FindLaw now moves to dismiss.

Background

FindLaw provides online advertising services to attorneys. One of its services is website development—aimed at helping attorneys increase their exposure to potential clients online. Ogletree is a law firm specializing in personal-injury matters. In 2012, it hired FindLaw to help develop three of its websites: *www.ogletreeabbott.com*, *www.1800jonesact.com*, and *www.complawyers.net* ("Ogletree Websites").

Between November 2012 and June 2013, FindLaw and Ogletree entered into a series of contracts to redesign and improve the "search engine optimization" (SEO) of the Ogletree Websites. Ogletree paid FindLaw $61,965.69 for its services. ... Ogletree was not satisfied with the revised websites and alleges that their quality and SEO deteriorated rather than improved. ... Ogletree alleges FindLaw did not utilize and migrate all of the existing indexed content and webpages from the original Ogletree Websites to the revised sites. For example, the number of indexed webpages was reduced from 612 pages to 184 pages on *www.ogletreeabbott.com*, from 598 to 81 on *www.1800jonesact.com*, and from 1,358 to 157 on *www.complawyers.net*. The more indexed pages with quality content on a website, the more opportunities there are for the website to be relevant to a user's search terms, potentially increasing the website's page ranking in Google and thus its visibility in the search results. ...

Dissatisfied with Findlaw's revisions to the Ogletree Websites, Ogletree stopped payment in September 2013. During a span of three weeks in November 2013, Ogletree removed the sites from Findlaw's servers and launched them on its own servers. Then, in an attempt to resolve the matter, it relaunched the sites from FindLaw servers. And when the parties did not reach resolution, it again removed them from FindLaw's servers and launched them on its own. In February 2014, Ogletree filed the instant action—asserting a deceptive trade practices claim. ... FindLaw now moves to dismiss the claim. ...

Fraud and Related Claims

Ogletree alleges FindLaw misrepresented its services to Ogletree—leading it to believe FindLaw would increase its websites' SEO and, in turn, increase its volume of business. Based on these alleged misrepresentations, Ogletree asserts claims for fraud, misrepresentation, and violations of the Minnesota and Texas Deceptive Trade Practices Acts—MDTPA and TDTPA, respectively. FindLaw makes several meritorious arguments for why these claims should be dismissed. But the court need address only one: Ogletree failed to plead them with particularity.

"[I]n alleging fraud or mistake, a party must state with particularity the circumstances constituting fraud or mistake." Fed. R. Civ. P. 9(b). "Conclusory allegations that a defendant's conduct was fraudulent and deceptive are not sufficient." *Schaller Tel. Co. v. Golden Sky Sys., Inc.,* 298 F.3d 736, 746 (8th Cir. 2002). Instead, a plaintiff must plead the "who, what, where, when, and how" of the alleged fraud in order "to enable the defendant to respond specifically and quickly to the potentially damaging allegations." *Drobnak v. Anderson Corp.,* 561 F.3d 778, 783 (8th Cir.2009). This heightened pleading standard applies to fraud claims as well as claims involving misrepresentation.

Thus, Ogletree must plead with specificity its claims for fraud, misrepresentation, and deceptive trade practices. *See, e.g., Trooien v. Mansour,* 608 F.3d 1020, 1028 (8th Cir.2010) (applying Rule 9(b) to misrepresentation claim); *DeVary v. Countrywide Home Loans, Inc.,* 701 F.Supp.2d 1096, 1110 (D.Minn. 2010) (applying Rule 9(b) to MDTPA claim); *Berry v. Indianapolis Life Ins. Co.,* 608 F.Supp.2d 785, 800 (N.D. Tex. 2009) (applying Rule 9(b) to TDTPA claim).

Ogletree has failed to meet this standard with respect to all three claims. Ogletree's Complaint alleges very few specific misrepresentations. Instead, Ogletree makes vague and conclusory allegations: "FindLaw has represented its goods or services have characteristics or benefits, which they do not have, represented that an agreement confers or involves rights, remedies, or obligations which it does not have or involve, or which are prohibited by law, and failed to disclose information concerning goods or services which was known at the time of the transaction." (These allegations do not pass muster under Rule 9[b].)

Even Ogletree's most specific allegations fall far short of the requisite particularity. Ogletree alleges FindLaw promised "more clients and more money" and "better results and more business." Allegedly, FindLaw also stated that it "produces results'" with "custom content"— developed by "expert copy writers" and a "dedicated team of attorney SEO experts." This is a step in the right direction, as Ogletree has at least put FindLaw on notice of the *content* of the alleged misrepresentations. Nevertheless, Ogletree provides no information about their *circumstances.* While a plaintiff may not need to plead all of the circumstances surrounding the fraud, it must plead at least a few. Here, Ogletree has not alleged who communicated these alleged misrepresentations, to whom, when, where, or how.

Accordingly, Ogletree's three fraud-related claims will be dismissed for failure to plead with particularity.

3. Proving a "Pure" DTPA Action Against Computer Vendors

Perez v. Hung Kien Luu

244 S.W.3d 444
(Tex. Ct. App.-Eastland 2007)

Rick Strange, Justice. This is a claim under the Deceptive Trade Practices Act (DTPA), Tex. Bus. & Com. Code § 17.41 et seq. Mario Perez filed a suit against Hung Kien Luu and MicroCache Computers, Inc.—contending that they violated the DTPA by refusing to sell him 100 hard drives at the advertised price of $1 each. The trial court conducted a bench trial.

I. Background Facts

MicroCache was a computer-related business. It maintained a website that listed for sale computer parts—including hard drives. Perez was a refinery operator for Shell Oil Refinery and repaired computers as a side business. The night of July 15, he was looking for hard drives on the Internet and went to MicroCache's website. He noticed that Seagate 146GB hard drives were listed for $1 each. Perez ordered 100 hard drives, paid MicroCache $228.25, and received a confirmation e-mail. The following day, he received an e-mail from Luu—a MicroCache officer—advising him that there was a system error and that his payment was being refunded. Perez e-mailed a response advising Luu: He did not want a refund. He wanted the 100 hard drives; and he expected delivery within ten days. Perez checked MicroCache's website again and saw that the hard drive's price was now $1,195 each.

MicroCache refused to sell the hard drives for $1, and Perez filed a lawsuit against Luu and MicroCache. The case was tried without a jury. The court found that Perez placed an order for 100 hard drives and paid MicroCache, that MicroCache's website had a pricing error, that the website advised customers that MicroCache had the right to correct any pricing error, that Perez was aware of this right, that MicroCache refunded Perez's purchase price upon learning of the pricing error, and that Perez accepted the credit. The trial court also found that MicroCache did not violate the DTPA and that neither MicroCache nor Luu was liable to Perez. Based upon these findings, the trial court entered a take-nothing judgment.

II. Issues

Perez challenges the trial court's judgment with six issues. Perez argues that the trial court's judgment is inconsistent with its findings of fact, that the trial court's finding that he was not deceived is based upon legally or factually insufficient evidence, that this finding conflicts with the trial court's other findings, that the trial court's finding that PayPal was acting as MicroCache's agent is based upon legally or factually sufficient evidence, and that the trial court erred by not entering judgment in his favor.

III. Discussion

A. Does the Trial Court's Judgment Conform with Its Findings of Fact?

Perez argues that the trial court's take-nothing judgment does not conform with its findings of fact because the court's findings do not negate at least one element of his claim or support every element of at least one affirmative defense and that the findings actually support his DTPA claims. Perez correctly notes that he was required to prove four elements to establish a DTPA claim: (1) that he was a consumer; (2) that the defendant(s) engaged in at least one of the laundry list items; (3) that he detrimentally relied on the false, misleading, or deceptive act or practice; and (4) that the false, misleading, or deceptive act or practice was a producing cause of his injury. *See Amstadt v. U.S. Brass Corp.,* 919 S.W.2d 644, 649 (Tex.1996).

Citing DTPA § 17.46(b), Perez alleged that MicroCache and Luu committed three laundry list violations:

1) representing that goods or services have sponsorship, approval, characteristics, ingredients, uses, benefits, or qualities which they do not have—§ 17.46(b)(5);
2) advertising goods or services with intent not to sell them as advertised—§ 17.46(b)(9); and,
3) representing that an agreement confers or involves rights, remedies, or obligations which it does not have or involve or which are prohibited by law—§ 17.46(b)(12);

Each of Perez's laundry list claims is based upon the hard drive's advertised price. Perez contends that the advertised price of $1 was a representation that (1) the hard drives had a *characteristic* (a $1 purchase price) and (2) that *an agreement confers or involves rights* (the right to purchase hard drives for $1). Perez argues: Since MicroCache refused to sell him 100 hard drives for $1 each, these representations were false. Perez also argues that he was not required to prove that MicroCache knowingly or intentionally made these misrepresentations and, therefore, that any pricing mistake is immaterial.

The Texas Supreme Court has held that a defendant may be liable for some laundry list violations, even if it did not know that the representation was false and it did not intend to deceive. *See Eagle Props., Ltd. v. Scharbauer,* 807 S.W.2d 714, 724 (Tex. 1990) (misrepresentations that do not necessarily constitute common-law fraud may be actionable under the DTPA). Knowledge or intent is required, only if called for by the language of the implicated laundry list item. *Pennington v. Singleton,* 606 S.W.2d 682, 689 (Tex.1980). However, the court has also held that legislative intent should be determined from the language of the entire act and not isolated portions. *Id.* at 686.

The DTPA contains four laundry list items specifically referring to advertising representations—Section 17.46(b)(9), (10), (17), and (18). Subsections (17) and (18) have limited applicability. Subsection (17) forbids advertising a sale by fraudulently representing that a business is going out of business. Subsection (18) forbids certain advertisements in connection with a prescription drug identification card. Subsections (9) and (10), conversely, are broadly phrased, apply to all advertising, and are generally implicated by price representations.

Subsection (9) prohibits advertising goods or services with intent not to sell them as advertised, and subsection (10) prohibits advertising goods or services with intent not to supply a reasonable expectable public demand unless the advertisement discloses a limitation of quantity. This type of conduct has been referred to as "bait and switch" advertising. *See Smith v. Baldwin,* 611 S.W.2d 611, 615 (Tex.1980) (describing bait advertising as attracting customers by advertising products at low prices and then switching them to another product at a higher price), and *Transmission Exchange Inc. v. Long,* 821 S.W.2d 265, 270 (Tex.App.-Houston [1st Dist.] 1991, writ denied) (describing the bait and switch technique). Both subsections require proof of intent and, in fact, are the only two laundry list items to use the word "intent."

Because the legislature assigned a higher burden of proof to the two laundry list items based upon general advertising representations and because the legislature worded those two items in a way that typically implicates price representations, we believe that the legislature did not intend to impose strict liability for advertising mistakes such as the one before us. We realize that courts have held that the DTPA imposes a duty on sellers to know if their factual representations are correct. *See, e.g., Lone Star Ford, Inc. v. McGlashan,* 681 S.W.2d 720, 723 (Tex.App.-Houston [1st Dist.] 1984, no writ). The cases that have discussed this principle, however, have involved a direct representation from the defendant to the plaintiff.

This does not mean that, merely because a representation is included in some form of advertising, subsections (9) and (10) are the exclusive avenues of relief. Representations beyond price and representations in addition to those in the advertising may violate other laundry list items. Additionally, a particular form or manner of advertising may lead to a different result. However, if the misrepresentation is limited to an item's price and that misrepresentation is made only in a general advertisement, we believe the legislature intended that a claimant prove an intentional misrepresentation to recover under the DTPA.

There was considerable evidence that the $1 price was a mistake. Luu testified that the website was new and that his programmer used a $1 purchase price to test it. The price was then mistakenly left at $1. Perez refused to concede the price was a mistake but did describe it as "a damn good deal." In fact, it was such a good deal that—even though he had only sold ten computers in the last five years, he ordered 100 hard drives when he saw the price. Because Perez was *required to prove intent* to establish an advertising misrepresentation under the DTPA and because the trial court found that the advertised price was a mistake, its take-nothing judgment is consistent with its findings.

Even if we are incorrect in our analysis and Perez was entitled to assert a claim under subsection (5) or (12) *without proving intent,* the trial court still correctly entered a take-nothing judgment. Perez understandably focuses on the website's initial price posting to define the operative representation. But Perez ignores the fact that the listed prices were not unconditional. The website advised customers that "[prices are for reference purposes only and are subject to change without notice. Micro[C]ache is not held responsible for any errors or discrepancies." Consequently, Perez was on notice when he ordered 100 Seagate hard drives that MicroCache could refuse to consummate the transaction if there was a pricing error. Because the $1 purchase price was a mistake and because MicroCache refunded Perez's money as soon as it realized the error, the trial court correctly found that Perez was not deceived. That finding is sufficient to establish that MicroCache did not commit a false, misleading, or deceptive act or practice. Perez's first and second issues are overruled.

B. Did the Trial Court Err by Finding that Perez Was Not Deceived?

Perez next argues that the trial court's finding—that he was not deceived—is based upon legally or factually insufficient evidence and that it conflicts with other fact findings. A trial court's factual determinations are reviewed for legal sufficiency under the same standards used to review a jury's verdict. *Anderson v. City of Seven Points,* 806 S.W.2d 791, 794 (Tex.1991). In considering a legal sufficiency challenge, we review all the evidence in the light most favorable to the prevailing party—indulging every inference in that party's favor. *Associated Indem. Corp. v. CAT Contracting, Inc.,* 964 S.W.2d 276, 286-87 (Tex.1998). In reviewing a factual sufficiency challenge, we consider all of the evidence and uphold the finding unless the evidence is too weak to support it or the finding is so against the overwhelming weight of the evidence as to be manifestly unjust. *Westech Eng'g, Inc. v. Clearwater Constructors, Inc., a Div. of Phelps, Inc.,* 835 S.W.2d 190, 196 (Tex.App.-Austin 1992, no writ).

The evidence is sufficient both legally and factually to support the trial court's finding that Perez was not deceived. We have previously found that the $1 purchase price was posted in error and that MicroCache's website notified potential customers that MicroCache had the right to correct a pricing error. This is sufficient to defeat a misrepresentation claim. Moreover, because MicroCache is not strictly liable for the pricing error, this finding is not in conflict with the trial court's other findings.

Perez argues that he was indisputably a consumer as defined by the DTPA. We agree. Also, section 17.50 allows a consumer to recover economic or mental anguish damages, but any recovery is conditioned upon proof of actual damage. *City of Marshall, Tex. v. Bryant Air Conditioning Co.*, 650 F.2d 724, 726 (5th Cir.1981). The benefit-of-the-bargain damage model compensates a DTPA claimant for the difference between the value as represented and the value actually received. *Leyendecker & Assocs., Inc. v. Wechter*, 683 S.W.2d 369, 373 (Tex.1984). The only representation Perez relied upon was the $1 purchase price. Thus, even if Perez were otherwise correct, his maximum damages under this theory would be only $100.

Additionally, Perez argues that the trial court's findings that he ordered and paid for the drives establish his reliance and damages. We do not agree, but collectively these are three of four elements that must be proven to establish a DTPA claim. Perez was also required to prove a laundry list violation. We have previously found that Perez was required to prove an intentional misrepresentation, which he did not do. And alternatively, because the pricing was qualified, MicroCache did not make a misrepresentation. This is sufficient to defeat a DTPA claim regardless of Perez's other proof. Issues three and four are overruled.

In his fifth issue, Perez contends that the trial court erred when it found that MicroCache and Luu were not liable to him. Perez argues that the trial court erred by finding that he was not "deceived" because none of the laundry list items specifically refer to or require proof of a deception. This is correct, but the DTPA requires proof of a "false, misleading, or deceptive act." Section 17.46(a). We have previously held that the trial court's finding that Perez was not deceived is sufficient to establish that the defendants did not commit a laundry list violation. *Cf. Eagle Props.,* 807 S.W.2d at 724 (finding in prior lawsuit that defendant did not misrepresent the bank's financial condition and the OCC's position on the challenged transaction barred a DTPA claim in a subsequent suit on this same basis). Perez's fifth issue is overruled.

The judgment of the trial court is affirmed.

UDTPA and DTPA "LAUNDRY LISTS"

Ohio's UDTPA § 4165.02 presents a laundry list of prohibitive practices; and, it presents representative illustration of the laundry lists in all UDTPAs. On the other hand, Texas's DTPA § 17.46(a) presents a more exhaustive laundry list of false, misleading, or deceptive acts or practices. Additionally, Texas's laundry list mirrors the lists of violations under other DTPAs.

Baldwin's Ohio Revised Code

Title XLI. Labor and Industry
Chapter 4165. Deceptive Trade Practices

§ 4165.02—Deceptive Trade Practices

(A) A person engages in a deceptive trade practice when, in the course of the person's business, vocation, or occupation, the person does any of the following:

(1) Passes off goods or services as those of another;

(2) Causes likelihood of confusion or misunderstanding as to the source, sponsorship, approval, or certification of goods or services;

(3) Causes likelihood of confusion or misunderstanding as to affiliation, connection, or association with, or certification by, another;

(4) Uses deceptive representations or designations of geographic origin in connection with goods or services;

(5) Lists a fictitious business name in a local telephone directory that is published on or after the effective date of this amendment, in circumstances in which all of the following apply:

(a) The person's fictitious business name is not registered as a trade name with, or its use as a fictitious name has not been reported to, the secretary of state under sections 1329.01 to 1329.10 of the Revised Code.

(b) The person's listed fictitious business name misrepresents the geographic location of the person, because that name includes a reference to a political subdivision or another geographic area of this state, the person does not have business premises in that political subdivision or other geographic area from which the person sells, leases, rents, or otherwise provides particular goods or services in this state, and the person's use of that name causes a likelihood of confusion or misunderstanding by consumers as to the geographic location with which the consumers are dealing in the purchase, lease, rental, or other provision of, or will be dealing in the resolution of problems that may arise in connection with, particular goods or services.

(c) The local telephone directory listing of the person's fictitious business name does not identify the political subdivision and, if the person is not located in this state, the state in which are located the person's business premises with which consumers are dealing in the purchase, lease, rental, or other provision of, or will be dealing in the resolution of problems that may arise in connection with, particular goods or services.

(d) Telephone calls to the local telephone number listed for the person's fictitious business name routinely are forwarded or otherwise transferred to business premises of the person that are located outside the calling area covered by the local telephone directory.

(6) Lists a fictitious business name in a directory assistance database on or after the effective date of

this amendment, the circumstances described in divisions (A)(5)(a) and (b) of this section apply regarding the person's listed fictitious business name, and telephone calls to the local telephone number listed for the person's fictitious business name routinely are forwarded or otherwise transferred to business premises of the person that are located outside the local calling area;

(7) Represents that goods or services have sponsorship, approval, characteristics, ingredients, uses, benefits, or quantities that they do not have or that a person has a sponsorship, approval, status, affiliation, or connection that the person does not have;

(8) Represents that goods are original or new if they are deteriorated, altered, reconditioned, reclaimed, used, or secondhand;

(9) Represents that goods or services are of a particular standard, quality, or grade, or that goods are of a particular style or model, if they are of another;

(10) Disparages the goods, services, or business of another by false representation of fact;

(11) Advertises goods or services with intent not to sell them as advertised;

(12) Makes false statements of fact concerning the reasons for, existence of, or amounts of price reductions;

(13) Advertises goods or services with intent not to supply reasonably expectable public demand, unless the advertisement discloses a limitation of quantity.

(B) In order to prevail in a civil action under section 4165.03 of the Revised Code that seeks injunctive relief or an award of damages and that is based on one or more deceptive trade practices listed in division (A) of this section, a complainant need not prove competition between the parties to the civil action.

(C) This section does not affect unfair trade practices that are otherwise actionable at common law or under other sections of the Revised Code.

(D) A telephone company, provider of directory assistance, publisher of a local telephone directory, or officer, employee, or agent of the company, provider, or publisher shall not be liable in a civil action under section 4165.03 of the Revised Code for publishing in any directory or directory assistance database the listing of a fictitious business name of a person who commits a deceptive trade practice that is listed in division (A) of this section unless the telephone company, provider of directory assistance, publisher of a local telephone directory, or officer, employee, or agent of the company, provider, or publisher is the person who committed the deceptive trade practice listed in division (A) of this section.

Vernon's Texas Statutes and Codes

Business and Commerce Code
Chapter 17. Deceptive Trade Practices
Subchapter E. Deceptive Trade Practices and Consumer Protection

§ 17.46—Deceptive Trade Practices Unlawful

(a) False, misleading, or deceptive acts or practices in the conduct of any trade or commerce are hereby declared unlawful and are subject to action by the consumer protection division under Sections 17.47, 17.58, 17.60, and 17.61 of this code.

(b) Except as provided in Subsection (d) of this section, the term "false, misleading, or deceptive acts or practices" includes, *but is not limited to*, the following acts:

(1) passing off goods or services as those of another;

(2) causing confusion or misunderstanding as to the source, sponsorship, approval, or certification of goods or services;

(3) causing confusion or misunderstanding as to affiliation, connection, or association with, or certification by, another;

(4) using deceptive representations or designations of geographic origin in connection with goods or services;

(5) representing that goods or services have sponsorship, approval, characteristics, ingredients, uses, benefits, or quantities which they do not have or that a person has a sponsorship, approval, status, affiliation, or connection which the person does not;

(6) representing that goods are original or new if they are deteriorated, reconditioned, reclaimed, used, or secondhand;

(7) representing that goods or services are of a particular standard, quality, or grade, or that goods are of a particular style or model, if they are of another;

(8) disparaging the goods, services, or business of another by false or misleading representation of facts;

(9) advertising goods or services with intent not to sell them as advertised;

(10) advertising goods or services with intent not to supply a reasonable expectable public demand, unless the advertisements disclosed a limitation of quantity;

(11) making false or misleading statements of fact concerning the reasons for, existence of, or amount of price reductions;

(12) representing that an agreement confers or involves rights, remedies, or obligations which it does not have or involve, or which are prohibited by law;

(13) knowingly making false or misleading statements of fact concerning the need for parts, replacement, or repair service;

(14) misrepresenting the authority of a salesman, representative or agent to negotiate the final terms of a consumer transaction;

(15) basing a charge for the repair of any item in whole or in part on a guaranty or warranty instead of on the value of the actual repairs made or work to be performed on the item without stating separately the charges for the work and the charge for the warranty or guaranty, if any;

(16) disconnecting, turning back, or resetting the odometer of any motor vehicle so as to reduce the number of miles indicated on the odometer gauge;

(17) advertising of any sale by fraudulently representing that a person is going out of business;

(18) advertising, selling, or distributing a card which purports to be a prescription drug identification card issued under Section 4151.152, Insurance Code, in accordance with rules adopted by the commissioner of insurance, which offers a discount on the purchase of health care goods or services from a third party provider, and which is not evidence of insurance coverage, unless:

(A) the discount is authorized under an agreement between the seller of the card and the provider of those goods and services or the discount or card is offered to members of the seller;

(B) the seller does not represent that the card provides insurance coverage of any kind; and

(C) the discount is not false, misleading, or deceptive;

(19) using or employing a chain referral sales plan in connection with the sale or offer to sell of goods, merchandise, or anything of value, which uses the sales technique, plan, arrangement, or agreement in which the buyer or prospective buyer is offered the opportunity to purchase merchandise or goods and in connection with the purchase receives the seller's promise or representation that the buyer shall have the right to receive compensation or consideration in any form for furnishing to the seller the names of other prospective buyers if receipt of the compensation or consideration is contingent upon

the occurrence of an event subsequent to the time the buyer purchases the merchandise or goods;

(20) representing that a guaranty or warranty confers or involves rights or remedies which it does not have or involve, provided, however, that nothing in this subchapter shall be construed to expand the implied warranty of merchantability as defined in Sections 2.314 through 2.318 and Sections 2A.212 through 2A.216 to involve obligations in excess of those which are appropriate to the goods;

(21) promoting a pyramid promotional scheme, as defined by Section 17.461;

(22) representing that work or services have been performed on, or parts replaced in, goods when the work or services were not performed or the parts replaced;

(23) filing suit founded upon a written contractual obligation of and signed by the defendant to pay money arising out of or based on a consumer transaction for goods, services, loans, or extensions of credit intended primarily for personal, family, household, or agricultural use in any county other than in the county in which the defendant resides at the time of the commencement of the action or in the county in which the defendant in fact signed the contract; provided, however, that a violation of this subsection shall not occur where it is shown by the person filing such suit that the person neither knew or had reason to know that the county in which such suit was filed was neither the county in which the defendant resides at the commencement of the suit nor the county in which the defendant in fact signed the contract;

(24) failing to disclose information concerning goods or services which was known at the time of the transaction if such failure to disclose such information was intended to induce the consumer into a transaction into which the consumer would not have entered had the information been disclosed;

(25) using the term "corporation," "incorporated," or an abbreviation of either of those terms in the name of a business entity that is not incorporated under the laws of this state or another jurisdiction;

(26) selling, offering to sell, or illegally promoting an annuity contract under Chapter 22, Acts of the 57th Legislature, 3rd Called Session, 1962 (Article 6228a-5, Vernon's Texas Civil Statutes), with the intent that the annuity contract will be the subject of a salary reduction agreement, as defined by that Act, if the annuity contract is not an eligible qualified investment under that Act or is not registered with the Teacher Retirement System of Texas as required by Section 8A of that Act;

(27) taking advantage of a disaster declared by the governor under Chapter 418, Government Code, by:

(A) selling or leasing fuel, food, medicine, or another necessity at an exorbitant or excessive price; or

(B) demanding an exorbitant or excessive price in connection with the sale or lease of fuel, food, medicine, or another necessity;

(28a) delivering or distributing a solicitation in connection with a good or service that:

(A) represents that the solicitation is sent on behalf of a governmental entity when it is not; or

(B) resembles a governmental notice or form that represents or implies that a criminal penalty may be imposed if the recipient does not remit payment for the good or service;

(28b) using the translation into a foreign language of a title or other word, including "attorney," "lawyer," "licensed," "notary," and "notary public," in any written or electronic material, including an advertisement, a business card, a letterhead, stationery, a website, or an online video, in reference to a person who is not an attorney in order to imply that the person is authorized to practice law in the United States.

(29) delivering or distributing a solicitation in connection with a good or service that resembles a check or other negotiable instrument or invoice, unless the portion of the solicitation that resembles a check or other negotiable instrument or invoice includes the following notice, clearly and conspicuously printed in at least 18-point type:

"SPECIMEN-NON-NEGOTIABLE";

(30) in the production, sale, distribution, or promotion of a synthetic substance that produces and is intended to produce an effect when consumed or ingested similar to, or in excess of, the effect of a controlled substance or controlled substance analogue, as those terms are defined by Section 481.002, Health and Safety Code:

(A) making a deceptive representation or designation about the synthetic substance; or

(B) causing confusion or misunderstanding as to the effects the synthetic substance causes when consumed or ingested; or

(31) a licensed public insurance adjuster directly or indirectly soliciting employment, as defined by Section 38.01, Penal Code, for an attorney, or a licensed public insurance adjuster entering into a contract with an insured for the primary purpose of referring the insured to an attorney without the intent to actually perform the services customarily provided by a licensed public insurance adjuster, provided that this subdivision may not be construed to prohibit a licensed public insurance adjuster from recommending a particular attorney to an insured.

(c) (1) It is the intent of the legislature that in construing Subsection (a) of this section in suits brought under Section 17.47 of this subchapter the courts to the extent possible will be guided by Subsection (b) of this section and the interpretations given by the Federal Trade Commission and federal courts to Section 5(a)(1) of the Federal Trade Commission Act [15 U.S.C.A. § 45(a)(1)].

(2) In construing this subchapter the court shall not be prohibited from considering relevant and pertinent decisions of courts in other jurisdictions.

(d) For the purposes of the relief authorized in Subdivision (1) of Subsection (a) of Section 17.50 of this subchapter, the term "false, misleading, or deceptive acts or practices" is limited to the acts enumerated in specific subdivisions of Subsection (b) of this section.

4. Proving a UDTPA "Laundry List" Action Against Domain-Name Owners and Registrants

To be sure, Texas, Illinois and other state legislatures have encouraged courts to construe UDTPAs and DTPA very liberally. For example, in *Price v. Philip Morris, Inc.* 848 N.E.2d 1, 32 (Ill. 2005), the Illinois Supreme Court stressed: "The Consumer Fraud Act was enacted in 1961 as a regulatory and remedial statute for the purpose of protecting consumers and others against fraud, unfair methods of competition, and unfair or deceptive acts or practices in the conduct of any form of trade or commerce. It is to be liberally construed to effectuate this purpose." And, in *Latham v. Castillo*, 972 S.W.2d 66, 68 (Tex.1998), the Texas Supreme Court reiterates: "The DTPA grants consumers a cause of action for false, misleading, or deceptive acts or practices." ... In our review of a DTPA claim, we must liberally construe and apply the statute to promote the underlying goals of the statute, which include protecting consumers against false, misleading, and deceptive business practices and unconscionable actions. *See* Tex. Bus. & Com. Code § 17.44(a).

Even more relevant, Texas DTPA § 17.46(b) reads: "[T]he term 'false, misleading, or deceptive acts or practices' includes—*but is not limited to*—the [enumerated] acts. And, Illinois UDTPA § 815 ILCS 510/2(a)(12) reads: "A person engages in a deceptive trade practice when, in the course of his or her business, vocation, or occupation, the person ... engages in *any other conduct* which similarly creates a likelihood of confusion or misunderstanding."

But consider the Texas Court of Appeal's brief analysis in *Willowbrook Foods, Inc. v. Grinnell Corp.*, 147 S.W.3d 492, 506-507 (Tex. Ct. App.-San Antonio 2004):

> In their response to the motion for summary judgment, plaintiffs merely make the general statement that their "summary judgment proof as outlined herein presents questions of fact on issues—including *but not limited to*—Defendant's failure to advise or warn Plaintiffs of assessment and proper use of its product." A plaintiff claiming nondisclosure under the DTPA must prove four elements: (1) a failure to disclose information concerning goods or services, (2) which was known at the time of the transaction, (3) if such failure was intended to induce the consumer into a transaction, (4) which the consumer would not have entered had the information been disclosed. Tex. Bus. & Com. Code § 17.46(b)(24) Accordingly, Defendant's motion—which states there is no evidence of any false, misleading, or deceptive act—specifically challenges these elements.
>
> In their affidavits, Plaintiffs list six instances of Defendant's failure to make certain "recommendations" or "indications" about its product. ... However, mere nondisclosure of material information is not enough to establish an actionable DTPA claim. Nondisclosure without evidence that a defendant had knowledge of the undisclosed information and intentionally withheld the information is insufficient to establish a violation of the DTPA. *Chandler v. Gene Messer Ford, Inc.,* 81 S.W.3d 493, 502 (Tex.App.-Eastland 2002). In order to recover damages under the DTPA for the failure to disclose material information, the plaintiff must also show that the information was withheld with the intent of inducing the consumer to engage in a transaction. *Robbins v. Capozzi,* 100 S.W.3d 18, 26 (Tex.App.-Tyler 2002). Here, plaintiffs did not meet their burden of bringing forth more than a scintilla of probative evidence that raises a genuine issue of material fact on the elements of their nondisclosure claim. Therefore, Emerson established its entitlement as a matter of law to summary judgment on this claim.

Are there exceptions to the "*any other conduct*" language which appears in many UDTPAs? Assuming that the answer is yes. Would such exceptions preclude solo or small-firm attorneys' ability to litigate technology-based disputes under a UDTPA? Consider the technology-based dispute in the next case and the court's analysis. Did the court construe the UDTPA generally and the "*any other conduct*" phrase liberally?

Juno Online Services v. Juno Lighting, Inc.

979 F.Supp. 684
(N.D. Ill. 1997)

Leinenweber, District Judge. Plaintiff Juno Online Service (Juno Online) sues defendant Juno Lighting, Inc. (Juno Lighting) seeking relief under Count IV. Defendant now moves to dismiss Counts IV for failure to state a cause of action and to strike all claims for monetary relief.

I. Background

The following information is taken from plaintiff's amended complaint. Juno Online—a Delaware limited partnership with its principal place of business in New York City—is an online provider with approximately 1.5 million subscribers. Juno Lighting—a Delaware corporation with its principal place of business in Des Plaines, Illinois—is a manufacturer and retailer of recessed and track lighting. Juno Lighting has used the Juno name in its logo since 1976 and holds two federal trademarks for the name "Juno."

The current dispute revolves around the Internet and the use of the domain name "juno.com." The Internet is a network of computers that are linked together, allowing computer users to share information and data. *See generally, Intermatic Inc. v. Toeppen,* 947 F.Supp. 1227, 1230-32 (N.D.Ill.1996). Each computer that is linked to the Internet contains a numeric address called an Internet protocol address, or IP address. The numeric IP address has four parts—each separated by a decimal point. An example of such an address would be 123.112.101.1. However, since it is easier to use, each computer is given an alphanumeric address—a domain name—that corresponds to the IP address. When an Internet user types in the domain name, the user's computer reads the name as the numeric IP address and contacts the appropriate computer. An example of such a domain name is "juno.com."

To send electronic mail ("e-mail"), the user addresses the message to the domain name of the recipient's e-mail provider. America Online, for instance, is an e-mail provider—whose domain name is "aol.com." Each user of the America Online service is given a user name to use with the domain name (*e.g.*,"harrysmith"). Therefore, if a person wants to contact Harry Smith—an America Online subscriber, the user would send an e-mail message to "harrysmith@aol.com." The computer would read "aol.com," translate this into the corresponding numeric IP address, and deliver the message to the America Online computer, which would then deliver the message to Harry Smith.

The domain name also functions as a "World Wide Web" address, if preceded by the letters www (*i.e.*, www.aol.com). Websites are pages of electronic information that a company, organization, or person wants to advertise to Internet users. Entities and people such as *Sports Illustrated*, Duke University, the National Basketball Association, and certain individual politicians have web sites that allow Internet users to look up information.

In December of 1994, Juno Online registered the domain name "juno.com" with Network Solutions, Inc. (NSI) and, subsequently, began providing free e-mail service to customers on April 22, 1996. Those who use Juno Online's e-mail service are given their own user name to use together with Juno Online's domain name (e.g., harrysmith@juno.com). According to Juno Online, its service has been quite popular—with 250,000 new accounts having been opened in January of 1997 alone. Juno Online currently services more than one out of every twenty United States e-mail addresses. Since July 5, 1995, Juno Online has also been using the World Wide Web address "www.juno.com" and, currently, its web page is "visited" thousands of times a day. By virtue of a government contract with the National Science Foundation, NSI is the exclusive registrar of Internet domain names. Therefore, once Juno Online registered the domain name "juno.com" with NSI, no other business or person could obtain that address.

NSI's general policy is to register a specific domain name to the first person or entity who applies for registration. However, in 1995, NSI instituted a "Domain Name Dispute Policy" that allows a third party to challenge a registrant's domain name—despite the "first come, first serve" general rule. According to the policy, to challenge a domain name, the third party must notify the registrant that the use of the domain name violates the third party's intellectual property rights. The third party must also file with NSI a certified copy of a trademark registration indicating that the third party owns a trademark that is the same as the contested domain name. If the domain name registrant cannot produce a similar trademark registration, NSI's policy requires it to suspend the use of the domain name until the issue is resolved. However, if either the registrant or third party files a suit against the other before the suspension takes effect, NSI allows the registrant to continue using the domain name and leaves it for the court to decide which party should be allowed to use the domain name.

In July 1995, D. E. Shaw & Co., L.P.—an affiliate of Juno Online—began applying for federal service mark and trademark protection for the word "Juno," as well as for various designs, slogans, and phone numbers related to "Juno." Juno Lighting sent a letter to Juno Online in June of 1996—stating its opposition to the Juno Online trademark applications. Juno Lighting also sent a letter to NSI on August 28, 1996, requesting that NSI cancel Juno Online's domain name "juno.com."

After NSI received Juno Lighting's letter, NSI sent Juno Online a letter dated September 19, 1996. It stated: Unless Juno Online transfers the domain name—"juno.com"—to Juno Lighting or filed a declaratory judgment action in federal court by October 26, 1996, NSI would suspend the operation of the domain name "juno.com." In response, Juno Online filed this action in the Eastern District of Virginia—naming Juno Lighting and NSI as defendants. ... Count IV involves Illinois's statutory unfair competition and deceptive trade practices laws.

II. Standard

In ruling on a motion to dismiss under Federal Rule of Civil Procedure 12(b)(6), the court must accept "the well-pleaded allegations in the complaint as true and draw all reasonable inferences in favor of the plaintiff." *Porter v. DiBlasio,* 93 F.3d 301, 305 (7th Cir. 1996). Dismissal is only appropriate absent a set of probative facts—which would justify plaintiff's relief. Where the court considers evidence outside the pleadings, the motion is treated as a motion for summary judgment. Fed. R. Civ. P. 12(B). Summary judgment will be granted only if, viewing the facts and inferences in the light most favorable to the non-moving party, the party moving for summary judgment proves the absence of a genuine issue of material fact and establishes its right to judgment as a matter of law. *Matsushita Elec. Indus. Co. v. Zenith Radio Corp.,* 475 U.S. 574, 587 (1986).

* * *

V. State Law Claims

In Count IV of the amended complaint, plaintiff alleges that defendant's "bad faith acts … constitute unfair competition and deceptive trade practices under the Illinois Deceptive Trade Practices Act, 815 ILCS 510/2, and the Illinois Consumer Fraud and Deceptive Business Practices Act, 815 ILCS 505/2." While plaintiff does not list the "acts" to which it is referring, the court can only conceive of two "acts" that could possibly support plaintiff's claim: (1) defendant having obtained the domain name "juno-online.com"; and (2) defendant having sent NSI a letter requesting that it cancel Juno Online's domain name "juno.com." Defendant argues that neither of these acts would support plaintiff's claims.

Under the Illinois Consumer Fraud and Deceptive Business Practice Act (ICFA)—815 ILCS 505/2, a person or corporation can be held liable for "unfair or deceptive acts or practices" used "in the conduct of any trade or commerce." According to the statute, "[t]he terms 'trade' and 'commerce' mean the advertising, offering for sale, sale, or distribution of any services and any property … and any other article, commodity, or thing of value." 815 ILCS 505/1(f).

While the Internet can be used for advertising and offering products or services for sale, plaintiff's amended complaint does not allege that defendant used the domain name to set up a web site that would have deceived consumers. In fact, plaintiff seems to have admitted otherwise in its brief. Merely obtaining a domain name—without setting up a web site or e-mail service—is not enough to constitute "trade or commerce." Furthermore, sending a letter to NSI and asserting rights to the trademark "juno" is also not the type of activity that comes under the definition of "trade or commerce."

As for its claim under the Illinois Deceptive Trade Practices Act (UDTPA)—815 ILCS 510/2, plaintiff relies on two subsections of the Act, subsections two and five. In relevant part, Illinois UDTPA §§ 815 ILCS 510/2 (2) and (5) read:

> A person engages in a deceptive trade practice when, in the course of his business, vocation or occupation, he … (2) causes likelihood of confusion or of misunderstanding as to the source, sponsorship, approval or certification of goods or services … [and] (5) represents that goods or services have sponsorship, approval, characteristics, ingredients, uses, benefits or qualities that they do not have or

> that a person has a sponsorship, approval, status, affiliation or connection that he does not have.

The Act also contains a catchall provision making it illegal to "engage in any other conduct which similarly creates a likelihood of confusion or of misunderstanding." 815 ILCS 510/2(12).

It is clear from the language of the statute and the accompanying comments written by The National Conference of Commissioners on Uniform State Laws that the aim of this law is to prevent misrepresentation via trademark or advertising. Within the twelve enumerated subsections of UDTPA § 2, there is an implicit—if not explicit—rule: Before a violation can occur, a defendant must make some form of a representation or do something to the public or to a potential buyer regarding a good or service. *Lynch Ford, Inc. v. Ford Motor Co., Inc.,* 957 F.Supp. 142, 147 (N.D.Ill.1997). The focus of this Act is on deception and "the existence of a likelihood of confusion." *See Balsamo/Olson Group, Inc. v. Bradley Place Ltd. Partnership,* 950 F.Supp. 896, 898 (C.D. Ill.1997) ("deception); and, *S Industries, Inc. v. GMI Holdings, Inc.,* 1996 WL 526792, at *3 (N.D. Ill. 1996) ("confusion").

However, as already discussed, plaintiff does not allege that defendant actually created a web page under the domain name "juno-online.com." Merely registering the domain name "juno-online.com" does not create a likelihood of confusion and certainly does not amount to deception. While the court is mindful of the fact that "a plaintiff need not prove ... *actual* confusion or misunderstanding" plaintiff still must show a *likelihood* of confusion or misunderstanding. Since defendant has not been accused of representing something to potential buyers or to the public, the court cannot infer such a likelihood.

Plaintiff has failed to state a claim under the UDTPA. As such, the court must dismiss Count IV of the complaint.

NOTES AND QUESTIONS

1) Leased Office Technologies, DTPA "Laundry List" Violations and Lessors' Liability. In *Innovative Office Systems, Inc. v. Johnson,* 906 S.W.2d 940, 947 (Tex. Ct. App.-Tyler 1995), Johnson leased an upgraded hardware system—a copier—from Innovative. The copier never functioned as represented. Johnson sued, claiming that Innovative committed several "false, misleading, or deceptive acts or practices" or "laundry list" violations under Texas DTPA §17.46(b): (2) Representing that the system had characteristics, uses, benefits, and qualities that it did not have; (3) Representing that the ... system was ... of a standard or quality, when it was not; (4) Advertising the ... system ... with an intent not to sell the components of the system as demonstrated or advertised; and (5) Failing to disclose to Johnson that the [software] program would not reach the market as early as promised. The court found: The lessor and agents misrepresented the availability of necessary software; and, the lessor's hardware was defective. In the end, the court concluded: "The evidence is legally and factually sufficient to support the court's findings that Innovative's actions were false, misleading, or deceptive."

2) Unsolicited Commercial Emails and Vendors' Liability under Deceptive Trade Practices Acts. In *Prukala v. Elle*, 11 F.Supp.3d 443, 446 (M.D. Pa. 2014), Hearst Communications—the publisher of *Elle Magazine*—sent a series of electronic mail messages to Christina Prukala's cellular telephone. The message encouraged Christina to purchase services from Hearst. The messages came from a third-party domain—making it difficult for Christina to block the e-mails. Christina sued Hearst under the Pennsylvania Unfair Trade Practices and Consumer Protection Law (UTPCPL) § 73 Pa. Stat. § 201–2(4)(xxi). This "catch all" section bars a seller of goods and services one from "engaging in any other fraudulent or deceptive conduct which creates a likelihood of confusion or of misunderstanding." And under the catch-all provision, "a showing of deceptive activity is sufficient to impose liability." *Wilson v. Parisi,* 549 F.Supp.2d 637, 666 (M.D. Pa. 2008). Still, to establish liability under the catch-all provision, "a plaintiff must present evidence showing: (1) a deceptive act that is likely to deceive a consumer acting reasonably under similar circumstances; (2) justifiable reliance; and (3) that the plaintiff's justifiable reliance caused ascertainable loss." *Slapikas v. First Am. Title Ins. Co.*, 298 F.R.D. 285, 292 (W.D. Pa. 2014). In *Prukala*, the court dismissed Christina's complaint because she failed to establish adequately that Hearst committed a "deceptive act" under UTPCPL.

B. TECHNOLOGY-BASED DISPUTES AND ATTORNEYS' UNCONSCIONABILITY ACTIONS UNDER UDTPAS AND DTPAS

Under the common law, a person may raise an unconscionability defense to prevent the enforcement of a contract. *Gaitan v. Mortg. Elec. Registration System,* 2009 WL 3244729, at *13 (C.D.Cal. 2009). A contract can be procedurally unconscionable. *See C & J Vantage Leasing Co. v. Wolfe,* 227 N.W.2d 65, 81 (Iowa 2011) ("Procedural unconscionability involves the advantaged party's exploitation of the disadvantaged party's unequal bargaining power, lack of understanding, and the use of convoluted language and fine print."). And the same contract can be substantively unconscionable. *See In re Marriage of Shanks,* 758 N.W.2d 506, 515 (Iowa 2008). *See also, Adler v. Fred Lind Manor,* 1103 P.3d 773, 781-82 (Wash. 2004) ("In some instances, individual contractual provisions may be so one-sided and harsh as to render them substantively unconscionable despite the fact that the circumstances surrounding the parties' agreement to the contract do not support a finding of procedural unconscionability.").

Additionally, the Uniform Commercial Code § 2-302(1) reads in pertinent part: "If the court ... finds [that a] contract or any clause [was] unconscionable at the time it was made, the court may refuse to enforce the contract, or it may enforce the remainder of the contract without the unconscionable clause, or it may so limit the application of any unconscionable clause as to avoid any unconscionable result."

Still, it must be stressed: Under the common law, the doctrine of unconscionability is an affirmative defense. It is not a theory of liability, cause of action, or theory of recovery. *Galvin v. First Nat. Monetary Corp.,* 624 F.Supp. 154, 158 (E.D.N.Y.1985). In addition, the UCC § 2-302(1) does not create an unconscionability cause of action. *See Best v. U.S. Nat. Bank of Oregon,* 714 P.2d 1049, 1056 (Or.Ct.App. 1986) (holding that the doctrine of unconscionability is not a basis for affirmative relief); and *Barnard v. Home Depot U.S.A., Inc.,* 2006 WL 3063430, at *3 n. 3 (W.D. Tex. 2006) (citing numerous cases for the proposition that neither the common law nor the Uniform Commercial Code allows affirmative relief for unconscionability).

On the other hand, consider the language in Florida Deceptive and Unfair Trade Practices Act § 501.204(1): "[U]nconscionable acts or practices ... in the conduct of any trade or commerce are ... unlawful." Similar language also appears in Nebraska Uniform Deceptive Trade Practices Act § 87-303.01(1)(2): "An unconscionable act or practice by a supplier in connection with a consumer transaction shall be a violation of [this Act]." And, Kansas Consumer Protection Act § 50-627(a)(b) states: "No supplier shall engage in any unconscionable act or practice, in connection with a consumer transaction."

Citing Florida's, Kansas's and Nebraska's deceptive trade practices statutes, may solo and small-firm practitioners commence an unconscionability cause of action—against sellers of law-practice technologies, internet service providers, website developers—and secure damages? The short answer is no. Generally, under DTPAs and UDTPAs, unconscionability is a defense. *See also*, David J. Federbush, *The Unclear Scope of Unconscionability in FDUTPA*, 74-AUG Fla. B.J. 49 (2000) ("The Florida Deceptive and Unfair Trade Practices Act ... does not define 'unconscionable' or provide standards for determining when a practice is unconscionable. ... FDUTPA's use of 'unconscionable'... poses a vagueness problem of constitutional dimension.").

There is, however, a major exception. Texas DTPA § 17.50(a)(3) allows a consumer to file a private unconscionability action and secure economic or mental anguish damages, if an unconscionable practice or act was the producing cause of the consumer's injury or loss. In this section, the cases and materials highlight the types of unconscionability claims that attorneys and other consumers in Texas have filed and may file against sellers of traditional- and virtual-office technologies and services.

NOTES AND QUESTIONS

1) Majority View—Procedural and Substantive Unconscionability Must Invalidate a Contract. Presently, a majority of state courts require litigants to prove both procedural and substantive unconscionability before invalidating allegedly unconscionable contracts. *See Roussalis v. Wyoming Med. Ctr., Inc.*, 4 P.3d 209, 246-47 (Wyo. 2000) (stressing that "most courts require a quantum of both [procedural and substantive unconscionability] and take a balancing approach in applying them"). Still, among the majority, significant divisions exist regarding whether "preponderance of evidence," "clear and convincing evidence," or "circumstantial evidence" is required to establish unconscionable conduct. *See Resource Management Co. v. Weston Ranch and Livestock Co.*, 706 P.2d 1028, 1043 (Utah 1985)(declaring that "a duly executed written contract should be overturned only by clear and convincing evidence"), *Gladding v. Langrall, Muir & Noppinger,* 401 A.2d 662, 665 (Md. 1979) (allowing circumstantial evidence to prove unconscionability), and *Worman v. FedEx Ground Package System Inc.,* 76 Pa. D. & C.4th 292, 300 (2005) (concluding that "plaintiff bears the burden of proving ... unconscionability, by a preponderance of the evidence.")

2) Minority View—Procedural or Substantive Unconscionability May Invalidate a Contract. State supreme courts are divided over whether procedural or substantive unconscionability may invalidate an assertedly unconscionable contract or clause. For example, Illinois and Missouri Supreme Courts have declared that a contract is unenforceable if it is procedurally *or* substantively unconscionable. *See Kinkel v. Cingular Wireless, LLC,* 857 N.E.2d 250, 263 (Ill. 2006) and *Brewer v. Missouri Title Loans, Inc.,* 323 S.W.3d 18, 22 (Mo. 2010). Conversely, Arizona, New York, Utah, and Washington Supreme Courts embrace a less liberal view: A contract is invalid and unenforceable, *only if* it is substantively unconscionable. *Maxwell v. Fidelity Financial Services, Inc.,* 907 P.2d 51, 59 (Ariz.1995)(declaring that "a claim of unconscionability can be established with a showing of substantive unconscionability alone, especially in cases involving either price-cost disparity or limitation of remedies."); *Gillman v. Chase Manhattan Bank, N.A.*, 534 N.E.2d 824, 829 (N.Y.1988) ("while determinations of unconscionability are ordinarily based on the court's conclusion that both the procedural and substantive components are present ... there have been exceptional cases where a provision of a contract is so outrageous as to warrant holding it unenforceable on the ground of substantive unconscionability alone"); *Resource Management Co. v. Weston Ranch & Livestock Co.*, 706 P.2d 1028, 1043 (Utah 1985) ("[G]ross disparity in terms—absent evidence of procedural unconscionability—can support a finding of unconscionability"); and, *Adler v. Fred Lind Manor,* 1103 P.3d 773, 781-82 (Wash. 2004) ("[We] hold that substantive unconscionability alone can support a finding of unconscionability.").

3) Texas Hybrid Unconscionability Doctrine. Under Texas law, the unconscionability doctrine is a two-prong test—containing elements of both substantive and procedural unconscionability. *See In re Palm Harbor Homes, Inc.*, 195 S.W.3d 672, 677 (Tex. 2006). However, it is less clear whether litigants must prove both procedural and substantive unconscionability before Texas courts will invalidate supposedly unconscionable contracts. *See In re Turner Brothers Trucking Co.*, 8 S.W.3d 370, 377 (Tex. Ct. App.-Texarkana 1999) (applying only a procedural unconscionability analysis and concluding that a contractual provision was unenforceable); *In re Halliburton Co.*, 80 S.W.3d 566, 572 (Tex. 2002) (declaring that Texas courts "may consider both procedural and substantive unconscionability" to evaluate the validity and enforceability of an arbitration provision); and *Shamrock Foods Co. v. Munn & Associates, Ltd.*, 392 S.W.3d 839, 847-848 (Tex. Ct. App.-Texarkana, 2013) (concluding that a successful unconscionability defense may be established by proving *only* substantive unconscionability).

---

1. Questionable Commercial Equipment Leases and Proving a "Grossly Unfair" Unconscionability Action Under Texas DTPA

Innovative Office Systems, Inc. v. Johnson

906 S.W.2d 940
(Tex. Ct. App.-Tyler 1995)

Holcomb, Justice. This is an appeal from a judgment that was entered in a Deceptive Trade Practices–Consumer Protection Act case. Jim Johnson d/b/a Electro Image (Johnson) sued Innovative Office Systems, Inc. (Innovative) to recover damages resulting from the lease of a color copier, computer equipment, and computer software.

Beginning in 1989, Johnson owned and operated Electro Image—a computer graphics business in Tyler. Electro Image is a service bureau that accommodates advertising agencies and corporate graphics departments that need high caliber artwork on printed materials, such as sales brochures.

Innovative sells and services office equipment. In January 1991, Innovative's Regional Sales Manager—Mike Dobbins ("Dobbins")—convinced Johnson to enter into a long-term lease for a new Canon color laser copier ("CLC–200"). Johnson used the Canon CLC–200 solely as a color copier. To produce high quality color graphics, Johnson created the original artwork in black and white, colored the black and white graphic by hand, and reproduced the original on the multi-color copier. Although Johnson considered this method undesirable, he was not aware that a more efficient, fully computerized color machine was available on the market.

In July 1991, the ceiling of Johnson's building fell on top of the CLC–200. Johnson contacted Innovative and began a series of conversations with Dobbins that resulted in Dobbins proposing that Johnson upgrade his equipment to an interfaced computerized color printing system. The system that Dobbins proposed included an upgraded copier, the Canon CLC–500 copier, an independent processing unit, a memory board, and a software package that was new on the market called SuperPrint. …

Johnson had reservations and concerns about the upgraded system, and Dobbins referred Johnson to Innovative President—Harry Farnham. Farnham had an "almost unlimited hardware capability" to determine the viability of any software that was new on the market. As part of his expertise, Farnham gave feedback to developers of software, such as Canon, on the effectiveness of any new software that entered the market.

To ensure that Innovative understood Johnson's expectations for the proposed new system, Johnson gave Dobbins a list of nine specifications of the factors that were important to Johnson if Johnson were to decide to upgrade his system. In turn, Dobbins gave all of Johnson's specifications to Farnham so that "[Farnham] would know exactly where we would be going with the software."

The nine specifications that Johnson considered important were:

1) The system had to be an integrated solution from one vendor;

2) The system had to operate on Windows 3.0;

3) The system had to enable the color laser copier as a scanner;

4) The system had to produce PostScript output;

5) The system must operate on Johnson's computer, an IBM PS/2 platform;

6) The system had to work with Johnson's large library

of PostScript Type I fonts;

7) The system must be suitable for a service bureau clientele and accept digital input from other IBM programs using industry standard formats;

8) The software solution must be upgradable should better hardware solution enter the market; and

9) The system had to be cost effective.

Johnson was satisfied with the performance of his CLC–200 copier; therefore, the upgrade to the CLC–500 was only attractive to him if there was a workable software solution to make his output less time consuming and more affordable. ... In reliance on the representations that the proposed system would, at a minimum, satisfy Johnson's nine basic specifications, Johnson signed a 65-month lease on the upgraded hardware.

In September 1991, Dobbins paid Johnson's expenses to attend a color laser copier software product fair and training seminar. At the software show, Johnson, Dobbins, and Farnham saw a demonstration of the software that would be compatible with Johnson's new system. The demonstration included two software packages, Colorbus and SuperPrint 3.0/Z–Script. Johnson testified that the demonstration was impressive and looked like everything Dobbins had told him it was going to be. ... That same day, Farnham and Dobbins introduced Johnson to Paul Peffer—a representative of Colorbus.

Peffer informed Johnson: The SuperPrint 3.0/Z–Script—that had been demonstrated—was not available at the show because the packaging and the instruction manual for the software had not been completed. Although the SuperPrint 3.0/Z–Script was not available, Peffer told Johnson that he could get the SuperPrint 2.0 software, which would produce a lower grade, but similar output as the SuperPrint 3.0/Z–Script. If Johnson agreed to order the 2.0 SuperPrint software, Peffer agreed to give Johnson a good price and agreed to ship the SuperPrint 3.0/Z–Script to Johnson "the minute that it was available" at no additional charge. Peffer represented to Johnson that the SuperPrint 3.0/Z–Script would be available in November of 1991.

At the conclusion of their discussion, Colorbus sold the software to Innovative, which then leased it to Johnson. The order form for the software was attached as a supplement to Innovative's original lease. The lease, as supplemented, attempted to obligate Johnson to make 65 monthly payments totaling $96,876 ... Johnson eventually assembled the system. ... But, the system never produced output at the level that had been demonstrated. At the software show demonstration, the proposed new process took only 12 minutes for the first copy. And thereafter, the machine would produce several copies per minute.

After spending "hundreds of hours—from October 1991 to January 1992— attempting to make the system work," Johnson finally "threw in the towel." Shortly thereafter, Johnson began having medical problems and was treated for an ulcer.

At trial, the court heard testimony from 13 witnesses and reviewed numerous exhibits. In entering a judgment in favor of Johnson, the court found that Innovative's conduct was unconscionable. As a result, the court awarded Johnson the following damages:

	Actual Damages
Lease Payments	$ 8,700.00
Expansion Costs	$ 8,434.00
Rent Differential	$ 10,615.00
Lost Profits	$ 96,586.00
Mental Anguish	$ 20,000.00
Pre-judgment Interest	$ 8,541.47
Attorney's Fees	$ 30,000.00
TOTAL	$ 182,876.47

	Statutory Damages
Mandatory Trebling	$ 2,000.00
Additional Damages	$ 100,000.00
TOTAL	$ 102,000.00

Scope and Standard of Review

On appeal, Innovative ... complains of the legal or factual sufficiency of the evidence to support the court's findings. In reviewing a legal sufficiency of the evidence challenge, we review only that evidence in the record which favors the challenged finding and any reasonable inferences that can be drawn therefrom. *Ben Fitzgerald Rlty. Co. v. Muller,* 846 S.W.2d 110, 119 (Tex.App.-Tyler 1993). Reviewing a challenge to the factual sufficiency of the evidence, we must consider all of the evidence in the record, and may set aside the finding and order a new trial only if the judgment is so against the great weight and preponderance of the evidence that the judgment is manifestly unjust. *Id.*

Regarding those findings for which Innovative had the burden of proof, the court must first examine the record for evidence and reasonable inferences that supports the trial court's failure to find, and ignore all evidence to the contrary. *Sterner v. Marathon Oil Co.,* 767 S.W.2d 686, 687 (Tex.1989). If there is no evidence to support the failure to find, the court may then examine the entire record to determine whether Innovative established the proposition as a matter of law. *Id.*

Sufficiency of the Evidence to Support the Trial Court's Findings on Liability

Innovative challenges the legal and factual sufficiency of the evidence to support the trial court's findings of liability. ... The evidence was sufficient to support the court's findings that Innovative's actions were unconscionable.

Under the DTPA—Tex.Bus. & Com. Code § 17.45 (Vernon 1987), "unconscionable action or course of action" is defined as an act or practice which, to a person's detriment:

> (A) Takes advantage of the lack of knowledge, ability, experience, or capacity of a person to a grossly unfair degree; or
>
> (B) Results in a gross disparity between the value received and consideration paid, in a transaction involving transfer of consideration.

To prove that Innovative's conduct was unconscionable, Johnson had to prove that the conduct resulted in unfairness that was "glaringly noticeable, flagrant, complete and unmitigated." *Kennemore v. Bennett,* 755 S.W.2d 89, 92 (Tex.1988). Unconscionability must be determined by examining the entire transaction, not merely the conduct prior to the execution of the lease. *Griffith v. Porter,* 817 S.W.2d 131, 136 (Tex.App.-Tyler 1991).

Innovative argues that Johnson wanted to be on the "cutting edge" of technology in the area of his specialty and that Innovative merely gave him the opportunity to take advantage of a new product on the market. Innovative further claims that it was just as misled as Johnson was by Colorbus's representations that the 3.0/Z–Script was coming on the market.

However, Dobbins and Farnham knew that Johnson needed a software program that was compatible with the upgraded hardware that Innovative had leased to Johnson. With this knowledge, Innovative sent written material to Johnson that contained numerous representations about the SuperPrint software that were misleading to Johnson.

Innovative knew that the SuperPrint 2.0 was significantly different from the SuperPrint 3.0/Z–Script. The box containing the SuperPrint 2.0 software specifically stated that the program provided "fast, beautiful/postscript-quality output." Farnham admitted that the representation on the software box was misleading. The box also represented that the SuperPrint 2.0 was compatible with Johnson's system, the IBM/PS–2 and Windows 3.0.

Evidence offered at trial revealed that the SuperPrint software had never been tested on an IBM/PS–2 computer. Johnson would not have leased the upgraded hardware had he not relied on Innovation's representations. The evidence was sufficient to support the court's findings that Innovative's actions were unconscionable. Point is overruled.

2. Questionable Commercial Equipment Leases and Proving a "Gross Disparity" Unconscionability Action Under Texas DTPA

Johnston v. McKinney American, Inc.

9 S.W.3d 271
(Tex. Ct. App.-Houston [14th Dist.] 1999)

Maurice E. Amidei, Justice. Dr. John P. Johnston and John P. Johnston, Inc. (Johnston) appeal from a money judgment entered against them in a suit by McKinney American, Inc. on an equipment lease. McKinney presented the following evidence at the bench trial. Mr. Jerome Epstein—president of McKinney—testified that no one from McKinney selected the computer equipment leased to Johnston. He stated: Ms. Judy Johnston—business manager for Johnston—told him that she met Teresa Rodriguez—chief officer for Amicus Computers—at a function and decided to employ Amicus to sell Johnston a computer and design a program for their business.

Amicus was not an agent, representative, partner, co-venturer, "or anything" with McKinney. Epstein stated that his company leased the computer equipment to Johnston, and that Johnston selected the equipment. He stated: He knew Johnston was going to use the equipment "generally" for financial transactions in his practice. McKinney assigned the lease to First City Bank after the first monthly rental payment by Johnston. An officer at the bank told Epstein that Johnston was paying slowly because "the computer program was not to their satisfaction." Johnston did not make the final payment of ten percent (10%) of the purchase price, or fair market value, which he had agreed to with McKinney in an addendum to the lease agreement. Johnston did not terminate the rental contract in writing as required by the lease agreement, nor did Johnston return the computer equipment to McKinney.

Judy Johnston—appellants' business manager—was the only witness for Johnston. In 1989, Ms. Johnston contacted Amicus Computers (Amicus)— a computer consulting firm—that advised her to lease "chiropractic specific" computer equipment and software from McKinney. Ms. Johnston completed a credit application with Amicus, and the lease agreement was later sent to Johnston by McKinney. McKinney bought the equipment from Amicus. The lease shows McKinney as the lessor of the equipment, Johnston as the lessee, and Amicus as the supplier of the equipment. The lease is dated May 11, 1989. And, in August 1991, Ms. Johnston noticed an increase in account receivables. Suspecting a computer problem, Ms. Johnston hired two computer consulting firms who advised her they could not diagnose the problem. Ms. Johnston called Mr. Epstein in August 1991, and Epstein told her that there was nothing he could do other than supply a lease on other equipment. In October 1991, Ms. Johnston contacted Amicus and was advised that the "problem was related to the print cue of the computer," and the computer "would hold no more than 100 claims." When the number of claims entered into the computer exceeded 100, the computer would lose them. In January 1992, Ms. Johnston bought new computer equipment and stored the Amicus equipment in her garage.

Over objection by McKinney, Ms. Johnston testified that they lost $33,376 in insurance claims as a result of the defective equipment. McKinney objected to her testimony about damages on the grounds that the disclaimer in the lease agreement exempted McKinney from any liability for defects in the computers and that Amicus was responsible for their problems. The objection was overruled by the trial court. Ms. Johnston also stated that she had paid a total of $24,171.30 in lease payments, and she continued making the payments after discovery of the defects because the bank owned the lease, and she felt obligated to the bank. Ms. Johnston called Mr.

Epstein to discuss a letter she received from him, indicating McKinney had not received a written termination notice and that the lease continued until terminated by written notice. Mr. Epstein told her: The lease provided for a payment of ten percent (10%) of the purchase price upon termination, or $1,714.00. She told Mr. Epstein she would not pay anything further and that he could pick up the equipment in her garage. ...

A. DTPA Unconscionability

The trial court entered a take nothing judgment against Johnston on his counterclaim. On appeal, Johnston contends: The trial court erred by failing to find that McKinney's conduct was unconscionable under the Deceptive Trade Practices Act (DTPA)—Tex. Bus. & Com. Code § 17.50(a)(3) (Vernon 1987). Specifically, Johnston contends: The trial court erred by failing to find that McKinney's conduct constituted an "unconscionable action or course of conduct" as defined by the DTPA. Alternatively, Johnston contends: The trial court erred by not entering any findings of fact on Johnston's DTPA claim of unconscionability.

1. Failure to File Findings and Conclusions

Johnston filed proposed amended findings and conclusions after the trial court entered its initial findings and conclusions. Johnston argues he cannot ascertain upon what facts and grounds the trial court based its judgment denying his DTPA gross-disparity unconscionability cause of action. The trial court did not rule on Johnston's amended findings and conclusions, and thereafter entered "corrected findings of fact and conclusions of law."

The court shall file any additional findings and conclusions *that are appropriate* within ten days after a request is filed. Tex. R. Civ. P. 298; *Tamez v. Tamez,* 822 S.W.2d 688, 692-93 (Tex.App.-Corpus Christi 1991). If the record shows that the complaining party did not suffer injury, the failure to make such additional findings does not require reversal. *Id.* Where refusal does not prevent the adequate presentation of the matter being complained of on appeal, no reversible error has occurred. *Id.* Appellant must show from the record that the trial court's refusal to file such findings and conclusions was reasonably calculated to cause and did so cause the rendition of an improper judgment. *Id.* If appellant requests findings directly contrary to, or inconsistent with, the original findings, the court need not make those requested findings. *Id.* Further, if the requested findings will not result in a different judgment, those findings need not be made. *Id.*

Johnston has not shown from the record how the trial court's refusal to file such findings and conclusions was reasonably calculated to cause and did cause the rendition of an improper judgment, nor have they shown they were prevented from adequately presenting their complaint on appeal. We find no evidence of injury to Johnston due to the trial court's refusing his request for additional findings and conclusions. *See Longoria v. Greyhound Lines, Inc.*, 699 S.W.2d 298, 305 (Tex.App.-San Antonio 1985). We overrule Johnston's contention that the trial court erred in not entering any findings on Johnston's DTPA claim of gross-disparity unconscionability.

2. Did McKinney's Conduct Constitute "Unconscionable Action or Course of Conduct" as Defined by the DTPA?

In issue one, Johnston challenges the legal and factual sufficiency of the evidence to support the trial court's implied nonfinding of McKinney's unconscionable action, and contend they have proved their DTPA gross-disparity unconscionability claim as a matter of law. Finding 11 was the only express finding of fact relating to appellants' gross-disparity unconscionability claim: "11. That Plaintiff made no representations of any nature to the Defendants relating to the computer equipment." The only conclusion of law concerning appellants' unconscionability claim was conclusion 5: "That the lease transaction between Plaintiff and Defendants was not unconscionable."

Johnston contends that section 17.45(5)(B) of the Texas Business and Commerce Code governs this case. That section provided the following at the time this suit was filed:

> "Unconscionable action or course of action" means an act or practice which, to a person's detriment ... (B) results in a gross disparity between the value received and consideration paid, in a transaction involving transfer of consideration.

Johnston argues that the only issue for the trier of fact was gross disparity. He claims: He established gross-disparity unconscionability as a matter of law. Therefore, the trial court erred by failing to find gross-disparity unconscionability as a matter of law. Johnston is attacking an adverse finding by the trial court on an issue for which he had the burden of proof. Because of this, he must "surmount two hurdles." *Sterner v. Marathon Oil Co.*, 767 S.W.2d 686, 690 (Tex.1989); *Taub v. City of Deer Park*, 912 S.W.2d 395, 397 (Tex.App.-Houston [14th Dist.] 1995) (*Sterner* applies to bench trials, such as this case and *Taub* wherein the fact-finders were the trial judges.). "First, the record must be examined for evidence that supports the [trial judge's] finding, while ignoring all evidence to the contrary." *Sterner,* 767 S.W.2d at 690. "Second, if there is no evidence to support the fact finder's answer, then, the entire record must be examined to see if the contrary proposition is established as a matter of law." *Id.*

Additionally, economic loss alone may support recovery. *Teague v. Bandy,* 793 S.W.2d 50, 54 (Tex.App.-Austin 1990). Where there is gross disparity between that delivered and that received, there is no requirement to show intent or a specific misrepresentation. *Id.* at 56–57. *See also Bekins Moving and Storage Co. v. Williams,* 947 S.W.2d 568, 580 (Tex.App.-Texarkana 1997); *Vick v. George,* 671 S.W.2d 541, 550 (Tex.App.-San Antonio 1983).

In *Teague,* 793 S.W.2d at 54, the court stated the rules that courts must follow when determining whether unconscionable actions result in gross disparity:

> The DTPA further provides that a consumer may maintain an action where any person's unconscionable action or course of action is a producing cause of the consumer's actual damages. Section 17.50(a)(3). An unconscionable action is one that, to the consumer's detriment, results in a gross disparity between the value the consumer received and the consideration paid in a transaction involving the transfer of consideration. *Chastain v. Koonce,* 700 S.W.2d 579, 583 (Tex.1985); section 17.45(5)(B). A consumer may maintain a DTPA cause of action for unconscionable conduct even if the seller made no specific misrepresentations. *Commercial Escrow Co. v. Rockport Rebel, Inc.,* 778 S.W.2d 532, 538 (Tex.App.–Corpus Christi 1989). Neither action requires a consumer to prove that the seller intended to deceive the consumer. *Chastain,* 700 S.W.2d at 583; *Smith v. Baldwin,* 611 S.W.2d 611, 616 (Tex.1980).

In the present case, Ms. Johnston testified: Johnston paid $24,171.30 to McKinney—in 45 monthly installments—as rent for the computer and software. She stated: "Not only did Johnston not get any benefit from it, but it cost $33,476.00 in lost income." She also testified that Johnston spent $2,000 for two computer experts to attempt to repair the equipment; they advised her they could not fix it. McKinney presented no evidence to refute this testimony. We find no evidence to support the trial court's implied finding: The lease transaction was not gross-disparity unconscionable. *Id.* We further find: There was no evidence to support the trial court's implied nonfinding of gross disparity between the value paid and received by Johnston.

We next determine if the contrary proposition was established as a matter of law. *Sterner,* 767 S.W.2d at 690. If the contrary proposition is established conclusively by the evidence, the point of error will be sustained. *Meyerland Community Improvement Ass'n. v. Temple,* 700 S.W.2d 263, 267 (Tex.App.-Houston [1st Dist.] 1985). Ms. Johnston proved that the equipment was effectively worthless and that it cost them $33,476 lost income and $2,000 for service calls—in addition to the $24,171.30 they paid in rent. No evidence was presented by McKinney to refute Ms. Johnston.

When the testimony of an interested witness is not contradicted by any other witness, or attendant circumstances, and the same is clear, direct and positive, and free from contradiction, in accuracies, and circumstances tending to cause suspicion thereon, it is taken as true as a matter of law. *Ragsdale v. Progressive Voters League,* 801 S.W.2d 880, 882 (Tex.1990). These are the tests that courts have traditionally applied to an interested witness's testimony—whether in summary judgment proceedings or in jury or nonjury trials—involving the question of whether a fact is established or negated as a matter of law. *Id.*

Accordingly, we find: Johnston has established gross-disparity unconscionability as a matter of law. And the contention—that the trial court erred in making an implied nonfinding of gross disparity—is sustained.

C. Technology-Based Disputes and Breach-of-Warranty Actions Under the Uniform Commercial Code and Deceptive Trade Practices Acts

Do Computer Purchasers Need Lemon Aid?

4 N.C. J. L. & Tech. 307

Rebecca Crandall

By 1993, all fifty states and the District of Columbia had passed lemon laws for cars. State legislatures passed these laws partially in response to considerable litigation over warranty disputes. Ten years later, the question of lemon aid resurfaces as at least three state legislatures consider whether computer purchasers, like car buyers, need protection.

Each year, millions of people purchase computers, and many of these consumers have difficulties with their new machines. ... In a January 2001 survey, *PC World* found that almost one out of eleven respondents bought computers that did not work upon first use. Of the 13.6 million desktop PCs sold in 2002, *Consumer Reports* found that about 1.9 million of them had serious problems within the first month of ownership; an estimated 544,000 of them were inoperable when buyers started the machines; and approximately 150,000 were lemons. This means that almost fifteen percent of computer purchasers in 1999 had to return and/or repair a new computer.

Because computers have become such a common part of daily life, federal and state legislatures should safeguard consumers by providing "lemon aid" for computer purchasers. Until statutory protections are in place to protect consumers from lemon computers, consumers can take steps to help protect themselves from computer manufacturers.

More generally, what can solo and small-firm attorneys do to protect their businesses from all types of defective office products as well as against ancillary services, until state and federal legislators enact a "uniform law"?

Under Article 2 of the Uniform Commercial Code. (UCC), practitioners may commence and secure various remedies under several theories of recovery. More specifically, if small law firms purchase allegedly defective computers, tablets, printers, smartphones or other electronic office products from vendors, those firms may file several breach-of-warranty claims under the UCC.

This section discusses the dispositions of cases in which consumers filed a breach of an express warranty action under UCC § 2-313, a breach of an implied warranty of merchantability action under UCC § 2-314, and a breach of an implied warranty of fitness action under UCC § 2-315. As you read findings, analyses and conclusions in the courts' opinions, consider two questions: Does the UCC provide enough protection for attorneys and other consumers who purchase allegedly defective office hardware? Does the UCC allow solo practitioners and other consumers to secure statutory remedies easily, efficiently and timely? May solo and small firm practitioners commence breach of warranties actions under a Deceptive Trade Practices Act or a Uniform Deceptive Trade Practice Act?

1. Defective Law Office Products and Proving a UCC § 2-313 Action—Breach of an Express Warranty

Visual Communications, Inc. v. Konica Minolta Business Solutions U.S.A., Inc.

611 F.Supp.2d 465
(E.D. Pa. 2009)

Anita B. Brody, District Judge.

This case arises from two broken color copiers. The defendant—Konica Minolta Business Solutions U.S.A., Inc., (Konica or KMBSUS)—manufactured the copiers and sold them to IKON Office Solutions, Inc. (IKON). The plaintiff—Visual Communications, Inc., (Visual)—leased the copiers from IKON and began using them. However, the copiers malfunctioned so often that Visual rented other copiers to replace them. Visual then sued Konica for breach of an express warranty ... under the Pennsylvania Uniform Commercial Code, 13 Pa. Cons. Stat. Ann. §§ 1101–9710. Jurisdiction exists under 28 U.S.C. § 1332. Before me now is Konica's motion for summary judgment under Federal Rule of Civil Procedure 56.

I. Background

In 2003, Konica and IKON entered into a contract in which Konica agreed to sell copiers to IKON for resale or lease to IKON's customers (Distribution Agreement). The contract contains the following provision:

> KMBSUS warrants that Product(s) and parts thereof delivered hereunder will meet the applicable Specifications for such Product(s) and shall be free from defects in material and workmanship for a period of one hundred eighty (180) days from the date IKON receives the Product(s). If, during such one hundred eighty (180) day period, KMBSUS is notified of any defect in the Product, then KMBSUS shall, within thirty (30) days of notification thereof and at KMBSUS's option, either repair, replace or credit IKON for such Product or component thereof.

The contract also provides that "IKON may pass through and assign any and all warranties, representations and indemnities provided by Konica hereunder to its customers for their benefit."

Visual designs and builds exhibits for trade shows, and makes presentations to prospective customers. In June 2005 and May 2006, Konica sold two color copiers to IKON pursuant to the Distribution Agreement. The copier sold in 2005 was the BP 500C, and the one sold in 2006 was the CPP 500. After each purchase, IKON leased the copier to Visual for a five-year term. Both lease agreements between Visual and IKON contain the following provision:

> We transfer to you without recourse, for the term of this Agreement, any written warranties made by the manufacturer with respect to the Equipment. Since we are a finance company and neither the manufacturer nor the distributor of the Equipment, **WE MAKE NO WARRANTIES, EXPRESS, OR IMPLIED, INCLUDING WARRANTIES OF MERCHANTABILITY OR FITNESS FOR USE OR FOR A PARTICULAR PURPOSE.** You acknowledge that you have selected the Equipment you are renting from us based on your own judgment and you hereby affirmatively disclaim reliance on any oral representations concerning the Equipment made to you.

In Konica's product literature, the BP 500C and CPP 300 copiers are called the Bizhub PRO C500 model. IKON's proposal to Visual dated June 16, 2005, states that this model "will handle up to 150,000 impressions per month." A print-out of Konica's website dated March 14, 2008, also indicates that this model has a "150,000-page monthly duty cycle."

Visual used the copiers immediately and found them unreliable from the start. Although Visual made on average fewer than five (5) thousand copies per month on one copier and fewer than fourteen (14) thousand copies per month on the other one, both copiers often jammed or made poor copies. Visual was forced to request service from IKON at least twice each month from January to August 2007. But servicing the copiers provided only temporary relief. Ultimately, Visual had to replace them. In September 2007, Visual leased two new copiers from Oce North America and tendered the old copiers to IKON for repossession.

On October 15, 2007, Visual sent an email to IKON alleging breach of warranty based on the copiers' malfunctioning. Visual also mailed a letter to Konica dated January 25, 2008, that contained the same allegations and included a draft complaint. This letter was the first notice that Visual gave Konica about any problem with the copiers. ...

Express Warranty

Visual claims that the copiers' malfunctioning breached an express warranty that each copier could produce 150 thousand copies per month. According to the UCC, "[a]ny description of the goods which is made part of the basis of the bargain creates an express warranty that the goods shall conform to the description." 13 Pa. Cons. Stat. Ann. § 2313(a)(2).

Visual offers two pieces of evidence to prove the alleged express warranty: (1) a print-out from Konica's website, and (2) a written proposal from IKON. Although both pieces of evidence contain an assurance that the Bizhub PRO C500 can produce 150 thousand copies per month, neither can prove the alleged warranty.

First, nothing in the record shows what Konica's website contained in 2005 and 2006 when Visual decided to rent the copiers. Instead, the offered printout is dated March 14, 2008. Because a statement in 2008 cannot have been a basis for bargains reached in 2005 and 2006, this evidence cannot prove the alleged warranty. Second, any express warranty created by IKON's proposal cannot be enforced against Konica—because this statement was made by IKON and not Konica.

Because Visual offers insufficient evidence to prove the alleged express warranty, I grant summary judgment as to the claim of breach of an express warranty.

NOTES AND QUESTIONS

1) Proof of an Express Warranty under the UCC § 2-313. With the exception of a few, most states have adopted section 2-313 of the UCC verbatim. Tex. Bus. & Com. Code § 2-313(a) states that a seller creates express warranties by:

> (1) Any affirmation of fact or promise made by the seller to the buyer which relates to the goods and becomes part of the *basis of the bargain* creates an express warranty that the goods shall conform to the affirmation or promise.
>
> (2) Any description of the goods which is made part of the *basis of the bargain* creates an express warranty that the goods shall conform to the description.
>
> (3) Any sample or model which is made part of the *basis of the bargain* creates an express warranty that the whole of the goods shall conform to the sample or model.

2) Privity of Contract and Standing to Sue Under Article 2 of the UCC. In *Visual Communications, Inc. v. Konica Minolta Business Solutions*, the court declared: "Any express warranty created by IKON's proposal cannot be enforced against Konica—because this statement was made by IKON and not Konica." Is this a general rule or an exception? *Compare*

Garcia v. Texas Instruments, Inc., 610 S.W.2d 456, 465 (Tex.1980) ("[P]rivity of contract is not a requirement for a Uniform Commercial Code implied warranty action involving personal injury.") and *Farm Bureau Mut. v. Combustion Research Corp.,* 715 662 N.W.2d 439, 443 (Mich. Ct. App. 2003) (finding that the lack of any contract between the injured party and seller did not remove the dispute from the confines of the UCC because privity of contract is not required), *with Williams v. Fulmer,* 695 S.W.2d 411, 413-14 (Ky. 1985) ("A claim of breach of warranty under Kentucky's Uniform Commercial Code ... is only viable when privity of contract exists between the commercial seller and the injured party or if the injured party is one of the persons described in KRS 355.2–318.5"); and *Rothe v. Maloney Cadillac, Inc.*, 518 N.E.2d 1028, 1029 (Ill.1988) (reiterating that under Illinois Uniform Commercial Code, privity of contract is typically a prerequisite to recover damages for breach of implied warranty).

3. Breach of Express Warranty Actions and Competing Standards of Proof. In Texas, a plaintiff must prove six elements to establish a breach of express warranty action: (1) the defendant sold services to the plaintiff; (2) the defendant made a representation to the plaintiff about the characteristics of the services by affirmation of fact, by promise, or by description; (3) the representation became part of the basis of the bargain; (4) the defendant breached the warranty; (5) the plaintiff notified the defendant of the breach; and 6) the plaintiff suffered injury. *Paragon General Contractors, Inc. v. Larco Const., Inc.*, 227 S.W.3d 876, 886 (Tex. App. Ct.—Dallas 2007), citing *Sw. Bell Tel. Co. v. FDP Corp.*, 811 S.W.2d 572, 576–77 & n. 3 (Tex. 1991) (embracing some UCC elements). Contrarily, Minnesota requires a complainant to establish three elements: (1) the existence of a warranty; (2) a breach of the warranty; and (3) a causal link between the breach and the harm. *Peterson v. Bendix Home Sys., Inc.*, 318 N.W.2d 50, 52–53 (Minn.1982). And under New Jersey law, a breach of an express warranty action has four elements: (1) proof a contract between the parties; (2) proof of a breach of contract; (3) proof of damages flowing from the breach; and (4) proof that complainant performed her contractual obligations. *Hemy v. Perdue Farms, Inc.*, 2011 WL 6002463, *23 (D.N.J. Nov. 30, 2011).

2. Defective Law Office Products and Establishing UCC § 2-314 and UCC § 2-315 Actions—Breach of Implied Warranty of Merchantability and Implied Warranty of Fitness for a Particular Purpose

David Nutt & Associates, P.C. v. First Continental Leasing Corporation

599 So.2d 576
(Miss. 1992)

McRae, Justice.

The transaction at issue is a classic three-party lease arrangement wherein the lessor purchased equipment specifically requested and selected by the lessee from a vendor/supplier and, in turn, entered into a lease agreement with the lessee. Attorney David Nutt—the lessee—had previously leased a computer system for his law offices from the lessor, First Continental Leasing Corporation in Hattiesburg. Seeking to upgrade the system, he wrote to First Continental on November 17, 1987—requesting financing for a new system and negotiation of a settlement of the existing lease. Nutt's correspondence indicates that he had selected both the equipment package and the vendor/supplier prior to contacting First Continental.

Following Nutt's instructions, First Continental purchased an IBM-AT Compatible/OS-2 Computer System from its designated vendor/supplier—Corporate Systems, Inc. On December 14, 1987, First Continental and Nutt entered into a lease agreement whereby Nutt would lease the IBM system purchased by the lessor for a four-year term—consisting of forty-eight payments at $665.65 per month.

The lease explicitly stated that the lessor makes no express or implied warranties; that any claims arising from problems with the equipment shall be made against the vendor/supplier; that notwithstanding any claims against the vendor/supplier, the lessee shall continue to make payments to the lessor; and that the lessor assigns to the lessee all rights it has against the vendor/supplier. It further provided that the lessee had no option to purchase the equipment or otherwise acquire title or ownership to it. The lessee was required to insure the equipment and keep it in good repair, and assumed the entire risk of loss or damage to the equipment.

The new system was apparently incompatible with the demands of Nutt's law practice. Accordingly, after seventeen months, Nutt ceased making payments to the lessor. On September 7, 1989, First Continental filed a complaint against Nutt—asserting that Nutt's failure to pay was a breach of the lease agreement. In his Answer, Nutt asserted—as an affirmative defense—that the lease was the functional equivalent of a sale and thus governed by Article 2 of the Uniform Commercial Code, codified at Miss. Code Ann. § 75-2-101, *et seq*.

Further, he counterclaimed that First Continental had breached the implied warranties of merchantability and fitness outlined in Miss. Code Ann. § 75-2-314 and § 75-2-315. On January 30, 1990, First Continental filed a motion for summary judgment. Following a hearing on the motion for summary judgment, the circuit court entered an order against Nutt in the amount of $25,236.18 on May 24, 1990. The judgment was amended on June 10, 1990—assessing Nutt further with post-judgment interest and the costs of litigation.

II.

Article 2 of the Uniform Commercial Code—codified at Miss. Code Ann. §§ 75-2-101 *et seq.*—includes provisions for implied warranties in contracts for the sale of goods. UCC § 75-2-314(1) provides for an implied warranty of merchantability. And, UCC § 75-2-315 outlined the implied warranty of fitness for a particular purpose. Nutt asserts: Looking at "the totality of the circumstances" surrounding his transaction with First Continental, the equipment lease was the "functional equivalent of a sale." Therefore, he contends: The Circuit Court erred in granting First Continental's motion for summary judgment—because there was a genuine issue of material fact regarding the nature of the transaction.

However, we have held: Article 2 warranties are not applicable in three-party lease transactions where the lessor is merely the financing arm of the transaction—separate and distinct from the seller, vendor or supplier of the equipment covered by the lease. *Capital Associates, Inc. v. Sally Southland, Inc.* 529 So.2d 640, 645 (Miss.1988). Our inquiry [must focus] on whether the lessor functionally occupied the role of a seller in the transaction. Scrutinizing the plain language of the statutes, we find that § 75-2-314 provides that: A warranty that the goods shall be merchantable is implied in a contract for their sale if the seller is a merchant with respect to goods of that kind. Further, UCC § 75-2-104 defines "merchant" as:

> "a person who deals in goods of the kind or otherwise by his occupation holds himself out to as having knowledge or skill peculiar to the practice or goods involved in the transaction or to whom such knowledge or skill may be attributed by his employment of an agent or broker or other intermediary who by his occupation holds himself out as having such knowledge or skill."

There is no evidence in the record to suggest that First Continental held itself out as having knowledge or skill in any area other than leasing and financing. … [T]he evidence in the record indicates: First Continental was also a financing lessor—assuming a role analogous to that of a lending bank with a perfected security interest in a customer's home or office computer.

Looking next at the implied warranty of fitness for a particular purpose, UCC § 75-2-315 provides:

> "Where the seller *at the time of contracting* has reason to know any particular purpose for which the goods are required and that the buyer is *relying* on the seller's skill or judgment to select or furnish suitable goods, there is an implied warranty that the goods shall be fit for such purpose."

By way of Nutt's November 17, 1987, letter and through his prior dealings with the lessor, it is apparent: First Continental knew at the time of the lease agreement that the computer system was intended for use in Nutt's law practice. However, there is no evidence whatsoever that Nutt relied on First Continental to select either the computer system or the vendor of its components. The selection of the system and its vendor/supplier—Corporate Systems, Inc.—clearly was Nutt's choice.

Thus, as a matter of law, the Article 2 implied warranties are not applicable. … Accordingly, we limit our holding to those three-party lease transactions where the evidence clearly shows that the lessor is an independent financing lessor, not the functional equivalent of a seller or an agent thereof …

IV.

Reiterating that the question of whether a lease is the functional equivalent of a sale is applicable only to two-party lease transactions and finding as a matter of law that the implied warranty provisions do not apply to an independent financing lessor, we affirm the decision of the circuit court and tax the appellant with the costs of this appeal.

NOTES AND QUESTIONS

1) UCC § 2-314—Implied Warranty of Merchantability; Usage of Trade:

(1) Unless excluded or modified (Section 2-316), a warranty that the goods shall be merchantable is implied in a contract for their sale if the seller is a merchant with respect to goods of that kind. Under this section the serving for value of food or drink to be consumed either on the premises or elsewhere is a sale.

(2) Goods to be merchantable must be at least such as

(a) pass without objection in the trade under the contract description; *and*

(b) in the case of fungible goods, are of fair average quality within the description; *and*

(c) are fit for the ordinary purposes for which such goods are used; *and*

(d) run, within the variations permitted by the agreement, of even kind, quality and quantity within each unit and among all units involved; *and*

(e) are adequately contained, packaged, and labeled as the agreement may require; *and*

(f) conform to the promise or affirmations of fact made on the container or label if any.

2) Competing Standards for Establishing a Breach of an Implied Warranty of Merchantability Action. In *Para-Chem Southern, Inc. v. Sandstone Products, Inc.*, 2009 WL 276507, *14 (Tex. App.-Houston [1st Dist.] 2009), the Texas Appellate Court in Houston stated that a plaintiff who files a breach of implied warranty of merchantability action must prove that (1) a product was defective for its purpose; (2) the alleged defect existed when the product left the defendant's possession; and (3) the alleged defect proximately caused the injuries and damages. In contrast, in North Carolina, a plaintiff must prove the following elements: (1) an implied warranty of merchantability attached to the sale and purchase of certain goods; (2) the goods were defective at the time of sale; (3) the defective goods caused the buyers injury and loss; and (4) damages were suffered as a result. *DeWitt v. Eveready Battery Co., Inc.*, 565 S.E.2d 140, 147 (N.C. 2002). And to prevail in a breach of warranty of merchantability action in Delaware, a plaintiff must prove: "(1) that a merchant sold the goods; (2) which were defective at the time of sale; (3) causing injury to the ultimate consumer; (4) the proximate cause of which was the defective nature of the goods; and (5) that the seller received notice of the injury." *Reybold Group, Inc. v. Chemprobe Tech., Inc.,* 721 A.2d 1267, 1269 (Del. 1998).

3) UCC Implied Warranty of Fitness for a Particular Purpose, Ill. Rev. Stat. 1985, ch. 26, § 2-315:

> Where the seller at the time of contracting has reason to know any particular purpose for which the goods are required and that the buyer is relying on the seller's skill or judgment to select or furnish suitable goods, there is unless excluded or modified under the next section an implied warranty that the goods shall be fit for such purpose.

4) Competing Standards for Establishing a Breach of an Implied Warranty of Fitness for a Particular Purpose. In *Divis v. Clarklift of Nebraska, Inc.*, 590 N.W.2d 696, 702 (Neb. 1999), the court outlined a "global" rule which requires a plaintiff to prove: (1) defendant made a warranty—express or implied—under §§ 2-313, 2-314, or 2-315; (2) goods did not comply with the warranty, i.e., the goods were defective at the time of the sale; (3) defective goods were the cause in fact and proximate cause of plaintiff's injury; and (4) damages. On the other hand, in *Norcold, Inc. v. Gateway Supply Co.*, 798 N.E.2d 618, 625–26 (Ohio Ct. App. 2003), the court required the plaintiff to prove: (1) the seller knew the buyer's particular purpose, (2) the seller had reason to know that the buyer was relying on the seller's skill or judgment to furnish or select the appropriate goods, and (3) the buyer relied upon the seller's skill or judgment.

---

3. Defective Law Office Products and Breach of Warranty Actions Under Uniform Deceptive Trade Practices Acts

Medeiros v. Lenovo

2016 WL 500503
(D. Mass. 2016)

Sorokin, J.

In this consumer goods case, Plaintiff Orlando Medeiros (Medeiros) sues on behalf of himself and a putative class against Lenovo of the United States, Inc. (Lenovo)—in connection with Lenovo's Yoga 2 Pro Laptop ("Yoga 2" or "laptop").

I. Facts Alleged

On or around October 16, 2013, Medeiros purchased a Yoga 2 through Lenovo's website. Lenovo advertised on its website that the battery life for the Yoga 2 was "Up to 9 Hours' Battery Life on a Single Charge." Medeiros alleges that "almost immediately" after he purchased the Yoga 2, he noticed that the battery life "did not come close to the advertised nine hours." He alleges further that he placed the laptop in "Power Saving" battery mode. But the laptop "continued to fall significantly short of the battery life Lenovo represented—typically lasting only four or five, or at most, six hours." ... Medeiros also quotes three customers who claimed on an online forum that they each obtained only about four hours of battery life.

Medeiros alleges that "numerous variables" contribute to battery life. These variables include ... the battery's energy storage capacity, the laptop's energy requirements, and the different configurations on a laptop, screen size, brightness settings, storage, and temperature. According to Medeiros, given these variables and the importance of battery life, "consumers generally rely upon manufacturer's representations concerning battery life in making purchasing decisions." Medeiros "brings this action on behalf of himself and all others who were damaged when they purchased a Yoga Pro 2—based on Lenovo's false and misleading representations as to the battery life." ...

According to Medeiros, prior to October 2014, there were "Terms and Conditions to which purchasers were required to agree before purchasing a laptop through Lenovo's website." Medeiros alleges, and Lenovo agrees, that the Terms and Conditions include a choice of law provision providing that North Carolina law applies to the contractual basis of the relationship.

The Terms and Conditions also provide that "Lenovo hardware Products are warranted under the Lenovo Limited Warranty accompanying each Lenovo hardware Product." That Limited Warranty, in relevant part, provides:

> WHAT THIS WARRANTY COVERS—Lenovo warrants that each Lenovo hardware product that you purchase is free from defects in materials and workmanship under normal use during the warranty period. The warranty period for the product starts on the original date of purchase as shown on your sales receipt or invoice or as may be otherwise specified by Lenovo. The warranty period and type of warranty service that apply to your product are as specified in "Part 3—Warranty Service Information" below. This warranty only applies to products in the country or region of purchase.

There is no allegation in the Complaint specifying the defect in materials or workmanship. There is no allegation attributing the less than promised battery life to anything. Medeiros alleges only that he was unable to attain nine hours of battery life.

* * *

The warranty then explains what a consumer can expect from Lenovo if a warranty claim is made:

> WHAT YOUR SERVICE PROVIDER WILL DO TO CORRECT PROBLEMS—When you contact a Service Provider, you must follow the specified problem determination and resolution procedures. The

> Service Provider will attempt to diagnose and resolve your problem by telephone, e-mail or remote assistance. The Service Provider may direct you to download and install designated software updates. Some problems may be resolved with a replacement part that you install yourself called a "Customer Replaceable Unit" or "CRU." If so, the Service Provider will ship the CRU to you for you to install.
>
> If your problem cannot be resolved over the telephone; through the application of software updates or the installation of a CRU, the Service Provider will arrange for service under the type of warranty service designated for the product under "Part 3—Warranty Service Information" below. If the Service Provider determines that it is unable to repair your product, the Service Provider will replace it with one that is at least functionally equivalent. If the Service Provider determines that it is unable to either repair or replace your product, your sole remedy under this Limited Warranty is to return the product to your place of purchase or to Lenovo for a refund of your purchase price.

There are no [evidence] in the Complaint [establishing that] Medeiros [tried] to obtain satisfaction under the warranty or that he sought to return his Yoga 2. Further, Medeiros does not allege that the remedies provided in Lenovo's written warranty fail of their essential purpose, or are otherwise unconscionable.

II. Discussion

A. Standard of Review

To survive a motion to dismiss under Rule 12(b)(6) of the Federal Rules of Civil Procedure, a complaint must contain sufficient factual matter, accepted as true, to "state a claim to relief that is plausible on its face." *Ashcroft v. Iqbal*, 556 U.S. 662, 678 (2009). The court "must take the allegations in the complaint as true and must make all reasonable inferences in favor of the plaintiff." *Watterson v. Page,* 987 F.2d 1, 3 (1st Cir.1993). "[F]actual allegations" must be separated from "conclusory statements in order to analyze whether the former, if taken as true, set forth a plausible, not merely a conceivable, case for relief." *Juarez v. Select Portfolio Servicing, Inc.*, 708 F.3d 269, 276 (1st Cir. 2013). This "highly deferential" standard of review "does not mean, however, that a court must (or should) accept every allegation made by the complainant, no matter how conclusory or generalized." *United States v. AVX Corp.*, 962 F.2d 108, 115 (1st Cir. 1992).

Dismissal for failure to state a claim is appropriate when the pleadings fail to set forth "factual allegations, either direct or inferential, respecting each material element necessary to sustain recovery under some actionable legal theory." *Berner v. Delahanty*, 129 F.3d 20, 25 (1st Cir.1997). "A district court must retain the power to insist upon some specificity in pleading before allowing a potentially massive factual controversy to proceed." *Assoc. Gen. Contractors of Cal., Inc. v. Cal. State Council of Carpenters*, 459 U.S. 519, 528 n.17 (1983). If a plaintiff has not sufficiently pled facts entitling him to relief, "this basic deficiency should ... be exposed at the point of minimum expenditure of time and money by the parties and the court."

* * *

C. The Complaint Fails to State a Claim Under North Carolina

Uniform Deceptive Trade Practices Act—Count I

To state a claim under North Carolina Uniform Deceptive Trade Practices Act (NC-UDTPA), plaintiff must show: (1) an unfair or deceptive act or practice; (2) in or affecting commerce, and; (3) which proximately caused actual injury to the plaintiff or to his business. *Dalton v. Camp*, 548 S.E.2d 704, 711 (N.C. 2001). In support of his NC-UDTPA claim, Medeiros alleges: Lenovo advertised that the battery life—for the Yoga 2—was "Up to 9 Hours' Battery Life on a Single Charge." But he insists that these representations "were false and unsubstantiated when made."

Lenovo moves to dismiss Count I on three grounds: (1) the alleged injury did not occur in North Carolina; (2) NC-UDTPA does not apply, because the crux of the dispute is contractual; and (3) the statement of "Up to 9 hours" is not actionable, as it would not deceive a reasonable consumer.

i. Place of Injury

Lenovo argues that in order to state a claim under NC-UDTPA, a plaintiff must allege that the injury occurred in North Carolina. The case of *Hometown Publ'g v. Kidsville News! Inc.*, 2014 U.S. Dist. LEXIS 179106, *15 (E.D.N.C. Oct. 3, 2014) provides an extensive historical explanation of the relevant case law and is on point. *Hometown* held: If "an in-state defendant's in-state conduct" injured a plaintiff, the complainant may bring a NC-UDTPA claim—although the injury *did not* occur in North Carolina. Lenovo is a North Carolina company and allegedly committed unfair and deceptive acts emanating from North Carolina. Under North Carolina law, the fact that the injury was allegedly sustained in Massachusetts does not prevent the claim from proceeding against Lenovo in Massachusetts.

ii. Count I Does Not State a NC-UDTPA Claim

In this case, the issue is whether a NC-UDTPA claim can withstand a motion to dismiss where: (1) the claim arises out of a breach of a consumer warranty based upon an alleged deceptive statement as to the product's performance; (2) the damage alleged is to the product itself; (3) the written warranty allocates the risk of loss; and (4) the written warranty is not alleged to be unconscionable or that it has failed of its essential purpose. Medeiros has not cited any factually analogous cases to support his claim: Under these circumstances, a NC-UDTPA claim can survive. Instead, he seeks to rely on general principles underlying his claim. Looking, however, to factually analogous cases, it is clear: General principles will not suffice, and courts have readily dismissed similarly pled complaints for the following reasons.

First, it is well settled in North Carolina: A mere breach of contract or breach of warranty does not, standing alone, constitute an unfair or deceptive trade practice. *See Ellis v. Louisiana–Pacific Corp.*, 699 F.3d 778, 784 (4th Cir.2012), and *Broussard v. Meineke Disc. Muffler Shops, Inc.* 155 F.3d 331, 346 (4th Cir.1998) (holding that it was reversible error to allow a UDTPA claim to go forward where claim was essentially just a breach of contract claim).

* * *

The requirement that substantial aggravating factors must be alleged is applicable to UDTPA claims arising out of a breach of warranty. ... *See also Yancey v. Remington Arms Co., LLC,* 2013 U.S. Dist. LEXIS 140397 (M.D.N.C. Sept. 30, 2013) (dismissing a NC-UDTPA claim where gun manufacturers allegedly warranted the safety of gun), and *Kelly v. Georgia-Pacific LLC,* 671 F.Supp.2d 785, 799 (E.D. N.C. 2009) (refusing to find an actionable NC-UDTPA warranty claim because plaintiffs could not prove substantial aggravating circumstances).

The requirement that a plaintiff allege substantial aggravating circumstances in a breach of warranty case is not easily overcome.

… Here, Medeiros alleges only that Lenovo warranted the battery life up to nine hours—although knowing that the battery life was substantially less than nine hours. Even assuming that Lenovo knew the battery life was not nine hours, the claim is still "indistinguishable from a run-of-the-mill breach of warranty claim." This is merely another way of alleging that Lenovo did not fulfill its promise to provide a laptop with a battery that would last up to nine hours. Medeiros's allegations do not state a plausible claim under NC-UDTPA …

For the reasons stated, Lenovo's motion to dismiss is allowed. Plaintiff's motion to amend the complaint is denied as moot. So Ordered.

4. Defective Law Office Products and Breach of Warranty Actions Under Texas Deceptive Trade Practices Acts

Henry Schein, Inc. v. Stromboe

102 S.W.3d 675
(Tex. 2003)

Justice Hecht delivered the opinion of the court.

Under Rule 42(b)(4) of the Texas Rules of Civil Procedure, the district court certified a nationwide class of some 20,000 purchasers of three dental practice management software products. There are members of this class in all fifty states. The five named plaintiffs and their counsel allege that the software was defective and was sold under false pretenses on which buyers relied. Some of their causes of action [are] breach of express and implied warranties and violations of the Texas Deceptive Trade Practices—Consumer Protection Act. Tex. Bus. & Com. Code §§ 17.41–.63.

I.

Henry Schein, Inc. and two subsidiaries—Easy Dental Systems, Inc. and Dentisoft, Inc. ("Schein")—produced and marketed three office management software applications for dental practices: "DOS-based "Easy Dental," "Easy Dental for Windows" and "Windows Easy Dental Lite." Shelly E. Stromboe, D.D.S. purchased the Windows software. Jeanne N. Taylor, D.D.S. purchased the DOS software. Stromboe and Taylor sued Schein on behalf of themselves and a class of all purchasers of the software in the nation. Stromboe and Taylor have filed separate petitions in the trial court.

Stromboe's petition alleges that in the process of opening her own dental office, she contacted Schein for advice about what management software program would be best for her. "In reliance on Schein's recommendation," Stromboe alleges: She selected "Easy Dental Lite." When she tried to use the software, she found that the program had numerous defects:

(a) inability to add a new insurance carrier;
(b) inability to properly print a fee list;
(c) inability to delete accounts;
(d) inability to activate or inactivate a patient's account;
(e) continual operating errors;
(f) inability to completely delete an appointment or replace an appointment with another patient's appointment;
(h) inability to add emergency information on a new patient;
(i) inability to properly credit accounts on the accounting software;
(j) inadequate space to fill in a treatment plan;
(k) electronic-claims processing problems;
(l) producing error messages on the computer;
(m) inability to save patients' notes;
(n) multiple inconveniences;
(o) inability to properly age accounts receivable; and
(p) a total lack of multi-tasking capabilities.

Stromboe contends that she complained to Schein—who admitted that the software was defective. But Schein also "steered" her to its more expensive product—"Easy Dental for Windows"—which she purchased. Stromboe alleges: She was required to have all of her data converted for the new program. In doing so, she lost time, records and production. Easy Dental for Windows also had bugs and defects which corrupted Plaintiff's data and made the system inoperable.

Stromboe's petition asserts the following causes of action:

a) breach of express warranties: "Defendants represented to Plaintiff Stromboe that its practice management software systems and products would satisfy Plaintiff's computer system and software needs to effectively manage and run a dental practice";

b) breach of an implied warranties merchantability—specifically—under Tex. Bus. & Com. Code § 2.314 (Texas UCC);

c) breaching express and implied warranties under DTPA § 17.50(a)(2);

d) violating DTPA §17.50(a)(1) and DTPA §17.46(b)—specifically—by:

(2) causing confusion or misunderstanding as to the source, sponsorship, approval, or certification of goods or services;

(3) causing confusion or misunderstanding as to affiliation, connection, or association with or certification by another;

(5) representing that goods or services have sponsorship, approval, characteristics, uses, and benefits that they do not have;

(7) representing the goods or services or of a particular standard quality or grade when they were of another;

(9) advertising goods or services with intent not to sell them as advertised;

(11) making false and misleading statements of fact concerning the reason for existence of or amount of price reductions;

(12) representing that services had been performed when services were not performed;

(22) failing to disclose information concerning goods or services that was known at the time of the transaction and with the intent to induce a consumer into a transaction which the consumer would not have entered into had the information been disclosed; and

(24) representing an agreement confers or involves rights, remedies or obligations which it does not have … or which are prohibited by law";

e) engaging in an unconscionable action or course of action—DTPA § 17.50(a)(3)— by committing "an act or practice which, to a consumer's detriment, takes advantage of the lack of knowledge, ability, experience, or capacity of the consumer to a grossly unfair degree"—DTPA § 17.45(5).

* * *

Plaintiff Stromboe also seeks to recover for herself and other Windows Class members actual damages incurred as a result of Defendants' unlawful practices and false, misleading and deceptive acts or practices under the DTPA. All of these acts were committed knowingly and/or intentionally and Plaintiff Stromboe and the other Windows Class members are entitled to recover additional damages of not more than three (3) times the amount of actual damages under the DTPA.

The damages sought for each individual Plaintiff and each individual member of the Windows Class—including interest, attorney's fees, costs, actual and additional damages and exemplary damages—are less than $74,000.00. … In the prayer of the petition, Stromboe requests for herself and all class members "actual, special and consequential damages, including attorney's fees," "exemplary damages," "actual damages" caused by the DTPA violations, "additional damages" under the DTPA, and "restitution of all money or property that Defendants have collected from Plaintiff Stromboe and the Windows Class."

* * *

Taylor's petition alleges: The plaintiffs purchased Schein's DOS software—"Easy Dental." And Defendant represented: Plaintiffs would have free, unlimited technical support." Taylor's petition asserts the following causes of action:

a) breach of contract;
b) breach of express warranties (none specified);
c) breach of implied warranties (none specified); and
d) breach of express and implied warranties under the DTPA § 17.50(a)(2).

The damage allegations in Taylor's petition are essentially identical to those in Stromboe's petition.

* * *

The trial court certified two subclasses—one of 5,000 Windows software purchasers, and 15,000 DOS software purchasers. In its order, the trial court found: "In light of the amount any individual Plaintiff could recover in this case, and the fact that Plaintiffs are owners and operators of small businesses, ... the economics of pursuing their claims individually would not be feasible."

Among the common questions of fact that the court identified for the *Windows class* were:

(1) whether members experienced any of the operational problems it had listed,
(2) whether advertisements and other communications were false, misleading, or deceptive,
(3) whether class members received the benefit of their bargain, and
(4) whether they suffered damages in reliance on Schein's misrepresentations.

Among the common questions of fact that the court identified for the *DOS class* were:

(1) whether misrepresentations were made,
(2) whether class members failed to receive the benefit of their bargain because they did not receive free technical support,
(3) whether they relied on and suffered damages from any misrepresentations, and
(4) whether they received unsolicited upgrades.

But, there was no evidence that all purchasers relied on the same or even similar representations by Schein. Some purchasers, for example, bought the software relying on the recommendation of friends and colleagues. There was no evidence all purchasers suffered problems of the same magnitude or incurred the same damages.

The court also found in its order that questions of law regarding essentially all of the legal theories asserted by Stromboe and Taylor were common to the class. Because class members reside in all fifty states, Schein offered evidence of the differences in state law that might apply to different class members. The trial court determined that Texas law would apply to all claims by all members because (1) all of the Windows software license agreements and some of the DOS software license agreements chose Texas law as the governing law, and (2) the software was designed, developed, programmed, and manufactured in Dallas, shipped from there, and partially marketed there. The court did not explain why either of these factors supported application of Texas law to class members' claims for *breach of implied warranties,* fraud, negligent misrepresentation, and violations of consumer protection statutes.

***

Schein took an interlocutory appeal from the trial court's certification order. ... The court of appeals observed that the trial court had been diligent in conducting a lengthy hearing on the plaintiffs' motion to certify the class, that the trial court had identified many common factual and legal issues, and that the evidence offered at the hearing showed that issues regarding Schein's conduct and the nature of its software would be common to the claims of all of the class members. ... The court of appeals was equally dismissive of Schein's argument that reliance is not a common issue but must necessarily be determined for each individual plaintiff. ... Schein petitioned this Court for review. ...

II.

Schein argues that the court of appeals' decision conflicts in two respects with ours in *Southwestern Refining Co. v. Bernal*, 22 S.W.3d 425, 430 (Tex.2000). For reasons we explain, we agree.

In *Bernal*, we held that it is improper to certify a class without knowing how the claims can and will likely be tried. A trial court's certification order must indicate how the claims will likely be tried so that conformance with Rule 42 may be meaningfully evaluated. "Given the plaintiffs' burden, a court cannot rely on [mere] assurances of counsel that any problems with predominance or superiority can be overcome." Schein argues that the court of appeals failed to hold the trial court's certification order to this standard. We agree. ... The court of appeals' conclusion that the certification order is proper conflicts with *Bernal*. ...

IV.

Rule 42(a) prescribes the following prerequisites for a class action:

> One or more members of a class may sue or be sued as representative parties on behalf of all only if (1)

> the class is so numerous that joinder of all members is impracticable, (2) there are questions of law, or fact common to the class, (3) the claims or defenses of the representative parties are typical of the claims or defenses of the class, and (4) the representative parties will fairly and adequately protect the interests of the class. Tex. R. Civ. P. § 42(a).

Rule 42(b)(4) provides that:

> An action may be maintained as a class action if the prerequisites of subdivision (a) are satisfied, and ... (4) the court finds that the questions of law or fact common to the members of the class predominate over any questions affecting only individual members, and that a class action is superior to other available methods for the fair and efficient adjudication of the controversy. The matters pertinent to the findings include: (A) the interest of members of the class in individually controlling the prosecution or defense of separate actions; (B) the extent and nature of any litigation concerning the controversy already commenced by or against members of the class; (C) the desirability or undesirability of concentrating the litigation of the claims in the particular forum; (D) the difficulties likely to be encountered in the management of a class action. Tex. R. Civ. P. § 42(b)(4).

Schein argues that the plaintiffs have failed to show that "the questions of law or fact common to the members of the class predominate over any questions affecting only individual members," as the rule requires. ... "The test for predominance is not whether common issues outnumber uncommon issues but ... whether common or individual issues will be the object of most of the efforts of the litigants and the court." *Bernal*, 22 S.W.3d at 434, quoting *Central Power & Light Co. v. City of San Juan*, 962 S.W.2d 602, 610 (Tex.App.-Corpus Christi 1998).

As we have noted, reliance is an element of five of the plaintiffs' causes of action: fraud, breach of express warranty—to a certain extent—and DTPA "laundry list violations." The burden on plaintiffs to prove reliance in order to recover on any of these theories is in no way altered by the assertion of claims on behalf of a class.

* * *

Thus, the 20,000 class members in the present case are held to the same standards of proof of reliance—and for that matter all the other elements of their claims—that they would be required to meet if each sued individually. This does not mean, of course, that reliance or other elements of their causes of action cannot be proved class-wide with evidence generally applicable to all class members; class-wide proof is possible when class-wide evidence exists. But evidence insufficient to prove reliance in a suit by an individual does not become sufficient in a class action simply because there are more plaintiffs. Inescapably individual differences cannot be concealed in a throng.

* * *

The plaintiffs contend that they have established "class-wide reliance" on misrepresentations made by Schein. But this is not supported by the record. It is true, as the plaintiffs say: There is evidence that Schein wanted purchasers to rely on its advertisements and other representations about its software products, as most marketers of any product would. But, there is no evidence that purchasers actually did rely on Schein's statements so uniformly that common issues of reliance predominate over individual issues. To the contrary, there is, for example, significant evidence that purchasers relied on recommendations from colleagues and others rather than any statements made directly or indirectly by Schein.

The trial court did not explain in its certification order how the plaintiffs can avoid individual proof of reliance or why the necessity for such proof would not defeat the predominance requirement for certification. Such an explanation would be an important part of the trial plan required by *Bernal*. The court of appeals premised affirmance of the order on the mistaken belief that reliance was not an element of the plaintiffs' principal causes of action.

The Fifth Circuit has recently observed: If "individual reliance is necessary to prove actual damages, a class action may not be certified on this issue." *Perrone v. General Motors Acceptance Corp.*, 232 F.3d 433, 440 (5th Cir. 2000). We need not and do not decide whether a class asserting a cause of action requiring proof of *reliance*, like the class alleged here, can ever be certified.

We hold only that the plaintiffs in this case have failed to show: Individual issues of reliance *do not* preclude the necessary finding of predominance under Rule 42(b)(4). … [Also] plaintiffs have failed to show that common fact questions regarding damages *predominate.*

* * *

The judgment of the court of appeals must be reversed. We cannot say, of course, that no class can be certified in this case. That matter must be decided by the trial court in the first instance. We conclude only that the certification order before us is improper. The case is therefore remanded to the trial court for further proceedings.

NOTES AND QUESTIONS

1) Texas Deceptive Trade Practices Act and Breach of Warranty Actions. Texas' DTPA §17.50(a)(2) reads: A consumer may maintain an action where any of the following constitute a producing cause of economic damages or damages for mental anguish—breach of an express or implied warranty.

2) Texas DTPA § 17.50(a)(2) Incorporates UCC § 2-313, § 2-314 and §2-315 Breach of Warranty Actions. Consider the Texas Supreme Court's analysis in *La Sara Grain v. First Nat'l Bank of Mercedes*, 673 S.W.2d 558, 564-566 (Tex.1984): DTPA § 17.50(a)(2) provides that a consumer may maintain an action if he has been adversely affected by the breach of an express or implied warranty. A consumer is defined as an "individual, partnership or corporation, or governmental entity who seeks or acquires by purchase or lease any goods or services." Tex.Bus. & Com.Code Ann. § 17.45(4). … The DTPA does not define the term "warranty." Furthermore, the act does not create any warranties; therefore, any warranty must be established independently of the act. *Cheney v. Parks,* 605 S.W.2d 640, 642 (Tex.Civ.App.—Houston [1st Dist.] 1980). Express warranties are imposed by agreement of the parties to the contract. *Rinehart v. Sonitrol of Dallas, Inc.*, 620 S.W.2d 660, 662-663 (Tex.Civ.App.-Dallas 1981; Tex. Bus. & Com. Code § 2.313 (Texas UCC). And implied warranties are created by operation of law and are grounded more in tort than in contract. *Humber v. Morton,* 426 S.W.2d 554 (Tex.1968). Implied warranties are derived primarily from statute, although some have their origin at common law. *See Kamarath v. Bennett,* 568 S.W.2d 658 (Tex.1978); *Jacob E. Decker & Sons, Inc. v. Capps,* 64 S.W.2d 828 (Tex. 1942). One statutory source of implied warranties is the Uniform Commercial Code. Tex.Bus. & Com.Code § 2.314 and § 2.315 (Texas UCC). ... A mere breach of contract is not a violation of the DTPA. *Ashford Development, Inc. v. USLife Real Estate Services Corp.*, 661 S.W.2d 933, 935 (Tex.1983). *See also*, *Southwestern Bell Telephone Co. v. FDP Corp.*, 811 S.W.2d 572, 576-77 (Tex.1991) ("Unlike a DTPA § 17.46(b) "laundry list" claim, an action for breach of warranty is not a creation of the DTPA.")

Vernon's Texas Statutes and Codes

Business and Commerce Code
Chapter 17. Deceptive Trade Practices Act
§ 17.505

§ 17.505. Notice; Inspection.

(a) As a prerequisite to filing a suit seeking damages under Subdivision (1) of Subsection (b) of Section 17.50 of this subchapter against any person, a consumer shall give written notice to the person at least 60 days before filing the suit advising the person in reasonable detail of the consumer's specific complaint and the amount of economic damages, damages for mental anguish, and expenses, including attorneys' fees, if any, reasonably incurred by the consumer in asserting the claim against the defendant. During the 60-day period a written request to inspect, in a reasonable manner and at a reasonable time and place, the goods that are the subject of the consumer's action or claim may be presented to the consumer.

(b) If the giving of 60 days' written notice is rendered impracticable by reason of the necessity of filing suit in order to prevent the expiration of the statute of limitations or if the consumer's claim is asserted by way of counterclaim, the notice provided for in Subsection (a) of this section is not required, but the tender provided for by Subsection (d), Section 17.506 of this subchapter may be made within 60 days after service of the suit or counterclaim.

(c) A person against whom a suit is pending who does not receive written notice, as required by Subsection (a), may file a plea in abatement not later than the 30th day after the date the person files an original answer in the court in which the suit is pending. This subsection does not apply if Subsection (b) applies.

(d) The court shall abate the suit if the court, after a hearing, finds that the person is entitled to an abatement because notice was not provided as required by this section. A suit is automatically abated without the order of the court beginning on the 11th day after the date a plea in abatement is filed under Subsection (c) if the plea in abatement:

(1) is verified and alleges that the person against whom the suit is pending did not receive the written notice as required by Subsection (a); and

(2) is not controverted by an affidavit filed by the consumer before the 11th day after the date on which the plea in abatement is filed.

(e) An abatement under Subsection (d) continues until the 60th day after the date that written notice is served in compliance with Subsection (a).

D. DTPA AND UDTPA AFFIRMATIVE DEFENSES

To be sure, when solo practitioners or small-firm attorneys raise various technology-based claims and commence UDTPA or DTPA actions, sellers of law-practice technologies and services must be aware: Some common-law affirmative defenses may not be used in DTPA-related trials. And there are many examples of state and federal courts' striking or rejecting certain procedural and substantive affirmative defenses. *See World Kitchen, LLC v. American Ceramic Society,* 2015 WL 3429380, *2 (N.D. Ill. 2015) (striking a First-Amendment defense in a UDTPA action); *Guessford v. Pennsylvania Nat. Mut. Cas. Ins. Co.,* 918 F.Supp.2d 453, 469 (M.D. N.C. 2013) (rejecting the doctrine of unclean hand as an affirmative defense in a UDTPA action); *Kuehnhoefer v. Welch,* 893 S.W.2d 689, 692 (Tex.App.-Texarkana 1995) (declaring that estoppel is not a defense and does not bar a DTPA action); and, *Shenandoah Assoc. v. J & K Prop., Inc.,* 741 S.W.2d 470, 496

(Tex.App.-Dallas 1987) (declaring that principles of ratification do not apply to DTPA claims).

On the other hand, defendants—who sell allegedly defective law-office products and services— may raise other affirmative defenses in DTPA or UDTPA trials. *See e.g., Ostrow v. United Bus. Machs., Inc.,* 982 S.W.2d 101, 105 (Tex. App.-Houston [1st Dist.] 1998) (declaring that the doctrines of accord and satisfaction may bar a DTPA action which arises out of a contract-based claim); *Johnson v. McLeaish,* 1995 WL 500308,*10 (Tex. App.-Dallas) (concluding that illegality and public policy violations bar DTPA actions); and, *Keriotis v. Lombardo Rental Trust,* 607 S.W.2d 44, 46 (Tex. App.-Beaumont 1980) (declaring that a statute of frauds prevents a consumer from commencing a DTPA cause of action).

This section presents a few cases—illustrating the types of "questionable" defenses that defendants have raised in DTPA and UDTPA trials. To be sure, the reported state and federal opinions do not present the universe of controversial procedural and substantive defenses, which have appeared in DTPA lawsuits.

1. State Courts' Personal Jurisdiction Over Out-of-State Internet Service Providers, Vendors, and Website Domain Owners

Hearst Corporation v. Goldberger

1997 WL 97097
(S.D.N.Y. 1997)

Peck, United States Magistrate Judge:

The issue before the court is whether the court has personal jurisdiction over defendant, because his Internet web site is accessible to and has been electronically "visited" by computer users in New York. Defendant has not contracted to sell or sold any products or services to anyone in New York as his "business" is not yet operational.

Hearst Corporation—owner and publisher of *ESQUIRE* Magazine—brought this trademark infringement action. Ari Goldberger—who established an Internet domain name and website, "ESQWIRE.COM"—is the defendant. Goldberger's website offers law office infrastructure network services for attorneys. But, such services are not yet available. Goldberger also provides legal information services. Goldberger lives in Cherry Hill, New Jersey, and works in Philadelphia.

Facts

Plaintiff Hearst and ESQUIRE Magazine

The Hearst Corporation and its predecessors-in-interest (Hearst) have published the well-known monthly, *ESQUIRE* Magazine since 1933. Hearst owns the trademark registration for the mark ESQUIRE for such goods. Hearst also has used the marks ESQUIRE or ESQ. or marks incorporating those terms on a variety of products and services. ... "Hearst is the owner of the domain names *viaesquire.com*, *esquiremag.com*, and *esquireb2b.com* which are registered with" Internic. The complaint alleges that Hearst's ESQUIRE and ESQ. marks "have acquired tremendous secondary meaning" and that those marks are "inherently distinctive, nonfunctional, strong and famous marks entitled to a very broad scope of protection."

Defendant Goldberger and His ESOWIRE and ESQ.WIRE Marks

Defendant Goldberger resides in Cherry Hill, New Jersey, and works as an associate at the Pepper, Hamilton & Scheetz law firm in Philadelphia. In 1992, Goldberger came up with the idea to "create an electronic law office infrastructure network that would provide individual attorneys—via computer—with legal support services equivalent to those available to lawyers practicing in large law firms." The scope of Goldberger's idea subsequently expanded to possibly include information services, such as the provision of reporting and commentary on legal issues. But, so far, this has been limited to his own case.

Goldberger decided to call his service "ESQ.WIRE1." And, on September 16, 1994, he applied to register that service mark with the Patent and Trademark Office. Hearst opposed Goldberger's application. The Trademark Office suspended its proceedings pending disposition of this lawsuit.

In September 1995, Goldberger registered the Internet domain name ESQWIRE.COM with Internic. In June 1996, Goldberger published a worldwide website on the Internet at the address http://www.esqwire.com. Goldberger has published his website through an Internet provider—Voice Net of Ivyland of Pennsylvania. Goldberger's website consists of a "home page." The latter briefly describes the types of services that Goldberger plans to offer. The home page also contains: (1) a summary of Hearst's activities against Goldberger in this lawsuit, (2) computer "links" to court filings, and (3) other documents related to this action.

Goldberger's home page describes Goldberger's planned services as follows:

> "ESQ.wirek will provide virtual-law-firm support services, legal information services and products to enable attorneys to practice law anywhere on the planet, with the simple click of a mouse. We are looking for attorneys in every jurisdiction in the world to become a part of this revolutionary virtual legal community. For more information, please e-mail esqwire@esqwire.com."

Goldberger does not consider this to be an advertisement for his services. But, he agrees: His website "could become a means to solicit [customers] when [he is] ready to start doing that." Although Goldberger has established his ESQWIRE web site, it is undisputed that he does not yet have any services or products to sell. And he has not sold any products or services in New York, or anywhere else for that matter. Goldberger specifically advised the court: "I have not sold anything or provided any service or product to anyone—nor have I been renumerated by anyone with any form of consideration with regard to the ESQWIRE.com site or the ESQ.WIRE business or name or anything."

It is further undisputed: New Yorkers have accessed Goldberger's ESQWIRE.com website. Goldberger's website also has been accessed by people from at least 20 other states and 34 foreign countries. In addition to Goldberger's Internet website, Hearst relies on additional contacts Goldberger has had with the media in New York *after* Hearst commenced this lawsuit. Goldberger has used ESQWIRE as e-mail address. After the commencement of this lawsuit by Hearst on May 15, 1996, Goldberger sent a few e-mails to media or lawyers in New York.

* * *

Procedural Background

Hearst brought this action on or about May 15, 1996 and raised seven causes of action—alleging that Goldberger:

(1) infringed on Hearst's registered ESQUIRE and ESQ. trademarks in violation of section

32 of the Lanham Act, 15 U.S.C. § 1114,

(2) violated § 43(a) of the Lanham Act, 15 U.S.C. § 1125(a)— "false designation of origin and false descriptions and representations of fact,"

(3) engaged in unfair competition under New York common law,

(4) violated § 43(c) of the Lanham Act, 15 U.S.C. § 1125(c)—by diluting Hearst's ESQUIRE and ESQ. trademarks,

(5) violated New York's Deceptive Trade Practices Act — N.Y. Gen. Bus. Law § 349.

On July 13, 1996, defendant Goldberger moved to dismiss for lack of personal jurisdiction or alternatively to transfer venue. Goldberger also moved to dismiss for failure to state a claim. …

Analysis

Legal Standards Applicable for A Motion to Dismiss for Lack of Personal Jurisdiction

A plaintiff's obligation to establish a basis for the court's personal jurisdiction over the defendant varies, depending on the procedural posture of the litigation. *Ball v. Metallurgie Hoboken–Overpelt S.A.*, 902 F.2d 194, 197 (2d Cir. 1990). … The court will construe the pleadings and evidence in Hearst's favor at this stage.

Hearst brings this action under the Lanham Act—the federal trademark law. The Lanham Act does not provide for national service of process. *See Hershey Pasta Group v. Vitelli–Elvea Co.,* 921 F.Supp. 1344, 1346 (M.D.Pa.1996). "In a federal question case where a defendant resides outside the forum state, a federal court applies the forum state's personal jurisdiction rules if the federal statute does not specifically provide for national service of process." *PDK Labs v. Friedlander,* 103 F.3d 1105, 1110 (2d Cir. 1997). *See also, Omni Capital Int'l v. Rudolf Wolff & Co.,* 484 U.S. 97, 104-105 (1987) (requiring a federal court to apply the forum state's personal jurisdiction rules in federal-question case if a defendant resides outside the forum state and "if the federal statute does not specifically provide for national service of process."). The court therefore turns to New York's jurisdictional statutes.

New York's Jurisdictional Statutes

CIVIL PROCEDURE LAW RULES § 301

CPLR § 301 provides, cryptically, that a "court may exercise such jurisdiction over persons, property or states as might have been exercised heretofore." Section 301 traditionally applies to persons actually present in New York and to corporations "doing business" in New York, "not occasionally or casually, but with a fair degree of permanence and continuity." *Hoffritz for Cutlery, Inc. v. Amajac, Ltd.,* 763 F.2d 55, 58 (2d Cir.1985) and *Beacon Enterprises, Inc. v. Menzies,* 715 F.2d 757, 762 (2d Cir.1983). ... The Court in this case, however, need not resolve the question of whether "doing business" jurisdiction applies to an individual person. Although Hearst's complaint asserts jurisdiction under CPLR § 301 as well as § 302 Hearst's brief in opposition to Goldberger's motion to dismiss does not rely at all on CPLR § 301 jurisdiction. Accordingly, the court finds that Hearst has waived any CPLR § 301 argument. *See, e.g., Abrahams v. Young & Rubicam Inc.,* 79 F.3d 234, 237 & n. 2 (2d Cir.).

CIVIL PROCEDURE LAW RULES § 302

New York "long-arm" statute—CPLR § 302(a)— provides:

> As to a cause of action arising from any of the acts enumerated in this section, a court may exercise personal jurisdiction over any nondomiciliary ... who in person or through an agent:
>
> (1) transacts any business within the state or contracts anywhere to supply goods or services in the state; or
>
> (2) commits a tortious act within the state; or
>
> (3) commits a tortious act without the state causing injury to person or property within the state ... if he
>
> > (i) regularly does or solicits business, or engages in any other persistent course of conduct, or derives substantial revenue from goods used or consumed or services rendered, in the state, or

(ii) expects or should reasonably expect the act to have consequences in the state and derives substantial revenue from interstate or international commerce. …

a. Goldberger's Internet Website

The present case does not involve a contract. It involves a tort or a trademark infringement surrounding commercial activity—Goldberger's Internet website. It is undisputed: Goldberger created and "published" his ESQWIRE web site from the Cherry Hill, New Jersey—a Philadelphia area, not New York. It is also undisputed: People located in New York have accessed or "visited" Goldberger's website. Further, it is undisputed that Goldberger has not sold any product or services. At most, his Internet web site is, an announcement of the future availability of his services for attorneys.

Goldberger's ESQWIRE Internet website thus is most analogous to an advertisement in a national magazine. Like an ad, Goldberger's Internet website may be viewed by people in all fifty states but it is not targeted at the residents of New York or any other particular state. New York law is clear, however, that advertisements in national publications are not sufficient to provide personal jurisdiction under § 302(a)(1). *See, Davidson Extrusions, Inc. v. Touche Ross & Co.,* 131 516 N.Y.S.2d 230, 232 (App. Div. [2d Dep't] 1987).

b. Goldberger's Post-Litigation E-mails and Other New York Contacts

Although Hearst mainly relies on Goldberger's Internet website, Hearst also points to the e-mail messages that Goldberger sent to or received from New York. Those e-mails—standing alone or in conjunction with Goldberger's Internet website—do not provide CPLR § 302(a)(1) personal jurisdiction over Goldberger for two reasons. First, the only e-mail communications with New York occurred after Hearst brought this suit. Only pre-litigation contacts are relevant to the jurisdictional question. *See Metropolitan Life Ins. Co. v. Robertson–Ceco Corp.,* 84 F.3d 560, 569 (2d Cir. 1996) and *Greene v. Sha–Na–Na,* 637 F.Supp. 591, 595 (D.Conn.1986) ("It is well-established that jurisdiction [must] be determined by examining the conduct of the defendants as of the time of service of the complaint."). …

Second, even if the court were to consider the post-litigation e-mails, the latter are analogous to sending letters to or communicating via telephone with people in New York. [One's sending letters or telephone communications] to people in New York is insufficient to establish personal jurisdiction under CPLR § 302(a)(1) or the due process clause—if the senders reside outside of New York. *See Robinson v. Overseas Military Sales Corp.,* 21 F.3d 502, 511 (2d Cir.1994) ("[An] isolated phone call is an insufficient basis for personal jurisdiction.") and *Fiedler v. First City Nat'l Bank of Houston,* 807 F.2d 315, 316-318 (2d Cir.1986) (ruling that three telephone calls and one mailing into New York are not sufficient for personal jurisdiction).

* * *

Conclusion

For the reasons set forth above, the court holds: Goldberger's out-of-state creation of an Internet website that is accessible in New York, standing alone, does not provide personal jurisdiction over defendant in New York. Pursuant to the parties' agreement, the case thus should be transferred to the United States District Court for the District of New Jersey, Camden Division.

NOTES AND QUESTIONS

1) Internet Webpages and Conflicting Long-Arm Jurisdiction Decisions. *Compare Bensusan Restaurant Corp. v. King,* 937 F.Supp. 295, 297 (S.D.N.Y.1996) (declaring that an Internet web page is not sufficient to establish long-arm jurisdiction in New York), *with CompuServe, Inc. v. Patterson,* 89 F.3d 1257, 1268-69 (6th Cir.1996) (finding personal jurisdiction in Ohio over a Texas Internet user who subscribed to an Ohio-based network service based and sold software over the Internet), and *Panavision Int'l, L.P. v. Toeppen,* 938 F.Supp. 616, 621-622 (C.D.Cal.1996) (finding that "Toeppen allegedly registered Panavision's trademarks as domain names with the knowledge that the name belonged to Panavision and with the intent to interfere with Panavision's business" and, concluding that personal jurisdiction was "proper because Toeppen's out of state conduct was intended to, and did, result in harmful effects in California.")

2) Abatement of Action: What is the distinction between an "abatement of action" and a "plea in abatement?" In *Hollingsworth* *v. Bagley,* 1872 WL 7390, *1 (Tex.), the Texas Supreme Court penned:

> The appellant brought suit in the district court against Cameron and Scott. No cost bond was required from the plaintiff. Pending the suit, both the defendants died, and the suit abated, and was never revived against the representatives of either of them. But the court permitted the officers of the court to have judgment against the plaintiff for the sum of twenty-two dollars and fifteen cents, on which execution issued on the twenty-eighth day of July, 1869; was levied on the land described in the petition; and it was sold to N. G. Bagley, the appellee, on the first Tuesday in August, 1869 ... *There can be no valid judgment where there are no proper parties to the record*; and after the death of the defendants, the officers of the court could not, as such, be substituted in a manner to entitle them to judgment in the original action against the plaintiff, for costs, although the plaintiff is undoubtedly liable to the officers of court for costs which he himself made in the action.

3) Plea in Abatement: In *Lipinski v. Lipinski,* 1995 WL 517333, *1 (Tex. App.-Hous. [14 Dist.] 1995)], the appellate court wrote the following:

> The essence of appellant's argument is that the trial court mischaracterized the plea in abatement as a plea to the jurisdiction. As such, the pleading was an ineffective substitute for challenging jurisdiction and should be disregarded. We disagree. Appellant's argument misconstrues the purpose behind a plea in abatement, which is utilized as a means of *suspending further action* in a lawsuit until the reason for the abatement has been removed. It is a not a plea in bar, such as *a plea to the jurisdiction.*

2. The Abatement of Internet-Service Subscribers' Deceptive Trade Practice Action

America Online, Inc. v. Williams

958 S.W.2d 268
(Tex. Ct. App.-Houston [14th Dist.] 1997)

Amidei, Justice. This is an interlocutory appeal from an order certifying a class in a DTPA action against appellant America Online, Inc. (AOL), an online computer services provider. *See* Tex. Civ. Prac. & Rem. Code Ann. § 51.014(3) (Vernon 1997). AOL presents an issue of first impression—contending the trial court abused its discretion by certifying a class during the mandatory abatement period provided by the DTPA when a plaintiff fails to give pre-suit notice to the defendant.

On December 1, 1996, AOL began offering a flat-fee plan instead of a per-minute rate for its online services. The resulting increased usage exceeded AOL's expectations and resulted in subscribers having difficulty obtaining access to AOL's network. AOL attempted to resolve customer complaints and on February 4, 1997, executed a negotiated agreement with the attorneys general of 45 states—including Texas. The agreement allowed subscribers to receive refunds or credits—the Assurance of Voluntary Compliance, or AVC.

Christy L. Williams and William M. Buss—the named plaintiffs in this action—filed a suit on January 24, 1997. They alleged that AOL violated the DTPA. Tex. Bus. & Com. Code §§ 17.041–.063. Specifically, appellees sought damages under section 17.50(b)(1). Tex. Bus. & Com. Code § 17.50(b)(1). AOL filed an answer on February 17, 1997. On February 26, 1997, appellees filed a motion to certify the class. AOL then filed a verified plea in abatement on March 12, 1997. It also filed a motion to dismiss the action pursuant to a forum selection clause in the subscriber agreements.

Appellees filed a response to AOL's plea in abatement on March 18, 1997—contending that pre-suit notice was unnecessary because AOL entered a potential settlement agreement with the Texas Attorney General's office. James Pearson—appellees' attorney—attached an affidavit that outlined the facts regarding filing, service, and the execution of the AVC. On April 2 and April 3, 1997, appellees filed their First and Second Amended Petitions, adding two additional plaintiffs and additional causes of action. On April

3, 1997, the trial court conducted a certification hearing. However, AOL objected to the court's consideration of certification during the automatic abatement period. ... The trial court executed its order certifying a class: "All AOL subscribers throughout Texas who were subscribers to AOL on December 1, 1996, or who became subscribers on that date or thereafter until and including April 1, 1997." After the court certified the class, it then abated the action for the applicable period after "proper DTPA notice."

Initially, appellees argue that only part of this action is appealable. Appellees understand that an order granting or denying class certification is appealable. *See* Tex. Civ. Prac. & Rem. Code § 51.014(3). However, appellees argue that AOL is also attempting to obtain review of an order granting or denying a plea in abatement. And an order on a plea in abatement is not an appealable order. *Harper v. Welchem, Inc.* 799 S.W.2d 492, 495 (Tex.App.-Houston [14th Dist.] 1990) ("An order that merely sustains a plea in abatement is interlocutory and not appealable."). When a plaintiff fails to give a statutory notice—a prerequisite to filing a lawsuit—and a defendant's timely request for an abatement is denied, the defendant is entitled to seek review of the court's denial by mandamus. *Hines v. Hash,* 843 S.W.2d 464, 469 (Tex.1992) (construing the DTPA notice provision). Alternatively, a defendant may wait and appeal the final judgment when seeking review of a denial of abatement. But the trial court's error must be harmful to obtain reversal. *Id.*

* * *

In this case, a proper review of the trial court's certification order requires us to consider the court's failure to abate the action until after it certified the class. ... In AOL's first point of error, it alleges: The trial court abused its discretion by certifying a class during the automatic and mandatory DTPA abatement period. *See* Tex. Bus. & Com. Code § 17.505(d). More specifically, AOL asserted: It was deprived of an opportunity to resolve plaintiffs' claims; and, the trial court had no authority to proceed during the abatement period.

"An abatement is a present suspension of all proceedings in a suit." *Permanente Med. Ass'n of Tex. v. Johnson,* 917 S.W.2d 515, 517 (Tex.App.-Waco 1996) (granting writ of mandamus when trial court only partially abated proceedings). "Suspend" means "to interrupt, to cause to cease for a time, to postpone, to stay, delay, or hinder, or to discontinue temporarily—but with an expectation or purpose of resumption." *Black's Law Dictionary* 1446 (6th ed. 1979). Abatement precludes a trial court and litigants from going forward on a case. *Martinka v. Commonwealth Land Title Ins. Co.*, 836 S.W.2d 773, 777 (Tex.App.-Houston [1st Dist.] 1992) (title insurer was judicially prevented from defending title during abatement period); *Lumbermens Mut. Cas. Co. v. Garza*, 777 S.W.2d 198, 199 (Tex.App.-Corpus Christi 1989) (discovery requests filed during the period of abatement were a legal nullity). The rationale for the 60-day abatement is to give the defendant 60 days to avoid litigation.

Our review of the trial court's decision is strictly limited to determining whether the court abused its discretion by granting the motion for class certification. *Morgan v. Deere Credit, Inc.*, 889 S.W.2d 360, 365 (Tex.App.-Houston [14th Dist.] 1994). A trial court does not abuse its discretion if it bases its decision on conflicting evidence. *RSR Corp. v. Hayes*, 673 S.W.2d 928, 930 (Tex.App.-Dallas 1984). A trial court *abuses* its discretion, however, when the court does not properly apply the law to the undisputed facts. Interpretation of a statute is a pure question of law over which the judge has no discretion. *Walker v. Packer*, 827 S.W.2d 833, 839-40 (Tex.1992) (a clear failure by the trial court to analyze or apply the law constitutes an abuse of discretion).

AOL argues that the trial court abused its discretion by failing to follow the express provisions of the DTPA for a mandatory abatement period. As a prerequisite to filing suit, a consumer must give at least sixty (60) days written notice—advising the defendant in reasonable detail of the consumer's *specific* complaint and the amount of damages. Tex. Bus. & Com. Code § 17.505(a). In 1995, the Texas Legislature amended the DTPA to require *automatic abatement* of a DTPA claim for sixty (60) days, if the plaintiff fails to give the requisite notice before filing suit. DTPA §§ 17.505(d), (e) provide:

> (d) The court shall abate the suit if the court, after a hearing, finds that the person is entitled to an abatement because notice was not provided as required by this section. A suit is *automatically abated without the order of the court* beginning on the 11th day after the date a plea in abatement is filed under [this act] if the plea in abatement:
>
> > (1) is verified and alleges that the person against whom the suit is pending did not receive the written notice as required by [this act]; and

(2) is not controverted by an affidavit filed by the consumer before the 11th day after the date on which the plea in abatement is filed.

(e) An abatement under Subsection (d) continues until the 60th day after the date that written notice is served in compliance with Subsection (a).

It is undisputed that appellees gave no pre-suit notice. Therefore, AOL asserts: The abatement automatically began on March 23, 1997, without the necessity of a court order. The court certified the class, and *then* ordered abatement—until sixty (60) days after notice on behalf of the entire class was given. … AOL contends the trial court should have abated the action—so the named plaintiffs could give notice as provided in section 17.505(a).

Appellees argue: The trial court was required to certify the class before abatement. Rule 42(c)(1) directs the trial court to determine whether an action is to be maintained as a class action "as soon as practicable." Tex. R. Civ. P. 42(c)(1). This rule has been interpreted liberally, and includes consideration of "all the relevant circumstances." *Franklin v. Donoho,* 774 S.W.2d 308, 314 (Tex.App.-Austin 1989). … Appellees also assert that the class must be certified for any notice to be meaningful.

* * *

We hold that the trial court abused its discretion by certifying a class action during the abatement period. We reverse the trial court's certification order and order the cause abated for sixty (60) days after the originally named plaintiffs give notice.

3. Discovery and DTPA Defendants' Right to Inspect "Stored Electronically Information" in Attorneys' Computers, Smartphones, and Cloud-Based Accounts

Ferron v. Search Cactus, L.L.C.

2008 WL 1902499
(S.D. Ohio 2008)

Gregory L. Frost, District Judge.

I. Background

[Plaintiff]—John W. Ferron—is an Ohio attorney. He uses various e-mail accounts. He has allegedly received a multitude of e-mails from Defendant—Search Cactus, L.L.C., a Michigan-based limited liability company. Defendant used the e-mails to make offers for unspecified free products and provide notifications of prizes that Plaintiff could claim. Plaintiff argues: The e-mail messages violate the Ohio Consumer Sales Practices Act (OCSPA) § 1345.02(A), in a variety of ways.

On January 18, 2007, Defendant filed a counterclaim against Plaintiff seeking declaratory judgment on four counts: (1) that a settlement agreement with Plaintiff from a prior lawsuit bars future lawsuits by Plaintiff against Defendant; (2) that Plaintiff is not a consumer for purposes of the OCSPA; (3) that the doctrine of res judicata bars recovery for damages; and (4) that Plaintiff's actions are fraudulent because Plaintiff caused e-mails to be sent to him for the purpose of increasing his damages.

Attorney Ferron use his home and office computers for storing and working with information—surrounding the representation of clients, lawsuits such as this action and other actions, and his personal life. Of these categories of information, the information related to the representation of clients … contains documents that are protected by the attorney-client privilege. The information that may be categorized as personal also has no relevance to this case and may be confidential in nature, e.g., banking and credit card information. However, the third category of information, i.e., information related to email and website advertising litigation is relevant and discoverable. *See* Fed.R.Civ.P. 26(b) (information is admissible or is reasonably calculated to lead to the discovery of admissible evidence).

In this court's opinion and order which granted in part and denied in part Defendant Search Cactus' motion for summary judgment, we held: "only the *unsolicited* emails that Plaintiff received at jferron@ferronlaw.com after April 3, 2006, may be used to support his claim under the Ohio Consumer Sales Practices Act. Thus, it is necessary for the parties to ascertain which of the emails Plaintiff received were unsolicited. As Defendants contend, Plaintiff's computer systems contain the only available documentary evidence that can show the pathways taken by Plaintiff to solicit the emails or the absence of those pathways.

II. Defendants' Discovery Requests

Defendants have requested an inspection of Plaintiff's computer systems, to secure relevant information that Plaintiff has not produced. ... Specifically, Defendant [wants] to inspect Plaintiff's computer systems to ascertain whether Plaintiff's ... receiving the emails and visiting the websites constituted a consumer transaction under the OCSPA, or whether Plaintiff's opening of the emails and any attempts to obtain free merchandise were part of a business designed to profit from email litigation. The parties agree: A forensic computer expert must be utilized to obtain or discovery information on Plaintiff's computer.

III. Analysis

The parties were unable to agree on a protocol for inspection of Plaintiff's computer's hard drives and requested another conference with this court to address the issue. At the April 14, 2008, telephone conference, this court considered the parties' arguments related to the inspection of Plaintiff's computers. The issues were (1) how to protect Plaintiff's confidential personal information that is stored on the computers—personal banking and credit card information, and (2) how to prevent Plaintiff from waiving the attorney-client privilege by allowing the information on the computers to be viewed by any third party.

The 2006 amendments to Rule 34 of the Federal Rules of Civil Procedure clarify "that discovery of electronically stored information stands on equal footing with discovery of paper documents." FED. R. CIV. P. 34 ADVISORY COMMITTEE'S NOTE ON 2006 AMENDMENTS. Consequently, without a qualifying reason, Defendants are no more entitled to access Plaintiff's electronic-information-storage systems than to access Plaintiff's warehouse which store paper documents. *See Scotts Co., LLC v. Liberty Mut. Ins. Co.,* 2007 U.S. Dist. LEXIS 43005, at *4-5 (S.D. Ohio 2007) (stressing "the 2006 Amendments to Rule 34 do not require a discovery order as a matter of course"); *Diepenhorst v. City of Battle Creek,* 2006 U.S. Dist. LEXIS 48551, at *10-11 (W.D. Mich. 2006).

Here, the court concludes: There are sufficient qualifying reasons to permit Defendants access to Plaintiff's computers. Plaintiff has apparently failed to fulfill his "duty to preserve information because of pending or reasonably anticipated litigation." Fed.R.Civ.P. 37 ADVISORY COMMITTEE'S NOTE ON 2006 AMENDMENTS. Plaintiff has not produced the relevant information. Moreover, that Plaintiff's computers contain the only available documentary evidence of his visits to the websites distinguishes this case from *Scotts* and

Diepenhorst. …

Plaintiff takes the position: He placed a proper litigation hold on electronically stored information relating to this case. Specifically, Plaintiff has represented: He has saved and preserved all of his commercial email since January 1, 2006. Plaintiff also represents to the court: No Defendant in this case has ever requested that he place a litigation hold on any other type of electronically stored information on his computers. Lastly, Plaintiff represents: He has never received any notice, stating that Defendant intended to inspect computers which Plaintiff uses to retrieve this information. …

Plaintiff's arguments are not well taken. Even if Plaintiff has preserved and saved his "commercial email," those actions do not sufficiently fulfill his duty: To preserve evidence, which "arises when the party has notice that the evidence is relevant to litigation or when a party should have known that the evidence may be relevant to future litigation." *Fujitsu Ltd. v. Federal Express Corp.,* 247 F.3d 423, 436 (2d Cir. 2001)). Further, Plaintiff's duty to preserve this information is independent of whether Defendants requested a litigation hold. *Kemper Mortgage Inc. v. Russell,* 2006 U.S. Dist. LEXIS 20729, at *3 (S.D. Ohio 2006) ("While [an] obligation may be enforced by court order or by a later sanction for spoliation, obviously the duty arises independent of any court declaration of the duty and indeed long before a court is available to make a declaration in the particular case.").

A. Confidential Personal Information

The parties and this court agree: Plaintiff's personal information is confidential and is irrelevant to this lawsuit. Defendants request a current mirror image of Plaintiff's computers' hard drives—contending that Plaintiff's removal of any information from the hard drives can unwittingly cause deletion of other, possibly relevant, information. …

To strike a balance between these competing interests, this court orders Plaintiff's forensic computer expert to produce mirror images of the hard drives on Plaintiff's computers and store the images safely. Plaintiff's forensic computer expert shall remove only Plaintiff's personal or confidential information—which cannot reasonably assist discovery in this lawsuit. Plaintiff shall disclose to Defendants the protocol that Plaintiff's expert used to remove the confidential information.

B. Attorney-Client Privileged Information

Plaintiff argues: If he is required to allow Defendants' forensic computer expert to review and copy Plaintiff's hard drives, the attorney-client privilege—attached to the information—will be lost. Plaintiff's makes that prediction, because a third party will review the otherwise privileged attorney-client information. This court disagrees. First, Plaintiff caused this issue to become problematic because of his failure to place a sufficient litigation hold on his computer systems. *Thielen v. Buongiorno USA, Inc.*, 2007 U.S. Dist. LEXIS 8998, at *8 (W.D. Mich. 2007) (ordering access to plaintiff's computer systems to determine whether plaintiff accessed defendants' website or a third-party website which advertised for defendant).

Second, Defendants have agreed to allow their forensic computer expert to review the information and allow Plaintiff to identify the privileged documents. Indeed, our sister district court ordered this exact protocol. *See Thielen,* 2007 U.S. Dist. LEXIS 8998, at *8-9 (ordering defendant to select a forensic expert to review and make a mirror image of the hard drive on plaintiff's computer and report findings under confidence to plaintiff's counsel before forwarding the findings to defendant's counsel).

Accordingly, this court orders Plaintiff to permit Defendants' forensic computer expert to make mirror images of Plaintiff's computer hard drives. ... The expert shall remove privileged information and provide all other information to Defendants.

United States Code

Federal Rules of Civil Procedure
Title V. Disclosures and Discovery
Producing Documents, Electronically Stored Information
Federal Rules of Civil Procedure Rule 34(a)

In General. A party may serve on any other party a request within the scope of Rule 26(b):

(1) to produce and permit the requesting party or its representative to inspect, copy, test, or sample the following items in the responding party's possession, custody, or control:

(A) any designated *documents or electronically stored information* — including writings, drawings, graphs, charts, photographs, sound recordings, images, and other data or data compilations—*stored in any medium* from which information can be obtained either directly or, if necessary, after translation by the responding party into a reasonably usable form; or

(B) any designated tangible things; or

(2) to *permit entry onto designated land or other property* possessed or controlled by the responding party, so that the requesting party may inspect, measure, survey, photograph, test, or sample the property or any designated object or operation on it.

Vernon's Texas Statutes and Codes

Business and Commerce Code
Chapter 17. Deceptive Trade Practices Act
§ 17.505

§ 17.505. Notice; Inspection.

(a) As a prerequisite to filing a suit seeking damages under Subdivision (1) of Subsection (b) of Section 17.50 of this subchapter against any person, a consumer shall give written notice to the person at least 60 days before filing the suit advising the person in reasonable detail of the consumer's specific complaint and the amount of economic damages, damages for mental anguish, and expenses, including attorneys' fees, if any, reasonably incurred by the consumer in asserting the claim against the defendant. *During the 60-day period a written request to inspect*, in a reasonable manner and at a reasonable time and place, the goods that are the subject of the consumer's action or claim may be presented to the consumer.

CHAPTER FOUR: Solo and Small-Firm Attorneys' Actions Under Federal Computer-Fraud, Anticybersquatting, Anti-Hacking, and Copyright Statutes

Advising Your Clients (And You!) In The New World of Social Media: What Every Lawyer Should Know About Twitter, Facebook, YouTube, & Wikis

Utah Bar Journal
3-JUN Utah B.J. 16
Randy L. Dryer

By March of 2010, there were 200 million blogs worldwide, 450 million people on Facebook, 27 million tweets every 24 hours, and 1.2 billion YouTube views each day. These staggering statistics reflect the explosive growth social media has experienced over the past three years, which growth is expected to continue unabated in the future.

Social media—blogs, wikis, social networking sites like Facebook and LinkedIn, multimedia sharing sites like YouTube and Flickr, and social tagging sites like Digg and Yelp—represents a revolutionary shift in the way we communicate. ... Social media is word of mouth on steroids and is beginning to morph from a fun and easy way to stay socially connected with friends into a dynamic and interactive way of doing business and practicing law. Businesses must now interact with their customers and other stakeholders in an entirely different way, and lawyers will have to adjust accordingly in the not too distant future.

As clients begin to adopt these new social media technologies, they will expect [their] lawyers ... to understand how these new communication platforms operate and what new legal risks are created. [This article identifies] the primary legal risks of utilizing social media—when businesses utilize social media ... [and] when lawyers use social media.

* * *

Traditional advertising laws—both federal and state—in general apply to online and social media advertising. Depending on the nature of the advertising and [its] social media platform, various federal and/or state laws may apply: Section 5 of the Federal Trade Commission Act—prohibiting unfair or deceptive acts or practices, including advertising; Section 43(a) of the Lanham Act—prohibiting unfair competition; the Digital Millennium Copyright Act—addressing copyright protections; Section 230 of the Communications Decency Act—protecting social media site providers from liability for user generated content), and the CAN-SPAM Act—governing email practices). …

Attorney web profiles should be regularly monitored for compliance with ethical rules. … Lawyers, under certain circumstances, may be responsible for the information contained on websites such as Martindale Hubbell, SuperLawyers, LinkedIn, and lawyer locator or rating sites. … The emergence of social media—in business and the practice of law—have opened up amazing new opportunities for marketing and connecting with customers and clients. It is not without legal risk, however, and *lawyers need to understand these risks*, not only for their clients, but for themselves, as well.

A. Improper Use of Website Trademarks, Misleading Advertisements and Attorneys' Right of Action under the Trademark (Lanham) Act of 1946

Allen v. IM Solutions, LLC

94 F.Supp.3d 1216
(E.D. Okla. 2015)

James H. Payne, District Judge. Before the court is Defendant Reed Elsevier Inc.'s motion to dismiss several counts in the class action complaint under Federal Rules of Civil Procedure 12(b)(6).

Background

This lawsuit arises out of pop-up advertisements for legal services that appear on Plaintiffs' websites. Plaintiffs Allen & Wiser, LLC and Blount Law Firm PLLC are law firms located in Oklahoma and Tennessee, respectively. Plaintiffs Anthony Allen and James Blount are lawyers and members of those respective law firms (collectively, Attorneys). According to the Complaint, Defendants IM Solutions (IMS) and LeadingResponse, LLC (RME) are limited liability corporations—engaged in the business of using the internet to generate leads for law firms to obtain potential clients. Further, according to the Complaint, Defendant Reed Elsevier Inc. (Reed) is the owner and operator of LexisNexis Martindale Hubbell, Lawyers.com, Attorneys.com and LawyerLocator. Defendant Internet Brands, Inc. (Internet Brands) owned and operated Nolo Legal divisions and over 150 web properties providing marketing services for lawyers and consumer-facing legal information.

The Complaint also alleges that Reed and Internet Brands created a joint venture combining its above-described business with Internet Brands' online marketing services. The Attorneys filed a class action against Defendants on June 3, 2014. In the Complaint, the Attorneys claimed that Reed violated the Trademark (Lanham) Act of 1946, 15 U.S.C. § 1125(a). For purposes of ruling on a motion to dismiss, the court considers the allegations of the Complaint to be true.

The Complaint alleges: IMS generates clients' leads by utilizing a "hidden browser plug-in." Unnamed "affiliates" place advertising—"adware" or "malware" plug-ins—on consumers' computers. The plug-ins cause a pop-up window to appear when a consumer visits the Attorneys' websites. If a consumer clicks on the first pop-up window, a second pop-up window appears—presenting a questionnaire about the legal services the consumer seeks. After completing the questionnaire and clicking "Speak to lawyers," the results are routed to Reed. And Reed places a telephone call to the consumer. Following the phone call, Reed sends an email to the consumer—referring them to IMS, who matches the consumer with a law firm. The Attorneys allege: This lead generating process improperly diverts potential customers away from the Attorneys' websites, allowing Defendants to capture the business.

The function of a motion to dismiss is to assess the legal feasibility of the complaint. *Ashcroft v. Iqbal*, 556 U.S. 662, 677 (2009). When deciding a motion to dismiss, the Court must accept all well-plead allegations as true and draw all reasonable inferences in favor of the pleader. *Id.* The Court need not accept as true unreasonable inferences, unwarranted deductions of fact, or conclusory legal allegations cast in the form of factual allegations. *Southern Disposal, Inc. v. Texas Waste Mgmt.*, 161 F.3d 1259, 1262 (10th Cir.1998). In other words, the complaint must contain the grounds upon which the claim rests through factual allegations sufficient "to raise a right to relief above the speculative level." *Bell Atl. Corp. v. Twombly*, 550 U.S. 544, 555 (2007). A plaintiff is obligated to amplify a claim with some factual allegations to allow a court to draw reasonable inference that the defendant is liable for the alleged conduct. *Ashcroft*, 556 U.S. at 677.

Discussion

The Trademark (Lanham) Act of 1946

Reed argues: Under no factual scenario could any claim arise under the Lanham Act. Specifically, Defendant Reed argues: The Attorneys do not allege that Reed *used* the Attorneys' service marks to confuse consumers, or *made any false or misleading* statements which confused consumers about the source of the information. Additionally, Reed argues: The pop-up advertisement ... does not constitute "use" within the meaning of the Lanham Act. According to Reed, the pop-up advertisement appears in a separate window and does not direct consumers away from the Attorneys' websites. In response, the Attorneys argue: The pop-ups were designed to cause prospective clients to believe: The advertisements were native to the Attorneys' websites. Therefore, the pop-ups confused consumers about the origin of the advertisement. Additionally, the Attorneys argue: Reed made misleading statements to consumers—referring to IMS as a "firm" and stating that IMS had been randomly selected.

This court finds that the Attorneys' Complaint fails to allege sufficient facts to state a claim against Reed under the Lanham Act. In order to establish a claim under section 43(a) of the Lanham Act, a plaintiff must assert: (1) the defendant causes confusion through improper use of a mark, or (2) the defendant causes confusion through by misrepresenting the origin or nature of advertised services. *General Steel Domestic Sales, LLC v. Chumley*, 2013 WL 1900562, *5-12, (D. Colo. 2013).

As an initial matter, the Attorneys have not alleged: Reed used the Attorneys' mark or marks, which would form the basis of a Lanham Act claim. In other words, the Attorneys fail to allege that Reed used plaintiffs' service mark—words, names, or symbols—to confuse consumers. *See 1–800 Contacts, Inc. v. Lens.com*, 722 F.3d

1229, 1238 (10th Cir. 2013) and, *1–800 Contacts, Inc. v. WhenU.com, Inc.*, 414 F.3d 400, 410 (2d Cir. 2005) (failing to finding a violation under the Lanham Act absent an improper use of a 1–800's trademark). The Attorneys attempt to distinguish the holdings of *1–800 Contacts* and *WhenU.com* by citing *Playboy Enterprises, Inc. v. Netscape Comm. Corp.*, 354 F.3d 1020, 1024-25 (9th Cir.2004). The holding in *Playboy*, however, is readily distinguishable: The defendant in the latter case was using the trademark words—"playboy" and "playmate"—to generate the offending advertisements. No such allegations have been made here. Without allegations that Reed used a service mark belonging to the Attorneys, there can be no violation under the Lanham Act.

Further, establishing "use"—within the meaning of the Lanham Act—is a threshold requirement: "[W]hile any number of activities may be in commerce or create the likelihood of confusion, no such activity is actionable under the Lanham Act absent use of a trademark." *WhenU.com, Inc.,* 414 F.3d at 411. The Attorneys have not satisfied, and cannot satisfy, the threshold requirement of "use." This court finds: The pop-up advertisement does not constitute "use" within the meaning of the Lanham Act. The pop-up advertisement appears in a separate window and does not divert or misdirect consumers away from the Attorneys' websites. *See WhenU.com, Inc.*, 414 F.3d at 411. Indeed, this court adopts the rationale of the *WhenU.com* court:

> Not surprisingly, 1–800 cites no legal authority for the proposition: Advertisements, software, or any other visual image—that can appear on a C-user's computer screen—must be authorized by the owner of any website that will appear contemporaneously with that image. – WhenU does not need 1–800's authorization to display a separate window—containing an ad—any more than Corel would need authorization from Microsoft to display its WordPerfect word-processor in a window contemporaneously with a Word word-processing window. *Id.* at 412

Since the Attorneys have failed to properly allege and prove "use," this court need not reach the issue: whether any of Reed's communications—with consumers—caused a likelihood of confusion, sufficient to state a claim under the Lanham Act. Even were the court to reach the "likelihood of confusion" issue, the Attorneys have failed to present sufficient facts to show: Reed made misrepresentations to consumers that would cause a likelihood of confusion. The Attorneys' assert: Reed made misrepresentations to consumers. "Reed told the prospect that we have matched you with the following firm ... when in fact, Reed essentially referred the prospect back to IMS." These statements, however, are irrelevant for establishing a Lanham Act claim because they have no bearing on whether the customer was confused about the origin of the pop-up advertisement.

The Lanham Act was intended to make actionable the deceptive and misleading use of marks. *Tenneco Auto. Operating Co. v. Kingdom Auto Parts*, 410 Fed. Appx. 841, 845 (6th Cir. 2010). Thus, there must be a causal connection between the challenged statement and the alleged consumer confusion which caused the harm. *Medison Am., Inc. v. Preferred Med. Sys. LLC*, 548 F.Supp.2d 567, 576 (W.D.Tenn.2007) ("In order to maintain an action under the Lanham Act, Medison must show that the Preferred Medical defendants made false or misleading statements of fact about Medison's productions.").

Viewing the facts as true and in the light most favorable to the Attorneys, the assertion that Reed violated the Lanham Act has not been sufficiently established. Furthermore, since the pop-up advertisements in this case do not constitute "use," no amendment can cure this pleading. Therefore, Defendant's motion to dismiss is granted in its entirety.

United States Code

Title 15. Commerce and Trade
Chapter 22. Trademarks
Trademark (Lanham) Act of 1946 and 1988
15 U.S.C. § 1125(a)

§ 1125(a)—Civil Action: False Designations of Origin, Descriptions and Dilution Forbidden

(1) Any person who, on or in connection with any goods or services...*uses* in commerce any word, term, name, symbol, or device, or any combination thereof, or any false designation of origin, *false or misleading description* of fact, or *false or misleading representation* of fact, which—

(A) is likely to *cause confusion*, or to cause mistake, or to deceive as to the affiliation, connection, or association of such person with another person, or as to the origin, sponsorship, or approval of his or her goods, services, or commercial activities by another person, or

(B) in commercial advertising or promotion, misrepresents the nature, characteristics, qualities, or geographic origin of his or her or another person's goods, services, or commercial activities,

shall be liable in a civil action by any person who believes that he or she is or is likely to be damaged by such act.

* * *

United States Code

Title 15. Commerce and Trade
Chapter 22. Trademarks
Trademark (Lanham) Act of 19461946 and 1988
15 U.S.C. § 1125(c)

§ 1125(c)—Dilution by Blurring; Dilution by Tarnishment

(1) Injunctive Relief—Subject to the principles of equity, the owner of a famous mark that is distinctive, inherently or through acquired distinctiveness, shall be entitled to an injunction against another person who, at any time after the owner's mark has become famous, commences use of a mark or trade name in commerce that is likely to cause dilution by blurring or dilution by tarnishment of the famous mark, regardless of the presence or absence of actual or likely confusion, of competition, or of actual economic injury.

(2) Definitions:

(A) For purposes of paragraph (1), a mark is famous if it is widely recognized by the general consuming public of the United States as a designation of source of the goods or services of the mark's owner. In determining whether a mark possesses the requisite degree of recognition, the court may consider all relevant factors, including the following:

(i) The duration, extent, and geographic reach of advertising and publicity of the mark, whether advertised or publicized by the owner or third parties.

(ii) The amount, volume, and geographic extent of sales of goods or services offered under the mark.

(iii) The extent of actual recognition of the mark.

(iv) Whether the mark was registered under the Act of March 3, 1881, or the Act of February 20, 1905, or on the principal register.

(B) For purposes of paragraph (1), "dilution by blurring" is association arising from the similarity between a mark or trade name and a famous mark that impairs the distinctiveness of the famous mark. In determining whether a mark or trade name is likely to cause dilution by blurring, the court may consider all relevant factors, including the following:

(i) The degree of similarity between the mark or trade name and the famous mark.

(ii) The degree of inherent or acquired distinctiveness of the famous mark.

(iii) The extent to which the owner of the famous mark is engaging in substantially exclusive use of the mark.

(iv) The degree of recognition of the famous mark.

(v) Whether the user of the mark or trade name intended to create an association with the famous mark.

(vi) Any actual association between the mark or trade name and the famous mark.

(C) For purposes of paragraph (1), "dilution by tarnishment" is association arising from the similarity between a mark or trade name and a famous mark that harms the reputation of the famous mark.

(3) Exclusions—The following shall not be actionable as dilution by blurring or dilution by tarnishment under this subsection:

(A) Any fair use, including a nominative or descriptive fair use, or facilitation of such fair use, of a famous mark by another person other than as a designation of source for the person's own goods or services, including use in connection with—

(i) advertising or promotion that permits consumers to compare goods or services; or

(ii) identifying and parodying, criticizing, or commenting upon the famous mark owner or the goods or services of the famous mark owner.

(B) All forms of news reporting and news commentary.

(C) Any noncommercial use of a mark.

(4) Burden of Proof—In a civil action for trade dress dilution under this chapter for trade dress not registered on the principal register, the person who asserts trade dress protection has the burden of proving that—

(A) the claimed trade dress, taken as a whole, is not functional and is famous; and

(B) if the claimed trade dress includes any mark or marks registered on the principal register, the unregistered matter, taken as a whole, is famous separate and apart from any fame of such registered marks.

* * *

United States Code

Title 15. Commerce and Trade
Chapter 22. Trademarks
Trademark (Lanham) Act of 1946 and 1988
15 U.S.C. § 1125(d)

§ 1125(d)—Cyberpiracy Prevention

(1) (A) A person shall be liable in a civil action by the owner of a mark, including a personal name which is protected as a mark under this section, if, without regard to the goods or services of the parties, that person—

(i) has a bad faith intent to profit from that mark, including a personal name which is protected as a mark under this section; and

(ii) registers, traffics in, or uses a domain name that—

(I) in the case of a mark that is distinctive at the time of registration of the domain name, is identical or confusingly similar to that mark;

(II) in the case of a famous mark that is famous at the time of registration of the domain name, is identical or confusingly similar to or dilutive of that mark; or

(III) is a trademark, word, or name protected by reason of section 706 of Title 18 or section 220506 of Title 36.

(B)(i) In determining whether a person has a bad faith intent described under subparagraph (A), a court may consider factors such as, but not limited to—

(I) the trademark or other intellectual property rights of the person, if any, in the domain name;

(II) the extent to which the domain name consists of the legal name of the person or a name that is otherwise commonly used to identify that person;

(III) the person's prior use, if any, of the domain name in connection with the bona fide offering of any goods or services;

(IV) the person's bona fide noncommercial or fair use of the mark in a site accessible under the domain name;

(V) the person's intent to divert consumers from the mark owner's online location to a site accessible under the domain name that could harm the goodwill represented by the mark, either for commercial gain or with the intent to tarnish or disparage the mark, by creating a likelihood of confusion as to the source, sponsorship, affiliation, or endorsement of the site;

(VI) the person's offer to transfer, sell, or otherwise assign the domain name to the mark owner or any third party for financial gain without having used, or having an intent to use, the domain name in the bona fide offering of any goods or services, or the person's prior conduct indicating a pattern of such conduct;

(VII) the person's provision of material and misleading false contact information when applying for the registration of the domain name, the person's intentional failure to maintain accurate contact information, or the person's prior conduct indicating a pattern of such conduct;

(VIII) the person's registration or acquisition of multiple domain names which the person knows are identical or confusingly similar to marks of others that are distinctive at the time of registration of such domain names, or dilutive of famous marks of others that are famous at the time of registration of such domain names, without regard to the goods or services of the parties; and

(IX) the extent to which the mark incorporated in the person's domain name registration is or is not distinctive and famous within the meaning of subsection (c) of this section.

(ii) Bad faith intent described under subparagraph (A) shall not be found in any case in which the court determines that the person believed and had reasonable grounds to believe that the use of the domain name was a fair use or otherwise lawful.

(C) In any civil action involving the registration, trafficking, or use of a domain name under this paragraph, a court may order the forfeiture or cancellation of the domain name or the transfer of the domain name to the owner of the mark.

(D) A person shall be liable for using a domain name under subparagraph (A) only if that person is the domain name registrant or that registrant's authorized licensee.

(E) As used in this paragraph, the term "traffics in" refers to transactions that include, but are not limited to, sales, purchases, loans, pledges, licenses, exchanges of currency, and any other transfer for consideration or receipt in exchange for consideration.

(2) (A) The owner of a mark may file an in rem civil action against a domain name in the judicial district in which the domain name registrar, domain name registry, or other domain name authority that registered or assigned the domain name is located if—

(i) the domain name violates any right of the owner of a mark registered in the Patent and Trademark Office, or protected under subsection (a) or (c) of this section; and

(ii) the court finds that the owner—

(I) is not able to obtain in personam jurisdiction over a person who would have been a defendant in a civil action under paragraph (1); or

(II) through due diligence was not able to find a person who would have been a defendant in a civil action under paragraph (1) by—

(aa) sending a notice of the alleged violation and intent to proceed under this paragraph to the registrant of the domain name at the postal and e-mail address provided by the registrant to the registrar; and

(bb) publishing notice of the action as the court may direct promptly after filing the action.

(B) The actions under subparagraph (A)(ii) shall constitute service of process.

(C) In an in rem action under this paragraph, a domain name shall be deemed to have its situs in the judicial district in which—

(i) the domain name registrar, registry, or other domain name authority that registered or assigned the domain name is located; or

(ii) documents sufficient to establish control and authority regarding the disposition of the registration and use of the domain name are deposited with the court. …

(D)(i) The remedies in an in rem action under this paragraph shall be limited to a court order for the forfeiture or cancellation of the domain name or the transfer of the domain name to the owner of the mark.

B. The "Fair Use" of Website Publications in Judicial Proceedings and Attorneys' Right of Action Under the Copyright Act 1976

Hollander v. Swindells-Donovan

2010 WL 844588
(E.D.N.Y. 2010)

Block, Senior District Judge.

Roy Den Hollander is an attorney, who appears *pro se*. Hollander sued two attorneys—Deborah Swindells-Donovan and Paul W. Steinberg—for copyright infringement under the Copyright Act of 1976, 17 U.S.C. §§ 101–803. Attorney Deborah Donovan moved to dismiss for lack of subject-matter jurisdiction and failure to state a claim. The court converted the motion to one for summary judgment and afforded the parties an opportunity to submit papers in support. Hollander cross-moved for summary judgment.

I.

Attorney Hollander authored six Essays, which convey his aggressively anti-"Feminazi" world view. He registered each essay with the United States Copyright Office (the "Office"). Hollander possesses certificates of registration for "A Different Time," "An Invisible Weapon," "Do Men Cause Wars," and "Some Differences: Men and Girls." The Office has not issued certificates for the remaining two essays—"Fear Corrupts" and "Two Sides."

He made the Essays publicly available on his website at some point in 2006 or 2007—when Steinberg made a copy. On October 19, 2007, Steinberg sent copies of the Essays to Donovan.

A. Attorney Deborah Donovan's Use of the Essays

Hollander's claims against Donovan arise from *Hollander v. Copacabana Nightclub, et al. ("Copacabana")*, in which Hollander alleged: The "Ladies' Night" promotions hosted by several New York City nightclubs discriminated against men in violation of the Fourteenth Amendment. Attorney Donovan represented defendant Lotus Nightclub. After a contentious status conference, Hollander moved to disqualify District Judge Miriam Cedarbaum. He asserted: Judge Cedarbaum's conduct had "created the appearance that she, whether true or not, is biased and prejudiced against men and creates a perception that she is not impartial in these proceedings." Attorney Deborah Donovan attached the Essays to Judge Cedarbaum's opposition to Hollander's motion and asserted: The Essays supported the argument that Attorney Hollander was "challenging Judge Cedarbaum's impartiality simply because the judge is female, not biased." Judge Cedarbaum denied Hollander's recusal motion and ultimately dismissed the *Copacabana* case because the defendants' offering of reduced-priced admission to females did not constitute state action. *See Copacabana,* 580 F.Supp.2d 335 (S.D.N.Y. 2008).

B. Attorney Paul Steinberg's Use of the Essays

Attorneys Deborah Donovan and Paul Steinberg's sordid history centers primarily on Steinberg's representation of Attorney Hollander's upstairs neighbor—William Fasano—and the object of a number of Hollander's lawsuits. Hollander's claims against Steinberg in this particular case, however, originated out of two New York state court actions. In *Hollander v. Fasano, et al. ("Fasano I"),* Hollander brought a defamation action against several parties for statements made in pleadings in a different action. Attorney Steinberg was a named defendant; and he also represented Fasano. When Hollander tried to add certain female acquaintances of Fasano as defendants, Steinberg submitted the Essays in opposition. Steinberg asserted: The content of the Essays—in light of Hollander's alleged "issues with gender identity," "obsession with Fasano's body," and assault of Steinberg— "addressed matters relating to [Hollander's] motivation in bringing suit."

In *Hollander v. Fasano ("Fasano II"),* Steinberg represented Fasano in a nuisance action brought by Hollander. After Hollander's complaint went unanswered, he moved for a default judgment. Steinberg opposed that motion, appending a verified answer and counterclaims which requested, *inter alia,* "protective orders ... to safeguard Mr. Fasano and others from potential physical harm by Mr. Den Hollander." In support of this request, Steinberg attached the Essays, asserting that their content—when considered with Hollander's alleged misdeeds—evidenced the danger that Hollander posed to his neighbors.

II.

Both Attorneys Donovan and Steinberg admit: They knowingly submitted Attorney Hollander's Essays as exhibits in a judicial proceeding. Accordingly, the issue before the court is whether

Attorneys Donovan and Steinberg's submissions constitute "fair use"—as a matter of law—under the Copyright Act of 1976, § 107.

A. Summary Judgment

"Summary judgment should be granted if there is no genuine issue as to any material fact and … the moving party is entitled to a judgment as a matter of law." *Blanch v. Koons,* 467 F.3d 244, 250 (2d Cir.2006), quoting Fed. R. Civ. P. 56(c). "Although fair use is a mixed question of law and fact," a court may "resolve fair use determinations at the summary judgment stage where there are no genuine issues of material fact." *Id.* A genuine dispute regarding material fact exists when "the evidence is such that a reasonable jury could return a verdict for the nonmoving party." *Anderson v. Liberty Lobby, Inc.,* 477 U.S. 242, 248 (1986). The "facts must be viewed in the light most favorable to the nonmoving party." *Scott v. Harris,* 550 U.S. 372, 380 (2007).

B. Subject Matter Jurisdiction

Donovan argues: Attorney Hollander's failure to present certificates of registration for "Fear Corrupts" and "Two Sides" deprives the court of subject-matter jurisdiction over infringement claims based on those essays. However, the record demonstrates: All six Essays were registered with the Office. Therefore, the court has jurisdiction over all of Attorney Hollander's infringement claims. *See In re Literary Works in Elec. Databases Copyright Litig.,* 509 F.3d 116, 122 (2d Cir.2007), citing 17 U.S.C. § 411(a).

C. Fair Use Under 17 U.S.C. § 107

Under the Copyright Act of 1976, the fair use of copyrighted works does not constitute "an infringement of copyright." The Act permits the reproduction of copyrighted works "for purposes such as criticism, comment, news reporting, teaching [and] research." 17 U.S.C. § 107. Determining whether a particular reproduction is a fair use requires the consideration of a number of statutory factors:

(1) the purpose and character of the use, including whether such use is of a commercial nature or is for nonprofit educational purposes;

(2) the nature of the copyrighted work;

(3) the amount and substantiality of the portion used in relation to the copyrighted work as a whole; and

(4) the effect of the use upon the potential market for or value

of the copyrighted work. *Id.*

These factors are not to be treated in isolation. "All must be explored, and the results weighed together, in light of the purposes of copyright." *Campbell v. Acuff-Rose Music, Inc.*, 510 U.S. 569, 577-78 (1994). Ultimately, the statute "calls for case-by-case analysis," and the lists of acceptable purposes and relevant factors are "illustrative and not limitative." *Id.* Defendants bear the burden of proving that the use was fair; however, defendants need not establish that each factor in § 107 weighs in their favor." *NXIVM Corp. v. Ross Inst.*, 364 F.3d 471, 476 (2d Cir.2004). Although neither the Supreme Court nor the Second Circuit has addressed fair use in the context of evidentiary submissions in judicial proceedings, other courts have.

Consistent with the case-by-case nature of the doctrine, those courts have not announced a *per se* rule. Instead, they have considered the uniqueness of each "fair use" question, guided by the four statutory factors where relevant. *See Bond v. Blum,* 317 F.3d 385, 395 (4th Cir.2003) (affirming a "fair use" finding where an alleged infringer introduced plaintiff's copyrighted manuscript as evidence in a child-custody proceeding); *Jartech, Inc. v. Clancy,* 666 F.2d 403, 407 (9th Cir.1982) (affirming a jury's finding of fair use where the alleged infringer introduced copyrighted films as evidence in a nuisance abatement proceeding); and, *Shell v. DeVries,* 2007 WL 4269047 (10th Cir.2007) (affirming a "fair use" finding where the alleged infringer copied "ten pages from plaintiff's website used it as evidence in unrelated litigation"). *But see Images Audio Visual Prod., Inc. v. Perini Bldg. Co., Inc.,* 91 F.Supp.2d 1075, 1082 (E.D.Mich.2000) (holding that the introduction of copyrighted photographs in an arbitration proceeding constituted copyright infringement where photos were copyrighted "specifically for the purpose of litigation").

D. Claims Against Attorney Deborah Donovan

Attorney Deborah Donovan's stated justification for submitting Attorney Roy Hollander's Essays to Judge Cederbaum appears somewhat disingenuous. The relevancy of the Essays to Hollander's recusal motion is dubious, and Attorney Donovan undoubtedly intended simply to prejudice Judge Cederbaum against Attorney Hollander. Nonetheless, the decisive factor bearing upon the issue of "fair use" in this case is clear: Attorney Deborah Donovan introduced the Essays into the judicial proceeding [to illustrate the state] of Attorney Hollander's mind. She did not attempt to produce a comparable or derivative work, nor did she use the Essays for their expressive content. Even though the Essays are indisputably creative and published, Attorney Donovan admits: She reproduced five of the six in their entirety, and her submission "[was] indifferent to [Attorney Hollander's] mode of expression." *See Bond,* 317 F.3d at 395 ("The copyright law was never designed to protect content as distinguished from mode of expression.").

Accordingly, Donovan did not exploit Hollander's copyrighted ideas or expressions, nor did she put the Essays to "the same intrinsic use" for which Hollander obtained the copyrights and for which he could "expect protection from unauthorized use." *Jartech,* 666 F.2d at 407. ... Moreover, given that Essays were submitted as evidence to illustrate the state of Hollander's mind, it is impossible to determine how their use in the judicial proceeding could affect the "men's rights groups" market for the Essays or impact their marketability. *See Bond,* 317 F.3d at 396–97 ("[I]f anything, [Attorney Deborah Donovan's use of Attorney Hollander's Essays as evidence] increases the value of the work in a perverse way, but it certainly doesn't decrease it.").

E. Claims Against Attorney Paul Steinberg

Although Attorney Steinberg embraced Attorney Donovan's arguments in his pre-motion letter and at oral argument, he did not formally join her motion, nor did he submit his own. Nevertheless, a district court has the power to *sua sponte* grant summary judgment "so long as the losing party was on notice that [he or] she had to come forward with all of her evidence." *Celotex Corp. v. Catrett,* 477 U.S. 317, 326 (1986).

The facts underlying the claims against Steinberg have been fully developed and are not in dispute. As with Donovan, Steinberg's purpose in introducing the Essays undoubtedly had less to do with their relevancy, which was questionable, at best, and more to do with poisoning the minds of the judges in *Fasano I and Fasano II.* Be that as it may, Attorney Steinberg also submitted the Essays to evince the workings of Hollander's mind. And Attorney Steinberg's use cannot realistically be viewed as negatively impacting Attorney Hollander's market for the Essays. Accordingly, the same rationale—which supports granting summary judgment for Attorney Deborah Donovan—compels the court to grant summary judgment for Attorney Steinberg.

Conclusion

Attorney Deborah Donovan's motion for summary judgment is granted, and Attorney Hollander's cross-motion is denied.

Summary judgment in favor of Attorney Steinberg is granted *sua sponte*. The complaint is dismissed in its entirety. So Ordered.

United States Code

Title 17. Copyrights
The Copyright Act of 1976
Chapter 1. Subject Matter and Scope of Copyright
17 U.S.C. § 107

§ 107. Limitations on Exclusive Rights: Fair Use

Notwithstanding the provisions of sections 106 and 106A, the fair use of a copyrighted work, including such use by reproduction in copies or phonorecords or by any other means specified by that section, for purposes such as criticism, comment, news reporting, teaching (including multiple copies for classroom use), scholarship, or research, is not an infringement of copyright. In determining whether the use made of a work in any particular case is a fair use the factors to be considered shall include—

(1) the purpose and character of the use, including whether such use is of a commercial nature or is for nonprofit educational purposes;

(2) the nature of the copyrighted work;

(3) the amount and substantiality of the portion used in relation to the copyrighted work as a whole; and

(4) the effect of the use upon the potential market for or value of the copyrighted work.

The fact that a work is unpublished shall not itself bar a finding of fair use if such finding is made upon consideration of all the above factors.

United States Code

Title 17. Copyrights
The Copyright Act of 1976
Chapter 4. Copyright Notice, Deposit, and Registration
17 U.S.C. § 411

§ 411. Registration and Civil Infringement Actions

(a) Except for an action brought for a violation of the rights of the author under section 106A(a), and subject to the provisions of subsection (b), no civil action for infringement of the copyright in any United States work shall be instituted until preregistration or registration of the copyright claim has been made in accordance with this title. In any case, however, where the deposit, application, and fee required for registration have been delivered to the Copyright Office in proper form and registration has been refused, the applicant is entitled to institute a civil action for infringement if notice thereof, with a copy of the complaint, is served on the Register of Copyrights. The Register may, at his or her option, become a party to the action with respect to the issue of registrability of the copyright claim by entering an appearance within sixty days after such service, but the Register's failure to become a party shall not deprive the court of jurisdiction to determine that issue.

(b) (1) A certificate of registration satisfies the requirements of this section and section 412, regardless of whether the certificate contains any inaccurate information, unless—

(A) the inaccurate information was included on the application for copyright registration with knowledge that it was inaccurate; and

(B) the inaccuracy of the information, if known, would have caused the Register of Copyrights to refuse registration.

* * *

(c) In the case of a work consisting of sounds, images, or both, the first fixation of which is made simultaneously with its transmission, the copyright owner may, either before or after such fixation takes place, institute an action for infringement under section 501, fully subject to the remedies provided by sections 502 through 505 and section 510, if, in accordance with requirements that the Register of Copyrights shall prescribe by regulation, the copyright owner—

(1) serves notice upon the infringer, not less than 48 hours before such fixation, identifying the work and the specific time and source of its first transmission, and declaring an intention to secure copyright in the work; and

(2) makes registration for the work, if required by subsection (a), within three months after its first transmission.

C. The Unauthorized Retrieval of Information on Attorneys' Protected Computers and Private Right of Action Under the Computer Fraud and Abuse Act of 1986

Bashaw v. Johnson

2012 WL 1623483
(D. Kan. 2012)

John W. Lungstrum, District Judge. Plaintiffs are former employees of defendant Attorney Jeremiah Johnson and/or defendant's law firm. Plaintiffs filed this diversity lawsuit alleging that Attorney Johnson required plaintiffs to wear skirts in the office. Then Attorney Johnson allegedly used an application on his iPhone and iPad to conduct video surveillance of the area beneath a particular desk in the office to secretly obtained video recordings of plaintiffs' legs, lower torsos and undergarments. Plaintiffs asserted several state law claims—invasion of privacy, outrage, and breach of fiduciary duty.

Attorney Johnson has counterclaimed—alleging that the former employees violated the Computer Fraud and Abuse Act of 1986, 18 U.S.C. § 1030 *et seq.* (CFAA). Specifically, Attorney Johnson contends that plaintiffs, accessed his iPhone and iPad—exceeding their authorization—and deleted data from those devices. This matter is presently before the court on plaintiffs-employees' motion to dismiss Attorney Johnson's counterclaim for failure to state a claim under Federal Rule of Civil Procedure 12(b)(6).

The Computer Fraud and Abuse Act Claim

Attorney Johnson's counterclaim asserts: One or more plaintiffs-employees violated the Computer Fraud and Abuse Act (CFAA) by accessing—without authorization or in excess of their authorization—Attorney Johnson's iPad, iPhone and one or more computers. Additionally, Attorney Johnson alleged that the former employees deleted unspecified data from those devices. According to Johnson, he has been damaged by the employees' actions; and the damages "would exceed" at least $5,000. The former employees move to dismiss this counterclaim. They assert that Attorney Johnson's claim fails in at least two respects: Johnson does not sufficiently establishes the nature of his damages within the meaning of CFAA; and he does not sufficiently allege and prove a qualifying "loss" within the meaning of CFAA.

CFAA is a federal statute that criminalizes certain activities in connection with computers. *See* 18 U.S.C. § 1030. Despite the criminal nature of CFAA, it provides a private civil cause of action under limited circumstances. *See* § 1030(g); *TriTeq & Sec. LLC v. Innovative Secured Solutions, LLC,* 2012 WL 394229, at *5 (N.D.Ill. 2012). Under § 1030(g), a civil action may be brought only if the conduct "involves 1 of the factors set forth in subclauses (I), (II), (III), (IV), or (V) of subsection (c)(4)(A)(i)." 18 U.S.C. § 1030(g). In other words, a plaintiff alleging a violation under § 1030(g) must allege the conduct involved one of the following factors:

> (I) loss to 1 or more persons during any 1-year period … aggregating at least $5,000 in value;
>
> (II) the modification or impairment, or potential modification or impairment, of the medical examination, diagnosis, treatment, or care of 1 or more individuals;
>
> (III) physical injury to any person;
>
> (IV) a threat to public health or safety; [or]

(V) damage affecting a computer used by or for an entity of the United States Government in furtherance of the administration of justice, national defense, or national security. *Id.* § 1030(c)(4)(A)(i)(I)-(V).

In his counterclaim, Attorney Johnson asserts that the former employees violated § 1030(g)—by violating § 1030(a)(2), (a)(4) and (a)(5). Each of these subsections, with some variation, prohibits accessing a protected computer without authorization and obtaining information from the computer.

According to the counterclaim complaint, each of these asserted violations are based on conduct—as required under § 1030(g)—involving an aggregated loss of at least $5,000. For each of these asserted violations, Attorney Johnson must allege a "loss" within the meaning of the CFAA. In addition, subsection (a)(5) contains an express "damage" requirement: Attorney Johnson must also adequately allege "damage" within the meaning of the statute for purposes of his subsection (a)(5) claim. *See TriTeq Lock,* 2012 WL 394229, at *5. Thus, to state a claim under § 1030(g) for violation of § 1030(a)(5) based upon § 1030(c)(4)(A)(i)(I), a plaintiff must allege both "damage" and a "loss" aggregating at least $5,000 in value. *Id.*

The CFAA defines "damage" as "any impairment to the integrity or availability of data, a program, a system, or information." 18 U.S.C. § 1030(e)(8). In construing this term, courts have determined that "damage" refers to "the destruction, corruption, or deletion of electronic files, the physical destruction of a hard drive, or any "diminution in the completeness or usability of the data on a computer system." *TriTeq Lock,* 2012 WL 394229 at *6. Attorney Johnson alleges: He "has been damaged." But he does not assert the nature of such damage. In his submissions on the motion, Attorney Johnson claims that he suffered damages because "data was erased."

However, in his submissions or counterclaim complaint, Attorney Johnson does not identify the data that was allegedly erased. This allegation essentially parrots the statutory language and is factually insufficient to satisfy the damages element of Attorney Johnson's CFAA claim. *See TriTeq Lock,* 2012 WL 394229, at *6 (plaintiff did not sufficiently allege "damage" for purposes of CFAA claim where complaint alleged only that defendant caused damage but failed to allege any facts "to give color to this bare assertion of damage"); *Ipreo Holdings LLC v. Thomson Reuters Corp .,* 2011 WL 855872, at *7 (S.D.N.Y. 2011) (the complaint must allege with some particularity "damage" as defined by the CFAA); *Fink v. Time Warner Cable,* 2009 WL 2207920, at *4 (S.D.N.Y. 2009) (dismissing CFAA claim under *Iqbal* where plaintiff alleged only that defendant caused damage by impairing the availability of data). For this reason, defendant cannot state a claim for relief under subsection (a)(5).

Similarly, Attorney Johnson has not adequately pled a qualifying "loss" for purposes of CFAA. Under CFAA, "the term 'loss' means any reasonable cost to any victim, including the cost of responding to an offense, conducting a damage assessment, and restoring the data, program, system, or information to its condition prior to the offense, and any revenue lost, cost incurred, or other consequential damages incurred because of interruption of service." 18 U.S.C. § 1030(e)(11). The majority of courts have construed the term "loss" to include only two types of injuries—costs such as lost revenues following interrupted computer service, and costs to investigate and respond to computer intrusion or damage. *See TriTeq Lock,* 2012 WL 394229, at *6-7 (collecting cases); and, *Trademotion, LLC v. Marketcliq, Inc.,* 857 F.Supp.2d 1285, 2012 WL 682465, at *6 (M.D.Fla. 2012).

In his counterclaim, Attorney Johnson has not alleged that he suffered any "loss" under CFAA. While he alleges that unspecified losses "would exceed" $5,000, he does not allege that he actually incurred losses in that amount. He does not allege or identify any investigative or response costs incurred as a result of the alleged CFAA violation. And he does not allege any lost revenues or other losses incurred due to any interruption in service. In his submissions, Attorney Johnson contends: Qualifying losses under the statute include "for example" the prorated salaries or wages of employees who spent time restoring a backup of deleted data or recreating lost work. But he does not suggest: His employees performed these tasks or that he incurred costs relating to such tasks.

Because he has not alleged any loss under the statute, Attorney Johnson cannot maintain a CFAA claim for violations of any of the subsections identified in his counterclaim complaint. This claim is dismissed in its entirety. Therefore, the plaintiffs-employees' motion to dismiss Attorney Johnson's CFAA counterclaim is granted.

United States Code

Title 18. Crimes and Criminal Procedure
The Computer Fraud and Abuse Act of 1986
Chapter 47. Fraud and False Statements
18 U.S.C. § 1030(a)

§ 1030(a). Fraud and Related Activity in Connection with Computers. Whoever—

(1) having knowingly accessed a computer without authorization or exceeding authorized access, and by means of such conduct having obtained information that has been determined by the United States Government pursuant to an Executive order or statute to require protection against unauthorized disclosure for reasons of national defense or foreign relations, or any restricted data, as defined in paragraph y. of section 11 of the Atomic Energy Act of 1954, with reason to believe that such information so obtained could be used to the injury of the United States, or to the advantage of any foreign nation willfully communicates, delivers, transmits, or causes to be communicated, delivered, or transmitted, or attempts to communicate, deliver, transmit or cause to be communicated, delivered, or transmitted the same to any person not entitled to receive it, or willfully retains the same and fails to deliver it to the officer or employee of the United States entitled to receive it;

(2) intentionally accesses a computer without authorization or exceeds authorized access, and thereby obtains—

(A) information contained in a financial record of a financial institution, or of a card issuer as defined in section 1602(n) of title 15, or contained in a file of a consumer reporting agency on a consumer, as such terms are defined in the Fair Credit Reporting Act (15 U.S.C. 1681 et seq.);

(B) information from any department or agency of the United States; or

(C) information from any protected computer;

(3) intentionally, without authorization to access any nonpublic computer of a department or agency of the United States, accesses such a computer of that department or agency that

is exclusively for the use of the Government of the United States or, in the case of a computer not exclusively for such use, is used by or for the Government of the United States and such conduct affects that use by or for the Government of the United States;

(4) knowingly and with intent to defraud, accesses a protected computer without authorization, or exceeds authorized access, and by means of such conduct furthers the intended fraud and obtains anything of value, unless the object of the fraud and the thing obtained consists only of the use of the computer and the value of such use is not more than $5,000 in any one-year period;

(5) (A) knowingly causes the transmission of a program, information, code, or command, and as a result of such conduct, intentionally causes damage without authorization, to a protected computer;

(B) intentionally accesses a protected computer without authorization, and as a result of such conduct, recklessly causes damage; or

(C) intentionally accesses a protected computer without authorization, and as a result of such conduct, causes damage and loss.

(6) knowingly and with intent to defraud traffics (as defined in section 1029) in any password or similar information through which a computer may be accessed without authorization, if—

(A) such trafficking affects interstate or foreign commerce; or

(B) such computer is used by or for the Government of the United States;

(7) with intent to extort from any person any money or other thing of value, transmits in interstate or foreign commerce any communication containing any—

(A) threat to cause damage to a protected computer;

(B) threat to obtain information from a protected computer without authorization or in excess of authorization or to impair the confidentiality of information obtained from a protected computer without authorization or by exceeding authorized access; or

(C) demand or request for money or other thing of value in relation to damage to a protected computer, where such damage was caused to facilitate the extortion;

shall be punished as provided in subsection (c) of this section.

United States Code

Title 18. Crimes and Criminal Procedure
The Computer Fraud and Abuse Act of 1986
Chapter 47. Fraud and False Statements
18 U.S.C. § 1030(c)

§ 1030(c). The punishment for an offense under subsection (a) or (b) of this section is—

(1) (A) a fine under this title or imprisonment for not more than ten years, or both, in the case of an offense under subsection (a)(1) of this section which does not occur after a conviction for another offense under this section, or an attempt to commit an offense punishable under this subparagraph; and

(B) a fine under this title or imprisonment for not more than twenty years, or both, in the case of an offense under subsection (a)(1) of this section which occurs after a conviction for another offense under this section, or an attempt to commit an offense punishable under this subparagraph;

(2) (A) except as provided in subparagraph (B), a fine under this title or imprisonment for not more than one year, or both, in the case of an offense under subsection (a)(2), (a)(3), or (a)(6) of this section which does not occur after a conviction for another offense under this section, or an attempt to commit an offense punishable under this subparagraph;

(B) a fine under this title or imprisonment for not more than 5 years, or both, in the case of an offense under subsection (a)(2), or an attempt to commit an offense punishable under this subparagraph, if—

(i) the offense was committed for purposes of commercial advantage or private financial gain;

(ii) the offense was committed in furtherance of any criminal or tortious act in violation of the Constitution or laws of the United States or of any State; or

(iii) the value of the information obtained exceeds $5,000; and

(C) a fine under this title or imprisonment for not more than ten years, or both, in the case of an offense under subsection (a)(2), (a)(3) or (a)(6) of this section which occurs after a conviction for another offense under this section, or an attempt to commit an offense punishable under this subparagraph;

(3) (A) a fine under this title or imprisonment for not more than five years, or both, in the case of an offense under subsection (a)(4) or (a)(7) of this section which does not occur after a conviction for another offense under this section, or an attempt to commit an offense punishable under this subparagraph; and

(B) a fine under this title or imprisonment for not more than ten years, or both, in the case of an offense under subsection (a)(4),3 or (a)(7) of this section which occurs after a conviction for another offense under this section, or an attempt to commit an offense punishable under this subparagraph;

(4) (A) except as provided in subparagraphs (E) and (F), a fine under this title, imprisonment for not more than 5 years, or both, in the case of—

(i) an offense under subsection (a)(5)(B), which does not occur after a conviction for another offense under this section, if the offense caused (or, in the case of an attempted offense, would, if completed, have caused)—

(I) loss to 1 or more persons during any 1-year period (and, for purposes of an investigation, prosecution, or other proceeding brought by the United States only, loss resulting from a related course of conduct affecting 1 or more other protected computers) aggregating at least $5,000 in value;

(II) the modification or impairment, or potential modification or impairment, of the medical examination, diagnosis, treatment, or care of 1 or more individuals;

(III) physical injury to any person;

(IV) a threat to public health or safety;

(V) damage affecting a computer used by or for an entity of the United States Government in furtherance of the administration of justice, national defense, or national security; or

(VI) damage affecting 10 or more protected computers during any 1-year period; or

(ii) an attempt to commit an offense punishable under this subparagraph;

United States Code

Title 18. Crimes and Criminal Procedure
The Computer Fraud and Abuse Act of 1986
Chapter 47. Fraud and False Statements
18 U.S.C. § 1030(e)

§ 1030(e). Definition of Terms. As used in this section—

(1) the term "computer" means an electronic, magnetic, optical, electrochemical, or other high speed data processing device performing logical, arithmetic, or storage functions, and includes any data storage facility or communications facility directly related to or operating in conjunction with such device, but such term does not include an automated typewriter or typesetter, a portable hand held calculator, or other similar device;

(2) the term "protected computer" means a computer—

(A) exclusively for the use of a financial institution or the United States Government, or, in the case of a computer not exclusively for such use, used by or for a financial institution or the United States Government and the conduct constituting the offense affects that use by or for the financial institution or the Government; or

(B) which is used in or affecting interstate or foreign commerce or communication, including a computer located outside the United States that is used in a manner that affects interstate or foreign commerce or communication of the United States;

* * *

(11) the term "loss" means any reasonable cost to any victim, including the cost of responding to an offense, conducting a damage assessment, and restoring the data, program, system, or information to its condition prior to the offense, and any revenue lost, cost incurred, or other consequential damages incurred because of interruption of service; and

(12) the term "person" means any individual, firm, corporation, educational institution, financial institution, governmental entity, or legal or other entity.

United States Code

Title 18. Crimes and Criminal Procedure
The Computer Fraud and Abuse Act of 1986
Chapter 47. Fraud and False Statements
18 U.S.C. § 1030(g)

§ 1030(g). Civil Action.

Any person who suffers damage or loss by reason of a violation of this section may maintain a civil action against the violator to obtain compensatory damages and injunctive relief or other equitable relief. A civil action for a violation of this section may be brought only if the conduct involves 1 of the factors set forth in subclauses (I), (II), (III), (IV), or (V) of subsection (c)(4)(A)(i).

Damages for a violation involving only conduct described in subsection (c)(4)(A)(i)(I) are limited to economic damages. No action may be brought under this subsection unless such action is begun within 2 years of the date of the act complained of or the date of the discovery of the damage. No action may be brought under this subsection for the negligent design or manufacture of computer hardware, computer software, or firmware.

D. Unauthorized Accessing and Rerouting Privileged Electronic Communications and Attorney's Private Right of Action Under the Stored Communications Act of 1986

Bovino v. MacMillan

28 F.Supp.3d 1170
(D.C. Colo. 2014)

Philip A. Brimmer, United States District Judge. This matter is before the court on a motion for summary judgment filed by David A. Bovino P.C. d/b/a Law Officers of Bovino & Associates, and Attorney David A. Bovino ("Attorney Bovino"). This court has subject matter jurisdiction pursuant to 28 U.S.C. § 1331 and § 1367.

Background

John H. MacMillan III was a descendant of the founder of Cargill Inc. — a United States-based food and manufacturing company. John MacMillan III married Patricia MacMillan and the couple had a son — Andrew Cargill MacMillan ("Mr. MacMillan"). John MacMillan III and Patricia MacMillan divorced and John MacMillan III died—leaving Mr. MacMillan as a beneficiary of a trust of significant value. The trust was administered by UBS Trust Company N.A. (UBS). Mr. Andrew MacMillan married Christina MacMillan ("Mrs. MacMillan") and the couple had a son.

Beginning in 2008, Attorney Bovino served as legal counsel for Mr. MacMillan. In 2010 and 2011, Mr. Bovino was retained to assist the transfer of trust assets from UBS to a different institutional trustee. Attorney Bovino and Mr. MacMillan also discussed "concerns over Andrew MacMillan's continuing his marriage" to

Mrs. Christina MacMillan. Attorney Bovino and Mr. MacMillan often communicated by email—via Mr. MacMillan's AOL account, and via Mr. Bovino's email account with the domain name *bovinolaw.com*.

For purposes of their motion, Attorney Bovino admits: Mrs. Christina MacMillan had permission to access Andrew MacMillan's account. However, the scope of that permission is disputed. Mrs. Christina MacMillan testified: Her husband—Andrew MacMillan allowed her to access his email by entering Andrew's email password into her computer. Christina MacMillan testified: "Andrew knew I could see his e-mails, too. He was fully aware of that." However, Mrs. Christina MacMillan also testified: Andrew MacMillan did not give her permission to forward emails to Andrew's mother—Mrs. Patricia MacMillan.

Mrs. Christina MacMillan admits accessing Mr. Andrew MacMillan's AOL account and viewing a January 7, 2011, email from Attorney Bovino—in which Mr. Bovino discusses concerns over Andrew MacMillan's continuing marriage to his wife, Christina. Mrs. MacMillan also admits: She accessed Andrew MacMillan's AOL account and viewed an email from Mr. Bovino dated February 2, 2011—in which Attorney Bovino discussed transferring trust assets from UBS to a different institutional trustee. At various times, Mrs. Christina MacMillan would access Mr. Andrew MacMillan's AOL account and forward Attorney Bovino's emails to Patricia MacMillan, UBS representatives and Christina's personal AOL account. Mrs. Christina MacMillan also admits: Sometimes, she deleted emails from Mr. Andrew MacMillan's email account.

On or about February 24, 2011, Mrs. Christina MacMillan created the domain name *bovinolaw.net*. Mrs. Christina MacMillan sent an email to Mr. Andrew MacMillan from a *bovinolaw.net* email address—pretending to be Attorney Bovino and stating: Attorney Bovino had changed his email address to *bovinolaw.net*. After creating the *bovinolaw.net* email address, Mrs. Christina MacMillan set up Mr. Andrew MacMillan's email to ensure: The emails that Attorney Bovino sent from his *bovinolaw.com* would be routed automatically to a spam folder. Then, Mrs. Christina MacMillan would review the diverted emails in Mr. MacMillan's spam folder, copy the emails' contents, and/or resend an email to Mr. MacMillan from the *bovinolaw.net* address. In one instance, Mrs. MacMillan admits: She altered the contents of Attorney Bovino's email before re-sending it to Mr. MacMillan from the *bovinolaw.net* address.

Mrs. MacMillan claims: She monitored her husband's emails out of concern for his mental state and decision-making ability. Mrs. Christina MacMillan testified: She believed Attorney Bovino knew her husband (Andrew) was vulnerable. And it was her intention to cut off communication between her husband and Attorney Bovino. According to a March 30, 2011, order from the 17th Judicial Circuit in and for Broward County (Florida), Mr. Andrew MacMillan was declared incompetent due to mental illness.

On May 10, 2011, Attorney Bovino, David A. Bovino P.C., and Mr. Andrew MacMillan filed this action against Andrew's mother—Mrs. Patricia MacMillan—in the District Court for Pitkin County, Colorado. On January 24, 2012, Mr. MacMillan—through his guardian ad litem—asked to be dismissed as a party. On January 25, 2012, the Court dismissed Mr. Andrew MacMillan from the case. On February 10, 2012, the remaining plaintiffs amended their complaint to add Mrs. Christina MacMillan as a defendant. On March 1, 2012, Mrs. Christina MacMillan removed the case to this Court. In the Second Amended Complaint, plaintiffs—Attorney Bovino and David A. Bovino P.C.—filed federal claims under the Lanham Act of 1946, the Computer Fraud and Abuse Act of 1986, the Stored Communications Act of 1986 and the Anticybersquatting Consumer Protection Act of 1999.

Plaintiffs move for summary judgment on the issue—whether Mrs. Christina MacMillan is liable under the Stored Communications Act of 1986 ("SCA"), 18 U.S.C. § 2701, *et seq.* Plaintiffs argue: Mrs. Christina MacMillan exceeded her authority by accessing Mr. Andrew MacMillan's AOL email account. And Mrs. Christina MacMillan prevented an intended party/addressee from accessing plaintiffs' emails. Mrs. MacMillan responds and argues: Plaintiffs lack standing to bring a claim under the SCA; and, Mrs. Christina MacMillan did not exceed her authorized access to Mr. MacMillan's AOL email account.

Analysis

A. Standing Under the Stored Communications Act of 1986

Mrs. MacMillan raises the issue of Attorney Bovino's standing to bring a claim under the SCA. Specifically, Mrs. MacMillan argues: Attorney Bovino did not suffer an "injury in fact." Therefore, he not an aggrieved person under the statute. Although it is not entirely clear, Mrs. Christina MacMillan also seems to claim: Attorney Bovino and the other plaintiffs lack standing under Article III of the United States Constitution. Plaintiffs argue: They have suffered an injury allegedly caused by Mrs. MacMillan's exceeding her authority—obtaining, forwarding, and altering privileged communications.

The Stored Communications Act is violated when a person: (1) intentionally accesses—without authorization—a facility through which an electronic communication service is provided; or (2) intentionally exceeds an authorization to access that facility; and thereby obtains, alters, or prevents authorized access to a wire or electronic communication while it is in electronic storage in such system. 18 U.S.C. § 2701(a). The SCA provides a right of action for persons "aggrieved by any violation of this chapter in which the conduct constituting the violation is engaged in with a knowing or intentional state of mind" 18 U.S.C. § 2707(a).

* * *

On the issue of whether they are "persons aggrieved" under the SCA, plaintiffs claim: "By admitting that she forwarded e-mails—between Attorney Bovino and his client—to the very individuals or entities about which the client sought legal advice, Defendant Christina MacMillan establishes the basis of Plaintiffs' grievance." Plaintiffs also state: They—a lawyer and a law firm—have Article III standing to prevent one's unauthorized obtaining, forwarding, altering and restricting access to attorney-client privileged emails.

Attorney Bovino correctly notes: When determining one's standing under Article III, a court should not confuse standing with merits. *See Initiative and Referendum Institute v. Walker,* 450 F.3d 1082, 1092 (10th Cir.2006). The Tenth Circuit observed in *Day v. Bond,* 500 F.3d 1127, 1137 (10th Cir.2007): "Practically speaking, *Walker* mandates: We assume—during the evaluation of the plaintiff's standing—that the plaintiff will prevail on his merits argument or that defendant has violated the law." The undisputed facts disclose: (1) Attorney Bovino and other plaintiffs were parties to communications that Mrs. Christina MacMillan viewed; (2) Mrs. MacMillan admits: She had no authority to forward privileged emails to third parties; (3) Mrs. Christina MacMillan accessed Mr. Andrew MacMillan's email account; and (4) Attorney Bovino addressed emails to Mr. Andrew MacMillan and Mrs. Christina MacMillan diverted those emails to [the] spam folder—before Mr. MacMillan could view them. Thus, the court finds: Attorney Bovino has shown injury in fact, which is sufficient to establish plaintiffs' standing to sue under Article III.

B. Mrs. MacMillan's Liability Under the Stored Communications Act

Attorney Bovino argues: Mrs. Christina MacMillan violated the SCA by forwarding, copying, printing, preventing access to, and altering emails that Mr. Bovino sent to Mr. MacMillan's AOL email account. Mrs. MacMillan does not dispute that her husband's AOL email account and email messages were "in storage"—at a "facility" which provides "an electronic communication service." 18 U.S.C. § 2701(a). Rather, Mrs. MacMillan argues: Her husband—Mr. Andrew MacMillan—gave her permission to access his AOL email account.

In part, the SCA was enacted "to protect privacy interests in personal and proprietary information and to address the growing problem of unauthorized persons deliberately gaining access to ... [private] electronic or wire communications." *Gen. Bd. of Global Ministries of the United Methodist Church v. Cablevision Lightpath, Inc.,* 2006 WL 3479332, at *3 (E.D.N.Y. 2006). Under the SCA, a person is not liable for conduct that is "authorized ... by a user of that service with respect to a communication of or intended for that user." 18 U.S.C. § 2701(c)(2). The existence and scope of authorization is generally a highly factual inquiry. *Global Policy Partners, LLC v. Yessin,* 686 F.Supp.2d 631, 636 (E.D.Va.2009).

Authorized access—in the electronic context—typically involves consideration of "the expected norms of intended use or the nature of the relationship established" between the holder of the communications and the authorized party. *U.S. v. Phillips,* 477 F.3d 215, 219 (5th Cir. 2007) (analyzing authorization under the Computer Fraud and Abuse Act (CFAA). *See also EF Cultural Travel BV v. Explorica, Inc.,* 274 F.3d 577, 581-84 (1st Cir.2001) (upholding a preliminary injunction based on "voluminous evidence" suggesting that the defendant likely violated the CFAA); *U.S. v. Morris,* 928 F.2d 504, 510 (2d Cir.1991) (affirming the jury's finding that defendant's unauthorized access violated CFAA).

* * *

Although the Tenth Circuit has not addressed the boundaries of authorized access under the SCA, other jurisdictions have interpreted the SCA—applying the common law doctrine of trespass. *See Theofel v. Farey–Jones,* 359 F.3d 1066, 1072-73 (9th Cir.2004) ("Just as trespass protects those who rent space from a commercial storage facility to hold sensitive documents, the Stored Communications Act protects users whose electronic communications are in electronic storage"); *Cablevision Lightpath,* 2006 WL 3479332, at *3 ("Computer hackers are defined as electronic trespassers."). Thus, some courts hold: "Permission to access a stored communication is not necessarily a valid authorization, if permission would not defeat a trespass claim in analogous circumstances." *Theofel,* 359 F.3d at 1073. Additionally, the SCA requires plaintiff to prove: The conduct or result was defendant's conscious objective. *Cardinal Health 414, Inc. v. Adams,* 582 F.Supp.2d 967, 976 (M.D. Tenn. 2008).

First, this court turns to the issue of authorization. Attorney Bovino admits: Mrs. Christina MacMillan had permission to access Mr. MacMillan's email account. Thus, Mrs. MacMillan's viewing Attorney Bovino's emails—whether or not they were marked "attorney-client privilege"—did not "exceed an authorization" under § 2701(a)(2). However, Attorney Bovino insists: Mrs. MacMillan exceeded the scope of her authorization by forwarding, copying, deleting, printing, diverting, and altering Mr. MacMillan's emails. Specifically, Attorney Bovino argues: Mrs. MacMillan knew she was "not authorized to forward e-mails, yet she intentionally forwarded e-mails to herself and intentionally printed e-mails." Attorney Bovino also argues that Mrs. MacMillan altered Mr. MacMillan's emails.

The SCA does not prohibit one's obtaining or altering emails without authorization. Instead, it prohibits one's obtaining or altering *access* without authorization. *Sherman & Co. v. Salton Maxim Housewares, Inc.,* 94 F.Supp.2d 817, 820 (E.D. Mich. 2000). The SCA prohibits unauthorized access—not "the *disclosure or use* of information gained without authorization." *See Wesley College v. Pitts,* 974 F.Supp. 375, 389 (D. Del. 1997) ("A person who does not provide an electronic communication service ... can disclose or use with impunity the contents of an electronic communication"); and, *Penrose Computer Marketgroup, Inc. v. Camin,* 682 F.Supp.2d 202, 211 (N.D.N.Y. 2010) ("[S]ection 2701 outlaws illegal entry, not larceny").

The SCA is, therefore, violated when "the trespasser gains access to information, which he is not entitled to see, not [when] the trespasser uses the information in an unauthorized way." *Int'l Ass'n of Machinists & Aerospace Workers v. Werner–Masuda,* 390 F.Supp.2d 479, 497 (D. Md. 2005). As a matter of law, Mrs. MacMillan did not exceed the scope of her authorized access—by forwarding or printing emails from Mr. MacMillan's AOL account.

Attorney Bovino also argues: Without having the requisite

authority, Mrs. Christina MacMillan routed Mr. Bovino's emails to Mr. Andrew MacMillan's spam folder and intentionally deleting certain emails. Mrs. MacMillan argues: Attorney Bovino has not produced any evidence to prove that her actions actually prevented or restricted Mr. MacMillan's access to Mr. Bovino's emails. Through her opposition to the summary judgment motion, Mrs. MacMillan admits: "She altered her husband's e-mail account to ensure that Bovino Law Firm's e-mails would go into Mr. MacMillan's spam folder."

However, Mrs. MacMillan's testimony on this subject contains numerous contradictions: ("Any emails that were forwarded to *bovino.net* [went] into the spam folder."). As a result, her apparent admission—all of plaintiffs' emails would be diverted to a spam folder—is actually an admission of the contradicting statements she made in her deposition. Initially Mrs. MacMillan testified: "I had Attorney Bovino's email so they would go into Andrew's spam and if I felt like they were appropriate, then I would copy them into the *bovino.net* and send them through. That was only one e-mail where that happened." She testified that only one or two emails ever went into the spam folder. ... It is unclear whether Mrs. MacMillan simply forwarded Attorney Bovino's emails to her *bovinolaw.net account*—which is not a violation of the SCA—or whether Mrs. MacMillan diverted Attorney Bovino's emails to Mr. MacMillan's spam folder.

A genuine dispute exists: whether Mrs. MacMillan exceeded her authorization by blocking her husband's access to Attorney Bovino's email. Therefore, Attorney Bovino and the other plaintiffs are not entitled to summary judgment on this issue. *See Seamons v. Snow,* 206 F.3d 1021, 1026 (10th Cir.2000) (holding that court may not resolve credibility issues in deciding a motion for summary judgment).

For the foregoing reasons, it is ordered that plaintiffs' motion for summary judgment is denied.

United States Code

Title 18. Crimes and Criminal Procedure
The Stored Communications Act of 1986
Chapter 121. Stored Wire and Electronic Communications and Transactional Records Access
18 U.S.C. § 2701

§ 2701. Unlawful Access to Stored Communications

(a) Offense—Except as provided in subsection (c) of this section whoever—

(1) intentionally accesses without authorization a facility through which an electronic communication service is provided; or

(2) intentionally exceeds an authorization to access that facility; and thereby obtains, alters, or prevents authorized access to a wire or electronic communication while it is in electronic storage in such system shall be punished as provided in subsection (b) of this section.

(b) Punishment—The punishment for an offense under subsection (a) of this section is—

(1) if the offense is committed for purposes of commercial advantage, malicious destruction or damage, or private commercial gain, or in furtherance of any criminal or tortious act in violation of the Constitution or laws of the United States or any State—

(A) a fine under this title or imprisonment for not more than 5 years, or both, in the case of a first offense under this subparagraph; and

(B) a fine under this title or imprisonment for not more than 10 years, or both, for any subsequent offense under this subparagraph; and

(2) in any other case—

(A) a fine under this title or imprisonment for not more than 1 year or both, in the case of a first offense under this paragraph; and

(B) a fine under this title or imprisonment for not more than 5 years, or both, in the case of an offense under this subparagraph that occurs after a conviction of another offense under this section.

(c) Exceptions—Subsection (a) of this section does not apply with respect to conduct authorized—

(1) by the person or entity providing a wire or electronic communications service;

(2) by a user of that service with respect to a communication of or intended for that user; or

(3) in section 2703, 2704 or 2518 of this title.

United States Code

Title 18. Crimes and Criminal Procedure
The Stored Communications Act of 1986
Chapter 121. Stored Wire and Electronic Communications and Transactional Records Access
18 U.S.C. § 2702

§ 2702. Voluntary Disclosure of Customer Communications or Records

(a) Prohibitions. Except as provided in subsection (b) or (c)—

(1) a person or entity providing an electronic communication service to the public shall not knowingly divulge to any person or entity the contents of a communication while in electronic storage by that service; and

(2) a person or entity providing remote computing service to the public shall not knowingly divulge to any person or entity the contents of any

communication which is carried or maintained on that service—

(A) on behalf of, and received by means of electronic transmission from (or created by means of computer processing of communications received by means of electronic transmission from), a subscriber or customer of such service;

(B) solely for the purpose of providing storage or computer processing services to such subscriber or customer, if the provider is not authorized to access the contents of any such communications for purposes of providing any services other than storage or computer processing; and

(3) a provider of remote computing service or electronic communication service to the public shall not knowingly divulge a record or other information pertaining to a subscriber to or customer of such service (not including the contents of communications covered by paragraph (1) or (2)) to any governmental entity.

(b) Exceptions for disclosure of communications.—A provider described in subsection (a) may divulge the contents of a communication—

(1) to an addressee or intended recipient of such communication or an agent of such addressee or intended recipient;

(2) as otherwise authorized in section 2517, 2511(2)(a), or 2703 of this title;

(3) with the lawful consent of the originator or an addressee or intended recipient of such communication, or the subscriber in the case of remote computing service;

(4) to a person employed or authorized or whose facilities are used to forward such communication to its destination;

(5) as may be necessarily incident to the rendition of the service or to the protection of the rights or property of the provider of that service;

(6) to the National Center for Missing and Exploited Children, in connection with a report submitted thereto under section 2258A;

(7) to a law enforcement agency—(A) if the contents—

(i) were inadvertently obtained by the service provider; and

(ii) appear to pertain to the commission of a crime; or

(8) to a governmental entity, if the provider, in good faith, believes that an emergency involving danger of death or serious physical injury to any person requires disclosure without delay of communications relating to the emergency.

United States Code

Title 18. Crimes and Criminal Procedure
The Stored Communications Act of 1986
Chapter 121. Stored Wire and Electronic Communications and Transactional Records Access
18 U.S.C. § 2707

§ 2707. Civil Action

(a) Cause of action—Except as provided in section 2703(e), any provider of electronic communication service, subscriber, or other person aggrieved by any violation of this chapter in which the conduct constituting the violation is engaged in with a knowing or intentional state of mind may, in a civil action, recover from the person or entity, other than the United States, which engaged in that violation such relief as may be appropriate.

(b) Relief—In a civil action under this section, appropriate relief includes—

(1) such preliminary and other equitable or declaratory relief as may be appropriate;

(2) damages under subsection (c); and

(3) a reasonable attorney's fee and other litigation costs reasonably incurred.

(c) Damages—The court may assess as damages in a civil action under this section the sum of the actual damages suffered by the plaintiff and any profits made by the violator as a result of the violation, but in no case shall a person entitled to recover receive less than the sum of $1,000. If the violation is willful or intentional, the court may assess punitive damages. In the case of a successful action to enforce liability under this section, the court may assess the costs of the action, together with reasonable attorney fees determined by the court.

* * *

(e) Defense—A good faith reliance on—

(1) a court warrant or order, a grand jury subpoena, a legislative authorization, or a statutory authorization (including a request of a governmental entity under section 2703(f) of this title);

(2) a request of an investigative or law enforcement officer under section 2518(7) of this title; or

(3) a good faith determination that section 2511(3) of this title permitted the conduct complained of;

is a complete defense to any civil or criminal action brought under this chapter or any other law.

(f) Limitation—A civil action under this section may not be commenced later than two years after the date upon which the claimant first discovered or had a reasonable opportunity to discover the violation.

E. Copyright Infringement, Removal of Copyright-Infringing Materials, and Subscribers' Private Right of Action Against Internet Service Providers Under the Digital Millennium Copyright Act of 1998

Ouellette v. Viacom

2011 WL 1882780
(D. Mont. 2011)

Jeremiah C. Lynch, United States Magistrate Judge. Plaintiff Todd Ouellette is proceeding *pro se* in this action. Under 28 U.S.C. § 1915(e)(2), a court must conduct a preliminary screening of plaintiff's allegations in *forma pauperis* proceeding. The court reviewed Ouellette's allegations in Count I of his Amended Complaint. By order entered February 7, 2011, the court concluded that those allegations state a cognizable claim for relief under the Digital Millennium Copyright Act of 1998.

II. Plaintiff's Allegations

Defendants are Google, YouTube, BayTSP, Audible Magic and Myspace. The allegations in Ouellette's Amended Complaint stem from his use of various internet websites—YouTube.com and Myspace.com—for the purpose of uploading, publishing or posting videos that he has produced. In general, Ouellette contends: Defendants have interfered with his ability and asserted legal right to post his videos on the internet.

Defendants' alleged interference, however, stems from accusations made against Ouellette. Defendants assert: Ouellette's videos infringe upon various copyrights owned by other parties—including some of the Defendants named in this action. Nonetheless, Ouellette alleges: Defendants have wrongfully accused him of infringing upon copyrights they own, have improperly removed his videos from the internet, and have refused to replace his videos on the internet as required by federal law. Ouellette's specifics are summarized below.

A. Count II

Ouellette alleges: Defendants Google, YouTube, BayTSP, Audible

Magic and Myspace improperly used "scanning software." Allegedly, the software located videos that Ouellette posted on YouTube and Myspace, and misidentified those videos as infringing upon existing copyrights. As a result, Ouellette's videos were removed from the internet, and "strikes" were imposed against Ouellette's YouTube and Myspace accounts.

Ouellette alleges: Defendants are liable, because they violated provisions in the Digital Millennium Copyright Act of 1998 (DMCA). He also asserts: Defendants are liable because they made misrepresentations regarding Quellette's supposed copyright violations, and violated Ouellette's "fair use rights." Ouellette further contends: Defendants "maliciously refused to restore Ouellette's 'Fair Use videos' to the internet."

B. Counts III-V

After Ouellette's videos were removed from the internet, Ouellette states: He submitted "substantially complete" notices to Defendants—Google and YouTube—in accordance with the DMCA. However, those companies refused to process Ouellette's counter notices, because minor errors appear in the notices. Ouellette asserts: He advised the Defendants that he suffers from a reading disability, which caused the minor errors.

Ouellette further contends: Defendants Google and YouTube's failure to process his DMCA counter notices violated his right to make fair use of others' copyright materials. And he asserts: After YouTube refused to process his counter notices, he sent counter notices to Defendant Viacom under the DMCA. According to Ouellette, Viacom refused to process those counter notices, and refused to comply with Ouellette's request: to retract its fraudulent assertion that Ouellette had violated its copyrights.

C. Count VI-VII

Ouellette alleges: Defendants Google and YouTube require subscribers to sign various provisions of a Terms of Service (TOS) agreement. According to Ouellette, those provisions are unfair or illegal. First, Ouellette contends the Defendants violated his rights under the ADA because the block lettering used in the TOS is impossible for him to read. And Defendants do not provide an audio version of the TOS as an alternative. According to Ouellette, the TOS unlawfully requires a subscriber to consent to an improper jurisdiction and venue; and the TOS bars his "fair use" right to download news videos for the purpose of critiquing those videos; the TOS permits Google and YouTube to violate DMCA's "safe harbor" provisions; and the TOS gives third parties the right to harass him and accuse him of copyright infringement.

Ouellette also alleges: Defendants Audible Magic and Myspace violate DMCA provisions. He asserts: Defendants employ "filter blocks" to remove copyright-infringing videos from websites on the internet–which fail to comply with the "takedown" procedures established in the DMCA. Additionally, Myspace allegedly refused to replace Ouellette's videos—thereby violating Ouellette's right to make fair use of others' copyright materials.

III. Discussion

A. Fair Use Doctrine

Ouellette's various claims allege Defendants have violated his right to make fair use of others' copyrighted materials. Ouellette's theory of liability, however, is not recognized under the law. The common law doctrine of fair use—now codified under the Copyright Act of 1976, 17 U.S.C. § 107—is only an affirmative defense to a claim of copyright infringement. It is not an affirmative right on which a cause of action may be premised. *See Eldred v. Ashcroft,* 537 U.S. 186, 219-220 (2003) (discussing the doctrine as a defense), and *Perfect 10, Inc. v. Amazon.com, Inc.,* 508 F.3d 1146, 1163 (9th Cir.2007) (same).

A defendant's fair use of copyrighted material is merely an exception to the copyright owner's exclusive rights to that material. *Hustler Magazine, Inc. v. Moral Majority, Inc.,* 796 F.2d 1148, 1151 (9th Cir.1986). Such fair use does not constitute an infringement of a copyright. 17 U.S.C. § 107. Because the fair use doctrine is only an affirmative defense, it does not afford a person an enforceable, guaranteed, or constitutionally protected right to engage in any particular use of another's copyrighted material. *See 321 Studios v. Metro Goldwyn Mayer Studios, Inc.,* 307 F.Supp.2d 1085, 1101 (N.D.Cal.2004) (recognizing that the fair use doctrine is not an affirmative right).

Ouellette's allegations that Defendants' conduct violated his alleged "fair use rights" are frivolous, and fail to state a claim on which relief may be granted. Those claims should be dismissed.

* * *

D. Digital Millennium Copyright Act of 1998

Ouellette claims the Defendants violated certain procedures mandated by the DMCA. However, the DMCA procedures on which

Ouellette relies do not create liability exposure for internet service providers, or other entities. The procedures do not create liability that does not already exist independent of the DMCA.

Title II of the DMCA was enacted as the Online Copyright Infringement Liability Limitation Act (OCILLA), 17 U.S.C. § 512. Its purpose is clear: to "facilitate cooperation among Internet service providers and copyright owners and "to detect and deal with copyright infringements that take place in the digital networked environment." *Ellison v. Robertson,* 357 F.3d 1072, 1076 (9th Cir. 2004)

The DMCA and OCILLA procedural mechanisms are designed to facilitate the identification and removal of material on the internet that infringes upon a copyright. If a copyright owner identifies an infringement, the owner may send a claim-infringement notice—a "takedown notice"—to the service provider. 17 U.S.C. § 512(c)(1)(C) and (c)(3). In response, the service provider must remove the infringing material from the provider's website. 17 U.S.C. § 512(c)(1)(C).

After issuing a takedown notice and removing material from the website, the service subscriber may challenge those actions by fashioning a counter notice. 17 U.S.C. § 512(g)(2)(C) and (g)(3). The subscriber may issue a counter notice—which informs the service provider that the material was improperly removed from the website." 17 U.S .C. § 512(g)(3)(C). After receiving the counter notice, the service provider must replace the subscriber's material on the website. 17 U.S.C. § 512(g)(2)(C).

The intent of the DMCA/OCILLA § 512 is to limit the liability of internet service providers. The purpose is not to create liability—which is precluded under existing independent theories of recovery. The statutory intent is "to provide greater certainty to service providers concerning their legal exposure for infringements that may occur in the course of their activities." *Ellison,* 357 F.3d at 1076. Congress chose not to rewrite or modify the existing doctrines that impose liability for copyright infringement—as those doctrines apply to the online world. Instead, Congress elected to create various "safe harbors" in five specific circumstances, or categories of activity, which limit internet service providers' liability for copyright infringement—liability that could be founded upon the existing doctrines of copyright infringement law. *Ellison,* 357 F.3d at 1076–1077

Thus, rather than establish new grounds for copyright-infringement claims against online service providers, the provider's liability must be established "under existing principles of law." *Ellison,* 357 F.3d at 1077. Under the DMCA, "safe harbors" do not affect the question of the provider's ultimate direct, vicarious, or contributory liability under copyright law. *Perfect 10, Inc. v. CCBill, LLC,* 488 F.3d 1102, 1109 (9th Cir.2007). The safe harbor provisions of 17 U.S.C. § 512 do not imply that a service provider is or is not liable.

Ouellette argues that Defendants are liable under two DMCA safe harbor provisions—the "takedown notice" and the "subscriber's counter notice" provisions. However, Ouellette's reliance—on the takedown and counter notice safe-harbor procedures—is misplaced. The Defendants' alleged compliance or non-compliance with the procedures does not provide a basis for liability. Again, liability may be imposed only under existing principles of law—which are independent of the DMCA's procedural requirements. Ouellette's allegations, however, do not invoke any independent theory of liability. Therefore, his claims founded upon the DMCA should be dismissed.

E. Misrepresentation under the DMCA

Ouellette alleges: Defendants Google, YouTube, BayTSP, Audible Magic, and Myspace made misrepresentations, asserting that Ouellette infringed upon certain copyrights. A defendant who insert misrepresentations in a DMCA takedown notice could be liable. 17 U.S.C. § 512(f). Ouellette's allegations, however, fail to state a claim of misrepresentation under 17 U.S.C. § 512(f). Ouellette does not allege Defendants made a misrepresentation in a takedown. To the contrary, Ouellette alleges: Defendants engaged in conduct "outside of the DMCA rules." Therefore, Ouellette's claims of misrepresentation should be dismissed.

IV. Conclusion

For the reasons stated, Ouellette's claims in Amended Complaint should be dismissed—as frivolous and for failure to state a claim on which relief could be granted. 28 U.S.C. § 1915(e)(2)(B)(i) and (ii).

The Digital Millennium Copyright Act of 1998

Pub.L. No. 105-304, 112 Stat. 2860
–Amending—
The Online Copyright Infringement Liability Limitation Act of 1990
Chapter 5. Copyright Infringement and Remedies
17 U.S.C. § 512(a)

§ 512(a)—Limitations on Liability: Transitory Digital Network Communications.

A service provider shall not be liable for monetary relief, or ... for injunctive or other equitable relief, for infringement of copyright by reason of the provider's transmitting, routing, or providing connections for, material through a system or network controlled or operated by or for the service provider, or by reason of the intermediate and transient storage of that material in the course of such transmitting, routing, or providing connections, if—

(1) the transmission of the material was initiated by or at the direction of a person other than the service provider;

(2) the transmission, routing, provision of connections, or storage is carried out through an automatic technical process without selection of the material by the service provider;

(3) the service provider does not select the recipients of the material except as an automatic response to the request of another person;

(4) no copy of the material made by the service provider in the course of such intermediate or transient storage is maintained on the system or network in a manner ordinarily accessible to anyone other than anticipated recipients, and no such copy is maintained on the system or network in a manner ordinarily accessible to such anticipated recipients for a longer period than is reasonably necessary for the transmission, routing, or provision of connections; and

(5) the material is transmitted through the system or network without modification of its content.

The Digital Millennium Copyright Act of 1998

Pub.L. No. 105-304, 112 Stat. 2860
–Amending—
The Online Copyright Infringement Liability Limitation Act of 1990
Chapter 5. Copyright Infringement and Remedies
17 U.S.C. § 512(c)

§ 512(c)—Limitations on Liability: Information Residing on Systems/Networks by Users

(1) In general. A service provider shall not be liable for monetary relief, or, except as provided in subsection (j), for injunctive or other equitable relief, for infringement of copyright by reason of the storage at the direction of a user of material that resides on a system or network controlled or operated by or for the service provider, if the service provider—

(A) (i) does not have actual knowledge that the material or an activity using the material on the system or network is infringing;

(ii) in the absence of such actual knowledge, is not aware of facts or circumstances from which infringing activity is apparent; or

(iii) upon obtaining such knowledge or awareness, acts expeditiously to remove, or disable access to, the material;

(B) does not receive a financial benefit directly attributable to the infringing activity, in a case in which the service provider has the right and ability to control such activity; and

(C) upon notification of claimed infringement as described in paragraph (3), responds expeditiously to remove, or disable access to, the material that is claimed to be infringing or to be the subject of infringing activity.

(2) Designated agent—The limitations on liability established in this subsection apply to a service provider only if the service provider has designated an agent to receive notifications of claimed infringement described in paragraph (3), by making available through its service, including on its website in a location accessible to the public, and by providing to the Copyright Office, substantially the following information:

(A) the name, address, phone number, and electronic mail address of the agent.

(B) other contact information which the Register of Copyrights may deem appropriate.

The Digital Millennium Copyright Act of 1998

Pub.L. No. 105-304, 112 Stat. 2860
–Amending—
The Online Copyright Infringement Liability Limitation Act of 1990
Chapter 5. Copyright Infringement and Remedies
17 U.S.C. § 512(f)

§ 512(f)—Misrepresentations

Any person who knowingly materially misrepresents under this section—(1) that material or activity is infringing, or (2) that material or activity was removed or disabled by mistake or misidentification shall be liable for any damages, including costs and attorneys' fees, incurred by the alleged infringer, by any copyright owner or copyright owner's authorized licensee, or by a service provider, who is injured by such misrepresentation, as the result of the service provider relying upon such misrepresentation in removing or disabling access to the material or activity claimed to be infringing, or in replacing the removed material or ceasing to disable access to it.

The Digital Millennium Copyright Act of 1998

Pub.L. No. 105-304, 112 Stat. 2860
–Amending—
The Online Copyright Infringement Liability Limitation Act of 1990
Chapter 5. Copyright Infringement and Remedies
17 U.S.C. § 512(g)

§ 512(g)—Replacement of removed or disabled material and limitation on other liability

(1) No liability for taking down generally.—Subject to paragraph (2), a service provider shall not be liable to any person for any claim based on the service provider's good faith disabling of access to, or removal of, material or activity claimed to be infringing or based on facts or circumstances from which infringing activity is apparent, regardless of whether the material or activity is ultimately determined to be infringing.

(2) Exception—Paragraph (1) shall not apply with respect to material residing at the direction of a subscriber of the service provider on a system or network controlled or operated by or for the service provider that is removed, or to which access is disabled by the service provider, pursuant to a notice provided under subsection (c)(1)(C), unless the service provider—

(A) takes reasonable steps promptly to notify the subscriber that it has removed or disabled access to the material;

(B) upon receipt of a counter notification described in paragraph (3), promptly provides the person who provided the notification under subsection (c)(1)(C) with a copy of the counter notification, and informs that person that it will replace the removed material or cease disabling access to it in 10 business days; and

(C) replaces the removed material and ceases disabling access to it not less than 10, nor more than 14, business days following receipt of the counter notice, unless its designated agent first receives notice from the person who submitted the notification under subsection (c)(1)(C) that such person has filed an action seeking a court order to restrain the subscriber from engaging in infringing activity relating to the material on the service provider's system or network.

(3) Contents of counter notification.—To be effective under this subsection, a counter notification must be a written communication provided to the service provider's designated agent that includes substantially the following:

(A) A physical or electronic signature of the subscriber.

(B) Identification of the material that has been removed or to which access has been disabled and the location at which the material appeared before it was removed or access to it was disabled.

(C) A statement under penalty of perjury that the subscriber has a good faith belief that the material was removed or disabled as a result of mistake or misidentification of the material to be removed or disabled.

(D) The subscriber's name, address, and telephone number, and a statement that the subscriber consents to the jurisdiction of Federal District Court for the judicial district in which the address is located, or if the subscriber's address is outside of the United States, for any judicial district in which the service provider may be found, and that the subscriber will accept service of process from the person who provided notification under subsection (c)(1)(C) or an agent of such person.

(4) Limitation on other liability. —A service provider's compliance with paragraph (2) shall not subject the service provider to liability for copyright infringement with respect to the material identified in the notice provided under subsection (c)(1)(C).

THE Digital Millennium Copyright Act of 1998

Pub.L. No. 105-304, 112 Stat. 2860
–Amending—
The Online Copyright Infringement Liability Limitation Act of 1990
Chapter 5. Copyright Infringement and Remedies
17 U.S.C. § 512(k)

§ 512(k)—Definitions

(1) Service provider.

(A) As used in subsection (a), the term “service provider” means an entity offering the transmission, routing, or providing of connections for digital online communications, between or among points specified by a user, of material of the user’s choosing, without modification to the content of the material as sent or received.

(B) As used in this section, other than subsection (a), the term “service provider” means a provider of online services or network access, or the operator of facilities therefor, and includes an entity described in subparagraph (A).

(2) Monetary relief. —As used in this section, the term “monetary relief” means damages, costs, attorneys” fees, and any other form of monetary payment.

F. Infringement of Website Domain Names and Law Firms' Private Right of Action Against "Cybersquatters" Under the Anticybersquatting Consumer Protection Act of 1999

Gioconda Law Group PLLC, v. Kenzie

941 F.Supp.2d 424
United States District Court
(S.D.N.Y. 2013)

J. Paul Oetken, District Judge. Plaintiff Gioconda Law Group PLLC (LawGroup) alleges cybersquatting, trademark infringement, unlawful interception and disclosure of electronic communications claims against Kenzie Arthur Wesley (Kenzie). Plaintiff has filed a partial motion for judgment on the pleadings with respect to Kenzie's alleged violation of the Anticybersquatting Consumer Protection Act of 1999 (ACPA).

I. Background

LawGroup is a professional limited liability company—duly organized under the laws of New York. It is engaged in the authorized practice of law—with a particular focus on brand protection and intellectual property. LawGroup has focused significant energies in recent years on combating piracy and counterfeiting on the Internet. Kenzie is a sophisticated computer programmer. He has multiple advanced degrees in computer programming—a Bachelor of Technology Degree in Computer Systems from BCiT and majors in Network Security Administration and Network Security Development. Kenzie's principal place of business is in Vancouver, British Columbia, Canada. And, on LinkedIn, he identifies himself as a "Cyber Security and Mobile App Developer."

LawGroup's general allegation reads: "This case presents the court with an identifiable Internet domain name cybersquatter and hacker. He has intentionally intercepted e-mail traffic intended for the LawGroup, a New York law firm which focuses on anti-counterfeiting and brand protection litigation." Kenzie denies this particular allegation. LawGroup alleges: "Domain name typosquatting is a well-known form of cybersquatting. It is used to capture web traffic when an Internet user accidentally misspells a legitimate domain name in his web browser." Kenzie agrees: This description is "essentially correct." But he emphasizes: The purpose of typosquatting can be either malevolent or benevolent.

Kenzie registered *GIOCONDOLAW.COM* ("the Infringing Domain Name" or "IDN")—"within the broader context of his responsible, good faith information security research into a significant e-mail vulnerability that is not currently well understood." On January 19, 2012, Kenzie registered the IDN on a third-party platform—Internet Registrar GoDaddy, Inc. When LawGroup discovered Kenzie's conduct, the firm sent e-mails to the *addressesinfo@giocondolaw.com* and *joseph.gioconda@giocondolaw.com*. A registered receipt e-mail system confirmed: Both e-mail messages were received at active mailboxes capable of receiving misdirected messages.

After LawGroup contacted Kenzie and informed him of the Complaint, Kenzie replied, in part:

> As for starting litigation against me, I am not clear what has caused you to assume that I would not be amenable to resolving your concerns and claims. My intentions with the domain name you are concerned about are transparent and above board—as they are part of my research into an email vulnerability that I have been studying since September 2011 and which I have been publicly discussing on my website ... I am doing nothing to cause any injury to your firm or any trademark rights you have, and would be glad to discuss those issues with you ... I have no objections to facilitating a transfer of the domain to you."

Kenzie has also registered the following eight domain names: *rnastercard.com*, *rndonalds.com*, *nevvscorp.com*, *rncafee.com*, *rnacvvorld.com*, *rnonster.com*, *pcvvorld.com*, and *qvvest.com*. Kenzie admits: He redirected each of these Internet domain names legitimate third parties' websites— "but not for avoiding detection."

* * *

On April 17, 2012, LawGroup received a registration number from the U.S. Patent and Trademark Office. The Service Mark—"Gioconda Law Group PLLC"—was registered in International Class 45 for intellectual property. Citing the ACPA, LawGroup alleges: (1) Kenzie registered an "Infringing Domain Name"; (2) the infringing name is virtually identifiably and/or confusingly similar to Gioconda Law Service Mark; and (3) LawGroup's mark was distinctive when Kenzie registered the Infringing Domain Name. Kenzie admits that the allegations are true. Additionally, LawGroup alleges: (1) "Kenzie registered and uses the Infringing Domain Name in bad-faith—intending to profit from the Gioconda Law Service Mark"; (2) "Kenzie has no bona fide noncommercial or fair use for the Gioconda Law Service Mark"; and (3) "Kenzie intends to divert consumers away from LawGroup for unlawful commercial gain, by creating a likelihood of confusion regarding the source, sponsorship, affiliation or endorsement of the Infringing Domain Name, and related e-mail addresses." Kenzie expressly denies these latter allegations.

In his Answer, Kenzie inserts several specific denials: (1) LawGroup has not suffered any actual damages; (2) he always acted in good faith; and (3) he "ensures that the contents of vulnerable e-mails are never read or disclosed to third parties, if he receives e-mails intended for an entity like LawGroup.

II. Discussion

A. Legal Standard Under the Anticybersquatting Consumer Protection Act of 1999

"To successfully assert a claim under the ACPA, LawGroup must demonstrate: (1) its marks were distinctive at the time the domain name was registered; (2) the allegedly infringing domain names are identical to or confusingly similar to LawGroup's mark; and (3) the infringer has acted in bad faith—intending to profit from that mark." *Webadviso v. Bank of Am. Corp.*, 448 Fed.Appx. 95, 97 (2d Cir. 2011) (citing 15 U.S.C. § 1125(d)(1)(a)).

Kenzie expressly admits: (1) He registered an Infringing Domain Name which "is virtually identical to, and/or confusingly similar to the Gioconda Law Service Mark; and (2) The IDN was distinctive when Kenzie registered the IDN. Therefore, the only issue is clear: whether Kenzie had a "bad faith intent to profit from that mark." 15 U.S.C. § 1125(d)(1)(A)(i). Any attempt to determine one's "bad faith intent to profit" under the ACPA raises important questions about the ACPA's scope. Consequently, an overview of the statute's purpose is required, given the potential difficulties of trying to apply traditional bad faith analysis to a case like this one.

1. The ACPA's Purpose

Cybersquatting involves non-trademark holders' registering well-known trademarks as domain names and selling the names to the trademarks' owners. Domain-name registrars do not determine whether requested domain names are registered trademarks. Therefore, it has been simple and inexpensive for persons to register companies' mask as domain names. In the end, mark owners are precluded from using their domain names. And often mark owners have paid "ransom" for their names. *Sporty's Farm L.L.C. v. Sportsman's Mkt., Inc.,* 202 F.3d 489, 493 (2d Cir. 2000). "Cybersquatting is the Internet's version of a land grab. Cybersquatters register well-known brand names as Internet domain names and force the rightful owners to pay for the right to use their own names in electronic commerce. *Interstellar Starship Services, Ltd. v. Epix, Inc.,* 304 F.3d 936, 946 (9th Cir.2002). Consequently, a cybersquatter "can reap windfall profits by laying claim to a domain name that he has no legitimate interest in or relationship to." *Harrods Ltd. v. Sixty Internet Domain Names,* 302 F.3d 214, 238 (4th Cir.2002).

Alarmed by a rising wave of cybersquatting in the 1990s, and concerned by the apparent inadequacy of preexisting laws, Congress enacted the ACPA in 1999. This law was passed "to protect consumers and holders of distinctive trademarks from cybersquatting." *Sporty's Farm,* 202 F.3d at 493. As the Senate Judiciary Committee explained: The ACPA was designed to "protect consumers and American businesses, to promote the growth of online commerce, and to provide clarity in the law for trademark owners. The ACPA prohibits bad-faith and abusive registration of distinctive marks with the intent to profit from the goodwill associated with such marks.

2. The ACPA's Requirement of a "Bad Faith Intent to Profit"

A key element of any ACPA violation is proof of one's "bad faith intent to profit." *See Interstellar Starship Services,* 304 F.3d at 946 ("A finding of 'bad faith' is an essential prerequisite to finding an ACPA violation."). The Second Circuit has noted: "Bad faith intent to profit" are terms of art in the ACPA, and they should not be equated necessarily with "bad faith" in other contexts." *Sporty's Farm,* 202 F.3d at 499 n. 13. To that end, the ACPA, 15 U.S.C. § 1125(d)(1)(B)(i) enumerates nine relevant factors for a bad faith inquiry:

(I) the trademark or other intellectual property rights of the person, if any, in the domain name;

(II) the extent to which the domain name consists of the legal name of the person or a name that is otherwise commonly used to identify that person;

(III) the person's prior use, if any, of the domain name in connection with the bona fide offering of any goods or services;

(IV) the person's bona fide noncommercial or fair use of the mark in a site accessible under the domain name;

(V) the person's intent to divert consumers from the mark owner's online location to a site accessible under the domain name that could harm the goodwill represented by the mark, either for commercial gain or with the intent to tarnish or disparage the mark, by creating a likelihood of confusion as to the source, sponsorship, affiliation, or endorsement of the site;

(VI) the person's offer to transfer, sell, or otherwise assign the domain name to the mark owner or any third party for financial gain without having used, or having an intent to use, the domain name in the bona fide offering of any goods or services, or the person's prior conduct indicating a pattern of such conduct;

(VII) the person's provision of material and misleading false contact information when applying for the registration of the domain name, the person's intentional failure to maintain accurate contact information, or the person's prior conduct indicating a pattern of such conduct;

(VIII) the person's registration or acquisition of multiple domain names which the person knows are identical or confusingly similar to marks of others that are distinctive at the time of registration of such domain names, or dilutive of famous marks of others that are famous at the time of registration of such domain names, without regard to the goods or services of the parties; and

(IX) the extent to which the mark incorporated in the person's domain name registration is or is not distinctive and famous within the meaning of subsection (c) of this section.

A leading treatise on the law of trademarks notes: The first four factors suggest an absence of a bad faith intent to profit from the goodwill of another person's mark. The next four factors indicate that bad faith exists. And the last factor might suggest the presence or absence of bad faith. 4 McCarthy on Trademarks and Unfair Competition § 25:78 (4th Ed.).

3. The Scope of One's "Bad Faith Intent to Profit"

The ACPA has the potential to encompass a broad array of online conduct; therefore, courts are "reluctant to interpret the ACPA's liability provisions in an overly aggressive manner." *Virtual Works, Inc. v. Volkswagen of Am., Inc.,* 238 F.3d 264, 270 (4th Cir.2001) ("The ACPA was not enacted to put an end to the sale of all domain names."). Consequently, courts have struggled to define the boundaries of a "bad faith intent to profit" because the ACPA expressly allows consideration of factors *beyond* the nine enumerated factors. *See* 15 U.S.C. § 1125(d)(1)(B)(i), and *Sporty's Farm,* 202 F.3d at 498 ("[W]e are not limited to considering just the listed factors when making our determination of whether the statutory criterion has been met. The factors are, instead, expressly described as indicia that 'may' be considered along with other facts.").

Thus, a number of courts—including the Second Circuit—have not strictly adhered to the statutory indicia. Instead courts have embraced a case-specific approach to find evidence of bad faith. *See Sporty's Farm,* 202 F.3d at 499 (concluding that Sporty's Farm intentionally acted in bad faith by examining "the unique circumstances of this case—which do not fit neatly into the specific factors enumerated by Congress." *Interstellar Starship Services,* 304 F.3d at 946–47. This "unique circumstances" approach to the bad faith inquiry is logical and in accord with the plain language of the ACPA. *See Sporty's Farm,* 202 F.3d at 499. It allows courts to secure the ACPA's core purpose even where a defendant has sidestepped the nine indicia. *See Newport News Holdings Corp. v. Virtual City Vision, Inc.,* 650 F.3d 423, 436 (4th Cir. 2011) (refusing to apply a "formalistic approach" and noting that doing so could "undermine the purpose of the ACPA").

B. Application

The only issue at this stage is whether LawGroup can prove enough facts to show that Kenzie's conduct was a violation under the ACPA—a "bad faith intent to profit." This analysis begins with the nine indicia of a "bad faith intent to profit" in the statute. 15 U.S.C. § 1125(d)(1)(B)(i). There is no evidence suggesting: Kenzie had rights in the domain name (Factor I). The domain name consists of a name that is commonly used to identify Kenzie (Factor II). Kenzie had prior use of the domain name in connection with the bona fide offering of goods or services (Factor III). Kenzie had a bona fide noncommercial, right to use the mark under the domain name (Factor IV). The absence of any admitted facts strongly augurs against a finding of bad faith intent to profit. However, Factors VIII and IX support a finding of bad faith. Kenzie admits: He has acquired at least eight other domain names with an intent to demand remuneration from the owner in exchange for the domain name. He also admits that LawGroup's mark is famous and distinctive.

The court concludes: Two of the nine weigh in favor of finding a bad faith intent to profit. That, however, is not enough. LawGroup can prevail on this motion for judgment on the pleadings—only if a more general assessment of the "unique circumstances" of this case demands a finding of bad faith. *See Sporty's Farm,* 202 F.3d at 499. Kenzie alleges: His conduct is part of a security-focused research agenda—looking for vulnerability in e-mail systems of the sort used by LawGroup. Kenzie states: He undertook this activity—acting in good faith—for noncommercial reasons. And Kenzie has arranged for domain names and e-mails to be transferred back to other entities situated similarly to LawGroup.

As an information security researcher, he believes: He is conferring numerous benefits on LawGroup and on the public by drawing attention to a significant vulnerability. He notes: There is no evidence that he has gained economic profit from his actions, made any other commercial use of the IDN, or attempted to sell the IDN back to LawGroup. Although a UDRP panel has condemned his behavior, it does not follow that Kenzie's conduct therefore runs afoul of the ACPA.

For the foregoing reasons, LawGroup's motion for judgment on the pleadings is denied.

NOTES AND QUESTIONS

1) Distinguishing Traditional Trademark Violation Claims and Trademark Claims Under the Anticybersquatting Consumer Protection Act. Traditional trademark law and the ACPA have distinct purposes. The respective claims and elements are different, too. Traditional trademark law restricts the commercial use of another's protected mark—to prevent one's confusing consumers about the source of a particular product. *New Kids on the Block v. News Am. Pub., Inc.*, 971 F.2d 302, 305-06 (9th Cir.1992); Cybersquatting liability, however, does not require commercial use of a domain name involving a protected mark. *Bosley Med. Inst., Inc. v. Kremer,* 403 F.3d 672, 681 (9th Cir. 2005). Moreover, to succeed on a claim for cybersquatting, a mark holder must prove "bad faith" under a statutory nine factor test. 15 U.S.C. § 1125(d)(1)(B). No analogous requirement exists for traditional trademark claims. *Lahoti v. VeriCheck, Inc.*, 586 F.3d 1190, 1202 (9th Cir.2009), citing *Interstellar Starship Servs., Ltd. v. Epix*, Inc., 304 F.3d 936, 946 (9th Cir. 2002).

2) Civil Liability Under the Anticybersquatting Consumer Protection Act. Cybersquatting means registering a domain name—associated with a protected trademark—either to ransom the domain name to the mark holder or to divert business from the mark holder. *Bosley Med. Inst., Inc. v. Kremer*, 403 F.3d 672, 680 (9th Cir. 2005) (quoting *DaimlerChrysler v. The Net Inc.,* 388 F.3d 201, 204 (6th Cir. 2004). The ACPA imposes civil liability for cybersquatting on persons that register, traffic in, or use a domain name with the "bad faith intent to profit" from that protected mark. 15 U.S.C. § 1125(d)(1)(A). Thus, the plain language of the statute prohibits the act of cybersquatting but limits when a person can be considered to be a cybersquatter. The statute makes no express provision for secondary liability. Extending liability to registrars or other third parties—who are not cybersquatters, but whose actions may have the effect of aiding such cybersquatting—would expand the range of conduct prohibited by the statute from a bad faith intent to cybersquat on a trademark to the mere maintenance of a domain name by a registrar, with or without a bad faith intent to profit.

PART II.
Technology-Based Claims and Actions Against Solo and Small-Firm Practitioners

CHAPTER FIVE: Disciplinary Proceedings Against Attorneys for Impermissibly Using and Accessing Computers and Using Websites, E-mails, and Social Media to Post, Download, or Share "Offensive" Messages, Photos, Documents, or Images

Every day, solo and small-firm practitioners use one or a combination of these technologies to (1) advertise legal services, (2) communicate with clients and various third parties, (3) post information or comments on message boards and social-media networks, (4) access information and data on the Internet or third parties' computers, (5) share and receive privileged information and confidential documents from clients, and (6) deposit and access funds in banking, trustee, and escrow accounts.

Therefore, it is important to stress: The American Bar Association (ABA) has fashioned MODEL RULES OF PROFESSIONAL CONDUCT. And numerous MODEL RULES—RULE 1.2(d), RULE 1.2(e), RULE 1.6(a), RULE 1.15(a), RULE 3.8(d), RULE 3.8(e)(1), RULE 5.5(b)(2), RULE 8.4(b), RULE 8.4(c) and others—are implicated when attorneys access without permission or employ law-practice technologies: desktop, laptop, and network computers; smartphones; short messaging services (SMS); multimedia messaging service (MMS); electronic tablets; office and cloud-based computing and printing systems; Internet websites and blogs, e-mails, social media, document sharing systems; and portable document format (PDF) software.

Consider, for example, RULE 1.6(a): "A lawyer shall not reveal information relating to the representation of a client unless the client gives informed consent." This is a "confidentiality of information" obligation. Arguably, an otherwise ethical solo practitioner can violate RULE 1.6(a) by inadvertently producing "metadata" during discovery. Or, after an attorney receives an electronic copy of a client's proposed memorandum of understanding, the attorney can generate metadata by revising the client's proposed memorandum. And if the attorney "innocently" e-mails the client's document to the counterparty, the attorney would have violated RULE 1.6(a).

What is metadata? When an attorney uses a computer to create a legal document, the computer's operating system and word processor track information about the file and build a data file. The latter file is called a "metadata." It contains the underlying file's name, creation date, size, location, and owner, as well as other information. *Gonzales v. City of San Jose*, 2014 WL 6687138, *2 n.7 (N.D. Cal. 2014). In addition, a client generates metadata when she uses a computer to create, download, and share electronically images, videos and spreadsheets. *U.S. v. Post*, 997 F.Supp.2d 602, 603 (S.D. Tex. 2014).

There is more. Metadata and metatags are produced when a client visits web pages. *Axiom Worldwide, Inc. v. HTRD Group Hong Kong Limited*, 2015 WL 8488653, *3 (M.D. Fla.). Metatags are HyperText Markup Language (HTML) codes—which appear in various forms. "Description metatags" describe a website that a client visited. *Cf. Promatek Industries, Ltd. v. Equitrac Corp.*, 300 F.3d 808, 810 n. 1 (7th Cir. 2002). "Keyword metatags" track and store keywords which appear on a web page. *Brookfield Communications, Inc. v. West Coast Entertainment Corp.*, 174 F.3d 1036, 1045 (9th Cir.1999).

Many, if not most, solo practitioners and small-firm attorneys have never heard the terms "metadata" and "metatags." Therefore, should a practitioner be "punished" for "innocently" or "negligently" sharing her client's metadata with a third party? The ABA and state disciplinary boards are divided over this question. On August 5, 2005, the ABA issued an opinion—*ABA Standing Committee on Ethics and Professional Responsibility Formal Opinion 06-442: Review and Use of Metadata*, SR045 ALI-ABA 1291, 1293 (2010). It reads:

> The MODEL RULES OF PROFESSIONAL CONDUCT do not contain any specific prohibition against a lawyer's reviewing and using embedded information in electronic documents, whether received from opposing counsel, an adverse party, or an agent of an adverse party. A lawyer who is concerned about the possibility of sending, producing, or providing to opposing counsel a document that contains or might contain metadata, or who wishes to take some action

> to reduce or remove the potentially harmful consequences of its dissemination, may be able to limit the likelihood of its transmission by "scrubbing" metadata from documents or by sending a different version of the document without the embedded information.

Conversely, some state bar associations declare: A lawyer has an *affirmative duty* to remove confidential metadata from an electronic document before sending the document to an opposing attorney. However, several bar associations only require solo and small-firm practitioners to implement *reasonably precautionary measures* to prevent an opposing attorney from "mining" confidential metadata in a client's document. *See APP. 2G Ethics Opinions Regarding Metadata,* 2015 WL 5622275, Elect. Disc. L. & Pract. 5622275 (C.C.H. 2015). Still, other state bar associations' opinions read: If a lawyer intentionally or unintentionally discovers confidential metadata in an opposing client's electronic document, the attorney *may not use* the information without securing the opposing lawyer's or client's consent.

How should a solo-practice attorney satisfy such conflicting professional obligations and decrease his likelihood of appearing before multiple disciplinary boards if the attorney practices in multiple jurisdictions or has a *virtual law practice*?

A. State Ethics Boards' Conflicting Legal and Ethical Standards for Determining Whether Attorneys Violated Model Rules of Professional Conduct

It is important to restate: Numerous ABA Model Rules—Rule 1.1, Rule 1.2(d), Rule 1.2(e), Rule 1.6(a), Rule 1.15(a), Rule 3.8(d), Rule 3.8(e)(1), Rule 5.5(b)(2), Rule 8.4(b), Rule 8.4(c) and others—are implicated when attorneys (1) access opposing attorneys' and clients' computers, electronic files and online accounts without permission, (2) employ various technologies to undermine courts' administration of justice, or (3) use social media and Internet blogs to defame or harass jurists. In particular, Comment 8—which accompanies MODEL RULE 1.1—reads in relevant part: "[A] lawyer should keep abreast of changes in the law [as well as] the benefits and risks associated with relevant technology."

"Many attorneys have violated various ethical guidelines and disciplinary rules." And given "the solitary nature of computer work," offending attorneys think that their deliberate and secret activities will never be discovered. *See* Jay M. Zitter, *Disciplining Attorney for Abuse or Misuse of Computer Technology Including Internet and E-mail Activities*, 46 A.L.R. 6th 365 (2009). Yet, there is a pressing question: What is the test or standard for determining whether a solo or small-firm attorney has violated an ABA technology-based rule?

Fairly recently, Brett Trout penned an article entitled "The Ethical Lawyer and the Tao of Technology," 48 Creighton L. Rev. 709 (2015). The following comment appears in the article:

> [T]he application of an ethical rule to a new technology makes a lawyer's life easier, by providing specific guidance. .... A [new] ruling can be problematic, however, [if] the ruling is overbroad and/or misinformed. [M]ost judges and ethics committee members—[who] apply ethical rules to new technology—are extremely well versed. But some [are] technological [naïve]. When issuing decisions involving new technology, less technologically sophisticated judges and ethics committee members may [adopt] broader, *vaguer*, and more conservative opinions to prevent more technologically sophisticated lawyers from trying to exploit flaws in a narrower, *more specific*, and more liberal opinion.

Nathan M. Crystal also presents an insightful analysis in his article entitled, "Criticism of Judges," 25-JAN S.C. Law. 10 (2014). Here is a synopsis:

> Disciplinary proceedings against lawyers—for criticizing judges—have been around for years. But the advent of the Internet and social media has increased the possibility of such proceedings. ... Civility rules are constitutional when applied to lawyers' criticizing other lawyers. *See In re*

> *Anonymous Member of the S.C. Bar*, 709 S.E.2d 633, 638 (S.C. 2011) (finding that the attorney sent an email to the opposing counsel—asserting that the latter's daughter used cocaine—and issuing a private letter of caution). … Incivility is not the only basis for [determining whether criticizing judges] is misconduct. Even when the criticism is temperate, it may be unethical under RULE 8.2(a) — "A lawyer shall not make a [false] statement … concerning the qualifications or integrity of a judge." This standard sounds very similar to the standard that the Supreme Court adopted in *New York Times Co. v. Sullivan*, 376 U.S. 254, 285-286 (1964). In *Sullivan*, the Court held: "In a libel action against a public official, a plaintiff must prove that the statements were made with "actual malice"—consisting of either knowledge of falsity or reckless disregard of whether they were true or false. Further, the plaintiff has the burden of proving "actual malice" by "convincing clarity"—which is generally understood to mean "by clear and convincing evidence." However, the vast majority of courts have [not embraced *Sullivan*'s "subjective" or "good faith" standard to establish a violation under] MODEL RULE 8.2(a). Instead, most courts have adopted an "objective" standard: Did the attorney have an "objectively reasonable basis" for making the statements?

Without doubt, whether to apply a subjective or an objective standard is a pressing question. But, state disciplinary boards and courts are also seriously divided over another question: whether a *mens rea* test should be used to establish an attorney's guilt or liability. An excellent discussion of this latter conflict appears in Nancy J. Moore's article, "Mens Rea Standards In Lawyer Disciplinary Codes," 23 Georgetown J. Legal Ethics 1 (2010). Here is a summary:

> Many ABA Model Rules of Professional Conduct have a specified *mens rea*, or mental state requirement—*e.g.*, RULE 1.4(a), RULE 3.3(a), RULE 4.3and RULE 8.2(a). … But many rules … do not specify any particular mental state requirement—*e.g.*, RULE 1.6, RULE 1.7(a), RULE 1.15(a), and RULE 7.1… What are we to make of the rules that have no *mens rea* requirement? Are they strict liability rules? … Even when a rule contains at least one

> *mens rea* requirement, it is often unclear whether the same or any *mens rea* requirement applies to other elements of the rule. Courts sometimes say: Rules that have no articulated *mens rea* requirement lack a "scienter requirement." But it is unclear whether they mean that the rule imposes strict liability or the rule does not [require evidence of the lawyer's having] acted intentionally or knowingly. …
>
> Courts sometimes characterize a rule as a "*per se* offense"—in which there is no "innocent behavior" or good faith excuse. … More typically, courts simply fail to address the mental state element in deciding whether a rule has been violated. Also, other confusions abound. Courts have failed to distinguish between negligence and mere inadvertence. … Given the attention that has been paid to *mens rea* issues in criminal law, it is surprising [to find] such confusion when similar issues arise in disciplinary enforcement. The primitive nature of the *mens rea* discussions—in the latter context—likely results from the manner in which disciplinary rules have evolved.

As you read each case in this chapter, answer the following questions: (1) Did the attorney employ a legal-practice technology that violated the spirit, intent or letter of the Model Rule?; (2) Which legal standard did the ethics board apply to determine whether an attorney was guilty?; (3) Which evidentiary standard did the state or federal court apply—a *circumstantial evidence*, a *preponderance of the evidence*, or a *clear and convincing evidence* standard?; (4) Was the "guilty" attorney censured or reprimanded?; (5) Was the "guilty" attorney's license suspended?; and, (6) Was the attorney disbarred?

Excerpts from the American Bar Association's Model Rules of Professional Conduct

Rule 1.1—Competence

A lawyer shall provide competent representation to a client. Competent representation requires the legal knowledge, skill, thoroughness and preparation reasonably necessary for the representation.

COMMENT [8]—To maintain the requisite knowledge and skill, a lawyer should keep abreast of changes in the law and its practice, including the benefits and risks associated with relevant technology, engage in continuing study and education and comply with all continuing legal education requirements to which the lawyer is subject.

Rule 1.2—Attorney-Client Scope of Representation and Allocation of Authority

(a) Subject to paragraphs (c) and (d), a lawyer shall abide by a client's decisions concerning the objectives of representation and ... shall consult with the client as to the means by which they are to be pursued ...

(b) A lawyer's representation of a client, including representation by appointment, does not constitute an endorsement of the client's political, economic, social or moral views or activities.

(c) A lawyer may limit the scope of the representation if the limitation is reasonable under the circumstances and the client gives informed consent.

(d) A lawyer shall not counsel a client to engage, or assist a client, in conduct that the lawyer knows is criminal or fraudulent. But a lawyer may discuss the legal consequences of any proposed course of conduct with a client and may counsel or assist a client to make a good faith effort to determine the validity, scope, meaning or application of the law.

Rule 1.6— Confidentiality of Information

(a) A lawyer shall not reveal information relating to the representation of a client unless the client gives informed consent, the disclosure is impliedly authorized in order to carry out the representation or the disclosure is permitted by paragraph (b).

(b) A lawyer may reveal information relating to the representation of a client to the extent the lawyer reasonably believes necessary:

(1) to prevent reasonably certain death or substantial bodily harm;

(2) to prevent the client from committing a crime or fraud that is reasonably certain to result in substantial injury to the financial interests or property of another and in furtherance of which the client has used or is using the lawyer's services. …

(c) A lawyer shall make reasonable efforts to prevent the inadvertent or unauthorized disclosure of, or unauthorized access to, information relating to the representation of a client.[1]

---

[1] ***Full Text: Client-Lawyer Relationship***
Rule 1.6 Confidentiality Of Information

(a) A lawyer shall not reveal information relating to the representation of a client unless the client gives informed consent, the disclosure is impliedly authorized in order to carry out the representation or the disclosure is permitted by paragraph (b).

(b) A lawyer may reveal information relating to the representation of a client to the extent the lawyer reasonably believes necessary:

(1) to prevent reasonably certain death or substantial bodily harm;

(2) to prevent the client from committing a crime or fraud that is reasonably certain to result in substantial injury to the financial interests or property of another and in furtherance of which the client has used or is using the lawyer's services;

(3) to prevent, mitigate or rectify substantial injury to the financial interests or property of another that is reasonably certain to result or has resulted from the client's commission of a crime or fraud in furtherance of which the client has used the lawyer's services;

(4) to secure legal advice about the lawyer's compliance with these Rules;

(5) to establish a claim or defense on behalf of the lawyer in a controversy between the lawyer and the client, to establish a defense to a criminal charge or civil claim against the lawyer based upon conduct in which the client was involved, or to respond to allegations in any proceeding concerning the lawyer's representation of the client;

(6) to comply with other law or a court order; or

Rule 5.5—Unauthorized and Multijurisdictional Practice of Law

(a) A lawyer shall not practice law in a jurisdiction in violation of the regulation of the legal profession in that jurisdiction, or assist another in doing so.

(b) A lawyer who is not admitted to practice in this jurisdiction shall not:

(1) except as authorized by these Rules or other law, establish an office or other systematic and continuous presence in this jurisdiction for the practice of law; or

(2) hold out to the public or otherwise represent that the lawyer is admitted to practice law in this jurisdiction.

(c) A lawyer admitted in another United States jurisdiction, and not disbarred or suspended from practice in any jurisdiction, may provide legal services on a temporary basis in this jurisdiction that:

(1) are undertaken in association with a lawyer who is admitted to practice in this jurisdiction and who actively participates in the matter;

(2) are in or reasonably related to a pending or potential proceeding before a tribunal in this or another jurisdiction, if the lawyer, or a person the lawyer is assisting, is authorized by law or order to appear in such proceeding or reasonably expects to be so authorized; ...

(d) A lawyer admitted in another United States jurisdiction or in a foreign jurisdiction, and not disbarred or suspended from practice in any jurisdiction or the equivalent thereof,

---

(7) to detect and resolve conflicts of interest arising from the lawyer's change of employment or from changes in the composition or ownership of a firm, but only if the revealed information would not compromise the attorney-client privilege or otherwise prejudice the client.

(c) A lawyer shall make reasonable efforts to prevent the inadvertent or unauthorized disclosure of, or unauthorized access to, information relating to the representation of a client.

may provide legal services through an office or other systematic and continuous presence in this jurisdiction that:

(1) are provided to the lawyer's employer or its organizational affiliates; are not services for which the forum requires *pro hac vice* admission; and, when performed by a foreign lawyer and requires advice on the law of this or another jurisdiction or of the United States, such advice shall be based upon the advice of a lawyer who is duly licensed and authorized by the jurisdiction to provide such advice; or

(2) are services that the lawyer is authorized by federal or other law or rule to provide in this jurisdiction.

(e) For purposes of paragraph (d), the foreign lawyer must be a member in good standing of a recognized legal profession in a foreign jurisdiction, the members of which are admitted to practice as lawyers or counselors at law or the equivalent, and are subject to effective regulation and discipline by a duly constituted professional body or a public authority.[m]

---

[m] ***Full Text: Law Firms And Associations***

Rule 5.5 Unauthorized Practice Of Law; Multijurisdictional Practice Of Law

(a) A lawyer shall not practice law in a jurisdiction in violation of the regulation of the legal profession in that jurisdiction, or assist another in doing so.

(b) A lawyer who is not admitted to practice in this jurisdiction shall not:

(1) except as authorized by these Rules or other law, establish an office or other systematic and continuous presence in this jurisdiction for the practice of law; or

(2) hold out to the public or otherwise represent that the lawyer is admitted to practice law in this jurisdiction.

(c) A lawyer admitted in another United States jurisdiction, and not disbarred or suspended from practice in any jurisdiction, may provide legal services on a temporary basis in this jurisdiction that:

(1) are undertaken in association with a lawyer who is admitted to practice in this jurisdiction and who actively participates in the matter;

(2) are in or reasonably related to a pending or potential proceeding before a tribunal in this or another jurisdiction, if the lawyer, or a person the lawyer is assisting, is authorized by law or order to appear in such proceeding or reasonably expects to be so authorized;

(3) are in or reasonably related to a pending or potential arbitration, mediation, or other alternative resolution proceeding in this or another jurisdiction, if the services arise out of or are reasonably related to the lawyer's practice in a jurisdiction in which the lawyer is admitted to practice and are not services for which the forum requires pro hac vice admission; or

Rule 7.1—Communication Concerning a Lawyer's Services

A lawyer shall not make a false or misleading communication about the lawyer or the lawyer's services. A communication is false or misleading if it contains a material misrepresentation of fact or law, or omits a fact necessary to make the statement considered as a whole not materially misleading.

COMMENT 1—This Rule governs all communications about a lawyer's services. ... Whatever means are used to make known a lawyer's services, statements about them must be truthful.

---

(4) are not within paragraphs (c) (2) or (c)(3) and arise out of or are reasonably related to the lawyer's practice in a jurisdiction in which the lawyer is admitted to practice.

(d) A lawyer admitted in another United States jurisdiction or in a foreign jurisdiction, and not disbarred or suspended from practice in any jurisdiction or the equivalent thereof, or a person otherwise lawfully practicing as an in-house counsel under the laws of a foreign jurisdiction, may provide legal services through an office or other systematic and continuous presence in this jurisdiction that:

(1) are provided to the lawyer's employer or its organizational affiliates, are not services for which the forum requires pro hac vice admission; and when performed by a foreign lawyer and requires advice on the law of this or another U.S. jurisdiction or of the United States, such advice shall be based upon the advice of a lawyer who is duly licensed and authorized by the jurisdiction to provide such advice; or

(2) are services that the lawyer is authorized by federal or other law or rule to provide in this jurisdiction.

(e) For purposes of paragraph (d):

(1) the foreign lawyer must be a member in good standing of a recognized legal profession in a foreign jurisdiction, the members of which are admitted to practice as lawyers or counselors at law or the equivalent, and subject to effective regulation and discipline by a duly constituted professional body or a public authority; or,

(2) the person otherwise lawfully practicing as an in-house counsel under the laws of a foreign jurisdiction must be authorized to practice under this rule by, in the exercise of its discretion, [the highest court of this jurisdiction].

B. Disciplinary Actions against "Deviant" Attorneys for Accessing Third Parties' Computers, Reading Emails and/or Gathering Privileged Information Without Permission

1. Disciplinary Actions Against "Deviant" Attorneys for Using "Innocent" Attorneys' "Protected" Passwords and Reading Privileged E-mails Without Authorization

In the Matter of Julia Ellis Brown

628 S.E.2d 885
(S.C. 2006)

Per Curiam:

While employed by the South Carolina Centers for Equal Justice (SCCEJ), Attorney Julia Ellis Brown used her office and home computers to access or attempt to access the email accounts of more than forty employees of SCCEJ and at least one member of the SCCEJ Board. Brown accessed the email accounts—using passwords either not voluntarily provided to her or not provided to her for the purpose for which she used them. Brown was not authorized to access these email accounts either by SCCEJ or by the individual users of the accounts.

Attorney Brown accessed the email accounts nearly every day from December 2002 until April 2004. Brown accessed her coworkers' email accounts to management activity and monitor anti-union sentiment during a unionizing effort that Brown initiated and supported. In particular, Brown was looking for information about the budget, management-meeting reports, and anti-union activities.

Brown read, downloaded, and disseminated some of the information contained in the email messages that she accessed during this period. Attorney Brown's reading, downloading, and disseminating of this information was not authorized by SCCEJ—the users whose email accounts she accessed—or the original parties to the email messages. Brown deleted some of the email messages. Some of the deleted email messages had not been read by the intended recipients. Brown was able to discern—from viewing the messages—which ones had and had not been read. The messages that Brown chose to delete contained anti-union information or sentiment. Brown's deletion of these email messages was not authorized by SCCEJ—the users whose email accounts she accessed—or the original parties to the email messages.

On or about March 29, 2004, Attorney Brown used her home computer to access the email account of the managing attorney in another office. She did not have authority—from either SCCEJ or the managing attorney—to access the account. Through that unauthorized access, Brown obtained a copy of an email message. An outside counsel—representing SCCEJ in connection with the union campaign—sent the email to the interim executive director of SCCEJ.

Attorney Brown disseminated the latter email to individuals working to unionize SCCEJ. Brown did not tell the individuals how she obtained the email message. At the insistence of those individuals, Brown forwarded the email to all of the SCCEJ employees who could vote in the union election. When she accessed the email and disseminated it, Brown knew that the original sender was an outside counsel, who was representing SCCEJ in the union matter.

Law

Attorney Brown admits: Her misconduct constitutes grounds for discipline under Rule 413 of the Rules for Lawyer Disciplinary Enforcement. Specifically Rule 7(a)(1) states: A lawyer shall not violate Rules of Professional Conduct or any other rules of this jurisdiction regarding professional conduct of lawyers. And, Rule 7(a)(5) reads: A lawyer shall not engage in conduct tending to pollute the administration of justice or to bring the courts or the legal profession into disrepute or conduct demonstrating an unfitness to practice law.

In addition, Attorney Brown admits: She has violated other provisions of the Rules of Professional Conduct, Rule 407. South Carolina Appellate Court Rule 8.4(a) reads: A lawyer shall not violate the Rules of Professional Conduct. Rule 8.4(d) states: A lawyer shall not engage in conduct involving dishonesty, fraud, deceit, or misrepresentation. And Rule 8.4(e) reads: A lawyer shall not engage in conduct that is prejudicial to administration of justice.

In this attorney disciplinary matter, Attorney Julia Ellis Brown and the Office of Disciplinary Counsel (ODC) have entered into an Agreement for Discipline by Consent pursuant to Rule 21 of the Rules for Lawyer Disciplinary Enforcement and Rule 413 of South Carolina Appellate Court Rules. In the Agreement, Attorney Brown admits misconduct and consents to the imposition of a confidential admonition, a public reprimand, or a definite suspension not to exceed two years. We accept the Agreement and impose a two-year suspension from the practice of law.

Conclusion

We accept the Agreement for Discipline by Consent and impose a two-year definite suspension from the practice of law. Suspension. Within fifteen days of the date of this opinion, Attorney Brown shall file an affidavit with the Clerk of Court—showing that she has complied with Rule 30 of the Rules for Lawyer Disciplinary Enforcement, and Rule 413 of South Carolina Appellate Court Rules. DEFINITE SUSPENSION.

Excerpt from the American Bar Association's Model Rules of Professional Conduct

Rule 8.4—Misconduct

It is professional misconduct for a lawyer to:

(a) violate or attempt to violate the Rules of Professional Conduct, knowingly assist or induce another to do so, or do so through the acts of another;

(b) commit a criminal act that reflects adversely on the lawyer's honesty, trustworthiness or fitness as a lawyer in other respects;

(c) engage in conduct involving dishonesty, fraud, deceit or misrepresentation;

(d) engage in conduct that is prejudicial to the administration of justice;

(e) state or imply an ability to influence improperly a government agency or official or to achieve results by means that violate the Rules of Professional Conduct or other law; or

(f) knowingly assist a judge or judicial officer in conduct that is a violation of applicable rules of judicial conduct or other law.

(g) engage in conduct that the lawyer knows or reasonably should know is harassment or discrimination on the basis of race, sex, religion, national origin, ethnicity, disability, age, sexual orientation, gender identity, marital status or socioeconomic status in conduct related to the practice of law. This paragraph does not limit the ability of a lawyer to accept, decline or withdraw from a representation in accordance with Rule 1.16. This paragraph does not preclude legitimate advice or advocacy consistent with these Rules.

---

2. Disciplinary Actions Against "Deviant" Spouses' Attorneys for Using "Protected" Passwords and Reading "Innocent" Spouses' Attorneys' E-mails Without Authorization

Lawyer Disciplinary Board v. Michael P. Markins

663 S.E.2d 614
(W.Va. 2008)

Per Curiam:

The facts of this case are not in dispute. Michael P. Markins objects to the sanctions recommended by a Hearing Panel Subcommittee of the Lawyer Disciplinary Board (Board) for violating the West Virginia Rules of Professional Conduct ("Rules"). Markins has been a practicing attorney since October 2001. At all times relevant, Markins was employed as an associate attorney at the *Law Firm of Huddleston Bolen, LLP* ("Huddleston"). Also, it is undisputed: In law school, Attorney Markins was an outstanding student—graduating near the top of his class. While at *Huddleston*, Markins was well thought of in the legal community and was on the firm's "Partnership Track."

His wife—also an attorney—was similarly employed at the *Law Firm of Offutt, Fisher & Nord* ("OFN"). In late October or early November of 2003, Markins began accessing his wife's OFN e-mail account without her permission or knowledge. The password to his wife's e-mail account was her last name. Similarly, the passwords to the e-mail accounts of all OFN attorneys was the individual account holder's last name. Markins testified that the purpose of reading his wife's e-mails was to secretly monitor her activities, because he believed she had become involved in an extramarital affair with an OFN client. Markins further testified: Initially, he improperly accessed only his wife's account and later, that of another attorney, an OFN partner. Eventually, however, Mankins's curiosity got the better of him, and he began accessing the e-mail accounts of seven other OFN attorneys. Obviously, Markins did so without the account holders' knowledge or permission.

When an OFN attorney began to suspect that her e-mail account had been improperly accessed, OFN retained Paul Law—a computer systems engineer— and launched an investigation. From Mr. Law's investigation, it was learned: On numerous occasions before November 7, 2003, until March 16, 2006, Markins gained unauthorized access to OFN e-mail accounts using three IP accounts: Markins's Huddleston IP account; Markins's residential IP account; and the IP account at the Hampton Inn in Beckley, West Virginia—where Markins had been monitoring a trial in which both Huddleston and OFN clients were being represented.

* * *

In March 2006, Markins's wife—who had been completely unaware of Markins's misconduct, told Markins that someone had been breaking into OFN e-mail accounts and that the firm was getting close to finding out who it was. Shortly thereafter, Markins revealed to his wife that it was he who had been improperly accessing the OFN e-mail accounts. ... Though she had learned of Markins's misconduct, she denied any knowledge of it. Immediately thereafter, Markins's counsel contacted partners at the firm to disclose Markins's actions. Both Markins and his wife were eventually terminated from employment by their respective law firms as a result.

Markins has consistently maintained that he has never disclosed to anyone any information he obtained from improperly accessing the various OFN e-mail accounts. He testified that he has never used any of the information in an improper manner; did not save any of the accessed e-mails onto his computer; and did not forward any of the e-mails to another person. Indeed, to date, there has been no evidence to the contrary. Markins testified that he is extremely remorseful for his actions, takes full responsibility for his misconduct, and has been cooperative during the course of this disciplinary proceeding and during OFN's investigation of the matter.

On the advice of counsel, Markins was examined by psychologist David A. Clayman, Ph.D., whose affidavit was submitted with Markins's Answer to Statement of Charges before the Board.

... According to Dr. Clayman, Markins would not have engaged in the misconduct herein described if it were not for the "significant emotional strain caused by concern for the integrity of his marriage." Dr. Clayman also stated: Markins was unlikely to repeat this or any similar conduct—given his professional and personal embarrassment, his family's strain and hardship, and his remorse.

On December 18, 2006, the Board filed a Statement of Charges against Markins, alleging violations of Rule 8.4(b) and (c) of the West Virginia Rules of Professional Conduct. Citing Rule 8.4(c), the Board asserted: "Markins engaged in the repetitive unauthorized access of [OFN] e-mail accounts by improperly using various e-mail account passwords assigned to various [OFN] attorneys." Under Rule 8.4(c), "[i]t is professional misconduct for a lawyer to ... engage in conduct involving dishonesty, fraud, deceit or misrepresentation."

Citing Rule 8.4(b), the Board asserted: Markins's repetitive unauthorized access of OFN e-mail accounts was a crime, violating West Virginia Code 61–3C–12. And the Board asserted that Markins's conduct adversely reflected on his honesty, trustworthiness or fitness as a lawyer. Under Rule 8.4(b), "[i]t is professional misconduct for a lawyer to ... commit a criminal act that reflects adversely on the lawyer's honesty, trustworthiness or fitness as a lawyer in other respects." The Board further alleged that there were "aggravating factors": "Markins's conduct involved multiple offenses. A selfish motive shaped Markins's pattern of misconduct, which were illegal acts.

Following the disciplinary hearing, the Board found that Markins violated Rules 8.4(b) and (c) and recommended the following sanctions:

1) Markins would be suspended from the practice of law for two (2) years;

2) After reinstatement, Markins's private practice would be supervised for one (1) year;

3) Markins would complete twelve (12) hours of CLE in ethics—in addition to the other ethics hours which are required to maintain an active license to practice law;

4) The additional twelve (12) hours would be completed before Markins was reinstated; and

5) Markins would pay the costs of the disciplinary proceedings.

Markins objects only to the recommended sanctions. Initially, Markins proposed that he be publicly reprimanded and be required to complete an additional six hours of CLE in ethics above his current requirements. During oral argument, however, he conceded: While a public reprimand may not be an appropriate sanction, the proper sanction should be something less than a two-year suspension of his law license.

Discussion

Our singular purpose in this matter is to determine the appropriate sanction. Rule 3.16 of the West Virginia Rules of Lawyer Disciplinary Procedure enumerates factors to be considered in imposing sanctions. It provides: "[When] imposing a sanction after a finding of lawyer misconduct, ... the [West Virginia Supreme Court of Appeals] or [Lawyer Disciplinary Board] shall consider the following factors: (1) whether the lawyer has violated a duty owed to a client, to the public, to the legal system or to the profession; (2) whether the lawyer acted intentionally, knowingly or negligently; (3) the amount of the actual or potential injury caused by the lawyer's misconduct; and (4) the existence of any aggravating or mitigating factors." *Office of Lawyer Disciplinary Counsel v. Jordan,* 513 S.E.2d 722-724 (W.Va. 1998).

Markins contends: There were mitigating factors that this court should consider before determining the sanction. According to Markins, he believed his wife was engaged in an extramarital affair with an OFN client; and OFN partners encouraged the affair. Thus, he secretly accessed his wife's OFN e-mail account and the accounts of other OFN attorneys while under extreme emotional distress—fearing he would lose his wife and family.

* * *

Presently, there is no evidence that Markins has used or misused the information he improperly accessed from OFN. Nevertheless, we must recognize that OFN has suffered negative consequences from Markins's actions. OFN was forced to expend valuable time and resources to investigate the matter and disclose the unfortunate events to its clients—opening itself up to potential lawsuits and professional embarrassment. Moreover, one is unable to predict or tangibly quantify the future impact of Markins's misconduct on OFN or on Markins's former law firm in terms of attracting new clients.

Finally, we recognize: The widespread use of e-mails—between and among attorneys and their clients—increases the likelihood that communications might be improperly infiltrated. Additionally, in this case, it was an attorney who repeatedly accessed other attorneys' confidential e-mails without the innocent attorneys' knowledge or permission. Thus, this court must ensure: Our sanction will effectively deter other attorneys and protect the public.

Accordingly, based upon the foregoing, we are compelled to adopt the recommendations of the Disciplinary Board.

NOTES AND QUESTIONS

1) The Multifaceted Purposes of Attorneys' Disciplinary Proceedings. In *Lawyer Disciplinary Bd. v. Taylor*, 451 S.E.2d 440, 445 (W.Va. 1994), the court stated: Attorneys' "disciplinary proceedings are not designed solely to punish the attorney." The proceedings are also designed "to protect the public, to reassure it as to the reliability and integrity of attorneys and to safeguard its interest in the administration of justice."

2) The Multifaceted Purposes of Disciplinary Punishment. Consider the court's observation *in Committee on Legal Ethics v. Walker*, 358 S.E.2d 234 (W.Va.1987): "[When] deciding on the appropriate disciplinary action for ethical violations, this court must consider not only what steps would appropriately punish, ... but also whether the discipline imposed is adequate to serve as an effective deterrent to other members of the Bar and at the same time restore public confidence in the ethical standards of the legal profession."

3) Sanctioning Attorneys for Listening to Third Parties' Voice-Mail Messages Without Permission. Consider the facts and analysis in *In re Schwartz*, 599 S.E.2d 184 (Ga. 2004). An offending attorney admitted: For nearly 14 months, he "accessed, listened to, and randomly deleted voice mail messages" on a law firm's voice mail messaging system—after the law firm discharged him. The attorney's conduct violated Georgia's Rules of Professional Conduct; and disbarment was an appropriate sanction. Nevertheless, the Supreme Court of Georgia agreed to accept the attorney's proposed sanction—an 18-month suspension of his law license. Certain mitigating factors persuaded the *Schwartz* court to embrace the attorney's proposal: (1) The attorney had "no prior or subsequent incidents of inappropriate behavior related to his professional conduct; (2) apparently, other members of the Bar respected the attorney; (3) the attorney was forthright when the State Bar confronted the attorney; and (4) the attorney demonstrated contrition and remorse.

---

3. Disciplinary Actions Against Attorneys for Using "Protected" Passwords to Access Lexis-Nexis, Westlaw, and Other Fee-Based Research Providers' Online Databases Without Permission

In re the Reciprocal Discipline of Everett Walton

287 P.3d 1098
(Or. 2012)

Per Curiam.

This is a reciprocal discipline proceeding pursuant to Oregon State Bar Rule of Procedure—BR Rule 3.5. Everett Walton is licensed to practice law in Oregon and in the State of Hawai'i. For approximately 14 months, Attorney Walton improperly used a Westlaw account password that belonged to the Republic of Palau. Walton's conduct violated Hawai'i Rules of Professional Conduct (HRPC). The accused entered into a stipulation for discipline with the Hawai'i Office of Disciplinary Counsel. Based on that stipulation, the Disciplinary Board of the Hawai'i Supreme Court imposed a public reprimand.

In March 2012, Hawai'i's Disciplinary Counsel provided the order and stipulation to the Oregon State Bar. Later, the latter Bar invited Walton to respond and provide any additional information that he wanted this court to consider in deciding reciprocal discipline. Walton submitted a reply and several exhibits. In August 2012, the Bar notified this court—under BR 3.5(a)—that Hawai'i had disciplined the accused. And it recommended that the accused be suspended from the practice of law in Oregon for six months. For the reasons stated below, we reject the Oregon Bar's recommendation.

In a reciprocal discipline proceeding, the order of discipline from another jurisdiction is sufficient evidence that the accused lawyer committed the misconduct described therein. *See* BR 3.5(b). Whether this court should impose discipline turns on two questions:

> (1) Was the procedure in the jurisdiction which disciplined the attorney lacking in notice or opportunity to be heard?
>
> (2) Should the attorney be disciplined by the court? *See* BR 3.5(c).

In this case, the Attorney Walton does not dispute that the Hawai'i disciplinary proceeding gave him notice and an opportunity to be heard, or that this court should discipline him for his misconduct in Hawai'i. Rather, he contends only that the appropriate sanction for his misconduct is a private reprimand. This court has rejected the practice of imposing a private reprimand, as distinguished from a public reprimand. *See In re Zumwalt*, 296 Or. 631, 634 n. 5 (1984). If the court imposes a reprimand, it is public. *See* BR 6.1(a)(ii). This court determines whether it should discipline an accused lawyer and in what manner after reviewing the judgment from other states' and the parties' submissions. *See* BR 3.5(e) and *In re Coggins*, 338 Or. 480, 483 (2005).

We therefore take the following facts from the Hawai'i stipulation for discipline and the accused's responses to the Bar and this court. Attorney Walton has been practicing law since 1977. In early 2001, he was appointed Special Prosecutor for the Republic of Palau's Office of the Special Prosecutor (OSP). In March 2007 and while still holding that position, Walton entered into a three-year contract with Thomson Reuters Corporation on behalf of OSP. The contract was for Internet legal research services—known as Westlaw. Under the contract, OSP agreed to pay a flat rate—about $1,170 per month for unlimited access to Westlaw until May 31, 2010. The contract included the following provision: "In the event Subscriber requests a Minimum Term in excess of one year as set forth in the Order Form, this Agreement may not be terminated prior to the expiration of such minimum term." Attorney Walton received two passwords that gave him access to OSP's Westlaw account.

In March 2008, Walton resigned from his employment as special prosecutor for OSP. But he knew: Under the Republic of Palau's hiring system, the position would remain unfilled for at least nine months. Therefore, before leaving that position, Walton contacted Thomson Reuters—trying to cancel the Westlaw contract. A Thomson Reuters representative informed Attorney Walton: The Company would not agree to terminate the contract for *any* reason before the May 2010 expiration date—because the monthly charges for the three-year contract were substantially discounted from the cost of a one-year contract.

Walton left Palau, returned to Hawai'i and began working as the managing attorney for the Legal Aid Society of Hawai'i. Walton continued to use OSP's Westlaw password while representing indigent clients in the Hilo office. He did not seek authorization from OSP or the Republic of Palau to do so. During that time, OSP continued to receive monthly statements from Thomson Reuters, which detailed Walton's monthly charges for using the Westlaw account. OSP forwarded those statements to the Director of the Bureau of National Treasury of the Ministry of Finance of the Republic of Palau—which, in turn, paid them.

In February 2009, the Republic of Palau named a new special prosecutor. In April 2009, the new special prosecutor attempted to cancel the Westlaw contract. Thomson Reuters denied the request to terminate the contract. In May 2009, a secretary in the special prosecutor's office sent an email to Walton and disclosed: The new special prosecutor was considering filing civil and criminal charges—as well as a Bar complaint—against Walton for his unauthorized use of OSP's Westlaw account. Attorney Walton immediately stopped using the account.

In July 2009, the new special prosecutor filed a complaint with the Hawai'i Office of Disciplinary Counsel and alleged: Without any authorization, Attorney Walton illegally accessed and used OSP's Westlaw account for his personal use after he left the position of special prosecutor. The complaint further alleged: Walton's conduct caused the Republic of Palau more than $20,000 in economic damages. The value of the used Westlaw services … was more than $45,000—based on per search and not flat rate charges. The complaint also alleged: Walton refused to pay for or reimburse the Republic of Palau for any of the Westlaw services that he had used. Finally, the complaint alleged: Walton's conduct violated HRPC 8.4(c)—which forbids dishonesty, fraud, deceit, or misrepresentation. The complaint also alleged that Walton violated HRPC 8.4(a)—which prohibits a lawyer's violating or attempting to violate rules of professional conduct).

Walton responded and asserted: (1) He did not use the Westlaw account for his personal use; (2) He used the password and account only to perform legal research for the indigent clients of the Legal Aid Society of Hawai'i; (3) His using of the Westlaw account did not cost the Republic of Palau any money whatsoever, given that the account could not be cancelled and the monthly fee was due and payable whether or not the account was used; (4) He had no intent to deprive the Republic of Palau of anything of value; and (5) The Republic of Palau implicitly consented to his using the Westlaw account by continuing to pay the monthly Westlaw invoices—which detailed the monthly usage on the account when no lawyer was working in OSP as special prosecutor. In addition, Walton pointed out: He had not generated a disciplinary record in more than 35 years as a lawyer, and he had freely admitted his usage of the Westlaw account.

In November 2011, the Attorney Walton signed a stipulation for discipline with the Hawai'i Disciplinary Counsel. Walton admitted that he violated HRPC 8.4(c) and HRPC 8.4(a)—by accessing and using OSP's Westlaw account for 14 months after he had resigned from OSP, and by refusing to pay or reimburse OSP or the Republic of Palau for any part of the Westlaw services that he had used. Walton stipulated that his substantial experience as a law practitioner was an aggravating factor. He also stipulated: His lack of a disciplinary record and his willingness to accept responsibility for his improper use of Westlaw services were mitigating factors. Finally, Walton and the Hawai'i Disciplinary Counsel agreed: A private reprimand was an appropriate sanction. As noted, the Hawai'i Supreme Court's Disciplinary Board accepted the stipulation. But the Disciplinary Board rejected the parties' recommendation for discipline—determining instead that a public reprimand was the appropriate sanction for the Walton's misconduct.

Notwithstanding Hawai'i's imposition of a public reprimand on the accused for his misconduct, the Bar now urges us to suspend Walton's ability to practice law in Oregon for six months. The Bar contends: By logging into a research service without permission or authority, using passwords provided to his former employer, using research services paid for by his former employer, and refusing to pay the provider for those services, Attorney Walton engaged in conduct involving dishonesty. And, the Bar insisted that Walton's misconduct reflected adversely on his fitness to practice law—which violates Oregon Rule of Professional Conduct (RPC). In particular, RPC 8.4(a)(3) provides: "It is professional misconduct for a lawyer to … engage in conduct involving dishonesty, fraud, deceit or misrepresentation that reflects adversely on the lawyer's fitness to practice law."

In addition, the Bar acknowledges: Walton did not stipulate that his conduct constituted a crime in Hawai'i. Still, the Bar contends: The stipulated facts—detailing the accused's unauthorized use of OSP's Westlaw account—are sufficient to establish that Walton committed a criminal act under Hawai'i's criminal code. The Bar does not specifically identify which provision or provisions of the Hawai'i Revised Statutes that Walton violated. Instead, the Bar suggests several provisions that might apply. Furthermore, the Bar argues that Walton violated Oregon RPC 8.4(a)(2)—which prohibits a lawyer from "committing a criminal act that reflects adversely on the lawyer's honesty, trustworthiness or fitness as a lawyer in other respects[.]"

Finally, the Bar contends: Walton's violating Oregon's Rules of Professional Conduct is a violation of RPC 8.4(a)(1)—which prohibits a lawyer from violating the rules of professional conduct by his own actions or through the acts of others. RPC 8.4(a)(1) reads: "It is professional misconduct for a lawyer to violate the Rules of Professional Conduct, knowingly assist or induce another to do so, or do so through the acts of another[.]"

We accept Attorney Walton's stipulation and the Hawai'i Disciplinary Board's conclusion: By using OSP's Westlaw password for Internet research without authorization, Walton engaged in conduct involving dishonesty. We find: Walton's conduct violated RPC 8.4(a)(3); and that violation constitutes a separate violation under RPC 8.4(a)(1). However, we reject the Bar's additional claim: Attorney Walton violated RPC 8.4(a)(2) by committing a criminal act. The Bar has the burden of establishing misconduct by clear and convincing evidence. *See,* BR 5.2. And, the Bar has not met that burden in this case. The State of Hawai'i did not prosecute Walton for any crime. However, that alone is not dispositive. But the Bar has not offered any legal analysis of cited provisions in Hawai'i criminal code. Moreover, it is not clear whether or not Walton's misconduct fits squarely within the proscriptions of those laws.

Thus, we turn to the question: What is the appropriate sanction Walton's violating RPC 8.4(a)(3) and RPC 8.4(a)(1)? In the case *In re Lopez,* 350 Or. 192, 198 (2011), this court stated: In reciprocal discipline cases, the court has an independent obligation to determine whether a sanction is warranted when a lawyer violates this state's professional rules. This court often concluded: The sanction that another jurisdiction imposes on an attorney is sufficient to vindicate Oregon's interests. But, we are free to impose a different sanction when appropriate. *Id.*

In determining the appropriate sanction, we consider both the American Bar Association's Standards for Imposing Lawyer Sanctions (1991, Amended 2005) (ABA Standards), and this court's cases. The ABA Standards direct courts to examine four factors to determine the appropriate sanction for a lawyer's professional misconduct: (1) the ethical duty violated, (2) the lawyer's mental state, (3) the actual or potential injury caused by the lawyer's misconduct, and (4) the existence of aggravating or mitigating circumstances. See, ABA Standard 3.0.

By engaging in conduct involving dishonesty, Walton violated his duty to the public—to maintain his personal integrity. ABA Standard 5.1. The ABA Standards provide: A lawyer acts with "intent" if it is the lawyer's "conscious objective or purpose to accomplish a particular result." ABA Standards at 7. A lawyer acts with "knowledge" if the lawyer acts with "the conscious awareness of the nature or attendant circumstances of the conduct but without the conscious objective or purpose to accomplish a particular result." *Id.*

The stipulation of discipline between Walton and Hawai'i Disciplinary Counsel does not recite any particular mental state. However, this court may infer from facts in the stipulation whether Walton used OSP's Westlaw password with the conscious objective to accomplish a particular result—to perform Westlaw research on OSP's account without paying for the service. We therefore find that Walton acted intentionally.

The Bar asserts: Walton's misconduct caused potential injury to OSP and actual injury to Thomson Reuters. The Bar does not explain how Walton's using the Westlaw password caused OSP potential injury. And we can see none. ... OSP was required to pay Thomson Reuters the same flat monthly fee whether or not its Westlaw account was used. ... More importantly, Walton used OSP's password to access Westlaw. And, as we have stated, OSP did not suffer any actual or potential harm.

Preliminary Sanction

We look to the ABA Standards for guidance to determine an appropriate sanction for conduct involving dishonesty, fraud, deceit, or misrepresentation. ABA Standard 5.1 provides, in part:

> Absent aggravating or mitigating circumstances, upon application of the factors set out in Standard 3.0, the following sanctions are generally appropriate in cases involving commission of a criminal act that reflects adversely on the lawyer's honesty, trustworthiness, or fitness as a lawyer in other respects, or in cases with conduct involving dishonesty, fraud, deceit, or misrepresentation:
>
> 5.11— Disbarment is generally appropriate when:
>
> (a) a lawyer engages in serious criminal conduct[,] a necessary element of which includes intentional interference with the administration of justice, false swearing, misrepresentation, fraud, extortion, misappropriation, or theft; or the sale, distribution or importation of controlled substances; or the intentional killing of another; or an attempt or conspiracy or solicitation of another to commit any of these offenses; or
>
> (b) a lawyer engages in any other intentional conduct involving dishonesty, fraud, deceit, or misrepresentation that seriously adversely reflects on the lawyer's fitness to practice."

> 5.12—Suspension is generally appropriate when a lawyer knowingly engages in criminal conduct which does not contain the elements listed in Standard 5.11 [disbarment] and that seriously adversely reflects on the lawyer's fitness to practice.
>
> 5.13—Reprimand is generally appropriate when a lawyer knowingly engages in any other conduct that involves dishonesty, fraud, deceit, or misrepresentation and that adversely reflects on the lawyer's fitness to practice law."

We observe that those standards are not a perfect fit in this case. We have concluded: Walton acted intentionally. But only one standard—ABA Standard 5.11—describes when disbarment is appropriate. ... That standard applies only when (1) a lawyer has engaged in "serious criminal conduct" or "other intentional conduct involving dishonesty," and (2) the conduct "seriously and adversely reflects on the lawyer's fitness to practice law." Although we have found that Walton acted intentionally, we have also concluded: The Bar has not established that Attorney Walton engaged in criminal conduct or serious criminal conduct. Moreover, we do not think that Walton engaged in conduct that seriously and adversely impairs his fitness. And, the Bar has not suggested that disbarment is an appropriate sanction in this case.

We therefore conclude that ABA Standard 5.11 does not apply in this case. ABA Standards 5.12 (suspension) and 5.13 (reprimand) refer to an accused lawyer's knowing his conduct involves dishonesty, fraud, deceit, or misrepresentation. In *The case of Flannery*, 334 Or. 224, 233 (2002) were emphasized: The principal difference between those two standards lies in the degree to which the conduct in question adversely reflects on the lawyer's fitness to practice law. Suspension is appropriate if the conduct seriously and adversely reflects on fitness. Otherwise, reprimand is appropriate.

We do not think that the accused's conduct reflects "seriously adversely" on his fitness to practice law. The accused was not charged with a crime. He did not benefit personally from his misconduct. The beneficiaries were the Legal Aid Society of Hawai'i and its indigent clients. And his misconduct did not cause any actual or potential harm. Those facts lead us to conclude that the accused's conduct does not "seriously" adversely reflect on his fitness to practice law, and ABA Standard 5.12 does not, by its terms, apply to the present facts. As a result, we determine preliminarily that the ABA Standard that most closely fits the conduct in this proceeding is Standard 5.13, which suggests that a public reprimand is an appropriate sanction.

Aggravating or Mitigating Circumstances

ABA Standards 9.22 and 9.32—respectively—list aggravating and mitigating factors that a court may consider to justify increasing or decreasing the court's preliminary sanction. Walton and the Hawai'i Disciplinary Counsel stipulated to the existence of one aggravating factor—Walton's substantial experience as a practicing attorney. ABA Standards 9.22(i). And there are two mitigating factors: (1) Walton's lack of a disciplinary record—ABA Standard 9.32(a), and (2) his willingness to accept responsibility for his improper use of Westlaw services—ABA Standard 9.32(e). The Bar agrees: This court may find those aggravating and mitigating factors, However, the Bar also argues: This court should find three additional aggravating factors: (1) Walton had a dishonest and selfish motive—ABA Standard 9.22(b); (2) Walton engaged in a pattern of misconduct—ABA Standard 9.22(c); and (3) Walton's indifference respecting making restitution, ABA Standard 9.22(j).

The Bar has not presented clear and convincing evidence that Walton used the OSP's Westlaw password … to achieve personal or financial gain. We find that the evidence in this proceeding does not support that aggravating factor. The Bar also asserts: Walton engaged in a pattern of misconduct. That is correct. Walton's misuse of OSP's Westlaw account continued for 14 months. However, the Bar has not pointed to any case in which this court has found a "pattern of misconduct," based on a single course of conduct, even a lengthy one. …

To summarize, we agree with the Hawai'i Disciplinary Board's findings of aggravating and mitigating factors. We conclude that the mitigating factors outweigh the aggravating factor. In addition, we have concluded: Walton's misconduct did not seriously or adversely reflect on his fitness to practice law; and the mitigating factors outweigh the aggravating factors. We are also persuaded that the conduct giving rise to this proceeding is unlikely to recur. Given those facts, and the fact that the Attorney Walton has an unblemished record for 35 years as a practicing lawyer, we are satisfied that a public reprimand will adequately protect the public.

The accused is publicly reprimanded.

NOTES AND QUESTIONS

1) Disbarment, Suspension or Reprimand for the Unauthorized Use of Computer Passwords. In *The Matter of Julia Ellis Brown*, the attorney admitted: On behalf of *union members*, she used another attorney's password and access her coworkers' email accounts without permission—reading, downloading, and disseminating information in the emails. Her law license was suspended for two (2) years. Did Attorney Brown commit a crime? Was she a thief? In *The Reciprocal Discipline of Everett Walton*, the attorney admitted: On behalf of *indigent clients*, he used a third party's password to access information in Westlaw's databases. Did Attorney Walton commit a crime? Was he a thief? His law license was not suspended. Instead, Walton only received a public reprimand. Can disparate punishments be harmonized?

2) The Unauthorized Use of Computer Passwords and Determining How Long to Suspend Attorneys' Bar Licenses. Once more, in *In the Matter of Julia Ellis Brown*, Attorney Brown read, downloaded and distributed third parties e-mails. And her law license was suspended for two (2) years. Was the length of Brown's suspension excessive, or unreasonable? Now, consider the lengths of the suspensions in the following cases: *In re Bennett*, 331 Or. 270 (2000) (the lawyer's license was suspended for *180 days*—after the attorney cashed and deposited checks from an opposing counsel in satisfaction of debt already paid, and after the attorney charged excessive fee and failed to refund a client's money); *In re Kimmell*, 332 Or. 480 (2001) (the lawyer's license was suspended for *six months* for shoplifting a jacket from retail store); *In re Summer*, 338 Or. 29 (2005) (a law license was suspended for *180 days* for attempting to recover proceed from separate insurers for his client's injuries); and *In re Unrein*, 323 Or. 285 (1996) (the lawyer's license was suspended for *120 days* after the attorney applied for and received unwarranted unemployment benefits on multiple occasions). Are the violations in *Bennett, Kimmell, Summer, and Unrein* more egregious than Attorney Julia Brown's using a password without permission to access, read and download third parties' personal e-mails?

3) "Patterns of Misconduct" and "Aggravating Factors"—The Search for Universal Standards: Again, in *The Reciprocal Discipline of Everett Walton*, Attorney Walton repeatedly and intentionally used a Westlaw password without permission. Still, the Oregon Supreme Court concluded: The Bar did not present *clear and convincing evidence* of Walton's using a third party's Westlaw password for Walton's "personal or financial gain." Additionally, according to the court, the Bar failed to establish: Walton engaged in criminal conduct or in conduct that seriously impaired his fitness to practice law. Clearly, Walton engaged in a "pattern of impermissible conduct." Was that an "aggravating factor"? What qualifies as an aggravating factor? *See In re McDonough*, 336 Or. 36, 44 (2003) (finding a pattern of misconduct where the lawyer repeatedly committed multiple criminal offenses); *In re Kluge*, 332 Or. 251, 263 (2001) (concluding that multiple misrepresentations on numerous occasions revealed a pattern of dishonesty and misconduct); *In re Haws*, 310 Or. 741, 753 (1990) (finding a pattern of misconduct where a lawyer failed to respond fully and truthfully to 12 separate state Bar inquiries regarding alleged violations); and *In re Luebke*, 301 Or. 321, 336, (1986) (finding a pattern of misconduct where the accused committed the same violations in two separate cases).

C. Disciplinary Actions Against Departing Attorneys and Partners for Impermissibly Accessing, Damaging and Vandalizing Law Firm's Computers and Network Servers

1. Actions against Attorneys for Deleting Privileged Computer Files without Authorization

Attorney Grievance Commission of Maryland v. Steven John Potter

844 A.2d 367
(Md. 2004)

Raker, Judge.

The Hearing Judge's Findings of Fact in the Disciplinary Proceeding

Steven J. Potter, *Esq.* is 39 years old. He graduated from law school in 1989 and was admitted to the Maryland Bar in 1990. After completing a judicial clerkship, he began to practice law as an employee with the *Law Office of Sheldon Braiterman*, P.A. In February 1992, he left his employment at *Braiterman*. From 1992–1997, Potter had his own practice. There is no evidence of any prior disciplinary complaints filed against the Potter during his 13 year tenure as a member of the Maryland Bar.

André R. Weitzman, *Esq.* has been a member of the Maryland Bar since 1979. Since 1992, Weitzman was a sole practitioner. From 1992 until July 1997, Weitzman and Potter had offices in the same building. During this time, Weitzman employed Potter as an independent contractor to work some of Weitzman's cases. Weitzman and Potter had fee-sharing agreements. From 1992 to July 1997, Weitzman and Potter did not have any disputes over those fee-sharing agreements.

From July 1997 until about July 26, 2001, Potter was an employee at the *Law Offices of André R. Weitzman* ("the law firm"). There is no writing—reflecting the terms of Potter's employment with the firm. Weitzman testified that the terms of Potter's employment called for a salary of $3,500 a month. In addition, Potter believed he was entitled to a percentage of the net proceeds, if any, from the law firm. Further, under the verbal terms of Potter's employment, Potter received a percentage of the fees generated. When Potter brought a client to the law firm, he received 50% of the fee generated by that client. After the fees were deposited into the law firm's bank account, Potter would receive his share of the fees, less withholding taxes.

While employed, Potter had an office. Potter kept files—those he was working on for the law firm—in his office. Weitzman testified that Potter was free to remove files from the office, if he needed to go to court or to take a file home. It was Weitzman's custom to retain client files while the representation was active and for at least five years thereafter. Potter brought two clients to the firm—Joseph Caldart and Lorrie Kazmar. ...The Caldart matter involved a worker's compensation matter and a third-party claim. Caldart signed a form agreement entitled "Power of Attorney and Contingent Fee Arrangement."...The clear and convincing evidence demonstrates: Potter provided legal services—on behalf of the law firm—for both Caldart and Kazmar.

On July 26, 2001, Potter advised Weitzman that he was resigning effective immediately. He decided to leave for several reasons: (1) Potter believed that Weitzman had not lived up to their agreement regarding Potter's share of the profits; and (2) Weitzman hired an inexperienced attorney—whose compensation mirrored Potter's compensation. Potter also thought that his salary was too low; and, he did not always agree with Weitzman's methods of operation.

* * *

Prior to his departure from the law firm, Potter accessed the law firm's computer and deleted files regarding the Caldart and Kazmar matters. The computer records included all documents prepared by the Potter and/or the firm's secretaries relating to these two matters. After Potter's departure, André Weitzman wrote a letter to Caldart. Weitzman threatened Caldart with a lawsuit, unless Potter paid a percentage of the fee earned in [the] case.

The Hearing Judge's Conclusions of Law

A Petition for Disciplinary Action was filed in the Court of Appeals—alleging that Potter violated Maryland Rules of Professional Conduct 8.4 (a), (b), (c) and (d). Rule 8.4 is entitled "Misconduct" and provides: It is professional misconduct for a lawyer to:

> (a) violate or attempt to violate the Rules of Professional Conduct, knowingly assist or induce another to do so, or do so through the acts of another;
>
> (b) commit a criminal act that reflects adversely on the lawyer's honesty, trustworthiness or fitness as a lawyer in other respects;
>
> (c) engage in conduct involving dishonesty, fraud, deceit or misrepresentation;
>
> (d) engage in conduct that is prejudicial to the administration of justice. …

Rule 8.4(b) of the Maryland Rules of Professional Conduct provides: It is professional conduct for a lawyer to commit a criminal act that reflects adversely on the lawyer's honesty, trustworthiness or fitness as a lawyer in other respects. The court finds that Petitioner has failed to demonstrate through clear and convincing evidence, that Potter committed "a criminal act that reflected adversely on his honesty, trustworthiness or fitness as a lawyer in other respects." The court acknowledges: It is not necessary for Potter to be charged or convicted of the criminal offense in order to find a violation of Rule 8.4(b) of the Maryland Rules of Professional Conduct. *Attorney Grievance Commission v. Garland*, 345 Md. 383, 394-95 (1997) (holding that there is no requirement that an attorney must be charged with or prosecuted for a crime to establish a violation of Rule 8.4(b)). Nevertheless, based on clear and convincing evidence, the court finds that Potter has not committed a criminal act that reflects adversely on his honesty, trustworthiness or fitness as a lawyer in other respects.

Petitioner attempts to show that Potter violated Section 7–104(a) of the Maryland Theft Statute, when Potter deprived Weitzman of the computer generated materials relating to the Caldart and Kazmar matters. Section 7–104(a) provides in relevant part:

> A person may not willfully or knowingly obtain or exert unauthorized control over property, if the person: 1) intends to deprive the owner of the property; 2) willfully or knowingly uses, conceals, or abandons the property in a manner that deprives the owner of the property; or 3) uses, conceals, or abandons the property knowing the use, concealment or abandonment probably will deprive the owner of the property.

The court finds: Under the facts and circumstances of this case, Potter did not have any intent to deprive Weitzman of client files and computer records. The client files were kept intact at all times; no part of any file has been lost or destroyed. The court further finds: While Potter's deletion of computer records may have been inappropriate and improper, Petitioner has failed to demonstrate by clear and convincing evidence, that the deletion of computer records under the facts and circumstances of this case constitutes a criminal act that reflected adversely on his honesty, trustworthiness or fitness as a lawyer in other respects.

Potter reasonably believed that the clients would follow him after leaving Weitzman's firm. At all times, Potter did what he believed was in the best interests of his clients. Indeed, had the clients instructed him to do so, Potter would have transferred the files back to Weitzman. Under the facts and circumstances of this case, the court finds: Potter did not commit a criminal act.

* * *

Maryland Court of Appeals' Jurisdiction Over Attorney Disciplinary Proceedings

This court has original jurisdiction over attorney disciplinary proceedings. *See Attorney Grievance Comm'n v. Harris,* 810 A.2d 457, 474 (Md. 2002). In the exercise of our obligation, we conduct an independent review of the record, accepting the hearing judge's findings of fact unless clearly erroneous. *See Attorney Grievance Comm'n v. Garfield,* 797 A.2d 757, 763-64 (Md. 2002). The factual findings of the hearing judge will not be disturbed if they are based on clear and convincing evidence. *See* Md. Rule 16–757(b) (providing that Bar Counsel has burden of establishing averments of the petition by clear and convincing evidence); *Attorney Grievance Comm'n v. Monfried,* 794 A.2d 92, 100 (Md. 2002). We consider the hearing judge's proposed conclusions of law *de novo.* *See Attorney Grievance Comm'n v. McLaughlin,* 493, 813 A.2d 1145, 1160 (Md. 2002).

Petitioner—Maryland Bar Counsel—filed an exception to Judge Berger's conclusion: Attorney Potter's conduct did not violate Maryland Rules of Professional Conduct 8.4(b), (c), and (d). The hearing judge erred *as a matter of law* and we sustain the Bar Counsel's exceptions. Potter's conduct was criminal conduct—which reflected adversely on his honesty, trustworthiness, and fitness as a lawyer. Potter's conduct was deceitful and prejudicial to the administration of justice.

Potter engaged in criminal conduct by deleting clients' files from the computer when he was not authorized to do so. We find by clear and convincing evidence that Potter's deleting the computer records violated Maryland Code § 7–302 of the Criminal Law Article. It provides: A person may not intentionally and willfully exceed that person's authorized access to a computer—with the intent to "alter, damage, or destroy all or any part of data or a computer program stored, maintained, or produced by a computer."

By exceeding his authorized use of the law firm's computer system, Attorney Potter violated § 7–302(c)(1). And he intended to alter and destroy part of the data stored on computer—which violates § 7–302(c)(2)(ii). Potter's deleting computer records was criminal conduct. And it reflects adversely upon his honesty and trustworthiness. Potter was authorized to use the law firm's computers to generate and store clients' documents. He did not have permission, however, to delete computer records without the consent of his employer.

Attorney Potter's fearing that Weitzman would interfere with Potter's continued representation of Caldart and Kazmar—after Potter left the law firm—did not authorize Potter to destroy the firm's computer records relating to those clients. Potter deleted the computer records at 1:00 a.m. or 2:00 a.m. on July 11, 2001—two weeks before Potter planned to quit his employment with the *Law Offices of Andre' Weitzman*. This surreptitious conduct—in the middle of the night—is strong evidence that Potter knew his conduct was unauthorized.

In addition to deleting computer records, Potter removed all of the "Caldart and Kazmar" files from the law firm. Judge Berger—the hearing judge—concluded: Potter did not violate Rule 8.4, because Potter was acting in the clients' interests. In finding no violation of Rule 8.4, the hearing judge focused on Potter's motive, rather than on his intent … The hearing judge erred, by concluding that the removal of the files was not a violation of Rules 8.4(c) and (d). Regardless of Potter's motive or his purported desire to protect the interests of the clients, Potter's conduct was dishonest and deceitful. As we have indicated, Potter had no authority to delete the records, and he knew that he had no such authority.

* * *

Maryland Court of Appeals' Sanctions

We now turn to the appropriate sanction to be imposed. Maryland's Bar Counsel recommends that Potter be suspended indefinitely from the practice of law—with the right to apply for reinstatement in one year.

The purpose of sanctioning an attorney is to protect the public rather than to punish the errant attorney. *See Attorney Grievance Comm'n v. Powell,* 800 A.2d 782, 789 (Md.2002). Attorney disciplinary proceedings also are conducted to deter other attorneys from violating the Rules of Professional Conduct. 800 A.2d at 789. The severity of a sanction depends on the particular facts and circumstances of each case—including consideration of any mitigating factors or aggravating factors. *See Attorney Grievance Comm'n v. Angst*, 800 A.2d 747, 755 (Md.2002). On occasion, when considering the appropriate sanction impose, we have referred to the ABA Standards for Imposing Lawyer Sanctions. *Attorney Grievance Comm'n v. Braskey*, 836 A.2d 605, 622 (Md. 2003). *See also* ABA Standards for Imposing Lawyer Sanctions, reprinted in ABA Compendium of Professional Responsibility Rules and

Standards, 338–39, 344 (1999). The Standards require answers to several questions:

(1) What ethical duty did the lawyer violate?

(2) What was the lawyer's mental state?

(3) What was the extent of the actual or potential injury caused by the lawyer's misconduct?

(4) Are there any aggravating or mitigating circumstances?

By deleting computer records, Potter committed criminal acts—intentionally and dishonestly. Although Potter knew that his actions were improper and illegal, he acted in an effort to facilitate his representation of the two clients and the hearing judge found that he had the clients' best interests in mind. ... There is no evidence in the record that the clients actually were harmed by Potter's conduct. ... [However,] Potter's unauthorized appropriation of the files and deletion of the computer records prevented Weitzman from adhering to this practice ... Weitzman potentially was harmed by not possessing any files or computer records relating to these two client matters.

* * *

Next, we consider several mitigating factors. Potter has no prior disciplinary record and has been a member of the Maryland Bar in good standing for thirteen years. Potter's actions appear to be an isolated incident, or at least do not constitute a pattern or course of conduct. Before Potter became employed with Weitzman's firm in 1997, Weitzman employed Potter for five years as an independent contractor. There are no allegations that Potter acted improperly from 1992 until 2001, when Potter engaged in the conduct that is the subject of this grievance proceeding. Finally, we accept the hearing judge's determination that Potter's underlying motive was "to represent competently the clients, not to be dishonest or deceitful."

A primary purpose of sanctions is to protect the public. We have stated: "The public is protected when sanctions are imposed that are commensurate with the nature and gravity of the violations and the intent with which they were committed." *Attorney Grievance Comm'n v. Awuah,* 697 A.2d 446, 454 (Md.1997). Thus, the appropriate sanction depends upon the facts and circumstances of each particular case, including consideration of aggravating and any mitigating factors. *See Attorney Grievance Comm'n v. Atkinson*, 745 A.2d 1086, 1092 (Md.2000).

Attorney Potter has violated Rules 8.4(b), (c), and (d). Notwithstanding the attorney's motive, lawyers in this State may not delete computer records or take client files from the law firm without authorization. After consideration of all the circumstances presented herein, we conclude: Attorney Potter's misconduct was sufficiently serious to warrant a suspension from the practice of law for a period of ninety (90) days. The suspension will commence thirty (30) days from the date of entry of this Opinion and Order. It is so ordered.

NOTES AND QUESTIONS

1) **Sanctioning Departing Attorneys Who "Vandalize" Law Firms' Computers and Network Servers.** Assume that an associate attorney in a large law firm decides to open a solo practice. But, before leaving the firm, he decides to "vandalize" the law firm's network computer or the server. What would be a proper sanction—disbarment, a suspension and/or a reprimand? For an answer, consider the plight of the former associate attorney in *The Case of Scott R. Porter*, 467 N.W.2d 825, 826 (Minn. 1991). After leaving the law firm, Porter returned and secured a key to the law offices from a staff member. In the course of events, Porter "vandalized four of the law firm's computers by erasing some files and damaging other files." Additionally, Porter stole the law firm's software, which was worth approximately $900. To repair the damaged computer files, the law firm "had to expend approximately 56 hours of staff time" and hired an outside computer programmer to reconstruct the law firm's computer files. What was Porter's penalty? The Director of Lawyers Professional Responsibility Board accepted Porter's recommended sanction—a public reprimand.

2) **Whether Attorneys in New York Are Automatically Disbarred for Violating Federal Computer Fraud Statutes.** Under New York's Judiciary Law § 90(4)(a) and (e), an attorney will be disbarred automatically if the attorney commits a felony under New York's or a federal criminal statute. *See also, In the Matter of Margiotta*, 60 N.Y.2d 147, 150 (1983). But consider the facts in *The Matter of Edwin E. Burks*, 861 N.Y.S.2d 208, 209 (A.D. 2008). The

"offending" attorney was a former prosecutor for the City of New Orleans. He prosecuted traffic violations. An undercover FBI agent—posing as a taxi driver—offered to give $1,000 if the prosecutor dismissed the bogus driver's traffic citations. After satisfying the oral contract, the attorney was convicted of a felony under a federal computer fraud statute, 18 USC § 1030(a)(4). Was he disbarred immediately? No. He was *suspended* from the practice of law—until he could *explain* "why a final order of suspension, censure or removal from office should not be made."

3) Attorneys' Sanctions for Violating Federal Computer Fraud Statutes in Louisiana. *In The Matter of Glenda Ann Spears*, 964 So.2d 293, 297 (La. 2007), several probationers wanted a release from probation and aftercare supervision. The probationers reported the same to their probation officer, who contacted Attorney Spears. For twelve months, the attorney altered the probationers' computer records, and encouraged a Louisiana court to release her "clients" from probation. Each probationer paid a $2,500 fee—which was split between the attorney and probation officer. The U.S. District Court for the Eastern District of Louisiana accepted the attorney's guilty plea. She committed two felonies: (1) computer fraud under 18 U.S.C. § 1030(a)(4), and (2) a conspiracy to commit computer fraud under 18 U.S.C. § 371. Louisiana's Office of Disciplinary Counsel determined that the attorney violated several professional rules of conduct—Rule 8.4(b), Rule 8.4(c), and Rule 8.4(d). The attorney's license to practice law in Louisiana was revoked. And she was permanently barred from being readmitted to practice law in Louisiana.

---

2. Actions Against Solo Attorneys for Deceptively Tampering with Law Firms' Computerized Files for Personal Financial Gains and Without Authorization

Attorney Grievance Commission of Maryland v. Keiner

27 A.3d 153
(Md. 2011)

Barbera, J.

On July 28, 2010, the Attorney Grievance Commission—acting

through Bar Counsel—filed a Petition for Disciplinary Action or Remedial Action (Petition) against Attorney Gregory Raymond Keiner. See Md. Rule 16–751. Bar Counsel charged Keiner with violating Maryland Lawyers' Rules of Professional Conduct (MRPC)—Rule 8.4 (Misconduct). In light of Maryland Rules 16–773 and 16–752(a), we referred the Petition to the Honorable Timothy J. McCrone of the Circuit Court for Howard County, to conduct an evidentiary hearing and make findings of fact and conclusions of law in accordance with Maryland Rule 16–757.

* * *

Judge Timothy J. McCrone's Findings of Fact and Analysis

Gregory Keiner was admitted to the Maryland Bar on December 18, 2002, and maintained his law practice in Baltimore, Maryland. From February 2003 until March 2009, Keiner was an associate attorney at the *Law Offices of Evan K. Thalenberg* ("law firm"). He was primarily a lead-paint litigator. As of 2008, Keiner's compensation at the firm was $268,700.

In 2008, Keiner decided to leave the law firm and become a solo practitioner. To facilitate his starting a solo practice, Keiner began altering and deleting clients' computer files and documents the law firm. He created the appearance that the client files had been closed, when in fact the files were still active. Keiner also drafted clients' termination letters—which were not sent to clients. Instead, Keiner put the letters in the firm's files—giving the false impression to members of the firm that the files had been closed.

* * *

Keiner's deception was discovered when a client contacted the firm and produced a letter from Keiner. The letter illustrated Keiner's rather than the law firm's letterhead. When confronted with the solicitation letter, Keiner wrote a letter to Thalenberg and admitted that he had altered computer records at the firm. John Kazmierczak—another attorney with the firm—was assigned the task of investigating files and cases that Keiner may have altered while working at the firm. ... Kazmierczak reviewed an electronic back-up system and discovered misleading entries in the firm's computer files. ... Keiner testified: He misrepresented his actions to avoid filing claims while working at the firm. He wanted to file the claims when he opened his solo practice. ...This court finds that Keiner revealed his misconduct to the firm only after the firm had become aware of Keiner's misconduct.

* * *

Keiner was terminated after his misconduct was discovered. Shortly thereafter, Keiner was voluntarily admitted to Howard County General Hospital and was found to be suffering from a depressive disorder and suicidal ideations. ... While the court finds that alcohol abuse and depression have no doubt adversely impacted Keiner, this court is not convinced that such difficulties resulted in Keiner's being unable to conform his conduct in accordance with the law and Maryland Lawyers' Rules of Professional Conduct.

Keiner was a very capable lawyer and was able to manage an extremely busy practice with considerable efficiency. Keiner was able to generate substantial income for the firm because of his skill and obvious attention to detail. The cause of Keiner's actions was a desire to keep for himself more of the income he had been generating for the firm. Of course, an ambition to improve one's financial circumstances is not a fault or defect. The manner in which such goals are pursued is key.

Keiner is clearly remorseful and has generally been very cooperative with Bar Counsel. The success Keiner has enjoyed in representing clients in the past leads this court to conclude that he must be a skilled advocate. To date, no client appears to have suffered pecuniary loss because of Keiner's misbehavior. And while Keiner's misbehavior came to light because of circumstances he had not anticipated, once discovered, Keiner was forthcoming. Several former clients, employers and opposing counsel have written letters of support on behalf of Keiner. This court further notes: The instant case represents the only allegation of misconduct ever reported against Keiner.

Judge Timothy J. McCrone's Conclusions of Law

Keiner's acts of altering and deleting documents and clients' computer files are criminal acts. They violate Maryland Criminal Law Code Ann. § 7-302. Those acts also violate Maryland Lawyers' Rules of Professional Conduct—Rules 8.4(a), (b), (c) and (d). Keiner's criminal conduct reflects adversely on Keiner's honesty, trustworthiness and fitness as a lawyer. Keiner's conduct was deceitful and prejudicial to the administration of justice—as Keiner carried out his deception after hours when others would not observe his actions. Keiner knew that his actions were inappropriate and unauthorized. Rules 1.4(a) and (b) require that an attorney communicate with his client regarding representation, including material changes in representation. Because Keiner failed to inform the firm's clients of his intentions, they were precluded from consenting to a potentially significant change in representation. Therefore, Keiner acted in a deceptive manner and exceeded the scope of his authority when he altered or deleted documents without his client's permission.

Rule 8.4 describes specific acts that constitute professional misconduct, including purposefully violating the MRPC, committing a criminal act that reflects negatively on a lawyer's honesty, and engaging in fraud, misrepresentation or conduct that is prejudicial to the administration of justice. In this case, Keiner knowingly violated the MRPC when he altered and deleted computer files—intending to solicit clients for his own law practice while he was still employed at *The Law Offices of Evan K. Thalenberg*. ... There is clear and convincing evidence that Keiner's misconduct violated Rules 8.4(a), (b), (c) and (d). In summary, the court finds that Bar Counsel has sustained each alleged violation of the Maryland Lawyers' Rules of Professional Conduct and Md. Code Ann., Crim. Law § 7–302.

* * *

Maryland Court of Appeals' Sanctions

At the hearing on the Petition, Bar Counsel "has the burden of proving the averments of the petition by clear and convincing evidence." Md. Rule 16–757(b). Keiner has the burden of establishing matters of mitigation or extenuation, if any, by a preponderance of the evidence. *Id.* Bar Counsel filed no exceptions to Judge McCrone's findings of fact or conclusions of law. Keiner takes no exception to Judge McCrone's conclusion that Keiner's conduct violated Rules 1.4 and 8.4. Indeed, Keiner throughout the disciplinary proceeding has conceded those violations.

Still, Keiner has noted exceptions to certain of the hearing judge's factual findings. He assails:

(1) The trial court's misidentification of Christian Tellefsen, M.D. and omission of Mr. Keiner's treating health care providers;

(2) The trial court's failure to acknowledge the circumstances surrounding Mr. Keiner's alcohol abuse and Mr. Keiner's continuing substance abuse treatment with James P. Quinn;

(3) The trial court's failure to consider the recommendation of the Peer Review Committee;

(4) The trial court's errors regarding the computer altered files;

(5) The trial court's failure to identify mitigating factors on behalf of Mr. Keiner; and

(6) The trial court's "error in making its ultimate conclusion"—*i.e.*, "that Mr. Keiner's behavior was not the result of depression and alcohol abuse.

* * *

[Generally, we overrule Keiner's exceptions to Judge McCrone's findings]. ... Keiner concedes: His conduct violates Rules 1.4(a) and (b), and Rules 8.4(a), (b), (c), and (d). And those violations are supported by clear and convincing evidence. Accordingly, our remaining task is to determine the appropriate sanction. ... Bar Counsel recommends disbarment as the appropriate sanction for Keiner's misconduct. Keiner urges this court to impose a period of suspension—arguing that he has established sufficient mitigation to obviate the need for disbarment. Keiner's intentional dishonesty was motivated exclusively by his desire for personal gain. And Keiner's "totality of the mitigation" argument does not establish "compelling extenuating circumstances" to prevent his disbarment. Accordingly, we order disbarment. It is so ordered.

Excerpt from the American Bar Association's Model Rules of Professional Conduct

Rule 1.15—Safekeeping Property

(a) A lawyer shall hold property of clients or third persons that is in a lawyer's possession in connection with a representation separate from the lawyer's own property. Funds shall be kept in a separate account maintained in the state where the lawyer's office is situated, or elsewhere with the consent of the client or third person. Other property shall be identified as such and appropriately safeguarded. Complete records of such account funds and other property shall be kept by the lawyer and shall be preserved for a period of [five years] after termination of the representation.

(b) A lawyer may deposit the lawyer's own funds in a client trust account for *the sole purpose* of paying bank service charges on that account, but only in an amount necessary for that purpose.

(c) A lawyer shall deposit into a client's trust account legal fees and expenses that have been paid in advance, to be withdrawn by the lawyer only as fees are earned or expenses incurred.

(d) Upon receiving funds or other property in which a client or third person has an interest, a lawyer shall promptly notify the client or third person.

(e) When in the course of representation, a lawyer is in possession of property in which two or more persons (one of whom may be the lawyer) claim interests, the property shall be kept separate by the lawyer until the dispute is resolved. The lawyer shall promptly distribute all portions of the property as to which the interests are not in dispute.

D. Disciplinary Actions Against Attorneys for Using Internet Chat Rooms, Online Video Conferencing, Social Media, Websites, and E-mails to Access or Share Pornographic Communications, Materials, and Images

1. Actions Against Attorneys for Violating Federal Child Pornography Statutes

Doe v. Boland

630 F.3d 491
(6th Cir. 2011)

Sutton, Circuit Judge.

Licensed to practice law in Ohio, Dean Boland specializes in technology-related legal issues. In February 2004, Boland downloaded innocent-looking images of the minor plaintiffs—Jane Doe and Jane Roe. He downloaded the images from a stock photo website, where photographers may upload images and viewers may download them for a fee. Boland digitally manipulated the pictures. In the end, the children looked like they were engaging in sexually explicit acts. For example, Attorney Boland took a picture of 5-year-old Jane Roe who was eating a doughnut and replaced the doughnut with a male penis. And he placed a picture of 6-year-old Jane Doe's face on the image of a nude woman, who was performing sexual acts with two adult males.

In March and April 2004, Boland used those images when he testified as an expert witness in two underlying state court criminal proceedings involving child pornography. In the underlying April 2004 proceeding, the defendant moved to dismiss the criminal charges against him, claiming that 18 U.S.C. § 2252(a)(4)(B) was overly broad and violated the First Amendment. The underlying defendant asserted: He could not determine whether a downloaded picture was "an actual or virtual image of a child," given the sophistication of modern computer-imaging technology. And in the underlying trial, the district judge allowed the defendant to present expert testimony regarding his First-Amendment defense at an evidentiary hearing.

During Boland's testimony, he displayed a series of "before-and-after" images that he had digitally altered. The aim was to show: It would be "impossible for a person—who did not participate in the creation of the image—to know whether or not the child in the altered photo was actually a minor. Boland showed an image of a nude adult woman and then showed how he could edit the image to make it look like a nude child. He also showed innocent images of Jane Doe and Jane Roe, followed by sexually explicit "morphed" versions of them.

Toward the end of the hearing, the prosecutors raised the possibility that Attorney Boland may have violated federal law by creating and possessing some of those "child pornography" images. The district judge disagreed, responding that Boland's photos were "prepared expressly at court order." But the judge admonished Boland to purge the images from the hard drive on his computer. Boland, however, did not remove the images from his hard drive. And later, Borland used the doctored images of the minors in two additional state-court proceedings while acting as an expert witness or counsel.

In May 2004, the FBI's Cleveland office started an investigation of Boland. FBI agents searched Boland's home and seized several electronic files. In April 2007, Boland entered into a pre-trial diversion agreement with the U.S. Attorney's Office for the Northern District of Ohio. Boland admitted: He violated 18 U.S.C. § 2252A(a)(5)(B) which prohibits one's knowingly possessing child pornography—a "visual depiction [that] has been created, adapted, or modified to appear that an identifiable minor is engaging in sexually explicit conduct." 18 U.S.C. § 2256(8)(C). In return for the government's agreement to defer prosecution for 18 months, Boland agreed to various conditions. One required him to make a public apology in the *Cleveland Bar Journal*, where he stated: "I do recognize that such images violate federal law."

In September 2007, the children and their guardians filed the current lawsuit against Boland under 18 U.S.C. § 2252A(f) and § 2255. Both federal provisions provide civil remedies for "any person aggrieved" and for minor victims who have suffered "personal injury" from a violation of 18 U.S.C. § 2252A(a). The plaintiffs also filed various state law claims.

The district court awarded summary judgment to Boland on the federal claims and opted not to resolve the state law claims. Finding a "difficult and troubling case," the court held: "It would not be fair" to impose "crushing damages" on Attorney Boland for his testimony in Oklahoma federal court. The court concluded that allowing the federal statute to permit liability could implicate a criminal defendant's Sixth Amendment right to counsel. The district court also observed: Boland "was responding to a federal court directive" when he created and possessed the images. Finally, the federal district court judge concluded: Liability under the federal statute would implicate "serious comity issues," because Ohio law provides immunity from state child pornography prosecutions for expert witnesses. The plaintiffs appealed.

II.

The question—whether or not federal child pornography laws exempt those who violate the law in the course of providing expert testimony—implicates three statutory provisions. The first provision establishes the standard of care. It reads: Any person who ... knowingly possesses, or knowingly accesses with intent to view, any ... computer disk, or any other material that contains an image of child pornography ... using materials that have been mailed, or shipped or transported in or affecting interstate or foreign commerce by any means, including by computer ... shall be punished as provided in subsection (b). 18 U.S.C. § 2252A(a)(5)(B).

Boland has no basis for denying that he (1) knowingly possessed, (2) a computer disk containing child pornography, (3) which was produced using materials that affected interstate commerce. In his deferred prosecution agreement, he stipulated: He "downloaded at least four ... images, from the Internet, depicting four ... real, identifiable minors in innocent poses," and then "digitally manipulated such images ... to appear that each of the ... minors was engaged in sexually explicit conduct." In his apology, he added: "I do recognize that such images violate federal law."

That leaves the civil remedy provisions. One clause—18 U.S.C. § 2252A(f)(1)—permits any aggrieved person to "commence a civil action for the relief" if prohibited conduct under 18 U.S.C. § 2252A(a) caused an injury. And the other provision—18 U.S.C. § 2255(a)—reads in part:

> Any person—while a minor—was a victim of a violation of section 2252A ... and who suffers personal injury as a result of such violation, regardless of whether the injury occurred while such person was a minor, may sue in any appropriate United States District Court and shall recover the actual damages such person sustains and the cost of

> the suit, including a reasonable attorney's fee. Any person as described in the preceding sentence shall be deemed to have sustained damages of no less than $150,000 in value.

* * *

A separate statute shows the extent to which Congress means business when it comes to enforcing the child pornography laws. The Adam Walsh Child Protection and Safety Act of 2006 states: In any criminal proceeding, child pornography "shall remain in the care, custody, and control of either the Government or the court." § 504—codified at 18 U.S.C. § 3509(m). Even though Criminal Rule 16(a)(1)(E) usually allows defendants to copy material documents in the government's possession, the Act requires federal courts to deny these requests when the materials contain child pornography. However, a defendant must have had "ample opportunity" to inspect, view, and examine the documents at "a Government facility." 18 U.S.C. § 3509(m)(2)(B). If Congress did not want defense counsel to view or to possess ... *existing* child pornography without governmental oversight, it is hardly surprising: Congress opted not to permit expert witnesses to create and possess *new* child pornography.

Without an exemption for this kind of expert testimony, Boland argues: A defendant's right to put on an effective defense under the Sixth Amendment would be hindered—requiring a narrowing of the civil-remedy provisions under the constitutional-avoidance doctrine. Neither premise of the doctrine applies. "[T]he canon of constitutional avoidance has no application in the absence of statutory ambiguity." *United States v. Oakland Cannabis Buyers' Co-op.*, 532 U.S. 483, 494 (2001). And no constitutional principle ... allows a criminal defendant to defend *one* criminal charge by urging his lawyer or witness to commit *another*.

* * *

Even when federal law allows participants in the criminal justice system to possess contraband, it does not allow the creation and possession of *new* contraband. *Cf.* 21 U.S.C. § 885 (immunizing federal, state and local officials from civil or criminal liability when they are "lawfully engaged in the enforcement" of federal drug laws). Individuals cannot defend criminal charges by having their lawyers or witnesses initiate *new* offenses. *Cf.* ABA Model Code Canon 7, DR 7–102 ("In his representation of a client, a lawyer shall not ... knowingly engage in ... illegal conduct.").

Nor do reasonable limits on defense counsel's access to the child pornography at issue in a criminal case, whether old or new, raise constitutional concerns. In *United States v. Paull*, the defendant argued that the absence of an exception in § 2252A for his counsel to possess child pornography violated his right to a fair trial. 551 F.3d 516, 524 (6th Cir.2009). Noting that the defendant had made "no allegations that the government used the law to disrupt his defense," we disagreed. *Id.* at 525. The defendant "could have worked with the district court and the government to ensure that he could put on the defense he wanted. But he chose not to." *Id.*; *see also United States v. McNealy,* 625 F.3d 858, 868 (5th Cir.2010) (restrictions on a defense expert's ability to possess child pornography do not violate the fair trial rights of defendant); *United States v. Shrake,* 515 F.3d 743, 745–46 (7th Cir.2008) (the Walsh Act does not violate a defendant's Fifth and Sixth Amendment rights).

Boland separately argues: The civil-remedy provisions do not apply because the Oklahoma district court—in the underlying case—allowed him to create and possess the images. But, that is not what happened. The judge in the underlying case did not *authorize* Boland to violate the pornography laws. And Boland did not seek permission to do so. Boland offered and obtained permission to present expert testimony and images. The purpose was to illustrate the difficulty of establishing that the underlying defendant knew that he possessed child pornography. ...

None of this authorized or required the creation or possession of *new* child pornography. Boland could have illustrated the difficulty of discerning real from virtual images by combining two innocent pictures into another innocent picture. Or, if Boland wished to use pornography to make the point, he could have morphed an image of an *adult* into that of a minor engaging in sexual activity. Boland indeed did the latter as part of his preparations. And had he stopped there, we would not be here. These images are not prohibited by federal law. 18 U.S.C. § 2252A(c). And they are protected by the First Amendment to the extent they are not obscene. *Ashcroft v. Free Speech Coalition,* 535 U.S. 234, 250-51 (2002).

Boland did something else. He morphed images of *minors* into pornography—images that "implicate the interests of real children." *Id.* at 242. The law expressly covers such images. 18 U.S.C. § 2256(8)(C). And, the reality that Boland himself did not "use" real children to produce the images makes no difference. § 2252A(c). ... Once Boland modified the images of the minors, he crossed the line between possessing lawful images and violating the statute.

* * *

Nor is this a case in which state law authorized Boland's conduct while federal law punished it. Ohio law provides immunity from state child pornography statutes if the images are used for "bona fide judicial purposes." *See* Ohio Rev.Code. Ann. § 2907.321(B)(1), § 2907.322(B)(1), and § 2907.322(B)(3). But this immunity does not help Boland. It applies, if there was a "bona fide" need to create and possess these images. And Boland has established such need, given other means to illustrate the difficulty of discerning real from virtual images. And it cannot be invoked in the Ohio courts in this setting. In *State v. Brady,* 894 N.E.2d 671, 677 (Ohio 2008), the defendant argued: The absence of an exemption for possessing pornographic images—under federal child pornography laws—precluded him from receiving a fair trial in state court for allegedly violating state child pornography law. Thus, Brady asked the court to dismiss his case. The Ohio Supreme Court disagreed, holding that it was "axiomatic that an expert's conduct must conform to the law." *Id.* at 679.

* * *

In view of these conclusions, we need not reach the other defenses that Boland has raised. … Boland, for example, argues: The children did not suffer "personal injury," as required under § 2255—because the parties have stipulated that each child does not know about the images. The fact that Congress has set such a sizeable damages threshold ($150,000) may suggest: The personal injury requirement is a serious one. He also argues: None of the plaintiffs can show they are "aggrieved" under § 2252A(f). And it is possible that constitutional defenses remain. We entrust the initial resolution of these issues to the capable hands of the district court judge.

For these reasons, we reverse the district court's judgment and remand the case for further proceedings.

2. Actions Against Attorneys for Using Online Chat Rooms to Solicit Sexual Favors from Minors and Share Pornographic Images, Messages, and Websites

Attorney Grievance Commission of Maryland v. Robert John Greenleaf

91 A.3d 1066
(Md. 2014)

Watts, J.

On November 8, 1979, this court admitted Robert John Greenleaf to the Bar of Maryland. Between 1987 and 2004, Greenleaf served as (1) an Assistant State's Attorney for Dorchester County, (2) an Assistant State's Attorney for Caroline County, (3) an interim State's Attorney for Caroline County, and (4) a Senior Assistant State's Attorney for Dorchester County. On January 6, 2004, Greenleaf became the Chief Deputy Clerk of the Court of Special Appeals. Greenleaf's office was located at the Robert C. Murphy Courts of Appeal Building.

On March 8, 2010, Detective Sergeant Louis Gary Yamin ("Yamin") of the Baltimore Police Department was working undercover for the Cyber and Electronic Crimes Unit. Yamin had a Yahoo Messenger account. The username was "ravens_ girl2003," which was connected to a Yahoo profile for a female named "Beth." On March 8, 2010, Yamin or "Beth" entered a Yahoo Messenger chat room entitled—"Maryland Romance." In the chat room, a person with the username "delmarvan19901" initiated a private chat with "Beth," who almost immediately sent the message: "14/f/balto. Md." The message identified the sender as a fourteen-year-old female in the Baltimore area. "delmarvan19901" began discussing sexual topics. "Beth" sent "delmarvan19901" two photographs that depicted a young teenage girl. "delmarvan19901" sent a photograph of himself.

In addition to sending the two photographs, "Beth" e-mailed "delmarvan19901"—who sent a reply e-mail. Yamin learned: Greenleaf was using the IP address from which "delmarvan19901" had sent the reply e-mail. The IP address belonged to the Maryland Judiciary. Yamin compared the photograph from "delmarvan 19901" with a photograph of Greenleaf from the Motor Vehicle Administration's database. Thus, it was established: While working as the Chief Deputy Clerk for the Court of Special Appeals,

Greenleaf used a state-owned computer in the Robert C. Murphy Courts of Appeal Building to communicate with "Beth."

Greenleaf believed that "Beth" was a fourteen-year-old or a fifteen-year-old girl. "Beth" repeatedly referred to her age and stated that she was a high school student. The hearing judge expressly rejected Greenleaf's allegation: He thought that "Beth" was an adult, who was "role-playing" and posing as a fourteen-year-old or a fifteen-year-old girl. On approximately one hundred fifty separate dates, Greenleaf and "Beth" e-mailed and/or chatted with each other. On nearly half of those dates, Greenleaf used his computer at the Robert C. Murphy Courts of Appeal Building to communicate with "Beth."

Greenleaf's and "Beth's" conversations were "consistently sexually explicit." For example, Greenleaf asked "Beth" to describe her pubic hair, sexual history, bra size, and whether she was taking birth control. Greenleaf often discussed arranging a meeting with "Beth" and described the sexual acts in which he wanted to engage with "Beth." Greenleaf "groomed" "Beth" for sexual activity by telling "Beth" that she seemed more mature than a fourteen-year-old or fifteen-year-old girl.

In December 2010, on four separate occasions, Greenleaf sent "Beth" links to pornographic videos. Greenleaf last communicated with "Beth" on January 25, 2011. Finally, in January 2011, Greenleaf was arrested and placed on administrative leave. On April 1, 2011, Greenleaf was permitted to retire from his position as the Chief Deputy Clerk of the Court of Special Appeals. On May 31, 2012, Greenleaf tendered a plea to a charge of attempting to violate Md. Code Ann., Crim. Law § 11–203 (Sale or Display of Obscene Item to Minor). Greenleaf received probation before judgment.

Greenleaf's actions came to the attention of the Attorney Grievance Commission. And on March 14, 2013, Bar Counsel filed a "Petition for Disciplinary or Remedial Action" against Greenleaf in this court, charging him with violating Maryland Lawyers' Rule of Professional Conduct (MLRPC), Rule 8.4. On March 18, 2013, this court assigned Attorney Greenleaf's discipline proceeding to the Honorable Paul M. Bowman of the Circuit Court for Kent County—the hearing judge. On July 25, 2013, the hearing judge conducted a hearing. On September 19, 2013, the hearing judge filed an opinion—including findings of fact and conclusions of law. The hearing judge concluded: Attorney Greenleaf violated Rules 8.4(a), (b), (c), and (d).

Standard Of Review

In an attorney discipline proceeding, this court reviews for clear error the hearing judge's findings of fact, and reviews without deference the hearing judge's conclusions of law. *See* Md. R. 16–759(b)(2)(B) ("The court shall give due regard to the opportunity of the hearing judge to assess the credibility of witnesses."); *Attorney Grievance Comm'n v. Reno,* 83 A.3d 781, 783 (Md. 2014) ("[T]his court reviews for clear error a hearing judge's findings of fact.]); Md. R. 16–759(b)(1) ("The Court of Appeals shall review *de novo* the [hearing] judge's conclusions of law."). This court determines whether clear and convincing evidence establishes that a lawyer violated the MLRPC. *See* Md. R. 16–757(b) ("The [Commission] has the burden of proving the averments of the petition by clear and convincing evidence.").

Discussion

A. Findings of Fact

The Commission does not except to any of the hearing judge's findings of fact. Greenleaf challenges the hearing judge's finding: Attorney Greenleaf believed that "Beth" was a fourteen-year-old or a fifteen-year-old girl. We overrule Greenleaf's exception, as the hearing judge did not clearly err, or err at all, in finding that Greenleaf believed that "Beth" was a fourteen-year-old or a fifteen-year-old girl. The record unequivocally demonstrates that "Beth": (1) identified herself as a fourteen-year-old girl; (2) repeatedly referred to her age; (3) stated that she was a high school student; and (4) sent two photographs that depicted a young teenage girl. Certainly, Greenleaf told "Beth": He thought she was a woman in her thirties. But, the hearing judge credited Yamin's opinion: Greenleaf made the statement as part of his grooming "Beth" for sexual activity, not because Greenleaf actually believed that "Beth" was a woman in her thirties.

The record is replete with evidence sufficient to establish that "Beth" identified herself as a fourteen-year-old girl; and, thus, there was sufficient evidence for the hearing judge to have independently rejected Greenleaf's claim to have believed Beth a "woman." Moreover, although a person must state that he or she is an adult to enter a Yahoo Messenger chat room, common sense dictates: A minor could enter a Yahoo Messenger chat room by falsely stating that he or she is an adult. We find no basis to disturb the hearing judge's express rejection of Greenleaf's allegation: He believed that "Beth" was an adult who was "role-playing" by posing as a fourteen-year-old or a fifteen-year-old girl.

In addition to excepting to certain findings of fact and attempting to establish mitigating circumstances, Greenleaf alleges additional facts: (1) he performed well as the Chief Deputy Clerk of the Court of Special Appeals; (2) at the time of his misconduct, he had just returned from sick leave, and was "troubled" at work because he had been transferred to a secluded office that was away from other employees; (3) he completed "mental health counseling" as a condition of probation; (4) he "suffered ignominy" because of his misconduct; and (5) he "has shown remorse" for his misconduct. The hearing judge did not find: (1) Greenleaf performed well as the Chief Deputy Clerk of the Court of Special Appeals; (2) Greenleaf suffered from any personal or emotional problems; (3) Greenleaf tried rehabilitation; (4) Greenleaf endured embarrassment; or (5) Greenleaf showed any remorse.

In *Attorney Grievance Comm'n v. Davy,* 80 A.3d 322, 333–34 (Md. 2013), we stated: Absent indications that a hearing judge failed to consider purported evidence of mitigating factors or the judge omitted purported evidence of mitigating factors from his opinion, this court may interpret the omission to mean that the hearing judge did not credit the purported evidence of mitigating factors. Here, the hearing judge neither credited nor rejected the alleged facts. The record demonstrates: The hearing judge allowed Greenleaf to testify on his own behalf and proffer at length.

We see no indication that the hearing judge did not consider Greenleaf's remarks. Given the nature of Greenleaf's proffer and testimony—*i.e.,* he performed well at work, he was in a secluded office, and he suffered embarrassment—it is evident that the hearing judge did not find this information to be mitigating. Even if the facts that Greenleaf alleges were accurate, it strains credulity that some of them—such as Greenleaf's work performance or his being moved to another office—would constitute mitigating factors. Thus, we do not adopt as mitigating factors the facts that Greenleaf alleges.

B. Conclusions of Law

The Commission does not except to any of the hearing judge's conclusions of law. Greenleaf excepts to the hearing judge's conclusion: Greenleaf violated CR § 3-324 (Sexual Solicitation of Minor). We overrule Greenleaf's exception and uphold all of the hearing judge's conclusions of law as to the MLRPC.

Maryland Lawyers' Rule 8.4(b)—Criminal Act

It is professional misconduct for a lawyer to ... commit a criminal act that reflects adversely on the lawyer's honesty, trustworthiness or fitness as a lawyer in other respects." MLRPC 8.4(b). Under CR § 3–324(b), "[a] person may not, with the intent to commit a violation of ... [CR] § 3–307[,] ... knowingly solicit ... a law enforcement officer posing as a minor to engage in activities that would be unlawful for the person to engage in under ... [CR] § 3–307[.]" Under CR § 3–307(a)(4), "[a] person may not ... engage in a sexual act with another if the victim is 14 or 15 years old, and the person performing the sexual act is at least 21 years old[.]" Under CR § 3–307(a)(5), "[a] person may not ... engage in vaginal intercourse with another if the victim is 14 or 15 years old, and the person performing the act is at least 21 years old."

Here, clear and convincing evidence supports the hearing judge's conclusion that Greenleaf violated MLRPC 8.4(b) by violating CR § 3–324(b). When he was at least twenty-one years old, Greenleaf knowingly solicited Detective Yamin—posing as "Beth," a fourteen-year-old or fifteen-year-old girl—for sexual acts and/or vaginal intercourse. For example, Greenleaf asked: "Beth, do you want to have sex with me?" Violating CR § 3–324(b) undeniably adversely reflects on a lawyer's fitness to continue to practice law. We reject Greenleaf's ludicrous contention: He did not violate CR § 3–324(b), because he did not intend to violate CR § 3–307 by immediately engaging in intercourse with "Beth" "then and there, but preparing for the *future*." CR § 3–324(b) simply requires: At the time of the solicitation, a person intends to violate CR § 3–307 at some point in the future—even if the person does not intend to immediately violate CR § 3–307.

Maryland Lawyers' Rule 8.4(c)—Dishonesty, Fraud, Deceit, or Misrepresentation

"It is professional misconduct for a lawyer to ... engage in conduct involving dishonesty, fraud, deceit, or misrepresentation." MLRPC 8.4(c). Here, clear and convincing evidence supports the hearing judge's conclusion. Greenleaf violated Rule 8.4(c) by using his computer at the Robert C. Murphy Courts of Appeal Building to communicate with "Beth." Greenleaf's using the computer at work to violate CR § 3–324(b) was conduct involving dishonesty. The Court of Special Appeals would neither expect, condone, nor excuse the use of a court's computer for soliciting sex with a minor.

That said, a lawyer may—at times—make incidental personal use of computer equipment in the workplace without violating MLRPC

8.4(c). However, Greenleaf use the Maryland Judiciary's computer equipment on multiple occasions—spanning almost eleven months ... In sum, it is the extensive use of the computer over a protracted course of time. ... Greenleaf secretly committed an offense in the workplace for which he knew his employment could be terminated. That causes us to conclude: His conduct constituted dishonesty in violation of Rule 8.4(c).

Maryland Lawyers' Rule 8.4(d)—Conduct Prejudicial to the Administration of Justice

"It is professional misconduct for a lawyer to ... engage in conduct that is prejudicial to the administration of justice." MLRPC 8.4(d). Generally, a lawyer violates Rule 8.4(d) where the lawyer's conduct negatively "impacts ... the public's perception ... of the courts or legal profession." *Reno,* 83 A.3d at 784. Here, clear and convincing evidence supports the hearing judge's conclusion: Greenleaf violated Rule 8.4(d). Greenleaf solicited for sexual acts a person whom he believed to be a fourteen-year-old or fifteen-year-old girl. Greenleaf was arrested and charged, and entered a plea to a charge of attempting to violate CR § 11–203. Greenleaf's misconduct tarnished the public's perception of both the legal profession and Greenleaf's employer, the Maryland Judiciary. Also, "[i]t is professional misconduct for a lawyer to ... violate ... the" MLRPC. Rule 8.4(a). Here, clear and convincing evidence supports the hearing judge's conclusion: Greenleaf violated MLRPC 8.4(a). As discussed above, Greenleaf violated MLRPC 8.4(b), 8.4(c), and 8.4(d).

C. Sanction

The Commission recommends that we disbar Greenleaf. Greenleaf asks that we reprimand him, or indefinitely suspend him from the practice of law—with the right to apply for reinstatement after one year. This court sanctions a lawyer not "to punish the" lawyer, but "to protect the public and the public's confidence in the legal profession." *Attorney Grievance Comm'n v. Worthy,* 84 A.3d 113, 119 (Md. 2014) (citation and internal quotation marks omitted). This court protects the public by: (1) deterring other lawyers from engaging in similar misconduct; and (2) suspending or disbarring a lawyer who is "unfit to continue" to practice law. *Attorney Grievance Comm'n v. Gerace,* 72 A.3d 567, 577 (Md.2013)

In determining an appropriate sanction, this court considers: "(a) the duty violated; (b) the lawyer's mental state; (c) the potential or actual injury caused by the lawyer's misconduct; and (d) the existence of aggravating or mitigating factors." American Bar

Association, *Standards for Imposing Lawyer Sanctions* ("ABA Standards") at III.C.3.0 (1992). *Aggravating* factors include: (a) prior disciplinary offenses; (b) dishonest or selfish motive; (c) a pattern of misconduct; (d) multiple offenses; (e) bad faith obstruction of the disciplinary proceeding by intentionally failing to comply with rules or orders of the [Commission]; (f) submission of false evidence, false statements, or other deceptive practices during the disciplinary process; (g) refusal to acknowledge wrongful nature of conduct; (h) vulnerability of victim; (i) substantial experience in the practice of law; (j) indifference to making restitution; [and] (k) illegal conduct[.] ABA Standards at III.C.9.22.

Mitigating factors include: (a) absence of a prior disciplinary record; (b) absence of a dishonest or selfish motive; (c) personal or emotional problems; (d) timely good faith effort to make restitution or to rectify consequences of misconduct; (e) full and free disclosure to [the Commission] or cooperative attitude toward proceedings; (f) inexperience in the practice of law; (g) character or reputation; (h) physical disability; (i) mental disability or chemical dependency including alcoholism or drug abuse when: (1) there is medical evidence that the [lawyer] is affected by a chemical dependency or mental disability; (2) the chemical dependency or mental disability caused the misconduct; (3) the [lawyer]'s recovery from the chemical dependency or mental disability is demonstrated by a meaningful and sustained period of successful rehabilitation; and (4) the recovery arrested the misconduct and recurrence of that misconduct is unlikely[;] (j) delay in disciplinary proceedings; (k) imposition of other penalties or sanctions; (l) remorse; [and] (m) remoteness of prior offenses. ABA Standards at III.C.9.32

* * *

Regarding the violated duty and Greenleaf's mental state, Greenleaf intentionally solicited for sexual acts "Beth," whom he believed to be a fourteen-year-old or fifteen-year-old girl. Greenleaf deliberately preyed on, and intended to violate, a person whom he believed to be under the age of consent. ... We are more than satisfied that disbarment is the appropriate sanction for Greenleaf's egregious misconduct. ... Greenleaf is, indeed, a sexual predator who is a danger to the public and is "unfit" to practice law.

For the above reasons, we disbar Greenleaf. It is so ordered.

3. Actions Against Attorneys for Using Third Parties' Computers to Access and Download Pornographic Images

In re Disciplinary Proceedings Against Todd J. Beatse

722 N.W.2d 385
(Wis. 2006)

PER CURIAM.

Attorney Todd J. Beatse was admitted to the practice of law in May 2000. At the times relevant to this matter, he was an assistant district attorney for Monroe County. On January 24 or 25, 2005, Attorney Beatse left his office to attend court hearings. While he was out of his office, the district attorney's office received notification that its computer system had to be shut down for maintenance purposes. When Attorney Beatse's secretary went to shut down his computer, she discovered pornographic images that had been downloaded from the Internet and minimized on the bottom of his screen.

Attorney Beatse told various individuals—including his supervisor, Monroe County District Attorney Daniel Cary: The images had come from his son's use of a home computer, that he had copied them onto a memory stick, and that he had loaded them onto his work computer to determine what files or websites his son had been accessing at home. This story was false. When the district attorney ordered an investigation of the matter, a review of Attorney Beatse's state-provided computer showed: During the preceding 55 days—29 of which Attorney Beatse had been at work, he had browsed pornographic Internet sites for 36 hours. Moreover, the investigation revealed that 12 of the 20 most visited sites were pornographic sites.

Ultimately, Attorney Beatse admitted: He lied to District Attorney Cary about his son having been the source of the pornography. Instead, Beatse had been improperly viewing pornography with his work computer, contrary to various state and local work rules. Attorney Beatse, however, stated: He had not viewed pornography after the discovery on January 24 or 25. This was false, because the audit of his computer showed: He spent over a half hour viewing pornography on January 26 and 27, 2005. Attorney Beatse was suspended without pay and given a disciplinary letter advising him that further misuse of the state computer system would lead to further disciplinary action.

While on disciplinary suspension, Attorney Beatse used the state e-mail system from his home computer to send a number of improper e-mail messages—including messages to two female government employees. One recipient was a court reporter. In those messages, Attorney Beatse made comments about having touched the breasts of a third Monroe County employee and about the court reporter's breasts. The court reporter also stated: Attorney Beatse had made a number of similar inappropriate oral comments about her breasts on previous occasions.

In addition to all of these comments, the audit of the computer system disclosed: Attorney Beatse had sent a number of e-mails about his sexual activities and other sexual topics. Attorney Beatse initially denied having sent sexually explicit e-mails using the state computer system, except when the sexual content was "part of a joke." This was not true. In light of these additional facts, the district attorney's office terminated Attorney Beatse's employment. After a period of not practicing law, Attorney Beatse now works as a private attorney.

The Office of Lawyer Regulation (OLR) filed a complaint against Beatse and alleged: By lying to his co-workers and his supervisor about the source of and reason for the pornography on his work computer, by lying about his continued viewing of pornography on his work computer after January 24 or 25, and by lying about sending and receiving sexually explicit e-mails, Attorney Beatse had engaged in conduct involving dishonesty, fraud, deceit or misrepresentation, in violation of Wisconsin Supreme Court Rules (SCR), Rule 20:8.4(c).

The second count of the OLR's complaint alleged: By making offensive comments to the court reporter about her breasts and by using the state e-mail system to send and receive numerous messages containing inappropriate sexual and other offensive content, Attorney Beatse violated the attorney's oath and the requirement to "abstain from all offensive personality," *see* SCR 40.15, thereby also violating SCR 20:8.4(g). Attorney Beatse filed an answer, pleading no-contest to the two counts in the OLR's complaint. He objected, however, to the OLR's request for a public reprimand, arguing that a private reprimand was sufficient discipline.

Russell L. Hanson was appointed as a referee and conducted a hearing on the appropriate sanction. The referee's subsequent report concluded: Attorney Beatse's no-contest pleas to the allegations were sufficient to find that the attorney had violated SCR 20:8.4(c) and SCR 20:8.4(g). Regarding the question of an appropriate sanction, the referee concluded that a public reprimand was warranted. The referee acknowledged: There were some mitigating factors in Attorney Beatse's favor: Attorney Beatse had already loss of his job. He had cooperated with the OLR in its investigation. And Beatse appeared to have genuine remorse for his misconduct.

On the other hand, the referee concluded: Attorney Beatse's conduct was so outrageous that it required public, rather than private, discipline. Additionally, it was disturbing that Beatse's lies caused his employer and co-workers additional work. Also, the referee stated: Attorney Beatse still did not fully understand that he did not have the right to comment on that person's anatomy, even if someone shares questionable or inappropriate stories with him.

After reviewing the record and in light of Attorney Beatse's no-contest plea, we adopt the referee's factual findings based on the allegations of the OLR's complaint. We also adopt the referee's legal conclusions: (1) Attorney Beatse violated SCR 20:8.4(c), by making multiple false statements, and (2) he violated his oath as an attorney, thereby violating SCR 20:8.4(g). We further agree: The repeated nature and seriousness of Attorney Beatse's misconduct warrants a public reprimand. Finally, we decide that Attorney Beatse should pay the costs of this proceeding, which were $6693.98 as of May 11, 2006.

It is ordered: Todd J. Beatse is publicly reprimanded for his professional misconduct. It is further ordered: Within 60 days, Attorney Todd J. Beatse must pay to the Office of Lawyer Regulation the costs of this proceeding. If the costs are not paid within the time specified and absent a showing of his inability to pay the costs within that time, Todd J. Beatse's license to practice law in Wisconsin shall be suspended until further order of the court.

E. Disciplinary Actions Against Attorneys for Using Websites, Internet Blogs, Social Media and E-mails to Threaten or Defame Judges, and to Influence Judicial Outcomes

Becoming A Competent 21st Century Legal Ethics Professor: Everything You Always Wanted To Know About Technology (But Were Afraid To Ask)

2015 Journal of the Professional Lawyer 75
Catherine J. Lanctot

In addition to teaching our students about the substantive content of the ethical rules governing litigation, we also focus on inculcating norms of professional behavior in dealing with opposing counsel, third parties, and the court. Careless use of social media by lawyers can generate unanticipated consequences. Law students must be alerted to the reality that once they enter the legal profession, long-standing habits of posting every detail of their lives online could come back to haunt them.

One example of unfortunate social media behavior was recounted by a judge who had received a request from a lawyer for a trial delay because of a "death in the family." The judge granted the delay but also decided to check the lawyer's Facebook page. She recalled: "There was a funeral, but there wasn't a lot of grief expressed online. ... All week long, this lawyer [was] posting about partying. One night drinking wine, another night drinking mojitos, another day motor biking." The judge ultimately denied a second request for postponement and reported the attorney to a senior partner at her firm. ..."

Lawyers who vent about judges or opposing counsel in social media may also find themselves in hot water. The lawyer who unwisely called a local judge an "evil, unfair witch" on his blog was reprimanded and fined by the Florida bar. In another case, an assistant state prosecutor posted a song parody to Facebook while awaiting a jury verdict in a trial, in which he referred to one of the participants as "weasle [sic] face," and criticized opposing counsel for purported ethical lapses. Although the attorney believed that his posting was private, its content was disclosed to others and became the subject of an investigation. The Chief Assistant State Attorney … described the incident as "immature" and "harmless joking." But he noted: The posting was a "training moment" for prosecutors to ensure that they maintain the public's trust. Similarly, two prosecutors in North Dakota were disciplined for Facebook postings that criticized jurors on [a] recent case as "12 idiots."

* * *

Judicial clerks may also generate problems through unprofessional use of social media. In 2012, a law clerk for the Kansas Court of Appeals attended a hearing on a controversial ethics complaint brought against State Attorney General. The law clerk live-tweeted through her personal Twitter account—referring to the Attorney General as a "douchebag," mocking his arguments, and making observations about the judges. After she lost her job, she attempted to justify her crass comments as "me saying dumb things." On January 13, 2014, a hearing panel concluded: Her tweets reflected bias and disrespect against a litigant and reflected badly on the courts. The panel recommended that she receive an informal admonition.

In June 2015, a law clerk for a New Jersey Superior Court judge resigned after posting disparaging remarks about an on-duty state trooper who died after a collision with a deer. The law clerk stated on Facebook: "I agree that it is sad and heart-wrenching for the family members left to suffer the consequences of the trooper's recklessness—especially for the deer family who lost a mommy or daddy or baby deer." After a two-week suspension, she resigned. [Also consider another arguably] less damaging, but equally unprofessional … incident: A judicial clerk … posted a series of status updates about an ongoing jury trial. One status report opined: "There's nothing like being hit on by jurors." A friend assured her: "Its ok if their [sic] hot!!! and have a good job!!!"

* * *

Although some lawyers might try to insulate themselves from these risks by avoiding all social media, the societal shift toward this means of communication suggests: This short-sighted strategy could backfire. In some contexts, failure to avail oneself of information that is readily available on social media might generate a separate ethics violation for lack of diligence. As one commentator has noted: "If more than half of divorce attorneys say that Facebook is their best source for online evidence, then failure to utilize the site as part of informal discovery may constitute a failure to perform due diligence. A divorce attorney who ignores Facebook and other social-networking sites as a source of possible evidence could be compared to a prosecutor who fails to conduct a criminal background check on a defendant's key alibi witness. Both may be in violation of MODEL RULE 1.3—"A lawyer shall act with reasonable diligence and promptness in representing a client."

1. ACTIONS AGAINST ATTORNEYS FOR USING SOCIAL MEDIA, E-MAILS, SMS/MMS MESSAGING, AND INTERNET BLOGS TO INFLUENCE JUDICIAL OUTCOMES IN CIVIL PROCEEDINGS

In re Joyce Nanine McCool

172 So.3d 1058
(La. 2015)

Knoll, Justice.

This disciplinary matter arises from formal charges filed by the Office of Disciplinary Counsel (ODC) against Attorney Joyce Nanine McCool, a Mandeville attorney. McCool is 52-years-old and was admitted to the practice of law in Louisiana in 2000.

Underlying Facts

Attorney Joyce McCool and Raven Skye-Maurer (Raven) were friends. Following Raven's divorce in 2006, she and her former husband were involved in a bitter child-custody dispute. Raven accused her ex-husband of sexually abusing their two young daughters—H. and Z. Raven unsuccessfully sought to terminate her ex-husband's parental rights in Mississippi before Judge Deborah Gambrell. McCool is not a member of the Mississippi Bar. And she was not admitted *pro hac vice* in Raven's Mississippi case. Still, McCool assisted Raven as a friend.

Additionally, McCool filed a petition in St. Tammany Parish on behalf of Raven's *new* husband—who sought to adopt H. and Z. The presiding judge—Judge Dawn Amacker—stayed the intrafamilyadoption proceedings, until the Mississippi dispute was resolved. Judge Amacker also declined to exercise subject matter jurisdiction—after responding to an emergency-custody motion that Attorney McCool filed on Raven's behalf. After Judge Amacker issued her ruling, McCool filed a writ application with the First Circuit Court of Appeal. It was denied. This court also denied the writs. *Maurer v. Boyd,* 68 So.3d 517(La. 2011).

Unhappy with Judge Gambrell's and Judge Amacker's respective rulings, McCool drafted an online petition. It was entitled "JUSTICE FOR [H] AND [Z]." Attorney McCool and Raven posted the petition on the Internet at Change.org—along with a photo of the two girls. Regarding the Mississippi proceeding before Judge Gambrell, the online petition stated:

> To Judge Deborah Gambrell: We, the undersigned, ask that you renounce jurisdiction in this matter to the Louisiana court, because the children have lived exclusively in Louisiana for the past three years. Their schools, teachers, physicians, therapists, little sister, brother and the vast majority of significant contacts are now in Louisiana. There is also an adoption proceeding pending in Louisiana over which Louisiana has jurisdiction. And in the interest of judicial economy, and the best interest of the girls, Louisiana is the more appropriate forum to oversee ensure [sic] the "best interest" of the girls are protected.
>
> If you refuse to relinquish jurisdiction to Louisiana, we insist that you remove the Guardian Ad Litem currently assigned to the case, and replace him with one that has the proper training and experience in investigating allegations of child sexual abuse in custody proceedings. We further insist that, in keeping [with] *S.G. v. D.C.,* 13 So.3d 269 (Miss.2009), you specifically define the Guardian Ad Litem's role in the suit. Require the new Guardian Ad Litem [to] prepare a written report. Require that the report be shared with all parties prior to a hearing. Require that all proceeding be conducted on the record, with advance notice and opportunity to be heard, and that an evidentiary hearing be conducted to review the allegations of child sexual abuse, and that no visitation be allowed until you have seen all of the evidence.

Regarding Judge Amacker and the Louisiana proceedings, the petition stated:

> To Judge Amacker: We, the undersigned, insist that you withdraw the unlawful stay of the adoption proceedings currently pending in your court. And, in accordance with La.Ch. C. art. 1253, [we request] a hearing ... with all due speed to allow the girls' stepfather to show why it is in the girls' best interest that they be adopted by him, thereby terminating all parental rights of the girls' biological father.

Attorney McCool re-posted the online petition on her blog site and in online articles that she authored. One of her articles included a photo of the two girls. In addition, McCool provided contact information for the judges' offices and the Louisiana Supreme Court. And she solicited and encouraged others to express their feelings to the judges and this court about the pending cases. She wrote:

> In spite of overwhelming evidence that the girls have been abused by their father, Judge Deborah Gambrell—the Chancery Court of Marion County, Mississippi—refuses to even look at the evidence. And Judge Gambrell has ordered the girls be sent to unsupervised visitation with their father. Judge Dawn Amacker—for the Parish of St. Tammany in Louisiana—also refused to protect the girls, even though she has the power and authority to protect them. ... Insist that Judge Amacker and Judge Gambrell do their jobs! ... Please sign the petition. Circulate it to all of your friends and families. Call Judge Amacker and Judge Gambrell—during the hours of 8:30 to 5:00 starting Monday, August 15—to ask why they won't follow the law and protect these children.
>
> Let them know you're watching and expect them to do their job and most of all, make sure these precious little girls are safe! Call the Louisiana Supreme Court and tell them: You want the law to protect these girls [phone number]. ... Let's turn this around and be H's hero. Please sign the Care2 petition and continue to call Judge Gambrell to ask her why she is unwilling to afford [H] and [Z] simple justice. You can sign the petition and lend your voice to this

> cause *here*. Or, you can contact directly. Contact information is: [provided contact information for the judges].

Two days before considering Raven's motion for contempt and to terminate her former husband's parental rights, Judge Gambrell's staff received an e-mail from Heather Lyons—a signer of the online petition. Ms. Lyons stated: She lived and voted in Forrest County, Mississippi. She would "be paying attention" to Raven's case—because "Judge Gambrell refused to hear evidence regarding child abuse and the father's likely molestation of the little girls. She has an obligation to protect our most vulnerable children." On behalf of Judge Amacker, an administrative assistant returned the petition to McCool, cautioning McCool's client against *ex parte* communications with the judge. Undaunted, Attorney McCool continued her online and social media campaign—disseminating the sexual abuse allegations and linking audio recordings in which Raven and her children discussed the alleged abuse.

* * *

McCool also used her personal Twitter account to promote the online petition and to draw attention to the audio recordings and the manner in which the judges were handling the cases. On August 16, 2011, the day of the Mississippi hearing, McCool tweeted 30 messages about the case and petition, including:

> I realize most of u think the courts care about kids but too often there's no walk to go with the talk: [*link to online petition*]. Shouldn't judges base decisions about kids on evidence?: [*link to online petition*]. GIMME GIMME GIMME Evidence! Want some? I got it. Think u can convince a judge to look at it? Sign this petition: [*link to online petition*]. Judges are supposed to know shit about ... the law ... Aren't they? And like evidence and shit? Due process? I am SO going 2 have 2 change jobs after this! ... I'm risking sanctions by the LA Supreme Court; u could be a HUGE help. Make judges protect [H] and [Z] from abuse by their father!

On August 24, 2011, McCool tweeted the following to a local investigative news organization: "focus ur lens on Y Judge Amacker won't protect these girls? And "ask Judge Amacker why she won't listen." Another tweet stated: "Judge Gambrell at it again—turned a 4 YO child over to a validated abuser—PLEASE TELL ME WHAT IT WILL TAKE FOR EVERYON [sic] TO SAY 'ENOUGH'?"

McCool's online articles and postings contain numerous false, misleading, and inflammatory statements about the manner in which Judge Gambrell and Judge Amacker were handling the pending cases. But McCool denies any responsibility for these misstatements, contending these were "Raven's perceptions of what had happened." Additionally, McCool insisted that she was simply "helping [Raven] get her voice out there."

* * *

Subsequently, McCool filed motions to recuse Judge Amacker in two matters unrelated to Raven's case. In response, Judge Amacker signed orders, stating she was "voluntarily recusing herself due to the possibility that the judge may be called as a witness" in disciplinary proceedings against McCool." Notwithstanding the judge's stated reasons for her recusal, McCool filed two more motions for recusal in which she stated: Judge Amacker had "voluntarily and *expressly admitted [her] extreme bias and conflict in recusing [herself]* in several other cases—which grounds are equally applicable in the case at bar."

On September 14, 2011, Judge Gambrell signed an order commanding McCool to appear and explain why she should not be held in contempt of court by disclosing information from a "sealed" record. McCool received a copy of the notice of the contempt hearing by regular United States mail. However, McCool did not appear, contending she was not properly served and the Mississippi court did not have jurisdiction over her. On October 6, 2011, Judge Gambrell signed an order holding McCool in contempt of court. In October 2012, Judge Gambrell rescinded the order of contempt.

The judge concluded: "Service of process was insufficient; and, although Attorney McCool has violated this court's order regarding the disclosure of audio transcriptions, this court has no authority to hold Joyce Nanine McCool in contempt of this court." In January 2013, Judge Gambrell *sua sponte* recused herself from further action in Raven's case—"in accordance with the Mississippi Code of Judicial Conduct, Canon 3 and to avoid the appearance of impropriety or bias.

Disciplinary Proceedings

In September 2011, Judge Gambrell filed a complaint against McCool with Louisiana Office of Disciplinary Counsel. In May 2014, the ODC filed one count of formal charges against McCool, alleging her conduct as set forth above violated the following Rules of Professional Conduct:

> Rule 3.5(a)—A lawyer shall not seek to influence a judge by means prohibited by law.
>
> Rule 3.5(b)—A lawyer shall not communicate *ex parte* with a judge during the proceeding;
>
> Rule 8.4(a)—Violating Professional Rules of Conduct is professional misconduct;
>
> Rule 8.4(c)—Dishonesty, fraud, or misrepresentation is professional misconduct; and
>
> Rule 4(d)—It is professional misconduct for a lawyer to engage in prejudicial act which undermine[s] the administration of justice.

Formal Hearing and Committee Report

After considering the evidence and testimony, the hearing committee made factual findings and determined McCool violated the Rules of Professional Conduct as follows:

Rules 3.5(a), 3.5(b), and 8.4(a)—McCool used the *internet, an online petition, and social media* to spread information, some of which was false, misleading, and inflammatory, about Judge Gambrell's and Judge Amacker's handling of and rulings in pending litigation. McCool circulated contact information for Judge Gambrell and Judge Amacker and solicited and encouraged others to make direct, *ex parte* contact with the judges to express their feelings about the pending cases, and attempted to influence the outcome of the pending cases. The clear intent of McCool's *online campaign* was an attempt to influence the judges' future rulings in the respective cases, and to do so through improper *ex parte* communication directed at the judges.

Rule 8.4(c)—McCool disseminated false, misleading, and inflammatory information *on the internet and through social media* about Judge Gambrell and Judge Amacker and their handling of these pending domestic proceedings. She also instructed others to sign and circulate an *online petition*, and to *call the judges* and let them know they are "watching" them and are "horrified" by their rulings. Finally, McCool made blatantly false statements about Judge Amacker in multiple motions to recuse.

Rule 8.4(d)—McCool used the *internet and social media* to influence Judge Gambrell's and Judge Amacker's future rulings in pending litigation. McCool's conduct threatened the integrity and independence of the court and was clearly prejudicial to the administration of justice. McCool also used *her Twitter account to publish tweets* linking the *audio recordings* of the minor children discussing alleged sexual abuse; to publish false, misleading, and inflammatory information about Judge Gambrell and Judge Amacker; and to promote the *online petition*, all of which was designed to intimidate and influence the judges' future rulings in the underlying proceedings.

The committee determined McCool violated a duty owed to the public and the legal system. She acted knowingly, if not intentionally. She caused actual and potential harm by threatening the independence and integrity of the judicial system, and causing the judges concern for their personal safety and well-being. The applicable baseline sanctions, therefore, range from suspension to disbarment.

* * *

Disciplinary Board Recommendation

The board determined: McCool violated duties owed to the public and the legal system by making false, misleading, and inflammatory statements about two judges. She did so as part of a pattern of conduct intended to influence the judges' future rulings in pending litigation. Considering the ABA's *Standards for Imposing Lawyer Sanctions* ("ABA Standards"), the board determined the baseline sanction is suspension. In *aggravation*, the board found a dishonest or selfish motive, a pattern of misconduct, multiple offenses, refusal to acknowledge the wrongful nature of the conduct, and substantial experience in the practice of law. In *mitigation*, the board found McCool has no prior disciplinary record.

After further considering McCool's misconduct in light of this court's prior jurisprudence, the board adopted the committee's recommendations: McCool should be suspended from the practice of law for one year and one day, required to attend Ethics School, and assessed with the costs and expenses of this proceeding. McCool filed an objection to the disciplinary board's recommendation. Accordingly, the case was docketed for oral argument pursuant to Louisiana Supreme Court Rule XIX, § 11(G)(1)(b).

Discussion

Bar disciplinary matters come within the exclusive original jurisdiction of this Court. La. Const. art. V, § 5(B). Consequently, we act as triers of fact and conduct an independent review of the record to determine whether the alleged misconduct has been proven by clear and convincing evidence. La. Sup.Ct. R. XIX, § 11(G); *In re: Banks,* 18 So.3d 57, 63 (La. 2009). While we are not bound in any way by the findings and recommendations of the hearing committee and disciplinary board, we have held the manifest error standard is applicable to the committee's factual findings.

Improper Ex Parte Communication

The ODC's allegations in this area relate to McCool's use of the *internet and social media* to disseminate information about the manner in which Judge Gambrell and Judge Amacker handled the child custody and visitation cases at issue, in an apparent attempt to marshal public opinion against these judges and attention from this court. …

We agree: The examples clearly and convincingly establish McCool solicited the public to contact the presiding judges and this court. Although McCool asserts "the admonitions in the petitions did nothing other than ensure that both parties would receive the same treatment—a hearing based on the law and evidence," the evidence shows she *used the internet and social media* to solicit and encourage others to make direct, *ex parte* contact with Judge Gambrell, Judge Amacker, and this court in an effort to influence their and our decisions in sealed, pending domestic litigations. … Accordingly, we find the evidence clearly and convincingly shows McCool's conduct in this regard violated Rules 3.5(a) and (b) and Rule 8.4(a) of the Rules of Professional Conduct.

Dissemination of False and Misleading Information

The ODC alleges McCool "disseminated false, misleading and/or inflammatory information through *the internet and social media* about Judge Deborah Gambrell and Judge Dawn Amacker in pending cases wherein McCool was counsel of record and/or had a personal interest." It further alleges McCool "also made false and misleading statements in multiple motions to recuse Judge Amacker."… McCool *posted audio recordings* of the minor children purportedly talking about abuse and stated: Judge Gambrell "once again refused to admit all of Raven's evidence, including these *recordings*. … [Also] McCool's *online posting and twitter feeds* are littered with misrepresentations and outright false statements.

Accordingly, we find: The evidence clearly and convincingly shows McCool's repeated false statements concerning Judge Amacker's "expressly admitted extreme bias" were not mere misrepresentations, but false statements knowingly and intentionally made. Accordingly, we find the evidence clearly and convincingly shows a violation of Rule 8.4(c).

Conduct Prejudicial to the Administration of Justice

Lastly, the ODC alleges McCool's overall conduct—*utilizing the internet and social media both* in an attempt to influence the judges and to expedite achievement of her goals in the case—was prejudicial to the administration of justice and violated Rule 8.4(d). … Though not as blatantly offensive as the blitzing itself, this result nevertheless prejudiced the administration of justice by causing undue delays in numerous time sensitive matters, some of which these judges had presided over for a long period of time. Therefore, we find McCool's overall conduct in this regard was prejudicial to the administration of justice in violation of Rule 8.4(d).

Sanctions

In determining a sanction, we are mindful disciplinary proceedings are not primarily to punish the lawyer, but rather are designed to maintain high standards of conduct, protect the public, preserve the integrity of the profession, and deter future misconduct. *Louisiana State Bar Ass'n v. Reis,* 513 So.2d 1173, 1177-78 (La.1987). The discipline to be imposed depends upon the facts of each case and the seriousness of the offenses involved considered in light of any aggravating and mitigating circumstances. *Louisiana State Bar Ass'n v. Whittington,* 459 So.2d 520, 524 (La.1984). Under Louisiana Supreme Court Rule XIX, § 10(C) and before imposing a sanction after a finding of lawyer misconduct, this court must consider four factors:

(1) whether the lawyer has violated a duty owed to a client, to the public, to the legal system, or to the profession;

(2) whether the lawyer acted intentionally, knowingly, negligently;

(3) the amount of actual or potential injury caused by the lawyer's misconduct; and

(4) the existence of any aggravating or mitigating factors.

As required, we consider each factor. ... First, we take umbrage with McCool's *online and social media activity*. She released the names of children, and she linked their audio child-abuse conversations—with their mother—and *posted their faces on the World Wide Web* for anyone to see. ... This evidence demonstrates both a level of intent and knowledge. ... [W]e likewise find: the evidence demonstrates McCool acted knowingly, if not outright intentionally, by disseminating false information on *social media/internet* ... [and encouraging the public to call] the presiding judges to express concern and outrage.

* * *

[And given McCool's] *internet and social media suavity*, she clearly was aware: The petition that she signed could and might very well be printed and sent to the judges and courts to whom the petition was addressed. ... The evidence shows McCool's conduct caused actual and potential harm to the independence and integrity of the judicial system and also caused the judges concern for their personal well-being. We also find her *exposure of the children on the World Wide Web* extremely harmful. ... Completely unapologetic for her misconduct, McCool made it abundantly clear she would *continue to use social media and blogs* to bring about the changes she sought in the underlying cases. McCool will not admit to any wrong doing whatsoever. ... This court will not tolerate McCool's defiant attitude and unapologetic actions, which make a mockery of our rules and traditions.

The only *mitigating factor* in this case is McCool's absence of a prior disciplinary record. While there is no Louisiana case directly on point with the manner in which McCool facilitated her misconduct— *i.e., through social media and the internet*, we do find the serious nature of her actions requires serious sanction. In these cases, we look to the ABA Standards for guidance in determining the baseline sanction. ABA Standard 6.32. The applicable baseline sanction under the ABA Standards ranges from suspension to disbarment.

* * *

Coupled with her complete lack of remorse and admitted refusal to simply allow our system of review to work without seeking outside interference, McCool's misconduct reflects a horrifying lack of respect for the dignity, impartiality, and authority of our courts and our judicial process as a whole. ... McCool's *social media campaign*—conducted outside the sealed realm of the underlying judicial proceedings constitutes—an intolerable disservice to these traditions and our judicial system.

Accordingly, we find her ethical misconduct warrants the highest of sanction—disbarment. It is ordered that Joyce Nanine McCool be and hereby is disbarred. Her name shall be stricken from the roll of attorneys and her license to practice law in the State of Louisiana shall be revoked.

Excerpt from the American Bar Association's Model Rules of Professional Conduct

Rule 3.5—Impartiality and Decorum of The Tribunal

A lawyer shall not:

(a) seek to influence a judge, juror, prospective juror or other official by means prohibited by law;

(b) communicate ex parte with such a person during the proceeding unless authorized to do so by law or court order;

(c) communicate with a juror or prospective juror after discharge of the jury if:

- (1) the communication is prohibited by law or court order;
- (2) the juror has made known to the lawyer a desire not to communicate; or
- (3) the communication involves misrepresentation, coercion, duress or harassment; or

(d) engage in conduct intended to disrupt a tribunal.

Becoming A Competent 21st Century Legal Ethics Professor: Everything You Always Wanted To Know About Technology (But Were Afraid To Ask)

2015 Journal of the Professional Lawyer 75

Catherine J. Lanctot

Prosecutors and Impartiality Concerns

Social media commentary on public events may also trigger concerns about impartiality if made by prosecutors. In the spring of 2015, a Michigan prosecutor posted about the ongoing rioting in Baltimore: "Solution. Simple. Shoot em. Period. End of discussion. I don't care what causes the protestors to turn violent. ... Regardless of the ... reason, this is [not] acceptable. Flipping disgusting." The post was immediately taken down after criticism.

In a somewhat different vein, a Missouri court recently expressed concern about a chief prosecutor who tweeted openly about the facts and circumstances of an upcoming criminal trial. Also days before jury selection, she stated in a tweet: "DNA hit linked him to 1992 rape of 11 yr old girl. 20 yrs later, victim now same age as prosecutor." She also tweeted while observing closing arguments: "I have respect for attys who defend child rapists. Our system of justice demands it, but I couldn't do it. No way, no how." The court of appeals did not overturn the conviction, but warned: "Extraneous statements on Twitter or other forms of social media, particularly during [a] ... trial, can taint the jury and result in reversal of the verdict. ... We are especially troubled by the timing of [the prosecutor]'s Twitter posts, because broadcasting such statements immediately before and during trial greatly magnifies the risk that a jury will be tainted by undue extrajudicial influences."

Similarly, an Iowa court postponed a jury trial for several months in response to a Facebook post by the lawyer for a plaintiff ... who was suing a former prosecutor for false imprisonment of her client. The lawyer posted: "I am going to trial on Monday in a case where the former county attorney in Madison County slept with his client and then beat her up. ... The case was being handled by another lawyer until he developed a conflict, so I have only been in it for a few weeks. I am really scrambling to get up to speed. It is one of those cases where I feel duty bound to take it because I have an obligation to my own profession. The Bar Association Grievance Commission recommended that his license be suspended for four years. The Supreme Court affirmed their findings, but reduced the penalty to 18 months. Yet, another example of why an all-white, all-male court really needs a woman. I hope a jury will be a little harder on him!" Opposing counsel immediately filed for a continuance based on concerns about influencing potential jurors, which was granted.

2. Disciplinary Sanctions Against Prosecutors for Withholding Exculpatory Electronic Evidence to Influence Judicial Outcomes in Criminal Proceedings

Lawyer Disciplinary Board v. Robert T. Busch

754 S.E.2d 729
(W.Va. 2014)

PER CURIAM.

This lawyer disciplinary proceeding against Richard T. Busch was brought to this Court by the Office of Disciplinary Counsel (ODC) on behalf of the Lawyer Disciplinary Board (Board). The Board's Hearing Panel Subcommittee (Subcommittee) determined that Mr. Busch committed numerous violations of the West Virginia Rules of Professional Conduct. Mr. Busch filed an objection to the recommendations, arguing that his conduct was merely negligent, not intentional. Based upon the parties' arguments to this court, we adopt the recommendations of the Subcommittee.

Factual And Procedural History

Mr. Busch was admitted to practice law by the West Virginia State Bar on April 23, 2002. Initially, Mr. Busch practiced law at his father's firm in Elkins, West Virginia. The conduct in question began in January 2009 during Mr. Busch's tenure as the Randolph County Prosecuting Attorney and ended with his resignation from the position on December 5, 2011. A background of the alleged misconduct is summarized herein.

Count I—Complaint Regarding Conduct in the Blake Case

J. Ronald Blake, Jr., and his wife—Judy Mae Blake—were the co-directors of the Community Response Foundation (CRF), a non-profit organization specializing in representative payee services for Social Security recipients. Mr. Blake died; and Mrs. Blake continued as CRF's director. A warrant was issued on December 4, 2009, for the arrest of Mrs. Blake for embezzlement. Subsequently, on December 7, 2009, a warrant was issued for all records and computers pertaining to the Blakes and the CRF.

A hearing was held before the Honorable Judge Jaymie Wilfong on April 7, 2010. It concerned a request from Appalachian Benefits Assistance, Inc.—the court-appointed conservator for the CRF. The conservator wanted an archival copy of the seized computers' records. Judge Wilfong granted the request. She wrote: "The computers must be turned over … to the State Police Crime Lab; and a complete archival record for each computer must be made and forwarded to Appalachian Benefits on an *expedited* basis." During a status conference, the contention was made: Mr. Busch—the county prosecutor—failed to comply with the directive in the April 8, 2010, order. In response, Mr. Busch made the following statement to the circuit court:

> [Sergeant Casto of the West Virginia State Police in Morgantown] is duplicating the hard drive. [He also is] while keeping it in the chain of custody so we can get that hard drive out and get it to Mr. Jory [counsel for Mrs. Blake] and to the benefit services group—the Appalachian Benefits. [It] has taken over the accounts.

Additionally, Mr. Busch proffered: "So, at this point, I tried to contact Sergeant Casto yesterday; and, I'm awaiting his response with regards to the status of if he's copied the hard drive or not. Essentially, that's where we are, Your Honor."

On July 22, 2010, a staff person in Prosecutor Busch's office asked about the location of the computers. The individual was advised that the computer equipment remained in the evidence—locker at the Randolph County Sheriff's Office. Additional communication occurred between Mr. Busch's staff and Sergeant Casto via e-mail messages on July 21 and July 22, 2010, concerning the computer hard drives and the duplication of the same. … Despite his awareness that the evidence remained in Randolph County and that his prior statements to the court regarding Sergeant Casto had been false, Prosecutor Busch took no remedial action to correct his prior misstatements to the court. Instead, memorialized the same in a draft order.

The following day, in response to receiving the proposed order from Mr. Busch, Defense Attorney Jory requested modifications. Specifically, Mr. Jory stated: "Not being computer literate, I interpret 'duplicate the hard drive' to mean that another hard drive should be produced. Nevertheless, it is the documents on the hard drive which Appalachian Benefits and I seek to obtain." Later, on July 30, 2010, Mr. Busch directed that the computer equipment be transported to the State Police Forensics Lab in Morgantown, West Virginia. By correspondence dated August 3, 2010, Mr. Busch advised the circuit court:

> The State's investigation may or may not include the said hard drives that are being provided to Appalachian Benefits Services. Therefore, the State is of the opinion: The Defendant is not entitled to copies of said hard drives at this time. Please advise how the Court wishes the State to proceed, through correspondence or by order.

By order entered August 24, 2010, the lower court ordered: "All documents in the seized hard drives must be printed; and copies must be duplicated and given to Appalachian Benefits Assistance, Inc., and the Defendant—on or before August 9, 2010."... By letter dated September 28, 2010, Defense Attorney Jory reminded Prosecutor Busch:

> Lest you forget, I am entitled to a copy of the hard drives. A court order exists stating that they shall be delivered to me. If you believe the order to be erroneous, you have an obligation to have it changed. Otherwise, you could find yourself in contempt of a court order. The ultimate issue is not, as you suggest, one of relevance.

* * *

The Grand Jury of Randolph County issued an eleven count indictment against Mrs. Blake. She was arraigned and a trial was set. Mr. Jory filed a motion to dismiss the case, citing Mr. Busch's prosecutorial misconduct, the prosecutor's failure to comply with the court's orders, and Mr. Busch's lies.

The circuit court found that Prosecutor Busch "deliberately refused to turn over documents as required;" made false statements to the circuit court hearing; attempted to shift the blame to others who were not responsible; failed to correct the false statements made to the court, hearing even after the court gave him an opportunity to correct the same by the issuance of a letter on October 12, 2010; and despite Mr. Busch's assertions to Mr. Jory, that the computer records were not germane, Prosecutor Busch subsequently acknowledged that he had never reviewed the records.

Count II—Complaint Regarding Conduct in the Faulkner Case

Autumn Ray Faulkner was indicted by the Randolph County Grand Jury on three counts of sexual abuse by a parent, guardian, custodian, or person in position of trust, and three counts of sexual abuse in the third degree. Ms. Faulkner's counsel of record—Attorney Mazzei—filed a "MOTION TO DISMISS INDICTMENT OR IN THE ALTERNATIVE TO SUPPRESS EVIDENCE ON ADDITIONAL GROUNDS." In relevant part, Attorney Mazzei claimed: The Prosecuting Attorney's Office refused to provide a video of the minor-child victim. The circuit court questioned Mr. Busch about this issue. And the prosecutor stated: He had never been in possession of the video. He had been in contact with the West Virginia State Trooper assigned to the case on multiple occasions. He believed that the West Virginia State Trooper had lost the evidence.

Judge Wilfong conducted a judicial review hearing. The state trooper testified: The video had never been "lost." A copy of the same was in his investigative file. Prosecutor Busch never contacted him about the video. Mr. Busch denied that he had blamed the trooper for losing the video. ... Attorney Mazzei reiterated his position: Based on Mr. Busch's course of misconduct, Ms. Faulkner's case should be dismissed with prejudice.

* * *

Judge Wilfong reported to ODC—allegations of misconduct by Mr. Busch. ... The ODC sent Mr. Busch a letter, directing him to file a response. He filed a verified response. And he resigned his position as Prosecuting Attorney of Randolph County on December 5, 2011. Mr. Busch avers that he has not practiced law since that date.

Statement of Charges

The Statement of Charges contains two separate counts: *Count I* involves Mr. Busch's actions in the *Blake* criminal case; and *Count II* relates to Mr. Busch's behavior in the Faulkner criminal case. In the *Blake* matter, Attorney Busch was charged with violating the following West Virginia Rules of Professional Conduct: Rule 3.1;

Rule 3.3; Rule 3.4; Rule 3.8; and Rules 8.4(c) and (d). It was alleged, in the *Faulkner* case, that Mr. Busch breached the same Rules of Professional Conduct as he had violated in the *Blake* case.

Taking into account both *mitigating* and *aggravating* factors, the Subcommittee recommended that Mr. Busch's law license be suspended for three years. Additionally, it recommended: Prior to petitioning for reinstatement, Mr. Busch should be evaluated by a licensed mental health provider. Prior to petitioning for reinstatement, Mr. Busch must complete an additional twelve hours of continuing legal education with a focus on ethics. Thus, this matter comes before this Court for review.

Discussion

We review this case with the recognition that the ODC is required "to prove the allegations of the formal charge by clear and convincing evidence." *Lawyer Disciplinary Bd. v. McGraw,* 461 S.E.2d 850 (W.Va.1995). The record before us fully supports the Subcommittee's determination and conclusion that Mr. Busch violated Rules 3.3, 3.4, 3.8 as well as Rules 8.4(c) and (d). ... The evidence illustrates: Mr. Busch's actions in the *Blake* and *Faulkner* cases also violated Rule 3.4 of the Rules of Professional Conduct. In *Blake*, Mr. Busch ignored requests made by Mr. Jory— Mrs. Blake's attorney—for the information contained on the computer hard drives. Significantly, Mr. Busch knowingly disobeyed the circuit court's order, requiring Mr. Busch to provide hard drive copies to Mr. Jory. Moreover, in the *Faulkner* case, Mr. Busch's misconduct unlawfully obstructed Ms. Faulkner's attorney's access to the recording of the alleged victim's statements. Therefore, the Subcommittee's findings that Mr. Busch violated Rules 3.4(a) and (c) in both cases will not be disturbed.

Next, the Subcommittee determined: Mr. Busch violated Rule 3.8 in both cases. Mr. Busch—as the elected Prosecuting Attorney—had a duty to make timely disclosures that "tend to negate" the guilt of the accused or mitigate the offense. In the *Blake* case, Mr. Busch was aware that the computer hard drives could possess exculpatory evidence. And he was under a court-ordered obligation to tender the same to defense counsel. Also, in the *Faulkner* case, Mr. Busch failed to provide a prior recorded statement of the alleged victim—despite his obligation to do so. Mr. Busch's refusal to comply with the court orders in the above-listed cases, as well as his failure to comply with these special duties as a prosecuting attorney[,] are violations of Rule 3.8.

Our analysis of the appropriate sanctions includes the well-settled principles that Rule 3.16 of the West Virginia Rules of Lawyer Disciplinary Procedure enumerates factors to be considered in imposing sanctions and provides as follows: (1) whether the lawyer has violated a duty owed to a client, to the public, to the legal system, or to the profession; (2) whether the lawyer acted intentionally, knowingly, or negligently; (3) the amount of the actual or potential injury caused by the lawyer's misconduct; and (4) the existence of any aggravating or mitigating factors." *Office of Lawyer Disciplinary Counsel v. Jordan,* 513 S.E.2d 722 (W.Va.1998). …

Amount of Real or Potential Injury

Mr. Busch was the chief law enforcement officer of Randolph County. And he repeatedly lied to the circuit court judge about the actions of law enforcement officers in the community. This pattern of misconduct not only caused actual harm to the legal system by undermining the community's perception of the justice system, but also endangered the jobs, pension plans, and credibility of the law enforcement officers who were portrayed as irresponsible by Mr. Busch. Further, Mr. Busch's misconduct could have affected the freedom of the defendants—especially when possibly exonerating evidence was not provided to them. As a matter of public harm, the dismissal of criminal cases merely because of prosecutorial misconduct is a waste of public funds, as well as a detractor from the public confidence in the office of the prosecutor. The amount of real or potential harm in this case was significant.

Presence of Mitigating and Aggravating Factors

The fourth and final factor in our analysis is the presence of mitigating and aggravating factors. "Mitigating factors in a lawyer disciplinary proceeding are any considerations or factors that may justify a reduction in the degree of discipline to be imposed." *Lawyer Disciplinary Bd. v. Scott,* 579 S.E.2d 550 (W.Va. 2003). Mitigating factors include: (1) absence of a prior disciplinary record; (2) absence of a dishonest or selfish motive; (3) personal or emotional problems; (4) timely good faith effort to make restitution or to rectify consequences of misconduct; (5) full and free disclosure to disciplinary board or cooperative attitude toward proceedings; (6) inexperience in the practice of law; (7) character or reputation; (8) physical or mental disability or impairment; (9) delay in disciplinary proceedings; (10) interim rehabilitation; (11) imposition of other penalties or sanctions; (12) remorse; and (13) remoteness of prior offenses. 579 S.E.2d 550.

Based on the evidence before the Subcommittee, the following mitigating factors were recognized: (1) upon the advice of counsel and prior to the commencement of impeachment proceedings, Mr. Busch voluntarily resigned his position as prosecuting attorney; (2) there was no prior disciplinary record; and (3) by and through counsel, Mr. Busch displayed a cooperative attitude toward the disciplinary proceeding. Mr. Busch argues that additional mitigating factors existed:

a) his lack of any prior service as prosecuting attorney and experience in handling criminal cases generally;

b) his attempt to ask the circuit court for guidance in both cases;

c) the absence of any dishonest or selfish motive;

d) the personal and emotional problems created for him as a result of his father's long-term illness and the loss of his father as a mentor and resource person;

e) his general anxiety disorder for which he has been treated for a number of years;

f) his general good character; and

g) the delay of over one year in these lawyer disciplinary proceedings from his final evidentiary hearing on July 27, 2012, until the issuance of the Subcommittee's report in August 2013.

"Aggravating factors in a lawyer disciplinary proceeding are any considerations or factors that may justify an increase in the degree of discipline to be imposed." *Scott, id.* The Subcommittee found the following aggravating factors in this case: (1) pattern of misconduct; (2) multiple offenses; (3) refusal to acknowledge wrongful nature of the conduct; (4) experience in the practice of law; (5) no additional penalty imposed upon Mr. Busch by the Judge in either the *Blake* or *Faulkner* cases for his misconduct; (6) lack of any interim rehabilitation in the execution of his duties as the prosecuting attorney after the *Blake* case; and (7) the fact that Mr. Busch was the elected prosecuting attorney, in a position of public trust, at the time of the misconduct.

Conclusion

Balancing the mitigating and aggravating factors in the instant case, we are convinced: The Subcommittee's recommendations—including a three-year license suspension—are appropriate. Mr. Busch ... engaged in egregious conduct as a public official. We find that Mr. Busch's pattern of misconduct, coupled with his habit of continuing his dishonest behavior even when provided opportunities to remedy the same, was a detriment to the public office, to the State of West Virginia as his client, to the public who deserved efficiency and protection from the public office, to the legal system, and to the legal profession. For those reasons, we adopt the recommendations as set forth by the Subcommittee.

Excerpt from the American Bar Association's Model Rules of Professional Conduct

Rule 3.8—Special Responsibilities of a Prosecutor

The prosecutor in a criminal case shall:

(a) refrain from prosecuting a charge that the prosecutor knows is not supported by probable cause;

* * *

(d) make timely disclosure to the defense of all evidence or information known to the prosecutor that tends to negate the guilt of the accused or mitigates the offense, and, in connection with sentencing, disclose to the defense and to the tribunal all unprivileged mitigating information known to the prosecutor, except when the prosecutor is relieved of this responsibility by a protective order of the tribunal;

(e) not subpoena a lawyer in a grand jury or other criminal proceeding to present evidence about a past or present client unless the prosecutor reasonably believes:

(1) the information sought is not protected from disclosure by any applicable privilege;

(2) the evidence sought is essential to the successful completion of an ongoing investigation or prosecution; and

(3) there is no other feasible alternative to obtain the information;

* * *

(g) When a prosecutor knows of new, credible and material evidence creating a reasonable likelihood that a convicted defendant did not commit an offense of which the defendant was convicted, the prosecutor shall:

(1) promptly disclose that evidence to an appropriate court or authority, and

(2) if the conviction was obtained in the prosecutor's jurisdiction,

(i) promptly disclose that evidence to the defendant unless a court authorizes delay, and

(ii) undertake further investigation, or make reasonable efforts to cause an investigation, to determine whether the defendant was convicted of an offense that the defendant did not commit.

(h) When a prosecutor knows of clear and convincing evidence establishing that a defendant in the prosecutor's jurisdiction was convicted of an offense that the defendant did not commit, the prosecutor shall seek to remedy the conviction.

[n]

---

[n] ***FULL TEXT: ADVOCATE***

RULE 3.8 SPECIAL RESPONSIBILITIES OF A PROSECUTOR

The prosecutor in a criminal case shall:

(a) refrain from prosecuting a charge that the prosecutor knows is not supported by probable cause;

(b) make reasonable efforts to assure that the accused has been advised of the right to, and the procedure for obtaining, counsel and has been given reasonable opportunity to obtain counsel;

(c) not seek to obtain from an unrepresented accused a waiver of important pretrial rights, such as the right to a preliminary hearing;

(d) make timely disclosure to the defense of all evidence or information known to the prosecutor that tends to negate the guilt of the accused or mitigates the offense, and, in connection with sentencing, disclose to the defense and to the tribunal all unprivileged

F. Disciplinary Actions Against Solo and Small-Firm Attorneys for Posting False and Misleading Social-Media, Website, and Internet-Blog's Advertisements

1. Actions Against Unlicensed and Suspended Attorneys for Advertising Legal Services on Law Firm's Websites

---

mitigating information known to the prosecutor, except when the prosecutor is relieved of this responsibility by a protective order of the tribunal;

(e) not subpoena a lawyer in a grand jury or other criminal proceeding to present evidence about a past or present client unless the prosecutor reasonably believes:

(1) the information sought is not protected from disclosure by any applicable privilege;

(2) the evidence sought is essential to the successful completion of an ongoing investigation or prosecution; and

(3) there is no other feasible alternative to obtain the information;

(f) except for statements that are necessary to inform the public of the nature and extent of the prosecutor's action and that serve a legitimate law enforcement purpose, refrain from making extrajudicial comments that have a substantial likelihood of heightening public condemnation of the accused and exercise reasonable care to prevent investigators, law enforcement personnel, employees or other persons assisting or associated with the prosecutor in a criminal case from making an extrajudicial statement that the prosecutor would be prohibited from making under Rule 3.6 or this Rule.

(g) When a prosecutor knows of new, credible and material evidence creating a reasonable likelihood that a convicted defendant did not commit an offense of which the defendant was convicted, the prosecutor shall:

(1) promptly disclose that evidence to an appropriate court or authority, and

(2) if the conviction was obtained in the prosecutor's jurisdiction,

(i) promptly disclose that evidence to the defendant unless a court authorizes delay, and

(ii) undertake further investigation, or make reasonable efforts to cause an investigation, to determine whether the defendant was convicted of an offense that the defendant did not commit.

(h) When a prosecutor knows of clear and convincing evidence establishing that a defendant in the prosecutor's jurisdiction was convicted of an offense that the defendant did not commit, the prosecutor shall seek to remedy the conviction.

Kentucky Bar Association v. Gee

363 S.W.3d 343
(Ky. 2012)

Opinion and Order.

The Kentucky Bar Association (KBA) recommends disciplinary action against Rebecca C. Gee—a/k/a Rebecca C. Meyer. She was admitted to the practice of law in the Commonwealth of Kentucky on October 11, 2002. Attorney Gee's bar roster address is located in Mount Orab, Ohio. This court suspended Ms. Gee from the practice of law in Kentucky on January 15, 2009 —for non-payment of bar dues for the year 2008–2009, and for non-compliance with continuing legal education requirements for 2007–2008. Ms. Gee has not been reinstated.

Ms. Gee is also a member of the Ohio Bar and is associated with the law firm of Megalaner 85 Associates, LTD in Cincinnati, Ohio. The law firm's website continued to represent: Ms. Gee was a member of the KBA even though she had been suspended from the practice of law on January 15, 2009.

On September 28, 2009, Ms. Gee provided legal representation to Richard Young. Mr. Young was a Kentucky resident involved in an automobile accident in Covington, Kentucky. In the course of this representation, Ms. Gee sent a letter on firm stationery to an insurance company that insured a vehicle involved in the accident. In the letter, she stated that she was asserting a claim for Mr. Young to the insurance company. On May 11, 2010, Ms. Gee was served a letter from the Office of Bar Counsel—informing her that she had engaged in the unauthorized practice of law and requesting a response. Ms. Gee did not file a response.

On July 9, 2010, the Executive Director of the KBA sent a letter via certified mail to Ms. Gee. But Ms. Gee again did not respond. On November 4, 2010, the Inquiry Commission issued a Complaint which was served on Ms. Gee by certified mail on November 6, 2010. Ms. Gee failed to respond to the Complaint. She was then sent a reminder letter and a second copy of the Complaint by certified mail which she signed for on December 1, 2010. However, she did not respond to the reminder letter or the Complaint.

On September 9, 2011, the Inquiry Commission of the KBA charged Ms. Gee with four violations of the Kentucky Rules of Professional Conduct. *Count I* charged her with a violation of Supreme Court Rules— SCR 3.130–3.4(c). Attorney Gee disobeyed the order of the

Kentucky Supreme Court—after suspending her from the practice of law in Kentucky. *Count II* charged her for violating SCR 3.130–5.5(a)—engaging in the unauthorized practice of law. She sent a letter—while her Kentucky license was suspended—to an insurance company. That letter presented a claim for a Kentucky resident for an accident occurring in Kentucky. *Count III* charged her for violating SCR 3.130–5.5(b)(2). Using her law firm's website and while her Kentucky license was suspended, Ms. Gee held herself out as a lawyer—who was admitted to practice law in Kentucky. *Count IV* charged: Ms. Gee violated SCR 3.130–8.1(b)—failing to respond to the Inquiry Commission Complaint through the Office of Bar Counsel and the Disciplinary Clerk.

Due to Ms. Gee's repeated failures to respond, the Board of Governors (Board) decided to treat this as a default case pursuant to SCR 3.210. The Board considered this matter on November 17, 2011. The Board unanimously found Ms. Gee guilty of all four counts and recommended: The suspension of her license to practice of law for sixty-one (61) days—consecutive to any other suspensions currently imposed.

Accordingly, it is hereby ordered that: (1) Rebecca C. Gee, a/k/a Rebecca C. Meyer is hereby found guilty of violating SCR 3.130–3.4(c); SCR 3.130–5.5(a); SCR 3.130–5.5(b)(2); and SCR 3.130–8.1(b). Further, Ms. Gee is ordered to immediately cease and desist listing or identifying herself, in any manner, as a Kentucky attorney.

Excerpt from American Bar Association's Model Rules of Professional Conduct

Rule 7.2—Advertising

(a) Subject to the requirements of RULES 7.1 and 7.3, a lawyer may advertise services through written, recorded or electronic communication, including public media.

(b) A lawyer shall not give anything of value to a person for recommending the lawyer's services *except* that a lawyer may

(1) pay the reasonable costs of advertisements or communications permitted by this Rule;

(2) pay the usual charges of a legal service plan or a not-for-profit or qualified lawyer referral service. A qualified lawyer referral service is a lawyer referral service that has been approved by an appropriate regulatory authority;

(3) pay for a law practice in accordance with Rule 1.17; and

(4) refer clients to another lawyer or a nonlawyer professional pursuant to an agreement not otherwise prohibited under these Rules that provides for the other person to refer clients or customers to the lawyer, if

(i) the reciprocal referral agreement is not exclusive, and

(ii) the client is informed of the existence and nature of the agreement.

(c) Any communication made pursuant to this rule shall include the name and office address of at least one lawyer or law firm responsible for its content.

---

2. Actions Against Attorneys for Posting Misleading Advertisements on the Internet

In re Zachary Steven Naert

777 S.E.2d 823
(S.C. 2015)

Per Curiam.

Attorneys Zachary Naert and Joseph DuBois are partners in Naert & DuBois, LLC—a law firm handling a variety of legal matters, including timeshare litigation. In 2013, Attorney Naert created a website for the firm—when the law firm opened in 2013. The website address did not contain the name of the law firm or any part of the names of the partners. In March 2013, Attorney Naert created a Google AdWords account—as part of the law firm's Internet marketing campaign.

Google AdWords is an Internet marketing technique in which the advertiser places bids for "keywords." When an individual uses Google to search keywords with match or approximates an advertiser's keywords, the search results may or may not include the advertiser's ad among other retrieved—nonadvertising or unpaid—websites. The advertiser pays Google, if the Internet user clicks on the advertiser's ad from amongst the search results.

When Naert & DuBois, LLC used Google AdWords, an advertiser's ad appeared under the heading "Ad related to [keyword or keywords]." At that time, ads for Google AdWords could appear amongst the search results with no visible designation or delineation of an area on the webpage specifically designated for advertisement.

Naert & DuBois, LLC, has filed a number of lawsuits on behalf of clients against a timeshare company (the Company). The Company and other individuals related to the Company are represented in various capacities by Attorney A, Attorney B, and Attorney C. The Law Firm of Naert & DuBois bids on the names of Attorney A, Attorney B, and Attorney C—as well as the name of the Company in its list of keywords for the firm's Google AdWords campaign. The firm's advertisement appeared in some Internet search results—in which Internet users entered one or more of the Attorneys' names in a Google search.

The firm's advertisement read as follows: *Timeshare Attorney in SC—Ripped off? Lied to? Scammed? Hilton Head Island, SC. Free Consult.* Sometimes the Attorneys' names appeared as the first result in the list of search results. And, at other times, the Attorneys' names appeared later in the list of search results. Naert & DuBois, LLC, paid for its advertisement each time an Internet searcher clicked on the firm's advertisement. Naert & Dubois terminated bidding on the use of the Attorneys' names prior to notice of the disciplinary investigation.

Attorney Naert admits: He is the attorney responsible for the Google AdWords campaign. He further admits the firm's advertisement did not contain *his name, Mr. DuBois' name, or the name of any other lawyer responsible for the advertisement's content.* Attorney Naert agrees: Using opposing counsels' names as keywords in an Internet marketing campaign—in a derogatory manner—violates provisions of the Lawyer's Oath.

Law

In this attorney disciplinary matter, Mr. Naert and the Office of Disciplinary Counsel (ODC) have entered into an Agreement for Discipline by Consent. Attorney Naert admits: He has violated the following provision of the Rules of Professional Conduct (RPC), Rule 407, South Carolina Appellate Court Rules (SCACR), and Rule 7.2(d)—any communication made pursuant to RPC Rule 7 shall include the name and office address of at least one lawyer responsible for its content. Attorney Naert further admits: He violated provisions of the Lawyer's Oath contained in SCACR Rule 402(k)—by taking the Lawyer's Oath, a lawyer pledges to opposing parties and their counsel fairness, integrity, and civility in all written communications and to employ only such means consistent with trust, honor, and principles of professionalism.

Attorney Naert also admits: He violated the following Rules for Lawyer Disciplinary Enforcement, Rule 413, SCACR: Rule 7(a)(1)—It shall be ground[s] for discipline for [a] lawyer to violate Rules of Professional Conduct; and Rule 7(a)(6)—It shall be ground[s] for discipline for lawyer to violate oath of office taken to practice law in this state and contained in Rule 402(k), SCACR.

Conclusion

We find that Attorney Naert's misconduct warrants a public reprimand. Within one (1) year of the date of this opinion, Mr. Naert shall attend and complete the Legal Ethics and Practice Program Ethics School and Advertising School and, no later than ten (10) days after the completion of the programs, submit proof of completion to the Commission. Public reprimand.

Excerpt from the American Bar Association's Model Rules of Professional Conduct

Rule 7.3—Solicitation of Clients

(a) A lawyer shall not by in-person, live telephone or real-time electronic contact solicit professional employment when a significant motive for the lawyer's doing so is the lawyer's pecuniary gain, unless the person contacted:

(1) is a lawyer; or

(2) has a family, close personal, or prior professional relationship with the lawyer.

(b) A lawyer shall not solicit professional employment by written, recorded or electronic communication or by in-person, telephone or real-time electronic contact even when not otherwise prohibited by paragraph (a), if:

(1) the target of the solicitation has made known to the lawyer a desire not to be solicited by the lawyer; or

(2) the solicitation involves coercion, duress or harassment.

(c) Every written, recorded or electronic communication from a lawyer soliciting professional employment from anyone known to be in need of legal services in a particular matter shall include the words "Advertising Material" on the outside envelope, if any, and at the beginning and ending of any recorded or electronic communication, unless the recipient of the communication is a person specified in paragraphs (a)(1) or (a)(2).

(d) Notwithstanding the prohibitions in paragraph (a), a lawyer may participate with a prepaid or group legal service plan operated by an organization not owned or directed by the lawyer that uses in-person or telephone contact to solicit memberships or subscriptions for the plan from persons who are not known to need legal services in a particular matter covered by the plan.

3. Actions Against Attorneys for Misrepresenting their Levels of Competency and Specialization in Internet Advertisements

In re Richmond's Case

872 A.2d 1023
(N.H. 2005)

Duggan, J.

William M. Richmond was admitted to the practice of law in New Hampshire in May 1996. This professional conduct matter arose from Richmond's representation and his involvement with the formation of an Internet start-up company—Environmental Showcase, Limited (ESL). In April 1999, Richmond represented Seaton Gras and Graham Bunce—a co-venturer in GES—in an involuntary bankruptcy action against GES. … While representing Gras and Bunce on their bankruptcy claim, Richmond also represented Bunce in a lawsuit brought against him by Stephen Barnes, another GES co-venturer, on an unpaid promissory note.

During the same period of time in 1999, Gras and Richmond formed ESL based upon an idea that Gras developed to provide a web portal to the environmental industry. Gras was the majority shareholder and chief executive officer of ESL, while Richmond was a member of the board of directors and the Chief Operating Officer (COO). Acting as COO and corporate counsel, Richmond filed ESL's articles of incorporation, drafted corporate by-laws and advised ESL on securities matters. Over the course of his involvement with ESL, Richmond never disclosed the potential conflict of interest stemming from his roles as COO, corporate counsel, board member and shareholder. Richmond failed to obtain the board members' written consent to serve as corporate counsel and did not advise the board to seek the advice of independent counsel regarding the potential conflicts.

In August 1999, on ESL's behalf, Richmond filed a form U-7 disclosure document with the New Hampshire Bureau of Securities Regulation (Bureau)—in order to conduct a sale of up to one million dollars of common stock. The website for Richmond's law firm suggested: He had experience in helping small businesses file direct public offerings, although Richmond had only drafted offerings that had never been filed. The Bureau completed an initial review of the form U-7 and commented on at least eighty-four items that required correction or additional disclosure. After further discussions with the Bureau, Richmond later withdrew the form U-7 on ESL's behalf. The Bureau conducted an investigation that resulted in a consent order in which Richmond, Gras and ESL admitted violating state securities laws by selling unregistered securities and selling securities without a license. ESL agreed to pay a $7,500 administrative fine and Richmond and Gras were ordered to cease and desist from further violations of the securities laws.

On March 6, 2003, the Supreme Court Committee on Professional Conduct (committee) filed a petition with this court requesting that William M. Richmond receive a six-month suspension from the practice of law. We referred the petition to a Judicial Referee for a hearing. The referee found that Richmond violated Rules of Professional Conduct 1.7(a) and (b)—by representing Gras and Bunce without adequately identifying the conflicts of interest and obtaining both clients' consent to the representation despite the conflicts.

The referee also found that Richmond violated Rules 1.7(a) and (b), 1.8(a) and 8.4(a)— by forming and operating ESL while serving as corporate counsel without disclosing the potential conflict of interest and obtaining a written waiver. Finally, the referee found that Richmond violated Rules 1.1(a) and (b), 7.1(a) and 8.4(a)— by issuing unregistered securities, inadequately preparing the form U-7 and misrepresenting his firm's legal services. The referee recommended that Richmond receive a six-month suspension from the practice of law and assessment of all expenses incurred by the committee.

* * *

Richmond argues that the referee erred by finding that the content of his firm's website violated Rule 7.1. Rule 7.1 prohibits a lawyer from making a "false or misleading communication about the lawyer or the lawyer's services." A communication is false or misleading if it "contains a material misrepresentation of fact or law." The referee found that Richmond's website advertised his expertise in financing and raising capital—even though "he did not have any special training or experience in securities law." Richmond testified: He had previously drafted, but never filed, a registration statement for the issuance of stock with the Bureau. Thus, the record supports the referee's finding that Richmond presented a material misrepresentation of fact in violation of Rule 7.1.

* * *

Having found that Richmond violated the Rules of Professional Conduct, we next consider the appropriate sanction. We first examine the recommended sanction for lack of competence. The referee found, and we agree: Richmond lacked the skill and knowledge needed to practice securities law. Richmond's numerous errors in conducting ESL's stock offerings and filing the form U-7 demonstrate his lack of knowledge about securities law practice. Furthermore, Richmond violated Rule 7.1 by misrepresenting the extent of his experience in this practice area on his firm's website. Throughout these proceedings, Richmond has maintained: He made reasonable efforts to educate himself about the regulatory process prior to filing the form U-7. The record, however, provides clear and convincing evidence that Richmond's lack of competence harmed ESL, resulting in withdrawal of the form U-7 and an administrative fine for violations of State securities laws.

* * *

Richmond is hereby suspended from the practice of law for six months. We remand to the referee to determine the costs associated with this case. Richmond shall have the right to resume the practice of law after the expiration of the suspension period upon compliance with all the terms and conditions of this order. *So ordered.*

Excerpt from the American Bar Association's Model Rules of Professional Conduct

Rule 7.4—Communicating Practice Areas and Specialization

(a) A lawyer may communicate the fact that the lawyer does or does not practice in particular fields of law.

(b) A lawyer admitted to engage in patent practice before the United States Patent and Trademark Office may use the designation "Patent Attorney" or a substantially similar designation.

(c) A lawyer engaged in Admiralty practice may use the designation "Admiralty," "Proctor in Admiralty" or a substantially similar designation.

(d) A lawyer shall not state or imply that a lawyer is certified as a specialist in a particular field of law, unless:

  (1) the lawyer has been certified as a specialist by an organization that has been approved by an appropriate state authority or that has been accredited by the American Bar Association; and

(2) the name of the certifying organization is clearly identified in the communication.

Excerpt from the American Bar Association's Model Rules of Professional Conduct

Rule 7.5—Firm Names and Letterhead

(a) A lawyer shall not use a firm name, letterhead or other professional designation that violates Rule 7.1. A trade name may be used by a lawyer in private practice if it does not imply a connection with a government agency or with a public or charitable legal services organization and is not otherwise in violation of Rule 7.1.

(b) A law firm with offices in more than one jurisdiction may use the same name or other professional designation in each jurisdiction. But identification of the lawyers in an office of the firm shall indicate the jurisdictional limitations on those not licensed to practice in the jurisdiction where the office is located.

(c) The name of a lawyer holding a public office shall not be used in the name of a law firm, or in communications on its behalf, during any substantial period in which the lawyer is not actively and regularly practicing with the firm.

(d) Lawyers may state or imply that they practice in a partnership or other organization only when that is the fact.

CHAPTER SIX: Attorneys' Constitutional and Civil Rights Actions Against State Disciplinary Boards for Restricting Attorneys' Internet, Website, E-mail, and Social-Media Communications and Advertisements

Regulating the Speech of Judges and Lawyers: The First Amendment and the Soul of the Profession

66 Fla. L. Rev. 961

Rodney A. Smolla

The speech of judges and lawyers operating within the legal profession is circumscribed to protect palpable functional interests, such as avoiding actual interference with the administration of justice, preserving the lawyer's obligations to maintain client confidences, or preventing misleading lawyer advertising or marketing. Where speech is limited for these reasons, the case for reduced First Amendment protection for judges and lawyers is theoretically coherent and practically straightforward. Restricting the speech of judges and lawyers in such circumstances fits comfortably within established First Amendment theory and doctrine.

When the basis for restricting speech drifts from such palpably functional rationales and ranges into the more idealistic and mythological values of the profession, the First Amendment justifications for such regulation become much less coherent and far more complicated. Values such as promoting respect for the rule of law, maintaining public confidence in the legal system, maintaining professionalism (a concept different than adherence to hard-law legal ethical rules), and safeguarding the dignity of the profession are aspirational. They are values embraced with great pride by most judges, lawyers, legal educators, and law students.

But to what extent do First Amendment theory and doctrine permit these values to serve as justifications for reducing the free speech protections that judges and lawyers would otherwise enjoy as private citizens?...

Self-Promotion by Marketing Lawyers

Self-promotion by lawyers engaged in advertising and marketing has caused the American legal profession no end of conflict since lawyer advertising was first declared constitutionally protected, at least to some degree, in *Bates v. State Bar of Arizona,* 433 U.S. 350 (1977). In *Bates*, the Court applied the special intermediate-scrutiny [commercial-speech standard to regulate] lawyers' advertising. ... [T]he government may regulate commercial speech when four conditions are met: (1) the communication is neither misleading nor related to unlawful activity; (2) the government asserts a substantial interest to be achieved by the regulation; (3) the restriction directly and materially advances the state interest; and (4) the regulation is no more expansive than necessary to advance the substantial governmental interest. ...

Advertising in the general marketplace is all about being self-promoting and self-laudatory, often with a healthy dose of hyperbole and puffery. Most states, however, prohibit forms of self-promotion and comparison to one's competitors in the legal profession. ... A number of prominent commercial speech decisions [provide less protection for lawyers' advertising and more protection for other advertisers] in the marketplace. ... A Virginia case—in which I was personally involved as an advocate—vividly demonstrates the tension between the First Amendment principles applicable in the general marketplace and the principles applied to the self-promoting speech of lawyers.

In *Hunter v. Virginia State Bar,* 744 S.E.2d 611 (Va. 2013), the Virginia Supreme Court [considered the Virginia State Bar's complaint] against Virginia attorney Horace Hunter. [The attorney] wrote a blog, entitled *This Week in Richmond Criminal Defense.* The blog was accessible to the general public both through a link on a website maintained by *Hunter & Lipton, P.C.* [and one could access Hunter's blog], without going to the law firm's website. Hunter's blog contained ... legal affairs [information] and judicial decisions. Some of the blog posts contained Hunter's commentary on national legal events—such as the controversy surrounding former Attorney General Alberto Gonzales and United States Attorneys' Offices. ... The Bar took the position: Hunter's blogs constituted advertising and was misleading. Hunter maintained:

His blogs were political speech and were entirely accurate descriptions of what transpired in public judicial proceedings—sprinkled with his own commentary and views.

Hunter also admitted: One of his motivations was self-promotion. And he conceded: The blog was a way of projecting a professional identity as a criminal defense lawyer—noting that "people want to know that you're more than just trying to sell services. They want to know who you are and what you stand for." Yet, Hunter insisted: He did not regard the blogs as "advertising" or as "soliciting business" in the normal sense of the term. To the contrary, his purpose was also political and ideological. …In Mr. Hunter's words:

> [I]t's intended to combat in large part the public perceptions that … people are *guilty until they're proven innocent*. There are shows out there like Nancy Grace and other things that you see … all the time—particularly on the Internet. Soon as somebody's arrested, okay, they're automatically guilty. And one of the things we do is try to combat that public perception. Even when we're talking about cases that I've dealt with personally, generally there's a comment at the end of the article that says something to the effect: [T]his case again demonstrates that just because somebody is charged doesn't mean they're guilty. Or what this case represents is the fact that this should have never been a crime in the first place. …

Hunter lost in the Supreme Court of Virginia—by a 5-2 vote. While the content of Hunter's speech may have been entirely political, his motivation was at least partly self-promoting and commercial. And this was enough to convince the Virginia court: His speech was misleading advertising, unless proper disclaimers were affixed to it.

Justice Donald Lemons—joined by Justice Elizabeth McClanahan—dissented. The dissent resisted the majority's willingness to draw a distinction between the blogs that described Hunter's own cases, and those that did not, as though the posts involving Hunter's own prior cases were not also laden with political content. Justice Lemons thus observed:

> Hunter's blog contains articles about legal and policy issues in the news, as well as detailed descriptions of criminal trials, the majority of which are cases

> where Hunter was the defense attorney. The articles also contain Hunter's commentary and critique of the criminal justice system. He uses the case descriptions to illustrate his views.

In reasoning that Hunter's discussion of his own prior cases constituted political speech, the dissenters stated: "As political speech, Hunter uses his blog to give detailed descriptions of how criminal trials in Virginia are conducted. He notes how the acquittal of some of his clients has exposed flaws in the criminal justice system." The United States Supreme Court, however, denied review.

A. First Amendment Actions Against Disciplinary Boards for Precluding Attorneys' Using the Internet and Social Media to Post Purportedly Political Speech

Gilsdorf v. Attorney Registration and Disciplinary Commission of Supreme Court of Illinois

2014 WL 3495734
(C.D. Ill. 2014)

Colin S. Bruce, District Judge.

Jerome Larkin is the Administrator for the Disciplinary Commission of the Supreme Court of Illinois (ARDC). On February 6, 2012, Larkin filed a two-count attorney disciplinary complaint against Attorney Jesse R. Gilsdorf. Larkin's specific charges and the underlying facts are discussed extensively in *People v. Fulmer*, 984 N.E.2d 591(Ill. Ct. App. 2013).

Underlying Facts in the Criminal Case—People v. Fulmer

On February 17, 2011, the state charged defendant—Angela D. Fulmer—with the Class 2 felony. Allegedly she knowingly delivered to a confidential source less than 50 grams of a substance containing hydrocodone—a Schedule II controlled substance. On February 28, 2011, Attorney Gilsdorf appeared on defendant's behalf; and, the trial court scheduled a preliminary hearing for March 29, 2011. On March 4, 2011, the state served discovery materials to Gilsdorf—consisting of numerous reports and a copy of a video. The latter allegedly shows Fulmer's delivering the controlled substance.

On March 29, 2011, defendant appeared with Gilsdorf, waived preliminary hearing, and entered a plea of not guilty. On April 12, 2011, the trial court postponed the trial until further notice. On April 20, 2011, the state filed a motion for sanctions for noncompliance with Rule 415(c). It reads:

> CUSTODY OF MATERIALS. Any materials furnished to an attorney pursuant to these rules shall remain in his exclusive custody and be used only for the purposes of conducting his side of the case, and shall be subject to other such terms and conditions as the court may provide. Ill. S.Ct. R. 415(c)

The state's motion alleged that on or about April 11, 2011, the contents of the video appeared for public viewing on YouTube. Additionally, the video was posted on Attorney Gilsdorf's Facebook page—under the heading, "Cops and Task Force Planting Drugs." The state's motion alleged that Gilsdorf was the only person who had custody of the copied video. The trial court conducted a hearing and asked Gilsdorf: How did the video get on YouTube? Gilsdorf responded: "I caused it to be placed there." He also acknowledged that the video was posted on his Facebook page, along with the following statement:

> Hey, one and all, want to see cops and their snitch planting drugs? This is the cop's video showing how their snitch brings drugs into a room, and after the victim leaves, putting [*sic*] the drugs in the middle of the table. Two parts because of space limits. Cops are the West Central Drug Task Force, Zack Orr, as seen in the video. Notice how the paperwork is all ready to be signed, even though they haven't even debriefed their snitch.

The Evidentiary Hearing Before ARDC Hearing Board

At the hearing, Gilsdorf was hardly apologetic for his actions—

claiming that they were necessary because of improper conduct by the State's Attorney and police. He explained: "Simply put, [this] acts as a check on possible abuse by the prosecution." At the conclusion of the hearing, the trial court found that Gilsdorf intentionally posted the discovered material [video] on the Internet—which violated Rule 415(c). As a sanction, the court directed Attorney Gilsdorf to remove the video from the Internet. Gilsdorf indicated that he would comply with the court's directive but would need some time to do so.

* * *

Attorney Walker R. Filbert entered his appearance on behalf of Attorney Gilsdorf and filed a second amended motion to reconsider the sanction order. Attorney Filbert asserted that Rule 415(c) violated the First amendment of the United States Constitution. ... The trial court denied the motions to reconsider. This appeal followed.

II. Analysis

At the evidentiary hearing before an ARDC Hearing Board, Gilsdorf argued: Posting the video was protected speech under the First Amendment to the United States Constitution. At the conclusion of the hearing, the Hearing Board recommended that Gilsdorf's law license be suspended for five months. Gilsdorf appealed the decision to the Review Board. Again, Gilsdorf argued that posting the video was protected speech under the First Amendment. The Review Board concurred in the Hearing Board's recommendation that Gilsdorf's law license be suspended for five months. Thereafter, Gilsdorf filed a petition before the Illinois Supreme Court. The petition argued, among other things: (1) the application by the ARDC of the Illinois Supreme Court rules violated the First Amendment, and (2) Gilsdorf's due process rights were violated when the ARDC brought up uncharged allegations during a hearing.

On March 14, 2014, The Illinois Supreme Court entered a final order denying Gilsdorf's petition. The court also ordered Gilsdorf's law license be suspended for five months, as recommended by both the Hearing Board and Review Board.

III. The Federal Complaint

On December 9, 2013, Gilsdorf filed a Complaint with this court. The complaint contained three counts. Count One alleged that the enforcement of the Illinois Supreme Court Rules by the ARDC violated the constitutional protection of free speech because the rules were not enforced against governmental actors and because the enforcement of the rules was unconstitutional. Count Two alleged that Gilsdorf's due process and fair trial rights were violated when the ARDC attempted to sanction him for matters that were dropped prior to and during the hearing and for matters the ARDC knew to be false. Count Three alleged that by sanctioning Gilsdorf, the ARDC threatens the right to effective assistance of counsel as guaranteed by the Sixth Amendment to the United States Constitution. Based on these violations, Gilsdorf requested injunctive and declaratory relief.

Federal Questions Analyses

ARDC argue: This court lacks subject matter jurisdiction to decide this case. At the onset of every case, this court must determine whether it has subject matter jurisdiction over the claims before it. *See Steel Co. v. Citizens for a Better Env't,* 523 U.S. 83, 94-95 (1998). If this court determines that it does not have jurisdiction over a claim, that claim must be dismissed. *See Johnson v. Merrill Lynch, Pierce, Fenner & Smith, Inc.,* 719 F.3d 601, 607 (7th Cir. 2013).

Here, ARDC argue: Gilsdorf's complaint is simply an attempt to have this court review the decision of the ARDC and the Illinois Supreme Court. Under the *Rooker–Feldman* doctrine, federal district courts lack jurisdiction to review judicial decisions of state courts. *See District of Columbia Court of Appeals v. Feldman,* 460 U.S. 462, 476 (1983); *Rooker v. Fidelitytrust Co.,* 263 U.S. 413, 415 (1923). Importantly, the Seventh Circuit has held that Illinois attorney disciplinary proceeding are judicial in nature. *Levin v. Attorney Registration and Disciplinary Com'n of Supreme Court of Illinois,* 74 F.3d 763, 766 (7th Cir. 1996). Therefore, absent specific authorization by Congress, a litigant cannot obtain collateral review of an ARDC decision in federal district court. *Levin,* 74 F.3d at 766.

A claim can be considered a collateral attack even if it was not argued in the state judicial proceeding. *Feldman,* 460 U.S. at 483–84. In order to determine if a claim is merely seeking collateral review, the court must ascertain whether the claim is "inextricably intertwined" with a state court decision. *Feldman,* 460 U.S. at 483-84 n. 16. The underlying inquiry for determining whether a claim is barred by the *Rooker–Feldman* doctrine is "whether 'the district court is in essence being called upon to review the state-court decision." *Levin,* 74 F.3d at 766.

Here, this court reads all three counts in Gilsdorf's complaint as requesting a review of Illinois' decision to suspend Gilsdorf's law license. Just like in *Levin,* all of Gilsdorf's claimed injuries stem from the application of allegedly unconstitutional Illinois Supreme Court Rules to his disciplinary proceedings. Gilsdorf has failed to allege any injury independent of those claimed in the ARDC hearings and the Illinois Supreme Court's decision to suspend his license.

Further, this court finds: Gilsdorf has simply contested his disciplinary proceedings, instead of offering a general challenge to the Illinois Supreme Court Rules at issue in his suspension. *See Feldman,* 460 U.S. at 486-87. Therefore, this court finds: Gilsdorf's claims are "inextricably intertwined" with the state's decision to suspend his license. As such, Gilsdorf's complaint amounts to an impermissible collateral attack of the Illinois Supreme Court's judgment in federal district court.

Conclusion

Based on the foregoing, this court finds: It does not have jurisdiction over any of the counts found in Gilsdorf's complaint. Therefore, ARDC's motion to dismiss is granted. And Gilsdorf's complaint is dismissed in its entirety. In dismissing the complaint, this court notes that Gilsdorf is not entitled to any injunctive or declaratory relief. It is therefore ordered.

NOTES AND QUESTIONS

1) **The Constitution and Commercial Speech.** In *Virginia State Bd. of Pharmacy v. Virginia Citizens Consumer Council, Inc.*, 425 U.S. 748, 770 (1976), the Court recognized: Commercial speech is protected under the First Amendment. Still, some regulation of commercial speech is "clearly permissible." But a state may not regulate speech to keep the public ignorant of truthful information. *Id.* Commercial speech is thus afforded less First Amendment protection than other constitutionally guaranteed expression. "For commercial speech to come within [the First Amendment's protections], it must concern lawful activity and may not be misleading." *Bd. of Trustees of the State University of N.Y. v. Fox,* 492 U.S. 469, 475 (1989). States may regulate non-misleading or potentially misleading advertising only if they show: (1) a substantial interest, (2) the regulation is narrowly drawn, and (3)

the interference is proportionate to the interest served. *Central Hudson Gas & Electric Corp. v. Public Service Commission,* 447 U.S. 557, 563-64 (1980).

2) The Constitutionality of Attorneys' Advertising Rules. The Supreme Court applied First Amendment protections to attorney advertising in *Bates v. State Bar of Arizona,* 433 U.S. 350(1977). Although stressing that advertising by attorneys' advertisements may be regulated in some ways, the Court stressed: Attorneys' advertising may not be subjected to blanket suppression. 433 U.S. at 383.

B. Federal Civil Rights Actions Against State Boards for Interfering With Attorneys' Commercial Speech—Advertising Types of Specialties and Services on the Internet

Loughlin v. Tweed

310 F.R.D. 323
(E.D. La. 2015)

Martin L.C. Feldman, District Judge.

Louisiana attorney Kearney Loughlin brings this suit against several defendants—Gregory Tweed, a deputy disciplinary counsel to the Office of Disciplinary Counsel (ODC); the Louisiana Attorney Disciplinary Board (LADB); Steven Tew, the Chair of the LADB; and Charles B. Plattsmier, Chief Disciplinary Counsel of the LADB. Loughlin alleged that defendants prosecuted him because he inserted certain information on his professional website. The Louisiana Office of Disciplinary Counsel filed a series of formal charges against Mr. Loughlin.

Gregory Tweed sent a letter sent to Loughlin on October 28, 2011. Tweed explained: Loughlin's website did not appear to comply with Louisiana's Rules of Professional Conduct, which govern attorneys' advertisements. The letter stated: "Our observation of the enclosed referenced web page indicates that your firm 'specializes in maritime personal injury and death cases.' However, no such specialty is recognized in this State. Also, the website states that the firm name is 'Loughlin and Loughlin.' However, it is our understanding: You are a sole practitioner and your wife is employed full time by the U.S. 5th Circuit." In response, Loughlin reported: "The only specialization referred to on the former web site was to my Certificate of Specialty in Maritime Law, which was issued by Tulane Law School." Loughlin believed he was in compliance with Louisiana's advertising rules.

In December of 2011, Tweed sent another letter to Loughlin advising him that the ODC had concluded as follows:

> Based upon our personal observation of the website in question, it appears that you have violated Rule 7.2(c)(5) of the Rules of Professional Conduct. Specifically, there is not now, nor has there ever been, a recognized specialty in the field of "maritime personal injury and death cases" as set forth on the main page of your website. While Tulane offers a degree program in Admiralty, this does not create a recognized specialty with the Louisiana Board of Legal Specialization. Even if this degree program did create a recognized specialty, there are formal requirements that must be adhered to in the advertisement, which were not a part of the webpage viewed by this office.

On February 2, 2012, the Office of Disciplinary Counsel brought formal charges against Loughlin on the advertising complaint. … The hearing was held on February 5, 2013, by a three-member committee of the Louisiana Attorney Disciplinary Board. Loughlin's constitutional claims arise from the proceedings at his disciplinary hearing.

* * *

The hearing committee found: Rules 7.2(c)(1)(B) and 7.2(c)(5) did not apply to websites. Still, Loughlin's using the word "specializing" violated former Rule 7.4. The committee recommended a public reprimand and ordered Loughlin to attend a continuing legal education program regarding lawyers' advertising. … Loughlin appealed the Board's ruling to the Louisiana Supreme Court. The State's high court dismissed all charges against him. The supreme court did not reach the constitutional issues. Loughlin then filed suit in this court under U.S.C. § 1983. He asserted: The attorney advertising rules were unconstitutional. And he sought to enjoin the defendants from enforcing them.

* * *

III. Section 1983 Claims

Title 42, U.S.C. § 1983 creates a damages remedy for the violation of federal constitutional or statutory rights under color of state law; it provides: "Every person who, under color of any statute, ordinance, regulation, custom, or usage, of any State ... subjects, or causes to be subjected, any ... person within the jurisdiction thereof to the deprivation of any rights, privileges, or immunities secured by the Constitution and laws, shall be liable to the party injured." To establish § 1983 liability, the plaintiff must satisfy three elements: (1) deprivation of a right secured by the U.S. Constitution or federal law, (2) that occurred under color of state law, and (3) was caused by a state actor. *Victoria W. v. Larpenter,* 369 F.3d 475, 482 (5th Cir. 2004)

Tweed responds to Loughlin's § 1983 claims by asserting qualified immunity. When a plaintiff seeks money damages from government officials for alleged violations of constitutional or statutory rights, officials sued in their individual capacities may invoke the defense of qualified immunity. Because it is an immunity from suit and not a defense to liability, courts are advised to resolve the issue "at the earliest possible stage in litigation." *Hunter v. Bryant,* 502 U.S. 224, 227, (1991)

"Qualified immunity shields government officials from civil damages liability," the U.S. Supreme Court has reiterated, "unless the official violated a statutory or constitutional right that was clearly established at the time of the challenged conduct." *Reichle v. Howards,* 132 S.Ct. 2088, 2093 (2012). In other words, qualified immunity "protects all but the plainly incompetent or those who knowingly violate the law, so we do not deny immunity unless existing precedent must have placed the statutory or constitutional question beyond debate." *Morgan v. Swanson,* 659 F.3d 359, 370–71 (5 Cir. 2011). "Qualified immunity balances two important interests—the need to hold public officials accountable when they exercise power irresponsibly and the need to shield officials from harassment, distraction, and liability when they perform their duties reasonably." *Pearson v. Callahan,* 555 U.S. 223 (2009).

* * *

The plaintiff claims: Tweed's actions violated his constitutional rights under the First and Sixth Amendments. The facts underlying the plaintiff's § 1983 claims are not in dispute: Tweed entered *"Kearney Loughlin, New Orleans, attorney"* into a Google search and retrieved a website entitled, "Loughlin & Loughlin." The website stated: "Loughlin & Loughlin is a plaintiff-oriented pure litigation firm specializing in maritime personal injury and death cases." Tweed took a screen shot of the webpage and submitted it to the ODC for screening. Based on the use of the word "specializing" on the webpage, the ODC opened a case against Loughlin—looking for potential violations of attorneys' advertising rules in Louisiana. ...

Tweed asserts: He is entitled to qualified immunity because his conduct was not objectively unreasonable in light of clearly established law at the time. Loughlin replies: Tweed is precluded from the defense of qualified immunity, because he was not performing a discretionary function of his office. And that is pivotal to this question.

Tweed's entitlement to qualified immunity turns on whether he was acting in his official capacity—as deputy disciplinary counsel or as a complaining witness when he submitted the screen shot of Loughlin's website to the ODC for screening. Tweed maintains: He discovered the website in the course of his investigation involving the contempt charges filed by the ODC against Loughlin on June 23, 2011—which were eventually dismissed. Loughlin responded to those contempt charges in August of 2011. Two months later, on October 13, Tweed discovered the alleged offending language on Loughlin's website after searching for his name on the Internet.

Louisiana Supreme Court Rule XIX § 4(B) vests the disciplinary counsel with the following powers and duties:

> (1) To screen all information coming to the attention of the agency to determine whether it concerns a lawyer subject to the jurisdiction of the agency because it relates to misconduct by the lawyer or the incapacity of the lawyer.
>
> (2) To investigate all information coming to the attention of the agency which, if true, would be grounds for discipline. ...
>
> (3) To dismiss or recommend probation, informal admonition, a stay, the filing of

formal charges, or the petitioning for transfer to disability inactive status with respect to each matter brought to the attention of the agency.

(4) To prosecute before hearing committees, the board, and the court discipline, reinstatement and readmission proceedings, and proceedings for transfer to or from inactive status.

Upon discovering the potential advertising violation on Loughlin's website, Tweed took a screen shot and submitted it to the ODC's screening department. Loughlin maintains that these actions make Tweed the "complaining witness" in the case. The court finds: Loughlin's characterization of Tweed as the "complaining witness" is misguided. Tweed was obligated by his duties as deputy counsel to investigate the contempt charges filed against Loughlin. It was not unreasonable for Tweed to search for Loughlin's name on the Internet.

Thus, Tweed was acting in his official capacity and not as a complaining witness. Loughlin fails to satisfy the two-part test for qualified immunity ... And, the defendants' justification for regulating the word "specialist" is to assure the public that a lawyer's claiming to be a specialist meets the standards the public expects of the lawyer. A simple acknowledgment of common sense. *Florida Bar v. Went For It, Inc.,* 515 U.S. 618, 628 (1995).

Therefore, *it is ordered* that Gregory Tweed's motion for summary judgment on the plaintiff's § 1983 claims is granted. *It is further ordered* that the defendants' motion for summary judgment on the plaintiff's claims that the Louisiana Rules of Professional Conduct are unconstitutional is *granted.* The plaintiff's claims are *dismissed with prejudice.*

C. First Amendment Actions Against State Boards for Precluding Attorneys' Using Various Technologies to Practice Law in Federal Courts

Surrick v. Killion

449 F.3d 52
(3d Cir. 2006)

Aldisert, Circuit Judge.

Robert Surrick was admitted to the Pennsylvania Bar in 1961, and to the Bar of the United States District Court for the Eastern District of Pennsylvania in 1966. On March 24, 2000, following disciplinary proceedings, Surrick was suspended from the Pennsylvania Bar for five years. The Eastern District of Pennsylvania ordered a reciprocal suspension for thirty months. Surrick "acted with reckless disregard of the truth when he leveled accusations of case fixing against certain jurists in a pleading filed in the Superior Court of Pennsylvania." *Office of Disciplinary Counsel v. Surrick,* 749 A.2d 441, 442 (Pa. 2000).

Surrick was readmitted to the Eastern District of Pennsylvania Bar on May 17, 2004. On August 16, 2004, the Pennsylvania Supreme Court issued its decision in *Office of Disciplinary Counsel v. Marcone,* 855 A.2d 654 (Pa. 2004)— involving disciplinary proceedings against another Pennsylvania attorney. Therein, the Pennsylvania Supreme Court held: A suspended attorney may not maintain a law office in the Commonwealth, and may not practice in Pennsylvania state courts—even if the attorney has been readmitted to practice law in federal district courts. *Marcone,* 855 A.2d at 668.

Surrick initiated a declaratory judgment action against Paul Killion—Chief Disciplinary Counsel of the Office of Disciplinary Counsel—and the named justices of the Pennsylvania Supreme Court. Surrick alleged: The decision in *Marcone* was contrary to federal law. And he reasonably feared that the Office of Disciplinary Counsel would administer sanctions, if he were to open a law office. Surrick asked the court to declare: He had a right to open a law office in Pennsylvania for the exclusive purpose of supporting his practice before the Eastern District of Pennsylvania. He also encouraged the court to issue a preliminary injunction—enjoining the Office of Disciplinary Counsel and the named justices from disciplining him for maintaining such an office.

Surrick's claims were predicated on the Supremacy Clause of the United States Constitution and the First Amendment. The Office of Disciplinary Counsel moved to dismiss Surrick's complaint—arguing that his claims were not ripe and his complaint failed to state a claim upon which relief could be granted. The District Court held hearings and Surrick disclosed: He wanted to open and maintain an office to support his practice before the federal courts. He intended practice in the medical malpractice field—suing those who bring "frivolous" malpractice lawsuits against doctors. He testified: Those lawsuits would be brought in federal court.

Relying on expert testimony, the Office of Disciplinary Counsel argued: Using modern technology, attorneys are now able to practice law without a traditional law office. The District Court granted limited declaratory relief in Surrick's favor and declared: Surrick "may open a legal office for the practice of law before the United States District Court for the Eastern District" of Pennsylvania subject to several pertinent conditions:

> (a) Plaintiff is authorized by the Eastern District's reinstatement Order to open and maintain a law office in Philadelphia, PA, solely for the practice of law before this court;
>
> (b) Plaintiff shall commence an application for reinstatement to the Bar of the Supreme Court of Pennsylvania by May 15, 2005;
>
> (c) Signs shall not appear on the outside of plaintiff's office building reflecting his federal practice;
>
> (d) Plaintiff shall not advertise his practice using outdoor advertisement or posters;
>
> (e) On all stationaries, business cards, files, websites, other documents or correspondence, plaintiff shall clearly state that his law practice is strictly limited to cases or controversies within the jurisdiction of the United States District Court for the Eastern District of Pennsylvania;
>
> (f) Plaintiff shall not provide legal advice or

consultation on state law matters and where appropriate will refer to other attorneys any state court cases or inquiries; and,

(g) Pursuant to his status as an admitted attorney before the Eastern District, plaintiff is authorized to represent clients on all matters within the jurisdiction of this court.

The District Court denied Surrick's request for injunctive relief, and declined to reach his First Amendment arguments. On May 13, 2005, Surrick submitted an application for reinstatement to the Pennsylvania Bar. The application was subsequently returned for being incomplete and defective. ...On May 24, 2005, the Office of Disciplinary Counsel filed a motion seeking relief from judgment under Rule 60(b) of the Federal Rules of Civil Procedure or, alternatively, a stay of the order pending appeal. On May 25, 2005, the District Court denied the motion "for lack of jurisdiction in light of the appeal." The District Court also stated: Even if it had jurisdiction, the motion would be denied as premature because Surrick had not been given adequate opportunity to cure any defects in his application.

II.

As an initial matter, the Office of Disciplinary Counsel argues that Surrick has failed to comply with the conditions imposed by the District Court's order and that his noncompliance renders this appeal moot. ... As discussed in more detail in Part VI, we agree with the Office of Disciplinary Counsel that Surrick has not complied in good faith with the District Court's order. Nonetheless, we conclude that this case is not moot at this stage.

III.

The Office of Disciplinary Counsel next contends that Surrick's complaint failed to assert a justiciable case or controversy as required by Article III of the United States Constitution and the Federal Declaratory Judgment Act, 28 U.S.C. § 2201. Specifically, it argues: This case is not ripe for adjudication, because the Office of Disciplinary Counsel has never threatened Surrick with discipline. The District Court disagreed, concluding that "the threat of potential contempt sanctions against [Surrick] is clear given any reasonable reading of the *Marcone* decision" and that Surrick has presented sufficient evidence "that the threat of contempt sanctions has caused him to forego his intended plans to open a law office within the Commonwealth of Pennsylvania."

* * *

The District Court was correct: The adversity of interest prong is satisfied here. … Accordingly, we conclude: The threat of sanctions is sufficiently real and substantial. … The Supreme Court has repeatedly stated: "One does not have to await the consummation of threatened injury to obtain preventative relief. If the injury is certainly impending, that is enough." *Pennsylvania v. West Virginia,* 262 U.S. 553, 593 (1923). … Surrick faces a real and substantial threat of sanctions in light of *Marcone* … A declaratory judgment will materially affect the actions of the parties. We therefore agree with the District Court that this case is ripe for adjudication. We turn now to the merits.

IV.

Although federal courts have traditionally used admission to the bar of a state court as a standard for initial admission to their bars, admission to practice law before a state's courts and admission to practice before the federal courts in that state are separate, independent privileges. *See Theard v. United States,* 354 U.S. 278, 281 (1957). Consistent with this settled proposition, the Court "has repeatedly emphasized … that disqualification from membership from a state bar does not necessarily lead to disqualification from a federal bar." *Frazier v. Heebe,* 482 U.S. 641, 647 n. 7 (1987). … The question in this case is whether a state may prohibit an attorney—admitted to the bar of a federal district court, but suspended from the state bar—from maintaining a legal office for the sole purpose of supporting a practice before the federal court.

The starting point for our analysis is the seminal case of *Sperry v. State of Florida,* 373 U.S. 379 (1963). In *Sperry*, the Court held: The State of Florida may not enjoin a local patent practitioner—who was not admitted to the State Bar of Florida—from preparing patent applications and other legal instruments that are filed solely in the United States Patent and Trademark Office. *Id.* at 385. …*Sperry* therefore stands for the general proposition: Where federal law authorizes an agent to practice before a federal tribunal, the federal law preempts a state's licensing requirements to the extent that those requirements hinder or obstruct the goals of federal law. *Id.*

***

We agree with the District Court: Maintaining a law office is "reasonably within the scope of the practice authorized" by 28 U.S.C. §§ 1654 & 2071 and the local rules. And state's regulating such conduct hinders Surrick's federal license to practice law. … Here, the District Court heard expert testimony on the ability of an attorney to practice law without a physical office and concluded:

> Despite technological advances in the practice of law—such as electronic filing and case research through internet subscriptions—physical space remains necessary for the representation of clients. A physical office space provides a location for confidential counseling with clients as well as room to store the necessary equipment—such as fax machines, legal text, telephones, paper files, typewriters and computers. [The latter technologies are required to properly manage] legal matters. Without a physical office location, the plaintiff would be effectively prohibited from "performing tasks which are incident to" litigating cases before the Eastern District. Citing *Sperry,* 373 U.S. at 404.

We agree with these findings. As both a practical and historical matter, the maintenance of a law office is incident to the practice of law. There is no precise formula for determining when a state regulation goes too far in burdening federal goals. *NW Cent. Pipeline Corp. v. State Corp. Comm'n of Kansas,* 489 U.S. 493, 515-519 (1989) (observing that some burden on federal goals does not result in preemption). Still, the direct effect of a state regulation's prohibiting an attorney from maintaining a law office is the frustration of his or her ability to practice before a federal court. Accordingly, we respectfully disagree with the Pennsylvania Supreme Court. And we conclude: The Eastern District of Pennsylvania's power to determine who may practice law before it preempts Pennsylvania law barring an unlicensed attorney from maintaining a law office.

* * *

We hereby affirm the declaratory judgment of the District Court with the following conditions: (1) Surrick will file a completed application for reinstatement to the Pennsylvania Bar, pay all costs required for reinstatement, enroll in the requisite number of CLE courses, and perfect all other requirements for reinstatement. … If Surrick chooses not to follow these conditions, he will violate a critical portion of the declaratory judgment. And, without any further order of this court, Attorney Surrick close his law office, until he is reinstated to practice law as a member of the

Pennsylvania Bar. *The mandate of this court will issue forthwith.*

CHAPTER SEVEN: Consumers' and Third Parties' Tort-Based Actions Against Attorneys

Under the common law, invasion of privacy, trespass to chattel, fraud and defamation are intentional torts. Consider these rules: An invasion of privacy occurs when a person intentionally intrudes into another person's place or conversation and violates the latter's reasonable expectation of privacy. *Hernandez v. Hillsides, Inc.,* 47 Cal.4th 272, 285 (2009); and a person is liable for trespass to chattel if the intrusion prevents a property owner from using his property or impairs the condition, quality. or value of the chattel. *CompuServe, Inc. v. Cyber Promotions,* 962 F. Supp. 1015, 1021-1022 (S. D. Ohio 1997). Generally, courts of law fashioned these rules to prevent a party from interfering with another party's *tangible* property or *physical* person.

On the other hand, a party is liable for committing common law fraud if he intentionally causes another person to rely detrimentally upon misrepresentations or omissions. *Tindle v. Birkett,* 171 N.Y. 520, 524–525 (1902). And liability for defamation will arise if (1) a party makes a false statement about a person and communicates the statement to a third party, and (2) the false statement decreases the aggrieved person's reputation or deters others from associating with the victim. *Lynch v. N.J. Educ. Ass'n,* 161 N.J. 152, 164-65 (1999). Clearly, these rules were not fashioned to prevent unwarranted interferences with a person's tangible property.

Increasingly, solo and small-firm attorneys are using highly sophisticated hardware and software technologies to access or "invade" the Internet—essentially a worldwide network of privately owned computers. The invasions allow attorneys to download other persons' intellectual property. The "invasions" also allow solo practitioners to upload potentially defaming statements and fraudulent communications. Still, other small-firm attorneys employ telecommunication devices to communicate and share documents with clients and third parties. And the latter devices also permit attorneys to transfer electronically fraudulent and defaming information to other persons' smartphones.

Of course, physical invasions of privacy and trespass to chattel can occur if practitioners use—without permission—their clients', employees', or partners' laptops or smartphones. Therefore, the question arises: whether solo and small-firm practitioners should worry about being sued for allegedly committing these intentional torts. Consider the following vignette:

> *Samuel, Adams and Moore* (SAM) is an extremely small, boutique law firm. SAM employed Derrick and purchased an iPhone and an iPad for Derrick to use "for business purposes." Shortly thereafter, Derrick synchronized the devices with his personal Apple account. The latter account was opened when Derrick worked for Jade-East. Derrick forgot to remove Jade-East's iPhone from the Apple account. Consequently, his private electronic data—sms, mms, photos—were sent to and synchronized with SAM's iPhone and iPad.
>
> Assume that SAM fires Derrick. And after seizing the iPhone and iPad, the small law-firm accesses, intercepts, monitors, reviews, stores, and uses Derrick's post-employment private electronic data and communications—without Derrick's consent. Also assume: (1) SAM accesses Derrick's text messages, which are stored on T-Mobile's—Derrick's cellular phone provider—network; and (2) the boutique law firm logs into his Apple account, reads Derrick's financial information and history, downloads personal information from Apple's cloud-based network, and shares Derrick's allegedly "pathetic financial state" with a new SAM employee.

Does Derrick have viable common-law actions—invasion of privacy, trespass to chattel, fraud and defamation—against the small law firm? If yes, would he prevail under each theory of recovery? Or would Derrick be compelled to file similar actions under various federal and state tort statutes? To be sure, these are timely and important questions. Why?

It has been strongly suggested: "The age of computer technology and cyberspace poses new challenges to legal principles. ... [T]he so-called Internet revolution has spawned a host of new legal issues as courts have struggled to apply traditional legal frameworks to this new communication medium. ... [Courts] must now grapple with proprietary interests, privacy, and expression arising out of computer-related disputes." *Intel Corp. v. Hamidi*, 71 P.3d 296, 330 (Cal. 2003) (Justice Mosk, dissenting), citing *Pavlovich v. Superior Court*, 29 Cal.4th 262, 266 (2002).

The cases and materials in this chapter illustrate how courts are "struggling" to apply both common-law and fairly new statutory theories of recovery to address client's and third parities' allegation: solo and small-firm attorneys use electronic and telecommunications devices and services to commit intentional torts.

A. Legal Technologies Invasion of Privacy Actions Against Attorneys

1. Electronic Communications, Invasion of Privacy, and Attorney's Liability Under the Common Law

Seidl v. Greentree Mortgage Company

30 F.Supp.2d 1292
(D. Colo. 1998)

Alan B. Johnson, Chief Judge. Most of the facts are undisputed although the significance of those facts is disputed. The following facts are undisputed except where noted. Defendant Greentree Mortgage Company (Greentree), is in the mortgage business. In December of 1996, it hired Mr. Mark Van Keuren, a sole proprietor conducting business under the name Modern Computing, on a one-time basis to advertise its mortgages by means of a bulk e-mail advertising campaign.

Greentree provided Van Keuren the body of the advertisement, which contains Greentree's 800 telephone number and its e-mail address "MFGTM@AOL.COM." The body of the advertisement provided by Greentree does not contain the disputed "localhost" address. Other than this one-time hiring, Greentree has no connection with Mr. Van Keuren. It paid him a flat fee to send the advertisement to a set number of E-mail users—during December of 1996 or January 1997. The time and manner of sending the email as well as the choice of recipients was up to Mr. Van Keuren who used his own equipment and his own mailing list.

When Mr. Van Keuren prepared Greentree's advertisement for e-mail, he placed the address "nobody@localhost.com" in both the "From" and "Reply to," or return, path fields. These path fields are identifiers for the computer system from which e-mail is delivered. It is undisputed that it was Mr. Van Keuren who chose the name for the "from" and the "reply to" path fields and who configured the e-mail headers to include them.

In January of 1997, Mr. Van Keuren sent out Greentree's advertisement soliciting business to thousands of e-mail addresses. All e-mails sent to inaccurate addresses "bounced-back, like return mail, to the localhost address Mr. Van Keuren had placed on the advertisement." Similarly, all recipients who clicked on the reply button automatically sent replies to the nobody@localhost address.

Plaintiff, Matthew Seidl, is a graduate student in computer science at a Colorado university. In 1995, Mr. Seidl registered "nobody@localhost.com" as a domain name for something named Wraith Interprises (Wraith). In his deposition, Mr. Seidl testified that Wraith is a d/b/a he developed but hasn't used.

Domain names are registered with Network Solutions, Inc. (NSI), an entity authorized by the federal government to keep track of all Internet addresses. The parties dispute the effect of such registration. Greentree says registration grants no exclusive rights to use a name. Mr. Seidl says it does. Greentree has submitted evidence that the "nobody@localhost.com" name Mr. Seidl registered is a generic name, like John Doe, conventionally not assigned to any real person and used as an addressing convention for e-mail or other network traffic for special purposes such as to loop back data. Often, mail software is configured to discard messages addressed to nobody. *Id.* Mr. Seidl testified in his deposition he registered the "nobody@localhost" name as gag or to keep a telemarketer from getting the name. Very early after registering it he began to receive misdirected replies.

In his Complaint, Mr. Seidl alleges: The "from" and "reply to" path fields of the e-mail headers on Greentree's advertisement were intentionally "misconfigured" or "forged" to contain the nobody@localhost address or domain name so that the misdirected mail would not "bounce back" to the sender. Mr. Seidl alleges that his computer received over 7,000 bounce backs from the Greentree e-mail advertisement. Mr. Seidl claims his computer memory was fully taxed by replies that were often profane and insulting and directed to him and that as a result of the incoming messages he was unable to use his computer for three days. Mr. Seidl also claims his reputation among the Internet community suffered because he was identified as the sender of the e-mail advertisement (the "spam").

Shirley Sostre is a Colorado attorney. Mr. Seidl and Ms. Sostre did not meet or communicate until after he began to receive the bounce backs from Greentree's e-mail advertisements in January 1997. Sending bulk e-mail advertising, or spam, is a controversial and much maligned practice—currently the subject of legislative action in Congress and various state legislatures.

Parties' Claims

A. Plaintiff's Claims Against Greentree

Plaintiff Seidl brings the following eight claims for relief against Greentree:

(1) violations of the Deceptive Trade Practices Act under Colo. Rev. Stat. § 6–1–105 alleging it was deceptive to imply that Seidl, through a domain name registered to Wraith, was somehow connected with the bulk e-mail;

(2) trespass to chattel (by tying up his computer for three days);

(3) negligence in breaching an asserted duty not to cause the owner of the nobody@localhost.com domain name damage;

(4) negligence per se for alleged violation of Colorado's Computer Crime Act, Colo. Rev.. Stat. § 18–5.5–102;

(5) negligent hiring alleging that Greentree should have determined that Mr. Van Keuren would not employ "unlawful" means to send the advertisement;

(6) violation of plaintiff's right of publicity by using Mr. Seidl's name (really Wraith's name) without consent;

(7) false light invasion of privacy alleging that Greentree made thousands of e-mail recipients believe Mr. Seidl was somehow connected with the junk e-mail because of the use of the domain name; and,

(8) violations of 47 U.S.C. § 227—the Junk Fax law by use of "telephone facsimile machine", which plaintiff contends

includes e-mail under the definition in the statute, 42 U.S.C. § 227(a)(2)(B). 1

B. Greentree's Counterclaims Against Plaintiff, Seidl, and His Lawyer, Sostre

Greentree brings seven counterclaims against Mr. Seidl and his **attorney**—Ms. Sostre. Greentree's first four counterclaims are brought under Title IX of the Organized Crime Control Act of 1970, the Racketeering Influenced Corrupt Organizations Act or RICO, 18 U.S.C. § 1962, alleging Ms. Sostre has conspired with her client in a scheme to extort money from innocent advertisers who use the Internet.

Greentree also brings the following counterclaims under Colorado law: libel per se alleging defamation by Mr. Seidl's and Ms. Sostre's publicity of claims against Greentree by use of press releases on the Internet, false light invasion of privacy and, interference with prospective contractual relations alleging Greentree lost business because certain persons chose not to do business with it as a result of the publicity of it as an organization that engages in spamming.

* * *

Sostre's and Seidl's Motions

False Light Invasion of Privacy

Greentree's sixth counterclaim is for false light invasion of privacy. Greentree contends that through the publication of the defamatory statements it was falsely associated with highly offensive conduct and as a result has had its privacy invaded by being placed in a false light.

The rule in Colorado is that, distinct from "a tort of defamation, which involves injury to reputation, invasion of privacy involves injury to the person, primarily through mental and emotional distress." *Bolduc v. Bailey*, 586 F.Supp. 896, 901 (D.Colo.1984). The court went on to hold that "the Court does not believe that an association of individuals, such as (the claimant), may claim collectively an invasion of privacy, particularly since the rule on damages appears on its face to refer to individual persons." *Bolduc*, 586 F.Supp. at 902; *Cf. McCammon & Associates, Inc. v. McGraw–Hill Broadcasting Company,* 716 P.2d 490 (Colo.Ct.App.1986) (affirming summary judgment in favor of corporate plaintiff on corporate defendant's claim of false light invasion of privacy without discussing whether claim may be maintained by corporation).

Greentree is not an individual; it is a limited partnership. Greentree attempts to avoid the rule announced in *Bolduc* by its contention that one of its limited partners is an individual. However, the limited partner whom Greentree identifies in its response as being painted in a false light is not the named party in this lawsuit.

Accordingly, the court finds and concludes that Greentree lacks standing as a limited partnership to bring a counterclaim against Ms. Sostre and Mr. Seidl for false light invasion of privacy and they are entitled to summary judgment dismissing this counterclaim. It is further ordered that counterclaim defendant Shirley Sostre's motion for summary judgment is granted.

2. Electronic Communications, Invasion of Privacy, and Attorney's Liability Under State Statutes

Habush v. Cannon

346 Wis. 2d 709
(Wis. Ct. App. 2013)

Lundsten, P. J.

This appeal concerns the right of privacy, as codified in Wis. Stat. § 995.50(2)(b), and the practice of using a person's name as a "keyword" search term in an Internet search engine. Here, the law firm Cannon & Dunphy bid on the search terms "Habush" and "Rottier" through Google, Yahoo!, and Bing search engines. Cannon & Dunphy—by successfully bidding on the names Habush and Rottier—assured that, when a person entered either name as a search term into one of these search engines, a link to Cannon & Dunphy's website would appear as a "sponsored link" above the "organic" link to the law firm of Habush, Habush & Rottier.

Attorneys Robert Habush and Daniel Rottier contend that, by successfully bidding on their names, Cannon & Dunphy violated § 995.50(2)(b) by using their names for advertising or trade purposes.

Background

Robert Habush and Daniel Rottier are trial attorneys and shareholders in the firm of Habush, Habush & Rottier. It is undisputed that Habush and Rottier are both well-known personal injury trial attorneys and their names have commercial and advertising value. Cannon & Dunphy is a law firm with a specialty in personal injury cases.

Internet search engines like Google, Yahoo!, and Bing produce at least three types of search results for Internet searchers: organic results, advertising results, and sponsored results. Organic results are lists of links to websites that are produced based on algorithms developed by each search engine. Advertising and sponsored results are produced by allowing advertisers to bid on and pay for the use of keyword search terms. When a search engine user enters keywords that have been bid on, lists of links to the websites of successful bidders are displayed in a special position on the user's web browser. "Advertising" results generally appear to the right of the organic search results. "Sponsored" results generally appear above the organic results and are usually set in background shading with the words "sponsored link" or "ad."

Beginning in 2009, Cannon & Dunphy bid on the keyword search terms "Habush" and "Rottier" through the search engines Google, Yahoo!, and Bing. This bidding assured that, in response to an Internet user's search of the terms "Habush" or "Rottier," links to the website of Cannon & Dunphy would appear as the first result above the organic results lists. Under the bidding arrangements, Cannon & Dunphy's successful bids mean that it pays the search engine companies each time an Internet user clicks on Cannon & Dunphy's sponsored links. The links to the Cannon & Dunphy website and the law firm's website itself contain no reference to the names Habush or Rottier.

Robert Habush and Daniel Rottier sued Cannon & Dunphy, William Cannon, and Patrick Dunphy (collectively Cannon & Dunphy). Habush and Rottier alleged that, by bidding on the keyword search terms "Habush" and "Rottier," Cannon & Dunphy used the names for advertising purposes without Habush's and Rottier's written consent in violation of WIS. STAT. § 995.50(2)(b). Habush and Rottier sought equitable relief in the form of an injunction, as well as attorneys' fees, pursuant to § 995.50(1)(a) and (c).

The parties filed cross-motions for summary judgment. The circuit court determined that Habush and Rottier must prove two elements: 1) there was an invasion of privacy under Wis. Stat. § 995.50(2)(b); and 2) that the invasion of privacy was done "unreasonably" within the meaning of § 995.50(1).

The circuit court concluded that Habush and Rottier succeeded in establishing the first element, that Cannon & Dunphy used the names Habush and Rottier for the purposes of advertising or trade by bidding on them as keyword search terms but did not establish the second element, that such an invasion was unreasonable. The court, therefore, granted summary judgment in favor of Cannon & Dunphy. While our analysis differs, we agree with what we understand to be the circuit court's pivotal reasoning—that the use of the names here is different in kind from the type of use the statute is intended to cover.

Discussion

Habush and Rottier argue that the undisputed facts show that Cannon & Dunphy violated Wis. Stat. § 995.50(2)(b). We begin with a brief summary of the disputed statutory provisions. Wis. Stat.§ 995.50(1) entitles anyone "whose privacy is unreasonably invaded" to equitable relief, compensatory damages, and reasonable attorney fees. Section 995.50(2) contains four alternative ways that a party's privacy might be invaded. The privacy right at issue here is § 995.50(2)(b), which provides:

> In this section, "invasion of privacy" means any of the following: ... the use, for advertising purposes or for purposes of trade, of the name, portrait or picture of any living person, without having first obtained the written consent of the person or, if the person is a minor, of his or her parent or guardian.

Thus, on its face, WIS. STAT. § 995.50(2)(b) requires only proof of the following: (1) "use ... of the name, portrait or picture of any living person"; (2) "use" that is "for advertising purposes or for purposes of trade"; and (3) "use" without "written consent." The parties, however, focus their attention on whether the term "unreasonably invaded" in § 995.50(1) adds an element of proof to this list.

Broadly speaking, the circuit court and Cannon & Dunphy take the position that "unreasonably invaded" is an additional requirement that both limits and defines the reach of § 995.50(2)(b). Habush and Rottier, on the other hand, contend that it would be "nonsensical to engraft ... an additional unreasonableness requirement on top of" the requirements already contained in the defined violations in the subsections of § 995.50(2), including the subsection at issue here, § 995.50(2)(b). Habush and Rottier seemingly assume that, if there is no additional "unreasonably invaded" element, it is obvious that

Cannon & Dunphy's use of their names is a violation of § 995.50(2)(b). In sum, the circuit court and the parties primarily see this case as turning on whether § 995.50(1), with its "unreasonably invaded" language, adds an additional element to § 995.50(2)(b). In our view, this framing of the issue needlessly complicates resolution of this particular dispute.

As Habush and Rottier point out, § 995.50(2)(b) is modeled after a New York statute that has no "unreasonably invaded" language. Consequently, apart from Habush's and Rottier's explanation as to why we should not read "unreasonably invaded" language as imposing an additional element of proof on a plaintiff suing under § 995.50(2)(b), Habush's and Rottier's argument effectively explains why, in their view, Cannon & Dunphy's keyword bidding constitutes prohibited "use" within the meaning of § 995.50(2)(b). In essence, we agree with Habush and Rottier that this latter topic is the key but disagree on the coverage of § 995.50(2)(b).

Accordingly, we direct our attention to the meaning of the term "use" in § 995.50(2)(b) and whether Cannon & Dunphy's actions constitute "use" within the meaning of that term. Our reframing of the issue does not prejudice Habush and Rottier. For example, although Habush's and Rottier's "incidental use" argument is placed in the context of a discussion of "unreasonably invaded," the substance of their argument is that we should read "use" in § 995.50(2)(b) broadly. Habush and Rottier write:

> The common-law doctrine of "incidental use" prevents the Subsection (2)(b) tort from being applied to minor or trivial uses of another person's name, or in publications with news or other literary or entertainment value, which do not exploit the commercial value associated with a living person's name. The words "unreasonably invaded" should not be construed any broader than necessary to keep these incidental uses from the statute's reach.

The gist of Habush's and Rottier's argument here, and elsewhere, is that use of any type should be covered if such use is an attempt to exploit the value of a name or image. This is an argument we fully address below.

In effect, our approach assumes without deciding that Habush and Rottier are correct that they need not meet an additional "unreasonably invaded" requirement. And, in the context of interpreting the term "use," we address all of Habush's and

Rottier's substantive arguments on the coverage of § 995.50(2)(b). Accordingly, from this point forward, we speak in terms of the meaning of "use," and sometimes cast the parties' arguments the same way.

Our interpretation of the word "use" in Wis. Stat. § 995.50(2)(b) is guided by the following statutory interpretation principles:

> This case presents a question of statutory interpretation, which we review de novo. The purpose of statutory interpretation is to determine what a statute means in order to give the statute its full, proper, and intended effect. "We begin with the statute's language because we assume that the legislature's intent is expressed in the words it used." Generally, language is given its common, ordinary, and accepted meaning. In addition, statutory language is interpreted in the context in which it is used, in relation to the language of surrounding or closely-related statutes, and interpreted to avoid absurd or unreasonable results.
>
> "If the meaning is plain, we ordinarily stop the inquiry." However, if a statute is ambiguous, we examine extrinsic sources, such as legislative history, to ascertain the legislative intent. A statute is ambiguous if "[t]he statute's ability to support two reasonable constructions creates an ambiguity which cannot be resolved through the language of the statute itself. [A] statutory provision is ambiguous if reasonable minds could differ as to its meaning." *Orion Flight Servs., Inc. v. Basler Flight Serv.,* 2006 WI 51, 16–17, 290 Wis.2d 421.

If our statutory interpretation analysis reveals ambiguity because we are presented with competing reasonable interpretations, it is our task to choose the more reasonable interpretation. *See, e.g., State v. Dartez,* 2007 WI App 126, 15, 16–17, 301 Wis.2d 499, (choosing the "more reasonable" interpretation of a statute); *Abbas v. Palmersheim,* 2004 WI App 126, 24, 275 Wis.2d 311 (choosing "the most reasonable interpretation" of a statute). Applying these statutory interpretation rules here, we conclude that the word "use" is ambiguous as applied to the facts in this case because the parties present two competing and reasonable interpretations of "use."

Habush and Rottier promote a reading of the statute that provides broad coverage. They contend that "use" in Wis. Stat. § 995.50(2)(b) covers any kind of use of a name or image if such use takes advantage of the commercial value of a person's identity. In support, Habush and Rottier point to common law indicating that an important purpose of the privacy right codified in § 995.50(2)(b) is the protection of an individual against the exploitation of his or her reputation for the benefit of another.

Habush and Rottier rely on the RESTATEMENT OF TORTS, and case law applying the RESTATEMENT, for the proposition that any use through which the user seeks to obtain the benefit of the "commercial or other values associated with the name" is an invasion of privacy. See RESTATEMENT (SECOND) OF TORTS § 652C, at 380 (1977) ("One who appropriates to his own use or benefit the name or likeness of another is subject to liability to the other for invasion of his privacy."); *AFL Philadelphia LLC v. Krause*, 639 F.Supp.2d 512, 529–32 (E.D.Pa. 2009)

Habush and Rottier argue that the only "uses" not covered by Wis. Stat. § 995.50(2)(b) are uses that are incidental. We understand their argument to be that "use" is not incidental if the use involves an attempt to benefit from the commercial or other value of a person's name or image. According to Habush and Rottier, because Cannon & Dunphy used the names Habush and Rottier in a manner that benefitted Cannon & Dunphy, the law firm used the names within the meaning of § 995.50(2)(b).

We conclude that this broad interpretation of "use" is reasonable because, as Habush and Rottier explain, it comports with an important purpose underlying Wis. Stat. § 995.50(2)(b).

Cannon & Dunphy argues that the legislature intended to cover only "use" that is visible to the public in the sense that the used name or image is "found in or on the defendant's product or solicitation for services." Under Cannon & Dunphy's reading of the statute, the law firm's use of the names Habush and Rottier is not a violation because the use is not visible in Cannon & Dunphy's sponsored links or its website. The "use" that Habush and Rottier complain about here is, according to Cannon & Dunphy, invisible. The allegedly improper "use" is merely a mechanism by which Cannon & Dunphy places its advertising near a link to information about Habush & Rottier. Cannon & Dunphy argues that this is a different kind of use than that to which the privacy right codified in § 995.50(2)(b) has historically applied.

We conclude that Cannon & Dunphy's interpretation is also reasonable because it is consistent with case law on which the statute is based and on case law interpreting statutory language that is comparable for our purposes. In every case brought to our attention by the parties and discovered in the course of our own research, the "use" of the name or image at issue was a visible part of some sort of promotion or product. *See, e.g., Hirsch v. S.C. Johnson & Son, Inc.*, 90 Wis.2d 379, 382, 280 N.W.2d 129 (1979); *White v. Samsung Elecs. Am., Inc.*, 971 F.2d 1395, 1396–97 (9th Cir.1992) (robot resembling game show personality Vanna White used in advertisement); *AFL Philadelphia LLC*, 639 F.Supp.2d at 518 (email address indicating former sales director's name as the sender of emails to fans of arena football team). ...

Because Habush and Rottier and Cannon & Dunphy have presented competing reasonable interpretations of the word "use" as it applies to the facts before us, we must choose the more reasonable interpretation. We conclude, in general terms, that the more reasonable interpretation is the one advanced by Cannon & Dunphy. But we do not adopt a comprehensive definition. Rather, our holding is limited to the particular "non-visible" type of use at issue here. In reaching this conclusion, we first examine the parties' discussion of the circuit court's "proximity" advertising examples, and then address additional arguments made by Habush and Rottier. ...

Conclusion

Based on the arguments before us and on our own attempt to find helpful authority, we conclude that the more reasonable interpretation of the word "use" in Wis. Stat. § 995.50(2)(b) is that it does not cover bidding on someone's name as a keyword search term. Accordingly, we further conclude that Cannon & Dunphy did not violate Habush's and Rottier's right of privacy under § 995.50(2)(b).

Judgment affirmed.

NOTES AND QUESTIONS

1) **Common Law Tort of Intrusion.** "A privacy violation based on the common law tort of intrusion has two elements. First, the defendant must intentionally intrude into a place, conversation,

or matter as to which the plaintiff has a reasonable expectation of privacy. Second, the intrusion must occur in a manner highly offensive to a reasonable person." *Hernandez v. Hillsides, Inc.,* 47 Cal.4th 272, 285 (2009). "The tort is proven only if the plaintiff had an objectively reasonable expectation of seclusion or solitude in the place, conversation or data source." *Shulman v. Grp. W Prods., Inc.,* 18 Cal.4th 200, 232 (1998)

2) The Tort of Invasion of Privacy of Intrusion. Generally, the tort can be one of four different types: (1) unreasonable invasion upon the seclusion of another; (2) appropriation of the other's name or likeness; (3) unreasonable publicity given to the others' private life; or (4) publicity that unreasonably places the other in a false light before the public. RESTATEMENT (SECOND) OF TORTS § 652D (1987)

3) Conflicting Decisions Regarding the Tort of Invasion of Privacy. California law recognizes four invasion-of-privacy categories: (1) intrusion upon seclusion; (2) public disclosure of private facts; (3) false light in the public eye; and (4) appropriation of name or likeness. *Shulman v. Group W Prods., Inc.,* 18 Cal.4th 200, 214 n. 4 (1998). Conversely, the Minnesota Supreme Court has refused to recognize a cause of action for invasion of privacy, concluding that it is not the function of a court to establish a new cause of action for invasion of privacy. *Hendry v. Conner,* 303 Minn. 317, 319, 226 N.W.2d 921, 923 (1975).

B. CLIENTS' AND THIRD PARTIES' "PHYSICAL" AND "ELECTRONIC" TRESPASS TO CHATTEL ACTIONS AGAINST ATTORNEYS

1. PHYSICAL TRESPASS INVOLVING HOME OFFICES AND COMPUTERS

Dalley v. Dykema Gossett, PLLC

287 Mich. App. 296
(Mich. Ct. App. 2010)

Gleicher, J.

In this action alleging several intentional torts, plaintiff—H. Scott Dalley—appeals a circuit court's order granting defendants summary disposition.

I. Facts and Underlying Proceedings

A. The Federal Case

This case finds its genesis in a dispute between an insurance company and its agent. On April 13, 2004, defendants Lincoln National Life Insurance Company and Lincoln Financial Advisors Corporation sued Rodney Ellis, a Lincoln agent, and Lucasse, Ellis, Inc. (Lucasse)—a company partially owned by Ellis—in the United States District Court for the Western District of Michigan. Lincoln's federal court complaint alleged fraud, breach of fiduciary duty, conversion, breach of contract, and tortious interference with business expectancies or relations. Defendants Dykema Gossett P.L.L.C. (Dykema) and John Ferroli—a Dykema member—represented Lincoln in the federal court action.

On April 15, 2004, a federal judge entered a temporary restraining order (TRO) prohibiting Ellis, Lucasse, and instant plaintiff Dalley from "deleting, erasing, destroying, shredding, secreting, removing, modifying, overwriting, replacing, or 'wiping'" any computer data or files containing information related to Lincoln's customers and financial records. The paragraphs of the TRO directly relevant to plaintiff's present intentional tort action provide as follows:

> Rodney D. Ellis and Lucasse, Ellis, Inc., all officers, owners, employees, principals, and agents of either of them who receive actual notice of this Order by personal service or otherwise, including but not limited to H. Scott Dalley, and all persons or entities acting in concert with any of them, are hereby ordered immediately upon service of this order to make available to a computer/data consultant retained by Plaintiffs all hard drives and other magnetic, optical or electronic media in the possession, custody, or control of any of them, including those hard drives and other magnetic, optical, or electronic media that they have the effective power to obtain, which contain any Lincoln Customer Records, for prompt non-destructive copying at Plaintiffs' expense. Plaintiffs shall minimize disruption to the producing person's business to the extent practicable. Plaintiffs shall return all hard drives and other magnetic, optical, or

> electronic media supplied pursuant to this Order within 24 hours, or such longer time as may be stipulated to or ordered by this Court. Plaintiffs' computer consultant shall maintain the copied data in a secure, locked location, and shall not review or inspect the data copied, or show it to Plaintiffs or their attorneys, until further order of this Court.
>
> Rodney D. Ellis and Lucasse, Ellis, Inc., all officers, owners, employees, principals, and agents of either of them, including, but not limited to, H. Scott Dalley, and all persons or entities acting in concert with any of them who receive actual notice of this Order by personal service or otherwise, are hereby ordered immediately upon service of this order to provide for prompt copying of, at Plaintiffs' expense, (i) any and all "notes" data, files or records of present or former customers of any Lincoln affiliate, and (ii) any and all "Alice Reports," "A–Roll" lists, and any other documents relating to any contemplated or processed change-in-employment status for any employees of the Henry Ford Health System with an account at any Lincoln affiliate.

On April 19, 2004, Lincoln's agents served plaintiff with the TRO in his Kentwood apartment, and with the assistance of personnel employed by defendant Guidance Software, Inc. (Guidance Software), copied all the data from all of plaintiff's computers. The events surrounding defendants' entry into plaintiff's apartment and the copying of his computer data form the basis of the instant lawsuit.

B. The State Court Complaint

Plaintiff commenced this action on April 18, 2007, by filing in the Kent Circuit Court a complaint against Dykema, Ferroli, Lincoln, and Guidance Software. Plaintiff subsequently filed a substantially similar first amended complaint, which describes in detail the circumstances surrounding defendants' conduct in serving the TRO and copying plaintiff's computer data. Because the allegations within the amended complaint supply the facts necessary to our resolution of this case, we turn to an examination of that pleading.

The amended complaint avers that in April 2004, plaintiff worked out of his apartment as an independent computer consultant for several small businesses, including Lucasse. The computers in his apartment provided the means to generate his livelihood and held confidential information concerning all his clients, such as their user identifications and passwords. Plaintiff, who suffers from AIDS, also stored on his computers highly personal information, medical records, photographs, and tax returns.

On April 19, 2004, plaintiff's doorbell rang and someone requested that plaintiff permit entry into his apartment building. Because plaintiff was not expecting visitors, he did not respond. At approximately 11:00 a.m., loud pounding on his door "jolted" plaintiff awake and he "realized that the men outside had managed to slip through the security system downstairs."

Plaintiff saw papers slid under his door, and he read them after the men had departed. The papers included the TRO, which "completely blindsided" plaintiff. Soon thereafter, plaintiff's telephone rang, but he did not answer it. The caller, Ferroli, left a message declaring that a federal court subpoena allowed him and others to enter plaintiff's apartment "to either take his computers and hard drives or copy what was on them." Plaintiff "reasonably believed that he could not let Ferroli simply walk out the door with the computers," and that "he had no choice and would go to jail" if he refused Ferroli access to his computers. Plaintiff thus "returned Ferroli's call and agreed to" allow Ferroli "to copy the information on his computers."

Ferroli and several Guidance Software employees arrived, and plaintiff "led the group to the master bedroom where he kept two computers and four hard drives and, having seen from the subpoena that the case had something to do with Lincoln and Ellis, pointed them to the one and only hard drive that would contain Lincoln data." But "[t]he intruders ... demanded everything." The Guidance Software personnel connected laptop computers to plaintiff's machines and transferred "every bit of information on all [plaintiff's] computers and hard drives." Only a "small percentage" of the information copied by the Guidance Software personnel related to Ellis, Lucasse, or Lincoln. The data transfer and copying process consumed 11 hours, during which period Ferroli "wandered in and out." In frail health and underweight, plaintiff "did not sleep for several days thereafter."

Four days after Ferroli and the Guidance Software technicians entered plaintiff's home, a Dykema attorney took plaintiff's deposition, urging him "to state on the record that he was suffering from AIDS[.]" As a result of illness, plaintiff had to complete the deposition later, by telephone from his bed. On July 1, 2004,

Lincoln's attorneys informed the federal judge in the Ellis case that plaintiff had violated the TRO. Despite this claim and similar allegations in Lincoln's federal court complaint, defendants never uncovered or presented any evidence of wrongdoing by plaintiff or Ellis. Defendants' actions "traumatized [plaintiff], devastated his best customer, and thereby destroyed [plaintiff's] business." According to the amended complaint, Lincoln bore vicarious liability for the conduct of Dykema, Ferroli, and Guidance Software, because these defendants "were Lincoln's agents and were acting within the scope of their agency."

The amended complaint sets forth five intentional tort claims including trespass .... All defendants sought summary disposition of plaintiff's claims pursuant to MCR 2.116(C)(8). Dykema, Ferroli and Guidance Software filed a separate motion seeking summary disposition under MCR 2.116(C)(10). In a written opinion and order entered on September 9, 2008, the circuit court granted defendants' motions under (C)(8) and dismissed the entirety of plaintiff's complaint. ...

II. Summary Disposition Analysis

A. Standard of Review

Plaintiff challenges the circuit court's grant of summary disposition in favor of defendants regarding all five counts of his complaint. This Court reviews de novo a circuit court's summary disposition ruling. A court may grant summary disposition under MCR 2.116(C)(8) if "[t]he opposing party has failed to state a claim on which relief can be granted." A motion ... tests the legal sufficiency of the complaint solely on the basis of the pleadings. When deciding a motion, this Court accepts all well-pleaded factual allegations as true and construes them in the light most favorable to the nonmoving party. A party may not support a motion ... with documentary evidence such as affidavits, depositions, or admissions. Summary disposition ... should be granted only when the claim is ... unenforceable as a matter of law." *Kuhn v. Secretary of State*, 228 Mich. App. 319, 324 (1998).

C. Trespass

Plaintiff next challenges the circuit court's ruling that his amended complaint "failed to state the element of unauthorized entry that is necessary for a claim of trespass." The circuit court reasoned that defendants "had a nonconsensual privilege to enter plaintiff's apartment for the purpose of" executing the TRO. In support of this conclusion, the circuit court cited this Court's decision in *Antkiewicz v. Motorists Mut. Ins. Co.*, 91 Mich. App. 389, 283 N.W.2d 749 (1979), and 2 Restatement Torts, 2d, § 210. Defendants suggest that because plaintiff refused to allow his computers to be taken from his apartment, the circuit court correctly determined that the TRO authorized entry of the apartment for duplication of the hard drives.

A trespass is an unauthorized invasion on the private property of another. *American Transmission, Inc. v. Channel 7 of Detroit, Inc.*, 239 Mich. App. 695, 705 (2000). In *Antkiewicz*, 91 Mich.App. at 396, 283 N.W.2d 749, the court explained that "[n]ormally, a public officer who is on the premises of another pursuant to legal authorization is not liable for trespass." The circuit court in this case recognized that defendants do not qualify as public officers, but opined that they possessed analogous powers under 2 Restatement Torts, 2d, § 210, which provides as follows:

> The privilege to execute an order of a court directing the actor to put a third person in possession of land of which another is in possession, or to do any other act on the land, carries with it the privilege to enter the land for the purpose of executing the order, provided that any writ issued for the execution of the order is valid or fair on its face.

Irrespective that Michigan has not adopted this section of the Restatement, we decline to apply § 210 here because it bears no relevance to the facts of this case. The TRO neither authorized defendants to take possession of plaintiff's land nor invested them with the authority "to do any other act on the land. ..." The TRO required plaintiff "to provide for prompt copying" of his computer data concerning Lincoln and permitted Lincoln's agents to copy the data, but it afforded defendants no right to enter plaintiff's apartment, either to obtain the computer hard drives or to accomplish the copying. Consequently, we reject as unfounded the circuit court's conclusion that the language of the TRO contemplated or authorized an entry into plaintiff's apartment.

Whether plaintiff consented to defendants' entry into his apartment presents a more difficult question. Plaintiff's amended complaint avers that he allowed defendants to enter his apartment on the basis of their misrepresentation that the TRO permitted them "to either take his computers and hard drives or copy what was on them." Michigan has not squarely considered whether—in an action for trespass—a misrepresentation utilized to secure a homeowner's consent to enter a private home vitiates the homeowner's consent.

In *American Transmission*, this Court considered a somewhat similar issue. The *American Transmission* plaintiffs sued a television station that had recorded the interactions between a decoy customer and the plaintiffs' transmission repair personnel.

The plaintiffs' complaint asserted that the defendants had committed a trespass when they "gained entry by concealing their true identity and misrepresenting their agent's relationship to them, ..." *American Transmission*, 239 Mich. App. at 699–700. This Court upheld the order granting summary disposition of the plaintiffs' trespass claim in favor of the defendants, finding that although the decoy customer "misrepresented her purpose, plaintiffs' consent was still valid because she did not invade any of the specific interests relating to the peaceable possession of land that the tort of trespass seeks to protect." *Id.* at 708. The Court emphasized that the decoy customer had entered only public areas of the plaintiffs' transmission shop and videotaped a "professional discussion. ..." *Id.* at 709. The decoy customer "did not disrupt the shop or invade anyone's private space, and the videotape she made did not reveal the intimate details of anybody's life." *Id.*

In *American Transmission*, 239 Mich.App. at 708, this Court cited favorably a case decided by the United States Court of Appeals for the Seventh Circuit, *Desnick v. American Broadcasting Cos., Inc.*, 44 F.3d 1345 (7th Cir. 1995). In *Desnick*, the Seventh Circuit ... rejected the contention that journalists posing as test patients at an eye surgery center had committed a trespass, reasoning that the test patients' entry did not invade any of the specific interests that the tort of trespass seeks to protect. The test patients entered offices that were open to anyone expressing a desire for ophthalmic services and videotaped physicians engaged in professional, not personal, communications with strangers (the testers themselves). The activities of the offices were not disrupted. ... Nor was there any [invasion of] a person's private space, ... as in the famous case of *De May v. Roberts*, 46 Mich. 160, 9 N.W. 146 (1881) (where a doctor, called to the plaintiff's home to deliver her baby, brought along with him a friend who was curious to see a birth but was not a medical doctor, and represented the friend to be his medical assistant). ... *Id.* at 1352

As the Seventh Circuit recognized in *Desnick*, important distinctions differentiate misrepresentations directed to gain entry to business concerns and those employed to enter a private home. The Seventh Circuit acknowledged that in a true trespass case, "there can be no implied consent in any nonfictitious sense of the term when express consent is procured by a misrepresentation or a misleading omission." *Id.* at 1351. The court posited the following illustrative example: "If a homeowner opens his door to a purported meter reader who is in fact nothing of the sort—just a busybody curious about the interior of the home—the homeowner's consent to his entry is not a defense to a suit for trespass." *Id.* at 1352. Nevertheless, the law sometimes deems effective in the trespass context a consent procured by misrepresentation.

The Seventh Circuit in Desnick explained the difference between the two classes of cases by contrasting the phony meter reader intruding into a home with a phony customer, reminiscent of the defendants in American Transmission:

> [T]he homeowner victimized by the phony meter reader does not want strangers in his house unless they have authorized service functions. The dealer's objection to the customer who claims falsely to have a lower price from a competing dealer is not to the physical presence of the customer, but to the fraud that he is trying to perpetuate.

A decision of the United States Court of Appeals for the Ninth Circuit, Theofel v. Farey–Jones, 359 F.3d 1066 (9th Cir. 2004), further illustrates that the character of a particular deceit remains critical to a determination of the implicated privacy interests. In *Theofel*, the plaintiffs cooperated with a faulty subpoena issued by the defendants, federal court litigants, and the Ninth Circuit considered whether the plaintiffs' cooperation operated as a consent to disclosure of otherwise protected information. The Ninth Circuit analogized to the common law of trespass and, citing *Desnick*, concluded that the plaintiffs had alleged facts that vitiated their apparent consent:

> A defendant is not liable for trespass if the plaintiff authorized his entry. But "an overt manifestation of assent or willingness would not be effective ... if the defendant knew, or probably if he ought to have known in the exercise of reasonable care, that the plaintiff was mistaken as to the nature and quality of the invasion intended."
>
> Not all deceit vitiates consent. "[T]he mistake must extend to the essential character of the act itself, which is to say that which makes it harmful or offensive, rather than to some collateral matter which merely operates as an inducement." In other

> words, it must be a "substantial mistake ... concerning the nature of the invasion or the extent of the harm." Restatement (Second) of Torts § 892B(2) cmt. g. [T]he theory is that some invited mistakes go to the essential nature of the invasion while others are merely collateral. Classification depends on the extent to which the intrusion trenches on "the specific interests that the tort of trespass seeks to protect." *Desnick,* 44 F.3d at 1352.
> ...
>
> Under this standard, plaintiffs have alleged facts that vitiate [their internet service provider] NetGate's consent. NetGate disclosed the sample in response to defendants' purported subpoena. Unbeknownst to NetGate, that subpoena was invalid. This mistake went to the essential nature of the invasion of privacy. The subpoena's falsity transformed the access from a bona fide state-sanctioned inspection into private snooping. The false subpoena caused disclosure of documents that otherwise would have remained private; it effected an "invasion ... of the specific interests that the [statute] seeks to protect." *Desnick,* 44 F.3d at 1352; *Theofel,* 359 F.3d at 1073–1074

The Ninth Circuit concluded that "[b]ecause defendants procured consent by exploiting a mistake of which they had constructive knowledge, the district court erred by dismissing based on that consent." *Id.* at 1075

"[T]respass is an invasion of the plaintiff's interest in the exclusive possession of his land. ..." *Adams v. Cleveland–Cliffs Iron Co.*, 237 Mich.App. 51, 59 (1999). Under the common law, a trespass on land violated the landowner's right to exclude others from the premises. Here, plaintiff's amended complaint avers that defendants obtained his consent to enter the apartment by representing that a "federal court subpoena" authorized their access to the inside of plaintiff's apartment, that defendants' entry constituted a trespass, and that "[t]hey intended to intrude on [plaintiff's] private property without authorization to do so."

We conclude that these averments adequately delineate a trespass claim and that defendants' alleged misrepresentations could reasonably be found to have vitiated plaintiff's consent to the entry of his apartment. Because the interest protected by the common-law tort of trespass is identical to that identified in plaintiff's amended complaint, this case more closely parallels the phony meter reader's entry into a residence than the decoy customers' entries into business premises.

Accordingly, we reverse the circuit court's grant of summary disposition in defendants' favor of the trespass claim.

NOTES AND QUESTIONS

1) **Common-Law Trespass to Chattel.** To make a viable claim for trespass to chattel, a property owner must establish that she had a possessory interest in the disputed chattel and that the tortfeasor (1) interfered with the owners' interest, (2) impaired the chattel's condition, quality, or value, (3) prevented the owners from using the chattel for a substantial amount time, or (4) caused bodily harm to the owner or to some person or thing in which the owners had a legally protected interest. *Universal Tube & Rollform Equip. Corp. v. YouTube*, Inc., 504 F.Supp.2d 260, 269 (N.D. Ohio 2007). Additionally, the interference must be "more than intermeddling." *Dryden v. Cincinnati Bell Tel. Co.*, 734 N.E.2d 409, 416 (Ohio Ct. App.1999), citing RESTATEMENT (SECOND) OF TORTS § 218 cmt. e (1965).

2) **Intangible Computer Damage is Trespass to Chattel.** Several courts have held that intangible damage to computers is a trespass to chattel. *Register.com, Inc. v. Verio, Inc.*, 356 F.3d 393, 404 (2d Cir.2004) (a trespass claim involving a defendant's using "search robots" to perform automated queries of the owner's database and depleting a sever capacity and increased the other risks); *eBay, Inc. v. Bidder's Edge, Inc.*, 100 F.Supp.2d 1058, 1071 (N.D.Cal.2000) (a trespass claim involving defendant's using an automated program to access and search eBay's auction database and compromising eBay's ability to use its server); and *Am. Online, Inc. v. LCGM, Inc.*, 46 F.Supp.2d 444, 451–52 (E.D.Va.1998) (a trespass claim involving a defendant's using an owner's computer network to transmit bulk emails).

3) **Intangible Computer Damage Does Not Quality as Trespass to Chattel.** Several courts have refused to find trespass to chattel where the intangible computer damage was speculative or minimal. *Intel Corp. v. Hamidi*, 71 P.3d 296, 309 (Cal. 2003)

(refusing to finding trespass to chattel after the plaintiff failed to prove that defendant's mass emails prevented the owner from using its computers "for any measurable length of time"); *Ticketmaster Corp. v. Tickets.com, Inc.*, 2000 WL 1887522, at *4 (C.D. Cal. Aug. 10, 2000) (denying a preliminary injunction where defendant's automated search robots used "very small" percentage of plaintiff's server space and plaintiff made "no showing that the use interferes to any extent with [its] regular business").

---

2. Law-Practice Technologies and Electronic Trespass

Sullivan v. Mericle

2013 WL 2552221
(N.D. Ohio 2013)

Donald C. Nugent, District Judge. *Pro se* plaintiff James D. Sullivan filed the above captioned action under the Stored Communications Act (SCA), 18 U.S.C. § 2707, against the Ohio Adult Parole Authority (OAPA), and OAPA Parole Officer Timothy Mericle. In the Complaint, plaintiff alleges the defendants exceeded the authority he gave them to access his email in violation of 18 U.S.C. § 2707. He seeks monetary damages.

Factual and Procedural Background

Plaintiff was on parole from a conviction for a sexual offense. After failing to complete a [Volunteers of America] program in Cincinnati, plaintiff was returned to Cleveland on February 22, 2011. He was placed under the supervision of Senior Parole Officer Timothy Mericle. Mericle imposed several conditions of supervision, including a blanket prohibition of using a computer. Plaintiff expressed some concern with this restriction so a meeting was arranged with a sexual offender specialist to determine if there was some way plaintiff could be given limited access to a computer.

At this meeting on March 2, 2011, plaintiff complained that the restriction impinged on his ability to seek employment, and indicated his resume was stored in his Yahoo! email account as an attachment to an email. Mericle offered to retrieve the resume for plaintiff if plaintiff agreed to provide his user name and password. Plaintiff contends he agreed to this arrangement and provided the information needed to gain access to his email account. He claims he also noted the specific location of the email with his resume appended as an attachment. He alleges an unknown parole officer took down the information and left the room.

She returned shortly thereafter with copies of his resume. He contends Mericle left the room a few minutes later and returned with copies of emails plaintiff sent from his Yahoo! account in violation of the terms and conditions of his parole. Mericle arrested plaintiff and charged him with a parole violation. After a hearing, plaintiff's parole was revoked and he was returned to prison. Plaintiff contends Mericle knowingly exceeded his authorization to access his Yahoo! account in violation of 18 U.S.C. § 2701 and § 2707.

Standard of Review

Although *pro se* pleadings are liberally construed, the district court is required to dismiss an *in forma pauperis* action under 28 U.S.C. § 1915(e) if it fails to state a claim upon which relief can be granted, or if it lacks an arguable basis in law or fact. A claim lacks an arguable basis in law or fact when it is premised on an indisputably meritless legal theory or when the factual contentions are clearly baseless. A cause of action fails to state a claim upon which relief may be granted when it lacks "plausibility in the complaint." *Bell Atl. Corp. v. Twombly,* 550 U.S. 544, 564 (2007). A pleading must contain a "short and plain statement of the claim showing that the pleader is entitled to relief." *Ashcroft v. Iqbal,* 556 U.S. 662, 677–78 (2009).

The factual allegations in the pleading must be sufficient to raise the right to relief above the speculative level on the assumption that all the allegations in the Complaint are true. The Plaintiff is not required to include detailed factual allegations, but must provide more than "an unadorned, the-defendant-unlawfully-harmed-me accusation." *Iqbal,* 556 U.S. at 678. A pleading that offers legal conclusions or a simple recitation of the elements of a cause of action will not meet this pleading standard. *Id.* In reviewing a Complaint, the Court must construe the pleading in the light most favorable to the Plaintiff. *Bibbo v. Dean Witter Reynolds, Inc.,* 151 F.3d 559, 561 (6th Cir.1998).

Discussion

As an initial matter, plaintiff fails to state a claim for relief against the Ohio Adult Parole Authority. The OAPA is an agency of the State of Ohio. The Eleventh Amendment provides state governments with immunity from suits brought in federal courts by their own citizens as well as by citizens of another state. ... In addition, plaintiff fails to state a claim upon which relief may be granted against Mericle. "Congress enacted the relevant provision of the SCA, 18 U.S.C. § 2701, to protect privacy interests in personal and proprietary information from the mounting threat of computer hackers 'deliberately gaining access to, and sometimes tampering with, electronic or wire communications' by means of electronic trespass." *See Devine v. Kapasi,* 729 F.Supp.2d 1024, 1026 (N.D. Ill.2010). Title 18 U.S.C. § 2701(a) provides:

> Except as provided in subsection (c) of this section whoever—
>
> (1) intentionally accesses without authorization a facility through which an electronic communication service is provided; or
>
> (2) intentionally exceeds an authorization to access that facility and thereby obtains, alters, or prevents authorized access to a wire or electronic communication while it is in electronic storage in such system shall be punished as provided in subsection (b) of this section.

Any person who is aggrieved by a violation of the statute may pursue a civil action for damages. Determining whether there was unauthorized access under the SCA is similar to determining whether there was trespass to property. *Cardinal Health 414, Inc. v. Adams,* 582 F.Supp.2d 967, 976 (M.D. Tenn. 2008). The difference between committing the tort of common law trespass and violating the SCA, is that intentional conduct is required to violate the SCA. The term "intentional" in this context is narrower than the dictionary definition of "intentional" and requires more than a finding that the offender engaged in conduct or caused a result.

To violate the SCA, "the conduct or the causing of the result must have been the person's conscious objective." *Butera & Andrews v. IBM Corp.,* 456 F.Supp.2d 104, 109 (D.D.C.2006). Furthermore, while SCA punishes the act of accessing a "facility through which an electronic communication service is provided" in an unauthorized manner, the SCA does not punish disclosing and using the information obtained through prohibited actions. *Sherman & Co. v. Salton Maxim Housewares, Inc.,* 94 F.Supp.2d 817, 820 (E.D.Mich.2000).

Plaintiff claims he gave his user name and password for his email account to an unknown employee of the OAPA. She took it and returned a short time later with copies of his resume. He contends Mericle remained in the room with him for a short time and then left the room. He returned with a copy of an email plaintiff had sent earlier that same day. As an initial matter, plaintiff does not allege sufficient facts to demonstrate that Mericle, and not the unnamed female OAPA employee, accessed the email in question.

Because the SCA does not prohibit disclosing or using the information in the email, plaintiff cannot state a claim against Mericle by merely alleging he came into the room with a copy of the email and used that email to revoke Plaintiff's parole. Plaintiff has not adequately pled facts to suggest Mericle personally accessed the email. Moreover, even if Mericle had accessed the email, there are no facts alleged suggesting he exceeded his authority to do so. Plaintiff acknowledges that he gave Mericle authorization to access his email account and provided him with his user name and password.

He contends however, that he only intended for Mericle to access the one email with his resume attachment. He does not specify where in his email this resume was found. When an email account is opened by a user, it generally opens to the inbox and shows the ... read and unread mail that has not been deleted by the user. An email that is received in the inbox will indicate if the user has responded to that email, and will show the date that the email was received.

Therefore, when the unnamed clerk or Mericle opened the email account to retrieve the resume, it would be immediately apparent from what was visible on the screen that plaintiff had accessed his email earlier in the day. When plaintiff gave his parole officers' permission to access his account, he could not reasonably expect them to ignore all readily visible evidence of a parole violation. The facts alleged do not support a violation of 18 U.S.C. § 2701(a).

Accordingly, this action is dismissed pursuant to 28 U.S.C. § 1915(e). The Court certifies, pursuant to 28 U.S.C. § 1915(a)(3), that an appeal from this decision could not be taken in good faith.

NOTES AND QUESTIONS

1) **Common-Law Electronic Trespass to Chattel.** An electronic trespass to chattels claim must be based on some connection to a physical object. *Universal Tube & Rollform Equip. Corp. v. YouTube,* Inc., 504 F.Supp.2d 260, 268 (N.D. Ohio 2007) (finding that a computer's hosting website would be a sufficient physical object).

2) **The Stored Wire and Electronic Communications and Transactional Records Access Act, 18 U.S.C. §§ 2701.** The SCA provides a cause of action against anyone who "intentionally accesses without authorization a facility through which an electronic communication service is provided ... and thereby obtains, alters, or prevents authorized access to a wire or electronic communication while it is in electronic storage." Under section 2707(a), "electronic storage" is defined as "temporary, intermediate storage ... incidental to ... electronic transmission," or "storage ... for purposes of backup protection."

United States Code

Title 18. Crimes and Criminal Procedure
Chapter 121. Stored Wire and Electronic Communications and Transactional Records Access
18 U.S.C. § 2701

§ 2701. Unlawful access to stored communications

(a) Offense. —Except as provided in subsection (c) of this section whoever—

(1) intentionally accesses without authorization a facility through which an electronic communication service is provided; or

(2) intentionally exceeds an authorization to access that facility;

and thereby obtains, alters, or prevents authorized access to a wire or electronic communication while it is in electronic storage in such system shall be punished as provided in subsection (b) of this section.

(b) Punishment. —The punishment for an offense under subsection (a) of this section is—

(1) if the offense is committed for purposes of commercial advantage, malicious destruction or damage, or private commercial gain, or in furtherance of any criminal or tortious act in violation of the Constitution or laws of the United States or any State—

(A) a fine under this title or imprisonment for not more than 5 years, or both, in the case of a first offense under this subparagraph; and

(B) a fine under this title or imprisonment for not more than 10 years, or both, for any subsequent offense under this subparagraph; and

(2) in any other case—

(A) a fine under this title or imprisonment for not more than 1 year or both, in the case of a first offense under this paragraph; and

(B) a fine under this title or imprisonment for not more than 5 years, or both, in the case of an offense under this subparagraph that occurs after a conviction of another offense under this section.

United States Code

Title 18. Crimes and Criminal Procedure Chapter 121. Stored Wire and Electronic Communications and Transactional Records Access 18 U.S.C. § 2707

§ 2707. Civil Action

(a) Cause of action. —Except as provided in section 2703(e), any provider of electronic communication service, subscriber, or other person aggrieved by any violation of this chapter in which the conduct constituting the violation is engaged in with a knowing or intentional state of mind may, in a civil action, recover from the person or entity, other than the United States, which engaged in that violation such relief as may be appropriate.

(b) Relief. —In a civil action under this section, appropriate relief includes—

(1) such preliminary and other equitable or declaratory relief as may be appropriate;

(2) damages under subsection (c); and

(3) a reasonable attorney's fee and other litigation costs reasonably incurred.

(c) Damages.—The court may assess as damages in a civil action under this section the sum of the actual damages suffered by the plaintiff and any profits made by the violator as a result of the violation, but in no case shall a person entitled to recover receive less than the sum of $1,000. If the violation is willful or intentional, the court may assess punitive damages. In the case of a successful action to enforce liability under this section, the court may assess the costs of the action, together with reasonable attorney fees determined by the court.

* * *

(e) Defense. —A good faith reliance on—

(1) a court warrant or order, a grand jury subpoena, a legislative authorization, or a statutory

authorization (including a request of a governmental entity under section 2703(f) of this title);

(2) a request of an investigative or law enforcement officer under section 2518(7) of this title; or

(3) a good faith determination that section 2511(3) of this title permitted the conduct complained of;

—is a complete defense to any civil or criminal action brought under this chapter or any other law.

(f) Limitation—A civil action under this section may not be commenced later than two years after the date upon which the claimant first discovered or had a reasonable opportunity to discover the violation.

(g) Improper disclosure.—Any willful disclosure of a "record," as that term is defined in section 552a(a) of title 5, United States Code, obtained by an investigative or law enforcement officer, or a governmental entity, pursuant to section 2703 of this title, or from a device installed pursuant to section 3123 or 3125 of this title, that is not a disclosure made in the proper performance of the official functions of the officer or governmental entity making the disclosure, is a violation of this chapter. This provision shall not apply to information previously lawfully disclosed (prior to the commencement of any civil or administrative proceeding under this chapter) to the public by a Federal, State, or local governmental entity or by the plaintiff in a civil action under this chapter.

CHAPTER EIGHT: Consumers and Third Parties' Contract-Based Actions Against Attorneys

Dealing with Debts: There Oughtta Be a Rule! (But There Isn't)

70-SEP Or. St. B. Bull. 9

Sylvia Stevens

Recently, I heard from an arbitrator—a respected trial lawyer of many years' experience—who was distressed: [He had] being "stiffed" when the lawyer for one of the parties ... refused to pay the arbitrator's fee. [The attorney argued] that he was unable to collect it from his client. My caller was certain: He had seen authority ... obligating lawyers to pay [professionals'] litigation expenses—those incurred on behalf of their clients. I replied that I was not aware of any such authority in Oregon ... I had always believed: [T]he issue was governed by agency law and was not a matter of professional regulation.

The caller's certainty of the existence of such a requirement nevertheless piqued my curiosity. ... I found a former OSB Opinion No. 307 from 1975: [A] lawyer's personal obligations are not within the bar's jurisdiction. ... There [is] no disciplinary rule governing the situation. [In] *Burt v. Gahan*, 220 N.E.2d 817 (Mass. 1966), a court reporting firm [filed a breach of contract action] against a lawyer—who had engaged [the reporting firm's] services for [a] client's hearing. In *Burt*, the issue was whether in the absence of an express agreement with the court reporting firm, the lawyer was responsible. The court found in the affirmative:

> While in a broad sense, counsel may be an agent and his client a principal, there is much more involved than mere agency. ... The attorney usually determines what steps are to be taken in his client's interest. And the acts of the attorney in the conduct of litigation are binding upon the client. We therefore deem the just and equitable rule of law: ...

> In the absence of express notice to the contrary, court officials and persons connected—either directly or indirectly—with the progress of the litigation, may safely regard themselves as dealing with the attorney, instead of with the client. *Burt v. Gahan*, at 818-19.

There [are] contrary decisions in ... other jurisdictions. But, the *Burt* court found them unpersuasive. ... *Burt v. Gahan* appears to [be] the beginning of a nationwide trend away from the historical rule: Attorneys are liable for clients' litigation expenses *only if* they expressly assume such liability. The "modern rule"—as expressed in *Burt*—is clear: [An] attorney will be liable unless responsibility is expressly disclaimed. *See, Free v. Lankford & Assoc., Inc.*, 643 S.E.2d 771,773-74 (Ga. 2007); *Williams v. N. Alabama Court Reporting Serv.*, 833 So.2d 622, 626-27 (Ala. 2001); and *Cahn v. Fisher*, 805 P.2d 1040, 1043-44 (Ariz. 1990).

[T]he authorities discussed above involve failure to pay court reporter fees. [However], the same principles would apply as well to fees for other services that lawyers engage *in connection with* representing a client. ... The potential for civil liability is clear. I am less confident that lawyers should be subject to professional discipline for nonpayment of "professional financial obligations"—except in the most egregious of cases where the lawyer has ignored a court order or engaged in dishonest conduct in connection with the transaction.

I do not mean to suggest: Lawyers should feel free to ignore these professional financial obligations. On the contrary, even if no discipline or even a civil claim ensues, failure to honor such obligations can do significant harm to the lawyer's reputation. ... If a lawyer knows a client will not be able to pay the costs unless the case has a successful outcome, then the lawyer should be prepared to assume the obligation herself or decline the case. There is no excuse for "stiffing" a professional colleague. And a lawyer who does so has only himself or herself to blame if the word gets around that the lawyer cannot be trusted.

In *Dealing with Debts,* the author did not discuss whether "*services in connection with representing a client*" includes lawyers' purchasing and employing various law-practice hardware and software technologies. But even more importantly, the commentator failed to discuss whether solo practitioners have *ethical* or "*professional financial obligations*" to pay "ancillary" debts—those associated with attorneys' purchasing and upgrading computers and other law-practice hardware, establishing and maintaining websites, or accessing and using cloud-based computing.

As of this writing, it is unclear whether solo and small-firm attorneys have a professional or an ethical duty to pay each and every "ancillary debt"—after ordering technology goods and services. On the other hand, under a common-law breach-of-contract theory of recovery, attorneys may be civilly liable for failing to pay debts—if disappointed technology vendors and service providers satisfy certain legal criteria or elements. In this chapter, a few selected cases illustrate some of the difficulties that allegedly "stiffed" vendors and service providers must overcome to prevail in a court of law.

A. Computer-Network-Integration Services, Attorneys' Debts and Vendors' Breach-of-Oral-Contract Actions Against Attorneys

LanQuest Corporation v. McManus & Darden LLP

796 F.Supp.2d 98
(D.D.C. 2011)

Beryl A. Howell, District Judge.

In this action, LanQuest Corporation seeks payment for computer-network-engineering, and consulting services provided to the law firm, McManus & Darden LLP. LanQuest is a Maryland corporation, and McManus operates in the District of Columbia. Pending before the court is LanQuest's motion for summary judgment on Count I, which seeks payment of an outstanding invoice in the amount of $90,541.40.

I. Background

According to the Complaint, the parties had an oral contract under which LanQuest would perform computer network engineering, integration, and consulting services ("IT services") for the McManus for ten years—from June 2000 through November 2010. LanQuest submitted invoices for the work it performed "from time-to-time." and those invoices were always paid. Consistent with past practice, LanQuest submitted an invoice—dated December 6, 2010 (the "Disputed Invoice"). The latter invoice covered IT services from July 2008 through November 2010. The Disputed Invoice totals $90,541.40. And McManus law firm has not paid it.

LanQuest believes it is entitled to summary judgment in the amount of the Disputed Invoice. McManus counters—arguing that summary judgment is inappropriate because there are disputed issues of material fact regarding the existence and terms of the alleged oral contract between the parties. Moreover, even if there were an enforceable oral contract, McManus has raised disputed issues concerning the LanQuest's performance under the contract.

II. Summary Judgment Standard

Pursuant to Federal Rule of Civil Procedure 56, a court will grant a motion for summary judgment "if the movant shows that there is no genuine dispute as to any material fact and the movant is entitled to judgment as a matter of law" based upon the pleadings, depositions, and affidavits and other factual materials in the record. Fed.R.Civ.P. 56(a), (c); *Tao v. Freeh*, 27 F.3d 635, 638 (D.C.Cir.1994). A court "need consider only the cited materials. But a judge may consider other materials in the record." Fed.R.Civ.P. 56(c)(3). The Court must view all inferences in a light most favorable to the non-moving party. *Tao*, 27 F.3d at 638 (citing *Anderson v. Liberty Lobby, Inc.*, 477 U.S. 242, 250-55 (1986)). The burden is on the moving party to demonstrate: There is an "absence of a genuine issue of material fact" in dispute. *Celotex Corp. v. Catrett*, 477 U.S. 317, 323 (1986).

Summary judgment is generally appropriate only after the non-moving party has been afforded an adequate opportunity to conduct discovery. *Hellstrom v. U.S. Department of Veterans Affairs*, 201 F.3d 94, 97 (2d Cir. 2000). A grant of summary judgment may be appropriate prior to discovery where the moving party can demonstrate: There is no disputed issue of material fact. "[T]he non-moving party must do more than simply show that there is some metaphysical doubt as to the material facts." *Bias v. Advantage Intern.*, Inc., 905 F.2d 1558, 1561 (D.C.Cir.1990). It must "provide evidence that would permit a reasonable [fact-finder] to find" in its favor. *Laningham v. U.S. Navy*, 813 F.2d 1236, 1242 (D.C.Cir.1987).

III. Discussion

In applying the summary judgment legal standard to the instant record, the court has considered the allegations in the Complaint and the declarations and affidavits presented by LanQuest and McManus. No discovery has yet taken place in this case. So the record consists solely of the documentary affidavits or declarations submitted in connection with this motion. As explained below, this record compels the conclusion: Genuine issues of material fact are disputed and summary judgment is not appropriate at this time.

In support of its motion for summary judgment, LanQuest's president—Mark Chambers— has submitted a lengthy affidavit. The document describes the historical relationship between LanQuest and McManus (and McManus's predecessor firm). LanQuest's position is straightforward: The parties had an oral contract, under which LanQuest would provide IT services. McManus disputes the existence of an oral contract—citing the lack of agreement between the parties on the material terms of their relationship.

McManus has attached two declarations in support of its position—the declaration of the managing partner of the firm—Eric Darden—and the declaration of a computer consulting expert, Victor Rezmovic. The two declarations present specific facts that raise genuine issues about whether LanQuest is entitled to $90,541.40.

McManus contests LanQuest's most fundamental assumption: There was a viable oral contract between the parties. Certainly, the parties agree: They had no written agreement, even after ten years of an ongoing relationship. McManus correctly cites District of Columbia law: A valid and enforceable contract requires both: (1) intention of the parties to be bound; and (2) an agreement regarding all material terms. *See Gaujacq v. EDF, Inc.*, 601 F.3d 565, 579 (D.C. Cir. 2010). *See also, Steven R. Perles, P.C. v. Kagy*, 473 F.3d 1244, 1249 (D.C. Cir. 2007) (a valid and enforceable contract must include the parties' intention to be bound and an agreement as to all material terms). The party asserting the existence of an oral contract has the burden of proving both requirements. *New Econ. Capital, LLC v. New Mkts. Capital Grp.*, 881 A.2d 1087, 1094 (D.C. 2005).

Additionally, a contract must be sufficiently definite regarding material terms—subject matter, price, payment terms, quantity, quality, duration, promises, and the performance to be rendered by each party. *EastBanc, Inc. v. Georgetown Park Assocs. II, L.P.*, 940 A.2d 996 (D.C. 2008). "All the terms contemplated by the agreement need not be fixed with complete and perfect certainty for a contract to [be enforceable]." *V'Soske v. Barwick*, 404 F.2d 495, 500 (2d Cir.1968)). To be enforceable, however, the contract terms must be "sufficiently definite so that the parties can be reasonably certain as to how they are to perform." *EastBanc, Inc.*, 940 A.2d at 1002. Moreover, "the terms of the contract [must be] clear enough for the court to determine whether a breach has occurred and to identify an appropriate remedy. ..." *Monument Realty LLC v. Wash. Metro. Area Transit Auth.*, 535 F.Supp.2d 60, 69 (D.D.C. 2008).

In this case, the parties agree about the price of LanQuest's IT services: LanQuest's rate was $110 per hour for services provided during normal business hours and $165 per hour for services provided outside of normal business hours. Other key terms appear to be hotly disputed—such as the terms of payment, the schedule of invoicing, the pre-approval condition from Eric Darden alone for any work performed, and the quality of the work performed.

In particular, McManus asserts: Pursuant to an understanding reached by the parties in November 2008, LanQuest had to bill the law firm monthly and was not authorized to do any work without Mr. Darden's approval. According to McManus, this understanding arose following a prior dispute between the parties that occurred in November 2008. At that time, LanQuest submitted *three invoices* for a substantial amount of money for work performed over the preceding two-and-a-half years. According to Mr. Darden, although the firm *paid that invoice*, he spoke to LanQuest's president—Mark Chambers—and made *clear certain terms for their continuing relationship*, including timely, monthly invoicing and pre-approval by Mr. Darden.

LanQuest seeks to have the oral contract enforced—based upon the "consistent course of conduct between the parties dating back to at least 2003." The law in this Circuit and the District of Columbia law support the general assertion: Even where there is a written contract, a party's course of conduct can constitute a waiver of specific contractual provisions and be relied upon by the parties as a modification of any enforceable contract that exists between the parties. *Nortel Networks, Inc. v. Gold & Appel Transfer, S. A.*, 298 F.Supp.2d 81, 88 (D.D.C. 2004) ("Intent to waive a known right need not be expressly stated but may be inferred from conduct inconsistent with an intent to enforce that right."). *See also, Radiation Sys., Inc. v. Amplicon, Inc.*, 882 F.Supp. 1101, 1103 (D.D.C. 1995) (a party's course of performance can modify the contracted terms of a lease agreement).

The problem for LanQuest in this case, however, is clear: The new conditions allegedly set out by Mr. Darden—in November 2008 for monthly invoices and pre-approval—were precisely intended to change the course of prior practices between the parties with new terms. Because, without such conditions, it was impossible for McManus & Darden to manage its business affairs and to manage the services allegedly provided by LanQuest.

The court need not decide whether or not there is an enforceable oral contract at this stage of the litigation. There are sufficient disputed issues of material fact involving the key terms of any such contract to make summary judgment inappropriate. *See Steven R. Perles, P.C.*, 473 F.3d at 1249–1250 (reversing the district court's finding that an oral contract existed, because the parties "did not agree on two essential elements of a services contract—the length of defendant's performance and defendant's chores).

Even assuming that an enforceable oral contract exists between the parties, the parties also dispute whether LanQuest breach the contract by (1) failing to comply with the billing schedule that Mr. Darden required, and (2) failing to provide necessary passwords and allowing unauthorized copying of the firm's data. Finally, there is a dispute over the accuracy and reliability of the Disputed Invoice and the total amount due under that invoice. McManus suggests that various entries on the invoice reflect either double billing or unauthorized services. Thus, even assuming the existence of an enforceable contract, summary judgment in the amount of the invoice would still be inappropriate at this stage.

IV. Conclusion

A number of material issues remain in dispute between the parties and preclude summary judgment. The McManus should have an opportunity for discovery and to present evidence bearing on the disputes of material fact it has raised. *See NRM Corp. v. Hercules, Inc.*, 758 F.2d 676, 684 (D.C. Cir. 1985) (reversing a grant of summary judgment in light of material questions raised by the defendant over scope of the agreement to modify the original contract). LanQuest's motion for summary judgment is therefore DENIED.

B. Exclusivity and Long-Term Technologies Contracts, Attorneys' Outstanding Debts, and Service Providers' Breach-of-Oral Contract Actions Against Attorneys

Certified Computer Solutions, Inc. v. Rieth & Antonelli Company

841 N.E.2d 866
(Ohio Mun. Ct. 2005)

Joan Synenberg, Judge.

Phil Muhlfelder is an independent computer consultant—doing business as Certified Computer Solutions, Inc. In January 2003, Rieth & Antonelli Company ("law partners")—a family law firm—responded to an advertising postcard sent by Muhlfelder. The Law Partners were having recurring problems with their client-billing software and were frustrated by the general slowness and unreliability of their office computer system. Muhlfelder met with the law partners. And, on January 8, 2003, he sent a written proposal to the attorney. The partners liked it and hired Muhlfelder to improve the office-computer system.

The parties did not have a written contract. But Muhlfelder testified: The law partners did not choose the optimal and most expensive solution that he suggested. However, he alleged that he did his best—given the decisions that the law partners made. Muhlfelder detected and removed many computer bugs and viruses that he found on the firm's computers. He also installed Microsoft Windows-XP software on several computers, installed RAM boards for additional memory capacity, recovered TimeSlips data lost when the system crashed, and replaced memory modules and several failing items of the law firm's hardware.

Codefendant attorney Dominic Antonelli testified that as far as he was aware, Muhlfelder did all of the work shown on the invoices that Muhlfelder submitted. The law partners also testified: Neither of them is particularly "computer literate." They heavily relied upon Muhlfelder's advice. As bad as things were before Muhlfelder began his work, they testified: The system was "a nightmare" afterwards.

The system slowed to a crawl, and the number of computer crashes or freezes was not significantly reduced.

By March 2003, law partners brought in Dean M. Boland to advise them. Boland is a lawyer in private practice and a principal of Boland Consulting, LLC—a law and technology consulting firm. A former assistant prosecuting attorney of Cuyahoga County, Boland has extensive computer and office-technology experience. And Boland has been qualified as an expert witness on questions of law and technology in United States district courts in Oklahoma and Texas, as well as in three Ohio courts of common pleas and one other Ohio municipal court. Also, Boland is a columnist for the *Cleveland Bar Journal* on law and technology. He has been an adjunct professor at Case Western Reserve University School of Law. And Boland has often taught Supreme Court-approved continuing-legal-education courses on law and technology. Boland strongly disagreed with much of what Muhlfelder had proposed.

In Boland's opinion, law partners' computer system was rapidly becoming obsolete: (1) it had reached its memory capacity and speed; (2) it was overburdened by demands; and (3) the computer system had to be replaced. Relying on Boland's advice, the law partners spent $8,060.55 to upgrade and improve the system. Given Boland's connections in the computer industry, the law partners enjoyed a hefty discount on their hardware and software purchases. Boland and a networking assistant—Paul Knapp—completed the project. And the law partners testified that they were very pleased with the system's performance thereafter.

At trial, on a motion of the defense and over Muhlfelder's objection, Boland was certified as an expert witness—under Evid. R. 702. Boland testified: In his opinion, Muhlfelder's proposals and work did not adequately addressed the law partners' concerns. Additionally, Muhlfelder's proposals and performance left the law firm—in some ways—worse off than they had been. Boland stated: Muhlfelder's installing Windows-XP software on the firm's aging computers was "like putting high-quality fuel in a Yugo."

At trial, the witnesses disagreed about (1) the nature of the law firm's computer problems, (2) when Muhlfelder began and finished his work, (3) whether or when he learned about the law partners' dissatisfaction, (4) whether or not the law partners fully understood or accepted Muhlfelder's advice, and (5) whether Muhlfelder accomplished what he was hired to do. But, it was clear: The law partners did not communicate the dissatisfaction wholly and candidly to Muhlfelder. The law firm kept paying Muhlfelder—long after Boland began his work. No written evidence was submitted, expressing either defendant's dissatisfaction with Muhlfelder's services. Over time, law partners paid $2,500 for Muhlfelder's work. Although Muhlfelder originally sought $2,815, he amended his complaint at trial—seeking $1,315. Law partners counterclaimed for $2,513.

Conclusions of Law

At trial, a court must determine the credibility of witnesses and the weight to be given the evidence. *In re Lieberman,* 125 N.E.2d 328 (Ohio 1955). The quality of evidence is more important than its quantity. If trial testimony or other evidence is in conflict, the court must decide which to believe and which to disbelieve. *State v. DeHass,* 227 N.E.2d 212 (Ohio 1967).

All of the witnesses in this case were generally credible. However, Muhlfelder's credibility suffered. He gave inconsistent testimony regarding his awareness of codefendant Richard Rieth's dissatisfaction with his work regarding the extreme slowness of the law firm's computer system after he installed Microsoft Windows-XP software and regarding his January 25, 2003, offer to accept a lump-sum payment of $1,000 in full satisfaction for what he believed the firm still owed him.

At the conclusion of the evidence and pursuant to Civ. R. 21, the law partners moved to substitute "Rieth & Antonelli Company"—the actual name of the law firm—for the four originally named co-law partners (Richard Rieth, Dominic Antonelli, and each doing business as the law firm). The court now grants it. All of Richard Rieth's and Dominic Antonelli's dealings with Muhlfelder were as partners of the law firm, not in their personal capacities. Muhlfelder was hired to assist the law firm, not these individuals. And the law firm is clearly the real party in interest. *W. Clermont Edn. Assn. v. W. Clermont Local Bd. of Edn.*, 426 N.E.2d 512(Ohio 1980).

It is a basic tenet of contract law: A binding agreement will not be valid unless the parties have had a meeting of the minds through the presentation of an offer by one side and an acceptance of that offer by the other. *Marshall v. Beach*, 143 Ohio App.3d 432, 436-437 (2001). There are three "paradigm elements essential to contract formation—i.e., offer, acceptance, [and] consideration." *Helle v. Landmark, Inc.*, 15 Ohio App.3d 1, 8 (1984). The interpretation of a contract is a matter of law. *Long Beach Assn., Inc. v. Jones,* 82 Ohio St.3d 574 (1998). When a contract is susceptible of two or more reasonable interpretations, the resolution of the ambiguity is an issue for the trier of fact. *Cent. Ohio JVS Dist. Bd. of Edn. v. Peterson Constr. Co.*, 129 Ohio App.3d 58 (1998). If the interpretation of a contract requires consideration of evidence extrinsic, that is also an issue for the trier of fact. *Davis v. Loopco Industries, Inc.*, 66 Ohio St.3d 64 (1993).

Regrettably, the parties had no written contract. As shown by the facts of this case, oral contracts are notoriously prone to dispute and misunderstanding, which is why the law strongly favors written contracts. Nevertheless, it is clear: The parties had an oral contract, with the requisite elements of offer, acceptance, and consideration. In attempting to comply with the terms of that contract, Muhlfelder did extensive work—which Rieth & Antonelli Company's partners deemed almost wholly unsatisfactory. However, he actually did the work. And defendant did not timely express its dissatisfaction. Muhlfelder did his best to meet defendant's expectations. But he may have been, as suggested by the defense at trial, in over his head and incapable of ever completing the job to defendant's satisfaction. Rieth & Antonelli Company's partners eventually did much of what Muhlfelder had suggested in the first place—using new rather than rebuilt or upgraded old computers and using apparently greater skill than Boland and his assistant.

When a vendor sues upon a contract and alleges performance that is denied by the consumer, it is incumbent upon the vendor to prove substantial performance of the contract according to its terms. *Enterprise Roofing & Sheet Metal Co. v. Howard Inv. Corp.*, 152 N.E.2d 807 (Ohio 1957). The vendor or supplier must establish—by a preponderance of the evidence—that performance was done to the satisfaction of the customer. And the customer is required to appraise the work as a reasonable person would.

The Cleveland Municipal Court has broad legal and equitable powers in the cases before it. In the court's view, Muhlfelder is entitled to keep the money that he has already been paid. But he has not proven—by a preponderance of the evidence—that he is entitled to more. Similarly, Rieth & Antonelli Company's partners have failed to prove by a preponderance of the evidence that the law firm is entitled to judgment on its counterclaim. Accordingly, judgment is granted for Rieth & Antonelli Company's partners on the complaint. Judgment is granted for Muhlfelder on the counterclaim. So ordered.

End-User Licensees of Computer Programs—Are They Allowed to Compete with Their Licensors?

13 Rutgers Computer & Tech. L.J. 297

Lance Rose

Thousands of computer programs change hands every year at all levels of commerce and industry—from programs that run automated car factories to programs for personal computers. ... apes. Almost all programs are transferred pursuant to written license agreements. ... Program licenses explicitly cover a number of subjects, including: limitations on the place and manner in which the program recipient ("end user") can use his copy, acknowledgments of the licensor's title to the program, trade secrets contained in the program, and warranty obligations and limitations.

In *SAS Institute, Inc. v. S & H Computer Systems*, 605 F. Supp. 816, 827-828 (M.D. Tenn. 1985), the court recognized a new, implicit obligation—potentially applicable to all end-user program licenses. The court held: The end user was not permitted to use a program ... as the basis for a new program to compete with another program marketed by the licensor, regardless of whether the new program violated any of the licensor's copyrights. The court held that the license agreement created an "implied covenant of good faith and fair dealing" under which the end user could not use the licensed program to compete with the licensor.

* * *

In the early 1980s, copyright protection quickly gained ground as a major means of asserting program ownership. The rising importance of copyright protection was largely due to the 1980 amendments to the Copyright Act which formalized copyright protection for programs. A definition of "computer programs" was added to § 101, Act of Dec. 12, 1980, Pub. L. No. 96-517, § 10(a), 94 Stat. 3015, 3028. And, in § 117, the owners of program copies were given certain rights so they could use those copies without technically violating the Copyright Act, § 10(b), 94 Stat. 3015, 3028.

Although a license between the program owner and the end user is not necessary for copyright protection, the practice of licensing programs has continued to the present. In the case of microcomputer programs sold over the counter at department stores or book stores, the license takes the form of a "shrink-wrap" or "tear-me-open" license. ... End-user license agreements today serve two main purposes for program owners. First, almost all program owners claim that their programs contain trade secrets requiring strict contractual regulation of program dissemination. Second, by "licensing" the end user to "use" a copy of the program, the owner retains much more control over the end user's activities than if he had sold the copy outright. ...

End-user license agreements are primarily a means for program owners to contractually exert greater control over program copies in the hands of end users than they would otherwise have if they were mere "sellers" of program copies. It is against this background that the implied covenant of good faith and fair dealing ... should be examined.

C. End-User License Agreements and Licensors' Breach-of-Contract Actions Against Solo Practitioners and Small-Law Firms

Out of the Box Developers, LLC v. LogicBit Corporation

2012 WL 5356282
(N.C. Super. Ct.)

Gale, Judge.

Out of the Box Developers, LLC (OTB) is a North Carolina limited-liability company. Its principal place of business is located in Cary, North Carolina. LogicBit is a Delaware corporation with a principal place of business in Cary, North Carolina. Rivera is a resident of Cary, North Carolina. He is also LogicBit's founder, sole owner, and Chief Executive Officer. Doan Law LLP ("Doan Law") and the Doan Law Firm LLP ("Doan Law Firm") are collectively the "Doan Defendants." Doan Law is a California limited-liability partnership. It owns, manages, and controls a consumer bankruptcy law firm with offices in various locations throughout

California. Doan Law Firm is alleged to be a California limited-liability partnership with multiple California offices.

OTB owns BK*express,* which is a system of customizations for another software product called "*Time Matters.*" LexisNexis owns and sells *Time Matters*—a law-firm practice management software. LexisNexis does not customize *Time Matters* for use in any particular practice area. Instead, LexisNexis recommends Certified Independent Consultants (CICs)—such as OTB—to provide law-practice-specific customizations. OTB's Managing Director—Tom Rowe—created BK*express* to customize the *Time Matters* software for use by consumer bankruptcy practitioners. The product is distributed in three versions, depending on a firm's size and desired customizations.

Stated generally, OTB's customization process involves an OTB representative's onsite injection of elements of "program data" into the "program tables" on the *Time Matters* system. OTB claims the program data is protected intellectual property. Defendants contend that the program data is merely a labeling system—utilizing common phrases such as "Debtor," "Chapter 7," and "Judge."

OTB's authority to customize *Time Matters* is governed by a master agreement between LexisNexis and OTB. LexisNexis licenses *Time Matters* to its users—pursuant to an End-User License Agreement (EULA). OTB's license for BK*express* is also with the end user. LexisNexis is not a party to that license.

In 2007, Doan Law was using *Time Matters*—under the terms of its LexisNexis EULA. Later, James Doan ("Mr. Doan") asked OTB to install BK*express.* Rowe oversaw the installation on Doan Law's computers and the training of Doan Law's staff. On September 30, 2008, OTB and Doan Law executed a standard OTB licensing agreement. The Licensing Agreement provides: BK*express* "is the confidential and proprietary property of OTB."

In January 2010, as the Licensing Agreement's initial term was nearing its end, Doan Law asked OTB to reduce its annual BK*express* licensing fee from $995 to $200 per user per year. OTB declined. And Mr. Doan began searching for an alternative to BK*express.* Mr. Doan identified *HoudiniEsq*— LogicBit's law-firm management system. At the time, the latter software had not been customized for use by consumer bankruptcy practitioners.

In early 2010, Doan Law installed the *HoudiniEsq* platform. OTB alleges: During the transition, Doan Law improperly transferred—to LogicBit and Rivera— a back-up copy (the ".bak File") of their *Time Matters* software with all of OTB's BK*express* customizations. OTB also alleges: The ".bak" file was used to develop a customized version of *HoudiniEsq* to compete with BK*express*. Defendants admit that the copy was made. But they contend: The copy was authorized and proper.

Doan Law, LogicBit, and Francisco Rivera worked to replicate BK*express's* functionality into the *HoudiniEsq* program. And, Mr. Doan admits: He used BK*express* to customize *HoudiniEsq* to perform the same functions—often having BK*express* open in front of him "to make sure that he was capturing every piece of data he had in the *Time Matters*/BK*express* system."

On March 22, 2010, Doan Law informed OTB that the Licensing Agreement would expire by its terms on April 23, 2010. On April 21, 2010, Rowe contacted Doan Law to schedule the removal of BK*express* from Doan Law's system— after the Parties were unable to reach an agreement to extend the Licensing Agreement on a prorated fee basis. Doan Law's IT provider—Roy Allen ("Allen")—migrated Doan Law's data from the *Time Matters* database into the *HoudiniEsq* platform. Doan Law suggested that OTB could uninstall the BK*express* customizations on or after May 3, 2010. Rowe indicates: He was prepared to remove the BK*express* customizations on May 5, 2010. But he was unable to do so, because Doan Law did not provide him with the information necessary to remotely access Doan Law's computer system. To date, OTB has not been allowed to uninstall BK*express* from Doan Law's system. Mr. Doan indicates: Doan Law has, however, not used BK*express* or *Time Matters* since the data migration to *HoudiniEsq*.

Analysis

OTB claims: Undisputed evidence establishes that Doan Law breached the Licensing Agreement by: (1) refusing to allow OTB to remove the BK*express* customizations from Doan Law's computer system when the Licensing Agreement expired; (2) transferring the *.bak* File to LogicBit and Rivera without OTB's prior written consent; and (3) reverse engineering BK*express* to customize *HoudiniEsq* for the purpose of competing with OTB.

Defendants assert that the court has no jurisdiction over these claims because: (1) OTB has no standing. Its license improperly limits the rights that Doan Law was given under its LexisNexis EULA; and (2) OTB's claims are preempted by the Copyright Act.

Defendants' Motion to Dismiss and Plaintiff's Motion to Strike

OTB Has Standing to Assert Breaches of Its Licensing Agreement

To have standing, a plaintiff must demonstrate injury in fact, causation, and the likelihood that the injury will be redressed by a favorable decision. *Lee Ray Bergman Real Estate Rentals v. N.C. Fair Hous. Ctr.,* 153 N.C.App. 176, 179 (2002). ... OTB has two agreements with LexisNexis—a "Certified Independent Consultant Agreement" and a "Solution Provider Agreement (Distributor)," which provide in pertinent part:

> [U]nder no circumstances may [OTB] grant licenses to use [*Time Matters*] ... on terms and conditions other than those set forth in the end user license agreements accompanying, embedded within [*Time Matters*] or otherwise displayed prior to allowing the customer to download, install, or use [*Time Matters*] (collectively, the "EULA").

OTB has standing to assert its claim, ... Defendants have not successfully demonstrated that OTB lacks standing to assert violations of its Licensing Agreement. To the extent that the motion to dismiss rests on this ground, it is denied.

Two of OTB's Claims Are Not Preempted by the Federal Copyright Act

Defendants assert: All of OTB's claims fall within the scope of the federal Copyright Act, 17 U.S.C. §§ 101 *et seq.*—meaning that OTB's exclusive claim is for copyright infringement. Defendants' essential argument is that OTB's claims are no more than variations on an assertion that Defendants created or transferred an unauthorized derivative work. Section 301(a) of the Copyright Act provides:

> All legal or equitable rights that are equivalent to any of the exclusive rights within the general scope of copyright as specified by Section 106 in works of authorship that are fixed in a tangible medium of expression and come within the subject matter of copyright as specified by sections 102 and 103 ... are

> governed exclusively by [the Copyright Act]. 17 U.S.C. § 301(a) (2006).

In pertinent part, Section 106 grants exclusive rights "(1) to reproduce the copyrighted work in copies or phonorecords; (2) to prepare derivative works based upon the copyrighted work; [and] (3) to distribute copies or phonorecords of the copyrighted work to the public by sale or other transfer of ownership, or by rental, lease, or lending." 17 U.S.C. § 106(l)-(3).

There is significant federal case law addressing preemption of state law claims by the Copyright Act. The case law is not always consistent, either between circuits or within the same circuit. *See generally,* 1 Melville B. Nimmer & David Nimmer, NIMMER ON COPYRIGHT § 1.01[B](1)[a] (2012). Stated as a broad general rule, a state-law cause of action is preempted by the Copyright Act if: (1) the cause of action falls within the subject matter of copyright law; and (2) the rights protected by state law are equivalent to any of the exclusive rights granted by the Copyright Act. *Rosciszewski v. Arete Assocs., Inc.,* 1 F.3d 225, 229 (4th Cir.1993).

Preemption does not depend on whether the owner has actually secured a registered copyright, although such a registration may be a predicate to filing a copyright infringement action. *See Innovative Med. Prods., Inc. v. Felmet,* 472 F.Supp.2d 678, 683 (M.D.N.C. 2006). Here, BK*express* falls within the subject matter of copyright law as an original work of authorship—fixed in a tangible medium. 17 U.S.C. § 102. Therefore, the determinative issue is whether OTB's state-law claims are equivalent to the "exclusive" rights granted under the Copyright Act. In *Rosciszewski,* 1 F.3d at 229-230, the Fourth Circuit articulated an "extra element" test, stated as follows:

> In order to ascertain whether a specific state cause of action involves a right equivalent to one of those identified in § 106, reference must be made to the elements of the state cause of action. State-law claims that infringe one of the exclusive rights contained in § 106 are preempted by § 301(a) if the right defined by state law "may be abridged by an act which, in and of itself, would infringe one of the exclusive rights. However, if an 'extra element' is required instead of or in addition to the acts of reproduction, performance, distribution or display, in order to constitute a state-created cause of action, ... here is no preemption, provided that the 'extra

> element' changes the "nature of the action so that it is *qualitatively* different from a copyright infringement claim."

North Carolina federal district court followed this test to determine whether North Carolina causes of action for trade secret misappropriation and unfair and deceptive trade practices based on such misappropriation are not preempted by the Copyright Act. *Forest2Market, Inc. v. Am. Forest Mgmt., Inc.*, 2008 WL 1820917 (W.D.N.C. Apr. 21, 2008).

As to breach of contract claims, federal circuits do not follow a uniform approach in determining whether the contractual promise—required to prove a breach of contract—is itself an "extra element" adequate to defeat preemption by the Copyright Act. Some circuits have held: The existence of a contractual promise in and of itself constitutes an extra element sufficient to avoid preemption. *ProCD, Inc. v. Zeidenburg.* 86 F.3d 1447, 1454 (7th Cir.1996); *Taquino v. Teledyne Monarch Runner,* 893 F.2d 1488, 1501 (5th Cir.1990), and *Acorn Structures, Inc. v. Swantz,* 846 F.2d 923, 926 (4th Cir.1988). Other decisions within the Fourth Circuit stated that breach-of-contract claims are preempted. *See Nichols Agency, Inc. v. Enchanted Child Care, Inc.,* 537 F.Supp.2d 774 (D.Md. 2008); *Madison Rover Mgt. Co. v. Bus. Mgt. Software Corp.,* 351 F.Supp.2d 436, 443–44 (M.D.N.C. 2005); *Brown v. McCormick,* 23 F.Supp.2d 594, 608 (D.Md. 1998); *Wharton v. Columbia Pictures Indus., Inc.,* 907 F.Supp. 144, 146 (D.Md.1995).

* * *

OTB's breach-of-contract claims—based on Defendants' alleged copying—raise more difficult preemption issues. Put simply, they more closely resemble a claim for copyright infringement. OTB asserts that Doan Law breached three provisions of the End-User Licensing Agreement: (1) Doan Law refused to allow OTB to remove the BK*express* customizations when the Licensing Agreement expired; (2) Doan Law gave LogicBit and/or Rivera an unauthorized copy of the BK*express* customizations; and (3) Doan Law improperly reverse engineered BK*express.* Each of these claims arises from Schedule 1 of the Licensing Agreement which provides:

> 3. *Limitations.* The System and Documentation (and all copies thereof) are licensed, not sold, and title to the System and Documentation and all copies thereof remains solely with OTB. The System may only be used by [Doan Law] to customize [Doan

> Law's] specific Lexis Software installation that is used in [Doan Law's] own business and not for any Improper Use. In this Agreement "Improper Use" means: … (v) any effort to reverse engineer, decompile, disassemble, or otherwise discover the operation of the System for the purpose of either competing with OTB, creating derivative works from the System, or creating software with similar functionality. …
>
> 6. *Ownership; Transfers and Other Restrictions.* [Doan Law] may not sell, rent, lease, lend, contract host (such as in an application service or hosing provider), or transfer any copy of the System, without the express prior written consent of OTB. You may not allow any other parties to provide the System to you under contract or application hosting, or other contract service, except by OTB, or an application or hosting provider that is an authorized distributor certified by OTB. …
>
> 8. *Term; End of Subscription License; General* … (ii) At the end of the subscription license period [Doan Law] shall cease all use of the System and shall permit OTB to access [Doan Law's] installation of the Lexis Software to remove all BK*express* functionality[.]

The first breach claim does not raise preemption issues, because removing customizations at the end of the license term does not fall within the subject matter of the Copyright Act. However, the second and third breach claims involve copying and fall within the scope of Section 106 of the Copyright Act. …

The court concludes that OTB's asserted breach of Schedule 1 Paragraph 6 of the Licensing Agreement—by furnishing a copy of the .bak File—is preempted. The act underlying the asserted breach would—without further proof—constitute copyright infringement. The claim is therefore preempted. Accordingly, Defendants' motion to dismiss OTB's claim for breach of Schedule 1, Paragraph 6 of the Licensing Agreement for lack of subject matter jurisdiction is granted.

Plaintiff's Motion for Partial Summary Judgment

Doan Law Breached the Agreement by Refusing To Allow Removal of Bkexpress

Defendants do not dispute that OTB has not been allowed remove the BK*express* customizations from Doan Law's system. Defendants rather defend OTB's breach of contract claim by asserting that any breach was immaterial or that allowing OTB to enforce its agreement would violate laws or public policy. While their arguments may later be effective in limiting any monetary damage OTB may be able to prove as a result of the breach, the uncontested evidence establishes that Doan Law has breached the Licensing Agreement by its refusal to allow the customizations to be removed. ... Accordingly, OTB's motion for partial summary judgment regarding the breach of Schedule 1, Section 8(ii) of the Licensing Agreement is granted.

There Are Material Issues of Fact Regarding OTB's Claim for Reverse Engineering

OTB contends that Defendants' own testimony supports granting OTB summary judgment on this claim. OTB points to Mr. Doan's deposition testimony that he used BK*express* to customize *HoudiniEsq* to perform the same functions, often having BK*express* open in front of him "to make sure that [he] was capturing every piece of data he had in the *Time Matters*/BK*express* system."

Defendants admit: Doan Law provided the .bak File to LogicBit and Rivera. And the latter wanted to ensure that Doan Law lost no functionality when changing to the *HoudiniEsq* platform. Again, the court is not persuaded that any public policy argument excuses violating the Licensing Agreement. But, a violation has not been proven by uncontested facts. More specifically, the record does not clearly show: Defendants actually incorporated OTB's protected customizations into *HoudiniEsq*. Instead, Defendants only used the .bak File to assure that Doan Law's client data was unlocked. The undisputed evidence demonstrates some degree of reverse engineering. But the evidence is disputed whether that the reverse engineering was of such a degree as to constitute developing a competitive product.

OTB's motion for partial summary judgment for violation of Schedule 1, Paragraph 3 of the Licensing Agreement is therefore denied. It is so ordered.

NOTES AND QUESTIONS

1) **The "Implied Covenant of Good Faith and Fair Dealing" Claim.** In *Gruenberg v. Aetna Ins. Co.*, 510 P.2d 1032, 106 (Cal. 1973), Justice Sullivan wrote: "There is an implied covenant of good faith and fair dealing in every contract." And if a breach occurs, the resulting action or theory of recovery may "*sound in both contract and tort.*" A majority of state supreme courts have embraced this rule. *See, e.g.*, *Cantwell v. City of Boise*, 191 P.3d 205, 213 (Idaho 2008) ("Idaho law recognizes a cause of action for breach of an implied covenant of good faith and fair dealing); *In re Hennepin Cnty. 1986 Recycling Bond Litig.*, 540 N.W.2d 494, 502 (Minn. 1995) ("Under Minnesota law, every contract includes an implied covenant of good faith and fair dealing ..."); and *Wood v. N.J. Mfrs. Ins. Co.*, 206 N.J. 562, 577 (N.J. 2011) ("[E]very contract in New Jersey contains an implied covenant of good faith and fair dealing that is, neither party shall do anything which will have the effect of destroying or injuring the right of the other party to receive the fruits of the contract[.]").

2) **The "Common Law Duty of Good Faith and Fair Dealing" Claim in Texas.** In *Natividad v. Alexsis, Inc.*, 875 S.W.2d 695, 697 (Tex. 1994), Justice Gonzalez wrote: "[T]his court has declined to *impose* an implied covenant of good faith and fair dealing in every contract. ... [But] we have recognized that a duty of good faith and fair dealing may arise as a result of *a special relationship* between the parties governed or *created by a contract.*" *See also, Jim Walter Homes, Inc. v. Reed,* 711 S.W.2d 617, 618 (Tex.1986): "The contractual relationship of the parties may create *duties under both contract and tort law.* The acts of a party may breach duties in tort or contract alone or simultaneously in both. The nature of the injury most often determines which duty or duties are breached. When the injury is only the economic loss to the subject of a contract itself, the action sounds in contract alone."

CHAPTER NINE: Consumers' Statutory Actions Against Attorneys' Deceptive and Unfair Debt-Collection Practices

Debt Collection in the Information Age: New Technologies and the Fair Debt Collection Practices Act

99 Cal. L. Rev. 1601

Colin Hector

Devilin Wilson— a friend of Melanie Beacham—received an unexpected message through his Facebook account. The man identified himself as "Jeff Happenstance." The message was straightforward: "Please have Melanie D. Beacham call" a specified phone number. Wilson responded, suggesting that he would relay Happenstance's request. But he noted: Since Beacham had her own Facebook account, it would be simpler for Happenstance to contact her directly. Happenstance thanked him for the reply, and did not message Wilson again. One month later, Beacham received a Facebook message from a person identifying himself as "Loxley Duffus." Duffus's message was much more pressing. The message stated that there was an "urgent" matter, provided a phone number to call, and asked Beacham to contact "Supervisor Duffus at MarkOne" by 6 p.m. that day.

Both messages were from a debt collector, and were aimed at inducing Beacham to repay a $362 car loan. But, instead of prompting a quick repayment, the unwanted online contacts led Beacham to file a civil suit in state court—alleging violations of state debt collection laws and intentional infliction of emotional distress. Beacham's suit marked the first time a debt collector had been sued based on a series of Facebook messages. While Beacham's suit may be the first, it almost certainly will not be the last. A growing number of similar lawsuits and media stories reveal: Debt collectors are increasingly turning to *emerging technologies* as a way to collect payments on defaulted debts.

In one case, a debt collector attempted to intimidate a putative debtor. [The collector stated that she saw] a picture of the consumer's "beautiful daughter" on the consumer's MySpace webpage. In another example, a Chicago lawyer reported that a young woman in a bikini had "friended" his client on Facebook. The account turned out to be a debt collector, who posted a message on the client's wall: "Pay your debts, you deadbeat." In yet another instance, a consumer alleged: A debt collector placed a message on his daughter's MySpace webpage, demanding that the daughter contact the debt collector and warning her that "[f]ailure to comply with this notice of surrender is a class 5 felony and carries a maximum penalty of imprisonment for two years plus all applicable surcharges."

Debt collectors' use of new communication mediums is not limited to the use of social networking websites. For example, debt collectors have also been experimenting with ways to integrate e-mail and mobile phone text messaging services into their overall collection strategy. One company that [sells debt collection technologies] claims: When a top-ten sub-prime mortgage lender "added text messaging to their existing communications efforts," the lender "saw increased payment rates by nearly 100% within five days of contact." Despite the potential effectiveness of new technologies, industry insiders have advised collectors to use caution—in order to avoid lawsuits like the one brought by Melanie Beacham.

Applying the Fair Debt Collection Practices Act to debt collectors' use of new technologies is a challenging endeavor. Congress passed the FDCPA in 1977—well before the advent of e-mail, Internet, mobile, and voicemail technologies. However, the provisions of the FDCPA have remained largely unchanged over the last thirty years.

To be sure, as a matter of law, federal courts have uniformly held: Lawyers *are not* debt collectors under the FDCPA—if attorneys' debt-collection activities constitute a *small percentage* of their revenues. *See Schroyer v. Frankel*, 197 F.3d 1170, 1172 (6th Cir. 1999) (finding that the law firm's debt-collection activities comprised less than 2% of firm's practice and concluding that the firm was not a debt collector); *Argentieri v. Fisher Landscapes, Inc.*, 15 F.Supp.2d 55, 60 (D. Mass. 1998) (finding that the attorney's debt-collection activities comprised .4% of firm's practice and declaring that the firm was not a debt collector); *Von Schmidt*, 9

F.Supp.2d at 102–103 (finding that the law firm's debt-collection revenue was only $807.79 and holding that the firm was not a debt collector); *Hartl v. Presbrey & Assoc.*, 1996 WL 529339 (N.D. Ill. 1996) (finding that the attorney's debt-collection activities comprised less than 1% of firm's practice and declaring that the firm was not a debt collector); and, *Nance v. Petty, Livingston, Dawson & Devening*, 881 F.Supp. 223, 225 (W.D.Va.1994) (granting the motion to dismiss after finding that the debt-collection comprised 1.07% of the firm's cases).

Still, an extremely large number of solo practitioners and small-firm attorneys form *contractual relationships* with debt-collection agencies—*sharing various traditional and emerging law-practice technologies. Cf. James v. Wadas*, 724 F.3d 1312, 1317 (10th 2013) ("In 1986, in response to the large increase in the number of attorneys' conducting debt collection, Congress repealed the attorney exemption. ... Congress intended for the FDCPA 'to cover any attorney who is *in the business* of collecting debts.' However, it offers little guidance on what constitutes the 'regular' collection of debts by an attorney or law firm.")

Consider, therefore, the following hypothetical: Jennifer—a solo-practice attorney—forms a *contractual relationship* with a debt-collection agency. And, under the terms of the agreement, third-party creditors send identical copies of delinquent debtors' files and outstanding accounts to both the collection agency and Jennifer. All parties use Digital Transaction Management Company's *DocuSign* software to transfer files as well as to share and sign various legal documents. Even more significantly, the solo-practice attorney and the debt-collection agency use the *same office technologies*—computers, social-media account, network printer, case-management programs, automated-dialing-telephones for calling delinquent debtors, e-mail accounts, and form-letters folding and processing machine.

Also assume: (1) The debt-collection agency generates and sends demand letters to delinquent debtors—using the *attorney's signature as well as the attorney's letterhead paper and envelopes*; and (2) After receiving one of the allegedly "deceptive and misleading" debt-collection letters, an agitated consumer-debtor sues Jennifer—rather than the debt-collection agency. Will the solo practitioner be liable under the Fair Debt Collection Practices Act or under a state fair debt collection statute for sending the allegedly "misleading" debt-collection letter? Will Jennifer be liable under the Uniform Deceptive Trade Practices Act of 1964 or 1969 (UDTPA) or under a Deceptive Trade Practices Act (DTPA) for engaging in deceptive debt-collection practices?

Again, as stressed in Chapter 3, every jurisdiction has enacted consumer-protection statutes. More specifically, some states have adopted the UDTPA. Texas and most states have modeled their DTPAs after the UDTPA. Generally, DTPAs have multiple functions. In some states, DTPAs are "intended to address unfair or deceptive trade practices that interfere with the promotion and conduct of another's business." *Grand Ventures, Inc. v. Whaley,* 632 A.2d 63, 64 (Del.1993). And, in other jurisdictions, DTPAs are designed to protect consumers against breaches of warranty and other false, misleading, and deceptive business practices. *See e.g., Pope v. Rollins Protective Servs. Co.,* 703 F.2d 197, 201 (5th Cir.1983).

Furthermore, in several states, consumer protection statutes have "tie-in" or "companion" statutes. *See Neuros Co., Ltd. v. KTurbo, Inc.,* 2013 WL 1706368, *2 (N.D. Ill.) (the court's finding a violation under a companion Illinois state statute); *Wright v. Jeckle,* 144 P.3d 301, 304 (Wash. 2006); and, Ed Walton, *DTPA "Tie-In" Statutes: A Practical Guide, in* STATE BAR OF TEXAS PROF. DEV. PROGRAM, ADVANCED DTPA/INSURANCE CONSUMER LAW COURSE (1994). Put simply, viable claims under so-called "tie-in statutes" may commence under and/or receive remedial action under a DTPA. For example, under Texas's DTPA, the Federal and Texas Fair Debt Collection Acts are "tie-in" statutes. *Cf. Bibolotti v. American Home Mortg. Servicing, Inc.,* 2013 WL 2147949, *7 (E.D. Tex. 2013). The federal act forbids debt collectors from employing "any false, deceptive, or misleading representation or means in connection with the collection of any debt." 15 U.S.C. § 1692e. The federal statute also prohibits any "false representation or implication"—stating that an individual is an attorney or stating that an attorney sent the communication. 15 U.S.C. § 1692e(3).

In this chapter, the cases and materials highlight some of the legal implications of solo and small-firm attorneys' forming contractual agreements with debt-collection firms. This chapter also outlines some of the procedural and substantive huddles that solo and small-firm attorneys must confront when defending themselves against consumers-debtors' lawsuits. But before examining the cases, consider the highly pertinent information and the short analysis in the next article.

A Rose Is A Rose Is A Rose—Or Is It? Fiduciary and DTPA Claims Against Attorneys

35 St. Mary's L.J. 823

James Parker, Jr., Thomas H. Watkins, and Rachel L. Noffke

In general, to recover under the DTPA, a plaintiff must establish that: (1) she was a consumer of the defendant's goods or services; (2) the defendant committed "false, misleading, or deceptive acts" in connection with the lease or sale of the goods or services or committed an unconscionable act; and (3) such acts were a producing cause of actual damages. ... It is axiomatic: Under the DTPA, a person must be a "consumer"—one who sought or acquired goods or services by purchase or lease. Moreover, the services must necessarily be the basis of the plaintiff's allegations. Thus, to the extent that a client directly seeks to obtain the services of a lawyer, there is no question: Clients can be consumers under the DTPA. Additionally, because privity is generally not required in a DTPA action against an attorney, a person need not actually seek to acquire the services from the lawyer before DTPA liability can attach. Thus, a plaintiff may be the "consumer" of the legal services, if a third party actually purchases the services for her benefit. ...

However, there are also a number of cases in which consumer status has been denied to persons attempting to sue attorneys under the DTPA. For example, in *Vinson & Elkins v. Moran*, 946 S.W.2d 381, 386 (Tex. App.-Houston [14th Dist.] 1997), the executors of an estate hired lawyers in connection with the administration of the estate. Later, the beneficiaries of the estate sued the lawyers for allegedly violating the DTPA. The executors claimed that they were the consumers of the lawyers' services. The court agreed. The estate beneficiaries benefitted incidentally by the executor's hiring the law firm. The attorneys assisted with the orderly administration of the estate. And the primary purpose of the attorneys' services was to assist the executors with the administration of the estate. Any additional benefit that the benefactors received "was merely incidental to the main purpose."

***

In 1995, the Texas Legislature enacted a number of changes to the DTPA. ... In Section 17.49(c)—entitled "Exemptions," the legislature provided that:

> Nothing in this subchapter shall apply to a claim for damages based on the rendering of a professional service—the essence of which is the providing of advice, judgment, opinion, or similar professional skill. This exemption does not apply to:
>
> (1) an express misrepresentation of a material fact that cannot be characterized as advice, judgment, or opinion;
>
> (2) a failure to disclose information in violation of Section 17.46(b)(24);
>
> (3) an unconscionable action or course of action that cannot be characterized as advice, judgment, or opinion;
>
> (4) breach of an express warranty that cannot be characterized as advice, judgment, or opinion; or
>
> (5) a violation of Section 17.46(b)(26).

Reviewing the above provisions, it is clear: The legislature intended to exclude claims for damages under the DTPA—based on the *rendering of a professional servic* . ... The difficulty is deciding what actions ... constitute nonactionable "advice, judgment or opinion," and what are actionable misrepresentations, warranties, or unconscionable conduct. Unfortunately, the cases decided after 1995 do not assist in developing a bright line test for attorneys' conduct.

A. Attorneys' Liability under State Consumer-Protection Statutes for Allegedly Employing Computers and Other Technologies to Harass Consumers-Debtors

1. Attorneys' Liability under Deceptive Trade Practices Acts

Kelly v. Palmer, Reifler, & Associates, P.A.

681 F.Supp.2d 1356
(S.D. Fla. 2010)

Edwin G. Torres, United States Magistrate Judge.

Civil theft recovery statutes have been enacted in all fifty states. Under the statutes, retail stores and other commercial entities may recoup losses sustained as a result of retail theft. Numerous retailers and commercial entities retained Palmer, Reifler & Associates, P.A. ("Palmer Law Firm" or "the firm") to collect civil damages and penalties from alleged shoplifters.

Plaintiffs—Veronica Kelly, Lil Simon, and Ron Baum or their children—received civil theft demand letters from the Palmer Law Firm. Plaintiff Kelly—who resides in Pennsylvania— received three letters from the firm in connection with an incident at J.C. Penney involving her minor child. The first letter stated: This Law Firm represents J.C. Penney concerning its claim ... in connection with an incident involving your child in their store 67 on 3/1/2008. Pursuant to "Damages in actions on retail theft" statute, 42 Pa.C.S.A. § 8308, J.C. Penney may proceed with a civil penalty action against you. *You may settle this matter by [paying] $202 within twenty (20) days of the date of this letter*. ... Payment should be made payable and mailed to [the Palmer Law Firm.]

The letter was signed by a lawyer admitted to practice law in Pennsylvania as "Of Counsel for the Firm." The second letter to Ms. Kelly noted her failure to pay ... and advised in pertinent part: Pursuant to the "Damages in actions on retail theft" statute, 42 Pa.C.S.A. § 8308, J.C. Penney may now proceed with litigation against you. *You may stop a lawsuit from being filed and settle this* *matter by making payment to us in the amount of $477.00 within ten (10) days of the date of this letter.* ... Should payment fail to be made, our client may ... file a lawsuit against you. ... If successful in any such litigation, we estimate that our client would [ask for] damages, attorney's fees and court costs in excess of the amount demanded herein. The third letter that Kelly received was similar to the second letter.

Plaintiff Simon received three letters in connection with an incident at Wal-Mart involving her adult child, Michael, who resides with her in Florida. The first two letters, sent by Wal-Mart, demanded payment of $200.00. The third letter was sent by the Palmer Law Firm and signed by James R. Palmer It was similar to the second letter. Simon paid $280 and received a written release. Plaintiff Baum received one letter from the Palmer Law Firm in connection with an incident at Macy's involving his minor child. He paid the $200 demand amount and received a written release.

The Palmer Law Firm has approximately 90 employees—six of whom are lawyers. The firm collaborates with attorneys in other states who provide various services: explaining local laws, reviewing cases, executing and sending certified demand letters, telephoning opposing parties and filing lawsuits. Natt O. Reifler—a partner at the Palmer Law Firm—reported that the firm sent over four million debt-collection demand letters between June 2004 and March or April 2009. The average was approximately 70,000 per week. The majority of people pay after receiving a demand letter. But some do not, and the total figure includes second and third letters as well as the initial demand letter.

The firm's demand letters are based on information provided to the firm by their retail clients—often but not always in an electronic format. ... Plaintiffs have sued to stop the Palmer Law Firm's practice of sending demand letters that are allegedly deceptive, unfair, and oppressive. According to plaintiffs, the purpose is "to harass, intimidate and coerce consumers into paying a large fine by threatening civil action by a local attorney—who has no intention of filing a suit, who has no involvement in the case). The Plaintiffs also assert: The Palmer Law Firm collects information from its retail clients and—utilizing sophisticated computer software—automatically generates misleading demand letters, calculates demand amounts, and affixes a local attorney's signature to the demand letter, all without an attorney's review.

Plaintiffs accuse the Palmer Law Firm of violating Florida's Deceptive and Unfair Trade Practices Act (FDUTPA), Fla. Stat. §

501.201, *et seq.* (Count V). ... The Palmer Law Firm moves for summary judgment in its favor on all of Plaintiffs' claims. Plaintiffs move for partial summary judgment on liability for violations of FDUTPA.

II. Analysis

Florida's Deceptive and Unfair Trade Practices Act Claims

1. Attorney's Conduct Under FDUTPA

The Palmer Law Firm contends: FDUTPA does not apply to attorneys' conduct. Thus, Plaintiffs' FDUTPA claims must be dismissed. The statute does not explicitly mention the legal profession in this context. And the firm acknowledges: To date, no Florida court has held that an attorney's conduct *will not* give rise to a FDUTPA claim. But, the firm cites decisions from courts outside of Florida. Those decisions hold that states' unfair trade practices acts do not apply to attorneys' conduct. Generally, the rationale in those cases is short: Lawyers are regulated by their state's highest court.

Therefore, acts committed by lawyers in the course of practicing law will not support claims of unfair trade practices. *See, e.g., Jamgochian v. Prousalis,* 2000 WL 1610750 (Del.Super.Ct. 2000) (holding that the punitive provisions of the Delaware Consumer Fraud Act did not apply to attorneys' conduct occurring within the practice of law given the state supreme court's inherent, constitutional, and statutory authority to discipline members of the state bar); and, *Cripe v. Leiter,* 703 N.E.2d 100 (Ill. 1998) (holding that Illinois's Consumer Fraud Act did not apply because the attorney-client relationship was the subject of regulation by the state supreme court). Alternatively, the firm suggests: If we determine there is insufficient Florida precedent on this issue, we should abstain from ruling and permit a state court to determine whether FDUTPA's apply to attorneys' conduct.

We are bound by Florida Supreme Court precedent on matters of Florida law. *See, e.g., United States v. Berdeal,* 595 F.Supp.2d 1326, 1328 (S.D.Fla.2009) (citing *Johnson v. Fankell,* 520 U.S. 911, 916 (1997) ("neither this Court nor any federal tribunal has any authority to place a construction in a state statute different from the one rendered by the highest court of that state") and *Cotton States Mut. Ins. Co. v. J.O. Anderson,* 749 F.2d 663, 667 (11th Cir.1984) (state courts have the inherent power "to construe their own statutes and federal courts are bound by that state interpretation").

In Florida, legislative intent is the polestar that guides the court's inquiry as to the meaning of a statute. *Knowles v. Beverly Enters.-Florida, Inc.,* 898 So.2d 1, 5 (Fla. 2005). Legislative intent is discerned primarily from the language of the statute. We must give statutory language its plain and ordinary meaning, and we may not "construe an unambiguous statute in a way which would extend, modify, or *limit,* its express terms or its *reasonable and obvious implications.*" *Holly v. Auld,* 450 So.2d 217, 219 (Fla.1984). It is fundamental that where the language of a statute is plain and unambiguous, there is no occasion for judicial interpretation. *Forsythe v. Longboat Key Beach Erosion Control Dist.,* 604 So.2d 452, 454 (Fla.1992).

* * *

We discern no ambiguity in FDUTPA—regarding whether attorneys per se are excluded from its provisions. They simply are not mentioned, and the firm has not offered any plausible basis for finding ambiguity under the present statutory scheme. In the absence of contrary precedent on this issue from the Florida Supreme Court, or even any guidance from Florida's district courts of appeal, we decline the Palmer Law Firm's invitation to read attorney conduct out of the statute based only upon an attorney's status under the law. *See generally* Fla. Stat. § 501.202(2) (the Florida Legislature expressed its intent that the provisions of FDUTPA be "construed liberally to promote" various policies including the protection of the "consuming public ... from those who engage in ... unconscionable, deceptive, or unfair acts or practices in the conduct of any trade or commerce."). ... We hold, therefore, that attorneys are not automatically exempt from the operation of the statute.

2. Consumer Engaged in Transaction Under FDUTPA

Plaintiffs claim that the Palmer Law Firm has violated and continues to violate FDUTPA by "mass mailing civil recovery demand letters to consumers nationwide." According to Plaintiffs, the "mass mailings" create false impressions: (1) The lawyers have evaluated each creditor's claim against each consumer-debtor; (2) The lawyers intend to file a lawsuit against each consumer-debtor on behalf of the retailer if each consumer-debtor fails to pay; (3) The lawyers are entitled to "pre-litigation attorneys' fees"; and (4) The lawyers are collecting a valid debt—rather than making a demand on an unadjudicated tort claim. The firm argued: The Plaintiffs are not consumers, who engaged in trade or commerce under the statute. Therefore, the Plaintiffs' FDUTPA claims fail *as a matter of law.*

FDUTPA prohibits "unfair methods of competition, unconscionable acts or practices, and unfair or deceptive acts or practices in the conduct of any trade or commerce." Fla. Stat. 501.204(1). The stated purpose of this act is to "protect the consuming public and legitimate business enterprises from those who engage in unfair methods of competition, or unconscionable, deceptive, or unfair acts or practices in the conduct of any trade or commerce." Fla. Stat. § 501.202(2). The statute does not define "unfair and deceptive act or practice." But, the provisions of the act must be "construed liberally." Fla. Stat. § 501.202. A practice is unfair under the FDUTPA, if it "offends established public policy." Or a practice is unfair, if it is "immoral, unethical, oppressive, unscrupulous, or substantially injurious to consumers." *PNR, Inc. v. Beacon Prop. Mgmt., Inc.,* 842 So.2d 773, 777 (Fla. 2003).

First, the Palmer Law Firm argues: Plaintiffs lack standing to maintain a claim, because they did not purchase services or goods from the firm. Therefore, they are not "consumers" and are precluded from suing under the FDUTPA. Several cases support the firm's argument: Only consumers may sue for damages under FDUTPA. *See, e.g., Kertesz v. Net Transactions, Ltd.,* 635 F.Supp.2d 1339, 1349-50 (S.D.Fla.2009) (holding that a non-consumer may not commence a claim for monetary damages under FDUTPA); *Cannova v. Breckenridge Pharm., Inc.,* 2009 WL 64337, at *3 (S.D. Fla. 2009) (dismissing a FDUTPA claim because the plaintiff failed to allege that he was a consumer); *Goodbys Creek, LLC v. Arch Ins. Co.,* 2008 WL 2950112, at **8-9 (M.D.Fla. 2008) ("Only consumers may bring private suit under FDUTPA.").

However, other cases hold that *non*-consumers may sue under FDUTPA. In those cases, the rationale is clear: The 2001 legislative amendments to § 501.211(2) broadened the scope of FDUTPA—authorizing any person or entity who suffered a loss as a result of an unfair or deceptive trade practice or act to bring a suit for damages. ... In 2001, the Florida Legislature replaced the word "consumer" with the word "person." Several courts have reasoned that this amendment "demonstrates an intent to allow a broader base of complainants ... to seek damages" under FDUTPA. *Niles Audio Corp. v. OEM Sys. Co., Inc.,* 174 F.Supp.2d 1315, 1320 (S.D. Fla. 2001) (holding that competitor could seek damages under the newly amended § 501.211[2]); and, *North Amer. Clearing, Inc. v.*

Brokerage Computer Sys., 666 F.Supp.2d 1299, 1309-10 (M.D. Fla. 2009) (declining to grant summary judgment merely because the plaintiff was not a consumer).

We agree with these latter cases: A non-consumer may maintain an action for damages under FDUTPA. Therefore, we find that the Palmer Law Firm is not entitled to summary judgment *merely* because Plaintiffs are non-consumers. Still, the law firm's motion for summary judgment must be granted, because Plaintiffs have not satisfied the "trade or commerce" element of FDUTPA. As noted earlier, FDUTPA prohibits unfair or deceptive acts or practices "in the conduct of any trade or commerce." § 501.204(1). The term "trade or commerce" is defined as "the advertising, soliciting, providing, offering, or distributing, whether by sale, rental, or otherwise, of any good or service, or any property, whether tangible or intangible, or any other article, commodity, or thing of value, wherever situated." Fla. Stat. § 501.203(8).

Plaintiffs contend: Their dealings with the Palmer Law Firm constituted "trade or commerce," because the firm sent demand letters – soliciting and offering a release in exchange for money. To support the argument, they cite *Sweringen v. New York State Dispute Resolution Ass'n,* 2006 WL 2811825 (N.D.N.Y. 2006) ("releasing legal claims for money constitutes a business that satisfies any 'trade or commerce' requirement"). *Sweringen* is not applicable to our analysis. … And, Plaintiffs' reliance on *Sweringen* is unavailing as the New York deceptive trade practices statute does not contain a "trade or commerce" element—which is expressly found in the Florida statute.

It is worth reiterating: The purpose of FDUTPA is to "protect the consuming public and legitimate business enterprises" from "unconscionable, deceptive, or unfair acts or practices *in the conduct of* any trade or commerce." § 501.202. The Palmer Law Firm's acts—conduct ostensibly occurring during the exercise of a legal remedy—had zero connection whatsoever to any "trade or commerce." There is scant authority in Florida on the issue of whether conduct occurring in the pursuit of legal remedies such as occurred here constitutes "trade or commerce" under FDUTPA.

* * *

We recognize that FDUTPA must be construed liberally. Yet, we find: Plaintiffs' attempt to include pre-suit demand letters—within the scope of the term "trade or commerce"—simply misses the mark. Under these facts, we will not hold: Soliciting or offering a release in exchange for money is the equivalent of soliciting or offering a "thing of value" under FDUTPA. There is simply no connection or nexus to trade or commerce between these parties through the firm's demand letters.

And absent that important nexus, the entire FDUTPA statutory scheme simply does not apply to these particular circumstances—even if a reasonable juror could find that the firm's conduct amounted to deceptive conduct. A contrary result would expose a great deal of pre-litigation tactics by attorneys to potential exposure under the statute—which is not contemplated by the statute.

Certainly, some lawyers may engage in trade or commercial transactions while acting as lawyers. Therefore, a lawyer's status per se is not a bar to relief. However, the particular conduct at issue here does not fall within the statute's umbrella. We have no choice, therefore, but to recommend that summary judgment be granted for the Palmer Law Firm on this issue and that the FDUTPA claims be rejected.

III. Conclusion

For the foregoing reasons, Defendant Palmer, Reifler & Associates, P.A.'s motion for summary judgment is granted. And the summary judgment will be entered in Defendant's favor and against each Plaintiff. Plaintiffs Veronica Kelly, Lil Simon, and Ron Baum's motion for partial summary judgment on liability for violating FDUTPA is denied.

---

2. Attorneys' Liability for Allegedly Using Misleading and Deceptive Standardized "Computer Generated" and "Robo Signed" Documents to Collect Delinquent Debt

Midland Funding LLC v. Brent

644 F.Supp.2d 961
(N.D. Ohio 2009)

Katz, District Judge.

Midland Funding LLC (Midland) and its affiliated companies are in the business of purchasing written-off debt from credit-issuers and collecting the debt in a variety of manners. Here, the questionable debt is a credit-card balance of $4,516.57. Allegedly, Andrea Brent (Brent) owes the debt. The original credit card was issued by Associates National Bank (Associates). Later, Citibank USA (Citibank) became the successor in interest. Ultimately, Midland Credit Management, Inc. (MCM)—a company closely affiliated with Midland—purchased the debt from Citibank.

After MCM purchased the debt, MCM employed Midland to collect the amount owed on the card. MCM attempted to collect the debt—trying, unsuccessfully, to contact Brent by mail and phone. Next, MCM referred the matter to the Law firm of Javitch, Block & Rathbone LLP (JBR law firm). On April 17, 2008, JBR law firm filed a debt-collection lawsuit against Brent in the Sandusky, Ohio Municipal Court. Brent answered, denying that she had an obligation to pay Citibank and Midland. Andrea Brent also filed federal statutory and common-law counterclaims against Midland and MCM. Again, MCM owns the debt and employed Midland to collect it.

Defendant Midland removed the suit to the Northern District of Ohio. MCM and Brent consented to the removal. On December 1, 2008, Brent filed an amended counterclaim against Midland and MCM. The amended counterclaim added a claim—alleging that Midland and MCM violated the Ohio Consumer Sales Protection Act, Ohio Rev.Code Ann. § 1345 *et seq.* (2008) (OCSPA). Both parties filed motions for summary judgment. …

Discussion

The Ohio Consumer Sales Protection Act was adopted in 1980. It offers a significantly wider set of protections for consumers. Ohio Rev.Code Ann. § 1345.01 *et seq.* The act regulates suppliers who engage in all sorts of consumer transactions. Most courts adopt the position that OCSPA covers debt collection, because it regulates violations that occur "before, during, *or after the transaction.*" § 1345.02. Brent alleges that Midland and MCM violated the OCSPA. In particular, Brent asserts: Midland and MCM used a false computer-generated affidavit to collect a debt and charge an interest rate higher than is allowable under law.

* * *

After purchasing Brent's debt from Citibank, Midland began to attempt to collect the debt. After sending two dunning letters to Brent and receiving no response, Midland instructed the JBR law firm to file a lawsuit. In the course of events, JBR law firm requested an affidavit to support the assertion that Brent owed the debt. Midland has a network computer system and the software program —"You've Got Claims"—is on the computer system. Attorneys at the JBR law firm as well as similarly situated attorneys other may access Midland's network computer and request supporting documents. The computer generates the documents.

Midland receives and fulfills about 200 to 400 requests for affidavits per day. Ivan Jimenez is one of Midland's ten "specialists." He works in the department that supports law firms. Jimenez personally signs between 200 and 400 affidavits per day. Typically, he finds stacks of requested affidavits on Midland's printer. He signs them and sends the affidavits—via internal mail—to the notary. ("Q: Where do your affidavits come from? A: [T]hey just come from the printer.") Using a program on the computer, Mr. Jimenez has the ability to check the accuracy of the information on the affidavit. And, he does. But, the percentage of examined affidavits is "very few and far between."

After receiving the signed JIMENEZ AFFIDAVIT from Midland, JBR attached it to Midland's complaint against Brent. The JIMENEZ AFFIDAVIT asserts: (1) Brent's debt is valid—she owes Citibank and Midland, a successor in interest); (2) Brent owes $4,516.57; (3) Brent's account is delinquent; and (4) She owes an outstanding 8% interest. On the other hand, when the JIMENEZ AFFIDAVIT is compared to Ivan Jimenez's deposition, it is apparent: The JIMENEZ AFFIDAVIT contains many falsehoods.

The JIMENEZ AFFIDAVIT reads: "I make the statements herein based upon my personal knowledge." It is apparent from the JIMENEZ DEPOSITION: Mr. Jimenez had no personal knowledge of Ms. Brent or her account. For instance, although Mr. Jimenez supports and works with ten law firms, the JBR law firm is not one of them. Thus, Mr. Jimenez would not have personal knowledge about any matter that JBR attorneys were handling. Mr. Jimenez was the affiant and signer—based entirely on the computerized information which was transferred to the printer. Mr. Jimenez never had any contact with Ms. Brent. ("Q: Did you ever have any contact with Ms. Brent, any business contacts at all? A: I did not personally.").

* * *

Although certain assertions in the JIMENEZ AFFIDAVIT are false and misleading, this court is not concluding that all information in the affidavit is incorrect. However, as a whole, the JIMENEZ AFFIDAVIT is both false and misleading. Moreover, it is unclear: Why would a business that specialized in the legal ramifications of debt collection use such a patently false standardized affidavit? Midland, MCM, or JBR could easily prepare an affidavit that achieved the same goals—without being misleading. Rather than basing the affidavit on false personal knowledge, they could base it on accurate records and data.

The Alleged Consumer-Debtor's Claim Under Ohio Consumer Sales Protection Act § 1345

Again, Ms. Brent alleges that Midland and MCM violated the Ohio Consumer Sales Protection Act. Ohio Rev.Code Ann. § 1345 *et seq.* (2008). In order for this to be true, the following elements must be present: (1) Midland and MCM must be "suppliers"; (2) Brent must be a "consumer"; (3) the act of collecting the debt must be a "consumer transaction"; and (4) Midland and MCM's acts must violate the OCSPA. *See* § 1345.01 (Defining supplier, consumer, and consumer transaction); *See also* § 1345.02 ("No supplier shall commit an unfair or deceptive act or practice in connection with a consumer transaction. Such an unfair or deceptive act or practice by a supplier violates this section whether it occurs before, during, or after the transaction.")

1. Whether Midland and MCM Are "Suppliers" Under the OCSPA

District courts in the Sixth Circuit have held: Although the OCSPA does not cover transactions between financial institutions and their customers, the OCSPA covers debt collectors who purchase debt. *See Williams v. Javitch, Block & Rathbone, LLP,* 480 F.Supp.2d 1016, 1024 (S.D. Ohio 2007) (finding no definitive authority that would exempt debt collectors under the act) ... For the purposes of the OCSPA, Midland and MCM are suppliers.

2. Whether Brent Is a "Consumer" Under the OCSPA

Once Midland and MCM are considered suppliers by the OCSPA, Brent is logically considered a consumer. The OCSPA defines consumers very simply as "a person who engages in a consumer transaction with a supplier." § 1345.01(D). Thus, Brent is a consumer for the purpose of the OCSPA.

3. Whether Collecting a Debt Is a "Consumer Transaction" Under the OCSPA

Logically, as courts have used the inclusive language of the OCSPA to consider debt collectors to be suppliers, they have also considered the act of collecting a debt to be a consumer transaction. The

OCSPA "prohibits a supplier of consumer goods from engaging in 'an unconscionable act or practice in connection with a consumer sales transaction ... before, during, or after the transaction.' Because the statute applies to acts or practices after a transaction has been completed, it may encompass debt collection." *Smith v. A.B. Bonded Locksmith, Inc.*, 143 Ohio App.3d 321 (2001).

Thus, the act of collecting a debt is considered a consumer transaction for the purposes of the OCSPA.

4. Violations of the OCSPA

The OCSPA prohibits "an unfair or deceptive act or practice in connection with a consumer transaction. And a supplier's unfair or deceptive act or practice violates this section whether it occurs before, during, or after the transaction." § 1345.02(A). As was discussed at length, the use of the false JIMENEZ AFFIDAVIT was unfair and deceptive. Therefore, Midland and MCM have violated the OCSPA by using the affidavit.

Midland and MCM's motion for summary judgment is denied. Brent's motion for summary judgment is granted: Midland and MCM violated the Ohio Consumer Sales Protection Act (OCSPA) by attempting to collect a debt with a false computerized affidavit. It is so ordered.

NOTES AND QUESTIONS

1) The Texas Debt Collection Act—Tex. Fin. Code Ann. §§ 392.404(a)(b) reads:

> (a) A violation of this chapter is a deceptive trade practice under Subchapter E, Chapter 17, Business & Commerce Code, and is actionable under that subchapter.
>
> (b) This chapter does not affect or alter a remedy at law or in equity otherwise available to a debtor, creditor, governmental entity, or other legal entity.

2) Proof of Actual Damages. To prevail under the DTPA—Tex. Bus. & Com. Code § 17.50(a), the Texas Debt Collection Act—Tex. Fin. Code § 392.403(a)(2), and the Federal Fair Debt Collection

Act—15 U.S.C. § 1692 *k* (a)(1), a plaintiff-consumer-debtor must build an unbeatable *prima facie* case.

3) Debt-Collection Claims, Arbitration and Federal Preemption. Courts have declared that causes of action under UDTPAs, DTPAs and debt-collection statutes fall within the scope of arbitration agreements. *See e.g., Jack B. Anglin Co., Inc. v. Tipps,* 842 S.W.2d 266, 270-71 (Tex.1992) (concluding that a DTPA claim is subject to arbitration, since the Federal Arbitration Act preempts DTPA's non-waiver provisions), and *In re Conseco Finance Servicing Corp.,* 19 S.W.3d 562, 570-71 (Tex. App.-Waco 2000) (concluding that the Debt Collection Act and DTPA claims were subject to arbitration, as they arose from or related to the contract).

4) Legal Consequences—Attorneys' Names and Facsimile Signatures on Computer-Generated, Debt-Collection Letters. Generally, attorneys' mass produced and computer-generated debt collection letters violate the fair debt collection statutes. *See e.g.,* Taylor v. *Perrin, Landry, deLaunay & Durand,* 103 F.3d 1232, 1237-1238 (5th Cir. 1997), and *Boyd v. Wexler,* 275 F.3d 642 (7th Cir. 2001) (finding that a three-lawyer firm mailed over 439,000 debt-collection letters over an-eight-and-a-half-month period and concluding that the consumers' files were reviewed before authorizing the letters). Retained solo and small-firm lawyers—who have no contractual relationship with a collection firm—must state clearly that they have no authority to fashion and send mass-produced and computer-generated debt-collection letters.

B. Attorneys' Liability under the Fair Debt Collection Act for Allegedly Employing Technologies to Harass Consumers-Debtors

1. Abuse of Shared Debt-Collection Technologies and Attorneys' Liability

Avila v. Rubin

84 F.3d 222
(7th Cir. 1996)

Terence T. Evans, Circuit Judge.

Raul Avila is a student loan debtor living in Connecticut. Van Ru Credit Corporation is a collection agency in Skokie, Illinois. Albert Rubin is an Illinois attorney. Although we were told at oral argument that Rubin and the Van Ru agency are separate, they actually seem to be as closely intertwined as lovers during an embrace. Here's the situation—from which we think that conclusion is justified.

Rubin founded Van Ru and owns 80 percent of its corporate stock. The remainder is owned by Van Ru's president—Rubin's son. Rubin is Van Ru's chief executive officer, draws a large salary from the company, and, until eight years ago, managed Van Ru's day-to-day collection activities. Rubin is involved in the creation and modification of form letters—the most critical part of the debt collection operation.

In addition to his duties at Van Ru, Rubin has a law office which he calls Rubin & Associates. Rubin & Associates is located on the third floor of the "Van Ru Building." The Van Ru Building is owned by Van Ru Credit Services, Inc. And Rubin owns 75 percent of this firm. Rubin & Associates splits the third-floor space of the building with Van Ru. Rubin & Associates is comprised of Rubin, one other attorney, and some 35 "legal assistant collectors." The primary business of Rubin & Associates is to send form letters to delinquent debtors—urging them to pay their debts and referring files of delinquent debtors to other attorneys for litigation.

Neither Rubin nor the other attorney in his office actually litigates in Connecticut. And it is unclear whether they litigate anywhere. Rubin & Associates receives all its business from Van Ru after Van Ru's efforts to collect debts are unsuccessful. Van Ru pays Rubin & Associates a monthly retainer for work that Rubin & Associates does on debtor accounts.

Rubin personally maintains offices in both the Van Ru and Rubin & Associates offices. Van Ru and Rubin & Associates use the *same computer system and internal account number* to identify files. Van Ru and Rubin & Associates also utilize the *same automated telephone dialing system* to call delinquent debtors. Employees from both entities sit next to each other when using the *same system*. Van Ru and Rubin & Associates receive mail at the *same post office box*. Van Ru and Rubin & Associates use the *same printer for their respective form letters*. The two also use the *same machine to fold and process form letters in preparation for mailing*.

The *mailing machine* processes Van Ru and Rubin & Associates letters *simultaneously*—resulting in stacks of mixed letters ready for mailing. Both Van Ru and Rubin & Associates' letters are placed in *identical envelopes*. The printer and mailing machine are operated by employees of Pegasus Data Systems—a company that shares the same address with Van Ru and Rubin & Associates. Rubin owns 50 percent of Pegasus.

Avila allegedly owes money on a student loan. His creditor is the Connecticut Student Loan Foundation. The foundation has a written contract with Van Ru and an oral agreement with Rubin for debt collection services. The foundation forwarded Avila's account for collection to Van Ru via *electronic data transmission*. Van Ru sent Avila two demand or "dunning" letters—attempting to collect the debt. Avila did not respond. Van Ru then "referred" Avila's account to Rubin & Associates. Rubin & Associates cranked out three dunning letters to Avila—using the attorney's letterhead paper. The five form letters are the basis for this suit. Raul Avila—as the class representative—filed a class action against Van Ru and Rubin. Now let's look at the letters.

* * *

Attorney Rubin reviews and approves the general form letters that Rubin & Associates send. He does not, however, personally prepare, sign, or review any of the letters sent to targets—including Avila. This is understandable: Rubin would probably be in the hospital with a severe case of writer's cramp if he did, because some 270,000 such letters go out each year. That, by the way, comes out to 1,062 per working day, 133 per working hour.

The letters from attorney Rubin are actually the product of a nonattorney "legal assistant collector"—who *directs the computer to generate a letter on Rubin's attorney letterhead.* Legal assistant collectors are provided with a training manual. Rubin developed the manual to help collectors to determine when an attorney's debt collection letter is warranted. According to Rubin, the collectors use their "skill, judgment, and training" to determine when a letter should be sent.

Avila filed this suit in the spring of 1994—claiming that the letters violated the Fair Debt Collection Practices Act (FDCPA), 15 U.S.C. § 1692 *et seq.*, and the Connecticut Unfair Trade Practices Act. CONN. GEN. STAT. § 42-110b. Eventually, the DTPA action was abandoned and class certification was granted. The parties filed joint motions for summary judgment. Avila's motion carried the day—as Rubin was held liable under §§ 1692g and 1692e(3) and (9) of the FDCPA. Van Ru was found liable as well under § 1692g. Following a bench trial on the issue of statutory damages, judgment was entered for Avila against Rubin for $84,983. Rubin and Van Ru appeal.

The rules for granting summary judgment and our standard of review are well-known and need not be repeated. Suffice to say that the facts are not in dispute and only questions of law are present which we review on a clean slate.

By law, a "validation notice" must be present in debt-collection letters. 15 U.S.C. § 1692g. Essentially, the notice must tell the target that she has 30 days to dispute the validity of all or a portion of the debt. If not disputed, the collector may assume that the debt is valid. We held in *Gammon v. GC Servs. Ltd. Partnership,* 27 F.3d 1254, 1257 (7th Cir.1994): Under the FDCPA, claims against debt collectors must be viewed through the eyes of the "unsophisticated consumer." We rejected a somewhat lesser standard—the "least sophisticated consumer." We reiterate our standard today.

* * *

The FDCPA § 1692e provides: A debt collector may not use any false, deceptive, or misleading representation or means in connection with the collection of any debt. Without limiting the general application of the foregoing, the following conduct is a violation of this section:

. ...

> (3) The false representation or implication that any individual is an attorney or that any communication is from an attorney.
>
> . ...
>
> (9) The use or distribution of any written communication ... which creates a false impression as to its source, authorization, or approval.

Avila contends: The three debt-collection letters are false, deceptive, or misleading representations, because the letters did not come "from an attorney"—as that term has been defined under the FDCPA § 1692e(3). Rubin's dunning letters implore Avila to pay his debt. And, as we noted, the form letters are mass-produced. Also, the letters are *mechanically signed* "Albert G. Rubin"—under his "attorney" letterhead. Additionally, as we noted, 270,000 letters of this sort were mailed in the year prior to the filing of this suit.

Clomon v. Jackson, 988 F.2d 1314 (2d Cir.1993) is the leading case on whether an attorney's mass-produced mailings violate the FDCPA. The facts in *Clomon* are similar to those presented here. In *Clomon,* a debt-collection agency mailed dunning letters to debtors after receiving *accounts on computer tape from the creditor.* An attorney was employed as a part-time general counsel for the agency. The agency's *computer system caused each letter to be printed, folded, and placed in an envelope for mailing.*

The *Clomon* plaintiff received six form letters from the agency. The first letter was sent on the letterhead of an "account supervisor." The remaining five were sent on the letterhead of the general counsel for the agency. Although the general counsel was an attorney and employed by the agency, the letters were not actually signed by the attorney. Instead, they bore the *mechanically reproduced facsimile of his signature.* The purported attorney's letters implored the debtor to pay up and threatened legal action if payment was not forthcoming. *Clomon,* 988 F.2d at 1316-17. The *Clomon* attorney personally approved the "form" of the letters. *Id.* at 1317. However, the attorney had no direct personal involvement in mailing the letters to the plaintiff or to any other debtor. In short, the attorney "never considered the particular circumstances of Clomon's case prior to the mailing of the letters." *Id.* at 1317.

The Second Circuit held: The debt-collection agency's using the attorney's letterhead and inserting the attorney's signature on the collection letters was sufficient to give the "least sophisticated" consumer the false impression that the letters were communications from an attorney. *Id.* at 1320. The letters were false and misleading, because the letters were not "from" the attorney in any meaningful sense of the word, although the attorney's name and signature were on them. The court also found and weighed other significant fact[s]: (1) the attorney did not review each debtor's file, (2) he did not determine when particular letters should be sent; (3) other parties recommended, approved and sent letters, (4) the *Clomon* attorney did not see the particular letters before they were sent; and (5) the attorney did not know the identities of the letters' addressees. *Id.*

Clomon establishes: An attorney—who sends dunning letters—must be directly and personally involved in the mailing in order to comply with the strictures of FDCPA. This may include (1) reviewing the individual debtors' files to determine if and when a letter should be sent, or (2) approving the mass mailing of debt-collection. *Clomon,* 988 F.2d at 1320. Given these requirements, *Clomon* concluded: "There will be few, if any, cases in which a mass-produced collection letter—bearing the facsimile of an attorney's signature—will comply with the restrictions imposed by section 1692e." *Id.* at 1321.

The undisputed facts in our case establish: Attorney Rubin has no real involvement in the mailing of dunning letters to debtors. Like the attorney in *Clomon,* he has a cozy relationship with the "referring" collection agency. Rubin is not personally or directly involved in deciding when or to whom a dunning letter should be sent. There is no true "judgment" being rendered here by a real attorney. Like the attorney in *Clomon,* Rubin did not review the debtor's file. He did not determine when particular letters should be sent. He did not approve the sending of particular letters based upon the recommendation of others. He did not see particular letters before they were sent. And he did not even know the identities of the debtors to whom the letters were sent.

Instead, at his deposition, Rubin said: Debt-collection letters are only brought to his attention for advice and guidance when there is "some unusual problem or something different [or] out of the ordinary comes up." Given these undisputed facts, the district court correctly concluded: Rubin violated FDCPA § 1692e(3) and (9), because his collection letters create the false and misleading impression that the communications were from an attorney when, in fact, they were not really "from" an attorney in any meaningful sense of the word .... A debt collection letter on an attorney's letterhead conveys authority. Consumers are inclined to more quickly react to an attorney's threat than to one coming from a debt collection agency. It is reasonable to believe that a dunning letter from an attorney threatening legal action will be more effective in collecting a debt than a letter from a collection agency.

* * *

The defendants make two final arguments. First, they claim that mass mailing is economically efficient and necessary in the debt collection industry. This argument has been rejected by several courts. In *Clomon,* the Second Circuit stated: "No mass mailing technique is permissible—regardless of how effective it might be—if the technique constitutes a false, deceptive, or misleading communication." *Clomon,* 988 F.2d at 1321. An attorney's signature implies: The attorney has formed a professional judgment about the debtor's case. These implications will frequently be false in a mass mailing situation.

Second, the defendants argue that holding Rubin liable will effectively condemn the use of paralegals and assistants in a law office. This argument is untenable. As the district court noted:

> Paralegals do not—or should not engage in the practice of law. Paralegals do not intake a new client, decide whether a lawsuit is warranted, prepare unreviewed pleadings, stamp the attorney's signature, and file the lawsuit without the considered approval of the attorney. Attorneys personally supervise and review paralegals' work, consider the case, and approve the recommendations or work.

Albert G. Rubin—acting *as* an attorney—was not the real "source" of the letters in this case. The true source of the "attorney" letters was the collection agent—*who pressed a button on the agency's computer*. "Albert G. Rubin & Associates, Ltd." is a collection agency—not a law firm in any real sense of the term. The "law firm" does not have a retainer agreement with plaintiff's creditor. No attorney—who works in the "law firm"—ever files a lawsuit or goes to court on behalf of a client. We agree with the district court and with the Second Circuit in *Clomon*. Rubin was on the wrong side of the FDCPA. Accordingly, the judgments of the district court are affirmed.

NOTES AND QUESTIONS

1) Allegedly False Communications, Federal Debt Collection Lawsuits. and the "Least Sophisticated Consumer" Standard. Courts employ the "least sophisticated consumer" standard to help determine whether an attorney-debt-collector has violated the federal act. *See Kistner v. Law Offices of Michael P. Margelefsky*, LLC, 518 F.3d 433, 438 (6th Cir.2008) and *Lewis v. ACB Bus. Servs., Inc.*, 135 F.3d 389, 400 (6th Cir.1998). This standard protects naive consumers and prevent liability for bizarre or idiosyncratic interpretations of collection notices. Courts "will not "countenance lawsuits based on frivolous misinterpretations or nonsensical interpretations of being led astray. *Jacobson v. Healthcare Fin. Servs. Inc.,* 434 F.Supp.2d 133 (E.D.N.Y.2006).

2) "Indefatigable" Debt Collection Technology—Aspect Telephony Computer Software System. Consider the court's observation in *Nelson v. Santander Consumer USA, Inc.,* 931 F.Supp.2d 919, 923-24 (W.D. Wis. 2013): Santander called Heather Nelson's cellular telephone number more than 1000 times over the course of a year—attempting to collect a debt on two vehicles that she had financed. To make the calls, Santander used Aspect Telephony System — a computer telephone software that routes and places inbound and outbound calls. Aspect stores telephone numbers, performs "predictive dialing" and permits "preview dialing." The predictive dialing feature allows the computer to schedule the dialing of numbers—using an algorithm to predict when an agent will become available to receive the next call. The preview dialing feature, allows an employee to choose a telephone number by clicking on a computer screen and the system calls it. The employees never called plaintiff by pressing numbers on a keypad. Again, between March 2010 and April 2011, defendant called Heather Nelson's mobile telephone 1026 times and left 116 prerecorded voicemail messages.

United States Code

Title 15. Commerce and Trade
Chapter 41. Consumer Credit Protection
Subchapter V. Debt Collection Practices
15 U.S.C. § 1692

§ 1692. Congressional Findings and Declaration of Purpose

(a) Abusive practices—There is abundant evidence of the use of abusive, deceptive, and unfair debt collection practices by many debt collectors. Abusive debt collection practices contribute to the number of personal bankruptcies, to marital instability, to the loss of jobs, and to invasions of individual privacy.

* * *

(e) Purposes—It is the purpose of this subchapter to eliminate abusive debt collection practices by debt collectors, to insure that those debt collectors who refrain from using abusive debt collection practices are not competitively disadvantaged, and to promote consistent State action to protect consumers against debt collection abuses.

2. Attorneys' Liability Under the Fair Debt Collection Act for Allegedly Employing Abusive Telephone Technologies to Harass Consumers-Debtors

Danow v. Borack

346 Fed. Appx. 409
(11th Cir. 2009)

PER CURIAM.

The Law Office of David E. Borack, P.A. ("Law Office") appeals from the final judgment entered against it. A jury returned a verdict in favor of Plaintiff Harry L. Danow. He claimed that the Law Office violated the Fair Debt Collection Practices Act (FDCPA), 15 U.S.C.

§ 1692c(a)(1)—by contacting him at an inconvenient location after he sent the Law Office a cease communications letter.

A district court has wide discretion to regulate the scope of counsel's arguments. *Goldsmith v. Bagby Elevator Co.,* 513 F.3d 1261, 1282 (11th Cir.2008). Regarding a counsel's allegedly improper opening or closing arguments, we also review the denial of a motion for a new trial to uncover an abuse of discretion. *Lanham v. Whitfield,* 805 F.2d 970, 972 (11th Cir.1986). We review *de novo* the district court's disposition of a motion for JNOV—reviewing "all the evidence, and the inferences drawn therefrom, in the light most favorable to the nonmoving party." And we recognize: If there is substantial evidence to oppose the motion, then such a motion must be denied and the case must be submitted to the jury. *Carter v. City of Miami,* 870 F.2d 578, 581 (11th Cir.1989). Finally, "we review the trial court's grant or denial of a motion for summary judgment *de novo*—viewing the record and drawing all reasonable inferences in the light most favorable to the non-moving party." *Patton v. Triad Guar. Ins. Corp.,* 277 F.3d 1294, 1296 (11th Cir.2002).

First, we are unpersuaded by the Law Office's argument: The district court abused its discretion by overruling an objection to Danow's counsel's prejudicial remarks during closing argument. We are reluctant to set aside a jury verdict because [of] a counsel's closing arguments. *Vineyard v. County of Murray, Ga.,* 990 F.2d 1207, 1214 (11th Cir.1993). "Statements made in oral arguments must be plainly unwarranted and clearly injurious to constitute reversible error." *Peterson v. Willie,* 81 F.3d 1033, 1036 (11th Cir.1996). In making this determination, we look to "the entire argument, the context of the remarks, the objection raised, and the curative instruction to determine whether the remarks were such as to impair gravely the calm and dispassionate consideration of the case by the jury." *Allstate Insurance Co. v. James,* 845 F.2d 315, 318-19 (11th Cir.1988)

During the trial, Danow claimed: The Law Office violated the FDCPA by contacting him at an inconvenient location—after he sent the Law Office a cease communications letter. 15 U.S.C. § 1692c(a)(1). In its defense, the Law Office argued: (1) Danow's letter did not give proper notice regarding whether or not he wanted to be telephoned at home; (2) the telephone calls did not violate the statute because they were intended to disclose that a debt collector or creditor may invoke specified remedies. § 1692c(c)(2); and (3) the Law Office satisfied the "bona fide error" defense. The latter requires "proof by a preponderance of the evidence" to establish: (1) the violation was not intentional; and (2) the violation "resulted from a bona fide error—notwithstanding the maintenance of procedures reasonably adapted to avoid any such error." § 1692k(c).

Explaining its "bona fide error" defense, the owner of the Law Office—David Borack—testified: He asserted that the firm's collection software allows the firm to place a "cease and desist" code on an account—which prevents unwarranted telephone calls. ... In rebuttal, Danow's lawyer attempted to cast doubt on the relevance and reliability of the computer records.

* * *

Moreover, after overruling the objection by the Law Office's counsel to the comments by Danow's counsel, the trial judge urged counsel to move on with his argument. Shortly thereafter, in the beginning of the jury instructions, the court instructed the jury: The lawyer's arguments are not evidence and should not be factored into the jury's deliberations. This occurred even though the Law Office failed to request a curative instruction from the trial judge.

On this record and given our reluctance to set aside a jury verdict based on comments made in closing argument, we conclude: The district court did not abuse its discretion—by denying the Law Office's motion for a new trial or by erroneously denying a motion for JNOV. We also reject the Law Office's claim that the district court erred by denying the Law Office's pre-trial motion for summary judgment. Accordingly, we affirm.

NOTES AND QUESTIONS

1) The Fair Debt Collection Practices Act and Elements of the "Bona Fide Error" Defense. A debt collector must knowingly make a misrepresentation in order to violate the FDCPA. Still, the debt collector may rely on the bona fide error defense to avoid liability. "A debt collector may not be held liable in any action ... if the debt collector shows by a preponderance of evidence that the violation was not intentional and resulted from a bona fide error notwithstanding the maintenance of procedures reasonably adapted to avoid any such error." 15 U.S.C. § 1692k(c). Furthermore, Congress did not require proof of intent in 15 U.S.C. §1692k(c). A successful bona fide error defense hinges on whether or not the debt collector fashioned and maintained procedures to avoid an error that was made.

2) Mass-Produced Electronic Documents and Robo-Signing Fraud. Consider some insightful observations in Jamie P. Hopkins's and Katherine A. Pustizzi's article— "A Blast From the Past: Are the Robo-Signing Issues that Plagued the Mortgage Crisis Set To Engulf the Student Loan Industry?", 45 U. Tol. L. Rev. 239, 239-40 (2014): In the fall of 2010, it was revealed that "tens of thousands of foreclosure filings across the nation were likely fraudulent—if not outright criminal. To combat the flood of paperwork required to proceed with the record number of foreclosure filings nationwide, banks, law firms, and other institutions resorted to a process known as "robo-signing"—using surrogates to sign foreclosure paperwork without any actual knowledge of the statements contained in the paperwork. ... Ultimately, the robo-signing scandal brought to light serious systemic problems within the U.S. debt collection industry ... In response to the widespread use of robo-signing during the foreclosure boom and the consequences thereof, state courts adopted rules specifically designed to confront the issue. Additionally, the federal government investigated the practice within large financial institutions, creating pressure on large financial institutions to cease the practice of robo-signing in foreclosure filings. ... This practice is also a concern in the context of student loans; defaults are approaching record highs nationwide, potentially spawning another massive debt collection boom. As student loans have become the second largest source of debt in the United States, totaling more than $1 trillion, the question must be asked, "Will robo-signing return in student debt collection proceedings?"

United States Code

Title 15. Commerce and Trade
Chapter 41. Consumer Credit Protection
Subchapter V. Debt Collection Practices
15 U.S.C. § 1692c

§1692c. Communication in connection with debt collection

(a) Communication with the consumer generally

Without the prior consent of the consumer given directly to the debt collector or the express permission of a court of competent jurisdiction, a debt collector may not communicate with a consumer in connection with the collection of any debt—

(1) at any unusual time or place or a time or place known or which should be known to be inconvenient to the consumer. In the absence of knowledge of circumstances to the contrary, a debt collector shall assume that the convenient time for communicating with a consumer is after 8 o'clock antemeridian and before 9 o'clock postmeridian, local time at the consumer's location;

(2) if the debt collector knows the consumer is represented by an attorney with respect to such debt and has knowledge of, or can readily ascertain, such attorney's name and address, unless the attorney fails to respond within a reasonable period of time to a communication from the debt collector or unless the attorney consents to direct communication with the consumer; or

(3) at the consumer's place of employment if the debt collector knows or has reason to know that the consumer's employer prohibits the consumer from receiving such communication.

(b) Communication with third parties

Except as provided in section 1692b of this title, without the prior consent of the consumer given directly to the debt collector, or the express permission of a court of competent jurisdiction, or as reasonably necessary to effectuate a postjudgment judicial remedy, a debt collector may not communicate, in connection with the collection of any debt, with any person other than the consumer, his attorney, a consumer reporting agency if otherwise permitted by law, the creditor, the attorney of the creditor, or the attorney of the debt collector.

(c) Ceasing communication

If a consumer notifies a debt collector in writing that the consumer refuses to pay a debt or that the consumer wishes the debt collector to cease further communication with the consumer, the debt collector shall not communicate further with the consumer with respect to such debt, except—

(1) to advise the consumer that the debt collector's further efforts are being terminated;

(2) to notify the consumer that the debt collector or creditor may invoke specified remedies which are ordinarily invoked by such debt collector or creditor; or

(3) where applicable, to notify the consumer that the debt collector or creditor intends to invoke a specified remedy.

If such notice from the consumer is made by mail, notification shall be complete upon receipt.

(d) "Consumer" defined. For the purpose of this section, the term "consumer" includes the consumer's spouse, parent (if the consumer is a minor), guardian, executor, or administrator.

CHAPTER TEN: Federal Statutory Actions Against Solo and Small-Firm Attorneys for Misrepresenting, Appropriating, Abusing, and Interfering with Protected Law-Practice Hard- and Software Technologies

Chapter Four presents a lengthy discussion of solo and small-firm attorneys' federal statutory claims. More specifically, attorneys sue a variety of parties for allegedly: (1) stealing or using attorneys' website trademarks without permission, (2) posting deceptive and unwarranted legal-services pop-up advertisements on attorneys' websites, (3) violating the "fair use" rule and using attorneys' copyrighted work—computer software programs—without permission, (4) illegally retrieving privileged and protected information on attorneys' computers, (5) using attorneys' protected passwords to gain access to fee-for-service databases like WESTLAW and LEXISNEXIS, (6) using law firms' registered Internet "domain names" without permission to confuse potential customers, (7) violating federal laws by improperly removing videos from attorneys' websites and refusing to replace the "confiscated" videos, and (8) "hacking" cloud-based storage systems and downloading attorneys' files and privileged attorney-client communications.

In Chapter Four, we also discover: To secure an assortment of remedies for allegedly sound federal claims, solo and small-firm attorneys are more likely to commence federal actions under one or a combination of the following statutes:

- The Trademark (Lanham) Act of 1946, 15 U.S.C. §§1051-1141 (2006);
- The Computer Fraud and Abuse Act of 1986, 18 U.S.C. § 1030 *et seq.*;
- The Stored Communications Act of 1986, 18 U.S.C. § 2701, *et seq.*;
- The Digital Millennium Copyright Act of 1998 — enacted as The Online Copyright Infringement Liability Limitation Act, 17 U.S.C. § 512 *et seq.*; and,

- The Anticybersquatting Consumer Protection Act of 1999, 15 U.S.C. § 1125(d)

But it is also important to stress: Citing purported violations under these same federal statutes, Internet service providers, opposing clients, opposing attorneys, website designers, domain-name owners, and website owners, as well as sellers of various law-practice goods and services have sued solo and small-firm practitioners. In this chapter, we will explore some of these latter controversies—focusing on some of the major procedural and substantive issues.

A. Federal Declaratory Judgment Actions against Attorneys to Resolve Ambiguities Under Federal Information Technology and Privacy Statutes

Webb Law Firm, P.L.L.C. v. Webb Law Firm, P.C.

2014 WL 4795159
(S.D. W.Va. 2014)

Thomas E. Johnston, District Judge.

The Webb Law Firm, PLLC—(Webb-PLLC)—is the Plaintiff in this case. And The Webb Law Firm, P.C.—(Webb-PC)—is the Defendant. Webb-PLLC is a West Virginia law firm principally located in Charleston, West Virginia. In early 2006, Charles "Rusty" Webb started the firm in Charleston. Webb-PLLC's law practice is limited to personal-injury and family law in southern West Virginia. Prior to forming his own firm, Mr. Webb practiced law in a two-man law firm—Giatras & Webb.

Webb-PC is a corporate intellectual-property law firm in Pittsburgh, Pennsylvania. Webb-PC registered the service marks "The Webb Law Firm" and "Webblaw.com" with the United States Patent and Trademark Office in the late 1990s. Webb-PC maintains that these marks are incontestable under federal trademark law. None of the members of Webb-PC's law firm bear the surname

"Webb." None of the Webb-PC's lawyers are licensed to practice law in West Virginia.

This dispute arises from Webb-PC's claim: Webb-PLLC uses "The Webb Law Firm" to market Webb-PLLC's legal services. The practice infringes on Webb-PC's service mark registrations. And the practice violates various provisions of the Lanham Act, 15 U.S.C. § 1111, *et seq.* and West Virginia state law. By letter dated July 17, 2013, Webb-PC's counsel advised Mr. Rusty Webb that Webb-PC owned the trademark registrations "The Webb Law Firm" and "Webblaw.com" for use in the category of "legal services."

The letter also indicated: There were previous communications between Webb-PC and Mr. Rusty Webb—concerning how Mr. Webb marketed his firm's legal services. The letter further advised Mr. Webb: "You are more prominently featuring the term 'The Webb Law Firm' in your marketing, including on your website. And it is our considered opinion that such increased use of 'The Webb Law Firm' infringes our firm's intellectual property interests and trademark registrations—in violation of the Lanham Act." Webb-PC requested that Mr. Webb cease and desist. ... In closing, Webb-PC's counsel requested that Mr. Webb respond within fifteen days or Webb-PC "will be forced to consider further legal recourse to protect our intellectual property."

Less than three weeks later, Webb-PLLC filed this lawsuit seeking a declaratory judgment that Webb-PLLC's use of "The Webb Law Firm, PLLC" does not violate the Lanham Act and does not constitute trademark infringement or unfair competition. Webb-PLLC also seeks a declaration that "The Webb Law Firm, PLLC" is not a reproduction, copy, counterfeit, or colorable imitation of Webb-PC's mark under the Lanham Act. Webb-PLLC further requests an injunction restraining Webb-PC from "further threats and harassment" and attorneys' fees. Webb-PC now moves for judgment on the pleadings under Federal Rule of Civil Procedure 12(c).

Discussion

The purpose of a Rule 12(b)(6) motion is to test the sufficiency of a complaint. Importantly, a Rule 12(b)(6) motion "does not resolve contests surrounding the facts, the merits of a claim, or the applicability of defenses." *Republican Party v. Martin,* 980 F.2d 943, 952 (4th Cir.1992). Applying these principles to this case, the conclusion is plain: Based solely on the matters contained in the Complaint and its exhibits, Webb-PC's motion lacks merit. The court will address each of Webb-PC's arguments in support of its motion in turn.

Webb-PLLC Has Not Conceded Liability on Any of Webb-PC's Counterclaims

Webb-PC argues that Webb-PLLC has admitted all facts necessary to a finding of liability for the *counterclaims* asserted by Webb-PC. The court disagrees. Webb-PC has alleged five counterclaims against Webb-PLLC: (1) service mark infringement in violation of 15 U.S.C. § 1114; (2) service mark counterfeiting in violation of 15 U.S.C. § 1114; (3) false designation of origin in violation of 15 U.S.C. § 1125(a); (4) service mark dilution in violation of 15 U.S.C. § 1125(a); and (5) common law service mark infringement.

Trademark infringement and false designation of origin claims share the same elements of proof. *Lamparello v. Falwell,* 420 F.3d 309, 313 (4th Cir.2005). To prevail under either cause of action, the trademark holder must prove: (1) it possesses a mark; (2) the [opposing party] used the mark; (3) the [opposing party's] use of the mark occurred "in commerce"; (4) the [opposing party] used the mark "in connection with the sale, offering for sale, distribution, or advertising" of goods or services; and (5) the [opposing party] used the mark in a manner likely to confuse consumers.

The Fourth Circuit has identified nine factors to guide a court's likelihood of confusion analysis: (1) the strength or distinctiveness of the plaintiff's mark as actually used in the marketplace; (2) the similarity of the two marks to consumers; (3) the similarity of the goods or services that the marks identify; (4) the similarity of the facilities used by the markholders; (5) the similarity of advertising used by the markholders; (6) the defendant's intent; (7) actual confusion; (8) the quality of the defendant's product; and (9) the sophistication of the consuming public. *George & Co. LLC v. Imagination Entm't. Ltd.,* 575 F.3d 383, 393 (4th Cir. 2009). Not all of these factors are equally important in any given case. Evidence of actual confusion is often paramount in the likelihood of confusion analysis.

Webb-PC is correct: Webb-PLLC admits that it used "The Webb Law Firm" mark in connection with its legal services. But Webb-PLLC insists: Webb-PC's demands are based on "one errant phone call from Beckley, West Virginia." These assertions do not, however, amount to a concession of liability by Webb-PLLC on any of Webb-PC's *counterclaims.* The core dispute in this case is whether Webb-PLLC's use of "The Webb Law Firm" to market its legal services constitutes use of the mark in a manner likely to confuse consumers. Webb-PLLC has plainly not conceded this important … For all these reasons, the court rejects Webb-PC's contention that Webb-PLLC has admitted all elements of Webb-PC's claims.

Webb-PC Is Not Entitled to Judgment on the Pleadings for Its Dilution Claim

Webb-PC argues that Webb-PLLC has conceded: (1) the mark "The Webb Law Firm" is famous, (2) Webb-PC owns a registered and uncontestable trademark to "The Webb Law Firm," and (3) there is evidence of actual confusion by the public. Therefore, Webb-PC contends that it is entitled to judgment on the pleadings with respect to its service-mark *counterclaim*. The court disagrees.

Section 1125(a) of Title 15 of the United States Code provides in pertinent part:

(1) Any person who, on or in connection with any goods or services … uses in commerce any word, term, name, symbol, or device, or any combination thereof, or any false designation of origin, false or misleading description of fact, or false or misleading representation of fact, which—

(A) is likely to cause confusion, or to cause mistake, or to deceive as to the affiliation, connection, or association of such person with another person, or as to the origin, sponsorship, or approval of his or her goods, services, or commercial activities by another person, or

(B) in commercial advertising or promotion, misrepresents the nature, characteristics, qualities, or geographic origin of his or her or another person's goods, services, or commercial activities, shall be liable in a civil action by any person who believes that he or she is or is likely to be damaged by such act. 15 U.S.C. § 1125(a)(1).

Section 1125(c)(1) states:

> Subject to the principles of equity, the owner of a famous mark that is distinctive, inherently or through acquired distinctiveness, shall be entitled to an injunction against another person who, at any time after the owner's mark has become famous, commences use of a mark or trade name in

> commerce that is likely to cause dilution by blurring or dilution by tarnishment of the famous mark, regardless of the presence or absence of actual or likely confusion, of competition, or of actual economic injury.

To state a *prima facie* dilution claim under Section 1125, the plaintiff must show the following: (1) the plaintiff owns a famous mark that is distinctive; (2) the defendant uses a mark in commerce that allegedly dilutes the famous mark; (3) a similarity between the defendant's mark and the famous mark gives rise to an association between the marks; and (4) the association is likely to impair the distinctiveness of the famous mark or likely to harm the reputation of the famous mark. *Rosetta Stone Ltd. v. Google, Inc.*, 676 F.3d 144, 168 (4th Cir. 2012).

As defined under 15 U.S.C. § 1125(c)(2)(A), a mark is "famous if it is widely recognized by the general consuming public of the United States as a designation of source of the goods or services of the mark's owner." "Dilution by blurring" is the "association arising from the similarity between a mark or trade name and a famous mark that impairs the distinctiveness of the famous mark." 15 U.S.C. § 1125(c)(2)(B).

Webb-PC correctly states: Webb-PLLC acknowledges that "The Webb Law Firm" and Webb-PLLC's website "rustywebb.com" are "famous marks and logos." The court disagrees, however, with Webb-PC's conclusion: Webb-PLLC admits that Webb-PC's registered trademark—"The Webb Law Firm"—is a famous mark, as that term is defined under 15 U.S.C. § 1125(c)(2)(A). Webb-PC's characterization of Webb-PLLC's allegation takes the allegation out of context. In any event, this is an issue better left to a fair contest on the merits. ...

Conclusion

For the reasons set forth above, the court denies in part and grants in part Webb-PC's motion for judgment on the pleadings and motion to strike; and the court denies the motion to the extent it seeks judgment on the pleadings. It is so ordered.

NOTES AND QUESTIONS

1) **The Federal Declaratory Judgment Act, 28 U.S.C. §§ 2201 and 2202.** Section 2201(a) provides in pertinent part: In a case of actual controversy within its jurisdiction ... any court of the United States, upon the filing of an appropriate pleading, may declare the rights and other legal relations of any interested party seeking such declaration, whether or not further relief is or could be sought. Any such declaration shall have the force and effect of a final judgment or decree and shall be reviewable as such.28 U.S.C.A. § 2201 (2010).

Section 2202 provides: "Further necessary or proper relief based on a declaratory judgment or decree may be granted, after reasonable notice and hearing, against any adverse party whose rights have been determined by such judgment."

2) **Removal of State Civil Actions to Federal Courts.** Under 28 U.S.C. § 1441(a), a litigant's right of removal is fairly clear. The provision reads: "Except as otherwise expressly provided by Act of Congress, any civil action brought in a State court of which the district courts of the United States have original jurisdiction, may be removed by the defendant or the defendants, to the district court of the United States for the district and division embracing the place where such action is pending."

3) **The Declaratory Judgment Act and Federal Courts' Jurisdiction.** The Declaratory Judgment Act does not confer jurisdiction upon federal courts. *Skelly Oil Co. v. Phillips Petroleum Co.*, 339 U.S. 667, 671 (1950). Consequently, federal courts' power to exercise jurisdiction over a controversy must come from an independent or another source. Federal courts may exercise federal-question jurisdiction under 28 U.S.C. § 1331. Diversity jurisdiction may be exercised under 28 U.S.C. § 1332. And, under 28 U.S.C. § 1367(a), federal courts may exercise supplemental jurisdiction over state-law claims and over claims that "form part of the same case or controversy"—assuming they evolved from a common nucleus of probative facts.

B. State Declaratory Judgment Actions Against Attorneys to Resolve Ambiguities Under States' Information Technology and Privacy Statutes

Riley v. Dozier Internet Law, PC

371 Fed. Appx. 399
(4th Cir. 2010)

Wilkinson, Circuit Judge.

Plaintiff-appellant Ronald J. Riley ("Riley") commenced this action to obtain a declaratory judgment that he was not liable to defendants-appellees John W. Dozier, Jr. ("Dozier") and Dozier Internet Law, P.C. ("DIL") for defamation or trademark infringement.

I.

Defendant Dozier is a Virginia lawyer and the founder of defendant DIL—a Virginia law firm that specializes in intellectual property law. Dozier maintains a website for his law firm at *cybertriallawyer.com*. The underlying dispute in this case arose when plaintiff Riley—a Michigan resident and head of a nonprofit corporation—created the website *cybertriallawyer-sucks.com*. As the name of the website suggests, cybertriallawyer-sucks.com was critical of Dozier and his law firm.

The first lawsuit was initiated in Virginia state court. In that suit, DIL sued Riley for trademark infringements— alleging that Riley's website infringed on the name "Dozier Internet Law, P.C.," a registered trademark with the Commonwealth of Virginia. In response to the state action, Riley filed his own lawsuit in the United States District Court for the Eastern District of Virginia. Riley brought the action against both Dozier personally and DIL.

In his complaint, Riley sought a declaratory judgment that his website neither defamed Dozier nor infringed on DIL's trademark. Riley also sought an injunction against any future claims of defamation or trademark infringement and damages caused by the attempted suppression of his website—including "nominal damages," "punitive damages ... in the amount of $1000," and "reasonable attorney's fees and costs."

Simultaneously with the filing of his complaint, Riley also attempted to remove the state court action to federal court. Upon motions by the defendants, the district court remanded the case back to the state court and dismissed the case. In dismissing, the district court explained: Even if it had subject matter jurisdiction over the case, it would "decline to adjudicate this case under the abstention doctrine established in *Burford v. Sun Oil Co.,* 63 S.Ct. 1098, 1107 (1943). The *Burford* Court found: The state court action would afford the parties "timely and adequate state court review," and federal adjudication would "be disruptive of state efforts to establish a coherent policy with respect to a matter of substantial public concern."

Riley promptly filed a motion to reconsider, which the district court denied. In doing so, the district court reiterated: Even if it had jurisdiction, it "must abstain from exercising jurisdiction"— this time citing *Employers Resource Management Co. v. Shannon,* 65 F.3d 1126, 1134-35 (4th Cir.1995). The decision in *Shannon* was based on the abstention doctrine of *Younger v. Harris,* 401 U.S. 37 (1971). The district court noted: "Virginia's interest in adjudicating claims involving a state-registered trademark is both clear and compelling; and the state-court proceeding affords Plaintiff an adequate opportunity to present his claims."

II.

Riley now appeals the district court's dismissal order—claiming that the court abused its discretion in abstaining.

A.

The Supreme Court held in *Brillhart v. Excess Ins. Co.,* 316 U.S. 491 (1942) and reaffirmed in *Wilton v. Seven Falls Co.,* 515 U.S. 277 (1995): When a plaintiff brings a declaratory judgment action, the district court enjoys discretion in deciding whether to assert jurisdiction over the action or abstain from hearing it. This discretion stems from the federal Declaratory Judgment Act—which expressly provides: District courts "*may* declare the rights and other legal relations of any interested party seeking a declaration." 28 U.S.C. § 2201(a). Given this "nonobligatory" language, the Supreme Court has explained: "In the declaratory judgment context, the normal principle—that federal courts should adjudicate claims within their jurisdiction—yields to considerations of practicality and wise judicial administration." *Wilton,* 515 U.S. at 288.

Thus, even when a court has jurisdiction, it "is authorized—in the sound exercise of its discretion—to stay or to dismiss an action seeking a declaratory judgment." *Id.* This court has likewise recognized the principle: "District courts have great latitude in determining whether to assert jurisdiction over declaratory judgment actions." *United Capitol Ins. Co. v. Kapiloff,* 155 F.3d 488, 493 (4th Cir.1998). A district court's discretion "is especially crucial when, as here, a parallel or related proceeding is pending in state court." *New Wellington Fin. Corp. v. Flagship Resort Develop. Corp.,* 416 F.3d 290, 297 (4th Cir.2005). In such cases, district courts have "wide discretion" to decline jurisdiction. *See Centennial Life Ins. Co. v. Poston,*88 F.3d 255, 257 (4th Cir.1996).

The Supreme Court and this court have provided district courts with general guidelines to aid their exercise of discretion. Broadly speaking, when deciding whether or not to stay or dismiss a declaratory judgment action when there is a related proceeding underway in state court, a district court should determine whether the controversy can be adequately "settled in the proceeding pending in the state court." *Wilton v. Seven Falls Co.,* 515 U.S. 277, 282 (1995). This requires the district court to weigh principles of "federalism, efficiency, and comity that traditionally inform a federal court's discretionary decision whether to abstain from exercising jurisdiction over state-law claims in the face of parallel litigation in the state courts." *Nautilus Ins. Co. v. Winchester Homes, Inc.,* 15 F.3d 371, 376 (4th Cir.1994). In making these determinations, a district court must strive to avoid "indulging in "gratuitous interference, by permitting the federal declaratory judgment action to proceed." *Wilton,* 515 U.S. at 283.

B.

In this case, we cannot say: The district court abused its discretion when it abstained from entertaining Riley's request for declaratory relief and allowed the dispute to proceed in the related suit already underway in Virginia state court. The district court's ruling was well within the discretion recognized by the Supreme Court in *Brillhart* and *Wilton.* It was likewise consistent with an application of the four *Kapiloff* factors to the facts of this case.

First, Virginia "has a strong interest in having the issues decided in its courts." *See Kapiloff,* 155 F.3d at 493–94. This case requires a determination of the liability of a Virginia resident and a Virginia law firm, involves intellectual property registered in Virginia, and demands an application of Virginia trademark law. *Cf. New Wellington Fin. Corp. v. Flagship Resort Develop. Corp.,* 416 F.3d 290, 297 (4th Cir.2005).

* * *

Second, the Virginia state court could likely "resolve the issues more efficiently" than this court. *See Kapiloff,* 155 F.3d at 493–94. As a general rule, "the first suit should have priority— absent the showing of balance of convenience in favor of the second action." *Ellicott Mach. Corp. v. Modern Welding Co.,* 502 F.2d 178, 180 n. 2 (4th Cir.1974). Here, the state suit was filed before the federal suit. The state proceeding is also further along than the federal action. This court's interference with the pending state court proceeding would produce inefficiencies by needlessly duplicating efforts, generating piecemeal litigation, and expending limited judicial resources.

Third, the Virginia state court proceeding and this federal court proceeding involve "overlapping issues of fact [and] law," *see Kapiloff,* 155 F.3d at 493-94. Both cases center on an identical core question: Does Riley's website infringe on DIL's trademark under Virginia trademark law? If the state court and this court were to simultaneously find facts related to alleged trademark infringement and make pronouncements on Virginia trademark law, the common issues involved here could easily result in an "unnecessary entanglement" between the two tribunals.

Fourth, the final *Kapiloff* factor weighs in favor of abstention insofar as Riley's federal suit appears to be "mere procedural fencing." *See Kapiloff,* 155 F.3d at 493–94. Procedural fencing occurs when, as in this case, "a party has raced to federal court in an effort to get certain issues that are already pending before the state courts resolved first in a more favorable forum." *Great Am. Ins. Co. v. Gross,* 468 F.3d 199, 212 (4th Cir. 2006). DIL sued Riley in state court. But he did not want to be in state court. So, Riley brought his own suit in federal court—requesting a declaration that he was not liable to DIL in state court. Such conduct is the sort of forum-shopping against which abstention seeks to guard. This attempted end-run around the removal statutes is strong evidence of "procedural fencing" and further weighs in favor of abstention.

C.

The proper route into federal court is under the removal statutes—not by a collateral attack on state proceedings under the Declaratory Judgment Act. When a federal court has subject matter jurisdiction over a suit brought in state court, a state court defendant may remove the case, guided by the comprehensive scheme Congress set out in the removal statutes. When, however, a state court defendant bypasses the removal mechanism and instead uses the Declaratory Judgment Act as his ticket into federal court, a district court is entitled to take that very fact into account in deciding whether or not to abstain.

III.

We hold only that the district court had discretion to abstain here and did not in these circumstances abuse its discretion in doing so. A peremptory reversal of the district court on these facts would entail serious risks, which we think it inadvisable to incur. Among other things, such a reversal would (1) rob *Brillhart* and *Wilton* of any meaningful effect, (2) encourage collateral attacks upon state court proceedings under the Declaratory Judgment Act—even where the state proceedings presented only questions of state law, (3) circumvent the removal statutes, (4) undermine the purpose of federal non-appealability provisions with respect to remands, (5) encourage gamesmanship by litigants in multiple forums—preliminary to any merits resolution of their cases, and (6) deny district courts the ability to assess the variable facts and circumstances that arise in these cases and that guide the sound exercise of trial court discretion. For all of the foregoing reasons, the judgment of the district court is hereby affirmed.

NOTES AND QUESTIONS

1) **Texas Uniform Declaratory Judgments Act—Tex. Civ. Prac. & Rem. Code § 37.004(a).** The act reads: "A person interested under a deed, will, written contract, or other writings constituting a contract or whose rights, status, or other legal relations are affected by a statute, municipal ordinance, contract, or franchise may have determined any question of construction or validity arising under the instrument, statute, ordinance, contract, or franchise and obtain a declaration of rights, status, or other legal relations thereunder."

2) **Distinguishing "Forum Shopping" and "Procedural Fencing".** Generally, forum shopping involves a litigant's selecting "a court with an eye towards gaining an advantage based on the forum's favorable substantive law or the avoidance of unfavorable law in an alternative forum." *Util. Workers Union of Am., AFL–CIO v. Dominion Transmission, Inc.*, 2006 WL 2794568 at *3 (W.D. Pa. Sept. 27, 2006). On the other hand, The Fifth Circuit has defined

"procedural fencing" as a plaintiff's commencing a declaratory judgment action before the declaratory judgment defendant is legally able to bring a state action. *The Sherwin-Williams Co. v. Holmes County*, 343 F.3d 383, 397 n. 7 (5th Cir. 2002). For example, requiring a defendant to exhaust administrative remedies would preclude the defendant's filing a state action.

C. Federal Statutory Actions Against Solo and Small-Firm Attorneys for Allegedly Using Owners' Protected Domain Names on the Internet

H. Jay Spiegel & Associates, P.C. v. Spiegel

652 F.Supp.2d 630
(E.D. Va. 2008)

James C. Cacheris, District Judge.

This case arises out of attorney Steven M. Spiegel's (Atty-Spiegel's) alleged infringement of H. Jay Spiegel & Associates, P.C.'s (Spiegel-PC's) trademarked domain name. Spiegel-PC filed a complaint on September 12, 2008—stating claims for trademark infringement and unfair competition under both federal and Virginia common law (the "Complaint"). The allegations in the Complaint are as follows.

Spiegel-PC is a Virginia professional legal corporation. It has operated continuously under its name since 1989. Spiegel-PC provides patent and trademark-related legal services. In January 1999, Spiegel-PC registered the domain name SPIEGELAW.COM with Network Solutions. The next month, Spiegel-PC established a website at that domain—WWW.SPIEGELAW.COM ("Spiegel-PC's Website")—and applied for federal registration of the domain name as a Service Mark for the provision of legal services. The application was assigned a serial number and registered on the Supplemental Register of the United States Patent and Trademark Office ("USPTO") on November 7, 2000.

After using the mark in interstate commerce for five consecutive years, Spiegel-PC filed an application to register it with the USPTO on the Principal Register. The application was assigned a serial number and entered on the Principal Register—as Registration No. 3,158,285—on October 17, 2006. In March 1999, a Lisa M. Spiegel—believed to be Atty-Spiegel's sister—registered the domain name SPIEGE*LL*AW.COM with Network Solutions. She did not create a website accessible at that address. In 2007 or 2008, Atty-Spiegel acquired ownership of the domain name. At some point in 2008, Atty-Spiegel created a website at WWW.SPIEGE*LL*AW.COM (Atty-Spiegel's Website).

Atty-Spiegel is a solo practitioner with a focus on employment law. Spiegel-PC and Atty-Spiegel each maintain a law office with an Alexandria, Virginia address. Spiegel-PC became aware of Atty-Spiegel's Website in July 2008—when an opposing lawyer sent Spiegel-PC an e-mail copied to Atty-Spiegel at Atty-Spiegel's website-based e-mail address. Upon discovery of Atty-Spiegel's Website, Spiegel-PC sent Atty-Spiegel a letter—demanding removal of the site from the Internet and asking Atty-Spiegel to convey his domain name to Spiegel-PC. Atty-Spiegel refused to do so. Spiegel-PC then filed this suit.

On October 28, 2008, Spiegel-PC submitted a motion for a preliminary injunction. Atty-Spiegel filed an opposition on November 10. Spiegel-PC's motion is before the court.

* * *

Analysis

Spiegel-PC requests a preliminary injunction forbidding Atty-Spiegel from using the domain name SPIEGE*LL*AW.COM. Granting the preliminary injunction would require the court to order Atty-Spiegel to shut down his website. "Preliminary injunctions are extraordinary remedies ... to be granted only sparingly and in limited circumstances." *MicroStrategy Inc. v. Motorola, Inc.,*245 F.3d 335, 339 (4th Cir. 2001). Whether a preliminary injunction should issue to preserve the *status quo ante litem* —during the adjudication of this claim—depends on the balance of hardship test set out in *Blackwelder*. *See* 550 F.2d at 194–95. A plaintiff must also make "a clear showing of irreparable harm as a condition" of his entitlement to a preliminary injunction.

A. Irreparable Harm to Spiegel-PC

The Fourth Circuit has noted: In Lanham Act trademark infringement cases, "a presumption of irreparable injury is generally applied once the plaintiff has demonstrated a likelihood of confusion—the key element in an infringement case." *Scotts Co. v. United Indus. Corp.,* 315 F.3d 264, 273 (4th Cir.2002). The *Scotts* court noted that the Fourth Circuit had never explicitly endorsed this presumption. The presumption has been applied in the Eastern District of Virginia, however, and was recognized as the general standard—if not outright embraced—by the Fourth Circuit in *Scotts. See* 315 F.3d at 273 n.3.

The Court will assume *arguendo* that applying the presumption would be appropriate if a likelihood of confusion exists. As explained below, however, even further assuming that Spiegel-PC could show a likelihood of confusion, Spiegel-PC is not entitled to a preliminary injunction under the *Blackwelder* balancing test. First, the balance of harms favors Atty-Spiegel—not Spiegel-PC. Second, Spiegel-PC's likelihood of success on the merits is uncertain. Finally, the public interest favors neither party.

B. Balance of Harms

Even after a party makes a "clear showing of irreparable injury absent preliminary injunctive relief, the *next* step for the court is to perform the *Blackwelder* balance of harms test. *Direx Israel,* 952 F.2d at 812. Thus, a showing of irreparable injury does not end the inquiry and does not automatically fulfill the *Blackwelder* balance of harms test in favor of Spiegel-PC. It is possible, after all, that the harm to a plaintiff without a preliminary injunction may be irreparable but of a miniscule amount. After a plaintiff makes a showing of irreparable injury, the court must still weigh the amount of likely harm to the plaintiff against the amount of harm likely to befall the defendant if the injunction issues.

1. Harm to Spiegel-PC

As noted above, the court assumes *arguendo* that Spiegel-PC has shown a likelihood of confusion between his mark and the domain name used by Atty-Spiegel—thus activating the presumption of irreparable harm. Spiegel-PC argues that the likelihood of confusion and the loss of goodwill caused by Atty-Spiegel's use of the domain name SPIEGE*LL*AW.COM create harm that outweighs any harm an injunction would cause Atty-Spiegel.

Spiegel-PC claims that they will suffer harm because their law practice—while physically based in Alexandria, Virginia—is international in scope. Many clients contact them through their website. Moreover, Spiegel-PC has devoted time and energy to creating and updating their website, which has existed continuously for more than eight years. The court agrees that Atty-Spiegel's use of the domain name SPIEGE*LL*AW.COM poses some threat to the goodwill that Spiegel-PC has built using their domain name.

The names are nearly identical. Some risk of confusion certainly exists. Individuals searching the Internet for Spiegel-PC could be misled or diverted by Atty-Spiegel's website. Additionally, persons who were given oral instructions to visit "WWW.SPIEGELAW.COM" could be confused about the website's spelling and stumble onto Atty-Spiegel's site instead of Spiegel-PC's. Spiegel-PC has submitted evidence that at least one individual was confused by the presence of Atty-Spiegel's Website.

The court takes seriously Spiegel-PC's allegations of present harm and potential future harm. However, on balance, the court is not convinced that Spiegel-PC will be harmed to a significant extent during the pendency of this litigation. First, Spiegel-PC operates a specialized legal practice—focusing on patent and trademark law. Atty-Spiegel practices employment law. A potential client searching for a patent lawyer named Spiegel and finding Atty-Spiegel's Website would quickly realize he located the wrong attorney. An individual who wanted to visit a website that he *heard* was WWW.SPIEGELAW.COM might visit WWW.SPIEGE*LL*AW.COM—another publicly-available website used by a solo legal practitioner with the surname "Spiegel."

In other words, the online presence of Atty-Spiegel does not pose a wholly novel threat to the ability of potential clients to locate Spiegel-PC's Website. While a "likelihood of confusion" may well exist as an element of trademark infringement under the Fourth Circuit's *Pizzeria Uno* test, the actual possibility that potential clients will be confused in a way that leads to serious harm to Spiegel-PC appears low. *Pizzeria Uno Corp. v. Temple,* 747 F.2d 1522, 1527 (4th Cir. 1984) (outlining a seven-factor test to determine whether a likelihood of confusion exists). In addition, the court has no indication that Atty-Spiegel has been attempting to "poach" Spiegel-PC's clients. Any such attempts would likely be counter-productive for an employment lawyer. Finally, the existence of a single mis-directed e-mail does not weigh heavily in Spiegel-PC's favor. Without more, the e-mail shows an isolated instance of confusion by a fellow attorney rather than large-scale confusion among Spiegel-PC's clients.

Spiegel-PC may be correct: The very existence of Atty-Spiegel's Website implicitly harms the goodwill of their business. Given the nature of this dispute, which involves similar-sounding but discrete Internet domain names, the court does not believe that the continued existence of Atty-Spiegel's website—while the litigation is pending—will impair the goodwill Spiegel-PC has in his business to a significant extent. Certainly, it would not outweigh the harm that shutting down Atty-Spiegel's website would cause Atty-Spiegel.

2. Harm to the Atty-Spiegel

Atty-Spiegel convincingly argues that an injunction forbidding him to use the domain name SPIEGE*LL*AW.COM presents a substantial likelihood of significant harm. Atty-Spiegel uses the website primarily in his capacity as class counsel in a civil rights class action lawsuit. Through the website, Atty-Spiegel is able to share information and communicate with members of the class. He claims to have spent eighteen months planning the website before its launch earlier this year. Shutting the website down, Atty-Spiegel argues, would cause "irreparable harm to him and to the public interest."

The court agrees: Shutting down Atty-Spiegel's website would disrupt, perhaps severely, Atty-Spiegel's law practice and harm the interests of the class action Spiegel-PCs he represents. The nature of a class-action lawsuit puts a premium on the ability of counsel to communicate with individuals who may be geographically diverse and, indeed, may never meet their attorney in person. Disrupting a major line of communication and information sharing between class counsel and a class of Spiegel-PCs poses a real threat to the ability of counsel to advocate in an effective and efficient manner.

3. Balancing the Harms

The continued existence of Atty-Spiegel's Website may cause some confusion to potential clients of Spiegel-PC. It may also leach some portion of the goodwill that Spiegel-PC has built up in his domain name. The court, however, does not believe that the actual amount of harm to Spiegel-PC is likely to be significant, at least during the time this lawsuit is pending. In addition, any harm Spiegel-PC will suffer going forward is speculative and difficult to quantify. Atty-Spiegel, on the other hand, would be immediately and severely harmed if the Court granted an injunction. An injunction would shut down his website and interrupt ongoing communications between Atty-Spiegel and numerous class-action clients. On balance, the harm to Atty-Spiegel outweighs the harm to Spiegel-PC.

C. Spiegel-PC's Likelihood of Success on the Merits

When the balance of harms favors the defendant, "a stronger showing on the merits is required" before a preliminary injunction will issue. *Rum Creek Coal Sales,* 926 F.2d at 359. In this case, the balance-of-harms test favors Atty-Spiegel. Unless Spiegel-PC can make a strong showing of a likelihood of success on the merits, the preliminary injunction must be denied.

In order to show trademark infringement and unfair competition under the Lanham Act and unfair competition under Virginia common law, Spiegel-PC must demonstrate: (1) evidence of ownership of a valid and protectable mark; (2) evidence of the use of the mark by an infringer; and (3) evidence of a likelihood of confusion. *See Lone Star Steakhouse & Saloon Inc.,* 43 F.3d at 930 n. 10 (4th Cir.1995) (noting that the elements for the federal and Virginia causes of action are "essentially the same"). S*ee also CareFirst of Md., Inc. v. First Care, P.C.,* 434 F.3d 263, 267 (4th Cir.2006). The court finds it unclear whether Spiegel-PC can show that their mark is protectable at this stage of the litigation, and so the overall likelihood of success is uncertain.

For the reasons stated above, the court will deny Spiegel-PC's motion for preliminary injunction.

D. Federal Civil RICO Actions Against Solo and Small-Firm Attorneys for Allegedly Conspiring to Appropriate Clients' Computer Software for Personal Use

Dauphinais v. Cunningham

2009 WL 4545293
(D. Conn. 2009)

Vanessa L. Bryant, District Judge.

Spiegel-PC—Douglas H. Dauphinais—brought this action *pro se* for damages under the Racketeer Influenced and Corrupt Organizations Act, 18 U.S.C. § 1961 et seq. (RICO) and the Connecticut Corrupt Organization and Racketeering Activities Act, Conn. Gen.Stat. § 53–393 et seq. (CORA). The Defendants are (1) Donald and Gertrude Cunningham—his former employers, (2) Somers Baptist Church, a local religious organization for which the Cunninghams have acted as deacon/deaconess or church officers, and (3) his former attorney—Phillip Steele.

I. Factual Background

Defendants Donald and Gertrude Cunningham are husband and wife. They own the Hanson Whitney Company, which formerly employed Spiegel-PC in the 1990s. While employed at Hanson Whitney, Dauphinais was a software developer—who specialized in computer software for manufacturing companies. He claims to have developed certain software on his own time and on his own computer. He also asserts: Hanson Whitney used the software, resulting in a large increase in profits for the Company.

According to Dauphinais, he asked the Cunninghams to help him to market his software. However, they declined. Instead, they allegedly bullied and threatened Dauphinais—calling him a "Damn Catholic." And they also allegedly threatened him, stating that he would receive "the worst of their (Baptist) three levels of punishment." Dauphinais quit his job at Hanson Whitney in May 1992. Hanson Whitney, however, continued to use Dauphinais's software exclusively.

After quitting his job at Hanson Whitney, Dauphinais experienced difficulties obtaining new employment. During October 1992, he applied for a systems-analyst position with Windsor Manufacturing Systems. After two interviews, Robert Chapman—the Company's Personnel Manager—informed Dauphinais that he had a job pending a check of his references. Dauphinais provided a reference. He was hired by Windsor, and his employment lasted from November through December 1992. In March 1993, Chapman phoned Dauphinais and informed him that Donald Cunningham was "blacklisting" him.

On June 30, 1993, Dauphinais filed a blacklisting complaint with the Connecticut Department of Labor (CDOL). In this complaint, Dauphinais alleged that Donald Cunningham gave him a bad reference and as a result he had been unable to secure employment. The CDOL Investigator handling the complaint interviewed Donald Cunningham on July 13, 1993. Cunningham stated that he had received one reference call from Windsor since Dauphinais left Hanson Whitney, and stated that he provided what he believed to be a fair and accurate assessment of Dauphinais's job performance to Chapman. ... Cunningham agreed in the future to only verify dates of employment, job title, and salary (if appropriate) unless he had written authorization to reveal additional information. Thereafter, the investigator provided a report of his investigation to Dauphinais and closed the file.

After receiving the CDOL's report, Dauphinais contacted the Hartford Legal Referral Service. He was referred to Attorney Phillip Steele. Steele met with Dauphinais and accepted his case at a rate of $210 per hour—along with a $1,000 retainer. At a subsequent meeting, Steele asked Dauphinais what he thought of Donald Cunningham. Dauphinais concluded that Steele had spoken to Donald Cunningham. During the same meeting, Steele convinced Dauphinais to represent himself and file a state-court action in order to save money. On October 5, 1994, Dauphinais filed a complaint in Connecticut Superior Court. He alleged that Donald Cunningham and Catherine Campbell—Controller for Hanson Whitney—made defamatory statements against him in order to interfere with his business relationship with Windsor, and negligently inflicted emotional distress upon him by making harassing telephone calls.

Attorney Steele "walked off" the case—which Dauphinais alleges is the result of his association with the Cunninghams. Thereafter, Dauphinais dropped his case in Connecticut Superior Court. He alleges that he received numerous harassing telephone calls from both Attorney Steele and Donald Cunningham—after Steele terminated his representation. Since that time, he has not been able to obtain an attorney to assist him in pursuing his claims. And, he has only been able to obtain sporadic employment. He does not claim that either of the Cunninghams spoke with anyone about him other than Chapman and the CDOL investigator.

* * *

Dauphinais further alleges: In July 2001, his son-in-law went to a Baptist Church and searched the computers attempting to locate software that Dauphinais had developed. ... Based upon the foregoing facts, Dauphinais alleges that the Cunninghams engaged in a scheme of bribery, extortion, and other criminal activities—in concert with the Baptist Church, Attorney Steele, and officials from CDOL to steal his computer software and blacklist him from finding employment.

II. Discussion

"The statute of limitations for a civil RICO claim is four years." *McLaughlin v. Am. Tobacco Co.,* 522 F.3d 215, 233 (2d Cir.2008). "The statute begins to run when the Spiegel-PC discovers or should reasonably have discovered the alleged injury." In support of his RICO claim, Dauphinais alleges: The Cunninghams engaged in a scheme to extort and bribe state officials, his prior attorney, and his own family—using their influence at the Baptist Church in order to appropriate his software and deprive him of employment opportunity. The majority of the RICO claim center on actions occurring in the 1990s. Apparently, Dauphinais is asserting: He discovered the alleged RICO scheme in 1993 or 1994—when the Cunninghams had bribed his then attorney—Phillip Steele. Therefore, the RICO claim appears to be time-barred as well.

However, even assuming that Dauphinais did not discover the alleged facts supporting his RICO claim until 2006, his claim must still be dismissed: The Complaint fails to allege a pattern of racketeering activity. Under 18 U.S.C. § 1962, "a person commits a RICO violation when he (a) invests income derived from a pattern of racketeering in an enterprise; or (b) controls an enterprise through a pattern of racketeering activity; or (c) participates in an enterprise through a pattern of racketeering activity; or (d) conspires to violate subsections (a), (b) or (c)." *Dempsey v. Sanders,* 132 F.Supp.2d 222, 226 (S.D.N.Y. 2001).

"As to what constitutes a pattern under RICO, the statute reads: "[It] requires at least two acts of racketeering activity – i.e., predicate acts—within a 10-year period." 18 U.S.C. § 1961(5). The Supreme Court subsequently narrowed the definition to require a showing of at least two racketeering predicates. ... A pattern is not formed by sporadic activity ... and a person cannot be subjected to the sanctions of [RICO] simply for committing two widely separated and isolated criminal offenses. Instead, the term "pattern" requires the showing of a relationship between the predicates and of the threat of continuing activity. It is this factor of continuity plus relationship which combines to produce a pattern. *H.J. Inc. v. Northwestern Bell Telephone Co.,* 492 U.S. 229, 239 (1989).

As to the relatedness requirement, predicate acts are "related" for RICO purposes when they "have the same or similar purposes, results, participants, victims, or methods of commission, or otherwise are interrelated by distinguishing characteristics and are not isolated events." *Schlaifer v. Nance & Co.,* 119 F.3d 91, 97 (2d Cir.1997). This requirement appears to be satisfied in this case, because Dauphinais alleges: All of the acts of extortion and bribery committed by the Cunninghams kept Dauphinais from using his software, while appropriating the software for their Company's exclusive benefit.

With respect to the continuity requirement, "Spiegel-PC in a RICO action must allege (1) an "open-ended" pattern of racketeering activity— past criminal conduct coupled with a threat of future criminal conduct, or (2) a "closed-ended" pattern of racketeering activity— past criminal conduct "extending over a substantial period of time." *Schlaifer Nance & Co. v. Estate of Warhol,* 119 F.3d 91, 97 (2d Cir.1997). "Essentially, courts have held that where a Spiegel-PC alleges a single scheme promulgated for the limited purpose of defrauding a single victim, continuity cannot be established." *Dempsey,* 132 F.Supp.2d at 228.

In this case, Dauphinais's RICO allegations consist of (1) quotations from various criminal statutes that may serve as predicate acts for purposes of RICO with the names of the Defendants inserted therein, and (2) general statements reflecting Dauphinais's belief that the Cunninghams bribed and extorted his former attorney, state officials, and members of his family, without any specific supporting facts. These are precisely the types of allegations that are insufficient to survive a motion to dismiss under the standard set forth by the Supreme Court in *Ashcroft v. Iqbal,* 556 U.S. 662, 678 (2009) ("A pleading that offers labels and conclusions or a formulaic recitation of the elements of a cause of action will not do. ... Nor does a complaint suffice if it tenders naked assertion[s] devoid of further factual enhancement.").

However, even construing Dauphinais's Complaint as liberally as possible and giving him the benefit of every doubt, his RICO claim still must fail because the "scheme" he alleges "is nothing more than a classic example of a single-victim, single-defendant fraud dressed up to resemble a multi-faceted RICO claim. It is simply not the type of activity constituting the "long-term criminal conduct" which Congress intended to target with the passage of RICO." *Dempsey,* 132 F.Supp.2d at 228–29. Accordingly, Dauphinais's RICO claim is dismissed.

Finally, the Defendants moved to dismiss Dauphinais's CORA claim—asserting that CORA does not permit a civil cause of action. CORA is purely a criminal statute and does not authorize a private right of action. *See Town of West Hartford v. Dadi,* 2002 WL 241462 (Conn. Super. Ct. 2002). *See also Cort v. Ash,* 422 U.S. 66, 80 (1975) (concluding that private cause of action does not exist under "a bare criminal statute, with absolutely no indication that civil enforcement of any kind was available to anyone"); *Burke v. APT Foundation,* 509 F.Supp.2d 169, 173 (D. Conn. 2007) ("criminal statutes ... do not provide a private right of action to civil litigants"). Therefore, Dauphinais's CORA claim is dismissed as well. Based upon the foregoing reasoning, the Defendants' motion for judgment on the pleadings is granted. It is so ordered.

PART III.
Common Law and Statutory Affirmative Defenses

INTRODUCTION

Consider the Utah Supreme Court's analysis in *Petty v. Clark,* 129 P.2d 568, 571 (Utah 1942): "A specific denial ... specifically points out and denies a particular allegation. ... A general denial—without attempting to point out particular allegations—denies every material allegation in the complaint which it will be necessary for the plaintiff to prove in order to recover." A close reading of the cases in Chapters 1–10 reveals: Solo and small-firm attorneys presented an assortment of general and specific denials, after various complainants filed common-law and statutory actions against the attorneys. Also, in the earlier chapters, one finds various defendants' raising similar general and specific denials—after solo and small-firm attorneys filed technology-based claims against those alleged tortfeasors or violators.

But, a general or specific denial is not an affirmative defense. Even more importantly, a defendant has the burden of *proving* an affirmative defense to prevent a court or jury from awarding a plaintiff's requested remedy or remedies. *Hinton v. McKee,* 329 So.2d 519, 520 (Miss. 1976). Furthermore, the list of affirmative defenses is long. Consider the court's observation in *City and County of San Francisco v. O'Flynn,* 2012 WL 968059, *10 n. 8 (Cal. Ct. App. 2012):

> In his first AMENDED ANSWER to the City's FIRST AMENDED COMPLAINT, O'Flynn raised the following affirmative defenses to the breach of contract claim: "no breach of contract"; "failure to join necessary and/or indispensable parties"; "cannot ascertain whether [the] agreement is written, oral or implied"; "enforcement is barred by the statute of limitations"; "enforcement is barred by statute of frauds"; "lack of consideration"; "no contract"; "enforcement is barred by modification, alteration and change of terms"; "contract is unlawful"; "contract is contrary to policy of express law"; "contract is contrary to good morals"; "plaintiff [breached] fiduciary and confidential duties"; "intentional misrepresentation"; "negligent misrepre- sentation"; "concealment or suppression of facts"; "constructive fraud"; "fraud in the execution"; "nonperformance ... by plaintiff"; "damages sought violate the rule

> against penalties"; "setoff"; "plaintiff has not suffered damages or injury"; "violation of the … sales act"; "laches"; and "mistake."

Yet, the *O'Flynn* list does not present the universe of statutory and common-law affirmative defenses. Some extremely important defenses are omitted. In this part of the casebook, the remaining chapters will cover some major affirmative defenses—which are likely to influence solo and small-firm attorneys' ability to prevail *as plaintiffs or defendants* in law-technology lawsuits.

CHAPTER ELEVEN: Law-Practice Technology Disputes, the Attorney-Client Relationship, and the Accompanying Defenses

A. THE FORMATION OF THE ATTORNEY-CLIENT RELATIONSHIP

Daniels v. DeSimone

16 Cal. Rptr.2d 615
(Cal. Ct. App. 1993)

Turner, P. J.

On or about February 28, 1979, Mr. Salvatore DeSimone and Mr. Dale D. Billips began practicing law as a partnership—*The Law Firm of Billips & DeSimone.* On February 13, 1986, Mr. Robert Daniels had a telephone conversation with Mr. DeSimone about a potential medical malpractice claim. The parties disagree as to whether Mr. Daniels was referred to the partnership or to Mr. DeSimone or Mr. Billips. In opposition to the summary judgment motion, Mr. Daniels declared he "was referred to the firm of Billips & DeSimone by an attorney who declined to represent [him]." However, Mr. Billips did not personally speak to the plaintiffs—Robert and Mitzie Jean Daniels.

On March 4, 1986, Attorney Ramsey—an associate of *The Law Firm of Billips & DeSimone*—wrote a letter to Mr. Daniels. It confirmed the conversation with Mr. DeSimone. Ms. Ramsey advised Mr. Daniels that he should forward copies of his medical records to "us" for review. On May 1, 1986, Mr. DeSimone and Mr. Billips agreed to terminate the partnership effective the same date. Mr. Billips and Mr. DeSimone "each went their separate ways." Ms. Ramsey continued to work with Mr. Billips. Under the terms of the dissolution agreement, the partners agreed to split the partnership files and share the proceeds regarding cases "wherein a suit had been filed."

On June 11, 1986, after the termination of the partnership, *The Law Offices of Dale D. Billips* filed a complaint for personal injuries on behalf of plaintiffs entitled, *Daniels v. St. Joseph's Medical Center* (Super Ct. L.A. County, No. NCC029824B). The complaint was signed by Ms. Ramsey on behalf of *The Law Offices of Dale D. Billips.* After the partnership dissolution, Ms. Ramsey worked exclusively for Mr. Billips and she "handled the entire case" on behalf of plaintiffs.

On October 3, 1986, Ms. Ramsey sent a letter to plaintiffs on behalf of *The Law Offices of Dale D. Billips.* The letter provided: "Pursuant to my conversation of October 2, 1986, with Mr. Daniels, enclosed is a retainer agreement in the above-captioned matter. Please review the agreement and if you have any questions concerning it, we can discuss them at our upcoming meeting." A copy of the unsigned retainer agreement indicated that *The Law Offices of Dale D. Billips* would be retained to represent plaintiffs.

On June 19, 1987, Mr. Billips became ill and was hospitalized. He went to Stanford University Hospital on November 9, 1987—where he received a heart transplant. He stayed at Stanford until October 12, 1988. He did not go into the office during the entire year of 1988. His condition ultimately led to a complete abandonment of his law practice. While Mr. Billips was in the hospital, Mr. DeSimone moved out of the office—which he and Mr. Billips had shared for over one and one-half years after the partnership was dissolved.

Before the partnership was terminated, Mr. DeSimone bought a computer. Ms. Ramsey prepared a diskette for every case that came into the office. When Mr. DeSimone moved from the offices he had shared with Mr. Billips, Mr. DeSimone took the computer diskette which contained information about plaintiffs' underlying medical malpractice action. Mr. Billips did not know anything about the Daniels diskette until April 1989. ... While Mr. Billips was ill, Mr. DeSimone handled the cases that had belonged to the partnership. Mr. DeSimone did not handle nor was he asked by Mr. Billips to do any legal work on the Daniels's case. Mr. DeSimone never agreed with Mr. Billips or plaintiffs to handle the medical malpractice action. According to Mr. Billips, plaintiffs' case fell "through the cracks."

On April 4, 1989, two months before the three-year statute ran, Mr. Daniels called Mr. Billips to inquire about the medical malpractice action. Mr. Billips advised Mr. Daniels to get another attorney because he was no longer practicing law. The underlying action was subsequently dismissed for lack of service and this suit for legal malpractice followed.

Robert and Mitzie Jean Daniels—Plaintiffs—filed the original complaint on March 3, 1990. The named defendants are Attorney Dale D. Billips, *The Law Offices of Dale D. Billips*, and Attorney Patricia Ramsey. The complaint alleged: Defendants negligently failed to timely serve an underlying medical malpractice and loss of consortium action. The medical-malpractice action was dismissed pursuant to Code of Civil Procedure § 583.210. On April 27, 1990, plaintiffs amended the complaint by designating Attorney Salvatore DeSimone and *The Law Firm of Billips & DeSimone*—fictitiously named—as defendants.

Mr. DeSimone answered the complaint and filed a motion for summary judgment. He alleged: (1) He had no duty to serve the underlying medical-malpractice complaint, because he was never their attorney; and (2) he did not proximately cause plaintiffs' injuries. The trial court granted the motion and entered judgment in favor of Mr. DeSimone. The plaintiffs filed a timely notice of appeal.

Discussion

There Are No Triable Issues of Material Fact

Plaintiffs argue that summary judgment was improper because triable issues of material fact remained as to whether Mr. DeSimone was liable for attorney malpractice. Plaintiffs assert that the underlying complaint was not served within three years after it was filed.

The elements of a cause of action for attorney malpractice are: (1) the duty to use such skill, prudence, and diligence as other attorneys commonly possess and exercise; (2) a breach of the duty; (3) a proximate causal connection between the negligent conduct and the resulting injury; and (4) actual loss or damage resulting from the attorney's negligence. *Budd v. Nixen,* 6 Cal.3d 195, 200 (1971). The court of appeal has noted: "[A]n attorney's duty to his or her client depends on the existence of an attorney-client relationship. If that relationship does not exist, the fiduciary duty to a client does not arise. Except for those situations where an attorney is appointed by the court, the attorney-client relationship is created by some form of contract, express or implied, formal or informal." *Fox v. Pollack,* 181 Cal.App.3d 954, 959 (1986).

Plaintiffs conceded in the trial court and here: At the point Mr. Billips filed the lawsuit, Mr. DeSimone owed them no duty. They nevertheless argue: Summary judgment was improper, because Mr. DeSimone had nonpartnership files moved into a storage facility. Mr. DeSimone forwarded the monthly storage bills to Mr. Billips. And Mr. DeSimone had possession of a computer diskette—which had some unidentified information on it concerning plaintiffs' suit. Again, the suit was filed by Mr. Billips. In other words, plaintiffs have admitted: When the complaint was filed on June 11, 1986, they were represented by Mr. Billips. But, they seek to hold Mr. DeSimone liable for attorney malpractice on the theory: By storing the files and taking possession of the diskette, Mr. DeSimone undertook to represent them in the underlying action.

The test for potential attorney malpractice under these circumstances was described by the Supreme Court as follows: "[T]he determination whether in a specific case [an attorney] will be held liable to a third person—not in privity—is a matter of policy and involves the balancing of various factors, among which are (1) the extent to which the transaction was intended to affect the plaintiff, (2) the foreseeability of harm to him, (3) the degree of certainty that the plaintiff suffered injury, (4) the closeness of the connection between the defendant's conduct and the injury, and (5) the policy of preventing future harm." *Lucas v. Hamm*, 56 Cal.2d 583, 588 (1961).

The question of duty is an "expression of the sum total of those considerations of policy which lead the law to say that a particular plaintiff is entitled to protection." *Peterson v. San Francisco Community College Dist.*, 36 Cal.3d 799, 805-806 (1984) Whether such a duty exists is initially a question of law and depends upon the balancing of a number of policy considerations for and against the imposition of liability under the particular facts of the case. *Goodman v. Kennedy,* 18 Cal.3d 335, 342 (1976).

Application of the above stated factors establishes that Mr. DeSimone owed no duty of representation to plaintiffs. No evidence was presented which established that Mr. DeSimone intended to affect plaintiffs by moving the files into storage during Mr. Billips's illness. And, there is no evidence regarding Mr. DeSimone's taking custody of the diskette. He possessed it. Under these circumstances, we conclude: Mr. DeSimone did not owe plaintiffs any duty to serve the complaint. The trial court properly granted the summary judgment motion. The judgment is affirmed.

NOTES AND QUESTIONS

1) An Expanded Analysis of the Attorney-Client Relationship. The basic question regarding the formation of an attorney-client relationship is clear: whether the purported client sought and received advice or assistance from an attorney regarding legal matters. *Newberry v. Cotton States Mutual Ins. Co.,* 242 Ga.App. 784, 785 (2000). The attorney-client relationship cannot be created unilaterally in the mind of the client. The alleged client's state of mind is not sufficient to create a confidential relationship. *Guillebeau v. Jenkins,* 182 Ga.App. 225, 230 (1987). Instead, a "reasonable belief" on the part of the would-be client that he/she was being represented by the attorney is necessary. *Calhoun v. Tapley,*196 Ga.App. 318, 319 (1990); *Guillebeau,* 182 Ga.App. at 231. A reasonable belief is defined as one which is reasonably induced by representations or conduct by the attorney. Calhoun *Guillebeau,* 182 Ga.App. at 230. The attorney-client relationship may be expressly created by written contract or may be inferred from the parties' conduct. *Horn v. Smith & Meroney, P.C.,* 194 Ga.App. 298, 299 (1990).

2) Virtual Law Offices and Redefining the Parameters of the Attorney-Client Relationship. The application of law technology is radically changing how attorney-client relationships are formed—which, in turn, determines whether or not an attorney may raise a successful attorney-client defense. Consider Timothy S. Faith's commentary in *Technology in the Practice of Law: Virtuality—The Lawyer That Is Almost Really There,* 47-DEC Md. B.J. 12 (2014). He writes: "In 2004, a 'virtual law firm [has] … the following criteria: (a) a stable core group of attorneys, (b) attorney collaboration with other specialized firms, (c) connected by technology, and (d) flexible staffing. … Today, attorneys often … provide some legal services *via a secure website.* Updated criteria for a virtual law practice could be summarized as an attorney [who] provides legal services securely through an *encrypted web portal* [and] uses a *click-wrap agreement* to initiate the attorney-client relationship."

The Attorney-Client Privilege: Does It Really Have Life Everlasting?

87 Ky. L.J. 1165

Richard C. Wydick

Thanks to prominent newspaper headlines in the summer of 1998, members of the American public may think: The secrets they share with their lawyers will remain secret forever and ever. The truth is not quite that simple. In *Swidler & Berlin v. United States,* 118 S. Ct. 2081 (1998), the Supreme Court declared: The attorney-client privilege continues to live after the client dies. But the Court did not say *how long* it lives, nor did the Court mention that the privilege lives longer in some places than in others.

Swidler & Berlin made headlines … because the cast of characters included [F]irst [L]ady Hillary Clinton, special prosecutor Kenneth Starr, and Vincent Foster—a White House lawyer who committed suicide in the middle of an investigation of supposed wrongdoing at the White House. In May 1993, someone ordered the firing of seven employees of the White House [T]ravel [O]ffice. The firing provoked congressional and other investigations, and Vincent Foster—a former law partner of Hillary Clinton—was the White House lawyer assigned to ride herd on the investigations.

On a Sunday morning in the summer of 1993, Vincent Foster went to the home of attorney James Hamilton, a partner in the private law firm of Swidler & Berlin. [Foster sought] legal representation in connection with the travel office matter. At the outset, Foster asked Hamilton whether their conversation would be privileged, and Hamilton assured him that it would be. During their meeting, Hamilton took several pages of handwritten notes. The word "privileged" is one of the first items to appear in these notes. Nine days after this meeting, Foster committed suicide.

In 1995, Starr started investigating whether certain people had lied or obstructed justice in the earlier investigations of the travel office matter. At Starr's request, a federal grand jury subpoenaed Hamilton's three pages of handwritten notes. Hamilton and his law firm asserted the attorney-client privilege on behalf of their deceased client—Vincent Foster. … [In the end], the Supreme Court held that lawyer Hamilton's handwritten notes were protected by the privilege even after client Foster's death. … The Court [reiterated]: "An uncertain privilege … is little better than no privilege at all."

B. Confidential Information and the Scope of the Attorney-Client Privilege Defense

Swidler & Berlin v. United States

118 S. Ct. 2081
(1998)

Chief Justice Rehnquist delivered the opinion of the Court.

Petitioner James Hamilton is an attorney. He made notes of an initial interview with a client shortly before the client's death. The Government—represented by the Office of Independent Counsel—now seeks his notes for use in a criminal investigation.

This dispute arises out of an investigation conducted by the Office of the Independent Counsel into whether various individuals made false statements, obstructed justice, or committed other crimes during investigations of the 1993 dismissal of employees from the White House Travel Office. Vincent W. Foster, Jr. was Deputy White House Counsel when the firings occurred. In July 1993, Foster met with petitioner Hamilton—an attorney at petitioner Swidler & Berlin. Foster sought legal representation concerning possible congressional or other investigations of the firings. During a 2–hour meeting, Hamilton took three pages of handwritten notes. One of the first entries in the notes is the word "Privileged." Nine days later, Foster committed suicide.

In December 1995, a federal grand jury issued subpoenas to petitioners Hamilton and Swidler & Berlin for, *inter alia,* Hamilton's handwritten notes of his meeting with Foster. Petitioners filed a motion to quash, arguing that the notes were protected by the attorney-client privilege and by the work-product privilege. The district court examined the notes *in camera* and concluded: The handwritten notes were protected from disclosure by both doctrines. The Court of Appeals for the District of Columbia Circuit reversed. We granted certiorari.

The Scope of the Attorney-Client Privilege Defense

The attorney-client privilege is one of the oldest recognized privileges for confidential communications. *Upjohn Co. v. United States,* 449 U.S. 383, 389 (1981); *Hunt v. Blackburn,* 128 U.S. 464, 470 (1888). The privilege is intended to encourage "full and frank communication between attorneys and their clients and thereby promote broader public interests in the observance of law and the administration of justice." *Upjohn* at 389. The issue presented here is the scope of that privilege—more particularly, the extent to which the privilege survives the death of the client. Our interpretation of the privilege's scope is guided by "the principles of the common law ... as interpreted by the courts ... in the light of reason and experience." Fed. Rule Evid. 501; *Funk v. United States,* 290 U.S. 371 (1933).

Common-Law Exceptions to the Attorney-Client Privilege Defense

The Independent Counsel argues: The attorney-client privilege should not prevent disclosure of confidential communications where the client has died and the information is relevant to a criminal proceeding. There is some authority for this position. The court of appeals below held: The privilege may be subject to posthumous exceptions in certain circumstances. And in *Cohen v. Jenkintown Cab Co.,* 238 Pa. Super. 456 (1976), the state appellate court recognized that the privilege generally survives death. But the court concluded that it could make an exception where the interest of justice was compelling and the interest of the client in preserving the confidence was insignificant. *Id.,* at 462–464.

Other than these two decisions, the cases' addressing the existence of the privilege after death—most involving the testamentary exception—uniformly presume the privilege survives, even if they do not so hold. See, *e.g., Mayberry v. Indiana,* 670 N.E.2d 1262 (Ind.1996); *Morris v. Cain,* 39 La. Ann. 712 (1887); *People v. Modzelewski,* 611 N.Y.S.2d 22 (1994). Several state supreme courts' decisions expressly hold: The attorney-client privilege extends beyond the death of the client, even in the criminal context. *In re John Doe Grand Jury Investigation,* 562 N.E.2d 69, 70 (Mass.1990); *State v. Doster,* 284 S.E.2d 218, 219 (S.C. 1981); *State v. Macumber,* 544 P.2d 1084, 1086 (Ariz. 1976).

* * *

"[T]he general rule with respect to confidential communications ... is that such communications are privileged during the testator's lifetime and, also, after the testator's death unless sought to be disclosed in litigation between the testator's heirs." *United States v. Osborn*, 561 F.2d 1334, 1340 (9th Cir. 1977); The rationale for such disclosure is that it furthers the client's intent. *Id.*, at 1340, n. 11. ... Given the language of Rule 501, at the very least the burden is on the Independent Counsel to show that "reason and experience" require a departure from this rule.

The Independent Counsel contends: The testamentary exception supports the posthumous termination of the privilege, because—in practice—most cases have refused to apply the privilege posthumously. He further argues: The exception reflects a policy judgment that the interest in settling estates outweighs any posthumous interest in confidentiality. He then reasons by analogy that in criminal proceedings, the interest in determining whether a crime has been committed should trump client confidentiality, particularly since the financial interests of the estate are not at stake.

But the Independent Counsel's interpretation simply does not square with the case law's implicit acceptance of the privilege's survival and with the treatment of testamentary disclosure as an "exception" or an implied "waiver." And the premise of his analogy is incorrect, since cases consistently recognize that the rationale for the testamentary exception is that it furthers the client's intent. There is no reason to suppose as a general matter that grand jury testimony about confidential communications furthers the client's intent.

Commentators on the law also recognize the general rule: The attorney-client privilege continues after death. Undoubtedly, various commentators have criticized this rule—urging that the privilege should be abrogated after the client's death where extreme injustice would result or as long as disclosure would not seriously undermine the privilege by deterring client communication. Despite the scholarly criticism, we think there are weighty reasons that counsel in favor of posthumous application. Knowing that communications will remain confidential even after death encourages the client to communicate fully and frankly with counsel. While the fear of disclosure, and the consequent withholding of information from counsel, may be reduced if disclosure is limited to posthumous disclosure in a criminal context, it seems unreasonable to assume that it vanishes altogether. Clients may be concerned about reputation, civil liability, or possible harm to friends or family. Posthumous disclosure of such communications may be as feared as disclosure during the client's lifetime.

In a similar vein, the Independent Counsel argues: Existing exceptions to the privilege—such as the crime-fraud exception and the testamentary exception—make the impact of one more exception marginal. However, these exceptions do not demonstrate that the impact of a posthumous exception would be insignificant. And there is little empirical evidence on this point. The established exceptions are consistent with the purposes of the privilege *United States v. Zolin,* 491 U.S. 554, 562-563 (1989). A posthumous exception in criminal cases appears at odds with the goals of encouraging full and frank communication and of protecting the client's interests. A "*no harm in one more exception*" rationale could contribute to the general erosion of the privilege, without reference to common-law principles or "reason and experience."

Here, the Independent Counsel has simply not made a sufficient showing to overturn the common-law rule embodied in the prevailing case law. Interpreted in the light of reason and experience, that body of law requires: The attorney-client privilege [must] prevent disclosure of the notes at issue in this case. The judgment of the court of appeals is *reversed.*

---

28 U.S.C.A.

Federal Rules of Evidence
Article V. Privileges

Rule 501. Privilege in General

The common law—as interpreted by United States courts in the light of reason and experience—governs a claim of privilege unless any of the following provides otherwise:

- the United States Constitution;
- a federal statute; or
- rules prescribed by the Supreme Court.

But in a civil case, state law governs privilege regarding a claim or defense for which state law supplies the rule of decision.

---

28 U.S.C.A.

Federal Rules of Evidence
Article V. Privileges

Rule 502. Attorney-Client Privilege and Work Product; Limitations on Waiver

The following provisions apply, in the circumstances set out, to disclosure of a communication or information covered by the attorney-client privilege or work-product protection.

(a) Disclosure Made in a Federal Proceeding or to a Federal Office or Agency; Scope of a Waiver. When the disclosure is made in a federal proceeding or to a federal office or agency and waives the attorney-client privilege or work-product protection, the waiver extends to an undisclosed communication or information in a federal or state proceeding only if:

(1) the waiver is intentional;

(2) the disclosed and undisclosed communications or information concern the same subject matter; and

(3) they ought in fairness to be considered together.

(b) Inadvertent Disclosure. When made in a federal proceeding or to a federal office or agency, the disclosure does not operate as a waiver in a federal or state proceeding if:

(1) the disclosure is inadvertent;

(2) the holder of the privilege or protection took reasonable steps to prevent disclosure; and

(3) the holder promptly took reasonable steps to rectify the error, including (if applicable) following Federal Rule of Civil Procedure 26(b)(5)(B).

(c) Disclosure Made in a State Proceeding. When the disclosure is made in a state proceeding and is not the subject of a state-court order concerning waiver, the disclosure does not operate as a waiver in a federal proceeding if the disclosure:

(1) would not be a waiver under this rule if it [was] made in a federal proceeding; or

(2) is not a waiver under the law of the state where the disclosure occurred.

(d) Controlling Effect of a Court Order. A federal court may order that the privilege or protection is not waived by disclosure connected with the litigation pending before the court—in which event the disclosure is also not a waiver in any other federal or state proceeding.

(e) Controlling Effect of a Party Agreement. An agreement on the effect of disclosure in a federal proceeding is binding only on the parties to the agreement, unless it is incorporated into a court order.

(f) Controlling Effect of This Rule. Notwithstanding Rules 101 and 1101, this rule applies to state proceedings and to federal court-annexed and federal court-mandated arbitration proceedings, in the circumstances set out in the rule. And notwithstanding Rule 501, this rule applies even if state law provides the rule of decision.

(g) Definitions. In this rule:

(1) "attorney-client privilege" means the protection that applicable law provides for confidential attorney-client communications; and

(2) "work-product protection" means the protection that applicable law provides for tangible material (or its intangible equivalent) prepared in anticipation of litigation or for trial.

C. The Attorney-Client Privilege Defense and the Scope of the Waiver and Work-Product Protection Exceptions

Shaub and Williams, L.L.P. v. Augme Technologies, Inc.

2014 WL 1033862
(S.D.N.Y. 2014)

James C. Francis IV, United States Magistrate Judge.

This is an action for the recovery of unpaid legal fees. Shaub & Williams, LLP (S&W) moves—pursuant to Rule 37 of the Federal Rules of Civil Procedure—to compel document production of attorney-client communications and attorney-work product from Augme Technologies, Inc. ("Augme"). S&W also files a motion to compel the depositions of Augme's current and former legal counsels—Tom Scott of Goodwin Procter LLP and Richard Sybert of Gordon & Rees LLP.

Background

Beginning in 2008, S&W represented Augme (as its predecessor, Modavox, Inc.) in litigation pursuing patent-infringement claims. In February 2011, Augme terminated S&W and retained Goodwin Procter as counsel in the patent cases. S&W formally withdrew from the underlying litigation in April 2011. On February 19, 2013, S&W filed a complaint against Augme alleging that it owed over $2 million in outstanding legal fees under a theory of *quantum meruit*.

Augme responded with two counterclaims—alleging legal malpractice and breach of contract. Augme also asserted a number of affirmative defenses. The legal malpractice counterclaim alleged: In the underlying patent litigation, S&W failed to resolve *discovery* issues in a proper and timely manner, "misunderstood" the patented technology in question, and "submitted poorly written claim construction briefs and incomprehensible motions." One affirmative defense alleged: S&W had been dismissed as counsel for Augme for good cause. A second asserted that S&W had engaged in excessive billing. And a third maintained that S&W was proceeding with "unclean hands."

On May 6, 2013, S&W filed a motion to strike some of the affirmative defenses and a motion to dismiss the counterclaims. While those motions were still pending, S&W filed a motion for summary judgment on the legal malpractice and breach of contract counterclaims. The motion for summary judgment was denied without prejudice as premature—since discovery had not been completed.

On February 14, 2014, the Honorable George B. Daniels, granted in part S & W's motions to dismiss Augme's counterclaims and strike its affirmative defenses. *Shaub & Williams, L.L.P. v. Augme Technologies, Inc.,* 2014 WL 625390 (S.D.N.Y. 2014). Judge Daniels dismissed Augme's legal malpractice counterclaim for failure to plead facts adequate to support causation. ... He also denied Augme's request for a leave to file an amended legal malpractice counterclaim and new counterclaims for breach of the implied covenant of good faith and fair dealing and breach of fiduciary duty. *Id.* at *1–3.

However, Judge Daniels sustained the counterclaim for breach of contract and permitted Augme to add facts alleging excessive billing. *Id.* at *6. Finally, Judge Daniels granted Augme's request to amend its affirmative defenses—the dismissal for good cause defense, and a breach-of-contract *defense.* On the other hand, Judge Daniels struck Augme's other defenses—laches, waiver, estoppel, and the doctrine of unclean hands. *Id.* at *7–9.

While these motions were pending, the S&W law firm submitted a production-of-documents request to Augme. The law firm also a subpoenaed attorney Goodwin Procter. The firm wanted "all documents, electronically-stored information, and things concerning communications"—between Augme and Goodwin Procter—regarding various topics of the underlying litigation, patent infringement analyses, document production, settlement negotiations, S&W's performance of legal services, compensation owed to S&W, and the continuation of S&W's services after Augme first contacted Goodwin Procter.

In July 2013, S&W, Augme, and attorney Goodwin Procter met several times to discuss the requests. In the end, Augme and Goodwin Procter rejected the requests—asserting that the requested information was protected by attorney-client privilege and the work product doctrine. In response, the S&W law firm filed the present motion to compel document production and depositions. ... S&W alleges that the dismissal of Augme's malpractice counterclaim has no impact here, because Augme "reasserts portions of its counterclaims for malpractice and breach of contract." Augme counters—asserting that there is presently "absolutely no reason to grant S&W's motion to compel, as it was based solely on discovery information relating to Augme's legal malpractice counterclaim and damages related thereto."

Discussion

Attorney-Client Privilege and the Waiver Defense

The attorney-client privilege protects from disclosure "(1) a communication between client and counsel that (2) was intended to be and was in fact kept confidential, and (3) was made for the purpose of obtaining or providing legal advice." *In re County of Erie,* 473 F.3d 413, 419 (2d Cir.2007). The privilege protects both the advice of the attorney to the client and the information communicated by the client that provides a basis for giving advice. *See Upjohn Co. v. United States,* 449 U.S. 383, 390 (1981. "[T]he burden is on a party's claiming the protection of a privilege to establish those facts that are the essential elements of the privileged relationship." *In re Grand Jury Subpoena Dated Jan. 4, 1984,* 750 F.2d 223, 224–25 (2d Cir.1984).

The attorney-client privilege may be waived— "when the defendant asserts a claim that in fairness requires examination of protected communications." *United States v. Bilzerian,* 926 F.2d 1285, 1292 (2d Cir.1991). "The key to a finding of implied waiver ... is some showing—by the party arguing for a waiver—that the opposing party *relies* on the privileged communication as a claim or defense or as an element of a claim or defense." *In re County of Erie,* 546 F.3d 222, 228 (2d Cir. 2008). Assertion of an advice-of-counsel defense is the "quintessential example" of an implied waiver. *County of Erie,* 546 F.3d at 228. Similarly, a defendant's asserting a good-faith defense—that implicates its state of mind—may also waive the privilege. *Id.* at 228-229. On the other hand, the fact that a privileged communication may simply be relevant to a claim or defense is insufficient to effect forfeiture of the privilege. *County of Erie,* 546 F.3d at 229.

The Work Product Doctrine

The work product doctrine "shields from disclosure materials prepared "in anticipation of litigation" by a party or its representative. *United States v. Adlman,* 68 F.3d 1495, 1501 (2d Cir. 1995), quoting Fed R. Civ. P. 26(b)(3). It is designed to protect "mental impressions, conclusions, opinions or theories concerning the litigation." *United States v. Adlman,* 134 F.3d 1194, 1195 (2d

Cir.1998). A document is prepared "in anticipation of litigation" if—"in light of the nature of the document and the factual situation in the particular case, it can fairly be said to have been prepared or obtained *because* of the prospect of litigation." *Id.* at 1202.

It is often asserted that the work product doctrine does not prevent disclosure of facts. *See,* 8 Charles A. Wright, et al., *Federal Practice and Procedure* § 2023 (3d ed. 2010) ("The work product concept furnishes no shield against discovery, by interrogatories or by deposition, of the facts that the adverse party's lawyer has learned."). However, the work product doctrine may protect from discovery notes taken by an attorney that reflect the results of an investigation undertaken in anticipation of litigation. *See In re Grand Jury Subpoena dated July 6, 2005,* 510 F.3d 180, 183 (2d Cir.2007) (holding that "fact work product may encompass factual material, including the result of a factual investigation"); *Chevron Corp. v. Donziger,* 2013 WL 3294820, at *1 (S.D.N.Y. 2013) ("[The work product doctrine] rests in part on the premise that each party to a lawsuit should do its own work, including its own investigation of the facts, without intruding into and benefitting from the efforts of its adversary.").

However, the work product doctrine is not absolute. It can be overcome by a showing of substantial need for production of the subject materials and the inability to obtain equivalent information from other sources. *See Adlman,* 134 F.3d at 1197, 1204.

Application

Before the issue of whether S&W is entitled to documents and communications that are otherwise protected by attorney-client privilege or work product doctrine even arises, the plaintiffs must prove that such information is "relevant to the defenses and counterclaims asserted by Augme." *Chen–Oster,* 293 F.R.D. at 561 ("The burden of demonstrating relevance is on the party seeking discovery."). Here, the plaintiffs have not provided sufficient explanation of why communications or documents exchanged between Augme and its attorneys are relevant to the claims, counterclaim, or affirmative defenses that are still at issue in this case.

The S&W attorneys claim: "Augme's assertion of privilege results from Augme's filing counterclaims for legal malpractice, breach of contract, breach of the implied covenant of good faith and fair dealing, and breach of fiduciary duty, against S&W." After Judge Daniels's ruling, however, the only surviving counterclaim is for breach of contract. And, contrary to S&W's interpretation, that counterclaim focuses on S&W's billing practices—not on any damages caused by S&W's representation that required correction by Goodwin Procter.

Augme continues to assert: The affirmative defense of dismissal for good cause is based on S&W's "failure to obtain or understand the relevant evidence needed for the underlying cases, drafting of incomprehensible briefs to the Court, unprofessional demeanor during hearings, excessive billings, and mishandling of experts." However, while this defense may raise some of the same malpractice-related issues as the dismissed counterclaim, it does not require proof of causation or damages that would implicate Goodwin Procter's corrective efforts.

S&W nevertheless argues: The dismissal of the malpractice claim does not alter the need to compel discovery of attorney client communications. Although S&W does not articulate clearly what privileged information it believes is relevant and discoverable, it focuses almost exclusively on disputes regarding the causation and damages elements of the (now dismissed) malpractice counterclaim. ... And even if S&W had established the relevance of the documents and communications they seek, they have not demonstrated: Augme waived the attorney-client privilege or disclosure is merited despite work product protection.

* * *

Furthermore, while Augme's affirmative defense dismissal for good cause—alleges that S&W misunderstood the underlying litigation, S&W fails to show why it needs "facts proving that S&W's alleged misunderstanding was wrong and facts supporting the allegedly 'correct' understanding of the technology." To the extent that Goodwin Procter or Gordon & Rees provided analysis to Augme, such information is protected by work product doctrine and S&W has not shown any substantial need for such information or evidence that it is unable to get it from a source other than communications between Augme and its attorneys.

Because S&W has not demonstrated that the requested communications are relevant, nor that they were relied upon as a basis for the remaining breach of contract counterclaim or remaining affirmative defenses, the motion to compel document production is denied.

D. Electronic Discovery, Employers' Motions to Compel the Production of Information, and the Scope of the Attorney-Client Privilege Defense

National Economic Research Associates, Inc. v. Evans

21 Mass. L. Rptr. 337
(Superior Ct. Mass. 2006)

Ralph D. Gants, Justice.

National Economic Research Associates, Inc. (NERA) and Marsh & McLennan Companies, Inc. —have moved to compel David Evans (Evans), LECG Corporation, and LECG, LLC (collectively, LECG) to disclose attorney-client communications between Evans and his private attorney. NERA contends that the attorney-client privilege never applied to these communications. Or, if it did, the privilege was waived when the communications were shared with third parties.

Background

NERA is a subsidiary of Marsh McLennan—a leading economic consulting firm. Until his resignation on March 15, 2004, Evans was one of NERA's more productive consultants. On December 9, 2002, and in order to exercise Marsh McLennan stock options, Evans executed a Non–Solicitation Agreement for Exercise of Stock Options. The solicitation contract renewed and extended his prior agreement for three years. Under the agreement, he promised not to solicit certain NERA employees, or solicit or perform services for certain NERA clients, for two years following the termination of his employment at NERA.

Before leaving NERA to join LECG, Evans conferred with his private attorney at the Law Firm of Nutter McClennen & Fish (Attorney Nutter). He wanted an opinion regarding various legal matters surrounding his departure from NERA and the commencement of his employment at LECG. Many of those attorney-client communications were conducted by e-mail. Specifically, Evans sent and received e-mails using his personal, password-protected, Yahoo e-mail account—rather than using his

NERA e-mail address. Evans often used an NERA-issued laptop to send and retrieve those e-mails.

Unknown to Evans, when one accesses information via the Internet using a private Yahoo account, a "screen shot" captures all accessed or retrieved information and stores it in a temporary Internet file on the computer's hard drive. Therefore, each attorney-client communication between Evans and Attorney Nutter was stored on the NERA-issued laptop's hard-disk drive. To be sure, the stored e-mail documents could not be retrieved easily using Windows Explorer or another browser. But a person with substantial computer expertise could retrieve them.

Evans left NERA and he returned the laptop to NERA. However, he deleted his personal computer files—those containing information about his divorce and finances. He even ran a computer program known as a "disk defragmenter." The latter program prevents one from recovering deleted personal files. Evans did not delete his Yahoo emails, those that were retrieved using the laptop. And he did not know: The e-mails had been stored on the laptop's hard drive. But, he purposely left his work-related files on the laptop's hard-disk drive.

After Evans's resignation, NERA retained a computer forensic expert to search the hard-disk drive of Evans's NERA-issued laptop. During the course of that forensic search, the expert retrieved various attorney-client communications—between Evans and Attorney Nutter. All of those communications were made via e-mails—using Evans' Yahoo account. None of the attorney-client communications were made using NERA's Intranet. And none were stored in documents that could be retrieved with Windows Explorer. After viewing and indexing the e-mails between Evans and Attorney Nutter, NERA's counsel instructed its computer forensic expert to retain the e-mails. But NERA's counsel did not review the communications, awaiting guidance from the court.

Discussion

To establish that the attorney-client privilege applies to certain communications, the party's asserting the privilege must establish: (1) the existence of an attorney-client relationship; (2) "the communications were received from a client during the course of the client's search for legal advice from the attorney;" (3) "the communications were made in confidence;" and (4) the privilege regarding the specific communications has not been waived. *In the Matter of the Reorganization of Electric Mutual Liability Ins. Co.*

Ltd. (Bermuda) ("Emlico"), 425 Mass. 419, 421 (1997). Here, NERA and Marsh & McLennan essentially contend: Evans cannot prove the third and fourth elements. More specifically, they assert: The hard-disk drive on Evans's NERA-issued laptop belongs to NERA and is subject to review by NERA.

Evans' use of the NERA-issued laptop was governed by the policies appearing in NERA's Policies and Procedures Manual ("Manual")—which was posted on NERA's Intranet. Marsh McLennan Code of Business Conduct and Ethics appears in the Manual. And under the section entitled "Computer and Communication Resources," it states that e-mails may be disclosed in litigation and e-mails "deleted in the ordinary course of business may be retrieved." The Manual also read:

> Any e-mail or voice mail sent or Internet site visited using Company resources is a reflection on the Company. Misuse of these resources can result in damage to the Company's reputation and even legal action. The personal use of e-mail, the Internet and telephones should be kept to a minimum for both productivity and financial reasons. All computer resources are the property of the Company. To the extent permitted by law and any applicable agreements, the Company may, from time to time and at its discretion, review any information sent or stored using these resources. Be aware that e-mails are not confidential and the Company may read them during routine checks.
>
> * * *
>
> Network administrators can read your [electronic] mail! Please use your Inbox as a temporary message store; delete your messages or (if you need to) archive them to the appropriate project directory after you have read them. Each Outlook installation has been set up to either delete or archive messages present in the Inbox and Sent Items folders.
>
> NERA does permit the use of Internet resources—dedicated or via dial-up—for personal use provided such use results in personal time savings that can be—at least partially—applied toward work. … Please note that all Internet access is logged by user and the logs are archived for at least 30 days. We do

> not make a habit of prying but any misuse of Internet resources can be easily traced.
>
> A log may be kept of users' network activities to monitor network usage. This may include logins, Internet sites visited, and electronic mail sent or received and telephonic and voice-mail usage. At times, it may be necessary for computer or law enforcement personnel to monitor network traffic or desktop activities, including electronic mail.

NERA contends: The warnings in the Manual provided reasonable notice to Evans; and, he should have known that the hard-disk drive on his issued laptop belonged to NERA and could be read by NERA. Therefore, NERA stresses: (1) Evans and Attorney Nutter's allegedly attorney-client communications (e-mails) were not made "in confidence"; and (2) Evans reasonably should have understood that NERA could read his e-mails.

Exceptions to the Attorney-Client Communications Defense

An attorney-client communication is not confidential and therefore not protected by the attorney-client privilege if:

(1) The communication was made in the presence of a third party who was not a necessary agent of the attorney or the client. *Commonwealth v. Rosenberg,* 410 Mass. 347, 354 n. 10 (1991); *or*

(2) The communication was intended to be private but the client reasonably should have understood—from the circumstances of the communication—that it might be overheard; *Commonwealth v. Petty,* 4 Mass. L. Rep. 611 (Mass. Super. Ct.1995) (attorney-client communication in busy clerk's office is not protected by privilege, because client could have no reasonable expectation of privacy when he chose to converse there); *or*

(3) The communication was made privately. But it was understood that the information communicated was to be conveyed to others. *Commonwealth v. Rosenberg,* 410 Mass. at 354 n. 10, 573 N.E.2d 949; *Peters v. Wallach,* 366 Mass. 622, 627 (1975).

Based on the warnings furnished in the Manual, Evans could not reasonably expect to communicate in confidence with his private attorney if Evans e-mailed his attorney using his NERA e-mail address through the NERA *Intranet*. The Manual plainly warned Evans that e-mails on the network could be read by NERA network administrators. The Manual, however, did not expressly declare that it would monitor the *content* of *Internet* communications. Rather, it simply declared that NERA would *monitor* the visited *Internet sites*. Most importantly, the Manual did not expressly declare, or even implicitly suggest: NERA would monitor the content of e-mail communications which were made when an employee used a NERA-issued laptop computer to access the Internet and used a personal e-mail account to communicate with third parties. In addition, NERA did not warn its employees, disclosing that NERA could read the content of Internet e-mail communications which were stored on an NERA-issued computer's hard drive.

On the other hand, NERA contends: Any reasonable person would have known that a program on the laptop would make a "screen shot" of all searches and communications including e-mails retrieved from a private password-protected e-mail account on the Internet—and store them in temporary files on the computer. This court does not agree that any reasonable person would have known this information. Certainly, until this motion, this court did not know: "Screen shots" of private e-mails are routinely stored on a computer's hard-disk drive.

Moreover, this court notes: The American Bar Association issued its Formal Ethics Opinion 99–413 on March 10, 1999, entitled "Protecting the Confidentiality of Unencrypted E–Mail." ABA Opinion 99 outlines the various ways in which third parties might access and read privileged e-mail communications. Nonetheless, the opinion concludes: "[L]awyers have a reasonable expectation of privacy when communicating by e-mail maintained by an [on-line service provider]," such as Yahoo. The ABA Ethics Opinion did not even mention the possibility: Such e-mails may be seen by anyone with access to the computer by examining the "screen shot" temporary file on the hard drive.

Evans cannot reasonably have understood that his attorney-client communications could be "overheard" by NERA. Evans has not waived this privilege. In *Emlico,* the Supreme Judicial Court clearly stated: The mere fact that an otherwise privileged attorney-client communication is overheard or inadvertently disclosed does not, by itself, constitute a waiver of the privilege. 425 Mass. at 422. "Thus, a client may be deemed to have met the burden of establishing that a privilege exists and no waiver has occurred if adequate steps have been taken to ensure a document's confidentiality." *Id.* at 423.

Here, Evans has met that burden. He did not engage in these attorney-client communications using NERA's Intranet. He used his private, password-protected Yahoo e-mail account that he accessed through the Internet. He did not forward these communications to his Intranet e-mail address. He did not save or store them as Word or WordPerfect documents in his My Documents (or equivalent) file on the NERA-issued laptop. He attempted to delete all personal documents on his NERA-issued laptop, before returning it. He even ran a "disk defragmenter" program—attempting to ensure that his personal documents could not be retrieved. The totality of these efforts are "adequate steps" to protect the confidentiality of his privileged communications with his Nutter attorney.

* * *

The bottom line is this: If an employer wishes to read an employee's attorney-client communications unintentionally stored in a temporary file on a company-owned computer—which were made via a private, password-protected e-mail account accessed through the Internet, not the company's Intranet, the employer must plainly communicate the following to the employee: (1) All e-mails are stored on the hard-disk drive of the company's computer in a "screen shot" temporary file; and (2) The company expressly reserves the right to retrieve those temporary files and read them. Only after receiving such clear guidance can employees fairly be expected to understand: Their reasonable expectation in the privacy of attorney-client communications has been compromised by the employer. For the reasons stated above, NERA and Marsh & McLennan's motion to compel the production of Attorney Nutter and Evans' attorney-client communications is denied.

E. Electronic Discovery, Spouses' Motions to Compel Production of Information, and the Scope of the Attorney-Client Privilege Defense

Schreiber v. Schreiber

29 Misc.3d 171
(N.Y. Supreme Ct.-Kings Cty. 2010)

Delores J. Thomas, J.

In this matrimonial action and pursuant to Rule 3102 of New York's Civil Practice Law and Rules (CPLR), Sarah C. Schreiber (Mrs. Schreiber) wants a court order that (1) compels Attorney Marc A. Schreiber *aka* Meir Aaron Schreiber (Attorney Schreiber) to produce the hard disk drive in a certain office computer and deposit it with the clerk of the court for a forensic examination, (2) permits Mrs. Schreiber's expert to copy the hard disk drive on site and deliver a copy of the same to the clerk of the court for safekeeping, and (3) prohibits Attorney Schreiber from conveying *any of the assets* which might be on the hard disk drive or a copy thereof.

Background

On December 7, 2007, the court denied Mrs. Schreiber's previous request for an immediate inspection of the hard disk drives in Attorney Schreiber's office computers. The court observed: "Inasmuch as this request for relief is not in the nature of pendente lite support, the issue of defendant's compliance is denied, with leave to renew, at either a subsequent compliance conference or in a separate motion. Moreover, inasmuch as the court already appointed an appraiser to value law practice, an order allowing Mrs. Schreiber to inspect the hard drive on Attorney Schreiber's computers may well be duplicative and unnecessary."

Thereafter, a court-appointed appraiser opined: The fair market value of Attorney Schreiber's solo law practice as of April 4, 2006, was $168,000. To reach that conclusion, the appraiser examined copies of defendant's Schedule C— "Profit or Loss From Business Sole Proprietorship"—for the years ended December 31, 2003-2005. The appraiser also interviewed Attorney Schreiber in his office, reviewed the bank statements provided by Mrs. Schreiber, and reviewed/searched publicly available financial publications and databases.

Because the underlying data were not audited, the appraiser cautioned: "Marc Schreiber represented to us that the information he supplied was complete and accurate to the best of his knowledge and that the financial information, as reported in the Law Practice's income tax returns, fairly reflects the Law Practice's results of operations and financial condition. *Information supplied to us has been accepted as correct without further verification, and we express no opinion on that information.*" (court's emphasis)

Mrs. Schreiber now renews her demand for the transfer of Attorney Schreiber's office computer hard disk drive so that her expert can make a "mirror image" of its contents. By this process, Mrs. Schreiber's expert would essentially create a "clone" of the subject hard disk drive—duplicating all programs, files, and other information contained therein, whether or not germane to this case. Mrs. Schreiber hopes to discover electronically stored evidence that Attorney Schreiber has not voluntarily produced during discovery.

In a March 9, 2010, stipulated order, the court directed: "On the consent of parties and pending a decision on the motion, Mrs. Schreiber shall pay Attorney Schreiber the cost of cloning the hard drive in his office computer within ten days. The original hard drive will be held by Attorney Schreiber's retained attorney—pending the court's decision on motion. Mrs. Schreiber's observers may be present when the hard drive is cloned. But they may not view it." Assuming that the stipulated order has been effectuated, Mrs. Schreiber is now essentially requesting an examination of all the computer files and file fragments on the cloned hard disk drive—the clone of Attorney Schreiber's office computer (the clone).

Mrs. Schreiber's Contentions

In support of her motion, Mrs. Schreiber asserts: Attorney Schreiber concealed his income and assets—attempting to avoid paying a fair share of the marital income and assets earned or acquired during the parties' 30-year marriage. Mrs. Schreiber also alleges: Attorney Schreiber misrepresented his income and assets in his August 2006 statement of net worth. And he testified falsely at his pretrial depositions—asserting that his annual income was approximately $50,000 and that he held no securities or cash. Mrs. Schreiber maintains: Despite her numerous attempts to obtain full and reliable information concerning these issues, Attorney

Schreiber has consistently declined to reveal his true financial condition.

Mrs. Schreiber further asserts: The documents obtained from Attorney Schreiber and third parties reveal that Attorney Schreiber has engaged in what she characterizes as "bizarre" financial activities:

(1) Attorney Schreiber utilized multiple and simultaneous professional escrow and stock brokerage accounts—which were held in his name individually or in the name of various for-profit and not-for-profit entities that may have been affiliated with Attorney Schreiber;

(2) He failed to file his income tax returns for the years 2006, 2007 and 2008;

(3) Attorney Schreiber did not receive any independent contractor tax forms from any of the lenders for whom he performed real estate closings. Rather, Attorney Schreiber deducted his legal fees from moneys that lenders deposited in his escrow accounts;

(4) He did not maintain a separate personal checking account. Instead he transferred any remaining funds from closings to his single operating account—which he utilized to pay both his business and personal expenses;

(5) Despite claiming that his annual income was only $50,000, Attorney Schreiber's total annual income each year from 2003 to 2009 exceeded $100,000, based on Mrs. Schreiber's analysis and extrapolation of existing (but incomplete) data;

(6) Notwithstanding his denial that he had no credit card accounts, he may have had several credit card account balances which he had been paying at least up until May 2008;

(7) Regardless of his claim to the contrary, he held multiple brokerage accounts in his name and in the name of his nominees or agents;

(8) It is likely that Attorney Schreiber may have concealed his assets in a corporate entity (known as Machne Menachem, Inc.) which was incorporated in July 1995 and filed for chapter 11 reorganization in December 2001; and,

(9) Attorney Schreiber may have stored assets in overseas accounts in Australia, Israel and Switzerland.

Based on the foregoing, Mrs. Schreiber posits: "Attorney Schreiber's mantra—that his legal practice is worthless and suffering from a declining economy—will be seen as false, when viewed in conjunction with the materials that Mrs. Schreiber uncovered as well as with those which are extremely likely to be on Attorney Schreiber's hard-drive. *These materials will show—upon information and belief, a thriving practice in which millions of dollars are routinely ferreted in and out of Attorney Schreiber's escrow accounts to effectuate business transactions and closings.*" (court's emphasis)

Attorney Schreiber's Opposition

In opposition, Attorney Schreiber contends: Mrs. Schreiber's request is unnecessary and burdensome, because Attorney Schreiber has supplied an affidavit, stating that he does not have any additional documents to share. Further, Attorney Schreiber characterizes Mrs. Schreiber's request for inspection of his computer hard disk drive as a groundless fishing expedition. Attorney Schreiber maintains: If Mrs. Schreiber has proof that Attorney Schreiber has concealed income and assets, she should present her evidence at trial. She should not attempt any further discovery based on her pure speculation and perhaps wishful thinking.

In addition, Attorney Schreiber avers: His statement of net worth was accurate. His annual net income has remained about $50,000. He has no assets, other than certain shares of stock which he purchased in 2009. In his affirmation in opposition, Attorney Schreiber explains why his law practice was worth only $168,000. And he defends the manner in which he conducts his business. He denies Mrs. Schreiber's allegations that he has concealed assets or misstated his income. Attorney Schreiber also asserts that he presently has no charitable or business accounts. He has no credit cards. And he has not been an active participant in Machne Menachem, Inc. for about 10 years.

He acknowledges that he has a securities brokerage account which was worth $68,481.68 on March 16, 2010. But he contends: The securities are his separate, nonmarital property. He indicates that he will submit an updated statement of net worth before trial required. He concludes: As a busy lawyer working long hours to eke out a small livelihood, he "simply does not have the time to go through each and every allegation dreamed up against him."

The Law

In matrimonial actions, "parties are entitled to full disclosure of all financial information concerning marital assets held during the marriage, including business records, real estate transactions, examinations of accounting procedures, financial records, and both hard copy and computer stored data" *Etzion v Etzion,* 7 Misc 3d 940, 943 (Sup. Ct.-Nassau County 2005). Domestic Relations Law § 236 (B) (4) (a) provides: "In all matrimonial actions and proceedings in which alimony, maintenance or support is in issue, there shall be compulsory disclosure by both parties of their respective financial states. No showing of special circumstances shall be required before such disclosure is ordered."

Under CPLR article 31, all of the discovery tools may be used in matrimonial actions. CPLR 3101(a) does not allow the affirmative defenses—"privilege," "attorney work product," or "material prepared for litigation"—to defeat a compulsory disclosure motion in matrimonial actions. In accordance with CPLR 3101(b), (c) and d), disclosure is proper and should be permitted. Nevertheless, the court is bound to "oversee the discovery process and to insure that undue prejudice and delay do not occur as the result of additional and/or potentially open-ended discovery, including unwarranted fishing expeditions" *Shumakh v Shumakh,* 21 Misc 3d 1142[A], *9 (Sup. Ct.- Kings County 2008).

* * *

In the context of disputes surrounding spousal maintenance or the equitable distribution of separate or community property, several courts have allowed *e*-discovery of various information on spouses' hard disk drives as well as the cloning of hard disk drives. *See Etzion v Etzion,* 7 Misc 3d 940, 943 (Sup. Ct.-Nassau Cty. 2005) (permitting the imaging of a defendant's hard disk drives to proceed, preventing a direct delivery of the clones to the plaintiff, and imposing limitations to protect the defendant's privileged materials); *R.C. v B.W.,* NYLJ, Apr. 3, 2008, at 26, col.1, 3 and 4 (Sup. Ct.-Kings Cty.) (reaffirming that electronic records and information are subject to disclosure, but declaring that a husband may not conduct "a fishing expedition" into his wife's computer if he was not looking for "financial documents, records, billing statements or bank statements"); and *Byrne v Byrne,* 168 Misc 2d 321 (Sup. Ct., Kings County 1996) (allowing a wife to confiscate her husband's employer-issued portable computer to review the husband's finances and personal business records and concluding that an employer-issued portable computer is akin to a filing cabinet—which may be accessed by the wife or husband in the marital residence).

Outside the matrimonial context, courts have been generally reluctant to sanction an intrusive examination of an opponent's computer hard disk drive as a matter of course. See *Melcher v Apollo Med. Fund Mgt. L.L.C.*, 52 AD3d 244, 245 (1st Dept. 2008); *Samide v Roman Catholic Diocese of Brooklyn*, 5 AD3d 463, 465 (2d Dept. 2004); and *Matter of Maura*, 17 Misc 3d 237, 247 (Sup. Ct., Nassau County 2007).

Discussion

The court finds: Mrs. Schreiber is not entitled to an unrestricted turnover of the computer hard disk drive—either in the form of the original hard disk drive or in the form of a clone. Unlike a typical discovery demand which targets particular information, Mrs. Schreiber's request is overbroad. It seeks general access as well as unlimited time to access the entirety of Attorney Schreiber's business and personal data on his office computer. Equally important, Mrs. Schreiber has proposed no discovery/issue resolution protocol. Accordingly, that branch of Mrs. Schreiber's motion—a request to compel the production of the hard disk drive in Attorney Schreiber's office computer—is denied … If Mrs. Schreiber wishes to renew, the sole object of her discovery will be a clone of the hard disk drive—the computer files and file fragments. The original hard disk drive will remain in possession of Attorney Schreiber's counsel.

In addition, if Mrs. Schreiber wishes to renew, her renewal must contain a detailed, step-by-step discovery protocol that would protect Attorney Schreiber's privileged and private material. The following is a proposed list of items such protocol should contain:

(a) DISCOVERY REFEREE: The parties will have until the renewal deadline to agree on an attorney referee, preferably someone with some technical expertise in computer science, to be appointed pursuant to CPLR 3104 (b) to supervise discovery (the referee).

(b) FORENSIC COMPUTER EXPERT: The parties will have until the renewal deadline to agree on a forensic computer expert who will inspect and analyze the clone (the expert). The expert will execute a confidentiality agreement (to be agreed upon by the parties) governing nondisclosure of the contents of the clone and its redelivery to Attorney Schreiber's counsel after completion of electronic discovery.

(c) FILE ANALYSIS: The expert will analyze the clone for evidence of any download, installation, and/or utilization of any software program, application, or utility which has the capability of deleting or altering files so that they are not recoverable (a drive-wiping utility). The expert will then (i) extract from the clone all live files and file fragments, and (ii) if the files on the clone have been deleted or altered using a drive-wiping utility, will also recover all deleted files and file fragments.

(d) SCOPE OF DISCOVERY: Mrs. Schreiber will list the keyword and other searches she proposes to have the expert run on the files and file fragments, subject to a reasonably short time frame (to be agreed upon by the parties) in which such files or file fragments were created or modified. Mrs. Schreiber is cautioned that she should narrowly tailor her search queries so as to expedite discovery and reduce the costs of litigation to the parties. To illustrate, a search query for *all* documents with an *.xls* (Microsoft Excel) extension created or modified within a three-year period preceding the commencement of this matrimonial action will not be permitted.

(e) FIRST-LEVEL REVIEW: The expert will run keyword or other searches on all of the extracted files and file fragments. After performing searches, the expert will export to CDs or DVDs a copy of the native files and file fragments which were hit by such searches, and will deliver such media to Attorney Schreiber's counsel to conduct a privilege review. An exact copy of the media delivered to Attorney Schreiber's counsel will be contemporaneously delivered by the expert to the referee. The expert will also concurrently deliver to the referee and to counsel for both parties a report (i) detailing the results of its searches, (ii) listing the file types for all files hit by the searches, with the file extensions and number of files for each, and (iii) stating whether or not it found evidence of the use of a drive-wiping utility.

(f) SECOND-LEVEL REVIEW: Within 20 days after delivery of the media containing the extracted files and file fragments, Attorney Schreiber's counsel will deliver to Mrs. Schreiber's counsel in electronic format (to be agreed upon by the parties) all nonprivileged documents and information included in the extracted files and file fragments, together with a privilege log which identifies each document for which Attorney Schreiber claims privilege and describes the nature of the documents withheld (but without revealing information which is itself privileged), so as to enable Mrs. Schreiber to assess the applicability of privilege.

(g) DISCOVERY DISPUTES: The referee will resolve any disputes concerning relevancy and privilege. Subject to the parties' agreement, the referee's determination will be final.

(h) COST SHARING: All costs for the expert will be borne by Mrs. Schreiber, subject to any possible reallocation of costs at the conclusion of this action. Mrs. Schreiber will indicate if she is willing to bear any other discovery-related costs and, if so, specify her proposed share.

(i) DISCOVERY DEADLINE: The parties should agree to a fast-track discovery schedule, subject to an outside 90-day deadline within which discovery should be completed.

(j) RETENTION OF CLONE: The discovery referee will keep the clone until the action is concluded, at which time the clone will be returned to Attorney Schreiber's counsel for disposal.

The court has looked at the overall circumstances of this case with an eye toward limiting disclosure to relevant documents and preserving the applicable privileges—both between Attorney Schreiber and his counsel as well as between Attorney Schreiber and his clients. A discovery protocol outlined above strives to achieve these fundamental goals.

Conclusion

That branch of Mrs. Schreiber's motion for an order pursuant to CPLR 3101—directing that the hard disk drive in a certain computer in Attorney Schreiber's office be confiscated and deposited with the clerk of the court for a forensic examination or, in the alternative, permitting Mrs. Schreiber's expert to copy such hard disk drive and to deliver a copy of same to the clerk of the court for safekeeping—is denied. She may leave to renew —upon responding to the deficiencies noted herein—within 45 days after the date of service of the instant decision and order with notice of entry.

That branch of Mrs. Schreiber's motion for an order directing Attorney Schreiber—once the subject hard disk drive or a copy thereof is delivered to the clerk of the court, not to convey any of the assets which may be identified on the subject hard disk drive or a copy thereof is—denied as premature.

United States Code

Rules of the United States Court of Federal Claims
Title V. Disclosures and Discovery
Rule 1. Scope and Purpose

These rules govern the procedure in the United States Court of Federal Claims in all suits. They should be construed and administered to secure the just, speedy, and inexpensive determination of every action and proceeding.

United States Code

Rules of the United States Court of Federal Claims
Title V. Disclosures and Discovery
Rule 26. Duty to Disclose; General Provisions Governing Discovery

(a) Required Disclosures.

(1) Initial Disclosure.

(A) In General. Except as exempted by RCFC 26(a)(1)(B) or as otherwise stipulated or ordered by the court, a party must, without awaiting a discovery request, provide to the other parties:

(i) the name and, if known, the address and telephone number of each individual likely to have discoverable information—along with the subjects of that information—that the disclosing party may use to support its claims or defenses, unless the use would be solely for impeachment;

(ii) a copy—or a description by category and location—-of all documents, electronically stored information, and tangible things that the disclosing party has in its possession, custody, or control and may use to support its claims or defenses, unless the use would be solely for impeachment;

(iii) a computation of each category of damages claimed by the disclosing party—who must also make available for inspection and copying as under RCFC 34 the documents or other evidentiary material, unless privileged or protected from disclosure, on which each computation is based, including materials bearing on the nature and extent of injuries suffered …

* * *

(C) Time for Initial Disclosures—In General. A party must make the initial disclosures at or within 14 days after the Early Meeting of Counsel unless a different time is set by stipulation or court order, or unless a party objects during the conference that initial disclosures are not appropriate in this action and states the objection in the Joint Preliminary Status Report. In ruling on the objection, the court must determine what disclosures, if any, are to be made and must set the time for disclosure.

(D) Time for Initial Disclosures—For Parties Served or Joined Later. A party that is first served or otherwise joined after the Early Meeting of Counsel must make the initial disclosures within 30 days after being served or joined, unless a different time is set by stipulation or court order.

(E) Basis for Initial Disclosure; Unacceptable Excuses. A party must make its initial disclosures based on the information then reasonably available to it. A party is not excused from making its disclosures because it has not fully investigated the case or because it challenges the sufficiency of another party's disclosures or because another party has not made its disclosures

* * *

(b) Discovery Scope and Limits.

(1) Scope in General. Unless otherwise limited by court order, the scope of discovery is as follows: Parties may obtain discovery regarding any nonprivileged matter that is relevant to any party's claim or defense—including the existence, description, nature, custody, condition, and location of any documents or other tangible things and the identity and location of persons who know of any discoverable matter. For good cause, the court may order discovery of any matter relevant to the subject matter involved in the action. Relevant information need not be admissible at the trial if the discovery appears reasonably calculated to lead to the discovery of admissible evidence. All discovery is subject to the limitations imposed by RCFC 26(b)(2)(C).

(2) Limitations on Frequency and Extent.

(A) When Permitted. By order, the court may alter the limits in these rules on the number of depositions and interrogatories or on the length of depositions under RCFC 30. By order, the court may also limit the number of requests under RCFC 36.

(B) Specific Limitations on Electronically Stored Information. A party need not provide discovery of electronically stored information from sources that the party identifies as not reasonably accessible because of undue burden or cost. On motion to compel discovery or for a protective order, the party from whom discovery is sought must show that the information is not reasonably accessible because of undue burden or cost. If that showing is made, the court may nonetheless order discovery from such sources if the requesting party shows good cause, considering the limitations of RCFC 26(b)(2)(C). The court may specify conditions for the discovery.

(C) When Required. On motion or on its own, the court must limit the frequency or extent of discovery otherwise allowed by these rules if it determines that:

(i) the discovery sought is unreasonably cumulative or duplicative, or can be obtained from some other source that is more convenient, less burdensome, or less expensive;

(ii) the party seeking discovery has had ample opportunity to obtain the information by discovery in the action; or

(iii) the burden or expense of the proposed discovery outweighs its likely benefit, considering the needs of the case, the amount in controversy, the parties' resources, the importance of the issues at stake in the action, and the importance of the discovery in resolving the issues.

(c) Protective Orders.

(1) In General. A party or any person from whom discovery is sought may move for a protective order. The motion must include a certification that the movant has in good faith conferred or attempted to confer with other affected parties in an effort to resolve the dispute without court action. The court may, for good cause, issue an order to protect a party or person from annoyance, embarrassment,

oppression, or undue burden or expense, including one or more of the following:

(A) forbidding the disclosure or discovery;

(B) specifying terms, including time and place, for the disclosure or discovery;

(C) prescribing a discovery method other than the one selected by the party seeking discovery;

(D) forbidding inquiry into certain matters, or limiting the scope of disclosure or discovery to certain matters;

(E) designating the persons who may be present while the discovery is conducted;

(F) requiring that a deposition be sealed and opened only on court order;

(G) requiring that a trade secret or other confidential research, development, or commercial information not be revealed or be revealed only in a specified way; and

(H) requiring that the parties simultaneously file specified documents or information in sealed envelopes, to be opened as the court directs.

(2) Ordering Discovery. If a motion for a protective order is wholly or partly denied, the court may, on just terms, order that any party or person provide or permit discovery. ...

United States Code

Rules of the United States Court of Federal Claims
Title V. Disclosures and Discovery
Rule 37. Failure to Make Disclosures or to Cooperate in Discovery; Sanctions

(a) Motion for an Order Compelling Disclosure or Discovery.

(1) In General. On notice to other parties and all affected persons, a party may move for an order compelling disclosure or discovery. The motion must include a certification that the movant has in good faith conferred or attempted to confer with the person or party failing to make disclosure or discovery in an effort to obtain it without court action. …

(3) Specific Motions.

(A) To Compel Disclosure. If a party fails to make a disclosure required by RCFC 26(a), any other party may move to compel disclosure and for appropriate sanctions.

(B) To Compel a Discovery Response. A party seeking discovery may move for an order compelling an answer, designation, production, or inspection. This motion may be made if:

(i) a deponent fails to answer a question asked under RCFC 30 or 31;

(ii) a corporation or other entity fails to make a designation under RCFC 30(b)(6) or 31(a)(4);

(iii) a party fails to answer an interrogatory under RCFC 33; or

(iv) a party fails to respond that inspection will be permitted—or fails to permit inspection—as requested under RCFC 34.

* * *

(e) Failure to Provide Electronically Stored Information. Absent exceptional circumstances, a court may not impose sanctions under these rules on a party for failing to provide electronically stored information lost as a result of the routine, good-faith operation of an electronic information system.

(f) Failure to Participate in Framing a Discovery Plan. If a party or its attorney fails to participate in good faith in developing and submitting a proposed discovery plan, the court may, after giving an opportunity to be heard, require that party or attorney to pay to any other party the reasonable expenses, including attorney's fees, caused by the failure.

Rise of The Robo-Form—Is This Doom for the Legal Profession?

37-MAY Mont. Law. 9

Cort Jensen

The ABA Tech Conference in Chicago this year was a strange mix of vendors' touting their digital wares, law tech geeks' sharing insights, and chants of doom about the future of the legal profession...First, a belief that too many lawyers did not know enough about technology—especially as it relates to discovery—to continue to practice. This is in an illusionary problem. Lawyers are smart and can learn. ... The second apocalyptic vision involved robo-forms and predictive coding.

Robo-forms are document creation tools that ask questions and use primitive artificial intelligence to guide a user to a completed document. Predictive coding applies basic artificial intelligence to presort or prioritize *e-discovery* documents. [Allegedly, the combination of these two technologies will spell] the "end of the legal profession" as we know it. ... At the heart of both technologies is the ability to do some legal "grunt" work faster, with fewer errors, and with less user knowledge of the law.

Robo-forms ... will decrease the amount of time a law practice needs to spend dealing with forms [and] decrease the [number] of lawyers needed to perform those functions. Robo-forms are primarily civil practice based ... and work best in situations where little courtroom litigation is anticipated. Small- and medium-size estate planning, family law, debt collection, real estate, and intellectual property: These are the areas of law that are being impacted the most. ... Many of these programs already come very near to the "practice" of law. ... Many of the systems require a law degree to use properly for any sort of real litigation *document preparation*. ... If your law practice is primarily filling in forms that people could have done themselves, then your practice days are numbered.

Predictive coding will likely not change the number of attorneys needed in any significant way. It allows an artificial intelligence to predict which *electronic* documents are most relevant for your search terms and organize documents together [if they] are merely versions of the same document or email thread. If used properly, predictive coding can massively simplify an attorney's responding to and dealing with *e-discovery*. To the extent that law firms have added attorneys to deal with large scale culling and sorting of *e-discovery* documents, this technology may allow them to scale back on hiring additional attorneys. [When this technology matures fully, it will permit] more traditional timelines and document review schedules for *e-discovery* cases.

Computers never get tired and are capable of reviewing the same document over and over again—looking for differences. Most of these systems still require someone—trained in the law—to "prime" the artificial intelligence. Someone must pre-classify a sample batch of documents for the case and then monitor the system to make sure it functions correctly. Employing this technology, you may need fewer attorneys to handle a large *discovery* case. But, attorneys must be well versed in both *discovery* and the particular software tool in order to complete predictive coding.

F. Electronic Discovery, the Internal Revenue Commissioner's Motions to Compel Production of Information, and the Scope of the Attorney-Client Privilege Defense

Pacific Management Group v. C.I.R.

2015 WL 3377839
(U.S. Tax Court)

Petitioners include numerous individuals affiliated with various entities—collectively, petitioners—that provided engineering services. In 1999 certain petitioners met with Attorney Ernest Ryder, who described an arrangement designed to minimize petitioners' federal income taxes. Petitioners eventually hired Mr. Ryder to implement this structure. The Commissioner of the Internal Revenue Service (IRS) contends that the structure lacked economic substance.

Before trial, the IRS served a subpoena duces tecum on Steven Dunning—an attorney who for many years had provided legal, corporate, and business advice to petitioners. Mr. Dunning appeared at the trial on January 12, 2015, and produced certain documents. He declined to produce numerous other documents—chiefly emails. He asserted that the excluded documents were protected by the attorney-client privilege.

Mr. Dunning supplied a privilege log entitled, "Attorney Client Privileged E-mail Log." This log consists of a table with four columns. Column 1—captioned "From"—lists the name of the person who sent the email. Column 2—captioned "To"—lists the name or email address of the person or persons to whom the email was addressed. Column 3—captioned "CC"—lists the name or email address of the person or persons who were copied on the email. Column 4—captioned "Email Date Sent"—indicates the date and time when the email was sent. The log is 55 pages long and covers about 2,000 emails.

The privilege log contains no other information. It does not state the subject of any email; it does not describe the contents of any email; it does not indicate whether documents were attached to any email or what the contents of any such documents were; and it does not describe the purpose for which any email or attached document was created. Petitioners offered no supplementary evidence at trial to support application of the attorney-client privilege to any particular email or document.

During the trial on January 20, 2015, the IRS filed the motion to compel and the parties presented oral argument. At the conclusion of the argument, the court indicated that it would grant the motion because the privilege log supplied by Mr. Dunning was inadequate to support privilege defense.

Discussion

Section 7453 of the Internal Revenue Code provides that Tax Court proceedings are conducted "in accordance with the rules of evidence applicable in trials without a jury in the United States District Court of the District of Columbia." The Federal Rules of Evidence—which incorporate the common-law rules of privilege—apply to proceedings in that court. *See* Fed. R. Evid. 501, 1101.

The attorney-client privilege applies to communications made in confidence (1) by a client to an attorney for the purpose of obtaining legal advice and (2) by an attorney to a client, where the communication contains legal advice or reveals confidential information regarding the client's request for advice. *Upjohn Co. v. United States*, 449 U.S. 383, 390 (1981). The burden of establishing that the attorney-client privilege applies to particular communications or documents rests with the party's asserting the privilege. *See Bernardo,* 104 T.C. at 682; *FTC v. Lukens Steel Co.,* 444 F.Supp. 803, 806 (D.D.C.1977).

In general, a "blanket assertion of the privilege will not suffice. Rather, the proponent must conclusively prove each element of the privilege. *In re Lindsey,* 148 F.3d 1100, 1106 (D.C.Cir.1998). Rule 45(e)(2) of the Federal Rules of Civil Procedure reads: "A person withholding subpoenaed information under a claim that it is privileged" must expressly make the claim and must also "describe the nature of the withheld documents, communications, or tangible things in a manner that, without revealing information itself privileged or protected, will enable the parties to assess the claim." *See also* Fed. R. Civ. P. 26(b)(5).

The Tax Court Rules of Practice and Procedure do not contain specific provisions addressing the issue presented here. Where "there is no applicable rule," the court may give "particular weight to the Federal Rules of Civil Procedure." Rule 1(b). *See Grandbouche v. Commissioner,* 99 T.C. 604, 616–617, 1992 WL 349739 (1992). In practice, this court has generally required the submission of a privilege log—whenever a party asserts the privilege over a large number of documents. *See Bernardo,* 104 T.C. at 683–684. *Cf. Avery Dennison Corp. v. Four Pillars,* 190 F.R.D. 1, 1 (D.D.C. 1999) (a privilege log is "the universally accepted means of asserting privileges in discovery in the federal courts").

A privilege log must present facts that establish each element of the claimed privilege—regarding each document. *Chevron Corp. v. Weinberg Group,* 286 F.R.D. 95, 98 (D.D.C. 2012), and *Alexander v. FBI,* 186 F.R.D. 102, 106-107 (D.D.C. 1998). An assertion of privilege requires, at a minimum, the identification of "the authors, dates of preparation, and subject matter of the documents, as well as facts establishing each element of the privilege claim." *United States v. W. Elec. Co., Inc.,* 132 F.R.D. 1, 3 (D.D.C.1990). Without an adequately detailed privilege log, neither a requesting party nor a court can adequately assess whether the privilege has been properly claimed or discern the proper scope of the claimed privilege. *United States v. Constr. Prods. Research, Inc.,*73 F.3d 464, 473-474 (2d Cir.1996).

An attorney's preparing [of] a privilege log must balance the need to show that specific communications are privileged against the risk of inadvertently waiving the attorney-client privilege by disclosing too much information. In assessing the adequacy of a privilege log, a court should be mindful of this consideration. *See* Fed.R.Civ.P. 26(b)(5)(A)(ii), 45(e)(2)(A)(ii). *Cf. First Am. Corp. v. Al–Nahyan,* 2 F.Supp.2d 58, 63 n. 5 (D.D.C. 1998) ("[A] party's resisting disclosure must produce some form of privilege log, although the degree of specificity required is dictated by the needs of the case.").

But where the privilege log supplies no information whatever about the subject of the allegedly privileged communications, the log is plainly inadequate. The log that Mr. Dunning supplied does not state the subject of any email; it does not describe the contents of any email; it does not indicate whether documents were attached to any email or what the contents of any such documents were; it does not describe the purpose for which any email or attached document was created; and it includes no facts indicating that any particular communication was intended to be confidential. Thus, it fails to establish each element of the attorney-client privilege.

Mr. Dunning is the corporate and general business attorney for petitioners and has long served as their trusted advisor. It is impossible to determine from the privilege log which of the communications to and from Mr. Dunning involve legal advice—as opposed to general business advice or transactional matters that do not entail legal advice. *See In re Lindsey,* 148 F.3d at 1106 ("[W]here one consults an attorney not as a lawyer but as a friend or as a business adviser or banker, or negotiator, the consultation is not professional nor the statement privileged."); and, *W. Trails, Inc. v. Camp Coast to Coast, Inc.,* 139 F.R.D. 4, 8 (D.D.C. 1991) ("Attorney-client communications concerning business matters are not within the attorney-client privilege.").

In sum, we find: Attorney Dunning and petitioners have failed to meet their burden of establishing that the attorney-client privilege properly applies to the documents listed in his privilege log. *See Mead Data Central, Inc. v. U.S. Dept. of Air Force,* 566 F.2d 242, 253 (D.C. Cir. 1977). Petitioners have adduced no other reason why these documents should not be produced. We will therefore grant IRS's motion to compel production of the documents in question. To reflect the foregoing, *an appropriate order will be issued.*

United States Code

Rules of the United States Court of Federal Claims
Title V. Disclosures and Discovery
Rule 16. Pretrial Conferences; Scheduling; Management

(a) Purposes of a Pretrial Conference. In any action, the court may order the attorneys and any unrepresented parties to appear for one or more pretrial conferences for such purposes as:

(1) expediting disposition of the action;

(2) establishing early and continuing control so that the case will not be protracted because of lack of management;

(3) discouraging wasteful pretrial activities;

(4) improving the quality of the trial through more thorough preparation;

(5) facilitating settlement; and

(6) assessing the utility of dispositive motions.

* * *

(d) Pretrial Orders. After any conference under this rule, the court should issue an order reciting the action taken. This order controls the course of the action unless the court modifies it.

(e) Final Pretrial Conference and Orders. The court may hold a final pretrial conference to formulate a trial plan, including a plan to facilitate the admission of evidence. The conference must be held as close to the start of trial as is reasonable, and must be attended by at least one attorney who will conduct the trial for each party and by any unrepresented party. The court may modify the order issued after a final pretrial conference only to prevent manifest injustice.

(f) Sanctions.

(1) In General. On motion or on its own, the court may issue any just orders, including those authorized by RCFC 37(b)(2)(A)(ii)-(vii), if a party or its attorney:

(A) fails to appear at a scheduling or other pretrial conference;

(B) is substantially unprepared to participate—or does not participate in good faith—in the conference; or

(C) fails to obey a scheduling or other pretrial order.

(2) Imposing Fees and Costs. Instead of or in addition to any other sanction, the court must order the party, its attorney, or both to pay the reasonable expenses—including attorney's fees—incurred because of any noncompliance with this rule, unless the noncompliance was substantially justified or other circumstances make an award of expenses unjust.

G. Electronic Discovery and Defending Against Allegedly Unconscionable Document-Production Orders

Navajo Nation v. United States

106 Fed. Cl. 753
(2012)

Allegra, Judge.

The parties filed a joint status report—discussing proposed *e*-discovery orders in this matter. In that report, the parties were unable to agree completely regarding the terms of those *e*-discovery orders. In light of the Court of Federal Claims Rules (RCFC) 1, 16, and 26 as well as Fed. R. Evid. 502(d), the court orders the following to facilitate discovery and avoid delays:

1. This order supplements this court's discovery rules and the provisions contained in the Confidentiality Agreement and Protective Order (CAPO) entered in this case on May 11, 2007.

2. Generally, the costs of discovery shall be borne by each party, subject to the provisions of RCFC 26(b)(2)(B) and (C), and 37.

Production of Electronically Stored Information ("ESI")

3. All documents that originally existed in native electronic form that are produced by the parties in this action shall be produced in electronic image form in the manner provided herein. Each document's electronic image shall convey the same image as the original document. Documents that present imaging or formatting problems shall be promptly identified by the receiving party; the parties shall meet and confer to attempt to resolve the problems.

4. All emails, email attachments, word processing documents (*e.g.,* Word, WordPerfect, etc.), presentation documents (*e.g.,* PowerPoint, Presentations, etc.), PDF documents, and TIFF documents shall be saved *electronically* or "printed" in a single page tagged image file format ("TIFF") image that reflects how the source document would have appeared if

printed out to a printer using the print settings that match how the document was last saved by the document's custodian. Email attachments shall be ordered to immediately follow the email to which each is attached. The parties shall produce a Concordance-compatible "load file," including an image cross-reference file, to accompany the images, which load file shall facilitate the use of the produced images by a document management or litigation support database system and shall identify document breaks for each document.

5. In responding to a discovery request propounded under the RCFC in this lawsuit, neither party is required to search for responsive materials from the following categories of ESI, absent a showing of good cause:

    a. Data in any electronic backup system for the purpose of system recovery or information restoration, including but not limited to, system recovery backup tapes, continuity of operations systems, and data or system mirrors or shadows, if such data are routinely purged, overwritten or otherwise made not reasonably accessible in accordance with an established routine system maintenance policy;

    b. Voicemail messages, instant messages—such as messages sent on AOL Instant Messenger or Microsoft Communicator—and text messages—such as cell-phone-to-cell-phone SMS messages, or other similar services including, but not limited to, Blackberry "PIN" messages;

    c. Data stored on a Personal Digital Assistant or smartphone (*e.g.*, Blackberry handheld), including electronic mail sent to or from such devices, as well as calendar or contact data, provided that a copy of such data is routinely duplicated elsewhere in a manner that would be subject to searching;

    d. Logs of calls made from cellular phones;

    e. Deleted computer files, whether fragmented or whole;

f. Temporary or cache files, including internet history, web browser cache, and cookie files, wherever located;

g. Server, system, or network logs;

h. Electronic data that is temporarily stored but not preserved by scientific equipment or attached devices in their ordinary course of operation, other than the data that is ordinarily preserved as part of any reports or analyses created by such equipment;

i. Messages that are posted on social media sites—including, but not limited to, Facebook—or on micro-blogging sites—including, but not limited to, Twitter; and

j. Data stored on printers, copy machines, or fax machines.

6. Each page of a document produced pursuant to paragraph 4, shall be electronically saved into a separate image file. If a document is more than one page, the order of the images constituting the document and any attachments and/or affixed notes shall be maintained as it existed in the original when creating the image file.

7. If an original document contains color, upon request of either party, the parties shall meet and confer regarding whether there is a reasonable need for that document to be produced in color images.

8. Each page of a document produced pursuant to paragraph 4, shall have a legible, unique page identifier ("Bates Number") *electronically "burned"* onto the image at a location that does not obliterate, conceal, or interfere with any information from the source document, preferably located at the bottom right hand corner of the document. There shall be no other legend or stamp placed on the document image unless a document qualifies for confidential treatment pursuant to the terms of the CAPO entered in this litigation, or has been redacted in accordance with applicable law or court order. In the case of confidential materials or materials redacted in accordance with applicable law or court order, a designation may be "burned" onto the document's image at a location that does not obliterate or obscure any information from the source

document. The Bates Number sequence shall be entirely alphanumeric, with no spaces or symbols.

9. Each such document image file shall be named with the unique Bates Number of the single-page TIFF image, followed by the extension ".tif."

10. The parties shall produce documents on CD–ROM, DVD, external hard drive (with standard PC compatible interface), or such other readily accessible computer or electronic media as the parties may hereafter agree upon (the "Production Media"). Each item of Production Media shall identify a production number corresponding to the production "wave" with which the documents on the Production Media are associated with (*e.g.,* "NN001" or "US001," "NN002" or "US002"), as well as the volume of the material in that production wave (e.g., "–001," "–002"). For example, if the first production wave by a party comprises document images on three hard drives, a party shall label each hard drive in the following manner: "NN001–001" or "US001–001," "NN001–002" or "US001–002," "NN001–003" or "US001–003."

    Additional information that shall be identified on the physical Production Media shall include: (1) text referencing that it was produced in No. 06–945L, (2) the producing party's name, (3) the type of materials on the media (*e.g.,* "Documents," "OCR Text," "Objective Coding," etc.), (4) the production date, and (5) the Bates Number range of the materials contained on the Production Media. In addition, the document custodian for each Bates Number range of materials shall be identified in a cover letter enclosing the Production Media.

11. The parties shall meet and confer regarding the format of production for databases and other dynamically stored ESI.

12. The parties shall meet and confer to determine whether certain files, including video files and audio files, shall be produced in native format. The parties agree to produce Excel and spreadsheet files in native format.

13. General ESI production requests *shall not include metadata*—absent a showing of good cause. However, the parties shall retain and preserve the original native electronic source documents in a manner so as to preserve

the metadata associated with these electronic materials in the event review of such metadata is warranted.

14. By preserving information for the purpose of any litigation on plaintiff's claims, the parties are not conceding that such material is discoverable in any litigation between the parties in this or any other lawsuit, nor are they waiving any claim of privilege.

15. Production of materials in compliance with this order also shall be deemed compliant with the requirements of RCFC 34.

Federal Rules of Evidence—Rule 502 and Privilege

16. The provisions of this order shall apply to all information produced in this litigation.

17. Pursuant to Fed. R. Evid. 502, the production of documents and data pursuant to this order shall not result in the *waiver* of the *attorney-client privilege* or *work-product protection* as to those documents and data. Also, the production of privileged or protected documents or data under this order shall not result in the waiver of the attorney-client privilege or work-product protection as to those documents and data in any other federal or state proceeding.

18. If the producing party determines that it has produced a document or data to which it wishes to assert a claim of privilege or protection, counsel for the producing party shall notify the recipient promptly of its claim. As part of the notification, the producing party's counsel shall identify, by Bates Number, the document as to which the producing party is asserting a claim of privilege or protection.

19. Upon receiving notice of a claim of privilege or protection by the producing party regarding a produced document or data, the recipient shall *segregate*, with promptness and in accordance with RCFC 26(b)(5)(B), the specified document or data, as well as any copies thereof, and the recipient shall not use the information in the specified document or data, except as provided by RCFC 26(b)(5)(B), until after the claim is resolved. If the court upholds—or if the recipient does not challenge within a reasonable time—the producing party's claim of privilege as to the produced document or

data, the recipient shall return or dispose of the specified document or data, as well as any copies thereof.

20. The recipient shall notify the producing party's counsel upon identification of any document or data which appears to be potentially privileged or protected. Such notification shall not waive the recipient's ability to challenge any assertion of privilege or protection made by the producing party as to the identified document. As part of the notification, the recipient shall identify, by Bates Number, the document or data at issue.

    The recipient shall *segregate* the specified document or data, as well as any copies thereof, from the other materials, and the recipient shall not use the information in the potentially privileged or protected document or data, except as provided by RCFC 26(b)(5)(B), for a period of 14 days after the date on which the recipient notifies the producing party's counsel. Within the 14–day period, or any other period of time agreed to by the parties, the producing party shall determine whether it will assert a claim of privilege or protection as to the identified document, and its counsel shall notify the recipient of its determination.

21. This order may be modified by the court for good cause. The court will be inclined to grant any modification jointly proposed by the parties.

CHAPTER TWELVE: Law Practice Technology Disputes and the Segregation of Damages, Attorney's Fees, and Costs Defenses

As discussed in Parts I and II of this casebook, solo and small-firm attorneys as well as opposing parties and the latters' attorneys commence actions under various common law theories of recovery. They also file mixed claims and counterclaims under state and federal-electronic communications and consumer-protection statutes: The Trademark-Lanham Act of 1946; Copyright Act of 1976; Computer Fraud and Abuse Act of 1986; Electronic Communications Privacy Act of 1986; Stored Communications Act of 1986; Electronic Communications Privacy Act of 1986; Copyright Infringement Act of 1990; Identity Theft and Deterrence Act of 1998; Digital Millennium Copyright Act of 1998; Anticybersquatting Consumer Protection Act of 1999; Internet False Identification Prevention Act of 2000; Fair Debt Collection Practices Act; Uniform Deceptive Trade Practices Act; and Deceptive Trade Practices Acts.

Under the statutes listed above, a "prevailing" party may receive various damages, "reasonable and necessary" attorney's fees and compensation for costs. *See e.g., Innovative Office Systems, Inc. v. Johnson*, 906 S.W.2d 940, 954 (Tex. Ct. App.-Tyler 1995) (finding liability under the common law and Texas Deceptive Trade Practices Act after a lessor's color copier, computer equipment, and computer software damaged lessee's office; awarding various damages—$146,335 for actual damages, $100,000 for additional damages, lost-profits damages; awarding compensation to cover relocation and rent-differential costs; and awarding $30,000 to cover reasonable and necessary attorney's fees).

Significantly, in *Newport News Holdings Corp. v. Virtual City Vision*, 650 F.3d 423, 441 (4th Cir. 2011), the Fourth Circuit stressed: "Our analysis of Anticybersquatting Consumer Protection Act's statutory damages is guided, in part, by their similarity to statutory damages under the Federal Copyright Act, 17 U.S.C. § 501(a). Both statutory damages provisions have similar structures and language. 17 U.S.C. § 504(c)(1) ("[A] copyright owner may elect at any time before final judgment is rendered to recover—instead of actual damages and profits—an award of statutory damages for all infringements involved in the action … in a sum of not less than $750 or more than $30,000 as the court considers just."

On the other hand, several common-law and statutory segregation doctrines or segregation defenses often determine whether or not "prevailing" litigants—solo and small-firm attorneys or opposing clients and third parties—will secure exorbitant or small damages, attorney's-fees, and indemnification-for-costs awards. For example, the *segregation of damages doctrine* requires a consumer to prove and segregate damages for each theory of liability. *See e.g., Barnett v. Coppell North Texas Court, Ltd.,* 123 S.W.3d 804, 820 (Tex. Ct. App.-Dallas 2003) (reiterating that the Texas DTPA requires a consumer to prove and segregate damages for each theory of liability and affirming the contractor's duty-to-segregate damages defense); and *Fields v. Wilber Law Firm, P.C.,* 383 F.3d 562, 565 (7th Cir. 2004) (holding that the consumers-plaintiffs sufficiently stated a claim under the Fair Debt Collection Practices Act—that survived a motion to dismiss because the debtor breached a contractual duty to segregate attorney fees).

Similarly, under the *segregation of attorney's-fees doctrine,* "prevailing" litigants must (1) segregate "recoverable" common-law or statutory claims from "non-recoverable" statutory or common-law claims; and (2) prove the amount of time that the attorney allocated, addressing and researching each set of claims. *See e.g., Randolph v. Dimension Films,* 634 F.Supp.2d 779, 799 (S.D. Tex. 2009) ("Randolph argues: Defendants have not segregated [the] time spent defending against the copyright claim … from the time spent defending against the Lanham Act and Texas Deceptive Trade Practices Act claims. … The Lanham Act—unlike the Copyright Act—only permits attorney's fee awards in exceptional cases. … A similarly strict standard applies to attorney's fee awards … under the DTPA.).

However, it is important to stress: If statutory and common-law claims are "so intertwined that it is impossible to differentiate" between them, a segregation of attorney's fees is not required. *See Gracie v. Gracie,* 217 F.3d 1060, 1069-1070 (9th Cir. 2000) (requiring the district court to apportion attorney's fees between Lanham Act claims and non-Lanham Act claims unless the claims are extremely intertwined and therefore making it impossible to differentiate between them).

Also, some common-law and statutory violations generate various costs—along with damages and attorney's fees. However, a plaintiff might incur costs even if a defendant did not violate a statute or the common law. Therefore, the law is clear: A successful litigant has a duty to segregate those two classes of costs, before a requiring a defendant to reimburse or compensate the plaintiff. *See e.g., Singer v. Pierce & Assoc., P.C.,* 383 F.3d 596, 598 (7th Cir. 2004) (declaring that a debt collector does not violate the Fair Debt Collection Practices Act, if the debt collector segregates court costs or attorney fees in the debt-collection letter). *But see, Nartron Corp. v. General Motors Corp,* 2005 WL 26991, *6 (Mich. Ct. App.) (rejecting Nartron's contention that GM had a duty to segregate its costs into classes—those "caused by" violations of discovery orders and those that would have been incurred in the absence of those violations).

Consider the universe of merchants, Internet service providers, technology companies, property and liability insurers, and financial institutions that allegedly have sold defective technologies or inferior services to solo and small-firm attorneys. Also, consider the long list of third parties and clients who might commence lawsuits—alleging that attorneys violated the laws outlined above or other statutes. Now, assume that the solo and small-firm attorneys sue their website developers, merchants, property insurers, or other providers of goods and services. And the latter parties file countersuits against the attorneys. May the respective classes of defendants use *successfully* one or a combination of the segregation doctrines to preclude or significantly reduce plaintiffs' requested damages, attorney's fees, and cost reimbursements? The cases and materials in this chapter provide some insight.

A. Plaintiffs' Duty to Prove Damages and "Reasonable and Necessary" Attorney's Fees

Arthur Anderson & Company v. Perry Equipment Corporation

945 S.W.2d 812
(Tex. 1997)

Cornyn, Justice.

In this accounting malpractice case, Perry Equipment Corporation (PECO) sued the accounting firm of Arthur Andersen for a faulty audit, which PECO relied on to purchase another company, Maloney Pipeline Systems. The audit favorably reported Maloney's financial condition when, in fact, the company was suffering substantial losses. Fourteen months after the sale, Maloney filed for bankruptcy. PECO sued for violations of the Deceptive Trade Practice Act, fraud, negligence, negligent misrepresentation, gross negligence, and breach of implied warranty. Based on the jury's verdict, the trial court rendered judgment for PECO. The court of appeals affirmed.

We address three issues presented by Arthur Anderson's application for writ of error. First, Arthur Andersen challenges PECO's consumer status because Maloney, rather than PECO, actually paid for the audit. Second, Arthur Andersen claims that the trial court failed to instruct the jury on the correct measure of damages. Third, Arthur Andersen contests the attorney's fees award, arguing that the percentage of recovery method is not a proper measure of attorney's fees under the DTPA, and that even if such fees were recoverable, no evidence supports the award.

I. Background

When PECO, a successful manufacturer of oil filters used in compressors for gas pipelines, decided to expand its business into the gas metering field, it looked into acquiring Maloney Pipeline Systems, one of three United States companies in the liquid metering market. In the mid-1980s, PECO began negotiating with Maloney's owner, Ramteck II. As a condition of the sale, PECO required an audit of Maloney's financial statements. Maloney retained Arthur Andersen to conduct the audit. Maloney eventually provided PECO financial statements audited by Arthur Andersen. The statements showed Maloney to be a profitable business. Relying upon this information, on August 23, 1985, PECO purchased the Maloney stock from Ramteck II, Inc. for $4,088,237.

Soon after the purchase, Maloney began to show signs of serious financial decline. For example, three months after the sale, Maloney ran out of cash and required a $400,000 advance from PECO to continue operating. PECO also attempted other emergency financial measures, but to no avail. Fourteen months after the sale, Maloney filed bankruptcy. PECO presented uncontradicted evidence at trial that the purchase price for Maloney was a total loss from which PECO realized no return and which PECO wrote off.

PECO's experts testified that Arthur Andersen's audit contained serious errors and otherwise failed to follow acceptable auditing procedures. One of the most significant errors, the evidence showed, was the failure to verify that contracts Maloney reported as complete were in fact complete or that Maloney's estimates of costs and percentage of completion for ongoing contracts were accurate. Maloney later incurred substantial losses on these contracts. One expert testified that the audit was one of the worst he had ever seen. Another expert, an auditing professor, stated that if a student submitted the work, he would have given the student a failing grade.

The jury found Arthur Andersen 51 percent at fault and PECO 49 percent at fault. The jury also found that Arthur Andersen had committed fraud, DTPA violations, and breach of warranty, but that it was not liable for negligent misrepresentation or gross negligence. The jury assessed damages of $5,449,468, including the $4,088,237 PECO paid for Maloney and $1,361,231 for other expenses incurred by PECO in its attempt to salvage the company. PECO elected to recover under the DTPA. The trial court credited Arthur Andersen with the two million dollars that Ramteck II had already paid PECO in settlement, and then awarded PECO a total of $9,297,601.20, including damages, prejudgment interest, DTPA additional damages, attorney's fees, and costs.

II. Proving One's Consumer Status

Arthur Andersen first contends that PECO is not a "consumer"—a prerequisite to recovery under the DTPA. The DTPA defines a consumer as one "who seeks or acquires by purchase or lease, any goods or services." Tex. Bus. & Com. Code § 17.45(4). In determining whether a plaintiff is a consumer, our focus is on the plaintiff's relationship to the transaction. *Amstadt v. United States Brass Corp.,* 919 S.W.2d 644, 650 (Tex.1996). As a condition of sale, PECO insisted that Maloney provide audited financial statements. Maloney hired Arthur Andersen for this specific purpose. PECO then relied on those statements in reaching its decision to purchase Maloney. Under these circumstances, we hold that PECO sought and acquired Arthur Andersen's services.

The next question is whether PECO sought and acquired these services *by purchase or lease,* inasmuch as it did not pay for the audit. Our decision in *Kennedy v. Sale,* 689 S.W.2d 890 (Tex.1985), controls this issue. There, we held that the DTPA does not require the consumer to be an actual purchaser or lessor of the goods or services, as long as the consumer is the beneficiary of those goods or services. *Id.*

The Texas Society of Certified Public Accountants, as amicus curiae, argues that a stock purchaser should not be considered a consumer simply because the corporation paid for an audit for the purchaser's benefit because virtually every external audit benefits third parties. Thus, any stock purchaser who reviews audited financial statements could bring a DTPA claim against the auditor. Our holding is not so broad. In this case, the audit was rendered in connection with the sale of Maloney and was specifically required by PECO and intended to benefit PECO. Arthur Andersen was aware that PECO had required the audit and would rely on its accuracy and knew the specific purpose for which it was conducted. We accordingly hold that PECO is a consumer under the DTPA.

Arthur Andersen also urges us to reject PECO's consumer status based on the decision in *Hand v. Dean Witter Reynolds Inc.,* 889 S.W.2d 483 (Tex.App.—Houston [14th Dist.] 1994, writ denied). In *Hand,* the plaintiff alleged that her stockbroker failed to purchase certain commodity option contracts after she requested that he do so. *Id.* at 487–88. After deciding that a commodity option contract is a right, not a "good," under the DTPA, *Id.* at 498, the court next considered whether the plaintiff was a consumer by virtue of her purchase of "services." The DTPA defines services as including "services furnished in connection with the sale or repair of goods." Tex. Bus. & Com. Code § 17.45(2). The court reasoned that the omission of any reference in the definition to services in connection with the sale of something other than a good indicated that services furnished in connection with the sale of intangibles did not fall within the definition of services under the DTPA. *Hand,* 889 S.W.2d at 498. The court then concluded: "The key to the [consumer status] determination is whether the purchased goods or services are an objective of the transaction or merely incidental to it." *Id.* at 500.

We believe that *Hand* confirms, rather than defeats, PECO's consumer status. Arthur Andersen's audit was not merely incidental to the sale of Maloney to PECO; it was required by PECO and was central to PECO's decision to consummate the purchase. Determining Maloney's financial condition was PECO's primary objective in acquiring Arthur Andersen's services. We therefore reject Arthur Andersen's contention that *Hand* defeats PECO's status as a consumer under the DTPA.

III. Measures of Damages

"Benefit-of-the-Bargain" and "Out-of-Pocket" Rules

Arthur Andersen next complains that the jury charge allowed the jury to award PECO the entire purchase price of Maloney, without instructing the jury to subtract the value of Maloney stock at the time of the sale. Arthur Andersen also contends that even if the court had properly instructed the jury, PECO failed to introduce any evidence that the stock was valueless at the time of sale, and thus failed to establish that it was entitled to the entire purchase price under either the "benefit-of-the-bargain" or the "out-of-pocket" measure of damages. PECO responds that in addition to direct damages, consequential damages are also recoverable under the DTPA. PECO thus argues that it is entitled to recover the purchase price as consequential damages.

Under the version of the DTPA in effect at the time PECO brought this action, a consumer could recover "the amount of actual damages" caused by the defendant's false, misleading, or deceptive conduct. TEX. BUS. & COM.CODE § 17.50(b)(1). The amount of actual damages recoverable is "the total loss sustained as a result of the deceptive trade practice." *Kish v. Van Note,* 692 S.W.2d 463, 466 (Tex. 1985) (citing *Smith v. Baldwin,* 611 S.W.2d 611, 617[Tex.1980]).

Actual damages are those damages recoverable under common law. *Brown v. American Transfer & Storage Co.,* 601 S.W.2d 931, 939 (Tex. 1980). At common law, actual damages are either "direct" or "consequential." *Henry S. Miller Co. v. Bynum,* 836 S.W.2d 160, 163 (Tex.1992). *See also,* RESTATEMENT (SECOND) OF TORTS § 549 (1977) (outlining measure of damages for fraudulent misrepresentation). Direct damages are the necessary and usual result of the defendant's wrongful act. They flow naturally and necessarily from the wrong. *See Southwind Aviation, Inc. v. Avendano,* 776 S.W.2d 734, 736 (Tex.App.-Corpus Christi 1989); *Anderson Dev. Corp. v. Coastal States Crude Gathering Co.,* 543 S.W.2d 402, 405 (Tex.Civ.App.-Houston [14th Dist.] 1976). Direct damages compensate the plaintiff for the loss that is conclusively presumed to have been foreseen by the defendant from his wrongful act.

Consequential damages, on the other hand, result naturally, but not necessarily, from the defendant's wrongful acts. *Haynes & Boone v. Bowser Bouldin, Ltd.,* 896 S.W.2d 179, 182 (Tex.1995); *Moore v. Anderson,* 30 Tex. 224, 230 (1867). Under the common law, consequential damages need not be the usual result of the wrong, but must be foreseeable. *See Mead v. Johnson Group, Inc.,* 615

S.W.2d 685, 687 (Tex.1981), and must be directly traceable to the wrongful act and result from it. *Airborne Freight Corp., Inc. v. C.R. Lee Enters., Inc.,* 847 S.W.2d 289, 295 (Tex.App.-El Paso 1992, writ denied). Of course, foreseeability is not an element of producing cause under the DTPA. *See Haynes & Boone,* 896 S.W.2d at 182; *Prudential Ins. v. Jefferson Assocs.,* 896 S.W.2d 156, 161 (Tex.1995). Still, if damages are too remote, too uncertain, or purely conjectural, they cannot be recovered. *See White v. Southwestern Bell Tel. Co., Inc.,* 651 S.W.2d 260, 262 (Tex.1983).

Under Texas common law, direct damages for misrepresentation are measured in two ways. *W.O. Bankston Nissan, Inc. v. Walters,* 754 S.W.2d 127, 128 (Tex.1988); *Leyendecker & Assocs., Inc. v. Wechter,* 683 S.W.2d 369, 373 (Tex.1984). Out-of-pocket damages measure the difference between the value the buyer has paid and the value of what he has received; benefit-of-the-bargain damages measure the difference between the value as represented and the value received. *Leyendecker,* 683 S.W.2d at 373. Under the DTPA, a plaintiff may recover under the damage theory that provides the greater recovery. *Id.* Both measures of damages are determined at the time of sale. *See Id.* at 373 (out-of-pocket damages are measured at the time of sale).

In this case, the jury was not asked to find direct damages at the time of the sale as well as consequential damages attributable to Arthur Anderson's misrepresentations. Rather, the jury was simply asked to consider the purchase price as part of the overall damages. PECO did present evidence that the purchase price was eventually a total loss. There was also evidence that Maloney was losing money at the time of the sale and continued to do so until it declared bankruptcy. What PECO did not establish, however, was how much of its loss occurred at the time of the sale and how much was attributable to subsequent events for which Arthur Anderson should bear legal responsibility. If subsequent losses were caused by Arthur Andersen's wrongful conduct and were not simply part of the risk a buyer of the business would have assumed, they may be part of PECO's consequential damages.

Subsequent losses, however, are recoverable only if the misrepresentation is a producing cause of the loss. *See Haynes & Boone,* 896 S.W.2d at 182. Without this limitation, an investor could shift the entire risk of an investment to a defendant who made a misrepresentation, even if the loss were unrelated to the misrepresentation. The basis of a misrepresentation claim is that the defendant's false statement induced the plaintiff to assume a risk he would not have taken had the truth been known. But to allow the plaintiff to transfer the entire risk of loss associated with his investment, even risks that the plaintiff accepted knowingly or losses that occurred through no fault of the defendant, would unfairly transform the defendant into an insurer of the plaintiff's entire investment.

Because the charge failed to instruct the jury on the proper measure of direct damages, the submission was reversible error. But, because we find some evidence that Arthur Andersen's misrepresentation was a producing cause of PECO's loss, we remand this case for a new trial. *See Spencer v. Eagle Star Ins. Co.,* 876 S.W.2d 154, 157 (Tex.1994) (holding that remand is proper when defective liability question is submitted); *Jackson v. Fontaine's Clinics, Inc.,* 499 S.W.2d 87, 90 (Tex. 1973) (remanding for new trial when defective damages question submitted); *Moulton v. Alamo Ambulance Serv., Inc.,* 414 S.W.2d 444, 449-450 (Tex. 1967) (affirming remand for new trial when defective damages question submitted).

We emphasize that a plaintiff's recovery of damages is limited not only by his own evidence, but also by the defendant's evidence of the plaintiff's failure to reasonably mitigate losses or evidence of intervening causes. *See Dubow v. Dragon,* 746 S.W.2d 857, 860 (Tex.App.-Dallas 1988, no writ). If a plaintiff's losses are attributable to his own mistakes or factors outside either of the parties' control, the defendant may be entitled to an appropriate limiting instruction to the jury.

IV. Attorney's Fees Award

Because we are remanding this case for a new trial, we turn now to Arthur Andersen's complaint that the trial court improperly awarded PECO attorney's fees calculated as a percentage of recovery.

Attorneys' contingency-fee contracts serve two main purposes. First, they allow plaintiffs who cannot afford to pay a lawyer up-front to pay the lawyer out of any recovery. Second, such contracts, because they offer the potential of a greater fee than might be earned under an hourly billing method, compensate the attorney for the risk that the attorney will receive no fee whatsoever if the case is lost. The lawyer in effect lends the value of his services, which is secured by a share in the client's potential recovery. Under some contingency-fee contracts, attorneys also agree to advance the out-of-pocket costs of the litigation. In such cases, the attorney not only risks loss of the fee, but also risks loss of actual expenditures.

Arthur Andersen complains: An award of contingency fees under a fee-shifting statute like the DTPA forces defendants to pay fees unrelated to the amount of work performed. While this is not always true, shifting these fees to the defendant presents two problems.

First, a contingent-fee award based solely on evidence of a percentage fee agreement between a lawyer and client may be determined without regard to many of the factors that should be considered when determining reasonableness. The DTPA allows recovery of "reasonable and necessary attorneys' fees." Tex. Bus. & Com. Code § 17.50(d). Factors that a factfinder should consider when determining the reasonableness of a fee include:

> (1) the time and labor required, the novelty and difficulty of the questions involved, and the skill required to perform the legal service properly;
>
> (2) the likelihood … that the acceptance of the particular employment will preclude other employment by the lawyer;
>
> (3) the fee customarily charged in the locality for similar legal services;
>
> (4) the amount involved and the results obtained;
>
> (5) the time limitations imposed by the client or by the circumstances;
>
> (6) the nature and length of the professional relationship with the client;
>
> (7) the experience, reputation, and ability of the lawyer or lawyers performing the services; and
>
> (8) whether the fee is fixed or contingent on results obtained or uncertainty of collection before the legal services have been rendered.

TEX. DISCIPLINARY RULES PROFESSIONAL CONDUCT 1.04, *reprinted in* TEX. GOV'T CODE, tit. 2, subtit. G app. (State Bar Rules, art. X, § 9); *see also Ragsdale v. Progressive Voters League,* 801 S.W.2d 880, 881 (Tex.1990).

While we do not doubt that many plaintiffs must contract for a contingent fee to secure the services of a lawyer, we do not believe that the DTPA authorizes the shifting of the plaintiff's entire contingent fee to the defendant without consideration of the factors required by the Rules of Professional Conduct. A contingent fee may indeed be a reasonable fee from the standpoint of the parties to the contract. But, we cannot agree that the mere fact that a party and a lawyer have agreed to a contingent fee means that the fee arrangement is in and of itself reasonable for purposes of shifting that fee to the defendant.

A party's contingent fee agreement should be considered by the factfinder. See TEX. DISCIPLINARY R. PROF. CONDUCT 1.04(b)(8), and is therefore admissible in evidence, but that agreement cannot alone support an award of attorney's fees under Texas Business and Commerce Code § 17.50(d). In other words, the plaintiff cannot simply ask the jury to award a percentage of the recovery as a fee because without evidence of the factors identified in DISCIPLINARY RULE 1.04, the jury has no meaningful way to determine if the fees were in fact reasonable and necessary.

Second, because the jury is not informed what the total amount of the judgment will be, the jury can only speculate about whether a percentage of that unknown recovery will represent a reasonable and necessary fee in that particular case. Rather than leave this question to speculation, the jury must decide the question of attorney's fees specifically in light of the work performed in the very case for which the fee is sought.

In light of these concerns, we hold: To recover attorney's fees under the DTPA, the plaintiff must prove that the amount of fees was both reasonably incurred and necessary to the prosecution of the case at bar, and must ask the jury to award the fees in a specific dollar amount, not as a percentage of the judgment.

For the foregoing reasons, we reverse the judgment of the court of appeals and remand this cause to the trial court for further proceedings consistent with this opinion

B. Disappeared and Damaged Law-Practice Technologies, Disputed Property-Insurance Claims, and the Segregation of Losses Defense

1. Insureds' Duty to Prove "Coverage" Under Business Owners Property Insurance Contracts

Schmidt v. Travelers Indemnity Company of America

101 F.Supp.3d 768
(S.D. 2015)

Timothy S. Black, District Judge.

Plaintiffs—Attorney Michael Schmidt and the Law Firm of Cohen, Todd, Kite & Stanford (CTKS)—allege that Travelers Indemnity Company of America (Travelers) breached the parties' contract and acted in bad faith when it refused to indemnify CTKS pursuant to an insurance policy. In addition to damages and attorney's fees, CTKS seek a declaration that the loss is a "covered loss" under the policy. And, therefore, Travelers owes Plaintiff CTKS a duty of indemnification.

CTKS and Travelers filed cross-motions for partial summary judgment.

II. Undisputed Facts

A. In Support of the Attorneys' Motion for Partial Summary Judgment

CTKS paid insurance premiums to Travelers in exchange for business owners insurance coverage under Policy No. 1–680–9A246743–TIA–11 ("Policy"). The Policy contains a "Computer Fraud" provision stating that insurance may be extended "to apply to loss of or damage to Business Personal Property resulting directly from the use of any computer to fraudulently cause a transfer of that property from inside the building at the described premises or 'banking premises': (a) To a person outside those premises; or (b) To a place outside those premises."

On February 21, 2012, while the Policy was in effect, Attorney

Schmidt received an email on his CTKS computer—requesting legal representation from a person residing in Japan and purporting to be Erick Carpenter ("Deceitful Carpenter"). CTKS and Deceitful Carpenter entered into a retention agreement via electronic mail. In exchange for a 25 percent contingent fee, CTKS agreed to represent Deceitful Carpenter—regarding his claims against North American Iron and Steel Company ("North American"). Via electronic mail, Deceitful Carpenter provided additional details to Attorney Schmidt regarding Deceitful Carpenter's claim against North American.

After entering the retention agreement, Schmidt drafted and addressed a demand letter to North American. He also forwarded the draft to Deceitful Carpenter—using CTKS's computer to craft and send the email. In response to Schmidt's email, Deceitful Carpenter approved the draft letter via electronic mail. On February 29, 2012, Schmidt sent the letter to North American via electronic mail using his CTKS computer. The letter demanded $378,000 and instructed North American to send the cash to Schmidt—Deceitful Carpenter's counsel.

Also, on February 29, 2012, a person purporting to be Edgar Marshall (Devious Marshall), responded via email and on behalf of North American to Schmidt's demand letter. Devious Marshall stated that North American would pay the balance of the outstanding $378,000—supposedly owed to Deceitful Carpenter—and would pay in two separate $189,000 payments. Attorney Schmidt conveyed the settlement offer to Deceitful Carpenter via electronic mail using CTKS's computer. Following these electronic communications, CTKS received a $189,000 cashier's check from North American on March 6, 2012. Via electronic mail, Deceitful Carpenter instructed Attorney Schmidt to wire $141,750—$189,000 minus CTKS's 25 percent contingent fee—to Deceitful Carpenter's account in Japan.

CTKS deposited the $189,000 cashier's check into CTKS's Interest on Lawyer Trust Account (IOLTA). On March 7, 2012, CTKS wired $141,750 to Deceitful Carpenter's Japanese bank. After wiring the $141,750, CTKS's bank disclosed that the deposited North American cashier's check fraudulent. CTKS received a second $189,000 cashier's check from North American on March 12, 2012; and it was also fraudulent. On March 14, 2012, more than a week after Plaintiffs wired the amount of $141,750 to Deceitful Carpenter's account, the person purporting to be Erick Carpenter sent an email—informing Attorney Schmidt that he would send a check for $141,750 to Attorney Schmidt.

CTKS has not received any reimbursement from the person or persons purporting to be Erick Carpenter or Edgar Marshall. CTKS filed a timely claim for its$141,750 loss with Travelers—asserting that the loss was covered under the Businessowners Property Insurance Contract. Travelers denied CTKS's claim

B. In Support of Travelers's Motion for Partial Summary Judgment

The Policy contains COMMON POLICY DECLARATIONS, a BUSINESSOWNERS PROPERTY COVERAGE SPECIAL FORM, and a LAWYER'S ENDORSEMENT. In the introductory paragraphs of the BUSINESSOWNERS PROPERTY COVERAGE SPECIAL FORM, it states:

> Throughout this policy the words "you" and "your" refer to the Named Insured shown in the DECLARATIONS [CTKS]. The words "we," "us" and "our" refer to the Company providing this insurance [Travelers].
>
> PARAGRAPH A—COVERAGE—We [Travelers] will pay for *direct physical loss of or damage to Covered Property* at the premises described in the DECLARATIONS caused by or resulting from a Covered Cause of Loss.
>
> COVERED CAUSES OF LOSS is a direct physical loss unless the loss is ... b. Excluded in PARAGRAPH B., EXCLUSIONS.
>
> COVERED PROPERTY is the type of property described in this Paragraph A.1., and limited in Paragraph A.2., Property Not Covered, if a Limit of Insurance is shown in the DECLARATIONS for that type of property.
>
> DESCRIBED PREMISES—CTKS's law offices at 250 E. 5th Street, Suite 1200, Cincinnati, Ohio.

III. Standard Of Review

A motion for summary judgment should be granted if the evidence submitted to the Court demonstrates that there is no genuine issue as to any material fact and that the movant is entitled to judgment as a matter of law. Fed.R.Civ.P. 56(c). *See Celotex Corp. v. Catrett,* 477 U.S. 317, 322 (1986); *Anderson v. Liberty Lobby, Inc.,* 477 U.S. 242, 247-248 (1986). The moving party has the burden of showing the absence of genuine disputes over facts which, under the substantive law governing the issue, might affect the outcome of the action. *Celotex,* 477 U.S. at 323.

All facts and inferences must be construed in a light most favorable to the party opposing the motion. *Matsushita Elec. Indus. Co. v. Zenith Radio Corp.,* 475 U.S. 574, 587 (1986). A party opposing a motion for summary judgment "may not rest upon the mere allegations or denials of his pleading, but … must set forth specific facts showing that there is a genuine issue for trial." *Anderson,* 477 U.S. at 248.

IV. Analysis

CTKS attorneys invoke three policy provisions in support of their motion for summary judgment on the coverage issue: (1) the Computer Fraud coverage extension; (2) the Business Personal Property provision; and (3) the Business Income and Extra Expense provision. Travelers argues: The provisions do not cover CTKS's loss. And, in any event, the "voluntary parting" and "default" coverage exclusions apply.

A. Rules of Contract Construction and Interpretation

The parties agree that Ohio law applies. Construing an insurance policy is a matter of law. *See Alexander v. Buckeye Pipe Line Co.,* 53 Ohio St.2d 241, 245-46 (1978). When interpreting an insurance contract, a court must give effect to the intent of the parties. *Hamilton Ins. Serv., Inc. v. Nationwide Ins. Cos.,* 86 Ohio St.3d 270, 273 (1999) (applying traditional rules of contract). A court must give words and phrases their ordinary meaning unless another meaning is apparent from the contents of the policy. *Westfield Ins. Co. v. Galatis,* 100 Ohio St.3d 216, 219 (2003) (applying the plain meaning rule). A court must give meaning to every paragraph, clause, phrase, and word. *Affiliated FM Ins. Co. v. Owens-Corning Fiberglas Corp.,* 16 F.3d 684, 686 (6th Cir.1994).

If provisions are reasonably susceptible of more than one meaning, they "will be construed strictly against the insurer and liberally in favor of the insured." *King v. Nationwide Ins. Co.,* 35 Ohio St.3d 208 (1988) (applying the ambiguity doctrine). However, provisions are to be strictly construed against the insurer only when they are ambiguous. *GenCorp, Inc. v. Am. Intern. Underwriters,* 178 F.3d 804, 818 (6th Cir.1999). "[T]he general rule of liberal construction cannot be used to create an ambiguity where one does not exist. If the terms of a policy are clear and unambiguous, a court must enforce the contract as written, giving words used in the contract their plain and ordinary meaning." *Monticello Ins. Co. v. Hale,* 284 F.Supp.2d 898, 901 (S.D. Ohio 2003).

B. CTKS Attorneys' Claimed Losses

Allegedly plaintiffs have suffered three distinct covered losses: (1) loss because the cashier's checks that they received from North American were fraudulent (*First Loss*); (2) loss because Plaintiffs wired $141,750 to Deceitful Carpenter (*Second Loss*); and (3) loss because Deceitful Carpenter failed to pay $141,750 to Plaintiffs as promised (*Third Loss*). Travelers argues that Plaintiffs suffered a single loss, which occurred when they wired $141,750 from CTKS's IOLTA account at Chase Bank to Deceitful Carpenter's bank account in Japan.

* * *

C. Establishing Coverage Under Property Insurance Contracts

The party who seeks to recover under an insurance policy generally has the burden of demonstrating coverage under the policy and proving a loss. *Chicago Title Ins. Co. v. Huntington Nat'l Bank,* 87 Ohio St.3d 270, 273 (1999). However, the insurer bears the burden of proving that an exclusion applies. *Cont'l Ins. Co. v. Louis Marx Co.,* 415 N.E.2d 315, 317 (Ohio 1980). Exclusionary language in insurance policies must be clear and exact. *See Lane v. Grange Mut. Cos.,* 45 Ohio St.3d 63, 65 (1989).

CTKS attorneys argue that their *First Loss* is covered under the insurance contract's BUSINESS PERSONAL PROPERTY provision. The BUSINESSOWNERS PROPERTY COVERAGE SPECIAL FORM provides:

> A. COVERAGE—We will pay for *direct physical loss* of or damage to Covered Property at the premises described in the Declarations caused by or resulting from a Covered Cause of Loss. Covered Property means the type of property described in this Paragraph A. …
>
> > b. Business Personal Property located in or on the buildings described in the Declarations or in the open (or in a vehicle) within 1,000 feet of the described premises, including "Money" and "Securities." …

> 4. Covered Causes of Loss—*risks of direct physical loss* unless the loss is Limited in Paragraph A.5 or Excluded in Paragraph B. "Exclusions".

According to Plaintiffs, they received bogus cashier's checks from North American and those are negotiable instruments are "business personal property"—specifically "securities." Also the attorneys argued that the terms "direct physical loss" and "covered cause of loss" are ambiguous.

There was no "direct physical loss of or damage to" the "checks." … This is *not* an instance in which cashier's checks were destroyed and lost in a fire. Since there is no evidence that the bogus cashier's checks were physically lost or damaged, the *First Loss* is not covered loss under the Business Personal Property provision.

D. Business Interruption and Extra Expense Coverage

Plaintiffs argue that their *Third Loss*—combined with the loss associated with the second fraudulent cashier's check—is covered under the "Business Income and Extra Expense" provision. The BUSINESSOWNERS PROPERTY COVERAGE SPECIAL FORM states in relevant part:

> A. COVERAGE … Business Income and Extra Expense is provided at the premises described in the Declarations … (a) Business Income means … Net Profit or Loss before income taxes … that would have been earned or incurred … and continuing normal operating expenses incurred, including payroll.
>
> We will pay for the actual loss of Business Income you sustain due to the necessary "suspension" of your "operations" during the "period of restoration." The "suspension" must be caused by direct physical loss of or damage to property at the described premises. The loss or damage must be caused by or result from a Covered Cause of Loss. …

* * *

"Suspension" is defined as "the partial or complete cessation of your

[CTKS's] business activities" or "[t]hat a part or all of the described premises is rendered untenable." "Operations" is defined as "your [CTKS's] business activities occurring at the described premises and the tenantability of the described premises."

Plaintiffs explain: As a consequence of electronically transferring $141,750 to Deceitful Carpenter's account in Japan and the dishonoring of the first bogus cashier's check, they incurred added expense. They had to deposit $141,750 into CTKS's IOLTA account. Plaintiffs claim that the loss of $141,750 is an "Extra Expense." The court cannot agree. Plaintiffs suffered no loss of income due to the necessary "suspension" of their "operations" *"caused by a direct physical loss of or damage to property at the described premises* [CTKS's law offices]." ... Plaintiffs presents no evidence of their business activities' partial or complete cessation. There is no evidence of the attorneys' losing business income or incurring extra expense as a result direct physical loss of or damage to property. The court finds that Plaintiffs' *Third Loss"* is not a covered loss.

E. Exclusions

Travelers assert that Plaintiffs' losses are clearly and unambiguously excluded from coverage under the Policy. ... The BUSINESSOWNERS PROPERTY COVERAGE SPECIAL FORM states in relevant

> B. EXCLUSIONS—2. We will not pay for loss or damage caused by or resulting from any of the following: i. Voluntary parting with any property by you or anyone else to whom you have entrusted the property. ... 1. Default on any credit sale, loan, or similar transaction.

* * *

The LAWYERS ENDORSEMENT OF THE POLICY "modifies insurance provided under the ... BUSINESSOWNERS PROPERTY COVERAGE SPECIAL FORM." And the following Coverage Extension is added by the LAWYERS ENDORSEMENT, PARAGRAPH B:

> *COMPUTER FRAUD*
>
> (1) When a Limit is shown in the Declarations for Business Personal Property at the described premises, you [CTKS] may extend that insurance to apply to loss of or damage to Business Personal Property *resulting*

directly from the use of any computer to fraudulently cause a transfer of the property from the inside the building at the described premises or "banking premises":

(a) To a person outside those premises; or

(b) To a place outside those premises.

(2) Paragraph B.2. does not apply to this Coverage Extension.

(3) The most we will pay under this Coverage Extension in any one occurrence is $10,000, regardless of the number of premises involved.

The LAWYERS ENDORSEMENT *does not provide that these exclusions are inapplicable* to the Computer Fraud Coverage Extension.

* * *

Courts considering exclusions similar to the instant "voluntary parting" exclusion have found that these exclusions are conspicuous, plain, and clear. *Martin, Shudt, Wallace, DiLorenzo & Johnson v. Travelers Indem. Co. of Conn.,* 2014 WL 460045, *3 (N.D.N.Y. 2014) (holding that the "voluntary parting" exclusion applied, despite the fact that the insured law firm was tricked into directing the wire transfer of funds to a fraudulent account).

CTKS attorneys argue: Fraud vitiated their ability to "voluntarily part" with the electronically transferred funds. They cite Ohio cases and law, which establish that a fraudulent induced payment is not a voluntary payment. However, those cases address only whether recovery may be had from the parties who received such payments and not whether the payors voluntarily *parted with* the funds. Accordingly, the court finds: The "voluntary parting" provision clearly excludes compensation for CTKS's *Second Loss.*

V. Conclusion

For the foregoing reasons, the court finds that Plaintiffs' asserted losses are not covered under the Business Property Insurance Contract. Accordingly, Travelers's motion for partial summary judgment is granted. CTKS attorneys' motion for partial summary judgment is denied. It is so ordered.

2. Insureds' Duty to Prove "Financial Losses" Under Commercial Property/Business Income Insurance Contracts

Zamplas Johnson, P.C. v. Cincinnati Ins. Co.

367 F.Supp.2d 1101
(E.D. Mich. 2005)

Taylor, District Judge.

In this case, the Plaintiffs/Counter-Defendants are Zamplas Johnson, P.C. and the Law Firm of Victoria, P.L.L.C. (collectively "Zamplas"). Both are Michigan corporations. Cincinnati Insurance Company (CPInsurer) is an Ohio corporation and the Defendant/Counter-Plaintiff.

The complaint alleges that CPInsurer breached its property insurance policy with Zamplas by failing to cover costs for *business income losses.* On September 18, 1998, Zamplas's law firm suffered damage to its telephone and computer network as a result of a lightning strike. Zamplas claims that CPInsurer owes an outstanding sum of $112,497.12 for property damages and accounts receivable losses. Allegedly, Zamplas was unable to make timely billings, because the firm's computers were damaged. Zamplas recovered $16,599.16 for their accounts receivable claim, bringing the total to $95,897.77.

Zamplas filed a four-count complaint and alleged: (1) CPInsurer materially breached the policy by failing to provide complete relief for the damages and work loss; (2) CPInsurer's bad faith handling of Zamplas's claim violated the Michigan Unfair Trade Practices Act (UTPA); and (3) CPInsurer was unjustly enriched. Zamplas contends that CPInsurer owes $95,897.77 in damages as well as $35,241.45 for interest, exemplary or punitive damages, and attorney fees.

CPInsurer filed a motion to dismiss and for partial summary judgment and argued: (1) An insured may not maintain a private cause of action under the UTPA, absent tortious conduct; (2) Michigan law does not recognize a bad-faith claim for unjust enrichment, and; (3) Zamplas's claims for exemplary or punitive damages and attorney fees are not recoverable for breach of an insurance contract and should be dismissed pursuant to Rule 12(b)(6). Further, CPInsurer filed a motion for partial summary judgment, arguing that the appropriate remedy for breach of contract is the mandatory statutory appraisal procedure pursuant to the policy provision and MCL 500.2833(m).

* * *

III. The Unfair Trade Practices Act Claim

Michigan legislators enacted the UTPA for the purpose of imposing penalties on insurers "who procrastinate or are dilatory in paying meritorious claims in bad faith." *Burnside v. State Farm Fire & Casualty Co.,* 528 N.W.2d 749, 753 (Mich. Ct. App 1995). Failure to pay proceeds on a timely basis is considered an unfair trade practice. And the violation may subject the insurer to the imposition of twelve percent (12%) penalty interest—starting sixty days (60) after Zamplas submits a satisfactory proof of a loss and the claim is not reasonably disputed. *See* MCLA 500.2006(1); M.S.A. 24.12006(1). The Sixth Circuit has determined: whether a claim is "reasonably in dispute" is a matter of law for a court to decide. *See All American Life & Cas. Co. v. Oceanic Trade Alliance Council Intern., Inc.,* 756 F.2d 474, 482 (6th Cir.1985).

Zamplas claims that CPInsurer delayed and failed to respond to its repeated inquiries in bad faith—triggering Zamplas's right to seek the UTPA penalties. Specifically, Zamplas contends that CPInsurer ignored the claim after Zamplas provided an amended request on September 15, 2000. Zamplas made two additional inquiries regarding the status of its claim on November 6, 2000, and January 3, 2001. CPInsurer ignored both. Again, on April 13, 2001, Zamplas inquired about the status of its claim. ... It was not until September 21, 2001, when CPInsurer asked Attorney Dennis Zamplas to submit to an examination under oath. ... Following the February examination, CPInsurer requested additional documents and scheduled a final meeting with the forensic accountant, which was not held until April 30, 2002. It is this series of delays and non-responsive conduct that forms the basis of Zamplas's claim for twelve percent (12%) interest under the UTPA.

* * *

Here, factual issues abound—regarding whether CPInsurer procrastinated and engaged in dilatory tactics on Zamplas's claim following Zamplas's September 15, 2000, letter. For the foregoing reasons, CPInsurer's motion to summarily dismiss Zamplas's claim under the UTPA is denied.

A. Interest on Lines of Credit

CPInsurer moved to dismiss Zamplas's claim for interest costs on two lines of credit Zamplas obtained to continue operating it law practice. Zamplas contends that the law firm had to borrow significant amounts of money as a direct result of CPInsurer's delay in addressing its claim. The alleged that they have incurred interest costs—$35,241.45. CPInsurer contends that interest costs—on a line of credit is an extra expense or consequential loss, which is expressly prohibited by the terms of the policy.
Zamplas—citing the same policy language as CPInsurer—contends that interest costs on lines of credit are covered under the "Business Income Loss" provision and is not an extra expense or consequential loss. Zamplas's comptroller testified: The firm had "[t]o borrow money for operations because of the loss of income—i.e., paying bills and making payroll, including overhead, rent, supplies, anything that's involved in running the law firm and making payroll." Zamplas further contends: The "Exclusions" section of the policy is contrary to the language providing coverage for this loss and should be strictly construed against the CPInsurer. *See Advance Watch Company Ltd., v. Kemper National Insurance Co.,* 99 F.3d 795, 800 (6th Cir.1996) ("whenever terms are ambiguous, courts are required to construe the language in the light most favorable to the insured").

The court finds that material fact issues exist regarding whether interest costs on lines of credit are expressly prohibited under the policy. Accordingly, CPInsurer's motion to summarily dismiss Zamplas's claim for interest costs on lines of credit is denied.

B. Accounts Receivable Losses

CPInsurer contends that Zamplas's claim for accounts receivable losses should be dismissed for failing to present any evidence substantiating the loss. Zamplas claims that it suffered accounts receivable losses. Allegedly, the law firm was unable to provide timely billing to its clients, given that lightning strikes damaged the firm's computers. CPInsurer contends: Zamplas's loss was caused by its failure to provide timely billing, since there was no actual damage to the accounts receivable records. *See e.g., Mendelson v. General Ins. Co. of America,* 455 F.2d 270, 271 (5th Cir.1972). The property insurer also contends: At best, losses for one's failing to provide timely billings are consequential losses, which are not covered under the property insurance contract.

In response, Zamplas contends: whether inaccessibility of accounts receivable records constitutes damage to those records is an issue of first impression for this court. The issue in *Mendelson* was whether the insurance company was required to pay the costs of reestablishing records of accounts receivable that were destroyed in a fire. Here, Zamplas seeks the costs of *accounts receivable losses.* Zamplas contends: The record does not contain enough facts to determine whether inaccessibility of computer records constitutes damage to accounts receivable records. We agree.

When factual disputes are established, a court "should refuse to grant summary judgment until the facts and circumstances have been sufficiently developed to enable the court to be reasonably certain that it is making a correct determination of the question of law." *NLRB v. Smith Indus., Inc.,* 403 F.2d 889, 893 (5th Cir.1968). Granting summary judgment is inappropriate when factual issues predominate and the non-moving party must be afforded the benefit of any reasonable doubt whether material issues of fact exist. *See Meridian Mutual Ins. Co. v. Hunt,* 425 N.W.2d 111 (Mich. Ct. App. 1998). Here, there are factual issues regarding whether the inaccessibility to the records constituted damage to accounts receivable records.

Accordingly, CPInsurer's motion to summarily dismiss Zamplas's accounts receivable losses claim is denied.

* * *

C. Exemplary or Punitive Damages

Zamplas requested "any punitive/exemplary damages that the court deems just and appropriate" for the CPInsurer's "bad faith" practices. Michigan does not recognize an implied contractual duty of good faith. Instead, the law requires a plaintiff to prove tortious conduct before awarding punitive and exemplary damages. *See e.g., Dahlman v. Oakland University,* 172 Mich.App. 502, 432 N.W.2d 304, 306 (Mich. Ct. App. 1988); and, *Kewin v. Mass. Mutual Life Ins. Co.,* 295 N.W.2d 50, 56 (Mich. 1980). Zamplas does not assert the following: (1) The property insurance contract contains a good-faith requirement; and (2) CPInsurer engaged in tortious conduct. *See Stockdale v. Jamison,* 416 Mich. 217, 223 (1982) (finding that where the express terms of the contract govern, questions of good or bad faith should not be considered). Therefore, CPInsurer's motion to summarily dismiss Zamplas's claim for punitive or exemplary damages is granted. It is so ordered.

3. Insureds' Duty to Prove "Coverage" Under Commercial Liability Insurance Contracts

Rob Levine & Associates Ltd. v. Travelers Casualty and Surety Company of America

994 F.Supp.2d 228
(D. R. I. 2014)

John J. McConnell, Jr., District Judge.

Plaintiffs are a law firm and two of its attorneys—Robert Levine and Benjamin Pushner (collectively, "Levine & Associates"). Levine & Associates advertise their services extensively on television and the internet. They use the tag line "Call A Heavy Hitter® Today!" Phyllis Stafford and Lynn Di Cristofaro—two Levine & Associates clients—filed a complaint in Rhode Island Superior Court against Mr. Levine and Mr. Pushner (the "Stafford Complaint"). The third count of the Stafford Complaint alleges a class action for "Deceptive Trade Practice" under R.I. Gen. Laws § 6–13.1–5.2.

Travelers Casualty and Surety Company of America ("Travelers") issued a liability insurance policy to Rob Levine & Associates. The contract provided Directors and Officers Liability coverage among other things ("D & O Policy"). The D & O Policy excludes the following from coverage: "Loss for any Claim based upon or arising out of any Wrongful Act related to the rendering of, or failure to render, professional services" (the "Legal Services Exclusion"). After receiving notice from Levine & Associates regarding the Stafford Complaint, Travelers denied coverage, citing on this policy exclusion.

Levine & Associates filed this action—seeking a declaratory judgment that they are entitled to coverage, a legal defense and indemnification, in connection with count three of the Stafford Complaint. This matter is before the court on cross-motions for summary judgment. Both parties seek summary judgment on the declaratory judgment claim, count one.

A. Legal Standard

Rhode Island courts interpret insurance policies by "applying the rules for construction of written instruments." *Allstate Ins. Co. v. Russo,* 641 A.2d 1304, 1306 (R.I.1994). *See Derderian v. Essex Ins. Co.,* 44 A.3d 122, 127 (R.I. 2012) (insurance policy terms interpreted in accordance with rules of construction governing contracts). "Contract interpretation presents a question of law, and is the court's responsibility." *Fashion House, Inc. v. K mart Corp.,* 892 F.2d 1076, 1083 (1st Cir.1989). "When a contract is unambiguous, [courts] review its terms in a *de novo* manner." *Papudesu v. Med. Malpractice Joint Underwriting Ass'n of Rhode Island,* 18 A.3d 495, 498 (R.I. 2011). In determining "whether a contract is clear and unambiguous, the document must be viewed in its entirety and its language be given its plain, ordinary and usual meaning." *Garden City Treatment Ctr., Inc. v. Coordinated Health Partners, Inc.,* 852 A.2d 535, 542 (R.I. 2004). When no ambiguity exists in the terms of an agreement, "judicial construction is at an end for the terms will be applied as written." *Monahan v. Girouard,* 911 A.2d 666, 672 (R.I .2006).

To determine if an insurance contract imposes a duty to defend, Rhode Island courts apply the "pleading test." *See Derderian,* 44 A.3d at 127. "That test requires the trial court to look at the allegations contained in the complaint, and if the pleadings recite facts bringing the injury complained of within the coverage of the insurance policy, the insurer must defend irrespective of the insured's ultimate liability to the plaintiff." The Rhode Island Supreme Court has explained that "when a complaint contains a statement of facts which bring the case within or potentially within the risk coverage of the policy, the insurer has an unequivocal duty to defend." *Employers' Fire Ins. Co. v. Beals,* 240 A.2d 397, 403 (R.I. 1968). A judge in this district deemed this standard the "potential-for-coverage standard" and noted that the R.I. Supreme Court has consistently applied it "in duty-to-defend cases" since 1968. *Emhart Indus., Inc. v. Home Ins. Co.,* 515 F.Supp.2d 228, 236 (D.R.I. 2007).

When an exclusion in an insurance policy is at issue, the analysis typically follows two steps. First, the insured "bears the burden of proving a prima facie case, including but not limited to the existence and validity of a policy, the loss as within the policy coverage, and the insurer's refusal to make payments as required by the terms of the policy." *Gen. Acc. Ins. Co. of Am. v. Am. Nat. Fireproofing, Inc.,* 716 A.2d 751, 757 (R.I.1998). "[A]ny doubts as to the adequacy of the pleadings to encompass an occurrence within the scope of the policy must be resolved in the insured's favor." *Allstate,* 641 A.2d at 1306. And second, if the insured sustains its initial burden, "[t]he insurer then bears the burden of proving the applicability of policy exclusions. ..." *Gen. Acc.,* 716 A.2d at 757.

B. Application

The parties have narrowed the court's work by submitting a joint statement of undisputed facts and limiting argument to whether Levine & Associates is entitled to defense in connection with the third count of the Stafford Complaint. The parties further focused their briefing on whether Travelers need not defend because this count is within the purview of the Legal Services Exclusion.

Applying the legal principles set forth above, the court examines the allegations in the third count of the Stafford Complaint, captioned "Deceptive Trade Practice Class Action." Count three's allegations include the following: "The Defendants deceptively advertise in all media in Rhode Island"; and "[t]he Defendants gave the false impression to Plaintiffs and presently give the false impression to future clients that [they] have special expertise in personal injury cases and disability cases and will recover more money than other Rhode Island lawyers."

The parties assume, and the court agrees, that Levine & Associates have met their initial burden to prove a prima facie case. *See Gen. Acc.,* 716 A.2d at 757. The contested question is whether Travelers has met its burden to demonstrate that the Legal Practices Exclusion precludes its duty to defend. The Legal Practices Exclusion states that "[t]he Company will not be liable for Loss for any Claim based upon or arising out of any Wrongful Act related to the rendering of, or failure to render, professional services."

Travelers first directs the Court's attention to the phrase "arising out of," a phrase that Rhode Island courts have interpreted broadly. Travelers references a R.I. Supreme Court case explaining that this phrase means "flowing from" or "having its origin in." *Id.* Travelers next focuses on the phrase "professional services," asserting that it is broadly interpreted by courts in other jurisdictions. Based on its interpretation of these two phrases, Travelers avers that the Legal Practices Exclusion "clearly and unambiguously excludes coverage for claims arising out [of] any wrongful act related to the rendering of or failure to render professional services." *Id.* at 14.

Travelers makes two additional arguments why the Legal Practices Exclusion applies: the Stafford Complaint's allegations of false and deceptive advertising are "inextricably intertwined with the rendering of professional services"; and the alleged false and deceptive advertising cannot constitute a Wrongful Act under the Legal Practices Exclusion unless Levine & Associates was hired by a claimant and then failed to provide services at the level advertised.

Levine & Associates counter that the Legal Practices Exclusion does not apply. They initially focus the Court's attention on the phrase "related to the rendering of ... professional services. Levine & Associates assert that count three of the Stafford Complaint involves allegations of misleading statements that are "related to *advertising,* not the actual rendering of legal services." Levine & Associates explain that the "plain, ordinary, and usual meaning" of the phrase "related to the rendering of, or failure to render, professional services," within the context of the D & O Policy, means "the actual performance of acts incident to particular professional services, for example, ... gathering medical records, negotiation of a settlement, filing complaints, and preparing discovery responses." According to Levine & Associates, the Wrongful Act was the "act of making misleading statements in advertisements" not the rendering of legal services.

The court looks to the plain and ordinary language of the Legal Services Exclusion: "arising out of any Wrongful Act related to the rendering of, or failure to render, professional services." The plain meaning of the word "render" is "to do; perform: to render a service"; "to do (a service) for another." *See Random House Dictionary of the English Language* 1631 (2d. ed., unabridged 1987); *Merriam–Webster Collegiate Dictionary* 1054 (11th ed. 2003). The plain and ordinary language in the Legal Services Exclusion therefore eliminates from coverage only conduct that relates to Levine & Associates providing legal services.

If the Court were to adopt the expansive reading of the Legal Practices Exclusion advocated by Travelers, then *any* conduct by Levine & Associations would be excluded from coverage since Levine & Associates' business is "related to the rendering of ... professional services." If this were the case, then the D & O Policy would be meaningless and provide no coverage. The court will not construe the contract to create such an absurd result. *See Dubis v. E. Greenwich Fire Dist.,* 754 A.2d 98, 101 (R.I.2000) (declining to construe unambiguous contract to "produce an absurd result").

Because the Stafford Complaint's third count alleges deceptive advertising and not wrongful acts in rendering professional services, the Legal Services Exclusion does not apply. Therefore, plaintiffs' motion for partial summary judgment as to Count I is granted. The court finds that the Legal Services Exclusion does not preclude coverage for the third count of the Stafford Complaint and Travelers has a duty to defend. Defendant's motion for summary judgment is denied. It is so ordered.

4. Insureds' Duty to Segregate Losses and Damages Under Property and Liability Insurance Contracts

Comsys Information Technology Services, Inc. v. Twin City Fire Insurance Company

130 S.W.3d 181
(Tex. Ct. App.-Houston [14th Dist.] 2003)

J. Harvey Hudson, Justice.

Comsys Information Technology Services, Inc. *f/k/a* Metamor Information Technology Services, Inc. *f/k/a* Comsys Technical Support Services, Inc. ("Comsys") appeals the denial of its summary judgment against Twin City Fire Insurance Company and Specialty Risk Services, Inc. f/k/a ITT Specialty Risk Services, Inc. (hereafter jointly referred to as "Twin City"). The court granted Twin City's summary judgment.

Comsys' predecessor—COREStaff, Inc.—purchased an Excess Temporary Employment Contractors Errors or Omissions Liability Insurance Policy from Twin City. The effective date of the policy was July 25, 1997, to July 25, 2000. The insurance contract's limit of liability was $5,000,000. It also had a self-insured retention limit of $250,000.

Texas State Low Cost Insurance, Inc. ("TSLCI") hired Comsys to develop and implement a project known as the "Computer Automated Records System (CARS) Migration Project." On August 4, 1997, TSLCI notified Comsys—alleging that Comsys's performance and supervision were inadequate and disclosing that TSLCI intended to file lawsuit against Comsys. On August 11, 1997, Comsys notified Twin City and the liability insurer acknowledged receipt of the notice. On September 11, 1997, TSLCI sued Comsys—citing problems with the computer project and listing several claims: negligence, gross negligence, negligent misrepresentation, DTPA violations, knowing DTPA violations, and breach of express and implied warranties. TSLCI also sought damages for overcharges, loss of revenue, and loss of good will. Comsys filed a counterclaim against TSLCI for unpaid work.

On February 11, 2000, Comsys settled the TSLCI suit at mediation for $275,000—plus forgiving $114,000 for unpaid work that Comsys had performed for TSLCI. Accordingly, Comsys sought recovery of approximately $139,000 under its Excess Temporary Employment Contractors Errors or Omissions Liability Insurance Policy. On March 28, 2000, Twin City denied Comsys' claim—asserting that Comsys settled the TSLCI suit without obtaining Twin City's consent. Comsys sued against Twin City—asserting claims for breach of contract, violations of articles 21.21 and 21.55 of the Texas Insurance Code, and breach of the duty of good faith and fair dealing. All parties moved for summary judgment. The trial court granted Twin City's motion for summary judgment, while denying Comsys' motion for partial summary judgment.

In its motion for summary judgment, Twin City asserted that Comsys was not covered under the policy, because (1) Comsys "settled the lawsuit with TSLCI without Twin City's consent," (2) "Many or all of TSLCI's claims and alleged damages are excluded under the policy," (3) "Comsys cannot meet its *burden of identifying what portion of the settlement, if any, was attributable to covered claims*," and (4) it was "not entitled to recover for the debt that it 'forgave' as part of the settlement." The trial court granted Twin City's motion for summary judgment without specifying the basis for its ruling.

Coverage Under The Policy

In its first point of error, Comsys contends: The trial court erred by granting the motion for summary judgment, because the policy expressly provides coverage for its claims.

In an insurance contract dispute, the initial burden falls upon the insured to establish coverage under the terms of the policy. *Venture Encoding Serv., Inc. v. Atlantic Mut. Ins. Co.,* 107 S.W.3d 729, 733 (Tex.App.-Fort Worth 2003). But, in a summary judgment context, Twin City had the burden to show that no material fact issues existed and that it was entitled to judgment as a matter of law. *Rhone–Poulenc, Inc. v. Steel,* 997 S.W.2d 217, 222 (Tex.1999). Once the defendant establishes that no genuine issue of material fact exists regarding an element of the plaintiff's claim, the plaintiff must present competent summary judgment evidence raising a fact issue on that element. *Guest v. Cochran,* 993 S.W.2d 397, 401 (Tex.App.-Houston [14th Dist.] 1999).

We take as true all evidence favorable to the nonmovant, and we make all reasonable inferences in the nonmovant's favor. *KPMG*

Peat Marwick v. Harrison County Hous. Fin. Corp., 988 S.W.2d 746, 748 (Tex.1999). When both sides move for summary judgment and the trial court grants one motion and denies the other, the reviewing court should review all summary judgment evidence, determine all questions presented, and render the judgment the trial court should have rendered. *Bradley v. State ex rel. White,* 990 S.W.2d 245, 247 (Tex.1999).

* * *

Waiver of the Consent Clause

Comsys contends: Twin City waived the settlement-without-consent provision when the insurer waited a month-and-a-half after the settlement to finally deny coverage. Alternatively, Comsys argues that Twin City is estopped to rely upon the consent provisions by its delay in deciding coverage. *See Minnesota Mut. Life Ins. Co. v. Morse,* 487 S.W.2d 317, 320 (Tex.1972); *Farmers Tex. County Mut. Ins. Co. v. Wilkinson,* 601 S.W.2d 520, 521 (Tex.Civ.App.-Austin 1980) (holding the doctrines of waiver and estoppel may operate to avoid conditions that would otherwise result in forfeiture of an insurance policy).

Waiver is an intentional relinquishment of a known right or intentional conduct inconsistent with that right. *Jernigan v. Langley,* 111 S.W.3d 153, 156 (Tex.2003); *United States Fid. & Guar. Co. v. Bimco Iron & Metal Corp.*, 464 S.W.2d 353, 357 (Tex.1971). Waiver can be established by either an express renunciation of a known right or by silence or inaction for so long a period as to demonstrate an intention to yield that known right. *Tenneco, Inc. v. Enterprise Prods. Co.,* 925 S.W.2d 640, 643 (Tex.1996). Waiver is generally a fact issue. However, if facts and circumstances are admitted or clearly established, it then becomes a question of law. *Motor Vehicle Bd. v. El Paso Indep. Auto. Dealers Ass'n, Inc.,* 1 S.W.3d 108, 111 (Tex.1999).

Twin City responds by asserting that the doctrines of waiver and estoppel cannot be used to create coverage where none exists by the terms of the policy. *See Texas Farmers Ins. Co. v. McGuire,* 744 S.W.2d 601, 602–03 (Tex.1988). Contrary to Twin City's assertion, however, Comsys does not raise waiver and estoppel as a vehicle to create coverage under the policy. Rather Comsys asserts: Twin City has waived or is estopped from relying on this forfeiture provision, by waiting until after a mediated settlement to deny coverage. Thus, the pivotal issue to be determined is at what point in the aforementioned proceedings did Twin City have a duty to determine coverage.

An insurer must, "within a reasonable time," either "affirm or deny coverage of a claim" or "submit a reservation of rights" to the policyholder. Tex. Ins. Code Ann. art. 21.21, § 4(10)(v). Under a general liability insurance policy, the insurer's duty to defend arises with the filing of a suit against its insured. And this duty to defend is determined by comparing the allegations in the pleadings with the language of the insurance policy. *National Union Fire Ins. Co. of Pittsburgh, Pa. v. Merchants Fast Motor Lines, Inc.,* 939 S.W.2d 139, 141 (Tex.1997). Thus, when the insurer has a duty to defend, it must decide the issue of coverage within a reasonable time after the filing of a suit.

However, the duty to defend and the duty to indemnify are distinct and separate duties. *Trinity Universal Ins. Co. v. Cowan,* 945 S.W.2d 819, 821–22 (Tex.1997). Unlike the duty to defend, the duty to indemnify is based on facts proven, not on pleadings. *Pilgrim Enter., Inc. v. Maryland Cas. Co.,* 24 S.W.3d 488, 492 (Tex.App.-Houston [1st Dist.] 2000). Thus, "the duty to indemnify only arises after an insured has been adjudicated, whether by judgment or settlement, to be legally responsible for damages in a lawsuit." *Collier v. Allstate County Mut. Ins. Co.,* 64 S.W.3d 54, 62 (Tex.App.-Fort Worth 2001). Thus, when the insurer has only a duty to indemnify, it must decide the issue of coverage within a reasonable time after judgment or settlement.

Here, the policy obligates Twin City to indemnify, but not defend Comsys. For example, the policy promises to pay on behalf of the insured "all sums which the insured shall become *legally obligated to pay as damages.*" Moreover, the policy states that the "*insured* against whom a 'claim' is made shall have the duty to defend any 'suit' seeking damages"; the "*insured* will ... have the obligation of paying any defense counsel selected by or on behalf of the insured and all defense costs"; and the insurer "shall not be obligated to assume charge of, participate in, or pay for the investigation or defense of any 'claim' or 'suit.'"

Notwithstanding these disclaimers, the policy also provides that if the suit is "reasonably likely" to result in damages in excess of the self-insured retention, Twin City has "the right but not the duty to assume control of the defense." Accordingly, if Twin City wanted to exercise its right to defend, it was obliged to decide coverage issues within a reasonable time after TSLCI filed its suit. On the other hand, if Twin City chose only to indemnify, it was obliged to decide coverage issues within a reasonable time after the settlement.

Here, the policy provides that no insured will, "except at [its] own cost, make or agree to any settlement for a sum in excess of the 'self-insured retention' without our consent." But Twin City could not unilaterally obstruct a settlement agreement, because the policy also provides that where the insured is willing to accept a settlement offer, and the insurer is not, the insurer "shall have the right to litigate in lieu of such settlement and will bear all 'claim expenses' subsequently incurred and any damages in excess of the amount for which the 'claim' could have been settled." Accordingly, under the terms of the policy, Twin City was obliged to either consent to the settlement agreement or assume the responsibility of defending Comsys. Twin City did neither.

An insurer may forfeit its right to control settlements when it violates its contractual obligation to an insured. If an insurer has breached its covenant, whether the breach is express or implied, the insured is free, despite limiting policy provisions, to protect his or her own interest in minimizing potential liability in excess of limits by agreeing to a reasonable good-faith settlement.

It is undisputed that Comsys asked Twin City to attend the mediation conference more than a week before it occurred. Twin City chose not to participate in the settlement negotiations. The only reason given by Twin City for refusing to attend the settlement conference was that it did not have sufficient time to investigate coverage issues. However, as we have already observed, there were no coverage issues to be resolved prior to settlement unless Twin City exercised its option to defend which it did not do during the two-and-a-half years in which the suit was pending. … As we have observed, remaining silent was not an option available under the terms of this policy. Twin City was required to either consent to the settlement or assume the defense.

Insureds' Duty to Segregate First-Party Property Losses and Third-Party Liability Claims

In light of our finding that *some of TSLCI's claims are covered under the policy and others are excluded,* Twin City contends Comsys failed to meet its burden to segregate the damages. Thus, Comsys is precluded from any recovery under the policy. An insured is not entitled to recover under an insurance policy unless it proves its damages are covered by the policy. *Employers Cas. Co. v. Block,* 744 S.W.2d 940, 944 (Tex.1988).

Under the doctrine of concurrent causes, when covered and non-covered perils combine to create a loss, the insured is entitled to recover that portion of the damage caused solely by the covered peril. *Allison v. Fire Ins. Exchange,* 98 S.W.3d 227, 258 (Tex.App.-Austin 2002); *Wallis v. United Servs. Auto. Ass'n,* 2 S.W.3d 300, 302-03 (Tex.App.-San Antonio 1999). The doctrine of concurrent causation is not an affirmative defense or an avoidance issue. Instead, it is a rule embodying the basic principle: Insureds are not entitled to recover under their insurance policies unless insureds prove that their *damage/loss* is covered by the policy. *Allison,* 98 S.W.3d at 258. The insured must present some evidence upon which the jury can allocate the *monetary damages* attributable to the *covered peril. Id.* at 258–59. Because the insured can recover only for *covered events,* the burden of segregating the *loss* attributable solely to the *covered event* is a coverage issue for which the insured carries the burden of proof. *Wallis,* 2 S.W.3d at 303. Otherwise, failure to *segregate covered and noncovered perils* is fatal to recovery. *Allison,* 98 S.W.3d at 259.

Comsys, however, argues: It had no duty to *segregate damages* in this case, because the policy is a *third-party liability insurance contract,* rather than a *first-party property insurance contract.* In *Warrilow v. Norrell,* 791 S.W.2d 515, 527-528 (Tex.App.-Corpus Christi 1989), the Corpus Christi Court of Appeals explained the difference between *liability* under a *first-party* policy and *liability* under a *third-party* policy:

> In Texas, if one force is covered and one force is excluded, the insured must show that the *property damage* was caused solely by the insured force, or he must separate the *damage* cause by the *insured peril* from that caused by the *excluded peril.* … [I]n the *third-party liability insurance* context, the right to coverage is established by traditional tort concepts of fault, proximate cause, and duty. By insuring for personal liability and agreeing to cover the insured for his own negligence, the insurer agrees to *cover the insured for a broader spectrum of risks.*
>
> Thus, the focus is on the insured's legal obligation to pay for *an injury or damage arising out of a certain occurrence,* and coverage should extend to an insured risk, negligence, which constitutes a concurrent proximate cause of the injury. *See State Farm Mutual Auto. Ins. Co. v. Partridge,* 514 P.2d 123, 130 (Cal. 1973) (involving concurrent causation as it applied to third-party liability insurance coverage and holding that "coverage under a liability

> insurance policy is equally available to an insured whenever an insured risk constitutes simply a concurrent proximate cause of the injuries."). By finding coverage, for an injury resulting from the insured's negligence, the reasonable expectations of the parties to the insurance contract are not frustrated. Our application of *Partridge* does not expand the insurer's potential liability, as would be the case in the *first-party property insurance* context.

Comsys urges us to adopt the position taken in *Warrilow*. On the other hand, Twin City argues: The doctrine of concurrent causes is *not limited to first party insurance* cases, but has been applied to *third party insurance* cases. We agree.

The greater weight of authority supports this conclusion. *See, e.g., Enserch Corp. v. Shand Morahan & Co.*, 952 F.2d 1485, 1494 (5th Cir.1992) (reversing and explaining that "we cannot allow an insured to settle allegations against it—some of which might be covered by its insurance, some of which might not—and then seek full indemnification from its insurer when some of that settled liability may be for acts clearly excluded by that policy"); *Society of Prof'ls in Dispute Resolution, Inc. v. Mt. Airy Ins. Co.*, 1997 WL 711446, at *7 (N.D. Tex. Nov.7, 1997) (allowing the insurer to contest coverage of certain claims where a settlement did not address whether the liability insurance contract covered any part of the liability); *Willcox v. American Home Assur. Co.*, 900 F.Supp. 850, 856 (S.D.Tex.1995) (reaffirming that damages recited in judgment or settlement of underlying lawsuit must be apportioned between covered and noncovered claims); *Winn v. Continental Cas. Co.*, 494 S.W.2d 601, 605 (Tex.Civ.App.-Tyler 1973) (finding no evidence of the insured's segregating allegedly covered civil-liability claims and non-covered criminal-liability claims).

Twin City maintains that because neither the memorandum of agreement nor the final settlement agreement between TSLCI and Comsys contains an apportionment of the settlement payment among the various claims and measures of damages, Comsys has failed to meet its burden. ... However, Comsys offered some evidence of allocation of damages. ... In its answers to interrogatories propounded in the underlying suit, TSLCI set forth amounts for some of the damages it sought. We conclude that Comsys has raised a fact issue with regard to allocation of damages in the settlement. ... *Some* of TSLCI's claims are covered under the policy. Further, because some evidence was offered regarding the allocation of damages under the settlement agreement, a fact issue exists regarding whether the sum of the covered claims exceeds the $250,000 self-insured retention.

Thus, summary judgment was inappropriate. The judgment of the trial court is reversed and the cause is remanded to the trial court for further proceedings consistent with this opinion.

C. Recoverable and Non-Recoverable Common-Law and Statutory Claims and the Segregation of Attorney's Fees Defenses

Aldous, P.C. v. Darwin National Assurance Company

92 F.Supp.3d 555
(N.D. Tex. 2015)

Sam A. Lindsay, District Judge.

The plaintiffs are attorney Charla Aldous ("Attorney Aldous") and Charla G. Aldous PC ("Aldous PC"). Attorney Aldous decided to purchase professional liability insurance for herself and her law firm. On March 1, 2010, Attorney Aldous purchased a professional liability insurance contract from Darwin National Assurance Company (Darwin).

In an underlying case, Attorneys Lisa Blue, Charla Aldous, and Steve Malouf (collectively "BAM")—associated with *The Law Office of Stephen Malouf*—provided legal representation for

Albert G. Hill III and his family ("Hill"). On February 15, 2011, BAM sued to recover attorney's fees. And Hill, in turn, sued them for breach of fiduciary duty, duress, breach of contract, fraud, and professional negligence (the *"Hill Lawsuit"*).

Attorney Aldous asked Darwin to hire Attorney Alan Loewinsohn of *Loewinsohn Flegle Deary LLC* ("LFD firm") to defend BAM against Hill's counterclaims. Attorney Loewinsohn helped BAM to fashion their affirmative claims and was familiar with the complexities of the case. On March 9, 2011, after exchanging multiple e-mails and phone conversations, the professional liability insurer agreed to retain the LFD firm to defend against Hill's claims. Darwin only agreed to the retain the LFD firm—subject to conditions in Darwin's reservation of rights letter ("RoR"). The RoR stated that BAM is "responsible for one-third (1/3) of Mr. Loewinsohn's reasonable and customary fees and expenses related to the defense of this counter claim and that we will not be covering any work done on behalf of the firms related to their affirmative claims in pursuing their attorney fees."

Attorney Aldous contend: Plaintiffs are entitled to summary judgment because Darwin breached the Policy by not paying all of the defense expenses. Plaintiffs also want a declaratory judgment—stating that "they are entitled to recover from Darwin at least all of the attorneys' fees and expenses incurred on their behalf by defense counsel." Darwin argues: It is required to pay only one-third of the attorney's fees incurred to defend against Hill's claims. The amount that it owes should not include attorney's fees for Plaintiffs' affirmative claims; and Darwin has paid an amount greater than what it owes.

Attorney Aldous eventually won her lawsuit against Hill and obtained a judgment. Plaintiffs additionally allege that Darwin wrongly represented that, once Aldous recovered judgment, Darwin was entitled to reimbursement for attorney's fees it had already paid. As part of its counterclaim, Defendant argues it is entitled to a portion of the judgment but that Plaintiffs refuse to pay.

***

III. Analysis

Plaintiffs assert that they are entitled to summary judgment on their breach of contract claim for two reasons. First, Plaintiffs argue that Darwin has a duty to pay for attorney's fees incurred in pursuit of Aldous's affirmative claims against Hill. They seek a declaratory judgment from the court stating that Aldous's affirmative claims were inextricably intertwined with the defense against Hill's counterclaims. Separate from asserting an obligation to pay for Aldous's affirmative claims, Plaintiffs also contend that Defendant breached its duty under the Policy by making improper deductions and wrongly allocating a 50/50 split between defensive claims and affirmative claims. The court addresses each of these contentions in turn.

A. Professional Liability Insurers' Duty to Defend

Plaintiffs contend: Darwin National Assurance Company had a duty to defend. Therefore, the insurer also had a duty to pay for legal services related to their affirmative claims "if the discrete legal services that supported Plaintiffs' affirmative claim also were required to defend even one of the counterclaims." Plaintiffs argue: "If a complaint potentially includes a covered claim, the insurer must defend the entire suit." *See Zurich American Ins. Co. v. Nokia, Inc.*, 268 S.W.3d 487, 491 (Tex.2008). The Fifth Circuit articulates this rule as follows: "When an insurer has a duty to defend, even where a claim falls partially within and partially outside of a coverage period, the insurer's duty is to provide its insured with a *complete defense.*" *Primrose Operating Co. v. National Am. Ins. Co.*, 382 F.3d 546, 559 (5th Cir. 2004).

The court is not impressed with Plaintiffs' citations—as none of the above-cited cases supports their arguments. Plaintiffs contend that these cases also create a duty to prosecute affirmative claims. Neither *Zurich* nor *Primrose* mentions anything other than an insurer's duty to provide a complete defense. That Defendant had a duty to defend does not give rise to an obligation to pay for Plaintiffs' affirmative claims. *Zurich* and *Primrose* do not stand for the proposition that a duty to defend one covered claim also gives rise to an obligation to pay for an insured's affirmative claims. Accordingly, Plaintiffs are not entitled to payment for fees associated with their affirmative claims.

B. Declaratory Judgment

Plaintiffs similarly argue: Darwin must pay for all of the expenses incurred "whether related to Plaintiffs' defensive or affirmative claims," because the attorney's fees relating to the claims are *inextricably intertwined and incapable of separation.* They seek a declaratory judgment: Plaintiffs are entitled to recover from Darwin all the attorney's fees and expenses incurred on their behalf by their law firm from the date they notified Darwin of the claim whether related to Plaintiffs' defensive or affirmative claims.

Plaintiffs' affirmative and defensive claims in the *Hill Lawsuit*—other than the negligence claim were inextricably intertwined—with the success or failure of each depending on the outcome of the other. Plaintiffs are entitled to a declaration that the fees and costs incurred in prosecuting their affirmative claims against the claimant from the date they notified Darwin of the claim are encompassed with Darwin's duty to defend.

C. The Duty to Segregate Recoverable and Non-Recoverable Attorney's Fees

In *Tony GulloMotors I, L.P. v. Chapa,* 212 S.W.3d 299, 313 (Tex.2006), the Texas Supreme Court concluded: "[If] discrete legal services advance both … recoverable and unrecoverable claims—[which] are so intertwined, they need not be segregated." This is a test for determining whether claims are inextricably intertwined. *See also In re Alonzo,* 540 Fed.Appx. 370, 373 (5th Cir.2013) ("Yet, interrelated or intertwined facts are not enough to trigger the exception. It is only when discrete legal services advance both a recoverable and unrecoverable claim that they are so intertwined that they need not be segregated.").

There are significant differences between the present action and the dispute in *Chapa*—which is relied on by Plaintiffs. *Chapa* involved an award of attorney's fees to the plaintiff for prevailing on her affirmative claims. *Chapa,* 212 S.W.3d at 310. *Chapa* ordered the plaintiff's attorney to segregate fees between the claims on which she prevailed and the claims on which she lost. Here, Plaintiffs' argument is qualitatively different from the arguments presented in *Chapa* and cases like it. These latter cases do not even address, and therefore cannot support, the proposition: A duty to defend also requires an insurer to pay for intertwined affirmative claims brought by the insured.

Even assuming that *Chapa* applies, it does not advance their argument. Plaintiffs argue that they "could not have prevailed on their affirmative claim without also defeating Hill III's counterclaim." Even so, this does not give rise to a duty to pay for Plaintiffs' affirmative claims. Stated differently, the converse of Plaintiffs' statement is not true; that is, to prevail against Hill's counterclaims to which Darwin has admitted its obligation to defend, BAM did not need to prevail on their affirmative breach of contract claim. Ultimately, the discrete legal duty to defend was capable of segregation.

Chapa refused to hold: The attorney's fees were inextricably intertwined. The court found that making such an argument "required [defendant's] attorneys to take a position inconsistent with [defendant's] underlying claims." 212 S.W.3d at 313. In *Chapa,* the defendant's attorneys previously argued that its *breach of contract and DTPA claims were separate.* And the court found: "Having prevailed in her argument that the claims are distinct, it is hard to see how she can also claim they are inextricably intertwined."

Here, Plaintiffs assert: "Because the counterclaim, affirmative defenses, and affirmative claims were all inextricably intertwined, success or failure of the affirmative and defensive claims depended on the outcome of the other." ... Plaintiffs attempt to have it both ways. When arguing against Darwin's 50/50 split between affirmative and defensive claims, they state, "Loewinsohn had already identified affirmative fee costs of $56,370 and $90,033.03 for March and April 2011."

Plaintiffs assertions do not align with the evidence in the record. Loewinsohn was able to segregate affirmative fees for March and April, and therefore the court cannot grant Plaintiffs' request for a declaration that "Plaintiffs are entitled to recover from Darwin *all the attorney's fees and expenses incurred* on their behalf by their law firm from the date they notified Darwin of the Claim forward whether related to Plaintiffs' defensive claims or affirmative claims." On this basis alone, Plaintiffs would not be entitled to 100% of the attorney's fees accrued, as Loewinsohn already established that a portion of the *work done is divisible.*

Plaintiffs have failed to establish that Darwin has any duty to pay for their affirmative claims. The Policy requires Defendant to pay for reasonable claim expenses arising from defense of a claim against its insured. The Policy imparts no duty on Darwin to pay for its insured's affirmative claims, and the court will not rewrite the Policy to find such a duty. Accordingly, the court will deny Plaintiffs' request for a declaratory judgment.

Show Me The Money! The Recoverability of Computerized Legal Research Expenses by the Prevailing Party in the Federal Circuits

36 Cap. U. L. Rev. 455
Sarah Wise

Computerized legal research expenses may be a foreign concept to a first year law student who is given unlimited "free" access to Westlaw and LexisNexis. But, these expenses are a major concern for competitive law firms. Computerized legal research is expensive and law firms incur these expenses in most lawsuits. Thousands of dollars are often spent researching on-line and the expenses add up after time. [Generally], computerized legal research expenses include fees charged to attorneys for time spent online using a commercial legal research service such as WESTLAW or LEXISNEXIS.

The yearly cost of a complete WESTLAW PRO in 2005 ranged from $13,512 for a one- or two-person firm, to $52,236 for a sixteen to twenty-person firm. Such *costs* increase the expense of modern litigation. The traditional system of legal research—once conducted solely in the library with the use of digests and reporters—has evolved into an efficient system of computerized research that can now be called a new standard of legal research. As a result, courts have ... the problem of determining whether the expenses associated with computerized legal research should be recoverable by a prevailing party in litigation. ...

The label given to computerized legal research expenses proves important because it determines whether or not a party will be reimbursed. If labeled as *costs*, the expense is awarded to *every* prevailing party in *every* case. If labeled as a *component of attorneys' fees*, the expense can only be awarded under a fee shifting statute. Further, if labeled as *overhead*, the expense would be unrecoverable to the extent that it was not already included in the attorney's hourly rate. And if labeled as a *related expense*, it would be recoverable as a reasonable expense separate from the attorney's hourly rate.

* * *

The English and American Fees/Cost Distinction and Rules

The early English practice was to completely reimburse the prevailing party to make them whole. The theory was that the prevailing party was the wronged party and should not be required to suffer the *expense of the litigation*. Under this practice, attorneys' fees were awarded as well as the *costs of litigation* to the prevailing party. In addition to having a basis in [equity], the English system of complete reimbursement was [fashioned] to discourage frivolous lawsuits by raising the potential liability of litigation. The English system [had] its pitfalls: [T]he poor were often discouraged from bringing meritorious lawsuits, because they could not afford the risk of losing and bearing the litigation expenses of both parties. Equally, the English system [did] not deter baseless claims from being filed by the extremely wealthy, or by the extremely poor—those incapable of paying costs.

[The English Rule] was brought to America and followed during the early part of the nineteenth century. However, the states soon started to abolish the rule of complete reimbursement. ... The traditional American Rule enables prevailing parties to recover their *costs*. But, absent specific statutory exceptions, prevailing parties must pay their own attorneys' fees. ... The American Rule reflects the desire to promote relatively easy access to the courts for all citizens and to reduce the threat of liability as an obstacle to pursuing or defending a lawsuit.

Several different arguments support the American Rule. First, litigation is uncertain and a person should not be penalized for defending or prosecuting a lawsuit. Second, the American Rule [allegedly] encourages settlement by requiring each party to be accountable for his/her expenses. ... Others argue that the American Rule fosters the development of the law itself, by encouraging counsel to develop new legal theories without fear of additional expenses if counsel did not prevail. ... A major criticism of the American Rule is that it puts a barrier in the way of making the successful party whole because the *costs* awarded do not include counsel fees. Others criticize the Rule because it should be assumed that the courts will get it right more often than not and, if that is the case, the innocent party should not have to pay for the litigation cost of vindicating its legal rights.

D. Attorneys' Burden to Prove the Reasonability and Reimbursability of Computer-Assisted Research

Wehr v. Burroughs Corporation

619 F.2d 276
(3d Cir. 1980)

Aldisert, Circuit Judge.

Karl C. Wehr had been employed as an engineer by the Burroughs Corporation since May 1967. He was discharged on August 1, 1975—ostensibly for unsatisfactory work performance—at the age of forty-four. Believing that he was a victim of age discrimination because of the company's expressed desire to replace some older employees with "young tigers," Wehr sought relief in district court in the form of lost wages, including both back and front pay, statutory liquidated damages, compensatory damages for pain and suffering, and attorneys' fees and costs. The jury returned a verdict of $126,760 in Wehr's favor for back pay and liquidated damages. And the court awarded $83,382.13 in counsel fees and costs. In the appeal, Burroughs contends that the district court erred in its interpretation and application of the liquidated damages provision of the Act.

II. Proving Liability Under the ADEA of 1967

The rights created by the Age Discrimination in Employment Act of 1967 (ADEA) are "enforced in accordance with the powers, remedies, and procedures" of specified sections of the Fair Labor Standards Act (FLSA), 29 U.S.C. § 626(b). Following the model of the FLSA, Congress has established two primary enforcement mechanisms within the ADEA. The Secretary of Labor may bring suit on behalf of an aggrieved individual for injunctive and monetary relief. In addition, private actions are authorized by the incorporated FLSA provisions together with § 7(c) of the ADEA, 29 U.S.C. § 626(c), for "such legal or equitable relief as will effectuate the purposes of" the ADEA. In a private action for damages under the ADEA, a plaintiff may initially recover lost wages. In addition, he may recover liquidated damages in an amount equal to the unpaid wages, *See* FLSA § 16(b), 29 U.S.C. § 216(b). However, recovery is allowed only when the violation is "willful." ADEA § 7(b), §9 U.S.C. § 626(b). In this respect the district court charged:

> Members of the jury, the Act provides that the plaintiff is entitled to liquidated damages if the defendant's conduct in violating the Act was willful. ... [Y]ou will have to determine whether the defendant's violation of the Act was willful. That is, did the defendant willfully use age as a determining factor in its decision to terminate plaintiff? What do we mean by "willfully"? An act is done willfully if it is done intentionally, deliberately and knowingly. Thus, an employer acts willfully in violation of the Act if the employer deliberately, intentionally and knowingly discharged the employee because of his age. In other words, if the employer intended to act consciously and intentionally in the discharge of the employee because of age, the employer acted willfully. The act of the employer must be

> intentional and cannot be an accident or it would not be willful.

Burroughs contends that the ADEA incorporates the good faith test of § 11 of the Portal-to-Portal Act of 1947, 29 U.S.C. § 260. From this Burroughs would infer: Procedurally, the final decision to award liquidated damages properly rested with the court rather than the jury. And substantively, the court should have considered whether Burroughs believed in good faith that it had a legitimate reason to discharge Wehr—notwithstanding the jury finding of age discrimination. We reject this contention. And for the reasons stated in *Loeb v. Textron, Inc.*, 600 F.2d 1003, 1020 (1st Cir. 1979), we determine that § 11 of the Portal-to-Portal Act is not incorporated into the ADEA.

III. Proving Liquidated Damages Under the ADEA of 1967

Burroughs second attack on the court's jury charge centers on the definition of the term "willful" in ADEA § 7(b). Burroughs contends that the proviso in ADEA § 7(b) that allows liquidated damages only upon a showing of a "willful violation of (the Act)" should be interpreted to mean that an employer is subject to liability for liquidated damages only if he intentionally violates the Act. The district court instructed the jury that "an employer acts willfully in violation of the Act if the employer deliberately, intentionally and knowingly discharged the employee because of his age." ... In sum, we find no reversible error in the trial court's jury charge on willful violation of the ADEA.

IV. Proving Liability for Computer-Aided Legal Research Costs

Also, in the appeal, Wehr's counsel complains that the court's award of attorneys' fees and costs was inadequate. Although ultimately awarded a total of $80,651.79, Wehr's counsel sought $161,879 in fees for the litigation on the merits, and $11,816.25 for time expended in preparing the fee petition. In addition, counsel requested reimbursement of $11,053.79 in *costs*. After Burroughs objected to the reasonableness of the proposed figures, the district court examined the documentation under the standards enunciated by this court in *Lindy Brothers Builders, Inc. v. American Radiator & Standard Sanitary Corp.*, 487 F.2d 161 (3d Cir. 1973) (*Lindy I*), *Lindy Brothers Builders, Inc. v. American Radiator & Standard Sanitary Corp.*, 540 F.2d 102 (3d Cir. 1976) (*Lindy II*), and their progeny. The court disallowed certain discrete amounts from the proposed lodestar and adjusted that figure downward. *See United*

Phosphorus, Ltd. v. Midland Fumigant, Inc., 205 F.3d 1219, 1233 (10th Cir. 2000) ("When determining what is a reasonable award of attorney fees, the district court must calculate the 'lodestar'—which is the reasonable number of hours spent on the litigation multiplied by a reasonable hourly rate."). It also declined to augment the lodestar by a multiplier. Counsel complain that by doing so, the district court misused its discretion.

On review, except for two modifications of the award mentioned below, we will affirm the district court's determination concerning fees and costs. And we reject counsel's various contentions regarding the court's exercise of discretion over whether to multiply the award. Indeed, it appears that this should not have been a difficult case for counsel. Yet it was over-prepared, over-discovered, and overtired by counsel for both sides. Significantly, in its instructions to the jury, the trial court recognized the absence of complexity in this case.

* * *

[W]e will modify the district court's award of costs because we disagree with the court's refusal to allow recovery for computer-aided legal research as a reasonable cost of litigation. We will allow recovery of these costs. Use of computer-aided legal research—such as LEXIS, WESTLAW, or similar electronic systems—is certainly reasonable, if not essential, in contemporary legal practice. Indeed, in at least one other case decided in this circuit, this type of cost has been awarded as a reimbursable expense. *See Pitchford Scientific Instruments Corp. v. Pepi, Inc.,* 440 F.Supp. 1175, 1178 (W.D. Pa.1977), aff'd without opinion, 582 F.2d 1275 (3d Cir. 1978). We think this is the better rule. But, we are careful to note: The amount of [computer-aided legal research] must be reasonable in order to be allowed. We conclude that the $440 requested by counsel in this case was reasonable.

Accordingly, the judgment of the district court will be affirmed and an additional $440 will be added to the district court costs.

NOTES AND QUESTIONS

1) **Jurisdictions' Holding that Electronic Research Is a Recoverable Cost.** *See Role Models Am., Inc. v. Brownlee*, 353 F.3d 962, 975 (D.C. Cir. 2004) (finding charges for computer

research are appropriate because those charges "save money by making legal research more efficient"*); Arbor Hill Concerned Citizens Neighborhood Ass'n. v. County of Albany*, 369 F.3d 91, 98 (2d Cir. 2004) (holding "the use of online research services likely reduces the number of hours required for an attorney's manual search, thereby lowering the lodestar, and that in the context of a fee-shifting provision, the charges for such online research may properly be included in a fee award"); *Case v. Unified Sch. Dist. No. 233 Johnson County, Kan.*, 157 F.3d 1243, 1257 (10th Cir. 1998) (finding that reasonable charges like Westlaw or LexisNexis fees should be included in the attorney's fee award if such expenses are usually billed in addition to the attorney's hourly rate"); *In re Hillsborough Holdings Corp.*, 127 F.3d 1398, 1400, 1404 (11th Cir. 1997) (allowing recovery for reasonable costs associated with computer-aided research because, according to the court, "they are often billed separately as expenses by reputable lawyers and law firms," such that "we doubt, therefore, that they can be held to be 'overhead' in some invariable, absolute legal sense"); *Wehr v. Burroughs Corp.*, 619 F.2d 276, 285 (3d Cir. 1980) (allowing computer research to be recovered because "[u]se of computer-aided legal research such as LEXIS, or WESTLAW, or similar systems, is certainly reasonable, if not essential, in contemporary legal practice").

2) Jurisdictions' Holding that Electronic-Research Expenses Are Not Recoverable Costs. *See Haroco, Inc. v. Am. Nat'l Bank & Trust*, 38 F.3d 1429, 1440-41 (7th Cir. 1994) (finding that electronic research qualifies as a portion of an attorney's fee rather than a separate cost); *Standley v. Chilhowee R-IV Sch. Dist.,* 5 F.3d 319, 325 (8th Cir. 1993) (stating "the law of this Circuit is that computer-based legal research must be factored into the attorneys' hourly rate, hence the cost of the computer time may not be added to the fee award"); *King v. JCS Enters.*, 325 F. Supp. 2d 162, 171-72 (E.D.N.Y. 2004) (holding that electronic research costs are not a separable cost to be awarded*); El-Fadl v. Central Bank of Jordan*, 163 F.R.D. 389, 391 (D.D.C. 1995) (concluding that computer-generated or manually performed legal research—using digests, legal texts, articles or books—is still research, which is more properly considered as part of an attorney's fee and not a cost").

3) Jurisdictions' Failing to Address Whether or Not Electronic Research Is a Recoverable Cost. *See Anderson v. Wilson*, 357 F. Supp. 2d 991, 1001 (E.D. Ky. 2005) (stating that "until the Sixth Circuit speaks definitively on this issue, the court finds no reason to disturb its prior ruling"); *Camargo v. Trammell Crow Interest Co.*, 318 F. Supp. 2d 448, 451 (E.D. Tex. 2004) (noting that the Fifth Circuit has yet to address whether electronic computer assisted research is a recoverable cost).

E. Computer Assisted Research Expenses and Conflicting Segregation of Costs and Attorney's Fees Defenses

Trustees of Construction Industry and Laborers Health and Welfare Trust

460 F.3d 1253
(9th Cir. 2006)

William A. Fletcher, Circuit Judge:

Plaintiffs/Appellants ("the Joint Trustees") prevailed in an action to collect delinquent benefit contributions owed to trusts established under the Employee Retirement Income Security Act ("ERISA"). The Joint Trustees then sought an award of "reasonable attorney's fees and costs of the action" under ERISA pursuant to 29 U.S.C. § 1132(g)(2)(D). The district court granted some of the requested fees. But it refused to allow any recovery for expenses incurred in the course of the litigation. The Joint Trustees appeal the district court's refusal to award these fees.

I. Background

On February 12, 2004, the district court granted the Joint Trustees' motion for summary judgment under 29 U.S.C. § 1145 for unpaid benefit contributions on behalf of nonunion employees. Because the Joint Trustees had prevailed on the merits of their claim, the court held that they were entitled to "reasonable attorney's fees and costs" under 29 U.S.C. § 1132(g)(2)(D).

The Joint Trustees initially requested attorney's fees and costs totaling $51,907.04. However, the district court found: The Joint Trustees failed to provide "sufficient information to determine whether the requested attorney's fees and costs are reasonable" under the twelve-factor test set forth in *Kerr v. Screen Extras Guild,*

Inc., 526 F.2d 67, 70 (9th Cir.1975). The court therefore ordered the Joint Trustees to provide "an affidavit including this information, as well as any additional information [they] deem germane to the Court's determination of reasonableness under the *Kerr* factors[.]"

The Joint Trustees submitted new affidavits in support of their request for attorney's fees and costs—now for a total amount of $55,064.88. One affidavit specified that their fees were calculated according to "normal billing rates," as follows:

> An additional affidavit specified the total number of hours billed, the hourly rate for each employee, and a "brief summation" of the work performed. The additional affidavit also specified litigation expenses, which it characterized as costs. These expenses were charges for *"electronic legal research, postage, photocopies, courier services, facsimile charges, long distance phone charges, and court reporter services."*

The district court refused to award fees for non-attorneys' work: "The court finds that Plaintiffs' attorney's fees are unreasonable to the extent they include the billings of law clerks, paralegals, and other non-attorneys. ... Accordingly, we reduce] Plaintiff's attorney's fees to $29,131 or to that amount of service actually performed by attorneys." The court also declined to award fees for any of the specified expenses. The Joint Trustees appealed.

II. Standard of Review

"This court reviews *de novo* any elements of legal analysis and statutory interpretation involved in an attorney fees decision." *Associated Gen. Contractors v. Smith,* 74 F.3d 926, 931 (9th Cir.1996). Where ERISA has been correctly interpreted, "we review a district court's award of mandatory attorneys' fees pursuant to § 1132(g)(2)(D) according to the deferential, clearly erroneous standard." *Parkhurst v. Armstrong Steel Erectors, Inc.,* 901 F.2d 796, 799 (9th Cir.1990); *see also Lads Trucking Co. v. Bd. of Trs. of the W. Conference of Teamsters Pension Trust Fund,* 777 F.2d 1371, 1373 (9th Cir.1985).

III. Discussion

ERISA provides for the mandatory award of attorney's fees to pension plans in successful actions to collect delinquent contributions owed under 29 U.S.C. § 1145. *Lads Trucking,* 777 F.2d at 1373–74. The statute reads: "In any action under this subchapter by a fiduciary for or on behalf of a plan to enforce section 1145 of this title in which judgment in favor of the plan is awarded, the court shall award [to] the plan. ... reasonable attorney's fees and costs of the action, to be paid by the defendant ..." 29 U.S.C. § 1132(g)(2)(D).

A. Segregation of Non-Attorneys' Fees

As we construe its order, the district court ruled *as a matter of law* under § 1132(g)(2)(D) that attorney's fees are not available to compensate work performed by non-attorneys such as law clerks and paralegals. The district court erred in so ruling. In *Missouri v. Jenkins,* 491 U.S. 274, 285 (1989), the Supreme Court held: Statutorily mandated "reasonable attorney's fees must compensate both attorneys and paralegals for their services. The Court reasoned in part:

> Clearly, a "reasonable attorney's fee" cannot have been meant to compensate only work performed personally by members of the bar. Rather, the term must refer to a reasonable fee for the work product of an attorney. Thus, the fee must take into account the work not only of attorneys, but also of secretaries, messengers, librarians, janitors, and others whose labor contributes to work product for which an attorney bills her client; and it must also take account of other expenses and profit. If the attorney's hourly rate already incorporates the cost of work performed by non-attorneys, then courts should not compensate for these costs as an additional "reasonable attorney's fee. The key is the billing custom in the "relevant market. Thus, fees for work performed by non-attorneys such as paralegals may be billed separately, at market rates, if this is the prevailing practice in a given community. Indeed, even purely clerical or secretarial work is compensable if it is customary to bill such work separately though such tasks "should not be billed at the paralegal rate, regardless of who performs them.

The principle established in *Jenkins* harnesses "the discipline of the market" to ensure that attorneys recover only those costs that are not already built into their hourly fees.

On remand, the Joint Trustees must show that it is the custom in the relevant community *to bill separately* for work performed by the non-attorneys. And the Joint Trustees must "produce satisfactory evidence—in addition to the affidavits of their counsel—that the requested rates are "in line with those prevailing in the community for similar services of lawyers of reasonably comparable skill and reputation." *Jordan v. Multnomah County,* 815 F.2d 1258, 1263 (9th Cir. 1987).

B. Segregation of Computer-Based Legal Research Expenses

The Joint Trustees contend: Their specified expenses—which are characterized as costs in their affidavit—are part of "reasonable attorney's fees" under § 1132(g)(2)(D). It is well established: Attorney's fees—under 42 U.S.C. § 1988—include reasonable out-of-pocket litigation expenses that would normally be charged to a fee paying client, even if the court cannot tax these expenses as "costs" under 28 U.S.C. § 1920. *See, e.g., Harris v. Marhoefer,* 24 F.3d 16, 19–20 (9th Cir.1994); *Davis v. Mason County,* 927 F.2d 1473, 1488 (9th Cir.1991); *United Steelworkers of Am. v. Phelps Dodge Corp.,* 896 F.2d 403, 407 (9th Cir.1990); *Chalmers v. City of Los Angeles,* 796 F.2d 1205, 1216 n. 7 (9th Cir.1986).

In this circuit, lower courts have applied the interpretation of attorney's fees in § 1988 to other fee-shifting statutes—in order to award expenses that do not fall within the scope of § 1920. *See, e.g., Griffeth v. Sheet Metal Workers' Local Unions & Councils Pension Plan,* 34 F.Supp.2d 1170, 1176 (D.Ariz.1998) (29 U.S.C. § 1132(g)(1)); *Aloha Tower Assocs. Piers 7, 8 & 9, Ltd. P'ship v. Millennium Aloha, Inc.,* 938 F.Supp. 646, 650 (D. Haw. 1996) (28 U.S.C. § 1447(c)); *Snell v. Reno Hilton Resort,* 930 F.Supp. 1428, 1434 (D.Nev.1996) (42 U.S.C. § 2000e–5(g)(2)(B)).

As in *Griffeth,* district courts outside this circuit have held: Although not all "reasonable out-of-pocket expenses of the kind normally charged to clients by attorneys" come within § 1920, "those expenses may in fact be recoverable as part of their reasonable attorney's fees" under ERISA. *Emmenegger v. Bull Moose Tube Co.,* 33 F.Supp.2d 1127, 1133 (E.D.Mo.1998) (§ 1132[g][1]); *see also Antolik v. Saks Inc.,* 407 F.Supp.2d 1064, 1079 (S.D. Iowa 2006) (§ 1132[g][1]); *King v. JCS Enters., Inc.,* 325 F.Supp.2d 162, 171 (E.D.N.Y.2004) (§ 1132[g][2][D]). *But see Perlman v. Swiss Bank Corp. Comprehensive Disability Protection Plan,* 990 F.Supp. 1039, 1044 (N.D.Ill.1998) (§ 1132[g][1]), *vacated by* 195 F.3d 975 (7th Cir.1999).

The Supreme Court has provided two guidelines addressing the scope of attorney's fees as applied to litigation expenses. First, "reasonable attorney's fees" do not include costs that have by tradition and statute been treated as a category of expenses distinct from attorney's fees. *See W. Va. Univ. Hosps., Inc. v. Casey,* 499 U.S. 83, 99–100 (1991). Second, "reasonable attorney's fees" include *litigation expenses* only when it is "the prevailing practice in a given community" for lawyers to bill those costs separately from their hourly rates. *See Jenkins,* 491 U.S. at 286–87. We note: There is a circuit split concerning whether *expenses for computer-based legal research* are compensable as "reasonable attorney's fees." The Eighth Circuit has held that "computer-based legal research must be factored into the attorneys' hourly rate. Thus, the cost of the computer time may not be added to the fee award." *Standley v. Chilhowee R–IV Sch. Dist.,* 5 F.3d 319, 325 (8th Cir.1993).

No other circuit has endorsed this view. Many have expressly held: In appropriate circumstances,

computerized research costs may be recovered in addition to the hourly rates of attorneys. *See, e.g., Arbor Hill Concerned Citizens Neighborhood Ass'n v. County of Albany,* 369 F.3d 91, 98 (2d Cir.2004) ("If the firm normally bills its paying clients for the cost of online research services, that expense should be included in the fee award."); *Invessys, Inc. v. McGraw–Hill Cos.,* 369 F.3d 16, 22 (1st Cir.2004) ("Computer-assisted research should be … reimbursed under attorney's fee statutes … so long as the research cost is in fact paid by the firm to a third-party provider and is customarily charged by the firm to its clients as a separate disbursement."); *Case v. Unified Sch. Dist. No. 233,* 157 F.3d 1243, 1257–58 (10th Cir.1998) ("Reasonable expenses incurred in representing a client in a civil rights case—such as WESTLAW charges—should be included in the attorney's fee award, if such expenses are usually billed in addition to the attorney's hourly rate.").

We believe that the growing circuit consensus reflects the Supreme Court's treatment of litigation expenses under attorney's fee statutes. Neither tradition nor statutory usage distinguishes computer-based legal research costs from attorney's fees. We therefore hold that reasonable charges for computerized research may be recovered as "attorney's fees" under § 1132(g)(2)(D) if separate billing for such expenses is "the prevailing practice in the local community." *Jenkins,* 491 U.S. at 287.

We therefore reverse the judgment of the district court and remand for further proceedings consistent with this opinion.

INDEX

CREDITS

Peter Lattman, "Mass Layoffs at a Top-Flight Law Firm," *Deal Book, The International New York Times*. Copyright © 2013 by The New York Times Company.

"Law School Solo Practice Incubators and Legal Residency Programs," Hanover Research. Copyright © 2012 by Hanover Research – Law School Administration Practice.

Jordana Hausman, Selection from 'Who's Afraid of the Virtual Lawyers? The Role of Legal Ethics in the Growth and Regulation of Virtual Law Offices,' *Georgetown Journal of Legal Ethics*, vol. 25. Copyright © 2012 by Georgetown University Law Center. Reprinted with permission.

John O. McGinnis and Russell G. Pearce, Selection from 'The Great Disruption: How Machine Intelligence Will Transform the Role of Lawyers in the Delivery of Legal Services,' *Fordham Law Review*, vol. 82, no. 6. Copyright © 2014 by Fordham Law Review. Reprinted with permission.

Brittany Stringfellow Otey, Selection from 'Millennials, Technology, and Professional Responsibility: Training A New Generation In Technological Professionalism,' *Journal of the Legal Profession*, vol. 37, no. 199. Copyright © 2013 by The University of Alabama School of Law. Reprinted with permission.

"Ouellett v. Viacom," Copyright in the Public Domain.

"Intel Corp v. Hamidi, 30 Cal. 4th 1342." Copyright in the Public Domain.

Amy Haywood and Melissa Jones, Selection from 'Navigating a Sea of Uncertainty: How Existing Ethical Guidelines Pertain to the Marketing of Legal Services over the Internet,' *Georgetown Journal of Legal Ethics*, vol. 14. Copyright © 2001 by Georgetown University Law Center. Reprinted with permission.

Andrew L. Askew, Selection from 'iEthics: How Cloud Computing Has Impacted the Rules of Professional Conduct,' *North Dakota Law Review*, vol. 88, no. 2. Copyright © 2012 by University of North Dakota/School of Law. Reprinted with permission.

Kenneth Sanney, Selection from 'Cyberjacking, Mousetrapping, and the FTC Act: Are Federal Consumer Protection Laws Helping or Hurting Online Consumers?,' *Vanderbilt Journal of Entertainment Law & Practice*, vol. 3. Copyright © 2001 by Vanderbilt University Law School. Reprinted with permission.

Randy L. Dryer, 'Advising Your Clients (And You!) In The New World of Social Media: What Every Lawyer Should Know About Twitter, Facebook, YouTube, & Wikis," *Utah Bar Journal*, vol. 23, no. 3. Copyright © 2010 by Utah State Bar.

Selections from 'Model Rules of Professional Conduct,' American Bar Association. Copyright © by American Bar Association. Reprinted with permission.

Catherine J. Lanctot, Selection from 'Becoming A Competent 21st Century Legal Ethics Professor: Everything You Always Wanted To Know About Technology (But Were Afraid To Ask),' *Journal of the Professional Lawyer*, vol. 75. Copyright © 2015 by American Bar Association. Reprinted with permission.

Rodney A. Smolla, Selection from 'Regulating the Speech of Judges and Lawyers: The First Amendment and the Soul of the Profession,' *Florida Law Review*, vol. 66, no. 3. Copyright © 2014 by University of Florida Law Scholarship Repository. Reprinted with permission.

Sylvia Stevens, Selection from 'Dealing with Debts: There Oughtta Be a Rule! (But There Isn't),' *Oregon State Bar Bulletin*. Copyright © 2010 by Sylvia Stevens. Reprinted with permission.

Lance Rose, Selection from 'End-User Licensees of Computer Programs—Are They Allowed to Compete with Their Licensors?' *Rutgers Computer & Technology Law Journal*, vol. 13. Copyright © 1987 by Lance Rose. Reprinted with permission.

Colin Hector, Selection from 'Debt Collection in the Information Age: New Technologies and the Fair Debt Collection Practices Act,' *California Law Review*, vol. 99, pp. 1602-1604. Copyright © 2011 by University of California Berkeley School of Law. Reprinted with permission.

Richard C. Wydick, Selection from 'The Attorney-Client Privilege: Does It Really Have Life Everlasting?,' *Kentucky Law Journal*, vol. 87, pp. 1165-1166. Copyright © 1999 by Kentucky College of Law. Reprinted with permission.

Cort Jensen, Selection from 'Rise of The Robo-Form—Is This Doom for the Legal Profession?,' *Montana Lawyer*, vol. 37, no. 8, pp. 9-10. Copyright © 2012 by State Bar of Montana. Reprinted with permission.

Sarah Wise, Selection from 'Show Me The Money! The Recoverability of Computerized Legal Research Expenses by the Prevailing Party in the Federal Circuits,' *Capital University Law Review*, vol. 36, pp. 455-457, 460-462. Copyright © 2007 by Sarah Wise. Reprinted with permission.

Legal Practice Technology and Law: Cases and Materials familiarizes readers with American Bar Association amended Model Rule 1.1 and added comment 8 in order to explain the risks of misusing technology in legal practice. The book teaches law students, as well as both newly minted and seasoned attorneys, how to avoid mistakes and the concomitant risk of suspension or disbarment. Readers learn the critical importance of staying current with the law and its practice regarding all legal-practice technologies.

This casebook discusses common-law and statutory rules that state and federal courts employ to resolve law-office-technology disputes, particularly the legal and/or ethical actions of solo and small-firm attorneys against clients, allegedly third-party victims, state disciplinary boards, and the designers, manufacturers, suppliers, and providers of technological goods and services.

Three important questions will be answered. Will virtual and technologically rich legal practices replace traditional brick-and-mortar law practices? What are the benefits and risks of solo practitioners' accelerated use of and reliance on law-practice technology? Can existing ethical rules be applied to resolve virtual-practice or law-office technology disputes? Thoroughly researched and expertly written, *Legal Practice Technology and Law* is ideal for courses that address the topic.

Willy E. Rice earned his J.D. at the University of Texas, Austin and his Ph.D. at the University of North Carolina in Chapel Hill, and pursued post-doctoral studies at Johns Hopkins University. Dr. Rice is now a professor of law at St. Mary's University School of Law in San Antonio, Texas, where he is a past recipient of the university's Distinguished Faculty Award for Excellence in Teaching. In a career spanning more than thirty years, he has researched, written about, and taught insurance and consumer rights laws and served as an expert for numerous plaintiffs and insurance defense law firms. Dr. Rice is a member of the Gerson-Lehrman Group of International Experts.

Printed by Libri Plureos GmbH in Hamburg,
Germany

9 781516 508242